D0773592

THE HISTORY OF
EUROPE

THE HISTORY OF
EUROPE

General Editor Dr JOHN STEVENSON

MITCHELL BEAZLEY

The History of Europe

Published in 2002 by Mitchell Beazley,
an imprint of Octopus Publishing Group Ltd
2–4 Heron Quays, London E14 4JP
Copyright © Octopus Publishing Group Ltd 2002

Executive Editor	Vivien Antwi
Executive Art Editor	Christine Keilty
Project Editor	Peter Taylor
Editor	Lindsay Porter
Designer	Peter Gerrish
Picture Researchers	Rosie Garai, Jenny Faithfull
Production	Kieran Connelly
Proofreader	Siobhan O'Connor
Indexer	Ann Parry

ISBN 1 84000 559 9
A CIP catalogue record for this book is available from the British Library.

General Editor Dr John Stevenson

Contributors

Ancient Greece	Peter Liddel
Ancient Rome	Josephine Crawley Quinn
Byzantium and the Rise of the West	Dr Peter Heather
The Middle Ages	Dr Andrew Bell
The Dawn of Modern Europe	Professor Andrew Pettegree
Absolutism and Enlightenment	Professor David Sturdy, Dr John Stevenson
The Age of Revolution	Dr John Stevenson
Nation-State and Empire	Chris Green
Europe at War	Matthew Williams
The Cold War in Europe	Martin Mevius
Towards a United Europe	Chris Alner

Typeset in Adobe Garamond, Gill Sans, Frutiger, Univers
Printed in China

Contents

Foreword

What is Europe? Where has it come from and where is it going? This book aims to answer these questions in the broadest possible terms. It takes its beginning with the early civilizations of the Aegean and traces the development of Europe in its different forms through to the present day. Europe has had many definitions and interpretations over the centuries, each of them reflecting a particular set of circumstances and influences. Europe has never been a single political, religious, or cultural unit through the more than two millennia covered in this book. It has always reflected a diversity of traditions and the inputs of other civilizations. The city-states of Greece and the grandeur of the Roman Empire – the fundamental building blocks of what we think of as European civilization – drew upon a rich inheritance of earlier achievements in government, economic life, and intellectual enquiry. Nonetheless, classical civilization made its unique and distinctive contribution to European development and, with the Christian epoch, was one of the two great forces shaping Europe as we know it today. The Europe of nation-states developed over the centuries to acquire its 20th-century identity, but this process was often fluid and varied with circumstances. Throughout this book, the aim has been to encompass not only the political and dynastic elements of Europe's history, but also to give full weight to its economic and social life, to its cultural achievements, and to the wider influence of Europe upon the rest of the world. In order to do so, a team of specialists has been assembled to provide analysis of the key political, economic, and cultural forces that have shaped Europe's history.

The history of the world at large has been profoundly influenced by the history of Europe, and increasingly, the wider world has influenced Europe in its culture and its taste. How a small continent came to spread the values of its civilization across the world, and what those values were, are explored in this book.

Dr John Stevenson, General Editor

The hands of God and Adam, a detail from from the ceiling of the Sistine Chapel. The Florentine artist Michelangelo was one of the outstanding figures of the Renaissance period in Europe. In 1508, he was commissioned by Pope Julius II to decorate the entire ceiling of the Sistine Chapel in the Vatican with frescoes. Working virtually single-handed, this vast undertaking took him over four years.

Introduction

The origin of Europe's name is unknown. Herodotus, the Greek historian, wrote of three continents – Europe, Asia, and Africa. The division of the world into three land masses was therefore very ancient, but Herodotus confessed that he did know why they had been given these names. In Greek mythology, Europa was the daughter of a Phoenician king with whom Zeus fell in love. Disguising himself as a bull, Zeus enticed Europa onto his back and galloped into the sea, taking her with him to Crete.

Little can be deduced from the myth except that the Greek word "Europa" may derive from the Phoenician for "evening land" – the land of the setting sun, or the West. The Greeks initially used Europe to mean central Greece, but soon it meant the whole of the Greek mainland and the entire land mass behind it to the north. The boundary between Europe and Asia was usually fixed at the River Don in Russia, but knowledge of lands north of Greece and west of Sicily was sketchy. Gradually, however, the Mediterranean seaboard of Europe was explored. Greeks and Phoenician traders passed beyond the Pillars of Hercules (the Straits of Gibraltar) to the Atlantic coasts of Europe. The land exploration of Europe was largely carried out by the Romans, who brought Spain, Gaul, and Britain into the early Roman Empire. The Balkans, the Alpine massif, and the Danubian lands were opened up by the conquests of later emperors. Roman traders rediscovered the amber route from Vienna to the Baltic, and the conquests of Trajan penetrated into the Carpathian lands; however, Roman knowledge beyond the Elbe was minimal and Scandinavia virtually unknown. The great sea beyond the Straits of Gibraltar – the Atlantic – was still assumed to encircle the whole world. The oldest medieval map – from the early 7th century – shows the three-part division of the world bounded by a great ocean. The first separate map of Europe dates from the early 12th century. Drawn up by Lambert, a canon of St Omer in France, it remains the earliest illustration of Europe as a separate geographical entity.

Defining Europe

Today, our geographical grasp of the continent is clearer. Conventionally, it is defined as the western part of the Eurasian land mass that forms one of the world's major land surfaces. Its boundary to the south lies at the Mediterranean, including the islands of Sicily and Crete. To the west, its boundary lies at the Atlantic Ocean and, to the north, at the Arctic Ocean and the Barents Sea. Its eastern boundary, however, is geographically indistinct. There are no great changes in flora or fauna to mark a point where Europe ends and Asia begins. Conventionally, the Ural Mountains, the Ural River, and the Caspian Sea are taken to denote the boundary between Europe and Asia. By convention, too, Turkey lies in Asia, with Europe ending at the Bosporus. The total land mass is about the same size as mainland USA but its coastline is more extensive than that of any other continent in proportion to its size. Accordingly, it has been said, Europe was built for seafarers, but it also could be said to be made for farmers and craftsmen. With much of it lying within the temperate zone and favoured by the Gulf Stream, it possesses abundant agricultural land, timber, and the essential raw materials for metalworking and, later, for industrialization.

This diversity is reflected in its history. Europe represents the expression of many traditions going back centuries. This book reflects the Europe we know today, made up of the nation-states that have emerged over the past four or five centuries. In some cases, they stretch the idea of Europe beyond the definitions of the geographers. Russia, extending right across to the Pacific, has always straddled Europe and Asia. The south-eastern boundaries of Europe, too, have always reflected ethnic and religious complexity, while contributing much to Europe's history. The Mediterranean – the cradle of ancient civilization – has been both a boundary and a highway at different points in Europe's past.

People make their own borders, and rivalries of politics, religion, and nationality have imposed barriers almost irrespective of geography. Historically, Europe has been open to conquest and migration, absorbing new cultures and ideas. Yet Europe has also been defined by more general characteristics, notably for what became understood as a distinctively European civilization. This was seen to derive from the ancient world, medieval

Christendom, the Renaissance, and the Enlightenment. This amalgam of ideas came to stand for European culture and was transmitted at the time of European dominance to the world at large.

The History of Europe attempts to weave the diverse traditions that make up the history of the continent into a coherent whole. It starts with the first recorded beginnings of European civilization in Greece. The Roman Empire unified many areas that were to form an integral part of what we now think of as Europe, but others lay beyond the reach of Rome. Much of Germany, central and Eastern Europe, Russia, and Scandinavia remained outside Rome's direct rule. The Roman Empire also included areas such as the Near East and North Africa, which were to become overlain by other cultures with the rise of Islam. Nonetheless, Rome laid foundations north of the Mediterranean that were to have a profound influence on the post-Roman world. The "barbarian kingdoms" of the West and the mutation of the Eastern Roman Empire into the Byzantine Empire meant that Rome's legacy was carried into the Middle Ages.

The role of religion

The rise of medieval Christendom served to unify and define Europe, although this unity had been challenged by the Arab conquests that brought the Muslim faith to the Balkans, Sicily, and Spain. In the north, the barbarian invasions and migrations eventually established themselves as Christian kingdoms, recognizing the religious supremacy of the popes in Rome. To the east, the Byzantine Empire and the Orthodox Church offered a rival Christian allegiance that was adopted by the Slavs and the early Russian state. In the Balkans and the eastern Mediterranean, these religious boundaries remained immensely fluid in the millennium that followed the fall of Rome. The Crusades cut right across the world of the Orthodox Greeks and the Byzantines and attempted to establish Christian kingdoms in the Holy Land. These attempts failed, and the boundaries of Christian Europe were once more pushed back. Indeed, under the power of the Ottoman Turks, it appeared that the boundaries of Christian Europe would be forced to give way as the Turks conquered Constantinople in 1453 and swept into the Balkans and the eastern Mediterranean. For more than two centuries, the boundary of Christian Europe in the Balkans and Mediterranean rested upon the military balance between the Christian powers and the Turks. The Ottoman threat was only blunted with their defeat at Lepanto in 1571 and their retreat from Vienna in 1683. Hungary, long in dispute between the Habsburg and Ottoman empires, finally fell back

into Christian control. Russia remained in conflict with the Turks for another century, with frontier areas still being contested into the 20th century.

Even as the Christian powers grappled with Ottoman Turkey, the unity of Christendom was being fractured. The Orthodox Churches remained separate and unreconciled to Rome. In the 16th century, the Reformation shattered the unity of medieval Christendom. Protestantism and the Catholic Counter-reformation were to plunge Europe into wars of religion, out of which arose states at least partly defined by religious adherence. Europe emerged as a series of nation-states, organized for international conflict under, in many cases, absolutist rulers.

Exploration and colonial expansion

A fresh dimension to European history came as Europe asserted itself overseas. Less than 40 years

A fresco from Naples depicts the Greek myth of Europa, a Phoenician princess who was wooed by the god Zeus in the form of a bull and carried off to Crete. On that island, she became his queen and the mother of the Minoan kings, founding the earliest civilization on European soil.

Europe in 2002

after the fall of Constantinople, Columbus made his first land fall in Hispaniola in the Caribbean, opening up the New World to Europe. The age of exploration created the first European empires in Latin and Central America, and European influence was soon being felt in Africa, the Indian Ocean, and the Far East. By the 18th century, European rivalries were fought out on a worldwide scale in the pursuit of trade, colonies, and influence. The Pacific was opened up and the remaining continents of Australia and Antarctica brought into European consciousness. Large tracts of the world became devoted to sustaining a European-driven trading system. Europeans transplanted millions of African slaves to the Caribbean and the Americas in one of the largest forced mass migrations in history. Rebels and convicts were also transported to far-flung parts of their empires, but Europeans also voluntarily transplanted themselves. The Spanish peopled the Latin American lands they conquered, followed by French and British settlements in North America. European trading posts dotted the coasts of Africa and Asia.

The age of revolution

European dynamism was not confined to colonial expansion. The Renaissance inspired new intellectual movements and led to challenges to established authority. The Enlightenment questioned ideas of absolutist government, and signs of resistance to rulers grew throughout the 18th century. The success of the American Revolution had a huge influence on Europe, priming it for the age of revolution that was about to burst forth.

The idea of democratic rights fused with the long-standing problems of the French monarchy to produce the French Revolution of 1789. Its consequences were to plunge Europe into a generation of warfare and almost six decades of revolutionary upheaval. French armies carried the ideas of liberty, fraternity, and equality throughout Europe, while Napoleon's successes seemed initially to herald a new era for subject peoples. The tide of counter-revolution, however, proved too powerful, and the Napoleonic Wars ended with the restoration of the powers that had been threatened by the upheavals emanating from France. Conservative political regimes were re-established, but were unable to prevent the re-emergence of liberalism that threatened the existing political order. At the same time, industrialization was creating huge social dislocations. Workers formed the first socialist movements, joining in the assault on the established order. Liberal sentiment proved strong enough to start the process of parliamentary reform in Britain and remove the restored monarchy in France. Elsewhere, the old order proved durable, with Russia resisting any glimmer of reform and Metternich skilfully maintaining the status quo in central and Eastern Europe.

Some national sentiments could not be denied. By 1870, a united Italy had emerged from the former conglomeration of states. In 1872, Prussia led the emergence of a unified German Empire. By the late 19th century, the European state system comprised a group of well-organized nation-states; however, stability was not assured. On the southern and eastern fringes of Europe, autocratic governments offered little scope for democratic advance. Russia remained a bedrock of conservatism, and economic reforms only served to show up the unyielding nature of the autocracy in the political sphere. Turkey was forced to relinquish more of its Balkan possessions, creating new states but also dangerous tensions, particularly in Austria-Hungary, where concession to nationalist sentiment could only lead to the dissolution of the state. Thus, at least two of the great European powers, Russia and the Austro-Hungarian Empire, were faced with serious internal difficulties by the early 20th century.

But Europe was more than simply a group of powerful states. The Industrial Revolution saw a rise in new technologies that allowed Europe to become the most powerful continent in the world. Europe asserted itself as never before, carving up Africa, large parts of Asia, and almost all of the Pacific into formal empires or spheres of influence. Europeans carried with them an innate belief in the superiority of their civilization, which was to have a profound influence on the non-European world.

In the early 20th century, Europe was to receive a shattering blow. World War I left more than 10 million soldiers dead, and three of the great European states profoundly altered. Austria-Hungary disintegrated, Russia's revolution led to the first communist government in history, and Germany was plunged into a depression from which Hitler and the Nazis would emerge. Europe's economies were plagued by unemployment and the loss of markets overseas, and the USA emerged as the world's most powerful economy. Hopes for a resolution of European rivalries were dashed by the effects of the Depression and the resentments aroused by the peace settlements of 1919. The rise of European dictators bent on revision of the peace settlements and territorial expansion drove Europe into a truly global war that reshaped the world.

World War II left a divided Europe. The former allies in the defeat of Nazism were now to fall out and confront each other in Germany. The USA's determination to ensure that communism did not make any further advances into Western Europe and Soviet determination to hold on to its own political system meant that for more than four decades after the end of the World War II, Europe was bisected by the Iron Curtain. Europe, once the dominant power, was now sandwiched between superpower rivals. Western Europe was now part of the NATO alliance, committed to defend itself against Soviet aggression. Eastern Europe became formally organized as the Warsaw Pact, a military alliance dedicated to maintaining a Soviet-style regime in countries under communist domination.

Towards a united Europe

From these two world wars came the idea of pooling the sovereignty of European nations into a single community. The Common Market was established in 1958, comprising France, Italy, West Germany, and the Benelux countries. Denmark, Ireland, and Britain joined in 1973, followed by Greece, Spain, Portugal, and Sweden. An affluent Europe was part of a "first world", sharing trade and culture with the USA and Japan.

Competition with the West had fateful results for Eastern Europe. Gorbachev's attempts in the 1980s to liberalize the USSR and allow the Eastern European satellites to decide their own fate produced the dissolution of the Eastern bloc. The two parts of Germany were reunited, and the USSR was split up into its constituent republics. Russia remained a nuclear superpower, but adapted painfully to the end of communist control. The return of fluidity to Europe's borders produced conflicts as well as resolutions. Borders were arbitrated by force, separations were sought, and warfare was brought to the Balkans as the former Yugoslavia descended into ethnic violence. As Europe moved closer to unity with the European Union, many Europeans remained acutely conscious of their ethnic and national identities.

Europe's culture is increasingly international. The impact of European civilization, so dominant in the centuries of expansion, is now being returned through the influences of immigrants, foreign cultures, and the "global village". Europe finds itself at the cultural crossroads of the world, with its long-standing connections with the world's other continents adding to its rich and diverse culture.

ANCIENT GREECE

2500–146 BC

3600 BC 2400 BC 1200 BC

POLITICS AND GOVERNMENT

*c.*3500 The beginning of urban settlements on the island of Crete, as permanent dwellings develop into village settlements.

1250 Traditional historical date of the Trojan War, narrated in Homer's *Iliad*.

*c.*1400 The palace at Knossos on Crete is destroyed.

1700–1200 Peak of Minoan and Mycenaean civilizations on Crete and mainland Greece. Agricultural and commercial societies thrive, directed towards providing for the royal palaces.

*c.*1200 The decline of Mycenaean civilization; the Dark Ages commence.

*c.*1125 Start of the Iron Age. Iron was used for the manufacture of weapons and tools. The use of iron gradually spread throughout Europe.

*c.*800 The era of the Greek colonization of the Mediterranean begins.

*c.*1100 According to legend, Dorian tribes from northern Greece return to the Peloponnese.

3600 2400 1200

SOCIETY AND CULTURE

*c.*1600 The rulers of Mycenae begin elaborate burials with luxury goods from around the Mediterranean.

*c.*2600–2000 The development of Cycladic marble sculpture.

*c.*1700–1400 The peak of the Minoan civilization, which started to decline from *c.*1200 BC.

*c.*3500–3000 The manufacture of bronze begins in the Cycladic archipelago of the Aegean Sea. This led to the Bronze Age period, *c.*3500–1125 BC.

*c.*1500–1200 The Linear B system of writing Greek develops. Greek writing later spreads around the Mediterranean world.

*c.*800 The Greeks begin to establish ports of trade around the Mediterranean.

*c.*1100 The development of the geometric style of vase painting.

*c.*1200–800 The Phoenicians of the Levant dominate Mediterranean trade. It is through contact with them that the Greeks begin to develop their alphabet.

16

3600 BC 2400 BC 1200 BC

431–404 The Peloponnesian War. Athens survives the ravages of plague, but is defeated in the war. The historian Thucydides writes a history of the war.

490–479 The Persian Wars, concluding with Greek victory and the foundation of the Delian Confederacy. The Delian Confederacy develops over the course of the 5th century into an Athenian empire.

358–276 The Macedonian Dynasty.

507 The democratic reforms of Kleisthenes herald the start of democracy at Athens.

229/8 The beginnings of Roman intervention in Greece, as Rome defeats Queen Teuta in the First Illyrian War.

594 Solon introduces social, political, and economic legislation in Athens.

211–197 The First and Second Macedonian Wars. Rome is victorious, and Greece becomes a Roman province.

146 The sack of Corinth marks the completion of Rome's conquest of Greece.

400

*c.***600** The introduction of coinage in Lydia, in Asia Minor.

*c.***570** Birth of the natural philosopher Xenophanes of Colophon.

*c.***525** The development of the red figure style of vase painting in Athens.

499–406 The golden era of Athenian tragedy.

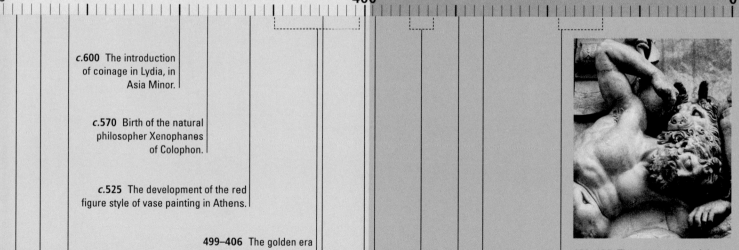

*c.***188–139** The construction of the Great Altar at Pergamum.

*c.***720** The development of the black figure style of vase painting in Corinth.

*c.***270** The poet Theocritus works in the court at Alexandria in Egypt, composing in the bucolic mode.

447 The Periclean building programme reaches its height with the construction of the Parthenon on the Acropolis.

297 The creation of the library and the museum at Alexandria.

*c.***750** Compilation of the Homeric poems to form the *Iliad* and *Odyssey*.

350–324 Athens undergoes an aesthetic revival with a building programme and scheme of religious, educational, and economic reforms.

776 Traditional date of the first Olympic Games, at Olympia in the Peloponnese.

387 Plato founds Academy in Athens.

399 Death of Socrates.

SOCIETY AND CULTURE

Much of the earliest Greek art preserved on vases consists of geometric patterns as well as illustrative scenes, as can be seen on this Attic vase of c.800 BC. Pottery finds not only provide a useful source for tracing the development of art, but can also be used to trace settlements and trade routes.

EARLY GREECE: 2500–750 BC

The period known as Early Greece covers a huge span of development, characterized by the rise and fall of the seafaring Cycladic civilization and the palace-based Minoan and Mycenaean cultures. These societies built networks of trade and artistic activity typical of later developed Greek civilizations.

Greek history can be divided into three periods: Early Greece (2500–750 BC), Archaic and Classical Greece (750–336 BC), and Hellenistic Greece (336–146 BC). Modern historians may have introduced these divisions, but they do reflect the most historically significant events, as well as changes to the type and amount of available ancient sources of information. The growth in the number and sophistication of these sources mean that the history of Greece is marked by an apparent acceleration in the succession of events. The period known as Early Greece is essentially "prehistoric", accessible largely through archaeological discoveries.

The Early Greek period is a long and diverse one. The sources for this era are patchy, however, so it is necessary to zoom in and out to look at developments that took place at different times in different areas of Greece. Today, our picture of Early Greece is more detailed than ever. As archaeological excavations took place over the 19th and 20th centuries, it became possible to trace the history of Early Greece further back and with more detail than was achieved by the Greek historians of the Classical and Hellenistic periods.

In about 3500–3300 BC, the inhabitants of islands in the Aegean Sea discovered how to make bronze from a mixture of copper and tin. Bronze became common at the end of the 3rd millennium BC, when trade connections ensured a supply of tin. The period c.3500–c.1125 BC has become known as the Bronze Age.

The earliest developed societies in Greece about which we have the most information are the Cycladic civilization (developed from c.3500 BC), the Minoan civilization of Crete (peaked 1700–1400 BC), and the Mycenaean civilizations located off mainland Greece (peaked 1600–1200 BC). In the last quarter of the 19th century, excavations at Knossos in Crete and Mycenae in the Argolid revealed significant remains of these prehistoric civilizations. These two cultures shared common elements in their systems of economy, government, and culture, and they provide some idea of the structure of early Greek communities.

Archaeological discoveries indicate that these societies centred on royal palaces, with groups of officials who supervised the labour of artisans and the flow of goods towards the palaces. These civilizations seem to have fallen into decline from about 1200 BC, as a result of dynastic rivalry and a breakdown in established lines of trade. The number of inhabited sites decreased, and those that remained in existence did so with a reduced population. It is reasonable to argue that the myths about the Trojan War in Homer's *Iliad* may reflect the upheavals that curtailed Mycenaean civilization. Greek myth tells also of migrations of populations after these upheavals. Myths such as these would form the basis for ideas about ethnic identity in the Classical period. A growth in the density of inhabited sites from the beginning of the 8th century BC may indicate a growth in population, coinciding with the formation of the Olympic Games, first held around 776 BC.

Environment and ecology are one part of the formative aspects of any society, and the civilizations of Early Greece are no exception. Mountains and the coast are the predominant features of the terrain, with only 20 per cent of the country consisting of flat land and the mainland having 4000 kilometres (2500 miles) of coastline. As the Greeks depended on agriculture and trade for survival, these features meant that Greek history was dominated by struggles for agricultural land and maritime supremacy.

Prehistoric Greece

The remains of Cycladic civilization and the Minoan and Mycenaean civilizations of Crete and mainland Greece provide some of the earliest and most spectacular traces of developed societies in Europe. Their civilizations were based on agriculture and trade. Mythical accounts of the Trojan War may reflect the upheavals that took place in the aftermath of the decline of these civilizations.

Minoan Crete

Some of the earliest farming sites in Greece have been identified on Crete, dating to around the beginning of the 7th millennium BC. Evidence suggests that populations concentrated in substantial settlements from around 3500 BC. These settlements shared features with those in the Asian Near East, such as regular street planning and a focus upon a public square or an important building. At the peak of its development around 1700–1400 BC, the population of Knossos, the largest city, may have reached around 1200.

In the early 15th century BC, all the palaces on Crete except at Knossos were destroyed: this may have been related to the power struggles with mainland Greeks over the island. Knossos was ruined several times, but the final destruction of the Knossos palace took place at around 1400 BC. The burning of the palaces baked clay tablets containing text written in a script known as Linear B. These texts provide us with detailed information about daily life in Knossos. For example, they relate that the herding of sheep was a major activity and that large numbers of women were employed in textile production. Rural farmers in the interior sent oil, wine, and grain as a tribute to the palaces of the rulers. From this emerges a picture of a society reliant on trade and agriculture for survival. As the Minoans had extensive trade contacts, other palace-civilizations on Crete arose at Phaistos, Mallia, and Zakros, locations connected to the rich rural interior as well as sea-trading routes.

Greece in the Bronze Age c.3500–1125 BC
This map illustrates some of the major Minoan and Mycenaean settlements in Greece during the Bronze Age, with a particular concentration of sites in the Argolid in the eastern Peloponnese. The very mountainous landscape of much of Greece meant that disputes over plains, which were especially valuable for agriculture, were a common cause of conflict.

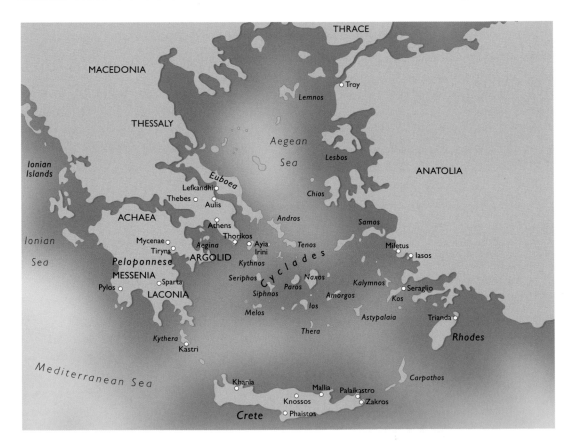

Mycenaean civilization

"Mycenaean civilization" refers not only to the society of prehistoric Mycenae, an important centre in the eastern Peloponnese, but also to a range of centres in mainland Greece, which developed by about 1600 BC. The 16th to 12th centuries BC saw a division of Greece into small kingdoms governed from fortified citadels and royal palaces. With the decline of Knossos from the 14th century BC, the major rival to the Mycenaeans vanished, and Mycenaean civilization reached its zenith, dominating the southern Aegean. As warriors and traders, their power spread to Crete around 1450 BC, and it is probable that the form of writing known as Linear B developed because of interaction between these two civilizations. In the 14th and 13th centuries BC, their decorated pottery vessels were exported throughout the Aegean and eastern and central Mediterranean, in exchange for copper from Cyprus and Sardinia, ivory from Syria, and other luxury items from Egypt.

Some of the most telling remains of Mycenaean civilization have emerged from the circular *tholos* tombs of the ruling classes. The items found in these burials, such as weaponry or remains of horses, indicate that they were a civilization highly concerned with military kudos. After a breakdown in traditional lines of trade and communication, dynastic unrest emerged during the 13th century BC, and Mycenaean civilization fell into decline.

The Dark Ages

The Mycenaean civilization in mainland Greece broke down some time around 1200 BC. For the four centuries following this collapse, writing seems to have vanished, and the changing nature of archaeological remains indicates that there was some hiatus in the development of communication between communities. This era is frequently known as the Dark Ages. However, archaeological excavations, such as those at Lefkandhi on the island of Euboea, central Greece, have revealed evidence of considerable opulence and trade with Cyprus and the Levant in the 10th and 9th centuries BC. One innovation that seems to have taken place in this period was the use of iron as the primary metal for weapons and tools, leading to the use of the term Iron Age for the period after 1125 BC.

The *Iliad* and history

During the Dark Ages, groups of stories narrating a heroic age were compiled to form Homer's *Iliad* and *Odyssey*. The *Iliad* tells stories revolving around a series of conflicts now known as the Trojan War, believed to have taken place around 1250 BC. The *Iliad* is best interpreted as a series of

Cycladic sculpture

The archipelago of the Cyclades, in the southern Aegean, was the home of a distinctive seafaring and farming civilization influential across the Aegean in the 3rd millennium BC. During the Bronze Age, the inhabitants became experts at carving stone, using supplies of marble from the island of Paros to produce female figurines. Examples have been excavated from tombs and are thought to represent goddesses placed there to protect the dead. Remains of paint on the figures suggest that they would have been more ornate than they now appear. Cycladic art reached Crete in its earliest period of civilization, c.2600–2000 BC.

myths, which developed over a period of time. The poems were collated in about 750 BC – some 500 years after the Trojan War. They reflect the Greeks' idea of their own past, but also provide information about the Mycenaean civilization, the Dark Ages, and the 8th century BC. It is important not to confuse the legendary aspects of the *Iliad* with historical fact, but it is valid to assume that a series of upheavals may have inspired the evolution of the story of the Trojan War.

The Trojan War

In the *Iliad*, the Trojan War is portrayed as the conflict between the Achaeans (Greeks) and the Trojans. Troy was a stronghold commanding the Dardanelles, a settlement founded in the Bronze Age. According to Homer, the cause of the conflict was the abduction of Helen, wife of the king of Sparta, by Paris, the son of the king of Troy. With the purpose of recovering Helen, a Greek force gathered under Agamemnon, the brother of the Spartan king Menalaus. They besieged Troy for nine years. In the 10th year, Achilles, the greatest of the Greek heroes, withdrew from the fighting after an argument with the Greek commander. The Trojans gained the better of the Greeks until Achilles returned, when he killed the Trojan commander Hector and routed the Trojans. According to Homer, Troy was obliterated and its women and children sold into slavery.

By representing the struggle of Greeks against non-Greeks, these poems had great significance for the Greeks of the Classical period. The *Iliad* and *Odyssey* acted as a source of Greek mythology, while also highlighting contradictions in values, such as the rules of war, the etiquette of gift-giving, and the clash of public and private commitments.

The Formation of Greek Identity   22–3 ▶
Poetry and Drama   36–7 ▶
Histories   42–3 ▶
The Foundation of Rome   60–1 ▶

The Formation of Greek Identity

The ancient Greeks thought of themselves not simply as Greeks, but also as members of ethnic groups. These interests were reflected in the myths surrounding migrations of these groups during the so-called "Dark Ages". Membership of an ethnic group inclined towards division, but a feeling of Greek identity developed with the beginnings of the Olympic Games.

The most socially and politically prominent ethnic identities in ancient Greece were those of the Dorians and the Ionians. In the Classical and Hellenistic periods, when individual city-states faced a threat, they could appeal for help from other Greek states on the grounds of these assumed ethnic affinities. These appeals were based upon a series of legends that seem to have developed as a response to changes in civilization at the end of the Mycenaean era. These legends told of a migration of the tribe of Dorians into the Peloponnese. This so-called Dorian invasion of Greece was once believed to be the cause of the Mycenaean

collapse, or the origin of historical Greece. More recently, historians doubt this because of the lack of archaeological evidence. Analysis of archaeological finds has indicated that considerable upheavals may have taken place in the 11th century BC, involving population movement across the Aegean. In reality, however, these were probably due to more complex factors than the mass emigration episode recounted by the myth.

The Dorian invasion

The myth of the invasion of the Dorians in the 11th century BC was based on their links to the most

According to mythology, the Dorians invaded from north-west Greece and settled the areas of Greece inhabited by populations who used the Doric dialect, many of whom may have migrated to western Asia Minor and formed the Ionian League, which met at the Panionium.

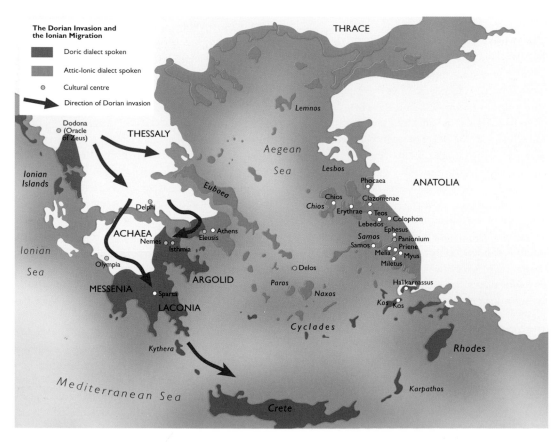

The Dorian Invasion and the Ionian Migration
- Doric dialect spoken
- Attic-Ionic dialect spoken
- Cultural centre
- Direction of Dorian invasion

THRACE · Lemnos · Aegean Sea · Lesbos · Phocaea · ANATOLIA · Chios · Clazomenae · Chios · Erythrae · Teos · Colophon · Lebedos · Ephesus · Samos · Panionium · Samos · Priene · Melia · Myus · Miletus · Halikarnassus · Kos · Kos · Rhodes · Karpathos · Delos · Paros · Naxos · Cyclades · Dodona (Oracle of Zeus) · THESSALY · Ionian Islands · Euboea · Delphi · Athens · ACHAEA · Eleusis · Nemea · Isthmia · Ionian Sea · Olympia · ARGOLID · MESSENIA · Sparta · LACONIA · Kythera · Mediterranean Sea · Crete

popular and widely worshipped of the Greek heroes, Heracles, and his sons. According to this story, known as the "Return of the Herakleidai", the offspring of Heracles were expelled from the Peloponnese. Hyallus, the eldest son of Heracles, attempted to lead them back, but the effort ended in his death. Thereafter they remained in central Greece, until the Delphic oracle informed them that the time had come to return to their ancestral lands. Soon afterwards, they migrated south to the Peloponnese. The 5th-century BC historian Thucydides attempted to rationalize the myth, telling us that the Dorians took over the Peloponnese "together with the Herakleidai". Indeed, there might be some element of truth in the story. It is possible that a heavily depopulated Argolid was taken over by Dorians who came from northern Greece, perhaps Thessaly, around the start of the 11th century BC. The Dorians extended their conquests to populate a large part of the Peloponnese, and they reached as far as Crete and the south-west corner of Asia Minor, including Halikarnassus. The residents of Messenia and Laconia were enslaved and, after the Dorian invasion, continued to inhabit their homeland as a servile race, known as *helots* (serfs) and *periokoi* (the "dwellers around"). Until 370 BC, they were subordinate to the citizens of Sparta, a city ruled by two kings who both claimed to be the descendants of Heracles.

The Ionian migration

Some myths ascribe the presence of Ionian Greeks in western Asia Minor to their expulsion from mainland Greece by the Dorians. One group of Ionians who were an exception to this rule were the Athenians, who appear to have remained steadfast in their homeland. Throughout their history, the Athenians took pride in being the indigenous inhabitants of their city, calling themselves *autochthons* – the "earth-born ones".

The first Olympic Games

The Olympic Games were as important to the ancient Greeks as they are to us today. As an event exclusively for Greek competitors, they became a gathering of great repute, sometimes taking on political overtones. Their foundation as a pan-Hellenic competition was highly significant in the formation of Greek identity as well as the city-state civilization of Greece.

Olympia was the site of the main sanctuary of Zeus in Greece, and it was situated in the valley of the river Alpheus in Elis, in the western Peloponnese. It is likely that contests at Olympia began in the Dark Ages, perhaps around 1000 BC,

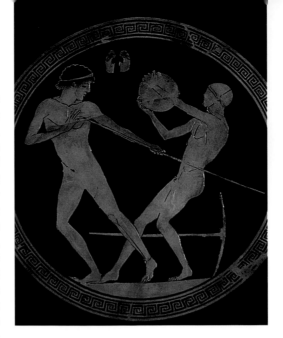

Many of the games practised in the modern Olympics have their roots in ancient games. This 4th-century cup depicts athletes with a javelin and discus.

but the traditional date for the first formal Olympic Games was 776 BC. Like the modern Olympics, these games took place every four years. For the first 50 years, the only athletic event was the *stade*, a 200-foot sprint that may have originally formed part of the entertainment at a religious festival. The Olympic Games at their fullest development included horse racing, wrestling, boxing, javelin throwing, the pentathlon, the long jump, and the discus.

Greek society and the Olympic Games

The Olympic Games were instrumental in highlighting or indeed perpetuating society's ranking at the time. Aristocrats and tyrants (usurping monarchs) were heavily involved in the Games, winning or reinforcing their positions through the acclaim of an Olympic victory. While the Olympic Games could serve to bring Greeks together under a sacred truce, and constituted an event that unified all Greeks for a common purpose, this did not preclude them being used for political purposes.

While the early Olympic Games were probably regional celebrations, they grew over the course of the 8th century BC into a pan-Hellenic festival. The Games, by excluding non-Greek "barbarians" who, in the Greek imagination, were unable to compete physically with the Greeks, contributed to the Greek idea of themselves as civilized, heroic, and athletic. Indeed, the Games were so important to the Greeks that exclusion for political reasons was an extreme insult to the city concerned. The Games also played an important role in the evolution of the identity of the city-states. Individuals would go to Olympia to display the wealth and resources of their particular city-state, as well as to display their individual skills. This was so successful that the Games were copied at Nemea, Delphi, and Isthmia, where pan-Hellenic games were established in the first third of the 6th century BC.

The Erechtheion was begun in
421 BC and finished in 407 BC.
As the most holy temple of the
goddess Athena on the Acropolis
in Athens, it housed a number of
cults. The temple's porch was
supported by a group of figures
known as the Caryatids. According
to mythology, they were named after
the city of Caryae in Laconia,
which had sided with the Persians
in the Persian Wars.

THE ARCHAIC AND CLASSICAL PERIODS: 750–336BC

The Archaic and Classical periods constitute what is frequently described as the golden age of Greek city-state civilization. Thanks to the evidence of classical writers, inscriptions, and other archaeological material, we are able to build up a multifaceted picture of these city-states. The culture, history, and politics of the period have shaped and continue to influence our modern world.

"Archaic" and "Classical" are terms used to describe the periods of Greek history between c.750–479 BC and 478–336 BC, respectively. These dates correspond to political developments, but are useful in pinpointing cultural developments, too. The Archaic period reveals the origins of the most prominent form of Greek civilization in the Classical period, the city-state (*polis*). As states formed civic cults – religious practices – of their own, they began to build sanctuaries relating to these cults, both in their city centres and on the borders of their territories. The religious processions that connected these two types of sanctuary, in combination with natural boundaries, helped define the areas controlled by these city-states. The city-state consisted of a territory comprising a peripheral agricultural zone and a city centre with an area for holding civic activities such as trials and political meetings. The city-state was closely identified with its citizen community, which shared obligations, privileges of participation, and a form of government. The associations of the city-state formed the background for most of the political and cultural developments of these periods. During the Archaic period, Greek civilization reached towards Italy and Sicily for purposes of trade and new resources, and settlements grew along the coast around the Black Sea. The Archaic period also saw the beginnings of democratic constitutions.

After the defeat of the Persians in the Persian Wars (490–479 BC), Greek identity became more consciously defined, as the differences between Greek and non-Greek ("barbarian") were emphasized. This period is frequently taken as the dividing point between the Archaic and Classical eras. The expulsion of the Persians from mainland Greece, the islands of the Aegean, and western Asia Minor opened the gates for Athenian expansionism. The Athenians formed the Delian Confederacy, which quickly developed into an empire. Throughout the 5th century BC, Athens became the focus of innovation in architecture, philosophy, and theatre. But the 5th century BC was also a time of conflict. The most important of these wars was the Peloponnesian War between Athens and its empire on one hand, and Sparta and its Peloponnesian and Dorian allies on the other.

After its defeat in the Peloponnesian War, Athens rebuilt its fortifications and political constitution, but was unable to re-create its empire. Over the course of the 4th century BC, as Athens, Thebes, and Sparta contended for ascendancy over Greece, the threat from the Macedonians in the north grew until their eventual defeat of the Athenians in 338 BC heralded the eclipse of "city-state" culture.

In the shadow of such events, the great historians Herodotus and Thucydides wrote their works, and Plato wrote the philosophical dialogues that raise questions still pertinent today. This period saw a golden age of the arts. Examples of sculpture and architecture still survive in the cities of the ancient world, while their legacy can be detected in modern architecture since the Renaissance.

Greeks on the Move

From the 8th century BC onwards, residents of the emerging city-states of mainland Greece formed communities in southern Italy and Sicily, and later, in the areas to the east of Greece. This process of colonization was linked to the development of trade across the Mediterranean and had an effect on the economic condition of the most important Greek cities.

Greek mobility

As traders and seafarers, Greeks were always on the move, so it was likely there would be some spread of their communities away from mainland Greece. "Colonization" in Greek terms represents a different phenomenon from the modern European process of a state sending out a group of settlers. The Greek process of colonization was less formal and could take place whenever a group of Greeks, whether traders, soldiers, or reprobates from their home city, settled in a given area. For instance, at the end of the 6th century BC, the Athenian general Miltiades ruled an area of the Thracian Chersonese as a fiefdom with a group of Athenian settlers. This place gradually became known to the Athenians as a colony. Accordingly, in the 350s BC, when threatened by the growing power of Philip II of Macedon, the Athenian politician Demosthenes described the Chersonese as Athens' property.

Cult ritual played an important part in the process of colonization. Colonists took with them fire from the sacred hearth of the mother city, in order to kindle a derivative flame in the colony. It was also usual for Greeks to consult the oracle at Delphi before beginning an expedition to found a colony, and a series of traditions relates the oracle's role in giving advice about the exact location and the population of such colonies. It is doubtful that these oracles were genuine: many of them were likely to have been inventions intended to justify the existence of the colony.

The colonists

The process of colonization frequently took place when disenfranchised groups of any one city-state moved to found a settlement or establish themselves in an existing settlement. Colonists could also be sent out by a community in order to rid itself of a surplus or undesirable population, as was the case with Taras in southern Italy at the end of the 8th century BC. A colonial settlement was founded there by a group of illegitimately born Spartans expelled from their home city after objecting to being deprived of their political rights. However, Sparta, the would-be mother city, retained close links with this settlement throughout the Classical period.

The colonies

Colonies arose most commonly at locations of commercial value. Thus the colonies at Taras and at the Chersonese were situated at points en route to supplies of grain. The same explanation could be applied to the Greek settlements on the Black Sea coast. In the second half of the 7th century BC, Milesians founded the first Greek settlements in this area. At the earliest point, these would have been trading settlements, with a population made up of both Greeks and indigenous residents. Archaeological discoveries reveal the effects of colonization on both Greek and local culture, with Greek pottery discovered alongside local treasures in the graves of the local aristocracy. Greeks in the colonies did not forget their homeland, with settlers in Sicily continuing to make dedications at the pan-Hellenic sanctuary of Olympia. Greek gods such as Apollo were worshipped in the colonies alongside local deities.

The colonization of the Mediterranean coincided with and was related to the development of trading links between Greece and its neighbours. From the end of the 9th century BC, the Greeks replaced the Phoenicians of the Levant as the most important trading partners of the Mediterranean, and trade became essential to the economies of Archaic and Classical Greece.

The beginnings of trade

The Greeks of the Mycenaean civilizations were heavily reliant on trade as a means of survival. The most prominent group of merchants in the Mediterranean between the 11th and the 9th centuries BC was the Phoenicians. They built up trading stations and then colonies in Cyprus, western Sicily, Spain, and North Africa, and reached the tin mines of Cornwall in England. Phoenician trade remained important throughout the Archaic

SCYTHIA
Tanais
Olbia
Panticapaeum · Phanagoria
Tyras
Istros
Pityus
Dioscurias
Tomi
Black Sea
Phasis
Odessus
Sinope
Mesembria
Amisus
Byzantium
Heraclea
Trapezus
Chalcedon
Abdera
Aenos
Sestos Cyzicus
Olynthus
Abydos
Potidaea
Thasos
Lampsacus
Mende
Torone
Corcyra
Assos
Ambracia
Cyme
Leucas
Chalcis
Phocaea
Eretria
Corinth
Athens
Miletus
ASIA MINOR
Aspendus

Agathe
Antipolis
Massalia
Nicaea
Emporiae
Po
Rhone
ITALY
Alalia
Rome
Danube
Neapolis
Hemeroscopion
Pithekoussai
Cyme
Posidonia
Metapontum
Apollonia
Elea
Taras
Heraclea
Sybaris
Croton
Himera
Mylae
Rhegium
Selinus
Zancle
Locri Epizephyrii
Acragas
Naxos
Gela
Catana
Camarina
Megara
Syracuse
Tigris
Euphrates
Mediterranean Sea

Barca
Apollonia
Tauchira
Cyrene
Euhesperides
Naukratis

**Greek Colonization
8th–6th Century BC**

● Ionian colonies

■ Dorian colonies

★ Aeolian colonies

period; however, from the 8th century BC, expansion ensured that the Greeks, and in particular the people of maritime cities such as Corinth and the cities of Euboea, became the most important trading partners in the Mediterranean. Through trading contacts, the Greeks adapted the Phoenician alphabet for their own purposes, a development contributing to the formation of the Greek alphabet as we know it today.

Trading posts

Trade and the search for valuable supplies of grain and metals were prime motivations of the Greek expansion from the 8th century BC onwards, and Greek colonies frequently served as trading posts (*emporia*). The first Greek colony in the West was on the Island of Pithekoussai off Campania. The discovery of Euboean pottery from around 770 BC, together with the discovery of iron-smelting works, suggests that the Greeks may have settled this area with the aim of gaining access to iron, which could be worked into weapons and armour. The Euboeans seem to have established trading posts at other places, such as Al Mina ("The Port") on the Orontes Delta in northern Syria and Naukratis on the Nile Delta. These societies differed from colonies in that they were entirely dedicated to the exchange of goods. The Greeks brought materials to Al Mina for transfer deeper into Asia Minor, and the mouth of the Orontes acted as the outlet for goods from inland Asia Minor.

Trade and agricultural reform

In Athens, the emergence of the state as a regulator of economic transactions is attested by the legislation of Solon, an Athenian politician and poet. In around 594 BC, Solon introduced a series of restrictions on commercial activity. These included measures affecting the export of goods, decreeing, for instance, that of all produce, it was permissible only to export olive oil. Solon seems also to have introduced legislation that both unified and divided the citizen-body of Athens. One of his acts was to abolish the group of sharecroppers known as the *hektemoroi*, men who rented land on the basis of returning one-sixth of its produce to the owner, possibly in return for protection by the powerful. Solon also abolished the custom of debt bondage, according to which citizens could fall into slavery if unable to pay debts. He also, however, introduced a four-stage class system that grouped men according to the amount of grain they produced each year. As political participation was based upon these class groups, political power became based on agricultural capacity.

In this way, Solon ensured that agricultural activity retained inextricable links with the class-system. This system reflected and perpetuated the idea that commercial activity was unsuitable for citizens. The stereotypical merchant of ancient Greece was a *metic*, a resident alien of a city who was liable to pay a tax in return for the privilege of residency. The Athenians preferred to think of themselves as farmers, rather than traders.

The locations of the Greek colonies founded across the Mediterranean in the Archaic period indicate the importance of the sea in the process of colonization. Most colonies were located on sea or trade routes and at places acting as ports.

The Ancient Economy

As trade developed in the Mediterranean over the 8th and 7th centuries BC, metal was introduced as a medium for exchange that would provide an accurate measure of value and a convenient means of storing wealth. Slavery was important in Mediterranean trade, and it played a significant role in the economies of ancient cities.

The origins of coinage

Archaeological and literary evidence indicate that coins were first utilized in western Anatolia. Measures of value pre-dated the existence of coinage: Homeric legends describe the use of cattle, slaves, and weapons. Over time, however, the Greeks, following the lead of the Egyptians and Mesopotamians, began to use metal as their predominant means of exchange. Initially, cumbersome iron spits were used as a means of transaction, and although the Spartans of the Peloponnese reputedly continued to use spits throughout the Classical period, the rest of the Greek world made use of coins.

In around 600 BC, coins came into use as a standard measure in western Anatolia, at the point where Greek cities of the Aegean coast and the inhabitants of the Lydian kingdoms of the interior of Asia Minor came into contact. Electrum was used for this earliest coinage, an alloy of gold and silver that occurs naturally in tributaries of the river Hermus to the west of the Lydian capital, Sardis. Electrum was soon replaced by coins of either silver or gold. The introduction of coins of tiny fractional value suggests that states began to recognize the value of coinage not only for inter-community trade, but also for small transactions such as the payment of mercenary soldiers.

The characteristics of coinage

The earliest coins consisted of lumps of standard weight, marked with a square punch-mark on the reverse. This form derived from the way the coins were minted. Molten metal was poured into

Our sources do not represent fully the kind of hardships that slaves or other manual labour who worked at mines must have undergone. On the contrary, this small clay plaque from Corinth illustrates a group of potters digging for clay while refreshment is lowered into the pit.

moulds to make blank discs; the discs were then placed on an anvil and struck with a die made from either toughened bronze or iron. As time went on, different states introduced characteristic markings on the front (obverse) of the coin, using motifs associated with their city. The Phocaians of Asia Minor used a seal (*phoke* in Greek), punning on the name of the city. The most famous Athenian coins depicted a helmeted head of Athena on the obverse, with an owl on the reverse together with the abbreviated name of the city. In later times, coins could be used as an expression of political events. Coins of the 340s BC from Taras show a boy raising his arms in appeal to a seated god identified by his trident as the sea god Poseidon; Poseidon inclines his head in sympathy. This image represented the appeal of the Tarantines, symbolized by the child, to the Peloponnesians, represented by Poseidon, for aid against enemy cities in Italy.

Coinage and politics

The imposition of coinage also became a means of imperialism. In the 420s BC, the Athenians issued a decree enforcing Athenian silver coins, weights, and measures upon the subject states of their empire. While this decree signified the political and economic dominance of the Athenians, it is unlikely that they were able to prevent the allied states from issuing their own coins; indeed, the minting of electrum coins was not banned. The Athenians took a great deal of pride in their silver coinage, linking its authenticity to their production of silver in Attica and, on a more abstract level, to the survival of their constitution. After a period of crisis at the end of the 5th century, when bronze and gold issues were used, the Athenians returned to silver coinage in the 4th century and passed a law outlining procedures for the testing of the currency.

The overseas slave trade

Two types of slave population were common in Archaic and Classical Greece. Indigenous slave populations, whose native land was under a state of occupation, existed in the Peloponnese. However, the majority of slaves in the Greek world were victims of war or civil strife, or had been sold on by merchants as part of a trade in slaves.

Slave-holding formed an important part of Greek society from the earliest times: the Linear B tablets from the Mycenaean palaces of the 13th to 12th centuries BC mention the use of slave labour within the kingdoms. The Homeric poems refer to male herdsmen and female domestic slaves, usually owned by the aristocracy. But it was only after the emergence of the city-state community that the division between citizen and slave became clearly defined. In the Archaic and Classical periods, slaves were more likely to be non-Greeks, and could take the name of their homelands. Hence "Carion" was a name for a slave of Carian origin. However, in the 5th and 4th centuries BC, the idea that non-Greeks were naturally subservient to Greeks exaggerated the divide between citizen and slave.

Enslavement

After Solon's reforms in Athens around 594 BC, citizens could no longer be sold into slavery in order to repay their debts, but there were other ways in which enslavement might take place. The first of these was through war: when the city of Melos was destroyed in the Peloponnesian War, its male inhabitants were killed and its women and children sold into slavery. Men captured by pirates were often enslaved. Another significant means of gaining slaves was through the slave trade, either by direct contact with eastern neighbours whose surplus populations were often sold or through unregulated and commercial activity. The historian Herodotus tells us the story of a certain Panionus of Chios, who made his living by procuring beautiful boys, castrating them, and taking them to Sardis and Ephesus, where he sold them at a high price. Panionus' activity was abruptly halted, however, when one of his eunuchs took revenge by forcing him to carry out castration on his own sons.

The uses of slaves

From the existing evidence, it is hard to tell whether slaves were an important source of agricultural labour. It is probable that hired labourers were used alongside slaves at the times of year that demanded the most intensive farm work. Slaves were just as likely to be employed in the cities as workers in the market place, while the city of Athens itself employed a group of Scythian archers who acted as a sort of police force. Probably the worst life for a slave was that of a labourer in the mines. In the late 5th century BC, it is known that some 20,000 slaves were employed in the Laurium silver mines in Attica, and these slaves escaped from the mines during the Spartan occupation of Decelea. Because of the racial mixture of much of the slave population of Greece, linguistic barriers hindered communication between slaves and consequently revolts were rare. However, this is not the case with the indigenous population of helots in Lacedaimonia, whose rebellious activities were a constant worry for their Spartan rulers.

The silver didrachm of the 4th century BC pictured here was worth 2 drachmai, an amount that an architect was paid in Athens in the 330s BC for one day's work. A manual labourer may have earned just one quarter of the amount.

Democracy Established

Important democratic innovations took place in the Peloponnese in the 6th century BC. It was in Athens, however, that democracy reached its fullest stage of development, moving from the rule of the popular assembly in the 5th century BC to the rule of law and sovereignty of the law courts in the 4th century BC.

ANCIENT GREECE   2500–146 BC

Ancient and modern democracy

Although modern democracy developed independently of the classical tradition, both the modern and ancient forms of democracy as a political system and ideology lay emphasis on the values of liberty and equality. However, the two have different modes of participation. Ancient democracy placed stress upon the direct participation of a limited group of citizens, through the attendance of popular assemblies. Modern democracies, for the most part, feature a larger citizen body, with government functioning according to the legislation of a parliament representative of the people.

Early democracies outside Athens

While democracy reached its furthest stage of development in Athens, the earliest democratic institutions were founded in Sparta, Athens' notorious rival in the 5th century BC. The Archaic Spartan constitution divided power between two kings, a board of elders, and the people. The

Pericles, the Athenian statesman, was said by the biographer Plutarch to possess almost perfect physical features, "with the exception of his head, which was rather long and out of proportion. For this reason almost all portraits show him wearing a helmet." The comic poets of Athens could not resist nicknaming him "pointy-head".

kings were from two families who, according to legend, derived from the sons of Heracles. The senior house, the Agiads, descended from the older son; the junior house, the Eurypontids, was descended from the younger. Citizens attended an assembly, which held the power to make decisions, although these could in practice be blocked by the kings and high-ranking officials (known as *ephors*). The Spartan constitution was anchored in these traditions, and popular government developed no further.

Democracy in Athens from the time of Solon

It was in Athens that democracy found its most fertile ground. In the 7th century BC, Athens was still ruled by a group of aristocrats, the *Eupatridai*, literally, "the well-fathered ones". Only gradually was their domination of Athenian politics reduced, and it never entirely vanished. Athenian democracy can be traced back to the reforms of Solon in 594 BC. What remains of Solon's poetry indicates that he took pride in having introduced written laws for the Athenians at their request. He introduced a four-stage citizen class system. Citizens qualified as such by virtue of birth and landownership. All citizens were allowed to take part in the popular assembly. The archonship, at that time the most important magistracy, was restricted to the two top classes. He also introduced a Council of 400, a senate that prepared the agenda for discussions which were to take place in the assembly. In this way, Solon located the focus of the political system upon the assembly and shifted the basis of qualification for office from aristocratic lineage towards agricultural production.

Kleisthenes' reforms

Despite these reforms, many aristocratic aspects of Athenian politics were untouched by Solon's legislation. Periods of tyranny and civil war continued until 507 BC, when Kleisthenes mobilized popular support and introduced a further series of democratic reforms. Kleisthenes was an Athenian politician from the famous Alcmaeonid family. His main action was to reorganize the citizenship body. Formerly, the Athenian citizen body had been divided upon the basis of four tribes native to the Ionians, with 100 representatives drawn from each tribe to constitute the Council of 400 introduced by Solon. But Kleisthenes deprived the Ionian division of political power and introduced instead 10 new tribes, of which each citizen was a member. It is possible that this reform aimed to disperse former spheres of aristocratic influence, although Kleisthenes' detractors argued that he aimed to augment the importance of his own Alcmaeonid clan through this new arrangement. Each citizen was also a member of one of the 140 *demes,* or villages, of Attica. Citizens were allocated to *demes* according to where they lived, and from 507 BC onwards their descendants retained identification with these *demes.* Many *demes* are known to have had an administration of their own: in this way, the Athenian democracy functioned on both city-state and local levels.

Ostracism

Kleisthenes is also believed to have introduced the institution of ostracism, first used in 487 BC. Each year, about halfway through the year, the question of the banishment of one citizen was raised in the assembly. If it were agreed that this should take place, an ostracism was held. Each citizen who wished to vote submitted to the assembly a piece of broken pottery (an *ostrakon*) inscribed with the name of the man he wanted banished. Providing that a total of 6000 votes were cast, the man whose name appeared on the largest number was banished for 10 years. This institution was initially intended as a safeguard against any man attempting to make himself tyrant; however, in practice, the institution was used as a means for powerful citizens to banish rivals. Evidence indicates that citizens were ostracized on the grounds of having collaborated with the Persians, religious offences, or, in one case, incestuous relations with his sister. The discovery of 190 *ostraka* dumped in a well, with the name of a prominent early 5th-century politician inscribed by only 14 different hands, has led to the theory that these *ostraka* had been prepared for circulation by conspiring opponents.

Athenian democracy after Kleisthenes

Democracy was far from secure in Athens after Kleisthenes. After his reforms, politics became divided upon ideological grounds, with one group of politicians appealing to popular support and offering further political reforms, and the other party appealing to the former aristocrats. While the

The Athenian assembly

The regular Athenian assembly in the Classical period took place on the Pnyx hill. Excavation of the site has revealed three stages in its development. Assemblies, perhaps from the time of Kleisthenes, made use of the natural contours of the hill, with the speaker addressing the crowd from the bottom of a semicircular auditorium. The second stage of development coincided with the introduction of payment for attending the assembly at the beginning of the 4th century BC, and included filling in the surrounding land to flatten the natural slope of the hill. The orientation of the speaker's rostrum (*bema*) was reversed to face inland, while the people faced the sea. In the third stage in its development, in the 340s BC, the capacity was enlarged from 6500 to 13,800.

leader of the aristocrats, Kimon, was outside Athens in 464 BC, the democrats seized the initiative. Under the leadership of Ephialtes, they removed the political powers of the board of former archons who met upon the hill of the Areopagus and who were drawn exclusively from the top two classes. Once this conservative body was rendered powerless, the floodgates were opened for more reforms, introduced during the period of Pericles' supremacy. The archonship was now opened to the third class of citizens, while the introduction of payment for service on the council, the fulfilment of a magistracy, or jury service meant that the poorer citizens of Attica were able to take a much more active role in democracy.

The development of Athenian democracy does not stop there. In the 5th century BC, sovereignty was possessed by the assembly. Democracy in the 4th century BC assumed a different shape, transferring sovereignty to the decisions of the law courts and written law. It is 5th-century BC democracy, however, that has most frequently captured the imagination of modern writers, as its development coincides with the most striking developments in other aspects of Greek civilization, such as architecture and drama.

Warfare in the 5th Century BC

War raged continuously in Greece throughout the 5th century BC. Many of these wars were minor border disputes, but two conflicts stand out in importance. The Greek victory in the Persian Wars led to the crystallization of Greek identity and was the origin of the Athenian imperial dominance of the Aegean Sea in the 5th century BC, while the Peloponnesian War eventually put an end to the Athenian Empire.

In 1955, the king of Greece uncovered a monument to Leonidas and the Three Hundred, who in 480 BC defended the pass of Thermopylae against the Persian invaders. This was located between the mountains and the sea, giving access to central Greece. The Persians, vastly superior in numbers, overcame the Greeks only after one Greek informed the Persians of an alternative route.

The origins of the Persian Wars

The Ionian Greeks inhabited western Asia Minor, an area that the Persian kings considered within their sphere of expansion. The Ionian Greeks had been subject to Persian rule since 546/5 BC. Further Persian expansion in the Black Sea area and Egypt led to increased taxation and conscription. Resenting this, in 499 BC, the Greek cities followed the Ionian revolt of the Milesian Aristagoras, deposing Persian governors and appealing to the Greeks of Europe for aid. The Athenians responded positively, sending an expedition that proceeded as far as Sardis, the headquarters of the Persian governorship, which they razed in 498 BC. The burning of the temple of Cybele incited the Persian king Darius to swear revenge.

After the subjugation of the Ionian Revolt in 494 BC, the Persians launched an attack on Greece in 490 BC. Having subdued many of the islands in the Aegean and forced the island of Euboea into surrender through a combination of force and treachery, the Persians landed at Marathon, on the north-east coast of Attica. But before they could advance to Athens, 10,000 Athenians and their Plataean allies advanced against the 20,000 Persians. After widening their line of attack, the Greeks ran towards the firing bows of the Persians. After success on their strong wings, the Greeks turned inwards to encircle the victorious Persian troops at the centre. The Persians fled to their ships, pursued by the Greeks.

Despite this defeat, the Persians were not deterred. The next Persian attempt of 480 BC was on a much bigger scale and was led by King Xerxes, son of Darius himself. Xerxes advanced across to Europe with some 100,000 men and up to 1200 triremes (ships). The Athenians, understanding the cryptic advice of the Delphic oracle to rely on "wooden walls" as a reference to wooden ships, built a navy with funds from the newly discovered mines at Laurium in Attica, and fled the city. Early Greek attempts at resistance were unsuccessful: the attempt to hold the pass between the mountains and the sea at Thermopylae in central Greece ended in the heroic death of the Spartan king Leonidas. But after the defeat of the Persian fleet at the battle of Salamis to the south of Attica and the defeat of the Persian infantry and cavalry at Plataea, the Persians began their retreat.

The aftermath of the Greek victory

After Plataea, the Spartans assisted the revolts from Persian rule of Chios and Samos, and helped defeat the Persian fleet off Cape Mycale in 479 BC. The Ionian Greeks appealed to the Spartans and then Athenians to liberate them from Persian rule. In a repetition of the events of 499 BC, only the Athenians responded positively. The Athenian response contributed to the emergence of the so-called Delian Confederacy, a league of states led by Athens. This alliance was based at the religiously significant island of Delos, and the pretext of the organization was to take revenge upon the Persian king in return for wrongs suffered by the Greeks. The Athenians went on to liberate cities of Asia Minor from Persian rule until the mid-460s BC. At some point in the middle of the 5th century BC, a peace agreement between the Persians and Greeks was made, but the rivalry for control of the Greek cities of Asia Minor was revived at the start of the 4th century BC. The continuing presence of the Persians as a threat of varying intensity served as a reminder to Greeks that their strength lay in pan-Hellenic unity.

The Peloponnesian War

The Peloponnesian War is the name given to a series of struggles between Athens and its allies on the one hand and Sparta and its allies of the Peloponnesian League on the other. The duration of the war saw some innovation in the techniques of warfare, but also coincided with a golden age of comedy and tragedy in Athens.

Rivalry between Athens and Sparta had been brewing ever since the formation of the Delian Confederacy by Athens and her allies. A period of

Athenian interventionism in the affairs of the Greek states is in striking contrast to Spartan introspection in the aftermath of the Persian Wars. From the period up to around 460 BC, the Spartans suffered trouble at home from their servile population, the helots, and disunity in their own organization of allies, the Peloponnesian League.

The historian Thucydides claims that the truest explanation for the outbreak of the Peloponnesian War was the Spartan fear of the growth of Athenian power. Athens' control of its allies grew between the end of the 460s BC and the outbreak of the Peloponnesian War. The treasury of the league was transferred from Delos to Athens in 454 BC, and by the start of the war its allies had become imperial subjects paying contributions to Athens. Thucydides describes complaints from the people of Aegina, Corinth, Megara, and Potidaea about Athenian intervention in their political affairs, adding further possible reasons for the outbreak of war.

The course of the war

At the outbreak of the war, when it became clear that the Spartans were about to invade Attic territory, Pericles advised the Athenians to withdraw within the walls of the city. This was an unorthodox means of resistance, and, partly as a consequence of the crowded conditions in the centre of Athens, a great plague broke out. At its worst in 430 BC, it damaged support for Pericles'

policy. Spartan attempts to invade Attica continued for the first five years of the war, until the Athenians captured a group of Spartan hostages on the island of Sphacteria in 425 BC.

After his death in 429 BC, Pericles' successors followed a more offensive war policy. However, after the death of the most belligerent generals on both sides, Cleon the Athenian and Brasidas the Spartan, the Peace of Nicias was agreed in 421 BC. The Athenians became involved in hostilities again after launching the overambitious Sicilian expedition in 415 BC. This ended in failure following the Spartan response to requests for aid from their Dorian kinsmen in Sicily. Between 413 and 404 BC, the Spartans placed a garrison within Attica at Decelea, making much of the Attic farmland inaccessible to the Athenians. The focus then shifted to strategic points on the Athenian grain-supply route from the Black Sea. The Peloponnesians built a fleet that blockaded Athens and caused its surrender after the battle of Aegospotami in 405 BC.

Thucydides' account of the Peloponnesian War focuses on many sociopolitical factors important to Greek life. Control of agricultural land and sea power; leadership, military tactics, and finances; ambition and the desire for revenge all were essential to the course of events during the war. Thucydides' insightful work is part of the cultural development that took place in Greece at the end of the 5th century.

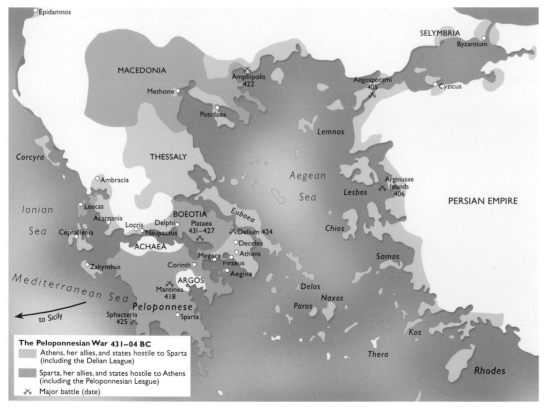

The Peloponnesian War 431–04 BC
- Athens, her allies, and states hostile to Sparta (including the Delian League)
- Sparta, her allies, and states hostile to Athens (including the Peloponnesian League)
- ✕ Major battle (date)

The Athenian policy in the Peloponnesian War was initially defensive, but also included a biannual invasion of the territory of Megara and raids on the Peloponnesian coast. The focus at the end of the war shifted towards the east, as the Peloponnesians attempted to cut off the grain supply of the Athenians, succeeding in their goal with their final victory at Aegospotami.

Philosophy and Religion

Over the course of the 5th century BC, owing to its cultural and political prominence, Athens became an important location on the circuit of the itinerant teachers of rhetoric, known as the Sophists. Socrates became famous for his conversations with these men, and his pupil Plato founded the Academy in Athens. While philosophy challenged many conventional beliefs, it did not undermine the vivacity of Greek religion.

Aristotle is best known as a philosopher who has been highly influential on Western thought. He started his career, however, as a member of the medical practice of the followers of Asclepius. His early interest in biology was reflected in his writings.

Zeus was the head of the gods and is illustrated on the right of this plaque reclining with a sceptre. In Homer, Zeus was represented as a "father" and as a "king", but never as a tyrant.

Philosophy in Archaic Greece

Philosophy is a Greek word, translated best as "devotion to knowledge". In its earliest stages of development, it did not require a specialized knowledge of any subject. Culture in the Archaic period had not undergone the process of specialization familiar to the modern world, where specific subjects become the domain of experts. The earliest Greek philosophers were poets simultaneously concerned with natural phenomena, cosmology, and theology. Philosophers of the Archaic period, known as the Pre-Socratics, attempted to explain natural phenomena and the world around them in comprehensible terms. Many of these philosophers came from the Ionian Greek towns of the west coast of Asia Minor, where Greek culture mingled with Near Eastern influences. Exposure to different cultural influences encouraged a more cosmopolitan outlook and a philosophical, relativistic approach to thinking. Perhaps the most radical of the Pre-Socratics was Xenophanes of Colophon. He lived in the 6th century BC and migrated to Sicily, where another centre of Greek philosophy was emerging. His relativistic approach to theology was novel. Stressing that human customs were based upon convention, he postulated that each culture recognized gods that reflected themselves, and so Thracians represented their gods as Thracians, Ethiopians their gods as Ethiopians, and so on. Xenophanes left a legacy of understanding that paved the way for the development of relativism and made important distinctions about the difference between belief and knowledge, a central tenet of Plato's *Republic*.

Philosophy in the 5th century and beyond

The skills of the Sophists were highly prized in the nascent democracy, where oratory and skilled debate were valued as tools for political participation. The most famous of the Sophists was Protagoras of Abdera, who was associated with the politician Pericles. Plato describes his contribution to the development of ethical theory, arguing that humans need institutions to survive in the world and that justice and temperance are necessary if these institutions are to survive.

Socrates' ethical system stressed the development of thought through discussion, and therefore he refused to write down any of his philosophy. The writings of Plato, Athens' most famous 4th-century philosopher, are based upon conversations supposed to have taken place between Socrates, Sophists, and other philosophers. Plato portrays Socrates as someone interested in discovering the usually flawed origins of others' beliefs. His investigations were based on the *elenchus*, a system of eliciting opinions and then proving these opinions to be flawed. Plato used this method as a springboard for his own ethical systems, including the ideal society described in his *Republic*. The work of Plato paved the way for the more empirical investigations of Aristotle, whose method had significance for much of Western philosophy.

Religion

Religion was part of everyday life in Greece. Each house had its own shrine, and sacrifices were made at important moments, such as just before a battle. These rituals and religious conventions played a vital role in the relationship between individuals and city-states.

The Greeks lacked any kind of sacred text or bible, and so there was no official religion that everyone had to follow, nor was there an idea of sin or redemption. Instead, Greek religion was embedded in the individual's consciousness through the myths concerning the "Pantheon" of 12 gods. The legends in the *Iliad* and *Odyssey* contributed to the formation of every Greek's idea of religion, portraying gods living in a society much like a human community. The list of these gods would sometimes vary, but usually included Aphrodite, Apollo, Ares, Artemis, Athena, Demeter, Dionysus, Hephaestus, Hera, Hermes, Poseidon, and Zeus. In addition to these, there were local deities who varied from state to state and groups of heroes who were even more specific to individual localities. These deities were associated with different aspects of daily life. Hephaestus, for instance, was the god of fire, blacksmiths, and artisans, while Demeter was the goddess of corn. Many of the festivals associated with her were celebrated at times of the year associated with agricultural activity: the Thesmophoria, a festival in her honour, took place in autumn before sowing time.

The relationship between individuals and the gods was important on both private and public levels. The most important part of Greek worship was sacrifice. Calendars of sacrifices were inscribed on stone and could include details of the time of year of sacrifice and the value of the animal to be sacrificed. After a sacrifice, the meat would be

Socrates

An Athenian citizen, Socrates was famous for questioning everything. Plato describes how his conversation and endless questions upset others' systems of belief. His encouragement of free thought annoyed many Athenians, and, in 399 BC, he was charged by three citizens with introducing new gods and corrupting the youth of Athens. In his trial, Socrates argued that his conversations were a blessing for the city, persuading people to perfect their wisdom. Although found guilty, he proposed that he be rewarded with free meals in the public building known as the *prytaneion*. Instead, his contemporaries condemned him to death by drinking hemlock.

shared among those present. Another important form of piety was expressed through cult oracles. Individuals would visit an oracle, such as the one at Delphi, for guidance on all kinds of issues. While many inquiries concerned religion or changes in cult practice, others were related to matters such as whether a wife might conceive a child on a journey or about health problems. Alternatively, city-states could claim the support of an oracle for a particular action, such as the foundation of a colony.

The Greeks used different cult names for their gods, which defined the nature or location of the worship. Hence Zeus *Agoraios* presided over the commercial life of the community, in particular that which took place in the *agora*, or market place. Greek religion was highly sensitive to social and political change: names such as *Eleutherios* (liberator) or *Soter* (saviour) were applied to the cult of Zeus to mark Athens' victory in the Persian Wars and survival after its defeat in the Peloponnesian War. Greek religion relied on human interpretation of responses and was associated with every aspect of life. For this reason, it remained a prominent part of daily life as it developed alongside the emergence of rational thought.

Poetry and Drama

Greek poetry was used in several contexts: on grave monuments, as prize inscriptions on vases, on dedications to the gods, and on victory commemorations. Poetry also played a didactic role in recording laws or even delineating ethics. The plays of the Classical period were written in verse and provided a publicly accessible medium for poetry.

Epic poetry

The term epic poetry describes verses that narrate stories about the deeds of heroes, men, and gods. Perhaps the best-known examples of epic poetry are Homer's *Iliad* and *Odyssey*. Epic poetry derived from an oral tradition of verse. Professional reciters, known as *rhapsodes*, were responsible for communicating this verse to the public. These men would recite the verses from memory at public festivals, where they would compete for prizes. Some of the earliest examples of writing coincide with this method of reciting from memory and consist of the scratched fragments of epic lines upon vases. These fragments mark the first stage in the development of a written form of poetry.

Lyric poetry

While some poets continued the tradition of Homer by composing epic narratives, others in the 7th and 6th centuries BC turned their attention to other forms of poetry, collectively known as lyric poetry. This was recited at harvests and wedding festivals, as paeans (songs of praise addressed to Apollo or Asclepius) and as dirges (lamentations), and at drinking parties. This type of poetry is usually classified as either monodic (solo) or choral. Monodic lyric poetry is believed to have originated in eastern Greece. Its subjects could include love, politics, war, and wine. Choral poetry was performed by a singing and dancing choir. This collective voice represented the community, and consequently most choral song was associated with worship. One particular type of lyric poetry was known as *dithyramb*, a

choral song in honour of the god of wine, Dionysus. During the Classical period, dithyramb was performed at several Athenian festivals.

Lyric poets held widely differing social attitudes. Some express a reaction against the aristocratic ideal of the epic poets. The poet Hesiod, a shepherd, wrote about the harsh life of farming in central Greece in *Works and Days*, while the poetry of the Ionian philosopher Xenophanes poked fun at the ostentatious dress-sense of his contemporaries. In contrast, during the 6th century BC, tyrants of Greek cities attracted poets to their courts, seeking to take advantage of the heroic ideal sometimes represented even in lyric poetry. The work of Pindar, reciting the achievements and strengths of aristocrats, falls into this category.

Poetry and politics

Throughout the Classical period, poetry was established as the medium through which sages could express models of heroic or ethical conduct. The Athenian law-giver Solon was thought to have inscribed his laws in prose, but many of the aims of his legislation, such as the appeasement of strife between rich and poor, are outlined in his poetry. The collective ideals of the community could be couched in poetry. In about 330 BC, the Athenian orator Lycurgus, finding that law provided insufficient guidelines for the conduct of a good citizen, quoted poetry in the prosecution of a citizen who had fled Athens during wartime. Drawing a contrast between the readiness of the accused to flee his city and nature's defence of its young, he quoted an unknown author: "Nor does the wild fowl let another's brood/Be laid within the nest that she has built". Although poetry in Greece was employed for political and religious purposes, its artistic merits remain appreciated today.

Drama

Greek drama was first and foremost a public art, and it is crucial to understand how it was performed to understand its importance to the community. Plays were performed in a public place and served to express, reinforce, and question certain social values, as well as drawing attention to society's shortcomings.

The origins of drama

Athenian plays were of three kinds: the dithyramb, the tragedy, and the comedy. Little survives of dithyramb today, but many comedies and tragedies survive more or less intact. The origins of Greek drama are obscure, but it may stem from a tradition of entertainment at festivals, suggested by depictions of Greek performers on vases from the 6th century BC. Greek drama owed many of its themes to Homer. Aristophanes parodied the myth of the abduction of Helen in Homer's *Iliad* by attributing the origin of the Peloponnesian War to the abduction of prostitutes. Greek dramatists made use of choruses, speeches, and conversations to put across different opinions to the audience. Plays could be set in the mythological past or the present.

Drama in context

Most surviving comedy and tragedy derives from Athens in the period after the Persian Wars. Groups of tragedies or comedies were performed at festivals, and afterwards the spectators would vote on which play they thought best. This popular element meant that plays often addressed subjects of particular relevance to their audience. However, tragedy rarely referred explicitly to specific events. Two exceptions to this rule are *The Capture of Miletus* by Phrynichus and *The Persians* by Aeschylus. Phrynichus' play was performed soon after the city of Miletus, helped by the Athenians in the Ionian revolt, had been captured and destroyed by the Persians in 494. This sensitive subject matter so upset the Athenians that they fined the playwright. In 472 BC, *The Persians* by Aeschylus (the earliest of the three famous tragedians, followed by Sophocles and Euripides) had a more appealing subject for the Athenians: the sea victory at Salamis in 479 BC. However, the theme of the tragedy is the defeat of the Persians, and, uniquely, the battle was described from the point of view of the Persian court, thus placing the tragic focus on the defeated enemy of the Greeks.

Over the course of the 5th century BC, tragedy evolved to address more complex issues, seen in Sophocles' most famous tragedy, *Antigone*, of 441 BC. In this play, following a civil war, Antigone, the daughter of the incestuous Oedipus and Jocasta, insists that her defeated brother must be buried in the customary way, to the objection of her uncle Creon, the tyrant of Thebes. Antigone's defiance of Creon's absolute authority leads the audience to dwell upon the position of women in

The Theatre of Dionysus at Athens

Theatres in Classical Greece were frequently located on the sides of hills, taking advantage of the naturally sloping sides for terraced banks of seating. The most important theatre of Classical Athens was situated at the base of the south slope of the Acropolis. As was common throughout the Greek world, the theatre was enclosed within a sanctuary of Dionysus. The processions forming part of the festival known as the *Great Dionysia* terminated here, transporting to the sanctuary the statue of Dionysus as well as loaves, phalli, bowls, and animals for slaughter. The assembly immediately after the festival would take place at the theatre.

Athens, as well as the clash of family interests against those of the State. Sophocles offered no explicit solutions to these contradictions: more questions were raised than answers given.

The poet Euripides sought even harder to question traditional Greek values. While his plays, like most Greek tragedies, were based upon well-known myths, Euripides introduced considerable elements of surprise and innovation to the familiar stories. This is illustrated in *Medea*, in which the title character, after being abandoned for a Corinthian princess by her husband Jason, takes vengeance upon him by killing their children. While Euripides did not invent this story, he did reinforce the shape of this myth through his dramatic retelling.

Aristophanes is the best-preserved writer of comedies in Greek antiquity. Again drawing on earlier myths, his comedies usually concern sex, the conflict between the young and the old or the rich and the poor, the difficulties of war, and the strange customs of the city compared to those of the countryside. With his deceptively whimsical themes, Aristophanes stood out for introducing to comedy serious artistic developments, as well satirical comment on politics and culture. In plays such as *The Acharnians* and *Lysistrata*, he made his leading characters critical of Athens' involvement in the Peloponnesian War.

The universal attraction of the questions posed and their adaptability to contemporary situations mean that the dramas produced in 5th-century Athens are still popular with modern audiences.

Imperial Life and Literature 82–3 ▶
Culture and Society 110–11 ▶
Literature 166–7 ▶
The Arts and Architecture 234–5 ▶

Art and Architecture

Greek art not only includes sculpture and vase painting, but also decorative jewellery, funerary decoration, and the design of buildings and monuments. A large proportion of sculpture was created by itinerant individuals or groups of workers, making it possible to outline trends that enveloped the whole Greek world, although, particularly in the sphere of vase painting, more local fashions can also be identified.

Illustrations on cups would sometimes reflect the contexts in which that vessel was used. This cup of c.450 shows a flute girl entertaining the aristocratic partakers in a symposium, or drinking party.

The Greeks developed more sophisticated methods of making bronze sculpture in the 8th century, using methods established in the Near East. Bronze statues created an entirely different effect to that of marble statues. Bronze reflects rather than absorbs light, and therefore a wider range of surface textures is possible. This shows particularly well in the sculpting of hair.

Vase painting

Many of the skills in vase painting developed during the Bronze Age were lost after the breakdown of Mycenaean civilization; however, the skill of pot making was never lost, and decorations rivalled those of the Bronze Age in sophistication. Between the 10th and 9th centuries BC, geometric designs were the most popular type of decoration.

Many of the earliest developments in Archaic Greek art were influenced by Eastern decorative arts, and plant and animal motifs replaced the geometric designs. The leading commercial city of the 6th century, Corinth, was also the leading innovator in pottery decoration.

Around 720 BC, a new technique known as "black figure" emerged in Corinth. The pot was made of naturally red clay. A black glaze matter was added where a figure was desired. Before firing, details could be scratched into the black glaze, then coloured with white or purple paint. By around 525 BC, Athenian potters, after imitating the techniques of the Corinthians, began to develop a method of their own, known as "red figure". In this style of decoration, the painter would decorate the pot with the black glaze solution in the places where a black background was required. After firing, red figures would appear in the areas where the black glaze had not been applied. The resulting red figure would then be decorated. This technique allowed for the development of more ornate decorations than the black-figure style.

Vases in the Archaic and Classical periods often depicted scenes from mythology and have been used to date the popularity of certain myths. From the mid-6th century BC, a cycle of Theseus' adventures appear on Athenian vases, suggesting that this mythical king of Athens was seen as a hero of the emerging democracy. Vases were used for storage and other practical purposes, but more decorative vases were given as prizes in sporting contests. Decorative pottery was also used by aristocratic drinking groups, forming part of the extravagant show of wealth that went on in these parties.

Sculpture

The other most prominent decorative art form was sculpture. From some time after 650 BC, the sculptures depicting skirted, striding male figures that were common in Egypt were adapted in Greece, and were known as *kouros* figures. Such figures, with their sleek, muscular forms, were not intended to represent individuals, but were an ideal type. They were used as offerings to the gods

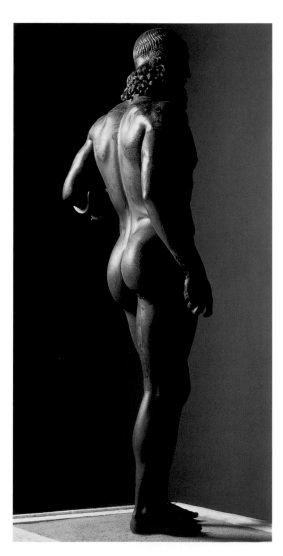

and as grave-markers. At the same time, a female version of these sculptures developed, known as the *kore* figure. These figures are more ornately decorated and sometimes hold out an offering.

In the Classical period, the standard *kouros* type vanished, and a new style of representation emerged. Characteristic features such as swinging hips, decorated hair, and turning heads all appeared on figurative sculpture in the period immediately after the Persian Wars. During the 4th century BC, sculpture is prominent in the adornment of grave-markers. These decorations are no longer representations of a generic human type, but illustrate personal achievements or interests, or wider civic virtues. One grave-marker depicts a little girl holding her pet doves, while another for an aristocratic horseman depicts him victorious on horseback. Greek sculpture reached its zenith in the Hellenistic period (336–146 BC), as sculptors developed more sophisticated means of decoration.

Architecture

Stone was used as a primary building material, and as a result a good deal of ancient Greek monumental architecture survives to this day. Buildings such as temples, sacred treasuries, theatres, and other public buildings were decorated with statues, giving rise to sculptural innovations.

A significant proportion of the ancient Greek monumental buildings that remain today had some sort of religious function as sacred treasuries – storehouses of dedications to the gods – or as temples. From the 6th century BC onwards, there emerged two clearly distinct styles of architecture for temples: the Doric and the Ionic. In the Doric style, columns were placed directly on the upper foundations of the building; Doric columns tapered upwards, with a convex curve. In the Ionic style, the columns were placed on bases which were then placed on the upper foundations. The columns were straight and more slender than the Doric, with more ornate bases and capitals.

The peak of the Doric style was reached in the mid-5th century BC. The Parthenon, a temple to Athena and a sacred treasury, was built upon the Acropolis in Athens in this style. In 447 BC, work on this building, which had originally begun before the Persian Wars, was recommenced as part of Pericles' plan to embellish the city with monumental architecture.

The decorative panels (*metopes*) on the front of the Parthenon illustrated popular scenes of Greek mythology, the battles of heroes and humans against Amazons, centaurs, giants, and Trojans. They represented the victory of the Greek forces of human reason over non-Greeks and monsters, and

perhaps alluded to the Persian Wars. The pediment illustrated divine scenes centring on Athena, representing her birth and her struggle with Poseidon for the control of Attica. The friezes illustrated scenes believed to be from the pan-Athenaic procession, which formed part of the four-yearly festival in honour of Athena and which culminated with the handing over on the Acropolis of the sacred robe (*peplos*) to adorn the statue of Athena *Polias* (Athena of the City). Viewed in their original position, around the top of the inner building (*ante*) of the Parthenon, they directed the viewer's attention to the central scene representing the delivery of the *peplos*.

Secular buildings

Pericles' building programmes were imitated in the second half of the 4th century BC by the politicians Eubulus and Lycurgus, who wanted to halt Athens' rapid decline after the destruction of the Second Athenian Confederacy in the Social War of 357–355 BC. During this period, work was carried out on temples and other religious buildings, but attention was also paid to the enlargement of the Theatre of Dionysus and the Pnyx (assembly place). Among the innovations was the construction of a huge warehouse for the storage of rigging, sails, and ropes for ships in Piraeus, known as Philon's Arsenal. Built between 337 and 330 BC, it was no ordinary warehouse, featuring provision for the maintenance of an air supply so that the nautical equipment would not moulder.

There is no doubt that innovation in Greek architecture advanced for practical as well as aesthetic reasons. However, the aesthetics of Greek sculpture and the Greek principles of proportion in architecture were to be highly influential during the Renaissance and beyond.

The Parthenon has served many uses over its 2500-year history. It was a church, then a mosque. With a new roof, it survived almost undamaged until 1687, when a gunpowder magazine stored in it exploded. Matters were made worse by the British aristocrat Lord Elgin's removal of the famous marbles. A new museum is to be built in Athens to display the sculptures of the Parthenon.

Architecture and Urbanism 84–5 ▶
Art and Architecture 98–9 ▶
Architecture 168–9 ▶
The High Renaissance 220–1 ▶

Science and Medicine

Greek science and medicine relied on the empirical method, forming rules on the basis of observation. This meant that scientific theories often arose in opposition to one another. Medical practitioners, too, were competitive and keen to promote their own theories.

Blood-letting and cupping was a form of treatment used up to the 19th century. This Greek plaque illustrates the blades, used to make the incisions for bleeding, and the cups, which were heated, and placed over the wound. As the air in the cup cooled, it drew blood from the wound as a result of the vacuum. The bleeding created would stop when the cup was removed.

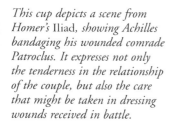

This cup depicts a scene from Homer's Iliad, *showing Achilles bandaging his wounded comrade Patroclus. It expresses not only the tenderness in the relationship of the couple, but also the care that might be taken in dressing wounds received in battle.*

The nature of Greek science

Greece in the Classical period for the most part lacked public libraries or laboratories, so the fundamentals of scientific thought were based on conversation and observation. Because of this, in its earliest stages science was inseparable from related disciplines such as philosophy, theology, and rhetoric. In his play *The Clouds,* Aristophanes illustrated one example of the fusion, or confusion, of the study of science and philosophy by parodying Socrates as a natural scientist, expert in "the air theory", who spent his time talking to the clouds. A more serious assessment of Greek scientists in this period recognizes their progress in theories of natural causality and rational proof, as well as scepticism about religious explanations of phenomena.

The natural sciences

One of the most important spheres of scientific progress in this period was in the field of explaining natural phenomena. In the 4th century BC, while doctors advanced rationalizing explanations

about the causes of disease, Theophrastus, who was a colleague of Aristotle, developed theories about the nature of plants. His work included classifications of plants depending on their parts, their qualities, the habitats in which they grew, and the course of their life. His work was based upon observation, and he was often critical of the ritual practices of "root cutters" and "drug sellers", who attributed the medicinal qualities of plants to magical powers. Although his work may have had some practical use, he was more concerned with rationalizing, observing, and defining phenomena than improving agriculture.

Mathematics and geometry

Architectural developments in the 5th and 4th centuries BC were heavily reliant on the progress of mathematics and geometry. One of the earliest thinkers to make important headway in the exploration of mathematics and geometry was the 6th-century BC Samian, Pythagoras. Tradition describes him as a philosopher, magician, and

priest, who dressed in a white robe, golden crown, and trousers. Through his mystical interest in numbers and music, he devised the geometric theory that bears his name to this day. He also contributed to the development of theories about musical harmony, and his school of successors, known as the Pythagoreans, continued his work. Other developments took place in the 5th century, with, for instance, the mathematician Zeno of Elea posing the "Achilles Paradox". This proposed that a quicker runner can never overtake a slower runner who starts ahead of him, as he must always first arrive at the place that the slower one has already occupied. His method of theorizing was based on attempting to contradict his contemporaries and illustrates well the competitive nature of the developing Greek sciences.

Medicine

Working along the same lines as the scientists and philosophers, Greek medical practitioners attempted to understand illnesses through reasoned explanation and observation, sometimes with an element of theology. Descriptions for the treatment of wounds sustained in combat are included in the Homeric epics, while the medical texts known as the *Hippocratic Corpus* provide evidence for the development of Greek medicine from the 5th century BC onwards.

While the Greeks may have learnt medical practice from the Egyptians, over time they outstripped them in skill. As early as the 6th century BC, Greek doctors were acclaimed throughout the Mediterranean. The Historian Herodotus relates a story in which the Persian king Darius I, in the late 520s BC, dislocated his ankle while dismounting a horse. The king immediately turned to Egyptian doctors; however, when these failed to cure his injury, he sought out a Greek doctor, Democedes, who was kept as a slave in his court. After curing the king, Democedes became highly esteemed at the court and renowned throughout the Greek world; he was even hired by the state of Athens.

Medical practitioners

In the 5th century BC, groups of medical practitioners became more common, the most famous of which was headed by Hippocrates of Kos. By the late 5th century BC, Hippocrates was well known as both a teacher and practitioner of medicine. The *Hippocratic Corpus* reveals the development of medical thought based on scientific enquiry and an interest in separating medical inquiry from the activities of faith-healers and other quacks. These works place a great emphasis on diet and exercise, and recognize the importance

Asclepius, the healing god

Although many of the writings of Hippocrates ruled out supernatural causes of particular diseases, Greek medical practice was inseparable from religion. The most famous healing cult in the Greek world was that of Asclepius, who had a sanctuary on the south slope of the Acropolis in Athens. Treatment was offered for all kinds of conditions, such as hair loss, blindness, lameness, parasitic afflictions, and snakebite. The patient would be sent to the shrine and would purify him or herself. Then, wearing a white robe and olive wreath, the patient would go to sleep on a bed of twigs or the hide of a sacrificial animal. He or she would receive dreams from the deity concerning healing. Frequently, medical treatment would follow the advice communicated in the dream.

of external environment in causing disease. The ancient interest in the ethics of medical teaching and practice is detailed in the Hippocratic Oath, which was used as a code of conduct by practising doctors and is one of the origins of the ethics of modern medical practitioners.

The Hippocratic approach is well illustrated in the treatise known as *The Sacred Disease*. This work is a critique of popular superstitions about the causes of epilepsy. The author is keen to stress that the disease is no more "divine" than any other disease, and he argues this by pointing to the fact that it is treatable. His argument does not preclude belief in the divine nature of disease: rather, he argues that no other disease has less claim to be divine than this one. The author's own explanation for the "Sacred Disease" is the flooding of the brain with phlegm – one of the four humours believed to affect health.

An interest in observation, cause, and diagnosis is evident in the theories of historians as well as those of the scientists of the 5th century BC, with Thucydides showing specific interest in medicine. He described in detail symptoms of the plague and aspects of contagion. Medical practice, we can deduce from his interest, was a well-respected practical and intellectual pursuit by the end of the 5th century BC.

Histories

The development of Greek historical writing is hard to trace, as most texts by Greek historians survive only in fragmentery form. Yet it is clear from the surviving works that the Greeks employed several important elements of historical inquiry. Research was carried out through conversation or through examination of written documents.

The origins of history

The first Greek historian was Hekataeus of Miletus, who played a part in the Ionian revolt. The celebrated opening words of his work reveal a great deal about the nature of his history: "I write these things, as they seem to me to be true. For the stories of the Greeks are many and ridiculous, it seems to me." Herodotus, writing in perhaps the 440s BC, described his work as *historia*, referring to the processes of questioning, enquiry, and research that he had gone through.

Herodotus' subject matter

Herodotus continued and extended interest in *historia*. Aiming to correct, update, and surpass the work of Hekataeus, Herodotus made the subject of his work the growth of the Persian Empire and the curtailment of its expansion by the Greeks. He takes as his starting point the causes of the conflicts between Greeks and non-Greeks. After surveying the traditional explanations of a series of mutual kidnappings, Herodotus goes on to give an account of the growth of Persian control of the Greek cities and the Ionian revolt. Herodotus' readiness to discuss the part played by women in social and political affairs is unique among ancient Greek historians.

While Herodotus' book is essentially an historical narrative, his interest in cause and consequence frequently leads his work into digressions in the form of fantastic tales. Sometimes Herodotus expresses his opinion on the truth of these stories, but more often he implies that they are important not because they were necessarily true, but because they were used as explanations of phenomena. For example, when relating the suicide of the Spartan king Cleomenes, Herodotus reports three alternative explanations for its cause, each representing some aspect of divine retribution. He reports that most Greeks thought it was punishment for his bribery of the Delphic oracle concerning the succession to the Spartan throne; that Athenians believed it was because he laid waste to some sacred ground at Eleusis in Attica; and that the Argives blamed it on his sacrilege in Argos. For Herodotus, therefore, the recording of beliefs and customs was essential to the recording and interpretation of actual historical events.

Greek depictions of Orientals show them dressed in flapped headdresses, patterned tunics, beards, and trousers, the latter of which was thought to be particularly un-Greek. This depiction was continued in Roman art, seen here in a Roman mosaic of the 2nd to 1st century BC. It illustrates the Battle of Issus between Alexander and Darius III, and is from the house of the Faun at Pompeii.

Herodotus the anthropologist

At other times, Herodotus provides anthropological insights, narrating the habits of the people central to the events he describes. The fourth book of his history is concerned with the Persian king Darius' attempt to subdue the nomadic Scythian tribes who lived to the north and east of the Danube and across southern Russia to the north of the Black Sea. Much of that book is spent describing the life and ways of the tribes resident in the lands beyond Scythia. He reports the existence of a race of peace-loving, bald-headed men, the Argippaians. These, he informs us, live from the produce of a particular fruit tree, which bears a fruit the size of a bean, containing a stone. This race also used the tree as a dwelling place. While ready to believe the authenticity of the lifestyle of the Argippaians, Herodotus was reluctant to give credit to the Argippaians' own stories of the existence of a race of men with the feet of goats or of others who hibernated. Herodotus' rejection of such stories provides the basis for the rationalizing scepticism of the next Greek historian whose work survives, Thucydides.

Thucydides

Thucydides was an Athenian general, exiled in 424 BC, who wrote a history of the Peloponnesian War. He left an unfinished work that went up to 410 BC. The history was intended as an "eternal possession", which would communicate Thucydides' belief about the human race: that it was reluctant to learn from its mistakes.

Thucydides is said to have burst into tears at a recitation of Herodotus' history. Whether out of pleasure or despair, the great impact that Herodotus' work had upon him is clear. Thucydides retained the theme of Herodotus' work – the build-up of power and its destruction – but, unlike Herodotus, he largely excluded women from his narrative. The most striking difference is that Thucydides aimed to remove the religious and mythological element of history and was more interested in the way that political beliefs or traits in human nature explained human action and the course of events. While this allowed for a more reasoned account of events, it led him to ignore the importance of cult practice as a motivating cause.

The content of the work

Thucydides' history begins with an account of early Greek history and introduces to the reader the importance of sea power, which was so vital for the growth of the Athenian Empire in the 5th century BC. The mixture of politics and war in the introductory section is representative of the

Thucydides' legacy

It is believed that Thucydides' history was read by later Greek and Roman historians, perhaps by the philosophers Plato and Aristotle, and also by later rhetoricians and critics. One later commentator of the 1st century BC, Dionysius of Halikarnassus even goes so far as to criticize Thucydides' style of writing as poetic, convoluted, and compact. Such comments are fair, but these very attributes allowed Thucydides to construct a history that analysed in depth the causes not only of the Peloponnesian War, but also of war in general, and the desire for power latent in human nature.

contents of the rest of the work, and it continues with his in-depth and two-layered analysis of the causes of the Peloponnesian War.

Much of the history consists of military narratives of the Peloponnesian War. These narratives are arranged in independent but related sections. For instance, the story of the disastrous Sicilian expedition of 415–413 BC seems independent from much of the rest of the history, but it stresses the usual themes of the work: the importance of naval technology, human greed, expansionism, and a failure to learn from the past. The gravity of Thucydides' writing reflected the very serious nature of his subject – war. His uses of documentary evidence and his focus on methodical theories of causation, human nature, inevitability, and the value of historical writing itself influenced the themes chosen by later historians such as Polybius.

The speeches

One of the most important elements of Thucydides' history is its speeches; their value cannot be overestimated. He states at the beginning of his history that the speeches reported "the necessary things" for the speakers to say, while adhering as closely as possible to what was actually said. He took the opportunity to adapt the content of the speeches for his own purposes, so if he wanted to paint a favourable picture of a character, he gave the impression that that character possessed foresight by ensuring his predictions turned out to be true. Pericles' funeral speech, a version of which was given at the funeral of those who had died in the first year of the Peloponnesian War, is frequently cited as one of the defining orations of Athenian democracy. In this speech, Pericles outlines his notion of the ideal community as one inspired by a combination of individual freedom and heartfelt duty to serve the State, an ideal shared and adapted by many modern Western liberal thinkers.

Warfare in the 5th Century BC   32–3 ▶
Republican Culture   72–3 ▶
Prehistoric Greece   20–1 ▶
Education and Learning   164–5 ▶

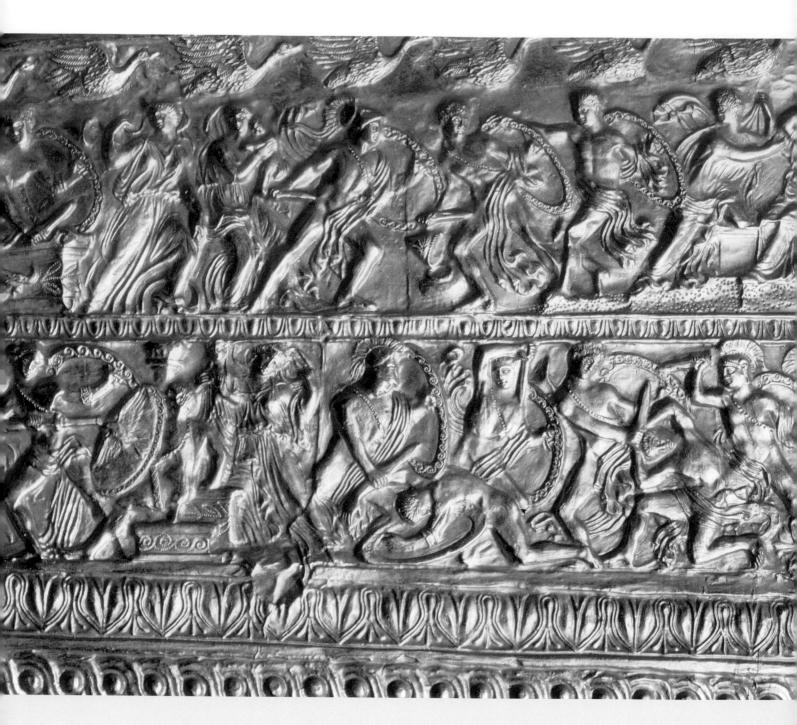

In 1977, three 4th-century
tombs were excavated at Aegae,
the burial place of the kings
of Macedonia. The frescos and
offerings in gold were of the
highest quality, and they
encapsulate the spirit of
conquest which contributed to
the Macedonian subjugation of
central Greece in the 330s BC.

THE HELLENISTIC PERIOD

The conquests of Philip II of Macedon had far-reaching consequences. By imposing Macedonian power over all Greece, Philip belittled the importance of the inter-state relations of the city-states of Greece. Thus his conquests marked the beginning of the eclipse of the city-state system which had been the most important method of political organization in Greece since the start of the 8th century BC.

The Hellenistic period is generally said to begin in 336 BC with the death of Philip II, king of Macedonia. From the 350s BC, Philip led Macedonia to a position of supremacy. Philip had taken advantage of Greek disunity to establish a hegemony over Greece that reached new peaks with his defeat of the Athenians at Chaironea in 338 BC. Alexander the Great, Philip's successor, strengthened the Macedonian grip over Greece and embarked upon a conquest of the Persian Empire. When he died in 323 BC, Alexander left an empire that stretched from Albania to India. Over the next 50 years, a struggle to win control of as much of this empire as possible ensued between Alexander's successors. By 276 BC, the Mediterranean was divided into three territorial states, each with a dynastic monarch. The Antigonids had control of the area known as Macedonia now including Greece, the Ptolemies held Egypt, and the Seleucids held the area that included Syria, Iraq, and Iran. Macedonia was the last of the areas to settle under a dynasty, that of Antigonus II Gonatas, who took control in 277/6 BC.

After the death of Philip, much of mainland Greece was subject to the rule of the Macedonian monarchy, and Greek inter-state diplomacy was no longer determined by relations between individual city-states. But another type of political organization now rose to prominence: the inter-state confederation. Of these, the Aetolian League grew in importance after the Aetolians of west-central Greece had been instrumental in the defeat of a Gaulish invasion in 280/79 BC. Another rival to the Macedonian control of Greece was the Achaean League, which became powerful in the 240s and 230s BC. However, after receiving Macedonian aid against the Aetolian League in the 210s BC, it allied with Macedonia, although under pressure it joined the Romans against Macedonia in 196 BC. Despite their evacuation of Greece in 194 BC, the Romans returned to make Macedonia a Roman province by 149/8 BC.

The Hellenistic period is often perceived as the story of the decline of Greek civilization to make way for Roman expansion. However, as interest in the period grew during the 19th and 20th centuries, it became clear that the era was significant not only as a link in the development of the ancient world, but also as a period of cultural innovation and the dispersion of Greek culture outwards from the Mediterranean basin. Some historians have seen the period as the time when Greek and Near Eastern cultures intertwined to form the background from which Christianity would arise. Although the military power of the Greek city-states contracted, the Greek way of life extended its geographical limits: a mark of this cultural expansion was the fact that Greek became the language of government from the shores of the Mediterranean to the borders of India.

The period saw intense activity in art, architecture, philosophy, and science. Alexandria became the centre of the scholarly world with the creation of its museum and library. Athens also remained important as a home of scholars and philosophers, and hundreds of small religious, professional, and social organizations developed there. Innovations in sculpture and technology took place in the wider Greek world. The Hellenistic period featured development, rather than decline, of lifestyles and political organizations, as the city-state was eclipsed rather than destroyed.

Alexander the Great

King Philip II of Macedon, under whom Macedonian power expanded into central Greece, was assassinated in the autumn of 336 BC in an atmosphere of domestic conflict and sexual jealousy. His son Alexander was proclaimed king, and he consolidated his position through a policy of military expansionism and by murdering his rivals.

Early life and the securing of Greece

Alexander III of Macedon was the son of Philip and Olympias, and was Philip's favourite for the succession. He was educated by Aristotle, and in his youth emerged as a precocious military talent.

After the murder of Philip, the Athenian assembly voted the privilege of a gold crown for Philip's assassin and entered into negotiations with one of Philip's former generals, Attalus, about over-throwing Alexander. Alexander's first task on the international front was to secure recognition of his succession throughout Greece. He marched south against the Thessalians, who soon admitted defeat and proclaimed Alexander their leader (*tagos*), as they had done earlier for Philip. He was also proclaimed leader of the League of Corinth, an organization of Greek states founded by Philip for the purpose of war against the Persians. In 335 BC, the Thebans rebelled against Macedonian leader-ship, but Alexander oppressed them by destroying their city and enslaving the population. Having established his supremacy of Greece, Alexander turned his attention to the war against Persia.

Alexander's Persian expedition

The idea of a pan-Hellenic expedition against Persia was not new. In the 4th century BC, the Athenian intellectual Isocrates urged the Greeks to proclaim Philip of Macedon leader of such an expedition against Persia. Philip made plans, seeing a conquest of Asia Minor as a potential source of wealth; when he died in 336 BC, a force of 10,000 men had already crossed the Hellespont. In 334 BC, Alexander led his force in the same direction. Consisting of over 30,000 infantry and 5500 horse-men, it was probably the largest expedition ever to depart from Greece. On landing at Elaious, he began by paying sacrifice at the tomb of Protesilaus, the first of the Greek heroes in the Trojan war to set foot in Asia Minor. By this sacri-fice, Alexander proclaimed his ambition to avenge the former misfortunes of the Greeks in Asia Minor.

Alexander first met the Persians in 334 BC at the river Granicus in north-west Asia Minor in a pitched battle. After a rout of the Persian cavalry, the Macedonian horsemen surrounded the foot soldiers of the Persians and their mercenaries. In

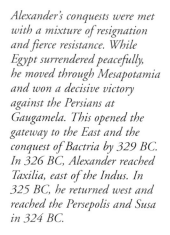

Alexander's conquests were met with a mixture of resignation and fierce resistance. While Egypt surrendered peacefully, he moved through Mesapotamia and won a decisive victory against the Persians at Gaugamela. This opened the gateway to the East and the conquest of Bactria by 329 BC. In 326 BC, Alexander reached Taxilia, east of the Indus. In 325 BC, he returned west and reached the Persepolis and Susa in 324 BC.

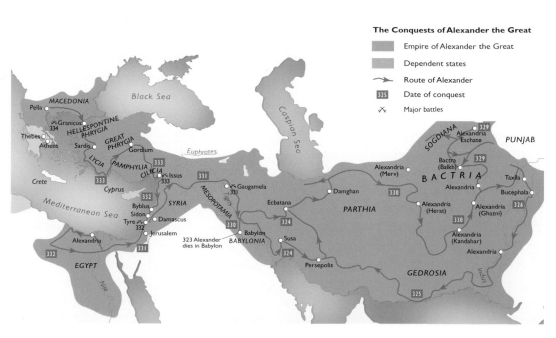

The Conquests of Alexander the Great

- Empire of Alexander the Great
- Dependent states
- → Route of Alexander
- [325] Date of conquest
- ✕ Major battles

Alexander's march across Asia Minor, Greek and non-Greek cities were treated in the same way: new governments were installed, and cities retained independence as long as they remained faithful to Alexander. By emphasizing its pan-Hellenic aspects, he attempted to secure unanimous Greek support for the expedition.

Alexander in the East

Alexander's expansion into Asia continued after Granicus, as he moved inland south towards Phrygia, Pamphylia, and Lycia. Having made Cilicia his base of campaign in 333 BC, he lured the Persian army to Issus, the town north of the coastal plain on the way to Syria. Alexander was able to reverse early losses, making use of the narrowness of the plain by instigating a cavalry charge from the right, prompting panic in the Persian lines. After victory at Issus, the cities of the eastern Mediterranean, Sidon and Byblus, surrendered. The ancient Phoenician port of Tyre on the Levant refused to capitulate and was captured by siege. Egypt surrendered peacefully in 333/2 BC, after which Alexander's forces turned to the East. They marched on Mesopotamia, and in 330 BC took Babylon and Persepolis, the native residence of the Persian kings in Persis. This city was destroyed in a fire allegedly started at a great drinking feast. But Persian resistance was not yet over: a provincial governor Bessus murdered Darius, proclaimed himself king of kings, and began a revolt against the Macedonians. Alexander appointed governors of his own to deal with this threat. He turned his attention to a march through Asia, crossing the mountains of the Hindu Kush by 327, reaching the Punjab by 326,

and making offerings to the gods at the mouth of the river Indus in summer 325 BC.

Forced to turn back by a revolt of his troops, Alexander left India for Persia in August 325. On his return, he went ahead with a purge of his generals, thus venting his anger at the curtailment of the Indian expedition on those around him. Despite failing health, he planned an expedition against the Arabians who had refused to honour him as a god. His hopes were dashed when he fell ill at a party hosted by one of his generals on 10 June 323 BC. His body, wounded and exhausted by constant warfare, was unable to ward off malaria.

Alexander's monarchy

Macedonia was an absolute monarchy under Alexander. Although the king was the traditional head of the Macedonian state, Alexander added refinements to the position. For instance, Alexander included the Persian tunic, diadem, and girdle in the dress of the king. By fusing Macedonian and Persian elements of royal government and making his monarchy acceptable to East and West alike, Alexander set a trend for the monarchs of the Hellenistic period.

By magnifying his victories over Indian tribes, and by founding a substantial number of cities across Asia, Alexander made himself the object of cult worship. The worship of Alexander was long lasting and was owed partly to the stories now known as the "Alexander Romance". These probably derived from a Greek source, and exist in a range of traditions, from Hebrew to Hungarian. The longevity of these myths is evidence of the success of Alexander's self-mythologizing.

Warfare in the 5th Century BC   32–3 ▶
Histories   42–3 ▶
Greece between Alexander
and the Romans   48–9 ▶
The Arab Conquests   96–7 ▶

Greece between Alexander and the Romans

Alexander's campaigns had the twin consequences of putting an end to the dominance of the Achaemenid clan in Persia, which had ruled the Near and Middle East for two centuries, and curtailing the importance of the Greek city-states in politics. Their replacement, however, was far from stable.

The Empire after Alexander

The period after Alexander's death to 276 BC saw a constant struggle between his successors to grab what they could of his vast empire. Soon after his death, a settlement at Babylon confirmed Perdiccas, head of Alexander's cavalry, as regent. The heirs to the throne were the mentally impaired and physically weak Philip Arrhidaeus, son of Philip II, and Alexander IV, Alexander's son by his Bactrian wife Roxane. By virtue of his Macedonian mother, Philip Arrhidaeus was the popular choice as heir among the Macedonian army. But for now, the power was out of the hands of the royal successors. Perdiccas the Regent offered to revive Alexander's policy of expansion, but his soldiers rejected this proposal. From this point, the age of Macedonian expansion was over. Perdiccas set about distributing areas of the Empire for the governorship of Alexander's former generals. Antipater was allocated the generalship of Greece, Ptolemy was given Egypt, Antigonus the One-Eyed was given western Asia Minor, and Lysimachus received Thrace. These four, along with Eumenes, sent to establish Macedonian control in Cappadocia and Paphlagonia in Asia Minor, became the most important men in the struggle for power.

The conflicts that began with the disputed succession of Alexander led to the division of his former empire between successor monarchs. This map shows the strongholds of the first generation of monarchs: Lysimachus (died 281 BC), Antigonus the One-Eyed (died 301 BC), Ptolemy (died 282 BC), Seleucus (died 281 BC), and Cassander (died 297 BC). Greece changed hands but witnessed the rise and fall of the Achaean and Aetolian Leagues before the Roman domination.

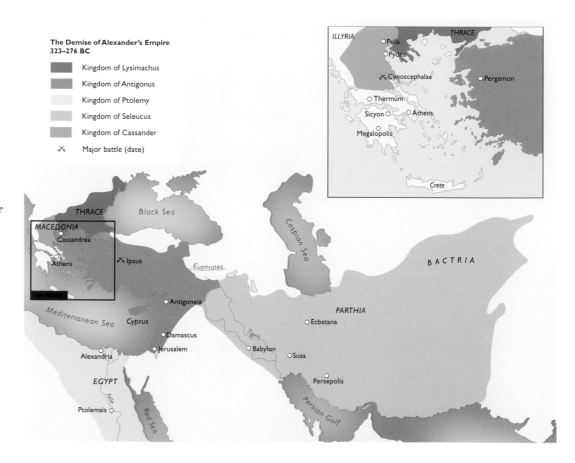

The Demise of Alexander's Empire 323–276 BC

- Kingdom of Lysimachus
- Kingdom of Antigonus
- Kingdom of Ptolemy
- Kingdom of Seleucus
- Kingdom of Cassander
- ⚔ Major battle (date)

The Wars of the Successors

The spark that began the Wars of the Successors naturally concerned Alexander. Ptolemy diverted Alexander's funeral cortege towards Egypt, claiming that Alexander had expressed a desire to be buried at his father's shrine. After resisting an invasion by Perdiccas, Ptolemy formed an alliance of generals against the regent. Soon afterwards, Perdiccas was murdered by his demoralized officers. By 316 BC, Antigonus the One-Eyed emerged as the dominant general, while his son, Demetrius the Beseiger, conquered the Greek states through siege warfare. Their success in conquering Greece, however, served to divide rather than unite. In 306 BC, after Antigonus had declared himself king, he was followed by Ptolemy, Seleucus, Lysimachus, and Cassander (the son of Antipater). In 301 BC, Antigonus' death at the battle of Ipsus in central Phrygia ended his dreams of succession. Between 301 BC and his death in 283 BC, Demetrius the Beseiger attempted to re-establish his father's position, but with little success. Only Antigonus Gonatas, Demetrius' son, established Antigonid power over Macedonia. With the Ptolemies holding power over Egypt and Seleucus over the area covered by Syria, Mesopotamia, and Iran, monarchy was established across the Mediterranean.

The Aetolian and Achaean Leagues

As the Hellenistic monarchies grew in power, Athens and Sparta formed an anti-Macedonian alliance which lasted until their defeat in the Chremonidean War by the Macedonians in 262/1 BC. But other states came together in unions made up of various city-states or tribal communities.

The Aetolian League was based on the tribal organization of the Aetolians centred at Thermum in west-central Greece. The Aetolian defeat of the invading Gauls at Delphi in 280/79 BC gave them prestige, and it also helped them to establish control over the Delphic Amphictyony, the organization devoted to the upkeep of the sanctuary of Apollo at Delphi. The festival of Zeus Soteria was reorganized into a pan-Hellenic, four-yearly festival, as a commemoration of their victory and in order to publicize their control of Delphi. Attracted by this success, distant states such as Chios and Vaxos in Crete joined the League. This increased membership allowed the organization to be an important player in the political development of Greece in the 3rd century BC.

Always rivals of the Aetolians, the Macedonians declared the Social War of 220–217 BC on behalf of their so-called Hellenic League, accusing the Aetolians of plundering sites in Greece. The Macedonians shocked the Aetolians by ravaging

Pyrrhus

Between 319 and 272 BC, Pyrrhus was the king of the Molossi, a group of peoples forming a tribal state in Epirus, in north-west Greece. Famous in antiquity for the greatness of his military innovation and bravery, Pyrrhus put an end to the dynastic troubles of the Molossi, conquered southern Illyria (modern Albania), established Ambracia as the capital of the state, and built fortifications and theatres. The origin of the so-called "Pyrrhic victory" lies in his notoriety for military successes achieved at high cost to his own army. He assisted the Tarantines in their struggle against Rome, and he invaded Macedonia and was briefly king there in 274 BC. Unable to consolidate any of his attempts, Pyrrhus died after being struck on the head by a tile hurled from a roof.

their federal sanctuary at Thermum. Never devoted to Greek independence for its own sake, the Aetolians became allies of the Romans in 212/11 BC. However, as a reaction against the restraint of their independence after the Second Macedonian War in 196 BC, they joined the Seleucids against Rome; they were never prominent again.

The original Achaean League, an organization based in the Peloponnese, was dissolved by the Macedonians in the early 3rd century BC, but was revived in 281/80 BC. The League became important in the mid-3rd century BC, after the Sicyonian Aratus brought his home city into the League. From 245 BC, he led the Achaean Confederacy in opposing Macedonian control, liberating Corinth and Athens. However, he joined with Philip V of Macedon for the Social War of the Hellenic League against the Aetolians. After the Romans began to appear in force in Greece, the Achaeans transferred their support to Rome. The Romans helped the Achaeans extend their control over the Peloponnese, but the alliance fell apart after the Spartans were dissolved into the League: their secession in 149/8 BC led to the Achaean War and the destruction of the League by Rome.

The Confederacies of the Greeks showed that they were capable of innovative political organization that resisted monarchy. The members of the Achaean League shared coinage and laws, as well as an assembly, common councils, and judges. An annually elected general served as commander in the battlefield. Thus, while the Hellenistic world saw a great expansion of Hellenism, the land mass of Greece itself remained an energetic centre of activity and political innovation.

Warfare in the 5th Century BC   32–3 ▶

Alexander the Great   46–7 ▶

Greece as a Roman Province   50–1 ▶

The Arab Conquests   100–1 ▶

Greece as a Roman Province

The coming of Rome happened in stages, by means of both diplomacy and warfare. Taking advantage of internal and external pressures on the Ptolemaic and Seleucid kingdoms, and the occasional readiness of the Greek cities and federal states to form alliances with it, Rome was able to establish absolute domination over Greece by 146 BC.

Early contacts

Military expansion was not the first contact that the Romans had with the Greeks. The presence of Greeks in Campania (west-central Italy) and the flourishing of trade routes meant that the Romans were exposed to Greek civilization from an early date. It was in defence of these trade routes that Roman intervention began in Greece.

Roman intervention in Greece began in the 280s BC, when Rome began to place colonies near the western shore of the Adriatic, thus opening the way for more Roman trade links with Epirus and Greece. From 280 BC, the Romans suppressed the rebellious movements of the city of Taras in southern Italy. With the fall of Taras in 272 BC, the Roman conquest of Italy was complete. The first direct Roman military intervention east of the Adriatic Sea was in the First Illyrian War (229/8 BC). This came as a response to the growth in power of the Illyrian kingdom under Queen Teuta, whose expansion became a threat to the stability of Roman communication and trade in the Adriatic Sea. A successful campaign left the Romans with a group of friendly states in the Adriatic area, and soon the Romans began to make defensive alliances with Greek cities on the east coast of the Adriatic. Their admission into the Isthmian Games of 228 BC indicated that Greek states accepted the Romans as honorary Greeks.

The First and Second Macedonian Wars

The next major Roman involvement on the Greek stage was in the First Macedonian War (211–205 BC). At a conference in Naupactus in 217 BC called to end the so-called Social War, the Aetolians expressed concern that the power in control of Italy posed a threat to Greece. From this point, according to the historian Polybius, Rome entered into diplomatic considerations whenever Greek leaders made war or peace with each other.

Philip V put an end to the Social War, and in 215 BC turned his attention west by making a pact with Rome's enemy Hannibal. In turn, in 211 BC, the Romans allied with the Aetolians. In the ensuing war against Philip V, the Romans showed their readiness to plunder and to enslave populations. The war ended after the Aetolians withdrew their effort; in the ensuing Peace of Phoenice, Athens and other Greek states were listed in a treaty as allies of Rome. It was the establishment of this relationship that gave Rome a reason to make demands in relation to the Macedonians' behaviour in Greece.

In late September 201 BC, two uninitiated Acarnanians wandered into the temple of Demeter at Athens at the time of the religious ceremonies known as the Eleusinian Mysteries, and the Athenians promptly put them to death for their sacrilege. The Acarnanians, allies of Philip V, appealed to the Macedonians, who in turn ravaged Attica. By this time, the Romans had already demanded that Philip not make war on the Greek cities, a demand made either from fear of Philip V or through covert expansionist aims. Philip had ignored the demand, and Rome intervened in the Second Macedonian War (200–197 BC). Throughout this conflict, the Romans maintained that they were fighting for the "Freedom of the Greeks" from Macedonian rule. After the defeat of Philip in a pitched battle at Cynoscephelae in 197 BC, the Romans proclaimed the freedom of the Greeks at the Isthmian games of 196 BC. While this freedom was subject to the constraints of Rome, and the declaration a piece of theatrical propaganda, the defeat of Macedonia did put an end to absolute Macedonian domination of the states of central Greece.

As the Romans asserted their power over the Aegean, the Seleucid monarch Antiochus III established dominance of coastal Asia Minor. Antiochus' crossing of the Hellespont and his contact with the Aetolians, combined with a rumour that he harboured ambitions to invade Italy, led to a renewal of the Roman presence in Greece from 192 BC. Between 191 and 188 BC, the Romans reconstituted the Delphic Amphictyony, under their own leadership. The defeat of the Seleucid king and his Aetolian allies by 189 BC served to reinforce Roman authority over Greece. From this time, the Romans subjected the Greek states to their ally King Eumenes of Pergamum, and the Romans were now able to deal with all Greek political problems in their own interest.

The Romans in Greece

The efforts of Perseus, Philip V's successor to the Macedonian throne, to revive Macedonia's power in Greece, combined with unrest in Greece, led to the outbreak of the Third Macedonian War in 171 BC. By 168 BC, at the battle at Pydna, Perseus was defeated, the Macedonian monarchy was abolished, and Macedonia was split into four republics. In 149 BC, a pretender to the throne led a revolt against Roman rule. However, this was quickly crushed and Macedonia reduced to a Roman province in 149 BC. Similarly in 146 BC, after the repression of the Achaean League, the Roman general Mummius razed Corinth, killed most of the men in the city, and sold the women and children into slavery. Democracies were abolished, and wealth became the requisite to qualify for government. Greece was placed under the rule of a Macedonian governor from Corinth, and it was made a separate province known as Achaia in 27 BC.

When Flamininus, the Roman general who defeated Philip V at Cynoscephelae, evacuated

Polybius

Vienna's neoclassical parliament building is flanked by statues of the great historians of antiquity. Polybius, from Megalopolis in the Peloponnese (c.200–118 BC), wrote a history of Rome's rise to power. He was active in the Achaean League as an envoy and was later involved in installing the Roman settlement of Greece in 146 BC. While his history shared with Thucydides' work a focus upon politics and war, he also included clear distinctions between "causes" and "beginnings", and observed the importance of chance on historic events. His legacy includes an image of Greek decline in the 2nd century BC and the power that the mixed constitution gave to Rome.

Greece in 194 BC, he took with him many works of art and treasure to mark his triumph. Similarly, the Roman defeat of the Macedonians in the Third Macedonian War brought the contents of the Macedonian Royal Library to Rome. As a result of such plundering, many portray Greece as a desolate place in the 2nd century BC. The historian Polybius describes this period as a time of depopulation and abandoned cities. In some ways this reflects a true picture; however, it did usher in the tremendous popularity of Greek culture with the Romans.

Carthage fell to the Romans and was razed at the same time as Corinth. In 1817, the painter J. M. W. Turner captured his impression of the destruction of Carthage in a scene bathed in the light of the setting sun.

Hellenistic Civilization

Greek civilization underwent considerable development in the period from 336–146 BC and beyond, and the Hellenistic period was characterized by remarkable social and cultural achievements. Many of the phenomena seen during this period pre-empt those that were to develop in Rome, and they illustrate the spread of Greek-style civilization across the Mediterranean.

The altar of Zeus found at Pergamum contains this scene of Gigantomachy, the fight against giants. This theme was a familiar one, appearing also on the metopes of the 5th-century Parthenon on the Acropolis, and might be interpreted as the visualization of the struggle of the known and reasonable against the unknown and irrational.

Technology

The expansion of the Greek world in the Hellenistic period led to new problems that inspired new solutions. Alexander, for instance, was particularly interested in canals for drainage after encountering them in Mesopotamia and in the use of dams to prevent silting. Irrigation became more common, and important innovations in agricultural equipment took place. The screw developed by Archimedes, an inventor and mathematican of the 3rd century BC, facilitated the workings of water-pumping devices for drainage and was also used in olive and grape presses. However, the application and availability of new goods and methods varied from city to city. Most of the city-states of Greece remained reliant on commercial imports and the donations of foreign benefactors for their food supply.

Sculpture

While social conditions varied, the cultural development of the Hellenistic world does show some uniformity. As sculptors would travel to centres where there was employment, it is difficult to establish regional trends in architecture or sculpture. There was a move away from the idealized forms of earlier sculpture as Alexander commissioned busts of himself with life-like features. A more individual style of portraiture developed as Alexander's successors followed his lead, commissioning sculpture to show aspects of their personalities as well as to reflect their positions of power. More life-like representation is also seen in everyday contexts. Small terracotta figurines, depicting ordinary people such as craftsmen, children, and the elderly were common throughout this period.

The famous 2nd-century BC frieze on the Great Altar at Pergamum is an exceptional example of Hellenistic sculpture. This features scenes of war between giants and the gods, a theme encountered in the 5th century BC on the metopes of the Parthenon. However, the frieze at Pergamum surpasses classical sculpture in its painstaking detail. The decorative detail on the figures and the variety of intricate surface textures depicting fur and feathers contribute to the power of the narrative. They also illustrate the height of stylistic virtuosity reached in Hellenistic sculpture.

Religion

The expansion and diversification of Greek culture in the Hellenistic period can be seen in records of religious practice, which illustrate an interchange between religious cults across the Mediterranean world. In Egypt, a Hellenized form of Egyptian religion developed when Ptolemy I called upon an Egyptian priest and an Athenian religious expert to fashion a new god as Alexandria's patron deity. The result was a god named Sarapis, who was identified by Hellenistic writers with the Greek gods Dionysus, Pluto, Zeus, and others. In Greece itself, deities adopted from elsewhere were

themselves transformed: the Egyptian goddess Isis, for example, became identified with Greek goddesses and assumed the Greek identity as a creator of the universe. Religious innovation coincided with preservation: in Athens, in the last third of the 4th century BC, there was a movement to preserve the traditional deities of the city, with the rebuilding of cult sanctuaries of the ancestors of the Athenians, such as Zeus and Athena Phratrios.

Poetry

Other disciplines combined revival with innovation. The poet Theocritus drew inspiration from the epic poetry of the *Iliad*, as well as from lyric poetry, but also invented a new genre known as *bucolic*, which refers to his rural sketches sometimes written in the Doric dialect. A Syracusan who worked at the royal palace from the 270s BC, he also composed poems praising the king. His *Idyll 17* is an example of this, reckoning King Ptolemy to be the first of mortals in the same way as Zeus was first of immortals.

Libraries

The first books in Greece were probably written on sheets of animal skin or panels of wood in the Archaic period, which were succeeded by the introduction of papyrus from Egypt towards the end of the 5th century BC. A major development was made in Pergamum in the 2nd century BC, when parchment was made from animal skins. The Hellenistic period also saw the creation of large buildings to be used as libraries. The two major libraries of the period were based at Alexandria and

Pergamum, but there were also important libraries at Athens. Founded and funded by the Ptolemiaic monarchy, the library at Alexandria held some 700,000 books by the 2nd century BC. At this time, a real interest in the preservation of classical culture can be seen: Ptolemy III, for example, borrowed manuscripts of the tragedies from Athens on deposit. However, he was more interested in keeping the texts than retrieving his money and refused to return them.

Philosophy

Philosophy underwent considerable development in this period, but its origins did not lie in the libraries alone. The group of philosophers known as the Cynics ("the dog-like") for their shamelessness were the followers of Diogenes. Diogenes believed that wisdom lay in action rather than thought. He spent his life as primitively as possible, eschewing possessions, living in a barrel, and surviving by begging. He was renowned for his belief in freedom of speech and actions, and he rejected traditional sexual customs. The philosophers known as the Stoics were not so far removed from the Cynics in their idea of liberty as the ability to live as one pleases. The founder of Stoicism, Zeno, agreed with the Cynics in declaring all general education useless. The Stoics were interested in logic, physics, and ethics. They argued that virtue is happiness, nothing except virtue is good, and that emotions are always bad. Some Stoics such as Epictetus created a literary form of the diatribe, the address concerned with moral exhortation given to a large outdoor audience.

Greek culture and Rome

The history of ancient Greece and its culture does not end with the Roman conquest. A visitor today to the ruins of any Greek city will see a large number of ruins of the Roman period, such as the 20,000-capacity theatre at Argos or the Tower of the Winds in Athens. The munificence of wealthy Roman individuals often financed these buildings, illustrating Greece's economic reliance on Rome. Levels of prosperity varied throughout Greece, and there was a movement in the population away from isolated rural settlements towards larger villages and cities. Despite the fact that Rome controlled Greece through the governors of Macedonia, Greece continued to be an area of self-administering communities, self-regulating with regard to their domestic affairs. Greece, and in particular Athens, remained a place of education and a haven for philosophers, where statesmen such as Cicero were educated in philosophy, and exiles went to muse over the injustices of life at Rome.

HELLENISTIC CIVILIZATION   **53**

ANCIENT ROME

753 BC–AD 476

754/3 Traditional founding of Rome by Romulus.

754–509 Legendary kings rule Rome and conquer Latium.

509 Traditional date of founding of the Republic by Brutus.

*c.*490–338 Wars with Latin League lead to Roman control of central Italy.

509–287 The Struggle of the Orders: the plebeians gradually wrest political and economic concessions from the patrician aristocracy.

264–146 Punic Wars between Rome and Carthage: In 241, the Romans takes Sicily; in 218, they defeat Hannibal and take much of Spain.

192–189 War against Antiochus III of Syria.

218–167 Macedonian Wars: Rome defeats Philip V and Perseus, and Flamininus declares the freedom of Greece at Corinth's Isthmian Games in 196, 50 years before the Romans raze Corinth to the ground.

390 The Gauls sack Rome.

| 800 BC | 700 BC | 600 BC | 500 BC | 400 BC | 300 BC | 200 BC |

*c.*600 The Forum valley is drained and laid out, beginning the urbanization of Rome.

451–50 The Twelve Tables are the first publication of Roman laws.

200–160 Plautus and Terence write the classic Roman comedies.

312 Via Appia built from Rome to Campania.

70–57 Ascendency of Pompey, who serves as consul in 70, breaks the pirates in 67, defeats Mithridates in 63, and secures the corn supply for Rome in 57.

73–71 Spartacus leads a massive slave revolt against Rome.

88–78 The age of Sulla, whose march on Rome sets off 10 years of civil war between Sullans and Marians.

49–46 Civil War between Caesar and Pompey; when Caesar wins he assumes dictatorial power at Rome. He is assassinated in 44 and the state descends into civil war.

31 BC–AD 14 Octavian finally defeats Antony and Cleopatra at Actium, and they commit suicide. He takes the name Augustus and becomes the first Roman Emperor.

91–88 The Italian allies make war on Rome and are eventually given Roman citizenship.

14–68 Julio-Claudian Dynasty: Tiberius, Gaius "Caligula", Claudius, and Nero.

98–192 Antonine Dynasty, including Trajan (r.98–117), the first emperor from the provinces, and the one who takes the empire to its greatest extent.

476 Last Western Emperor Romulus Augustulus driven out by Goths and abdicates. The Greek-speaking, Eastern Empire survives as Byzantium until 1453.

193–235 Severan Dynasty; Septimius Severus (193–211) is the first African emperor. In 212, his son Caracalla grants Roman citizenship to almost all the freemen in the empire.

293 Empire divided into two halves – east and west – each with an emperor (an Augustus) and a deputy (a Caesar).

312 Constantine unites the Roman Empire, and makes Constantinople the capital in 330.

395 Empire again split into eastern and western halves.

410 Sack of Rome by Alaric the Goth.

| 100 BC | 0 | AD 100 | AD 200 | AD 300 | AD 400 | AD 500 |

80 The Colosseum is completed in Rome. It becomes Rome's most popular stadium. First amphitheatre is built at Pompeii.

70–43 Career of Cicero: politician, writer, rhetorician, and philosopher.

31 Augustus and Agrippa begin a building programme that transforms Rome, including the Augustan Mausoleum, the Pantheon, and the Ara Pacis.

87–8 The height of 1st-century poetry. Virgil (70–19) writes the epic of Rome, the *Aeneid*.

35–65 Seneca publishes Stoic philosophy and political drama.

123 Hadrian's Wall is built. It is the only permanent defensive border in the empire.

80–140 The Age of the Satirists: the corruscating Juvenal (58–140) and exuberant Martial (40–102).

79 Eruption of Vesuvius destroys Pompeii and Herculaneum.

64 Great Fire of Rome. Execution of Christian apostles Peter and Paul at Rome.

324 Christianity becomes a recognized state religion.

250–310 Climax of the persecution of Christians.

A view across the Roman Forum towards the Colosseum, past the round temple of Vesta, and the surviving columns of the temple of Castor and Pollux. The Forum was the political and social centre of Rome for the seven centuries from the Period of the Kings to the death of Julius Caesar.

THE ROMAN REPUBLIC: 509–44 BC

During its first seven centuries, Rome grew from a set of hilltop villages to the largest city in the Mediterranean, commanding the obedience and fear of almost all the known world. This growth took place amidst continuing conflict – both external conflict with other powers and internal conflict at the heart of the state itself.

In the centre of the new city lay the Roman Forum. This provided the stage on which the political dramas of the period were performed, and to tell the story of this urban space is to relate the history of Rome itself.

When the first settlers arrived on the hills that would later become Rome, they buried their dead in the swampy valley. It was drained during the Period of the Kings c.600 BC and quickly began to fill with temples, precincts, sanctuaries, and shrines, as the new city acquired both citizens and territory through war.

The last king of Rome was expelled in c.509 BC with the help of the army and the people, and two consuls were elected to lead the state. An integrated complex of political institutions grew up in the Forum. The new Republic required a Senate House, public assembly area, and a rostrum, where magistrates could address the people. After a long struggle between the plebeians and patricians, there was also a bench for the plebeian tribunes, who had won the right, and the duty, to protect the people from the excesses of their rulers.

The Forum also became a showplace for the noble families, whose funeral processions wended their way there. The funerals would end with addresses from the rostrum by relatives of the deceased on the history and glory of the family and sometimes with great gladiatorial contests in the middle of the Forum.

As Rome's power in Italy grew, its citizens were in a constant state of military alert. The temple of Janus in the Forum was a reminder of war at home: by tradition, its gates were closed only in peacetime, and they remained open (with one brief respite) throughout the entire Republican period. Roman troops ventured further and further afield in the Mediterranean, and the wealth and glory of empire were brought right into the heart of the city. Statues of victors, collections of spoils, and foreign art jostled for space amid the monumental new buildings erected by generals along the route of their triumphal processions.

But empire also brought popular discontent to Rome, and the plebeian tribunes played a central role in battles in the Senate, and with the people, over land, political rights, debt, and food shortages. From the mid-130s BC, Tiberius and Gaius Gracchus fought for their radical reforms from the rostrum, before their deaths at the hands of senators.

The dictator Sulla increased the power of the Senate at the expense of the people, but his attempt to silence the tribunes failed. During the last decades of the Republic, the Forum witnessed rioting, occupations, and barricades. Pompey and Caesar vied for the support of the people and the army. In the fevered revolutionary atmosphere of the 50s BC, the last great popular tribune, Clodius Pulcher, was murdered; in a parody of an aristocratic funeral in more peaceful times, his supporters displayed his body on the rostrum before cremating him in the Senate House, burning it to the ground.

These battles of great men for individual power foretold a new era at Rome. Caesar built a new Senate House, obliterating the public assembly space, and then began work on an entirely new Forum. His funeral in the old Forum in 44 BC marked the very end of its glory: his successors in power, including Mark Antony and the future emperor Augustus, would later use its rostrum to display the remains of hundreds of victims of their persecutions.

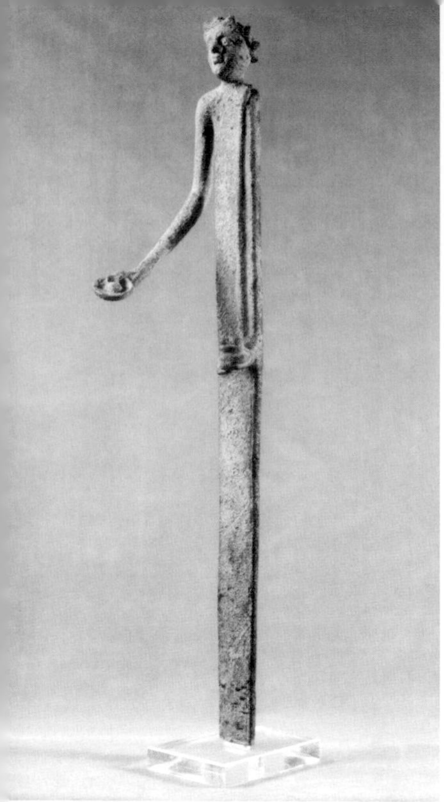

The Etruscans were Rome's most powerful neighbours. A wealthy, cosmopolitan federation of towns grew up north of the Tiber, flourishing from the 8th to 6th centuries BC, with an artistic tradition that rivalled their military reputation. As with this bronze male figurine, their sculpture often betrays the influence of the eastern Mediterranean, as well as local traditions.

The Foundation of Rome and the Period of the Kings

Traditionally, the rise of Rome begins with the fall of Troy. Aeneas, a Trojan prince, escaped the burning city, holding his infant son by the hand and carrying his father on his back. They set off on an odyssey through the Mediterranean which eventually led to the shores of Italy and the kingdom of the Latins, where Aeneas married a local princess.

Legends of early Rome

The historical origins of Rome are shrouded in legends such as the one above. They are found in versions told almost a millennium after the first archaeological traces of settlement on those hills around 1000 BC. These tales were retold and reshaped over the years by Greek scholars and by Italy's travelling story-tellers and performers.

Romulus and Remus, it is said, were descendants of Aeneas, twin brothers of mixed Trojan and Latin blood. They were born to Rhea Silvia, a princess of Alba Longa condemned to life as a virgin priestess when her uncle usurped her father's throne. Despite this precaution, she became pregnant, apparently by the god Mars. After their birth, her uncle threw her into prison, and the infants were placed in the Tiber to drown. There they were discovered by a she-wolf, who suckled them until they were found by the king's shepherd. He and his wife raised the boys as herdsmen. When Remus, now a young man, was jailed on a charge of cattle-rustling, he was recognized by his grandfather Numitor, the rightful king. The truth out, the brothers reinstalled Numitor on the throne before leaving to found a city at the place they had once been left to drown, where seven hills surrounded a crossing of the Tiber. There they quarrelled over the right to govern the new city, and in the fight Remus was killed. Romulus fortified the Palatine hill and became the first king of Rome. The traditional date for the city's foundation is 753 BC.

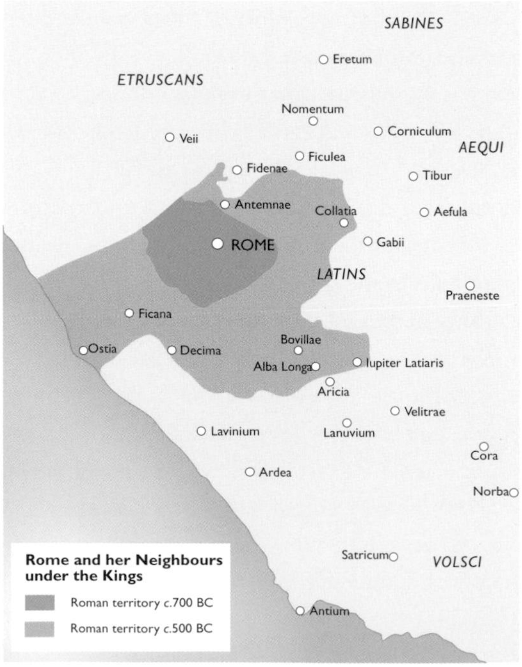

SABINES
ETRUSCANS
Eretum
Nomentum
Corniculum
AEQUI
Veii
Ficulea
Fidenae
Tibur
Antemnae
Collatia
Aefula
ROME
Gabii
LATINS
Praeneste
Ficana
Ostia
Decima
Bovillae
Alba Longa
Iupiter Latiaris
Aricia
Velitrae
Lavinium
Lanuvium
Cora
Ardea
Norba
Satricum
VOLSCI
Antium
Rome and her Neighbours under the Kings
Roman territory c.700 BC
Roman territory c.500 BC

Rome's early territory in the immediate vicinity of the city expanded during the Period of the Kings to fill the prosperous and productive lowlands of Latium between the Sabatine Mountains to the north and the Alban Hills to the south. Despite skirmishes, the hill towns and tribes of central Italy were not yet threatened by the fast-growing city in the plain.

The beginnings of Rome

In order to amass a population for his fledgling city, Romulus opened the gates to the homeless, the poor, the criminals, and the slaves of nearby communities. This marked the beginning of Rome's traditional openness to outsiders. He organized the population into tribes and chose 100 senators as a council of advisers.

The new city and its unsavoury inhabitants were viewed with deep suspicion by the Latin communities in the area and the Sabines to the north-east, and they refused to intermarry with the Romans. In need of wives for his citizens, Romulus invited these neighbours to a festival. They came, curious to see the new town, and they brought their families. On a pre-arranged signal, young Romans seized the women and carried them off. This act of treachery led to war. Romulus gradually defeated the surrounding communities and invited the inhabitants to move to Rome, reuniting many of the women with their families and increasing the extent of Roman territory. The Sabines were the last to attack Rome; the Sabine women threw themselves between their husbands and fathers on the battlefield and begged them to make peace. The two populations merged, and the Sabine king Tatius ruled jointly with Romulus. By the time Romulus died, Rome was a thriving local power.

Perhaps the most famous statue from Roman antiquity, the "Capitoline Wolf" is actually an Etruscan bronze sculpture dating from around 500 BC. It stands almost a metre (3 ft) tall. The she-wolf was the symbol of Rome from an early stage, although this statue may not be intended to recall the myth of Romulus and Remus: no doubt because the story of Romulus and Remus was so central to Roman mythology, the twin boys were added to the sculpture during the Renaissance.

The legendary kings

The legends of the regal period tell us little about what actually happened in early Rome, but they do reveal a great deal about Roman self-identity and self-understanding as a military and religious community. The Roman character, at least as it was later understood, was based on centuries of military glory, collective piety, and a curious combination of aggression towards neighbouring peoples and generosity to defeated foes. The stories of Romulus' reign reflected and perpetuated an image of Rome as an inclusive city, where initiative and courage counted for more than origins and enemies were incorporated rather than destroyed.

The kings who were supposedly elected to follow Romulus are also ciphers, fictions with which the Romans explained the origins of their political and religious institutions. Priesthoods, rituals, and the sacred calendar are ascribed to Romulus' peace-loving successor Numa Pompilius (r.715–672 BC), who was, like Tatius, a Sabine; political institutions such as the Senate House are attributed to Tullus Hostilius. In the same spirit, the religious regulations governing declarations of war and treaties are said to be the work of Ancus Marcius. Archaeologists have found evidence of trade with the rest of Italy and with Greece, of craft production, and of increasing prosperity in Rome from this period (c.750–600 BC).

The Etruscan kings

The last kings of Rome, the household of an Etruscan immigrant of Greek descent, presided over the urbanization of the city until 509 BC. Although we do not know if the Tarquins really ruled at Rome, the military and engineering projects attributed to them are genuine. Monumental building, trade, contacts abroad, and the influence of the Greeks and the Etruscans increased dramatically in this period. The stories of these kings are full of the boldness and ingenuity of the women around them, a reflection of the high standing that women had in Etruscan society.

As the story goes, Tarquin the Elder came to Rome with his wife Tanaquil to seek his fortune, befriended Ancus Marcius, and was elected to succeed him on his death in 616 BC. He waged war on the Latins, drained the marshy valley to create the Forum, and laid the foundations for the great temple on the Capitol to Jupiter, Juno, and Minerva before the old king's sons assassinated him. Tanaquil's cunning saw to it that they would not succeed him. She told the people that her husband was merely wounded and that their son-in-law, Servius Tullius, would act as regent while he recovered. By the time the truth was known, the young man had entrenched his position.

Trying to avoid the fate of his father-in-law, Servius had his own daughters, both named Tullia, married to two of Tarquin's descendants. Another Tarquin, an arrogant man, married a dutiful daughter; his milder brother Arruns married an ambitious one. Both matches were unhappy, and the bolder pair arranged the murders of their respective spouses and married. Tarquin began canvassing the support of the aristocrats, who felt that Servius was too generous in distributing land to the citizens, and staged a coup. He ruled from 534–510 BC, retaining the throne through fear, and came to be known as Tarquin the Proud.

The Early Republic and the Struggle of the Orders

Tarquin the Proud was a successful general, but he ruled without reference to the people or the Senate. He operated at home through a mixture of murder, exile, and confiscation of property for the rich and forced labour for the poor. The nobles rebelled against him, and a republic was established on the banks of the Tiber.

The end of the monarchy

The constitutional revolution at Rome may have been sparked by palace or aristocratic intrigue, or the intervention of an Etruscan leader, but the Romans themselves told the story of the rape of Lucretia, whose husband Collatinus was a relative of the king. Lucretia was famed for her virtue. One night, when the king and all the nobles were away on campaign, Sextus, the king's son, visited her house in Collatia, near Rome, and raped her at knife point. She summoned her father and husband, and made them promise to avenge her. They proclaimed her innocence, but she insisted that she should not be an example of unchastity and killed herself. Collatinus had brought with him the king's nephew Brutus, who until that moment had feigned stupidity to avoid assassination. Brutus took charge of the situation and marched on Rome. Moved by Lucretia's plight and reminded of their own suffering, the people rallied to him. When Tarquin returned to Rome, he found the gates barred against him. Inside the city, two consuls were elected to replace the king: Brutus and Collatinus. Tradition dates the founding of the Republic to 509 BC.

The early Republic

The early years of aristocratic rule in Rome were lean ones for the new Republic. A treaty with Carthage traditionally dated to the first year of the Republic in 509 BC recognized Roman suzerainty in Latium, but within a decade Rome was once again at war with the Latins. With, according to legend, aid from the gods Castor and Pollux, the Romans triumphed at the battle of Lake Regillus in 493 BC, and the Romans and the Latin towns made a treaty granting their citizens the right to intermarry, conduct business, and transfer their citizenship. Peace with the Latins lasted for at least a century, but the surrounding mountain peoples went on the offensive and took much of the territory the kings had won. Rome soon lost the southern half of

Latium to the Volscians and was harassed by raids from the Sabines in the north and the Aequi, a highland tribe to the east. On occasion, the enemy threatened Rome itself. There was also ongoing conflict between Rome and the Etruscan city of Veii, just 16 kilometres (10 miles) to the north.

Alongside the loss of power in central Italy came trouble at home. Foreign contacts and trade dried up by the second quarter of the 5th century BC. There is no evidence of monumental building for about 75 years, with few temple dedications and a decline in the quantity and quality of artistic production. This is probably not due to the political changes; the same phenomena is also apparent in the cities of Etruria, Latium, and southern Italy, and the incursions from the mountains reflect migrations of peoples causing havoc all through Italy.

The "Struggle of the Orders"

In these difficult times, the Roman aristocracy was split between a patrician minority supposedly descended from Romulus' first 100 senators and a larger group of plebeians, of more recent wealth and status. The patricians controlled religious offices and the power of veto over decisions taken by the people. In the first years of the Republic, the consulship could be held by plebeians, but the patricians monopolized it from the 480s BC. The first Roman law code, published c.450 BC, confirms the schism: among the provisions was a ban on intermarriage between plebeians and patricians.

The plebeian families fought this inequality by refusing on occasion to fight on Rome's behalf. They withdrew to hills outside the city on a regular basis, only returning when their demands were met. There were small victories for the plebeians, including the right to elect tribunes to represent them. At some point these tribunes acquired the power of veto over any magistrate or law. It was not until 367 BC, however, that a law was passed re-opening the consulship to the plebeians. In 300 BC, the priestly colleges were divided between the two orders; in 287 BC, the decrees of the plebeian tribal assembly became binding.

Although the "Struggle of the Orders" was a dispute among the elite, the plebeian assembly and tribunes also represented the city's lower classes. These peasants and artisans must have suffered during the troubles of the 5th century BC. They would have gained little from the political

Was Rome democratic?

Only free male citizens could vote, and their votes were not equal. The junior magistracies were elected in the Tribal Assembly, where each tribe had one vote. There were 15 tribes for rural voters and only four for city dwellers, so the system was weighted towards the more conservative rural population. The consul and the other senior magistrates were elected by the Centuriate Assembly. Here voters were allotted to "centuries" within five property classes, and each century had one vote. The wealthiest class had an overall majority of centuries and began the voting. The election ended once a majority was reached, so the votes of the lower classes were rarely needed. With the introduction of the secret ballot in the late 2nd century (depicted on the coin above), the average citizen could cast his vote in greater safety.

concessions made in that century, but in 367 BC there is evidence of credible laws passed to relieve debt and protect the access of the peasants to land. Most importantly, debt bondage was abolished in 326 BC, and Roman citizens could no longer be enslaved for falling into debt. This flurry of legislation suggests either that the woes of the poor worsened in the 4th century BC or that they had learnt to voice their discontent. In any case, a more lasting solution to their problems was sought in the establishment of colonies throughout Italy.

This depiction of a census comes from an altar dedicated on the Campus Martius in Rome by the consul Domitius Ahenobarbus in 122 BC. The citizens are being registered on lists by the official on the left. The census took place every five years, and was followed by a ritual purification ceremony.

Rome in Italy

Military fortunes began to improve at the end of the 5th century BC for the Romans and their Latin allies. They clawed back southern Latium from the Volsci, founded a number of colonies there, and introduced pay for soldiers. In 396 BC, Veii fell to Rome after a long siege and was destroyed.

Annexation and colonization

With the fall of Veii, the Romans adopted a new strategy. They annexed its territory and divided it among the Roman people. By settling citizens on new land, they not only quieted discontent among the rural population, but also ensured that these peasants could meet the property qualification to serve in the army. Around this time, Rome imposed a property tax on its citizens to fund military operations and instituted indemnities for defeated enemies. These changes put the army on a more secure footing; however, things would get worse before they got better. The Gauls attacked and sacked Rome in 390 BC, almost capturing the Capitol itself – and this time it was the Romans who had to pay a large indemnity in order to persuade them to leave.

Rome recovered quickly from the Gallic sack, and military policy became more aggressive. Rome continued to make war on the mountain peoples, annexed more land, and began to found colonies in Etruria. This added to the difficulties of the Etruscans, who had lost their holdings in southern Italy in the 5th century BC and were now trapped between the newly powerful Romans in the south and the Gauls in the north. Roman activity was gaining notice outside Italy, too: in 348 BC, another treaty with Carthage viewed Rome as a military, colonial, and trading power, and as a potential threat to Carthaginian interests in all these areas.

Citizenship and expansion

The rapid expansion of Rome alarmed its allies, and the Latins sometimes sided with the mountain peoples against the city. In 341 BC, the Latins united against Rome, but they were comprehensively defeated in 338 BC. Many Latin communities were directly incorporated into Roman citizenship, much of their land was annexed, and the ancient League of the Latins was broken forever.

Rome now turned its attention south, where the Samnites had been attacking and occupying Greek and Etruscan cities, also weakened by class conflict, for almost a century. Roman progress was rapid. Their first intervention in the region had come in 343 BC, when the besieged city of Capua appealed for help against the Samnites. Roman armies lifted the siege, and in 340 BC the Capuan aristocracy were granted Roman citizenship. The remainder of the Campanians received a form of the citizenship in 338 BC. They did not receive the right to vote, but they did incur the responsibilities of taxation and military service. Rome made further strategic alliances: in 326 BC, for instance, the Romans came to the aid of the aristocratic faction at Naples against the Samnites, who were supported by the Neapolitan masses. The first Roman colonies south of Latium were established in 334 and 328 BC, and many more were to follow.

These local conflicts escalated into several full-scale wars between the Romans and the Samnites. The final battle came in 295 BC, when the Samnites, in alliance with the Gauls, Etruscans, and Umbrians, made one last effort to resist Roman hegemony. After defeating this coalition, Rome was unquestionably the biggest power in Italy. Some of the Greek cities in the south held out a little longer, and democratic Tarentum (the Roman name for

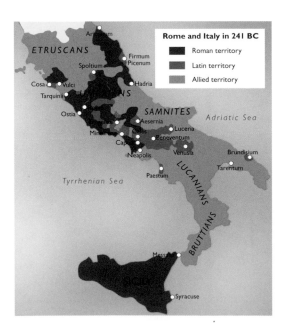

By the middle of the 3rd century Italy was a patchwork of communities of Roman citizens and "allies". Although all were effectively subject to the government at Rome, the different classifications and privileges given to the various towns and peoples were one of the reasons why they developed little solidarity against their common overlord.

Map labels:
Rome and Italy in 241 BC
- Roman territory
- Latin territory
- Allied territory

ETRUSCANS · Arretium · Firmum Picenum · Spoletium · Cosa · Vulci · Hadria · Tarquinii · Ostia · SAMNITES · Aesernia · Luceria · Minturnae · Cales · Beneventum · Capua · Venusia · Neapolis · Brundisium · Paestum · Tarentum · LUCANIANS · Tyrrhenian Sea · Adriatic Sea · BRUTTIANS · Messana · SICILY · Syracuse

The Roman amphitheatre at Capua in Campania. Capua was one of the first cities in southern Italy to ally itself with the Romans, in 343 BC. The alliance was valuable to both sides, and the first major Roman road in Italy, the Via Appia, was built from Rome to Capua in 312 BC. It was a major blow to Rome when the city defected to Hannibal in 216 BC.

Taras) the longest of all. The Tarentines summoned the Greek war hero Pyrrhus of Epirus to their aid – the first foreign general to fight on Italian soil – but he, too, was defeated by a Roman army in 275 BC.

Roman hegemony

The Romans conquered Italy in several different ways. They annexed land to the city, incorporated communities into different forms of Roman citizenship, and established colonies throughout the peninsula. They appeased their own lower classes with land, booty, and the benefits of civic prosperity such as aqueducts and roads, and they forged alliances with aristocratic factions in other cities. Most Italians, on their defeat or surrender, became allies of Rome, rather than citizens. They were liable for military services – and shared in the profits of war. As in the incorporated towns, the aristocracies of these allied communities could rely on Roman help if they experienced domestic troubles. Italy became a patchwork of Roman citizens, colonies, and allies, and soon Sicily beckoned.

The First Punic War

Sicily was divided between Greek cities in the west and Carthaginian foundations in the east. But in 288 BC, the Mamertines, a rogue band of mercenaries from Campania, had taken control of the Sicilian city of Messana just across the straits from Italy. They caused a great deal of trouble for the Greeks and Carthaginians on the island, and in the end the Syracusans besieged them in their city. One faction at Messana appealed to Carthage for help, while the other appealed to Rome. The Carthaginians arrived first and installed a garrison. At Rome, the consuls put the question of intervention to a vote of the people (dwelling, it is said, on the material gains of war). The Romans voted to send an army to Messana in 264 BC, and the conflict escalated. With the troubles of Messana soon forgotten, Rome and Carthage were at war with one another in the first of the conflicts known as the Punic Wars.

This war for Sicily was long and fought largely at sea. The Romans were not seafarers, which initially put them at a disadvantage. It was only when they captured a Carthaginian war ship that they were able to build their own on the same model. Three times they lost an entire fleet at sea. Eventually, the Romans forced a truce in 241 BC. The Carthaginians were to withdraw from Sicily entirely, leaving Rome with its first province outside the mainland, and to pay a large indemnity. Carthage was immediately confronted with a bitter rebellion by its own mercenaries and African subjects. The Romans took advantage of the city's distress to demand that they also cede the island of Sardinia. The Carthaginians could not refuse, but never forgot the injustice. With the coming of Hannibal, the Romans would regret their greed.

The Conquest of the Mediterranean

The First Punic War brought the Romans into the Mediterranean; victory in the Second Punic War against the might of Hannibal led to their domination of the entire region. Their rise was rapid. The Greek politician and scholar Polybius claimed that in less than 53 years (220–167 BC), they brought almost the whole of the inhabited world under their rule.

The Hannibalic War

Deprived of Sicily and Sardinia, the Carthaginians turned their attention towards Spain. By the time Hannibal became leader of the forces in Spain in 221 BC, a large portion of the peninsula was under Punic control. For their part, the Romans went to war against Queen Teuta of Illyria, claiming that she sponsored piracy in the Adriatic, and took steps to pacify the Gauls who were threatening their northern frontier.

The two states came to blows again over Hannibal's siege of Saguntum, a city on Spain's eastern coast. The Romans claimed this city as an ally, and claimed further that Hannibal was breaking previous treaties both by attacking this city and by advancing so far north in Spain. The Carthaginians disputed these claims, and the city

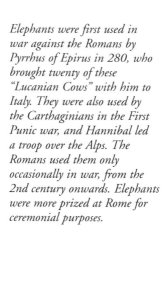

Elephants were first used in war against the Romans by Pyrrhus of Epirus in 280, who brought twenty of these "Lucanian Cows" with him to Italy. They were also used by the Carthaginians in the First Punic war, and Hannibal led a troop over the Alps. The Romans used them only occasionally in war, from the 2nd century onwards. Elephants were more prized at Rome for ceremonial purposes.

fell to Hannibal after eight months. Rome sent envoys to Carthage, demanding that they surrender their champion. When the Carthaginians refused, the envoys declared war. The Romans assumed that they would fight this war in Spain and sent one consular army there, with another to Carthage itself. To their astonishment, Hannibal set out overland for Italy.

After a difficult march over the Pyrenees and the Alps, during which many of his soldiers, horses, and elephants perished, Hannibal defeated hastily recalled Roman armies at Trebbia and Trasimene in northern Italy. He moved through the peninsula, bypassing Rome, and in 216 BC he won a devastating victory at Cannae in the south: the Romans lost more than 70,000 men in one day.

Hannibal found many allies, both among the Gauls in the north of Italy who had been resisting Rome for several years and among the Greek and Italian cities in the south who now rebelled against their overlord. Hannibal's boldest alliance was with King Philip V of Macedon in 215 BC – Philip was also interfering with Roman interests in the Adriatic. When a treaty between the two was discovered by the Romans, they declared war on Macedonia as well. As they were fully occupied with the war with Hannibal, this war was fought largely by Greek allies on their behalf and reached an impasse in the last years of the 3rd century BC.

After their comprehensive defeats on the battlefield, the Romans pursued a policy of avoiding direct confrontation, on the advice of the general Fabius Cunctator, who was known as the "Delayer" because of his military tactics. They harried the Carthaginian troops, recovered cities in the absence of Hannibal's army, and gradually clawed back control of Italy. At the same time, they captured Carthaginian strongholds in Sicily and Spain. With Hannibal eventually confined to

"Carthago delenda est"

Carthage recovered swiftly from the Hannibalic War and began territorial skirmishes with Rome's Numidian allies. The great orator Marcus Porcius Cato never lost an opportunity to insist upon the continuing danger of the Carthaginians. He dropped fresh African figs from his toga in the Senate House, in order to demonstrate how quickly their ships could reach Rome, and he customarily ended every speech he made on any subject with the words "Carthago delenda est" ("And Carthage must be destroyed"). Cato died just after Rome went to war with Carthage for the third time in 149 BC. He missed the complete destruction of the city in 146 BC, in which the inhabitants were sold into slavery and the city razed. The site of Rome's ancient enemy was ceremonially cursed, and Rome took over Carthage's territory in Africa.

the far south of the peninsula, the Romans went on the offensive and took the war to Africa, with Hannibal hard on their heels. The great Roman general Scipio eventually defeated Hannibal's forces there at the battle of Zama in 202 BC, earning the nickname "Africanus".

Now that the Carthaginians had been forced out of Spain, the Romans took some areas of the peninsula under their direct control. From 197 BC, they made a permanent military and administrative commitment, sending out annual praetors to two separate regions, Nearer Spain and Hither Spain. As in Sicily and Sardinia, the presence of Roman troops and officials enabled the Romans to exploit the area's mineral and agricultural resources, as well as to claim tribute from its inhabitants. Although formal Roman colonies were not established, the new opportunities attracted Italian merchants and businessmen to the areas.

Wars in the East

With victory over Carthage secured, hostilities were now resumed with Macedonia, and Philip was defeated at Cynoscephalae in 197 BC. At first, instead of creating provinces in the eastern Mediterranean, the Romans consolidated their hegemony through alliances and political intervention. Building on the diplomatic success of their earlier victory over Illyria, whose pirates had threatened Greeks in the Adriatic as well as Italians, they now posed as liberators of the Greeks from Macedonia. At the conclusion of the war with Philip, the Greek general Flamininus appeared at the Isthmian Games at Corinth in 196 BC and declared that the Greek cities

henceforth would be free of garrisons and tribute, and subject to their own laws. It was said that the Greeks' jubilation was so loud that birds fell out of the sky.

The Romans returned to the East in 192 BC to take on the Syrian king Antiochus III after he defied their order to free Greek cities in Asia. That war ended in defeat for Antiochus, but the freedom of the Greeks was to be conditional. Rome established oligarchic governments in some cities and encouraged them in others. The Senate expected all disputes in the East to be referred to them, and all Roman commands to be obeyed, even by the Hellenistic kings. Philip V's son Perseus tried to reinvigorate Macedonian influence in Greece and received a great deal of popular support, but was defeated by Rome in 167 BC. Roman hegemony was complete: when Antiochus IV of Syria invaded Egypt in the same year, he was met by a Roman envoy who handed him instructions from the senate to leave the country. Antiochus said that he would consider the request, whereupon the Roman drew a circle around him with a stick and ordered him to remain inside the circle until he had made a decision. Antiochus agreed to leave.

The Romans made another military intervention in the East in the early 140s BC, when a revolt in Greece brought about a war with the Achaeans, leading to the Roman destruction of Corinth in 146 BC, the same year that Carthage was finally destroyed. Over the next decades, the Romans gradually formalized their hegemony overseas, sending governors and standing armies, making laws, planting colonies, and distributing or selling land in their control.

Politics and Discontent in Rome and Italy

The new empire brought great riches to Rome, but it also brought suffering and dissent. The wealthy, the lower classes, and Rome's allies in Italy all had grievances, and these disputes erupted into the violence that would dominate the last century of the Republic.

Corruption and competition

The rewards of empire were enormous. As well as taxes imposed on the provinces in the west, there were war indemnities, hundreds of thousands of slaves, and a great deal of booty. The booty from Carthage in 146 BC was more than enough to finance a spectacular aqueduct, the Aqua Marcia, the Republic's most expensive building project. The Roman people also benefited from new roads and the abolition of property tax in 167 BC.

Much of the new wealth, however, ended up in the hands of the elite. As well as senators, this included the *equites*, members of the upper class who did not pursue political careers – their name comes from their original function as cavalry in the Roman army. Legitimate means of enrichment were abundant, but illegitimate means became ever more attractive as wealth became the only way to demonstrate honour and prestige. Bribery and corruption were rampant, especially among provincial governors and their staff.

Members of the elite competed to display their wealth and win the political favour of the people. They erected public buildings, put on great spectacles, and lived extravagantly. The more conservative senators became concerned by this individualism and attempted to stifle these excesses by passing laws against luxurious private entertainment and dress. They also regulated access to public office, instituting minimum ages, compulsory intervals between offices, and a ban on holding the consulship more than once.

Rome's businessmen, drawn from the *equites*, did well from building contracts at Rome and the operation of industry and taxation in the provinces. But tensions developed with the Senate over the terms of these contracts, and the *equites* also resented their exclusion from the courts, where only senators could be jurors.

The land crisis

Discontent among the elite was nothing compared to growing rancour among the lower classes, especially the rural peasantry who made up the army. The unceasing warfare that had won Rome its empire had forced Roman soldiers to spend years abroad on campaign. Their farms often collapsed in their absence, forcing them to abandon or sell the land. During the 2nd century BC, the newly enriched elite bought up far more public land than the law permitted. The peasants who had farmed this land had nowhere to go.

Roman rule spread swiftly around the Mediterranean after their victory in the first war against Carthage. Although that power was initially exercised largely through diplomacy, administrative and military forms of overseas government became an increasingly important tool during the 2nd and 1st centuries BC.

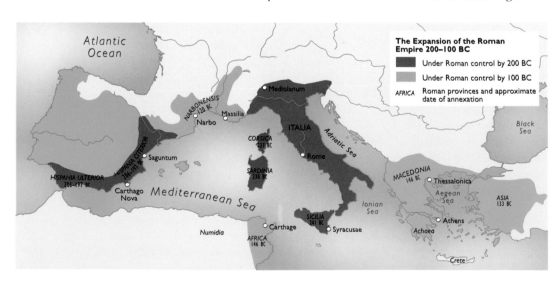

A banquet from a wall painting found at Pompeii, on the bay of Naples. Life for the wealthy in Roman Italy was a far cry from the dirt, disease, and overcrowding suffered by most of the urban poor. As the rich took over agricultural land and built country villas, peasants were forced off their land and often into the cities.

753 BC–AD 476

ANCIENT ROME

It was not only Romans who were suffering: the Italians also fought for Rome and lost their land, and they were now increasingly treated as subjects rather than allies by the Romans, liable to plunder, persecution, and interference in local affairs.

The downtrodden looked to the plebeian tribunes for help, and this era saw an unprecedented increase in the power and visibility of these tribunes. As social concerns came to the fore at Rome, politicians became known as *populares* ("for the people") or *optimates* ("for the best").

Tiberius Gracchus

Tiberius Gracchus, grandson of Scipio Africanus, was elected tribune in 133 BC. He attempted to alleviate rural poverty with a bill that would compel large landowners to give up public land they held in excess of the legal limit. This land would then be redistributed to the poor. In his speeches, Tiberius claimed to be the champion of those "who fought and died to win luxury for others".

Many senators were opposed to the plan, and persuaded one of the other nine tribunes to veto it. In return, Tiberius removed the tribune from office. He successfully resubmitted his proposal to the people and set up a commission to begin dividing up the public land. In the same year, King Attalus of Pergamum bequeathed Rome his kingdom, which became the province of Asia, and his property. Tiberius proposed to divert the new resources to the people, to provide equipment grants for his settlers. Enraged, his opponents took matters into their own hands when he stood for re-election the next year. As the people voted, the senators beat Tiberius and more than 300 supporters to death, before throwing his body into the Tiber.

Gaius Gracchus

Ten years later in 123 BC, Tiberius's younger brother Gaius was elected tribune, and he renewed the battle for reform. He passed laws for further land distribution, the foundation of new colonies, subsidized grain, restrictions on military service, the recruitment of the *equites* to the juries, and the protection of provincials from the corruption of Roman magistrates. He also proposed the extension of Roman citizenship to the Latins and voting rights to the Italians, but this did not pass – the Romans were keen to protect their privileges. The Senate opposed Gaius as implacably as they had his brother, and once again politics ended in violence. In 122 BC, Gaius killed himself just outside Rome, pursued by a senatorial mob.

Marius' army

The last great popular politician of the 2nd century BC chose practical innovation over confrontation. Gaius Marius was a distinguished soldier, a Roman citizen from an Italian town, and a "new man" – he had no senatorial ancestors. He won his first consulship in 107 BC by denouncing the corruption and luxury of the elite, and he amassed forces to defeat King Jugurtha of Numidia by enlisting volunteers as well as the traditional conscripts. He settled his soldiers – Roman and Italian – in veteran colonies. Thus, he won the favour of the people and created an army that was loyal primarily to him rather than the state. The Romans elected him consul again in 104 BC when a German attack seemed imminent. Over the next five years of successful warfare against the Germans he was annually re-elected, a break with Republican tradition that would prove ominous.

The Age of Pompey, Caesar, and the Civil Wars

The complaints of the Italians and Roman peasants went unheeded by the Senate, which now found itself under attack. The provinces threatened rebellion. Slave revolts had shaken Sicily, and unemployment and food shortages were driving the urban poor to violence. Powerful individuals with client armies dominated the last decades of the Republic, dismantling its institutions and fighting over its remains.

Julius Caesar emerged as the victor from the military and ideological battles of the late Republic. A patrician who capitalized both on his family's supposed descent from Aeneas and the goddess Venus, and their more recent connection by marriage to the "new man" Gaius Marius, he also gained popularity with the army during his lengthy and lucrative campaigns.

The Italians, frustrated by their meagre success in obtaining land grants and voting rights, and inconvenienced by the new colonies and settlers that land reform had scattered throughout Italy, agreed among themselves to do away with Roman exploitation altogether. They planned to replace the current regime with a federal state, Italia. Fighting broke out in 91 BC and spread throughout central and southern Italy; this war was the first for centuries to pit Roman and Italian troops against each other. It took Rome three years to conciliate the combatants with promises of citizenship.

Powerful generals and client armies

In the meantime, Mithridates, the king of Pontus on the Black Sea, had invaded Roman territory in Asia in 88–84 BC. He was welcomed as a liberator by many of the provincial subjects, who were suffering extortion by Roman officials as well as taxation and interference by the state. In Rome, the people wanted to award the command against Mithridates to Marius; the majority of the Senate preferred Marius' old deputy in Numidia, Sulla. Both generals resorted to military force. Sulla marched on Rome, drove Marius out of the city, and imposed martial law. After Sulla left with his army in order to face Mithridates, Marius recaptured Rome and was elected to a seventh consulship; however, he died before he could set out in pursuit of his rival.

Sulla eventually made a lucrative peace with Mithridates and once more marched on Rome. By 81 BC, he was in control of the city, whereupon he revived the ancient office of the dictatorship, in which supreme power was awarded to an individual by the Senate at times of national crisis, traditionally in order to complete a specific task and for a very short time (six months at most). As sole ruler, Sulla reorganized the magistracies and deprived the tribunes of their powers. He killed more than 90 of his enemies in the Senate after

publishing their names on proscription lists. The loyalty of his soldiers was not forgotten, and he settled them in veteran colonies before retiring from public life in 79 BC.

The tactics of Marius and Sulla were a glimpse of things to come. Roman soldiers, once reluctant to abandon their farms and families for years for Rome, were eager to fight for individual generals who bought their loyalty with shares of booty and land grants. The generals enjoyed unprecedented power and freedom of action through "special commands" awarded for years at a time.

The two men who would overshadow the last three decades of the Republic both used popular rhetoric to gain personal power. Pompey the Great

The Trials of Cicero

In 58 BC, five years after Cicero had Catilina's supporters put to death, Clodius passed a bill exiling magistrates who executed citizens without trial, with retrospective effect. The great lawyer fled to Greece rather than face trial. His house on the Palatine was burned down, and the site became a shrine to Liberty – although he did engineer a recall to Rome a year later. After equivocating between Pompey and Caesar in the civil wars, Cicero's final moment of glory came after Caesar's assassination when he vehemently attacked the excesses of Mark Antony in public speeches. He was swiftly killed by the new regime, and his head and right hand were cut off and displayed on the rostrum in the Forum.

restored the powers of the tribunes during his first consulship in 70 BC – a consulship that he had obtained without holding previous office. He went on to eradicate the pirates who threatened the city's grain supply, appointed to this special command for three years by the people against the wishes of the Senate. Pompey spent the late 60s BC defeating a fresh invasion of the eastern provinces by Mithridates and afterwards devoted several years to annexing territory for Rome and founding cities: activities that led in some quarters to suspicions that he desired kingship himself. The wealthy aristocrat Julius Caesar also won the favour of the people, not least by funding generous entertainment, public works, and extensive electoral bribery. He obtained the consulship in 59 BC and set out on a spectacular decade-long conquest of Gaul, in which perhaps a million Gauls died and another million were enslaved.

Debt, hunger, and violence

Rome faced enormous troubles during these decades. There were rebellions in Spain, as well as in the East. A Thracian gladiator, Spartacus, started a revolt in southern Italy in 73 BC, which quickly spread from the gladiatorial schools to slaves and many of the free poor. It took the Romans two years to defeat this massive insurrection.

More Romans had lost their land as a result of the recent warfare in Italy, and debt had become endemic. Violence, riots, and political assassinations were part of everyday life. Two aristocrats emerged as lightning rods for discontent. Sergius Catilina led agitation for land redistribution and debt cancellation in 63 BC and was hounded out of the city amid accusations of arson and conspiracy by the moderate consul Cicero. Catilina raised an army and was killed in battle, whereupon Cicero persuaded the senators to execute those suspected of co-conspiracy. The poor found another champion – and Cicero another enemy – in Clodius Pulcher, a libertine with links to both Pompey and Caesar. Clodius had himself adopted into a plebeian family in order to be eligible for election to the tribunate of 58 BC, where he passed measures to provide free corn for the people.

The final confrontation

Clodius was killed in a brawl with a rival in 52 BC; in the same year, in yet another departure from Republican tradition, Pompey was appointed sole consul. Pompey and Caesar had hitherto maintained an uneasy alliance. Both had bypassed the Senate in order to take legislation to the people and to make foreign policy decisions, and both had earned vast wealth from their conquests. But now Caesar wanted a second consulship to mark his triumphant return from Gaul, and Pompey co-operated with the Senate to block it. War was inevitable, with both men claiming that they were defending the Republic against tyranny. In 49 BC, Caesar and his army crossed the Rubicon, which marked the boundary of his province, to march on Rome. The civil war that followed was fought all over the Roman Mediterranean: Pompey led the "Republican" resistance army to defeat in Greece in 48 BC. He was murdered in Egypt, and his supporters were hunted down in Africa and Spain. By 46 BC, Caesar was consul and dictator at Rome. He reformed the Senate and the magistracies, founded colonies for his veterans and for the urban poor, and was worshipped as a god. In 44 BC, still consul, he declared himself dictator for life. This was a step too far, and Caesar was assassinated by a conspiracy of senators on the ides of March.

Republican Culture

In contrast to the Greeks' elegant theatres and athletics, Roman entertainment was raw and often bloodthirsty: gladiator shows in the Forum, chariot races at the Circus Maximus, and pantomime in temporary theatres. With the conquest of Greece, more sophisticated and literary entertainments emerged, but they never displaced the thrill of the race and the fight for ordinary Romans.

This mosaic panel from Pompeii shows a group of actors with their chorus master rehearsing for a satyr play, complete with masks, costumes, and musical instruments. Satyr plays were originally performed in Greece as light-hearted finales to the trilogies of tragedies that playwrights composed for dramatic competitions.

There were four different types of gladiators: The Murmillo, with a fish's crest on his helmet, the Samnite, with an oblong shield and a short sword, the Retinarius, who carried a net and a trident, and the Thracian, who had a round shield and curved sword.

Games and festivals

Funded in part by the state, in part by individual magistrates, Roman games were held in honour of religious festivals. They featured chariot races as far back as the Period of the Kings, and the best-known racing arena was the Circus Maximus, which could hold 150,000 spectators. The teams in the races were known by their colours: first white and red, later joined by blue and green. Up to twelve chariots competed over seven laps. Mime artists and dancers were later added to the celebrations; later still, plays were also performed, although they do not seem to have been written down or circulated separately. Literary drama, along with history and epic, developed out of contacts with Greeks in the period of Roman expansion.

The Greek conquest of Roman culture

"Captive Greece took her savage conqueror captive, and brought the arts into rustic Latium." So the poet Horace described the extraordinary appeal of all things Hellenic to the Romans of the later Republic. While Greek culture was never unknown to the Romans, it became increasingly fashionable as they conquered the Mediterranean. Roman commanders learnt Greek and learnt to appreciate Greek art and life, often bringing Greek artworks – painting, sculpture, and bronzes – back to Rome as part of their booty.

The first poets and playwrights to record their work in Latin wrote in the Greek epic genre about Roman history and heroes, and translated Greek plays for the Roman stage. Plautus and Terence adapted Greek comedies for Roman religious festivals and funeral games in the early part of the 2nd century BC and were the first Latin writers whose work survives in more than fragments. Both relied heavily on misunderstandings, mix-ups, and farce for their comic effect. Life is turned upside down in their domestic dramas: prostitutes are virtuous, and cunning slaves routinely save their masters from trouble. Although some of the details are "Romanized", it is likely that the Greek setting and the topsy-turvy plots gave the plays an aura of escapism. Potentially subversive elements in the population – especially slaves and women – could run riot, but only in Greece, and only on the stage.

While the people watched these dramas, which were usually performed in temporary theatres or temples, the Roman elite competed to build temples and public buildings in the Greek style and to adorn their country villas with Greek works of art, commissioning copies if necessary. The culmination of this competitive Hellenism came in 55 BC, when Pompey built Rome's first permanent stone theatre in the Campus Martius.

Greeks in Rome

Greeks themselves began to arrive in Rome in large numbers, as craftsmen, doctors, and artists,

The Vestal Virgins

As young girls, Vestal Virgins took a 30-year vow of chastity. These priestesses were charged with the care of the sacred fire in the temple of Vesta in the Forum, which guaranteed the preservation of the city. They led unusually public and independent lives for women, under no man's control, with special seats at banquets and the games, and the power to spare condemned criminals. They were regarded as sacrosanct: if someone so much as bumped into a Vestal's litter, he would be put to death. And if a priestess was found to have broken her vow of chastity, she was buried alive.

but also as refugees, slaves, and prisoners of war. The historian Polybius was taken to Rome as a hostage in 167 BC, and it was there that he wrote his 40-volume history in Greek of the Roman rise to power in the Mediterranean. On a famous occasion in 155 BC, philosophers representing the Stoic, Sceptic, and Peripatetic schools in Athens came to Rome as a delegation. Carneades the Sceptic drew large crowds to his public speeches, where he argued persuasively in favour of justice one day and, on the next, equally convincingly against it. Marcus Porcius Cato, the grand old man of Roman politics, was disgusted. He considered Greek philosophers dangerous windbags and had the delegation sent away as quickly as possible.

The new cosmopolitanism was certainly not welcomed by everybody. Historians and orators regularly blamed the troubles of the late Republic on the effects of the conquest of the East, either pointing to the corruption of Roman troops by oriental luxury or, more practically, to the effects of sudden unprecedented wealth on the upper classes. But Hellenism did not entirely suppress the old culture of Rome. As well as Greek adaptations, Roman drama had a strong homegrown tradition of contemporary political commentary and satire, and Latin authors concerned themselves with practical matters such as agriculture and law, as well as the new arts of history and philosophy. Cato himself wrote a treatise on farming, in addition to one of the first historical works in Latin, on the origins of Italian communities.

Latin poets often combined Greek genres and techniques with Roman themes and experience. The "Hellenistic" poets of the last decades of the Republic used Greek models and techniques to create experimental poetry about the daily lives and love affairs of dissolute and disillusioned Roman youth. The results were both extremely erudite and iconoclastic. While this poetry did not avoid commentary on the harsh realities of war or the corruption of contemporary politics, it does give us a glimpse of a world in which these matters compete for attention with sex, friendship, and learning. The best-known of these poets was Catullus, who is remembered for political commentary and miniature epics, as well as obscene poems set in the brothels and backstreets of Rome. Many of his poems are about his unhappy love affair with the mysterious Lesbia, rumoured to be a pseudonym for Clodia, the notorious sister of the tribune Publius Clodius.

Gladiatorial contests

Catullus and his fellow poets did not provide entertainment for the masses. Far more popular were the gruesome gladiator shows that had been held in the Forum since the middle of the 3rd century BC. These contests pitted prisoners of war, condemned criminals, and professional fighters against each other in a fight to the death, although the crowd could – and often did – save the life of a defeated man. During the Republic, they were always held as part of funeral celebrations.

Beast contests were also popular, with creatures from all over the Empire, including lions, panthers, crocodiles, and elephants, fighting other animals or unfortunate criminals. Romans could see the fruits of their overseas expansion in these shows, both in the financial resources they required and in the exotic prisoners and animals they displayed.

*The Augustan poet Virgil sits between
Clio, the Muse of History, (left) and
Melpomene, the Muse of Tragedy
(right). Virgil's* Aeneid, *an epic poem
on Roman origins and identity, was
a double-edged commentary on the
new world order.*

THE ROMAN EMPIRE: 44 BC–AD 476

By the time of Augustus (27 BC–AD 14), Rome was a huge, chaotic city of perhaps a million people, citizen and slave. Water was scarce, famine a constant threat, sanitation poor, and disease rife. Augustus brought some measure of order to the city, just as he enlarged and organized the Roman Empire, and his successors sought to emulate his example. Life at Rome would never be calm, but it could be controlled.

The institutions of the Republic had grown increasingly outmoded, and with the advent of monarchical power came a shift at every level of society from the collective to the individual. The emperor himself ruled with the authority that had once belonged to a college of magistrates, while the voting power of the people first diminished, then disappeared. Freedom of association was tightly regulated. Power was concentrated in the household of the ruler, who was the source of legislation, adjudicated disputes, and granted privileges to individuals and cities. Rome's citizens old and new had wider horizons, but quieter voices.

Once again, these changes were reflected in the monuments and public spaces of the city itself. Aristocratic competition in building gave way to imperial munificence. The Republican Forum, once the crossroads of the politics and people of Rome, was quickly rendered obsolete. The temples, shrines, and legends of the Forum became a museum to Rome's past, as well as a monument to the imperial family, with new temples and arches erected to celebrate their achievements.

The political functions of the old Republican Forum moved to a series of monumental fora built by the emperors, where the state religious and military ceremonies were now held, and to the imperial palaces. Julius Caesar had begun to build a new Forum abutting the Republican Forum to the east. It was finished by Augustus, who built his own alongside, surrounding a ground temple with statues.

The Campus Martius (Field of Mars) was the plain in the crook of the Tiber outside the city walls, where armies used to gather and where Pompey had built Rome's first theatre amid temples dedicated by triumphant Republican generals. Now the emperors adorned this quarter with theatres, baths, gardens, and temples. One political institution – a new voting hall – was built there by Agrippa in 15 BC. But the popular vote meant little even by then, and the hall later became an arena for gladiators.

Augustus had kept a relatively modest house on the Palatine hill, above the old Forum. His successors, by contrast, erected vast imperial palaces there, and Domitian's palace still dominates the hill today. The various areas of the city had once been united and drawn together by the Republican Forum, open on all sides, where both the nobility and the poor came together in a political context. Now the Republican Forum was a space that separated the palaces, the imperial fora, and the popular delights of the Campus Martius. By dispersing the population, the emperors controlled the city and suppressed potential conflict.

Later emperors abandoned Rome, sometimes spending their whole reigns in the provinces. Citizenship was extended to the entire Empire in 212, but it was no longer a guarantee of participation in political life and was instead a symbol of a relationship with the emperor. Like the city, the Roman Empire never achieved true stability, and what peace and security there was came at the price of tyranny. Religious and political suppression helped to keep the system alive, but could not prevent its decline nor the increasing discontent of the lower classes and subject peoples. The result was that, by the 5th century, the entire Western Empire was easy prey to the Goths and Vandals.

Augustus Caesar

If Julius Caesar's assassins were hoping to restore senatorial authority, they were too optimistic. The surviving consul, Mark Antony, quickly marshalled the support of the people and the army. The Senate fell back on the young Octavian as their champion, and 13 more years of civil war racked the Mediterranean as Caesar's adopted son gradually eliminated all his rivals to power.

When Caesar was assassinated, his great nephew and adopted son, Octavian, was just 18 years old. With Cicero's support, the young man was appointed to the Senate and given extraordinary powers to protect the state. Once he had gained control of the Roman army, he intimidated the Senate into allowing his election as consul and almost immediately cut a deal with Mark Antony. Along with Lepidus, a governor of Gaul, the two generals established an uneasy "triumvirate". The people awarded the three men special constitutional powers to set the state in order. They appointed magistrates, confiscated land for their veterans, and carried out proscriptions, offering money in exchange for the heads of their enemies.

Octavian gained a reputation as the most hard-hearted and bloodthirsty of the three, although it was Antony who finally defeated Caesar's assassins in Macedonia in 42 BC.

Antony and Cleopatra

Octavian and Mark Antony divided the Mediterranean between them, with Octavian taking the western provinces and Antony the east, where he met Cleopatra. The queen of Egypt already had a child by Julius Caesar, and twins by Antony now followed. His subsequent marriage to Octavian's sister Octavia may have consolidated the triumviral alliance, but it does not seem to have diminished his affection for the Egyptian queen. By 36 BC,

Cleopatra VII was the last of the Ptolemaic rulers of Egypt, and the first to learn Egyptian. Inheriting the throne at the age of 18, she became very popular with her subjects and successfully opposed Roman annexation for 20 years. She was celebrated more for her intellect and conversation than her beauty.

Antony's relationship with Cleopatra and an unsuccessful campaign against the Parthians had tarnished his reputation in Rome. At the same time, Octavian consolidated his position there when his general Agrippa defeated Pompey's outlaw son Sextus, who had been blockading Roman grain ships in the Mediterranean.

Octavian forced Lepidus into a permanent retirement, and his relationship with Antony broke down. Propaganda became open war in 32 BC, when Octavian had Antony's powers as *triumvir* revoked in Rome and declared war on Cleopatra. Antony refused to desert his queen, but the royal couple both deserted the decisive battle of Actium in 31 BC and fled to Alexandria, where they committed suicide.

The restoration of the Republic

Octavian now ruled alone. In 27 BC, he handed power back to the Senate and the people, retaining the consulship for himself. In return, the Senate voted him the title "Augustus", a word which had religious connotations, and he was awarded supreme command over the provinces of Spain, Gaul, Syria, and Egypt, which contained almost all the Roman legions. In 23 BC, he went further, giving up the consulship and refusing the title of dictator when the people of Rome pressed it upon him. But these changes were superficial: Augustus remained in control of the state not only by virtue of a grant of tribunician power, and thus the right to propose or veto any legislation, but also because of his special command in the provinces. He called himself the *princeps* – the first man.

The Senate still met, although Augustus revised the membership. He cut their workload by restricting the number of meetings and decreeing that only those selected by lot to ensure a quorum need attend. Elections also took place with the *princeps* making his preferences known, at first by canvassing in the Republican tradition, but later by simply posting a list. No rivals were permitted, but many nobles were taken into his circle. His brilliant general Agrippa was his most trusted adviser and became almost a partner in government, left in charge of affairs at Rome while Augustus spent long periods in his provinces.

Pax Augusta

It is unlikely that anyone was fooled by the Republican rhetoric, but the peace and plenty of the Augustan era ensured his popularity with the Roman people. Civil war ended, and Italy began to recover. Augustus now compensated for his bloody youth with ostentatious clemency towards his enemies. He restored aqueducts and bridges, gave land

to his veterans, and dispensed cash handouts to the poor. The Augustan peace must have seemed a welcome respite from Republican freedom.

Wars were fought far from Rome. Augustus professionalized the army, and he pacified and enlarged the empire he had inherited. He established dozens of colonies abroad and reformed the taxation and census systems so that even more provincial wealth was chanelled to the capital. The expansion met resistance, and the last decade of Augustus' life saw serious revolts in the provinces.

The problem of succession

Augustus married Livia Drusilla in 39 BC, a second marriage for both. It was a devoted partnership, although childless. Augustus brought a daughter, Julia, from his previous marriage, and Livia a son, Tiberius, who became a successful general and politician. Julia was married to Agrippa, while Tiberius was married to Agrippa's daughter Vipsania. On Agrippa's death, however, Julia and Tiberius were forced to marry. The pair detested each other, and Julia's extramarital adventures became embarrassing to her father, who had her exiled in 2 BC. Tiberius had retired from public life to the island of Rhodes in 6 BC, in part to escape his wife, but also because of his stepfather's promotion of Julia's sons by Agrippa, Gaius, and Lucius. Augustus adopted the boys and gave them public commands. Both died young. Augustus had to recall Tiberius and, to Livia's delight, adopted him.

This large onyx gem dates from the first decade AD, and unites the Augustan themes of dynasty, piety, and empire. Augustus as Jupiter is being crowned by Oikoumene, the "known world". Alongside him are Livia as the goddess Roma and (far left) the future emperor Tiberius. Below, Roman soldiers are erecting a trophy over barbarian prisoners.

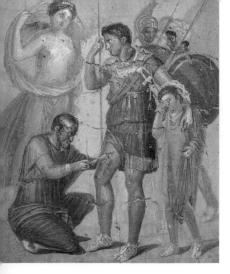

Augustan Culture

The people of Rome were fast losing their political authority – and with it their practical role as Roman citizens. Augustan propaganda sought to reinforce the notion of a communal citizen identity and introduced practical means to do so. Romans followed the same clock and calendar, and worshipped at the same altars, under the common authority of one man – Augustus.

This 1st century AD fresco from Pompeii shows a scene from Book 12 of the Aeneid *where the doctor Iapyx is tending to Aeneas, who has been wounded in battle. Aeneas's mother Venus looks on anxiously in the background, and Aeneas's son Ascanius weeps on the right.*

Augustus filled Rome with new temples, monuments, theatres, and baths, shifting the focus of urban activity away from the Republican political centre into the Campus Martius, previously the army's assembly ground. Augustus boasted that he had found Rome a city of brick and left it a city of marble.

The image of Augustus

Augustus distanced himself from the horrors of civil war and looked instead to Rome's past. He revived old customs and invented new ones. With new laws on marriage, adultery, extravagance, and bribery, he advocated a return to traditional morality. He even barred those not wearing the traditional toga from entering the Forum. In 17 BC, the Secular Games were held, a festival that traditionally marked the passing of an era at Rome. This time it officially designated a new golden age, where peace and the traditions and values of the past would once again predominate.

Augustus transformed the city with architectural projects that celebrated the themes of his reign: peace, fertility, order, and piety. In 28 BC, Augustus built a massive family mausoleum in the northern part of the Campus Martius. He later added a giant sundial, which also operated as a calendar, to celebrate victory over Egypt. The sundial's pointer was an Egyptian obelisk, underlining the importance of the Empire as an integral part of the Roman order. The final part of the complex

was an altar to Augustan Peace, which the Senate voted to him in 13 BC to commemorate victories over the Gauls and the Germans.

The altar featured the founders of Rome – Aeneas and Romulus – as well as the goddesses Roma and Mother Earth. The imperial family, magistrates, and the people were depicted participating in a sacrificial procession, each group accorded its proper, supporting role within the new order. It is telling that this triumphal monument officially commemorated peace rather than war, and it depicted Augustus himself not as a general, but as a sacrificing priest. The continuity, stability, and authority of the new regime was symbolized by the stories depicted on the altar.

The period of Augustan Peace was followed by a new stage of expansionism. In 2 BC, Augustus built his own Forum. This monument was dominated by a grand temple to Mars the Avenger, and a statue of Augustus stood between serried ranks of individual Roman heroes. This new bellicose authoritarianism stood in stark contrast to – and was made possible by – the earlier emphases on peace and order.

Augustus, son of the Divine Julius

Augustus became *pontifex maximus* (chief priest) in 12 BC, and he accumulated many supplementary priesthoods besides. Religion was a cornerstone of the Augustan programme, with ostentatious veneration of both Olympian and traditional local gods existing alongside a nascent ruler cult. Julius Caesar had been deified on his death, and his adopted successor never missed an opportunity to remind the Romans that he was the son of a god.

Augustus blurred the boundaries between the human and the divine. Official state prayers were addressed to his *genius* (spirit), and temples were dedicated to him in the provinces. Ruler cult was not new in the eastern Mediterranean, but temples to Augustus are also found in the West. In

Map labels:
- Mausoleum of Augustus
- Horologium of Augustus
- Ara Pacis
- Aqua Virgo (Agrippa)
- Aqua Marcia
- Aqua Julia (Agrippa)
- Pantheon of Agrippa
- Portico of Pompey
- Baths of Agrippa
- Saepta Julia (voting enclosure)
- Theatre of Pompey
- Portico of Octavia
- Tabularium
- Forum of Julius Caesar
- Forum of Augustus
- Portico of Livia
- Theatre and Crypt of Balbus
- Amphitheatre of Statilius Taurus
- Republican Forum
- Servian city wall (c. 4th BC)
- Theatre of Marcellus
- Temple of Jupiter Capitolinus
- Aqua Alsietina
- Temple of Apollo on the Palatine
- Circus Maximus
- Aqua Appia (c. 4th BC)
- Tiber
- Porticus Aemilia (warehouse)

Augustan Rome
- Pre-Augustan
- Augustan
- Augustan administrative region

Family values

Augustan legislation to encourage legitimate marriage and reproduction among upper-class Romans demonstrates the way in which private life became a public concern in this period. Marriage and divorce were formalized and adultery was criminalized. If a man refused to divorce his adulterous wife and prosecute her, he could be prosecuted for living off immoral earnings. Penalties were introduced for those who did not marry, and rewards given for having children. The new laws were not very popular or successful. The knights demonstrated against them, and senators' wives discovered a useful loophole: they avoided penalties for adultery if they registered with city officials as prostitutes.

Italy, he was more reticent, although he did build and restore many temples, including one to Apollo that interconnected with his house on the Palatine. He moved the ancient cult of Vesta into the house itself. It must have come as no surprise that, on his death, Augustus, too, was proclaimed a god.

Political literature

The golden age was hailed by contemporary poets, many of whom were supported and funded by Maecenas, who was a close friend of the *princeps*. Horace may have been the closest to being a court poet; Augustus commissioned him to write the choral ode to be sung by children at the Secular Games, the *Carmen Saeculare*. In other poems, Horace thanks Augustus for delivering Rome from the horrors of civil war and the threat of rule by a decadent oriental queen. According to Horace, Augustus "guards the Italian state with arms, and graces it with morals".

The epic poet Virgil often echoes these sentiments. In his *Aeneid* (19 BC), an oracle predicts that Augustus will carry Rome's rule forward to Africa and India. Jupiter announces that he has set the Romans no boundaries in space or time, but given them an empire without end. Despite the friendship between Virgil and Augustus, however, his tale of the wanderings of Aeneas on his way from Troy to Italy is not simple propaganda. The poet explores the tensions in the new era, celebrating it and questioning it at the same time.

Aeneas is Rome's wise and dutiful hero, described as the first of a line of great leaders which culminates with the rule of Augustus himself. When he escapes from Troy to Carthage, he and his men are rescued by the Carthaginian queen Dido, and the pair fall in love. Yet he soon abandons her to follow his divine calling to found a city in Italy. Dido commits suicide, and Aeneas' ships sail out in sight of her blazing funeral pyre. The reader is left to contemplate whether love and citizen duty can be compatible; whether piety requires a lack of pity. Dido is not the only victim of Aeneas' (and thus Rome's) success; the Italian kings must also make way for the new leader, and in the last lines of the poem pious Aeneas completes his mission by slaughtering the courageous Rutulian king Turnus in a moment of passionate cruelty and rage. Order is fragile, Virgil seems to be warning us, and peace has its costs.

The Early Empire

On his deathbed, Augustus counselled Rome to keep the Empire within its present limits. His successors followed this advice for almost a century. There was plenty to occupy them at Rome, where their unconstitutional position was never formalized. With no clear right to govern, they relied instead on a combination of populism, force, and fear.

The Julio-Claudian dynasty

By the time Augustus died in AD 14, Tiberius had already been awarded long-term tribunician power and authority greater than any other magistrate except the *princeps*. The succession was not in doubt, although Tiberius himself claimed to be reluctant. Nonetheless, he began as a conscientious and hardworking ruler, concerning himself with the problems of the Italians and the provincials, and refusing to have temples dedicated to him. An old-fashioned man fond of learning and suspicious by nature, he did not ingratiate himself with the Senate or the Roman people in the manner of his predecessor. Elections were transferred to the Senate from the popular assemblies, but the emperor's wish dictated the results of the election.

The question of the succession tortured the Julio-Claudian dynasty from Augustus to Nero. Tiberius had two heirs: his son Drusus and his nephew Germanicus, whom he had adopted. Germanicus died in AD 19, claiming that he had been poisoned on the emperor's orders, and Drusus died in 23. This latter tragedy seems to have destroyed Tiberius' spirit, and three years later he retired to Capri with his household, giving up on most state business. His closest confidant was the head of his imperial guard, the unpopular Sejanus, who now became his only link with Rome and exercised almost imperial power there. Sejanus was to fall foul of the emperor, however, and was killed in 31.

Thereafter, Tiberius devoted himself to a life of leisure and, later writers alleged, extraordinary vice. He was joined on Capri by Germanicus' son Gaius "Caligula", a youth already notorious for an unusually close relationship with his own sister. Gaius took to the pleasures available on the island with enthusiasm.

During the reign of Trajan, the Roman Empire surrounded the whole of the Mediterranean, and encompassed most of continental Northern Europe and Britain. A complex bureaucracy and a large army maintained stability in these regions for a significant period of time, although Trajan's attempt to incorporate areas even further east failed almost immediately.

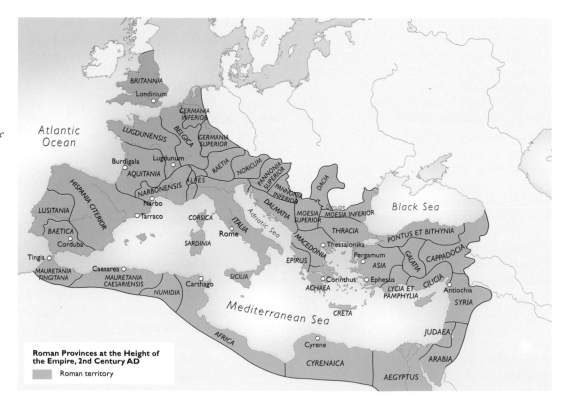

Roman Provinces at the Height of the Empire, 2nd Century AD

Roman territory

When Tiberius died in 37, Gaius was named heir in his will. He was the first emperor to declare himself divine in his own lifetime, and he installed a life-sized golden statue in a shrine to himself, which every day was dressed in clothes to match his own. He briefly returned the elections to the people; however, he treated the Senate with outright contempt, and it may be this that led to rumours that he was planning to award a consulship to Incitatus, his favourite horse. His short reign was ended by assassination in 41.

The senators attempted to reclaim power, but the imperial guard forced them to accept Germanicus' brother Claudius. His physical disabilities and diffidence caused many to perceive him as weak, yet Claudius seems to have been a competent emperor. It was under his rule (although not his command) that the first significant territorial gains since the Augustan period took place, with the conquest of southern Britain in 43. Claudius was poisoned in 54 by his fourth wife, his niece Agrippina, in order to ensure the succession of her son Nero.

The new emperor was young, popular, and immensely brutal. He murdered his stepbrother Britannicus in 55, and his mother in 59. In 62, he divorced then murdered his wife Octavia and married his mistress Poppaea, whom he kicked to death in 65. This was the same year that he forced his tutor, the philosopher and playwright Seneca, to commit suicide. Nero's public life became increasingly dissolute and confiscations fuelled his wildly expensive tastes. When a great fire destroyed much of Rome in 64, he took advantage of the devastation by building an enormous palace in the centre of the city, the Golden House. Judea revolted in 66, and in 68 the governors of Gaul and Spain organized a revolt of their armies. Nero panicked and killed himself. The Julio-Claudian dynasty had wiped itself out.

The Flavian dynasty

The Year of Four Emperors took place in 69, when events demonstrated that outsiders could become Roman emperors. Four provincial governors in succession seized power, the last being Vespasian, an obscure senator who had been appointed by Nero to put down a Jewish revolt in 66. Vespasian was a disciplinarian, and he quickly solidified his position. His son Titus captured Jerusalem and was the officer responsible for the burning of the Temple in 70. His brief but happy rule after the death of his father in 79 BC ended with his own death in 81 BC; there were rumours that his younger brother Domitian had poisoned him. Domitian then commenced

Bread and circuses

Roman politicians traditionally won popular support with distributions of grain or cash, and extravagant public games. In the Julio-Claudian period, the emperors came to monopolize these activities. Vespasian and his sons asserted their popular credentials after the megalomania of Nero's reign by building the Colosseum where the Golden House had stood. Trajan established a new formula for public welfare in Italy – the alimentary scheme – whereby capital improvement mortgages were issued to farmers from the imperial treasury at a fixed 5% interest rate. The proceeds were distributed to poor children in the locality – 16 sesterces for boys and 12 for girls.

a reign of terror. Constant denunciations and treason trials led to several attempted revolts, and he was finally stabbed to death in a plot that involved his wife.

Emperors by adoption

Domitian's successor, Nerva (r.96–8), was nominated by the Senate, and he founded a tradition of adopting an heir from among the promising senators, which proved to be a stable, less bloody way of organizing the succession. His choice was the Spanish-born Trajan, a renowned general and the governor of Upper Germany.

Trajan's accession was so uncontroversial that he did not even come to Rome for more than a year. He was a diplomatic and just ruler, but he was also ambitious and turned again to expansion. In 106, Trajan annexed Dacia (the region that is roughly modern Romania) with its gold mines, and in the same year he established the province of Arabia. Trajan's greatest success of all came in 115 when the provinces of Assyria and Mesopotamia were created. Yet even before his death in 117, revolts were under way among the Jews and Mesopotamians, and the Empire began to shrink again; however, it was quite appropriate that the largest extent of the Roman Empire should have been won by its first provincial emperor.

Imperial Life and Literature

Tacitus called the accession of Trajan "the dawn of this most happy age". After the reign of Domitian, the return of free speech with the new emperor came as a great relief to writers and politicians. By now, no one dreamt of a restored Republic; an emperor was a necessary evil to ensure peace and good emperors a rare delight.

The best history is often written by those with an awkward relationship to power: Polybius was a Roman hostage, Sallust a disgraced senator, and Seneca combined teaching, philosophy, and playwriting with a career in politics until his ex-pupil Nero forced him to commit suicide for alleged involvement in a plot on the emperor's life. The historian Tacitus was a politician during the reign of Domitian, whom he thought worse even than Nero, for "even Nero looked away, and did not gaze upon the atrocities he ordered". Tacitus appointed himself the historian of the households that ruled the Roman Empire, preserving them in vivid colour and biting prose. The books dealing with Domitian are now lost, but Tacitus' own collaboration seems to haunt his writing.

If Tacitus recorded the lives of the imperial family, the writings of his friend Pliny, who was a consul in 100 and governor of Bithynia from 110–12, paint a broader canvas of upper-class Roman life. Pliny wrote nine books of letters in the first decade of the 2nd century, intended for publication. As well as the conventional praise of Trajan, his major themes are land and the extraordinary wealth of the Roman elite. At a time when the average daily wage of a labourer was around 3 sesterces, and a soldier earned 1200 sesterces a year, Pliny had no difficulty raising 3 million sesterces to buy another estate, although he complains at the same time of financial problems. The minimum property requirement for a senator in the imperial period was 1 million sesterces.

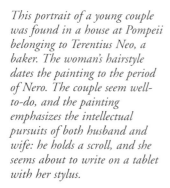

This portrait of a young couple was found in a house at Pompeii belonging to Terentius Neo, a baker. The woman's hairstyle dates the painting to the period of Nero. The couple seem well-to-do, and the painting emphasizes the intellectual pursuits of both husband and wife: he holds a scroll, and she seems about to write on a tablet with her stylus.

Most income came from land. Pliny himself had several estates and rented land to tenant farmers. The early Empire was a time of rural prosperity and increasing population in Italy, although tenants had little security and relied on the goodwill of the landowners. Intensive cultivation made marginal land viable for agriculture, and there is evidence of a great variety of farmhouses, villas, and ranches throughout the peninsula. Vines and olives, which required space, investment, and a good supply of seasonal labour, were a popular choice for farmers, demonstrating the stability of rural life. Agricultural slavery was also widespread, especially in the centre and south of the peninsula.

Pompeii

Pliny is also the chronicler of seaside life in the Bay of Naples, where the wealthy kept holiday villas in addition to their country homes outside Rome and their agricultural estates. The towns around the bay were wealthy resorts, servicing visitors and the local elite in bars, baths, and brothels in the shadow of the volcano Vesuvius, thought to be long extinct. One local character was Pliny's uncle, known as Pliny the Elder, who wrote a vast encyclopedia of knowledge, including science, ethnography, and geography. Such subjects were fashionable in the 1st century AD, codifying the new knowledge from the Empire just as the provinces themselves were being organized.

Pliny the Elder was commander of the fleet at Misenum on the northern tip of the bay when Vesuvius erupted. The younger Pliny recounts the events of 24 August 79, describing how his mother drew his uncle's attention to an unusual cloud that was forming over the bay. Ash and stones were raining down from the mountain, and the elder Pliny sprang into action, leading boats to the rescue of the fleeing population. They were forced to put in at Stabiae as the eruption worsened. Flames were shooting out of the volcano and the ground was shaking. By the morning, the sky was black with soot. Pliny the Elder was overcome by the smoke and died alongside more than 20,000 residents of Pompeii, Herculaneum, and Stabiae, most of whom were drowned in lava or mud.

Vesuvius both destroyed and preserved Pompeii, burying the town in volcanic lava and creating an astonishing record for posterity of the daily life of this bustling city, stopped dead in an instant. Modern visitors to the Bay of Naples can walk around Pompeii's fancy houses, shops, and restaurants, marvel at the town's open spaces and gardens, and sit in the theatre and amphitheatre alongside crowds of tourists: nowhere else is the

world of the ancients closer to us. Household effects can be inventoried, business records and graffiti still read, and an incomparable picture of small-town Italian life emerges. We learn that merchants and freedmen had increasing economic influence in the town at the expense of local landowners, that overall business was in something of a decline, that electoral competition was rife, with graffiti and notices recording endorsements, and that a prostitute cost two asses (half a sestertius).

Poverty existed even in a town such as Pompeii, but it was dwarfed by the scale of destitution in Rome. There were job opportunities in the capital for labourers, and artisans and small businesses could flourish, with women as well as men finding ways to make money from crafts and selling goods at markets. Yet much of the urban population was crowded into rickety apartment blocks, expensive to rent, easy to burn, and quick to collapse. Homelessness was common, and the state welfare of grain and cash distributions did not reach those who needed it the most. Outside the monumental centre, open sewers ran through the streets, and the public water supply was inadequate to the needs of the population. Disease was endemic. Unfortunately, the only first-hand accounts of conditions are from the protected pens of the elite. Martial wrote exuberant and often scurrilous poems about Roman life and characters, while courting rich and powerful patrons, especially the emperor Domitian. His contemporary Juvenal's satires are often darker, but also ironic: he complains with a typical sneer of the "thousand dangers of the savage city": the fires, building collapses, and "poets reciting in August".

The last moments of some of Vesuvius's victims have been preserved in tragic detail. Lava buried this young Pompeian woman alive as she fled the volcano, and then hardened around her. When the city was excavated many centuries later, although her body was long gone, the space it had created in the lava remained. This cast and others like it are displayed at Pompeii, and serve as a counterpoint to the deserted buildings.

Architecture and Urbanism

The cities of the Roman provinces prospered in the 2nd century AD. Growth, wealth, and magnificent public architecture reflected the new importance of provincial politicians and soldiers in the Roman Empire, as well as the increasing "globalization" of politics, trade, and culture in the Mediterranean world.

The new architecture

Roman architecture was heavily influenced by Greek building styles, but new developments and inventions gave it a different character. In particular, the use of arches, concrete, and sophisticated vaulting techniques meant that Roman architects, unlike their Greek counterparts, were at least as concerned about internal space as external structure. Towards the end of the Republic, the building trade adopted standardized industrial production techniques, and under the early emperors Romans learnt how to combine reliable concrete with weight-relieving brick arches in order to build domes. These became the hallmark of ostentatious Roman imperial architecture. Hadrian's Pantheon, built in the 2nd century and still standing in the middle of the Campus Martius, is a perfect example of the new possibilities. From the outside it is a conventional square-fronted temple, but that is only the porch. The classical columns lead to an echoing rotunda lit through an opening at the top of a vast dome. The art of the dome was lost for a millennium before the Renaissance, and the diameter of the Pantheon's dome was unequalled until the construction of the CNIT building at La Defense in Paris in the 1950s.

Alongside new techniques, distinctive versions of Greek building forms developed in the Roman period. Theatres were enclosed and were given substructures, wide stages, and façades; bath-houses acquired central heating and elaborate architectural elements; and Greek *agoras* (market places) were surrounded by colonnades to make Roman forums. Etruscan and Italic forms also formed important ingredients in Roman architecture. Roman temples, like Etruscan ones, had a high podium and steps only at the front; and wealthier Romans retained the traditional Italian house, built round an open-air atrium.

"Roman"-style theatres spread across the provinces during the Empire. This spectacular example from the city of Sabratha in Tripolitania (modern Libya) is 92 metres (322 ft) wide, and 108 columns adorn the wall which served as a backdrop for the performances. The front rows were reserved for local magistrates and other dignatories.

Although these building forms are associated with Rome, they did not develop in the city itself. The earliest "Roman" theatres, baths, amphitheatres, and even domes are found around the Bay of Naples, although more monumental versions were soon built in the capital. New architectural and urban forms developed almost simultaneously in Italy, Gaul, and Africa, with Rome sometimes lagging a little behind. The only building form which is first encountered in Rome is the basilica, a large covered hall, often used for state or legal affairs. It is recognizably related to the Greek *stoa*, a covered colonnade, but different in function. The first basilica was built in Rome in the 2nd century BC, and with the forum and temples it became the trademark of a "Roman" town.

Urbanism in the Roman world

From the 1st century AD, the cities of the Roman world came to have more and more in common. As well as similar public buildings, there is evidence for shared tastes in pottery, food, dress, and many other aspects of culture. These changes can be seen as part of broader economic and social developments, including industrial production, more extensive trade, and better communications. Provincial elites were also connected with each other through the new political and military opportunities available in the Roman imperial system.

Great differences persisted between the regions, and strong continuities remained with pre-existing cultures. Agoras and gymnasia remained common in the East; Gallic or Celtic architectural features were prevalent in the West. African buildings and town plans were often of recognizably Carthaginian inspiration. In the same way, the local gods retained a great many of their "native" characteristics even if they adopted Roman names, and local languages often outlived Latin. Towns were more likely to develop the new "Mediterranean" culture the larger they were, the closer to the sea, and the more politically and commercially important. Cultural life in rural areas, by contrast, did not change much at all.

Urbanization in itself was often seen by the ancients as a sign of Roman influence and control. Cities were a mark of civilization, and ancient authors can give the impression that Roman colonialism introduced the urban form to backward nomadic natives in Britain, Gaul, and Africa. In fact, cities usually pre-existed the coming of the Romans. This was true not only in the Greek East, and on the coast of the Mediterranean, but also in the West and the interior. The urban forms may have looked different in these places, but the functions remained the same.

Hadrian's Wall

The continuous barrier across the north of England is unique, the only permanent defensive frontier in the Roman Empire. It was built between 126 and 122 AD and abandoned around the end of the 4th century. The wall is 3 metres (10 ft) thick and 4 metres (15 ft) tall, with a wide ditch a few metres to the north. There are fortified gateways every Roman mile, and 12 major forts straddle the wall. Much of it survives today, and the forts have yielded a great deal of evidence of the lives of ordinary soldiers posted overseas. This includes reports, accounts, and, most fascinating of all, many private letters. Elsewhere, frontiers were flexible, and forts were mainly used to channel and control communications. Hadrian's Wall divided Roman from barbarian land, and it was probably of more symbolic than military importance: it could not have withstood an army.

Colonization and cultural change

Roman expansion created many opportunities for elite cultural convergences, but those convergences did not follow the Roman frontier. Settlements in Gaul and Britain shared architectural and cultural features with contemporary Italian towns long before they became Roman territory. Conversely, when Roman colonists were added to existing populations in the provinces, the physical effect on the town was often negligible, with new buildings imitating the local style rather than the imperial one. Cities outside the Roman Empire could have much more "Roman" architecture than many within it: Lepcis Magna on the African coast had a forum, Italian temples, and an Italian-style theatre with a dedication to the Roman emperor in the Augustan period, even though it did not officially become a Roman town until at least the time of Vespasian (*c*.69–79). Septimius Severus, the first emperor from Africa (193–211), was a native of Lepcis Magna, and it was he who rebuilt the city. He gave it a Hellenistic colonnaded street with Roman arches and a new Roman forum and basilica with decorative touches in an Asian style. These Eastern influences on architecture in an African city built by a Roman emperor perfectly exemplify the complexity of imperial culture.

Religions and Rome

When Polybius encountered Roman state religion, he was cynical: "I believe that it is fear of the gods that holds the Roman state together." Religion was so theatrical in Rome and so embedded in public and private life that he suggested these "invisible terrors and pageantry" were a tool used by the elite to control the mob.

The lives and loves of the traditional Roman pantheon of gods were a favourite subject in Roman art. In this fresco from a house at Pompeii, Venus, the goddess of love, is marrying Mars, the god of war.

The Roman gods

Religion was a structural part of Roman life and politics, and Polybius's words show how bewildering this was to an educated Hellenistic Greek. Even he, however, admitted that Roman magistrates never broke religious oaths. From a Roman perspective, Cicero put it differently: because candidates from the same political elite filled both the priesthoods and the magistracies, religion was upheld by the proper administration of the state, and vice versa.

No votes took place in Rome without favourable auspices, meetings had to be held in ritual spaces, and state festivals were all linked to religious celebrations. Priests were attached to specific state functions rather than individual gods in most cases, and they were consulted by the Senate about all the matters of ritual, prodigy, and sacred law that had a direct effect on political activities. The people were integrated into the relationship between religion and the state as well: priests were elected in the late Republic, and even before that various religious

decisions had to be endorsed by popular vote. Private religion was also important: domestic altars, rural shrines, and curse tablets – small lead sheets imploring gods to take revenge on an enemy – all demonstrate the way in which a respect for supernatural forces was an intrinsic part of Roman life.

The Roman state gods were partly adopted from the Greek pantheon and partly from local and Italian traditions. The most important Roman gods were the "Capitoline Triad" of Jupiter, Juno, and Minerva, whose temple on the Capitol was dedicated in the first year of the Republic. But as polytheists, the Romans saw all gods as manifestations of the same divine powers and were open to accepting new gods into the official cult, especially at times of national crisis. They were even quicker to identify gods from the provinces with Roman deities, and religious freedom was a notable feature of the Roman Empire. Even when the local gods came to be worshipped under their Roman names, they retained many of their characteristics.

This map of bishoprics, church councils, and other Christian communities shows how far the religion had spread by the time the Emperor Constantine converted to Christianity in 310. It was more popular in the East than the West and very much an urban religion; however, Christians could be found in every corner of the Roman world.

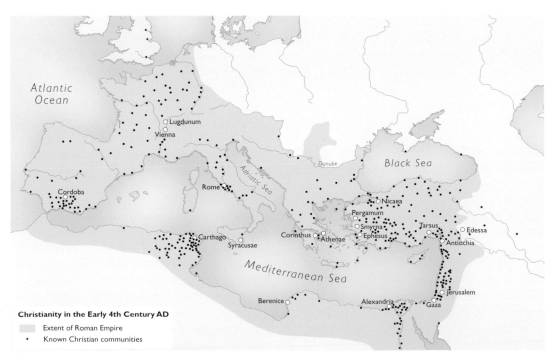

Christianity in the Early 4th Century AD

Extent of Roman Empire

•   Known Christian communities

After Augustus, all emperors were made *pontifex maximus* (chief priest), and so religious and political authority were no longer the province of one class, but of one man. Emperors were declared divine when they died and provincial subjects were expected to show proper reverence for the cult of the imperial family and the *genius* of the emperor, as well as their own gods.

Mystery religions from the East made their way to Rome and were usually tolerated by the authorities. The Egyptian cult of Isis became popular even among the elite, and Isis was eventually incorporated into official religion by the emperors. Mithras was a Persian god with a lower-class appeal, worshipped mostly in underground shrines by soldiers. Although these religions were secretive, they were not incompatible with official religion; a devotee of Isis could also sacrifice to Jupiter. Problems only arose when foreign gods demanded exclusive rights to their worshippers.

Rome and the Jews

Judea was another example of religion and state intertwined. Military and political alliances with the Romans meant that the Jews and their client kings were given a lot of leeway in interpreting the imperial cult, and a sizable Jewish community grew up in Rome itself. Judea became a province in 6 AD, but it was never completely pacified, and corrupt governors did not help the Roman cause. Resistance movements started among the poor, and rural leaders became the focus of popular discontent. In this context, Jesus was put to death by the Roman authorities. Whether or not he himself was a political revolutionary, he had amassed a large following both in Galilee and in Jerusalem, and therefore presented a credible threat to the stability of the Roman province.

The spread of Christianity

The followers of Jesus believed that he had been resurrected after his death, and they gradually distanced themselves from other types of Judaism and began to recruit among gentiles. The cult spread throughout the cities of the Mediterranean, though it remained very small, and its adherents tended to be of low social status. Christians in Rome attracted little attention from the authorities, with one notorious exception: Nero arbitrarily made them the scapegoats for the Great Fire of 64 and executed a number of them, burning some to death as torches for his garden. Later Christian writers claimed that St Peter and St Paul were among the victims.

The Christians demanded allegiance to one god, and their faith forbade the worship of others,

The Bishop of Hippo

The greatest of all the Church fathers, Augustine of Hippo (354–430), is best known today for his extraordinary *Confessions*, a long, autobiographical prayer. Memorable moments include his meditation on his youthful theft of some unripe pears, his adolescent prayer to "Grant me chastity, Lord, but not yet!", his Christian mother Monica's frequent weeping, and a vision in a garden in Milan which prompted his baptism by the local bishop Ambrose. Abandoning his common-law wife, Augustine returned to his native North Africa, becoming Bishop of Hippo in 395 and completing his vast book *The City of God against the Pagans* in 426.

which did not sit comfortably with the Romans' religious toleration. They often refused to swear by the *genius* of the emperor, and their allegiance to him was therefore suspect. Nonetheless, persecution was very limited until the mid-3rd century, and it was almost always in response to specific local circumstances. A few hundred names are recorded altogether, although the "Passions" of these martyrs, written on the eve of their executions, are compelling. In North Africa, St Perpetua was among a small group of Christians mauled by wild animals in the amphitheatre before being executed in 203. In her Passion, she describes her devotion to her new religion. Martyrs were good for Christianity; they encouraged converts and popular support. Around the time Perpetua died, the bishop Tertullian declared that blood of the martyrs was the seed of the Church.

Under the 3rd-century emperors Decius and Diocletian, with the values of the Empire under strain, Christians were imprisoned and executed in larger numbers for their refusal to participate in the religious and military apparatus of the state. The emperor Constantine brought relief. After a vision and omens in 310, he began to worship the Christian god, gave legal privileges to individual Christians and to priests, and built many churches, giving Christianity a prestige and official acceptance previously lacking.

Given the growing popularity of the Christian cult, this conversion may have been political in its motivation. Nonetheless, it had a profound effect. Other religions were practised in the Roman world for centuries, and not all later emperors worshipped the Christian god. But by the mid-4th century, Christianity was as influential a part of the Roman Empire as the pagan gods it had largely supplanted.

The Decline and Fall of the Roman Empire

Despite the prosperity of the 2nd century, the Roman Empire began to show weakness. Although rebellions and invasions were contained by the Roman army, it proved impossible to preserve the unity of the Roman world. The award of universal citizenship in 212 did nothing to stop the disintegration, and the Empire soon lost its metropolis.

This porphyry statue depicts the four rulers of the Roman world under the system introduced by Diocletian in 293: an emperor (an "Augustus") and his deputy (a "Caesar") for both halves of the unwieldy Roman Empire. They are depicted identically except that the ones on the left of each pair sport beards, indicating their superior status.

Fragmentation of the Empire

Septimius Severus (r.193–211), who came to power during serious civil warfare, was the last of the emperors to aim seriously at further conquest. After a career spent mainly in the provinces, he died attempting to conquer Scotland. His 3rd-century successors, of whom there were 20 in 50 years, tended to meet violent ends in civil warfare. Most were army commanders from different regions, and they faced not only internal competition, but also invasions from the east and north. Dacia was ceded to the Goths, but the Romans retained the greater part of their Empire. In response to rebellions and invasions, the imperial administration became more bureaucratic and authoritarian on a local level.

Without fresh conquests, Rome lost its supply of slaves and booty. Without a reliable, cheap source of slave labour, traditional agriculture and industry were in jeopardy. Prices rose sharply, and, in the absence of new technology, production decreased. The rising cost of transport encouraged localization of markets in all but luxury goods. Taxes and rents were paid in kind rather than cash. Cities declined, construction stopped, and the rural population had to cope with the devastation of war and the disease that followed in its wake. There were uprisings in the countryside.

The reforms of Diocletian

Diocletian (r.284–305) formalized the fragmentation of the Empire and by doing so checked it temporarily. He divided the provinces into smaller, more manageable units, and he brought an end to the constant internecine warfare among the army commanders by dividing the imperial power between two Augustuses. These were to rule as equals, one in the East and one in the West, with two Caesars as deputies and presumptive heirs. This institution, known as the *tetrarchy*, provided the basic pattern for imperial rule during the last

centuries of the Western Empire. It was frequently modified, however, and it did not prevent civil war breaking out again on Diocletian's death.

Diocletian increased the size of the army in order to strengthen the Empire's defences and tried to reverse the process of decentralization in some respects. All the new soldiers and administrators had to be paid, and so Diocletian reformed and regularized the taxation system. He attempted to fix maximum prices and wages, and to create a unified currency across the provinces; however, these measures were out of keeping with the times and were largely ignored. The fact that Diocletian only made one brief visit to Rome shows how much had changed.

Diocletian's most lasting innovation was in the realm of agriculture and rural life, where he is credited with the establishment of the colonate, a distinctive tenancy arrangement that directly prefigured medieval serfdom. *Coloni* were tenant farmers who leased land from larger owners or from municipalities in return for rent in cash or, as time went on, crops. As part of his taxation reform, Diocletian tied peasants to the places they were registered. Now that slaves were scarce and expensive, landlords gleefully enforced this rule on their tenant farmers to ensure a permanent source of labour and rent at no ongoing cost to themselves. The rural population had no escape route, and this added to the misery brought by increased taxation and oversight. The world of the peasant farmer grew smaller and more wretched.

Constantine to Theodosius

After several more years of civil war, another strong leader emerged in the Augustus of the West, Constantine the Great (r.307–37). In 324, he defeated the other Augustus and temporarily reunited the Empire under a single ruler. He founded the city of Constantinople in 330. It showcased his wealth and Christianity, and symbolized the new importance of the eastern half of the Empire. Meanwhile, the Western capital was moved from Rome itself to Milan.

Constantine's successors in the 4th century faced down renewed invasions from the Germans, and Persia made large gains in Roman territory in the East. The Goths, under pressure themselves from the Huns, crossed the Danube in 376, and they defeated the Roman army at Hadrianople in 378.

Theodosius the Great became Augustus of the East in 379. He fought the Goths without success, then made an alliance with them, giving them land in the Black Sea provinces. In 386, he treated with Persia, again ceding disputed land. Theodosius was a fervent Christian and banned pagan religion, further entrenching the relationship between the Catholic Church and the Roman state. He left his two sons as the Augustuses of East and West. In the East, the Roman Empire recovered, especially under Justin and Justinian, but by the 6th century, there were new rulers in the West.

The final years of the Western Empire

The various Gothic peoples in the Roman Empire united under Alaric as the Visigoths in the early 5th century, and they moved west from the Balkans and the Black Sea. The Western Roman government retreated from Milan to Ravenna. The Visigoths sacked Rome in 410, then carved out their own kingdom in Gaul and Spain. Worse was

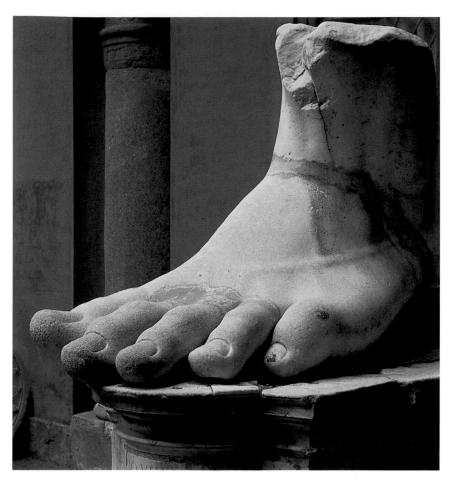

to follow: the Vandals went to North Africa in 429 and had captured it entirely by 442. At the same time, the rural peasantry was staggering under the weight of taxation, and the colonate and sporadic revolts had become continuous guerrilla warfare against local commanders and officials.

The Western Empire did not so much fall as peter out. In what was left of the Roman administration, Visigoths attained high commands and influence. The last Western emperor, Romulus Augustulus, was forced to abdicate by the Visigoth king Odoacer in 476. The Goths reunited Italy, Spain, and southern Gaul, cultivated the Church and the Eastern emperors, and ruled with Roman-style administration. It is unlikely that the provincial population knew or cared that their rulers were no longer Roman; Rome itself was long gone.

The Romans were the first to unite Europe in a common citizenship, and their legacy endures. Their language, their roads, and their laws are some of the foundations of modern Europe, building on older traditions and built on in turn by the cultures that took their place. Every generation has reinvented its Roman inheritance: poets, soldiers, tyrants, revolutionaries, and architects have all found something Roman to claim as their own.

This enormous foot belongs to a colossal seated statue of the emperor Constantine, from his Basilica in the Forum. Made at the beginning of the 4th century, the complete work would have been over 9 metres (30 ft) high.

THE DECLINE AND FALL OF THE ROMAN EMPIRE **89**

BYZANTIUM AND THE RISE OF THE WEST

500–1000

POLITICS AND GOVERNMENT

527–65 Reign of Justinian I, Emperor of East Rome, whose conquest policies and massive artistic patronage created the Byzantine Golden Age.

*c.*580–620 Slavic occupation of the Balkans and beginnings of Slavic domination between the Carpathian Mountains and the Baltic Sea.

535 Byzantine general Belisarius invades Southern Italy. The Byzantines complete the conquest of Italy by 555.

632–655 Islamic Arab conquests of the old Persian Empire, and of the Near East and Egypt from Byzantium destroy the ancient world order which saw Europe dominated by the Mediterranean.

493–526 Theoderic, King of the Ostrogoths in Italy, preserves many Roman institutions and values.

714–41 Reign of Charles Martel reunifies Francia after the collapse of Merovingian unity in the 7th century.

400

575

*c.*630 Sutton Hoo ship burial in East Anglia; amongst its treasures is fabulous jewelry in the Hiberno-Saxon style.

SOCIETY AND CULTURE

*c.*480–550 St Benedict of Nursia, monastic founder and writer of the single most influential monastic guide – *The Rule of St Benedict.*

*c.*580–632 Life and teachings of Muhammad in Arabia generates the Islamic religion.

597 Arrival in England of the Roman mission, led by Augustine of Canterbury. Opens new era of spreading the Gospel in Europe.

*c.*700 production of the *Codex Amiatinus* in Northumbria, with fabulous illuminations in a realistic, classicizing style.

679–754 St Boniface, the "Apostle of Germany", missionary and Church reformer who spreads the Gospel in Germany and the Low countries until his martyrdom.

*c.*732–87 First Iconoclasm in Byzantium.

538 Inauguration of the rebuilt, domed Church of Hagia Sophia in Constantinople sets new standard for Christian architecture in the Mediterranean.

*c.*740–804 Alcuin of York: leading Christian scholar of hi[s] day and one of the architects of the revival of learnin[g] under Charlemage – the Carolingian Renaissance

51 Creation of the Papal States.

771 Charlemagne is crowned sole king of the Franks. He conquers Lombardy and is crowned King of the Lombards in 774. In 772, he embarks on the conquest of Saxony, which was completed in 802.

793 The sack of the island monastery of Lindisfarne marks the opening of fierce Viking raiding upon Western Europe.

911 Licensed settlement of the Vikings of Rollo around Rouen on the Seine: the first act in the creation of the Duchy of Normandy.

888 Deposition of Charles the Fat marks the end of the Carolingian imperial period in the West.

865–78 The first Viking great army in England conquers Northumbria, Mercia, and East Anglia.

1066 William of Normandy conquers England to create new cross-channel superstate in Western Europe.

962 Imperial coronation of Otto I in Rome marks the creation of the Holy Roman Empire based on the Duchy of Saxony.

983 Revolt of the Elbe Slavs against Saxon domination.

0   925   1000

750 onwards Introduction of manorialized agriculture in Western Europe increases total output, but cements social divides between landlords and peasants.

789 The *Admonitio Generalis* marks Charlemagne's efforts to reform Christian observance in the areas under his rule.

c.860 Cyril and Methodius create the first written version of Slavic to translate the Bible.

814–43 Second Iconoclasm in Byzantium.

c.830 Classicizing illustrations of the Utrecht Psalter.

c.820–50 Great era of Carolingian Church construction: huge basilicas with apses and towers at each end such as St. Riquier and as advocated in the paradigmatic Plan of St Gall.

909/10 Foundation of the monastery of Cluny in Burgundy opens new era of monastic federations operating independent of lay patrons and answering to the Pope.

c.920–89 Christianization of new states of Slavic Europe: Bohemia, Poland, and Kievan Russia.

1054 The Great Schism marks a culmination of papal self-assertion.

Byzantine emperors saw themselves as appointed by God to rule the entire world. This silver dish produced on the 10th anniversary of the reign of Emperor Theodosius I celebrates unbreakable, divinely inspired imperial order. The emperor sits in state holding the orb that symbolizes his authority over the earth.

BYZANTIUM: APOGEE AND DECLINE

In AD 500, Byzantium – the eastern half of the Roman Empire – was emerging triumphantly from a very difficult century. Its Western Roman counterpart had fallen in the 5th century, and its own territories had been repeatedly invaded. Yet with the 6th century, Byzantium entered an era of renewed prosperity, first under Anastasius, then under an uncle and nephew, Justin and Justinian.

In this era, Byzantium asserted itself as a major Mediterranean power, its territories stretching over Greece and the Balkans, across Asia Minor as far as the Caucasus, and through the Middle East. However, difficulties remained. In the east, Persia, its traditional foe, was also enjoying respite from northern threats, and, internally, imperial politics remained unstable. Nonetheless, 6th-century emperors, particularly Justinian, were able to mobilize the powerful resources of this state to launch a new era of greatness. Two of the barbarian kingdoms that had replaced the Western Roman Empire – the Vandals and the Ostrogoths – were destroyed, bringing North Africa and Italy under Byzantine control. Dissensions in the kingdom of the Visigoths were also exploited to add parts of southern Spain.

Culturally, this period of Byzantine greatness is famous for the emergence of a new Christian art, manifesting itself in the magnificent domed churches that still stand in Istanbul. Decorative mosaic for church walls also evolved, and all the established art forms – ivory, metalwork, textiles – were deployed to the praise of the Christian God.

The peak of Byzantine greatness was not to last. After Justinian's death, it was damaged by the rise of the nomadic Avars in the north and renewed conflict with Persia. Disaster, however, was to come from an unexpected quarter – the Arabian peninsula – and when Byzantine–Persian coexistence collapsed into world war in the early 7th century, the resulting weakness of the two empires was exploited by the newly united power of Islamic Arabia. By 651, the Persian Empire had been extinguished and Byzantium stripped of its richest territories. By the end of the 7th century, Byzantium had ceased to operate as an imperial power and became an unwilling satellite of the Islamic world. When Islam was united, Byzantium had to struggle to survive. However, it did so for another 800 years, and its influence on the course of European history was immense.

Between 527 and 565, the Emperor Justinian added enormous tracts of territory, but much more was lost to the Arabs and others. Reduced drastically in size by 651, the Empire was forced to refinance its armies by granting them heriditary landholdings in the themes of Asia Minor.

The Rise and Fall of Byzantium in the 6th–7th Century AD

Byzantine Empire 527

Byzantine Empire 565

Territory always under Byzantine control

The Renewal of Empire

The late 5th and early 6th centuries saw the dawn of a new era in Byzantine history. The external and internal threats of the previous century had been overcome, and the economy was booming. The problem lay in politics: ever since the end of the Theodosian dynasty in 451, one childless emperor had been replaced by another.

Between 491 and 517, power was exercised by the able Anastasius; however, on his death, his adult nephews were passed over in favour of a well-connected guards officer, Justin I. Justin was also childless, but he had his own highly ambitious nephew Justinian, who, over the next decade, so entrenched himself in power that he was able to succeed his uncle in 527.

In Roman thought, "victory" represented the seal of divine approval upon any reign. Needing to secure his position, military adventurism was thus a natural choice for Justinian to make, and he

The Emperor Justinian victorious. Christ, portrayed at the top of this ivory, makes the mounted Justinian (surrounded by female embodiments of victory) dominant over the entire world, whose different peoples – note the varieties of costume and animals – bring him their tributes, bowing down before him in submission.

immediately picked a fight with Persia, which was the traditional enemy of Constantinople. After initial successes, Byzantium suffered a major defeat at the hands of the Persians in 532, and Justinian was forced to pay for the humiliating "Endless Peace". Defeat inspired plotting against him, and attempts were made to replace Justinian with the nephews of Anastasius during the Nika riot. After a week of violence in which most of central Constantinople was burned down and 20,000 people (including Anastasius' nephews) killed, Justinian only just held on to power. He decided to gamble on still more military adventurism, sending a small expeditionary force under Belisarius to Vandal North Africa, which was in the middle of its own succession dispute. Against all expectations, the Vandals were decisively defeated, and the entire kingdom was conquered between 532 and 534. The rewards for Justinian were huge. He was politically unassailable, and a massive victory parade was held to display the captured enemy and all his gold.

The next acquisition was also painless. Sicily was conquered from the Ostrogoths in 535 with minimal opposition, but this was only a prelude to the main assault. Belisarius, again, landed in southern Italy in the spring of 536, and by 540 seemed to have won a great victory when the Gothic king Wittigis surrendered. But only some of the Goths had been defeated; most had simply gone home in what was more of a truce than a peace. The Persians, too, were becoming worried by the extent of Justinian's success in the West, and they launched a massive raid towards the Mediterranean in the summer of 540, sacking the city of Antioch. When Belisarius and some of his troops were withdrawn from Italy, the undefeated Goths revolted. This established a pattern for the next decade, with Persian affairs making it impossible to defeat the Goths decisively. Only in 551, when peace was again negotiated with Persia, could a large army under Narses be sent to Italy. By 553, Italy was finally in Byzantine hands. Justinian had also taken advantage of a civil war in the Visigothic kingdom to conquer a thin strip of territory in southern Spain.

Internal affairs

Justinian was equally energetic internally. Here his greatest achievement lay in the field of law. By the early 6th century, legal authority reposed in a confused mass of expert opinions given between the 1st and 3rd centuries, and a host of ill-edited imperial rulings. Under the leadership of Tribonian, everything was pulled together by 535 into one simplified code: The *Corpus Juris Civilis* (*Body of Civil Law*). In Church affairs, Justinian

Mosaic of Justinian from Ravenna
The famous mosaics of St Vitale in Ravenna, Italy, are a contemporary representation of the Emperor Justinian and his court. It has often been claimed that he came to the throne determined to reconquer the lost Roman lands in the West, but his armies attacked the Persians first, and only turned west when this war failed. A chain of victories followed in North Africa, Sicily, Italy, and Spain; however, they came at a price. The historian Procopius eventually condemned Justinian: "He made a desert and called it peace." Historians remain divided as to whether the gains were worth the cost.

tried to end the monophysite dispute, a debate over how to understand the mixture of the human and divine in the person of Christ, revolving around the definition of faith agreed at the Council of Chalcedon in 451. By Justinian's reign, two separate parties with their own bishops, priests, and church organization existed, and there was little he could do to resolve the schism. His other reforming efforts were geared to the problem of raising money to finance both his huge campaigns and a vast building programme. These certainly aroused hostility among certain taxpayers, but there is no sign that they caused serious damage to the economy.

The balance sheet

In time, Justinian's new North African provinces became useful parts of the Byzantine Empire, their revenues more than paying for the costs of their conquest and upkeep. The same was true of Sicily. Shortly after Justinian's death in 565, however, large parts of mainland Italy fell to the Lombards, and the Gothic war had been very damaging to the Italian economy. Justinian's reign also saw an outbreak of plague, and much of the Eastern Empire was to fall into Arab hands in the 630s. The suggestion is often raised, therefore, that the plague and conquests had between them overstretched imperial resources. The later losses of territory were born of quite different circumstances, however, and large areas of Italy remained useful parts of the Byzantine Empire for centuries, despite the losses it suffered. The 6th-century plague also seems to have been too minor a phenomenon to have caused serious dislocation. Overall, North Africa, Sicily, and southern Italy, at least, were important strategic gains, and the great Arab successes occurred three generations after Justinian's death and were not of his making.

Art and Architecture

The later 5th and 6th centuries were an era of huge artistic and architectural achievement in the Byzantine Empire. The booming economy provided funds for artistic patronage of all kinds and on every scale, from huge imperial monuments to smaller-scale local activities. This was the period, too, when traditional Graeco-Roman artistic forms merged with newer cultural concerns to generate a properly Christian art.

Architecture

Some of the Emperor Justinian's buildings survive intact, above all the Church of Hagia Sophia in Istanbul; others are known from archaeological investigation, with a long account of them written by Procopius in the *Buildings* of 561. In religious architecture, Justinian's reign was marked by the development of a distinct Christian structural style: the domed church. Large churches had previously been constructed as basilicas, the standard rectangular form used for most large Roman public buildings. In the 6th century, starting with the Church of Saints Sergius and Bacchus in Constantinople in 530, such churches were increasingly replaced with domed structures, either of wood or masonry, and resting on squinches or more advanced pendentives. The apogee of this new form was achieved in the rebuilding of Hagia Sophia (previously a basilica) between 532 and 537. The architects were able to suspend the top of the dome a staggering 56 metres (182 ft) from the floor and create a vast space beneath. Repairs had subsequently to be made because of earthquakes, but the new church was a triumph and set the form for all the major constructions of the 6th century, such as San Vitale in Ravenna and the pilgrimage Church of St John the Baptist in Ephesus.

Secular building was not ignored. Most cities already had a stock of forums, baths, circuses, and council buildings, but these had to be maintained, and, where new settlements were founded, or earthquakes intervened, they were built from scratch. Justinian turned his birthplace in the Balkans (Justiniana Prima, now Caricingrad) from a village into a classical city. After the Persian sack of 540, likewise, Antioch underwent a magnificent reconstruction, with porticoed main streets and fora. But in the midst of all the splendour, there was a sense of threat. Much of the construction recorded in Procopius' *Buildings* was of fortresses. Every major city had huge fortifications, the countryside was dotted with refuge centres, and chains of castles and watchtowers guarded the frontiers.

The Arts

A handful of beautifully illuminated manuscripts survive from this era of Byzantine greatness, above all the *Vienna Genesis* and fragments of the *Cotton Genesis*. These used to be seen as the tip of a vast iceberg of lost artistic achievement, but are now understood to be items produced for very special purposes. Such manuscripts would have been extremely rare even in their own time. The first flowering of a specifically Christian art involved a much wider range of media than the illuminated book. The ancient art of lifesize (or greater) statuary in three dimensions fell into disfavour and was replaced by the bust. Otherwise, a full range of traditional media continued to be employed. Carved ivory was used to provide covers for imperial

Hagia Sophia. Justinian's revolutionary domed church design created a central open space of breath-taking size and beauty. Richly decorated, and lit by countless windows and lamps, this became the setting of spectacular liturgies and imperial ceremonies. In the East, it replaced the basilica as the classic form for church buildings.

Golden, luminescent mosaic decoration had emerged by the 6th century as a central feature of Byzantine Christian art. In this example from the south vestibule of Hagia Sophia, the Virgin and Child are framed by two emperors. Constantine offers them the original Hagia Sophia he built in the 4th century, Justinian the still surviving church of the 6th century.

letters of appointment, particularly to the highest dignitary of state, the consulship. Many consular diptychs survive, carved in high relief, in a realistic, classicizing fashion. Ivory was also employed in many religious contexts, whether carved as part of reliquaries or in such prestigious items as the so-called ivory throne (perhaps in reality a book rest) of Bishop Maximian from 6th-century Ravenna.

Equally wide use was made of silver. Gifts of fine silver were often made by emperors to their loyal officials to commemorate great events. The "David Plates", discovered in Cyprus, are a striking survival. These were issued by Emperor Heraclius to celebrate his astonishing comeback victory against the Persians in the 620s – David's victory over Goliath having perhaps provided the original inspiration – and illustrate episodes from the Biblical king's life. Most of the silver to survive from this era, however, was originally church plate: chalices, pattens, ewers, and candlesticks. Churches were not only endowed with rich silver, but also extraordinary textiles. Some examples from Egypt survive in fragments.

The new Christian art also flourished on the walls of churches themselves. Hagia Sophia was decorated only with bare mosaic crosses, but, elsewhere, Byzantine churches were evolving their standard cycle of mosaic decoration, which sought to make the inside of the church representative of the entire Christian cosmos. Christ and the Virgin Mary were represented only at the highest physical points, at the apex of the dome. The next level was occupied by the angels and the panoply of heaven, and, finally, closer to eye level, human saints. The earliest surviving example of the full cycle comes from the rotunda of St George from Thessalonica (dating *c*.450–500). Variations on the basic scheme were possible: in San Vitale in Ravenna, after the destruction of the Ostrogothic kingdom, the famous pictures of the Emperor Justinian and the Empress Theodora and their courts were placed between heaven and earth. As in so many other areas, the era of Byzantine greatness set a standard for Eastern Christian art which was followed throughout the Middle Ages.

Patronage

To flourish to such an extent, Christian art required massive patronage. Hence, larger projects were funded by the state. Justinian and other emperors followed the pattern established by Constantine two centuries before in channelling building funds and tax revenues towards grandiose structures such as Hagia Sophia. Many smaller churches were built through local efforts. The great and recently excavated Church of St Polyeuktos in Constantinople was the brainchild of one great aristocrat – Anicia Julia – in the 520s. Smaller churches were built and decorated by local bishops, priests, and aristocrats, with mosaics sometimes recording their efforts, as in the Church of Saint Demetrius in Thessalonica. The same was true of all church silver, several pieces of which are engraved with the name of their donors. Much of the public and private patronage which used to be expended upon the classical city was now redirected towards Christian art.

Hellenistic Civilization   52–3 ▶
Architecture and Urbanism   84–5 ▶
Culture and Society   110–11▶
The Carolingian Renaissance   130–1 ▶

The Arab Conquests

In the mid-7th century, a new force suddenly appeared to change the course of European history. Muhammad's new religion united the previously divided tribes of the Arabian peninsula. The military force unleashed was powerful enough to destroy the Persian Empire entirely, reduce Byzantium to a fraction of its former strength, and definitively separate the northern and southern shores of the Mediterranean.

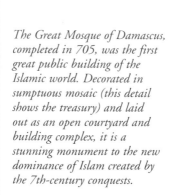

An Umayyad-period desert palace, combining mosque, baths, and a decorated dining hall, at Qusayr Amra in Jordan. In entertainment complexes such as these, 7th- and 8th-century caliphs courted the Bedouins who were the source of the military power which allowed them to conquer Persia and most of Byzantium.

The Great Mosque of Damascus, completed in 705, was the first great public building of the Islamic world. Decorated in sumptuous mosaic (this detail shows the treasury) and laid out as an open courtyard and building complex, it is a stunning monument to the new dominance of Islam created by the 7th-century conquests.

Within the Arabian peninsula, important structural transformations worked themselves out in the late Roman period. Up to the early 3rd century, this had been a world of very small political units, consisting of mixed populations of agricultural producers and nomadic Bedouin. These steppe and savannah regions, on the fringes of the true desert, then came to form a southern front in the ongoing great-power confrontation between Byzantium and Persia. To secure the southern front, both empires recruited, armed, and paid client Arab forces. By process of competitive escalation, the allied groups became ever larger, until by the 6th century both sides were dealing with just one Arab entity each: the Byzantines with the Ghassanids and the Persians the Lakhmids. The constituent smaller groups continued to exist within these confederative umbrellas; however, both the Lakhmids and Ghassanids were powerful enough to pursue their own agendas, which were sometimes threatening to the imperial powers. In the early 580s, the Emperor Maurice destroyed the power of the Ghassanids by military action. But the clock could not be turned back. The tribes of Arabia had become used to working in larger alliances.

Great-power conflict

Many shorter term events also contributed to the Islamic revolution. Throughout the 6th century, competition between Persia and Byzantium was endemic and had been so since the 3rd century. Fighting was limited, however, to raids for prestige and profit, and the occasional siege. In the later 6th century, the conflict ran out of control. In 602, the Byzantine Emperor Maurice was murdered and his son, Theodosius, fled to the Persian Shah Chosroes. Chosroes had previously been restored to the throne by Maurice and tried at first, it seems, to repay the favour, invading Byzantium on Theodosius' behalf. His aims, however, escalated. Chosroes' unprecedentedly successful conquest of Egypt, Palestine, and Syria by the mid-610s convinced the Persian to attempt the total conquest

of Byzantium. In 626, his forces moved as far as Chalcedon on the southern side of the Bosporus, and their Turkic-speaking nomadic Avar allies, now based on the Hungarian Plain, were outside the land walls of Constantinople to the north. The Byzantines, however, still ruled the waves, and their enemies were unable to unite. The Emperor Heraclius, in the meantime, launched a counter-offensive from the north-east, which outflanked and defeated the Persian army. Chosroes was deposed in 628. Heraclius' victory was in essence a draw, brought about by exhaustion on both sides.

Muhammad and Arabia

This draining war gave the Prophet Muhammad an opportunity to add another key ingredient to the revolution brewing inside Arabia. In creating his new religion, Muhammad took elements from Judaism and Christianity, both of which had been present within Arabia from the 4th to the 6th centuries, and refashioned them into an entirely new mix. Muhammad's message, preserved in the

Piero della Francesca's 15th-century rendering of Heraclius' struggle against Chosroes, from the apse of the Church of San Francesco in Arezzo. Heraclius overcame heavy odds to defeat the Persians and return the True Cross to Jerusalem, but the struggle exhausted both empires and paved the way for the Islamic conquests.

Koran, presented him as the culmination of the Jewish prophetic tradition transmitted via the Old Testament and the necessary successor to Jesus. Muhammad proclaimed that all the faithful should form one political community and set about uniting the Arab world behind him. Within Arabia, his message and military leadership, eventually based at Mecca in the Hijaz, provided a political superstructure independent of Byzantium or Persia. The new unity led to unprecedented military success, providing healthy profits to those participating in the new enterprise. During Muhammad's lifetime, military activity was directed towards uniting the peninsula and preying on its fringes. After his death in 632, his successors looked outwards to the richer prizes available in Persia and Byzantium.

Here, the postwar weakness of these empires played a critical role. Muhammad's religion and authority had created an Arab entity of unprecedented power. Yet it is unlikely that Arabia would have conquered so much had its imperial neighbours not been so devastated by their great war. Victory over the Byzantines at Yarmuk in 636 allowed the Arabs to capture Syria and Palestine. Egypt was conquered in the 650s. In the meantime, similar gains had been made in the Persian Empire, with the last Shah, Isdigerdes III, defeated and killed in 651, by which time the Arab conquests stretched over all of the territory now covered by Iraq and Iran. The Byzantine emperors survived, but only just. Two major Arab sieges had to be fought off in the 670s and 710s, and the Empire was only a shadow of its former self. By the year 700, its North African provinces had also been lost to Islamic conquest, reducing Byzantium to between a quarter and a third of its former size. By the early 8th century, the Muslim world stretched from India to the Pyrenees, with the bulk of Visigothic Spain falling into its hands in the 710s.

A satellite state

The consequences for Byzantium could not have been more profound. It became a second-rank regional power at the eastern end of the Mediterranean, confined to the southern Balkans and northern and western Asia Minor. In the face of constant Arab raiding, its economy suffered so much that former large cities shrank into refuge fortresses. The population of late 7th- and 8th-century Constantinople likewise collapsed to one-tenth of what it had been in its 6th-century heyday. Byzantium became an unwilling satellite of the Muslim world. When the latter was united, Byzantium could only suffer, and it was only when Muslim unity collapsed in the late 9th and 10th centuries that a limited Byzantine expansion could follow. When the Seljuk Turks reunited the world of Islam in the 11th century, Byzantium quickly shrank back to its now core territories in north-western Asia Minor and the Balkans. For Europe as a whole, the rise of Islam brought the ancient world order to an end. The conquests divided the Mediterranean world in two and freed the rest of Europe to chart its own historical course.

This fabulously ornate initial page introduces the Gospel of St Mark in the 8th-century Book of Kells. It is a perfect example of the Hiberno-Saxon pictorial style of the Dark Ages, which combined interlacing, abstract monsters, and geometric patterns into explosions of multicoloured decoration.

THE BARBARIAN KINGDOMS

By AD 500, the Western Roman Empire was no more than a memory. A broader Roman legacy was still alive, however, in territories around the rim of the Mediterranean, where Roman landowners survived alongside barbarian armies. They preserved Roman governmental systems and Roman cultural values in their Christianized form. In Anglo-Saxon England and north-eastern Gaul, the Roman legacy was rejected. In some areas, Latin education was not maintained, and Christianity was thrown over in favour of pagan religious cult.

Over the next two centuries, the differences between northern and southern kingdoms in the post-Roman west were eroded. Justinian's campaigns destroyed two of the Mediterranean states – the Ostrogothic and Vandal kingdoms – and, in the longer term, a pattern of dual evolution set in. The northern territories came to accept parts of the Roman value system, turning to Christianity and trumpeting the civilizing importance of written law. Further south, Roman value systems survived, but not the structures of centralized Roman rule. A simpler kind of state, with rudimentary low-yield tax structures and small unspecialized bureaucracies, became the norm in both north and south. Political power was switched from the centre to the localities.

These changes also had very significant cultural effects. The late Roman world was characterized by extensive literacy among the secular aristocracy, due to years of private education. This allowed the elite to participate in the lucrative bureaucratic careers of the Roman world. As these careers disappeared, so did the willingness of elite parents to pay for education, and it quickly became the preserve of the Church. At the same time, new cultural modes were introduced by the immigrant barbarian elites and began to coexist alongside such classicizing cultural elements as were preserved by the Church.

Simultaneously, east-central and eastern Europe was undergoing a massive revolution of an entirely different kind. Up to about AD 500, Europe as far east as the river Vistula, the outer arc of the Carpathian mountains, and their eastern

approaches north of the Black Sea were all dominated by Germanic-speaking groups. From that date, Slavic-speakers spread from their original homes in the wooded steppe zone of the East European plain. In the later 6th and 7th centuries, they came to dominate most of Greece and the Balkans and swept through central Europe. By the time that written sources start to cover these regions in the 9th and 10th centuries, all of Central and Eastern Europe from the Elbe to the Volga was divided between different Slavic tribes. How this revolution was achieved continues to be debated, but it clearly involved the Slavicization of indigenous populations.

The Successor States
⁓ Approximate frontiers of barbarian kingdoms
→ Lombard invasion 568

By AD 500, Roman Europe had been carved up between a host of successor states. These states were built around the military might of intrusive "barbarian" groups, but incorporated, to differing degrees, Roman land-owning elites who had survived the Empire's fall. Over the following two centuries, boundaries were redrawn as the kingdoms quarrelled among themselves and struggled against Byzantium and the rising power of Islam.

Kingdoms of the Mediterranean Rim

After the deposition of the last Roman Emperor in the West, Romulus Augustulus, in 476, the successor states established around the Mediterranean coast preserved for at least the next half a century Roman culture and institutions to a quite surprising degree. In the long run, however, important structural changes in their political economies meant that their Roman character was destined to disappear.

The Codex Argenteus *of Ulfila's Gothic Bible translation is a stunning symbol of the imperial and Gothic culture of Ostrogothic Italy. It was produced in Ravenna in the early 6th century for King Theoderic, on purple-dyed parchment in gold and silver inks. The vellum is so fine that it may have been made from the skin of unborn calves.*

The Vandals of North Africa have become synonymous with mindless destruction and were more aggressive than many of the groups who founded successor states. As the international UNESCO excavations at their capital of Carthage have shown, however, they preserved much of the fabric of the classical city, as well as the theatre and other traditional aspects of gracious Roman living.

The first-generation successor states to the Western Roman Empire – Visigothic southern Gaul and Spain, the Burgundian kingdom of the Rhone valley, Ostrogothic Italy, and even Vandal Africa – were all born with the ruins of the Roman West smoking around them, and they continued to see themselves as part of a wider Roman world. They all maintained one fundamental institution of Roman government: large-scale taxation of the agricultural economy. This included maintenance of the administrators and record keeping at the local level (all land was registered in local city archives) necessary to make taxation work. They also maintained much of the framework of Roman law and incorporated a numerically dominant, culturally distinct Roman population, some of whose elite elements continued to enjoy access to positions of power. As part and parcel of the latter process, the kingdoms all accepted the established

Roman value system, which saw literary education and written law as essential to a civilized society. Maintaining a Roman legal system was thus an ideological statement, as well as a practical instrument of government, and most of these kings encouraged the written use of Latin at their courts. Even the kings of Vandal Africa wanted to be praised in Latin verse, and it was under their rule that much of the *Latin Anthology*, a definitive selection of older poetry, was compiled.

These kingdoms were all, however, based around the military power of the immigrant groups after whom they were named. Integrating the latter into existing Roman societies posed a number of common problems. First and foremost, the new kings needed to reward the loyalty of the immigrant soldiers who had put them in power. They did this initially through grants of landed estates, mostly found by reallocating publicly owned

assets, supplemented by annual salaries paid from existing Roman tax revenues. Only Vandal Africa saw large-scale expropriations of private property. In the Ostrogothic and Visigothic kingdoms, the immigrants were settled in a series of concentrated clusters at strategically important points. These clusters in part reflected pre-existing groupings within the larger force and allowed some continuity of identity and custom to be maintained.

A second problem area was that of religion. The immigrants were all Christian, but held to a variant form – so-called Arianism – regarded as heretical by the Catholic Romans. In Africa, the Vandal kings periodically persecuted the Catholics, confiscating churches and other assets, refusing to allow the appointment of bishops, and even attempting to make the population adopt their Arian version of Christianity. Elsewhere, however, tension was minimal. Theoderic built Arian churches in his capital Ravenna, but these coexisted with Catholic ones, and the king enjoyed, for the most part, good relations with the Roman Church. He was even called upon to settle a disputed election to the papacy and was judged to have acted equitably.

History

A new strategic order evolved only slowly in post-Roman Europe. Up to the 520s, the dominant power was the Ostrogothic kingdom of Theoderic. Between 508 and 511, he took direct control of the Visigothic kingdom, adding it to lands that he had already acquired in the Balkans. He also established hegemony over the Burgundian and Vandal kingdoms, and an alliance system, with himself as the dominant partner, which stretched north into central Germany. He consider himself to have re-established the Western Roman Empire, and one of his Roman subjects hailed him as "Augustus" in an inscription celebrating economic expansion in northern Italy. But Theoderic's grand edifice did not survive his death in 526. The Visigothic and Ostrogothic kingdoms separated again, and the Burgundians and Vandals had already exploited the king's declining years by attempting to throw off Ostrogothic hegemony. The situation was transformed by Justinian, whose conquests wiped the Vandal and Ostrogothic kingdoms from the map. This allowed the Franks to swallow up the Burgundian kingdom in the 530s and the Lombards to move into Italy in 568. By c.580, of the sub-Roman kingdoms of the Mediterranean rim, only the Visigoths survived.

Structural transformation

These political changes took place on top of more structural transformations. Most important of

Mosaic of Theoderic's palace

Theoderic, the Ostrogothic king of Italy, was determined to present himself as a legitimate Roman ruler. He continued to use the old Roman capital of Ravenna and operated a Roman palace complex there. In his Arian cathedral, St Apollinare Nuovo, Theoderic had his palace depicted in mosaic, together, originally, with himself in full Roman panoply. After Justinian's conquest, the king's figure was removed from the central arch. Theoderic was entirely typical of the successor state kings of the Mediterranean rim in seeing himself as part of a larger, still-living Roman world and as presenting a Roman face to his many Roman subjects.

all, original distinctions between Roman and immigrant, especially at elite level, steadily eroded. In a world of volatile international relations, kings needed military service above all. Romans, therefore, quickly moved from administration to military service, where there were rich rewards. Latin culture had originally been transmitted among these Roman elites, for whom it gave access to jobs in the bureaucracy. Previously, they had also been willing to pay relatively large amounts of tax because it paid for a professional army. Once they were fighting in their own defence, they ceased to be so willing, and tax gradually played a less important role in post-Roman state structures. Intermarriage and other alliances between Roman and immigrant elites also became common, as they were present at the same royal courts. These changes were happening everywhere, but came to fruition in the Visigothic kingdom. By the 7th century, the lifestyles of the secular aristocracy concentrated on martial endeavour, and the power of the central state declined alongside its tax revenues. Cultural fusion was brought to completion by the conversion of the remaining Arian Visigoths to Catholicism at the Third Council of Toledo in 589.

Northern Worlds 500–700

The new imperial power of Western Europe emerged not from the kingdoms of the Mediterranean rim, but from further north. Here Roman ideals were lost or rejected as new immigrant elites built political systems based on warmongering and the exchange of rich gifts, rather than Latin and the efficient bureaucratic exploitation of resources.

Beyond the Mediterranean rim, there was an outright rejection of Roman ideologies. In England, all Roman villas ceased to be occupied from the early 5th century onwards, and many of them were violently destroyed. In the towns of Roman Britain, too, evidence of occupation quickly disappears in the 5th century. Among the now largely rural population, the extensive cemetery evidence shows that, by the mid-5th century, new, Germanic cultural norms had come to prevail. From around 480–520, the same could

be said of northern Gaul, too, most particularly in areas north and east of Paris.

In the past, the appearance of these new cemeteries was taken to prove that the native population had been expelled by the mass intrusion of immigrants: Angles and Saxons from the Low Countries, southern Denmark, and England; and Franks from east of the Rhine in northern Gaul. In England, there certainly was some immigration. A first major influx occurred in the 440s; however, migration was still occurring in the mid- to late

The tomb of Clovis in the monastery of St Denis in Paris, as reinterpreted in the 13th century. Responsible for turning the Franks into one of the great powers of the post-Roman West, Clovis united previously independent warbands into one force and began to integrate them with the sub-Roman population of his new kingdom by converting to Catholicism.

6th century. The cremation burials of eastern England, in particular, clearly belong to an intrusive population of immigrant Angles. The end result was the total replacement of native Celtic languages with various Germanic dialects and the appearance of Anglo-Saxon kingdoms right across the English countryside. Some of the occupants of these new cemeteries were not true migrants, but individuals of Romano-British and Gallo-Roman descent, who accommodated themselves to new Anglo-Saxon and Frankish norms to prosper in changed circumstances. This makes the extent of immigration hard to estimate, but does not obscure the underlying point. Outside the Mediterranean, the old ideals of Roman civilization, such as Latin, Christianity, written law, town dwelling etc, were firmly rejected.

The rise of the Merovingians

The most important political development of the later 5th and 6th century in north-western Europe was the rise of the Frankish Merovingian dynasty. In the Roman period, the Franks were divided into a number of small warbands, but the disappearance of imperial power allowed them to unite in the reigns of a father and son: Childeric (d.482) and Clovis (r.482–511). Childeric operated as a Roman client; Clovis exploited the fall of Rome to create a dominant kingdom. By 485, he had defeated Syagrius, a Roman potentate, to add Paris and Champagne to his father's power base in Belgium. The unification of the previously fragmented Franks then gave him sufficient military power to conquer south-western Gaul from the Visigoths, establish hegemony over the Burgundians of the Rhone valley, and undertake a series of conquests east of the Rhine. These brought the German tribe of the Alamanni, in particular, under his control. Further expansion was temporarily halted by the power of Theoderic, but, after Justinian's destruction of the Ostrogothic kingdom, expansion picked up again. The Burgundians were finally conquered in the early 530s, and Frankish hegemony stretched out over all the peoples of what is now Germany: from the Saxons in the north, to the Bavarians in the south. An important side effect was that the wealth of conquest flowed into the courts of Merovingian kings, and in the later 6th century – after a gap of 75 years – they started to affect some of the trappings of Roman imperial power. Latin culture was encouraged, and efforts were made to govern both civil and ecclesiastical society by means of written law and to erect a more substantial system of taxation.

The limits of power

Behind this Romanizing façade, however, there were fundamental differences between the Frankish

Sutton Hoo

Excavated in the 1930s, the Sutton Hoo burial site brought to life the non-Roman world of northern Europe. Instead of wearing togas and hanging about in forums, the elite of post-Roman Britain buried their dead in boats surrounded by fantastic treasure. Among the items discovered was the famous Sutton Hoo Helmet. Constructed of leather underneath, iron plates provided the wearer's head with all-round defence, while rich gold and silver inlays marked out his status. It was made for a king of East Anglia, quite likely the Redwald mentioned in Bede's *Ecclesiastical History*.

kingdom of the early Middle Ages and the Roman Empire. The Franks were running a structurally weaker state with less power collected at the centre and, correspondingly, more left in the localities. The army was composed of armed local landowners, tax structures (giving the state independent financial muscle) were much weaker, the localities did not in general look to kings for written rulings, and the kings did not run the vast court bureaucracy. Frankish kings could offer court jobs to a few tens of landowners at most, where the Western Roman emperors had employed more than 10,000. In general, therefore, Frankish kings were not as powerful as their Roman forbears, unless they were engaged in military expansion, which brought them extraordinary sources of wealth to distribute.

In the 6th century, when there were plenty of wealthy and not too powerful neighbours to conquer, Merovingian kings became very rich indeed. In the 7th century, however, the supply of suitable neighbours dried up, and kings found themselves in increasing difficulties when it came to controlling powerful subordinates. By 700, the great Merovingian Empire had fragmented. The satellite powers east of the Rhine (Thuringia, Saxony, Bavaria, and Alamannia) re-established their independence, and the central Gallic lands fragmented into separate power blocks. North-east Gaul, north-west Gaul, Burgundy, and Aquitaine all saw their own local ducal dynasties usurp most of the powers of the last Merovingian kings. Right across Western Europe both inside and beyond the old Roman frontier, states of a homogeneous non-Roman structure had emerged. The highly centralized Roman Empire gave way to early medieval kingdoms, the kings of which functioned much more on the basis of the purchased consent of local landowners.

The Rise of the Slavs

Following on from the fall of Rome, the 6th and 7th centuries witnessed another huge revolution in the European political landscape. Emerging from the woods of the east, many small Slavic groups spread across vast tracts of the continent, occupying lands as far west as the river Elbe. At the same time, social and economic transformations began which would eventually lead to the emergence of Slavic states.

Slavic origins

The origins of Europe's Slavic-speakers was a highly political issue throughout the 19th and for most of the 20th century. Western Slavic scholars insisted that the Slavs had always been a major presence in central Europe, arguing that, in the Roman period (when no Slavs are mentioned in what is now Poland and the Czech and Slovak republics), Slavs had nonetheless inhabited these territories "submerged" under the domination of a minority Germanic-speaking population. Russian scholars took the alternative view that Slavs had originated in mother Russia and that the "Slavicness" of central Europe in medieval and modern times was the result of migration. Only

with the fall of the Berlin Wall in 1989 has greater objectivity entered the discussion, the issue being decided largely in favour of the Russian view.

Slavs are first mentioned in literary sources in the 6th century AD, at which point they inhabited regions around the northern edges of the Carpathian Mountains from the southern Vistula to the Black Sea. Recent archaeological research has made a convincing identification of these groups with two related archaeological systems of the same date: the Prague-Korcak and Penkovka cultures. Early Slavs emerge from these remains as Iron Age subsistence farmers, distributed in grouped clusters of small villages composed of 10 to 20 simple log cabins, often partly sunk into the ground for extra protection against the weather. They used only handmade pottery and some very simple iron tools: a plain ard plough, for instance, which scraped narrow trenches for seed. At this point, a Slavic-speaking population in the Carpathian region was a new phenomenon. It had moved into the area only in the latter part of the 5th century, as the Hunnic empire of Attila collapsed to create a power vacuum. All the evidence suggests that Slavs migrated there from areas further north and east in the wooded Steppes zone of what is now southern Russia and the Ukraine.

Slavic spread

Further migrations then spread Slavic-speaking groups right across central Europe, from the Baltic to the Aegean. Byzantine literary sources describe their takeover of the Balkans, where the nomadic Avars played a crucial role. From *c.*560 onwards, the Avars put together a powerful empire on the Hungarian Plain, which mounted a series of campaigns into Byzantine territory. This caused huge damage, particularly in the reign of Heraclius, when the Emperor was primarily occupied with his war against Persia. As a direct result, Slavic groups moved south across the river Danube and then inserted themselves alongside the indigenous Roman population in large parts of the Balkans,

A critical moment in the Slavs social and economic development came in the 8th century when their early handmade pottery was replaced by wheel-made wares such as this example from None Zaluku. This reflects the major increase in agricultural productivity that supported both specialist producers and the militarized elites around whom the first Slavic states would form.

even into the Peloponnese. Further north and west, the spread of Slavic-speakers has to be reconstructed on the basis of archaeological evidence alone. By the 9th century, when Carolingian authors first show detailed knowledge of the Slavic world, all of central Europe east of the Elbe was Slavic-speaking, whereas, up to c.550, territories between the Elbe and the Vistula, at least, had been Germanic-speaking. Between c.550 and 800, therefore, Slavs had come to dominate vast areas of Europe.

In part, this was accomplished through direct migration. The use of pottery of the Penkovka and particularly Prague-Korcak types spread west through central European uplands as far as the Elbe in the 6th and 7th centuries. Similar pottery – known as *Sukow* – also spread through the northern plains of what is now Poland and eastern Germany at more or less the same time. No literary sources describe these events, but the pottery remains probably reflect the initial Slavic takeover of these lands, which, in the Roman period, had been Germanic-speaking. Further east, similar processes were also unfolding in the Russian forest world. By the 9th century, Slavic-speaking groups here had spread northwards from the Kiev region as far as Lake Ilmen, taking over a landscape which, to judge by place and river names, had originally been occupied by speakers of Baltic languages.

Slavicization

The creation of Slavic Europe involved not just migration, but also, as with post-Roman Britain, the absorption of indigenous populations into new patterns of life. Now that consensus has finally begun to emerge over origins, the big debate in early Slavic studies now revolves around the questions of how many Slavic migrants moved into central Europe in the early Middle Ages and the extent to which the Slavicization of Europe was based on cultural accommodation among an existing central European population. In the past, answers were again highly political. Scholars in Cold War East Germany "found" Slavic- and Germanic-speakers living side by side on the same sites, mimicking the ideology of Germano-Slav co-operation that legitimized the state which employed them. More recent work has shown, however, that the handful of "proof sites" usually cited in support of such views were actually occupied sequentially by Germanic and Slavic groups, not simultaneously. The most useful information comes, in fact, from pollen diagrams, which show whether the basic pattern of agriculture in a given area was disrupted or not in the era of Slavic takeover. Where it was disrupted, then migration was probably significant.

While the coverage of such diagrams is far from comprehensive, it does show a mixed pattern. Slavicization was not a simple or singular process, but the product of both migration and acculturation, in different combinations in different localities.

Nor did transformation cease at the initial point of takeover in the later 6th or 7th centuries. In the 8th and 9th centuries, the archaeology of central Europe throws up Slavic pottery types (such as the Leipzig, and Tornow) of a much more sophisticated kind, characterized by a much wider range of forms, better firing, and, eventually, the use of the wheel. Agricultural exploitation also became much more intense, with more effective soil-turning ploughs and crop-rotation schemes coming into use. This greater economic productivity in turn spawned a larger population and the general development of more sophisticated political structures. These further processes culminated in the appearance of the first Slavic states of the 9th and 10th centuries.

Of all the cities of the Balkans, only Thessalonica survived the Slavic onslaught. According to a contemporary text, the Miracula of St Demetrius *(here pictured in a 12th-century icon), this was entirely due to the saint's intervention. It was believed that the saint prevented the city's capture in 586, 614, 633, and again in 680.*

Northern Worlds 106–7 ▶
The Ottonians 120–1 ▶
The Christianization of Europe 128–9 ▶
New States in Eastern Europe 406–7 ▶

Culture and Society

The early Middle Ages saw new cultural norms in Europe. Landowning aristocrats ceased to be trained intensively in Latin language and literature, and the Christian Church became the repository of classical learning. Only those texts were preserved, however, which were perceived to be of value for Christian purposes, and an entirely different oral culture of battle poetry was enjoyed by the secular warrior elites.

Cultural ideologies

In the Roman world, education in Latin language and literature was fundamental to being a civilized human being. Literature contained countless examples of people behaving well and badly, and was a moral database from which the civilized individual could learn to temper the barbarian desires of the body by exercising the rational influence of the mind. Literature also taught the individual to accept the civilizing influence of written laws, which were held to guarantee equal protection for all. The conversion of Rome to Christianity had prompted only minor adjustments to these long-held ideas. Some old texts fell out of use as Christian commentators such as Augustine (especially in his *De Doctrina Christiana*) added the Bible to the literary canon of vital works. But a religion with the Ten Commandments and Leviticus deep within its own ideological structure only served to reinforce the idea that written law set superior societies apart from inferior ones.

Many successor states received a Roman legacy in the form of an established landowning elite, and most embraced these Christianized Roman cultural ideologies. The *Variae* letter collection of the Ostrogothic king Theoderic stressed at every opportunity the importance of written law and classical literature, and Theoderic established some state-funded teaching posts. The Burgundian and Visigothic kingdoms, likewise, established their own functioning systems of written law. Further north, the Franks produced a more symbolic law code – *Lex Salica* – which does not seem to have been much used in practice, but showed that the Franks belonged to the club of civilized states. In the second half of the 6th century, a classical poet from Italy, Venantius Fortunatus, found an enthusiastic Gallic audience for his work, comprising both Roman and Frankish aristocrats who wanted to be written about in old-style Latin verse. As Christianity spread, the emphasis on written law continued to be transmitted, and Anglo-Saxons, Alamannis, and Bavarians all produced symbolic law codes upon joining the new Christian world.

Literacy and education

Literacy among the secular aristocracy was widespread in the late Roman world. Parents paid

Ezra's book cupboard from the *Codex Amiatinus*

The stunning *Codex Amiatinus* was produced in Bede's monastery of Monkwearmouth-Jarrow, Northumbria, Britain, in the early 8th century. It contains richly coloured, highly naturalistic classicizing illuminations in realistic style which clearly went back to classical models. These models had probably been brought north in the collection of materials acquired in Italy by the monastery's founder, Benedict Biscop, in the 660s. The picture of Ezra, with his manuscripts collected in a cupboard, is an accurate depiction of an early medieval scholar at work. The manuscript was a luxury item. The vellum alone was made from the hides of 1700 cows.

for their children to receive 10 years of private education with a private teacher of language and letters – the grammarian. They were willing to do so because such an education was necessary for elite status and led to lucrative careers in the Roman imperial bureaucracy. In the post-Roman world, these careers disappeared as administrative structures reverted to a much simpler level. As a result, elite parents, even of Roman descent, became unwilling to pay for such an intense education, and the grammarians went out of business. After c.475, there was none north of the Alps, and they disappeared even from Italy after c.550. The post-Roman elite, including barbarian royal families, still learnt to read some Latin, but not to write it, and they usually learnt within their families, where women became the chief educators. More intensive literacy was confined to the Church, and, in c.500, many church leaders suddenly realized that the old educational structures were disappearing. In order to reverse this process, individual bishops started to collect libraries of important books and to establish schools within their households, to train their clergy in the literacy essential to Christianity. *The Institutes of Divine Learning* of Cassiodorus, a later 6th-century list of crucial works, was particularly influential, but there was no general pattern. The quality of post-grammarian education depended upon local initiative, with the 6th-century Merovingian, 7th-century Visigothic, and 8th-century Anglo-Saxon Churches showing particular excellence.

Art and architecture

Little architecture of the post-Roman period survives intact, making it difficult to establish general trends. In northern Francia and Anglo-Saxon England, building in stone ceased altogether, and even royal centres (such as Yeavering in Northumbria) were entirely wooden constructions. In these areas, Roman cities fell largely out of use. Further south, change was less marked. Some of the existing Roman public buildings were maintained, and new constructions in stone, particularly of churches, continued. Most of these early medieval structures were later rebuilt, although some smaller Visigothic churches still survive. The size and sophistication of construction between the 6th and 8th centuries has often been underestimated; however, as state structures brought in smaller amounts of taxation, fewer funds were available for grand architectural programmes than in the Roman period.

Artistic activity throughout this period presents a similarly mixed picture. Classical realism continued to exert considerable influence, and it was seen

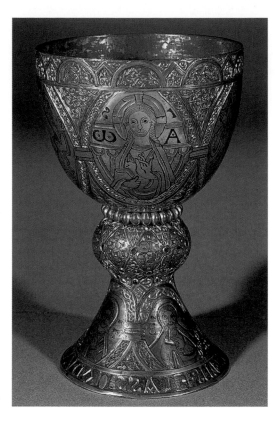

Early medieval elites were highly militarized, but also deeply pious, and the metalworking skills that produced weapons and high-status jewellery were also turned to religious subjects. This stunning gold and silver chalice was presented to the monastery of Kremsmunster by Duke Tassilo of Bavaria and his wife Liutpirc in 770.

most strongly closer to the Mediterranean. The fact that so many older manuscripts were destroyed in the Carolingian period (751–987) makes it difficult to estimate the extent of artistic activity and the predominant styles in the earlier medieval era. Further north, alongside occasional examples of the classicizing pictorial style such as the *Codex Amiatinus*, a more abstract art, the so-called Hiberno-Saxon style, was also flourishing. This was characterized by fantastic interlacing monsters and abstract patterns, and it was often used as illustration, as on the initial pages of the late 7th-century *Lindisfarne Gospels*. It manifested itself in other media: on the great standing stones of Anglo-Saxon England, such as the Ruthwell Cross, and on metalwork, such as that found at Sutton Hoo. The latter also points us towards a world that we can only begin to grasp: the rich metalwork seems to have been made by post-Roman kings to distribute to their supporters, a material expression of the generosity that was expected of them.

These elites and their kings also had their own oral culture of heroic poetry, where treasures such as those at Sutton Hoo were celebrated. *Beowulf* is a surviving example, but this tradition occasionally coincided with other forms. The Ruthwell Cross is not only decorated with Hiberno-Saxon motifs, but also inscribed with *The Dream of the Rood*, a Christian poem on the Crucifixion expressed in Anglo-Saxon poetic form.

On Christmas Day 800,
Charlemagne was crowned
emperor in St Peters in Rome,
reviving the concept of empire
in Western Europe. This bronze
equestrian statue in miniature,
produced in about 870,
celebrates his glory. It portrays
him with the orb that
symbolized, after Roman
models, his world domination.

NEW EMPIRES OF THE WEST

In the period *c.*700–1000, new imperial powers emerged in a post-Roman West freed from Mediterranean domination. The greatest of these empires was that of the Frankish Carolingian dynasty. In the 8th century, it united all of Francia west of the Rhine, then added Germany up to the Elbe, most of Italy, and a large part of central Europe. The title of emperor was revived on Christmas Day 800 to crown the achievements of its greatest member: Charles the Great – Charlemagne.

Carolingian domination was built on the exploitation of extraordinary sources of wealth, rather than on developed governmental institutions. When the wealth ran out, as it did in the 9th century, the basic situation that had evolved in the post-Roman West still applied: power tended to move from the centre to localities. In the 9th and 10th centuries, this was reinforced by two longer term developments. First, in the manorialized estates, landlords evolved a more intensive form of agricultural exploitation that allowed them to generate a much greater income from the same area of landed holding. As kings had no general rights to tax their landowners, the latter grew in power and wealth compared to their kings. At the same time, defensive armour and castle-building was making military activity an elite profession and distancing landlords from lesser mortals. A dominant, militarized landowning oligarchy thus came to power in the localities. Where kings lost access to outside sources of wealth, as in West Francia (now France) from the later 9th century, this oligarchy came to establish its almost complete independence of monarchical centres.

In East Francia (now Germany), the Carolingian line ran out earlier, but centralized government survived. In the first half of the 10th century, through Henry I and his son Otto I, the ducal line of Saxony advanced first to royal, then imperial status. This success was based partly, like the Carolingians, on having extraordinary sources of wealth to fund the acquisition of supporters, but also on providing effective leadership against the nomadic Magyars who had moved into the Hungarian Plain in the 890s. Otto led the east Franks to final victory over the Magyars in 955, then brought both Italy and the newly emerging Slavic monarchies of central Europe into his political orbit.

Scandinavian populations also came to play a major role in European history in this period. By 800, they had developed the naval technology to form closer ties with the rest of Europe. Some traded, while others – the Vikings – raided and eventually, from c.850, formed larger armies in order to conquer areas for settlement. Further east in northern Russia, Scandinavian traders extracted furs and slaves, and quickly discovered the river routes that allowed them to sell their goods in the rich markets of the Islamic Near East. As a whole, the Viking period generated a wide range of effects. Many new trading relationships were established, new settlements were established in England and northern France, and new states – both in Scandinavia itself and in Russia – came into existence.

From one of the settlements, that around Rouen, Normandy was to emerge: the last of the new western empires. In the 10th century, the Scandinavian rulers of Rouen united other Viking groups behind them and played politics in the wider arena of West Francia. By 1000, they had proclaimed themselves dukes of Normandy, and, in 1066, in the person of William the Conqueror, stepped up to become kings of a state that spanned the Channel. Lesser Normans were also highly active, moving vigorously into Celtic Britain and, above all, southern Italy, to create a wider Norman empire.

Charlemagne's Empire

On Christmas Day 800, Charlemagne entered St Peters in Rome as King of the Franks and left it as Emperor of the West. He would later say that had he known what Pope Leo III was about to do, he would have stayed outside. This was an obligatory show of modesty. Charlemagne and his advisers had been working towards the imperial title for a decade.

Charlemagne's silver coinage set a standard for all of Western Europe and is a sign of increasing monetary exchange. This silver penny, minted at the trading port of Quentovic (near modern Boulogne), was also used to celebrate his new imperial status, styling him imperator (imp) *and* augustus (aug)*, the characteristic titles of Roman emperors.*

Charlemagne's palace complex at Aachen in North Rhine-Westphalia was modelled on the great palace in Constantinople, but with important modifications. Both had thrones in their main Churches, but where Byzantine emperors sat in the east behind the high altar, Charlemage deliberately placed himself more modestly in the west, criticizing their claims to rule "with God" as hubris.

The Rise of the Pepinids

By 700, the kingdom of the Merovingian Franks had fragmented. Charlemagne's ancestors first rose to prominence as the dominant aristocratic dynasty in one of its now largely autonomous regions: north-eastern France and Belgium (known as Austrasia). The new dynasty's rise to more general dominance was secured by Charlemagne's grand-father Charles Martel. Securely in control of Austrasia from 714, he defeated in 719 a coalition of rivals from the other regions of Francia: north-western France (known as Neustria), Aquitaine, and Burgundy. By the time of his famous victory over the Muslim Arabs at Poitiers in 732, he had reunited Francia and begun to restore its hege-mony east of the Rhine. After the death of his Merovingian figurehead, Theoderic IV, in 737, Charles also operated for his last years as an entirely independent ruler, although he stepped back from claiming the royal title. Charles was succeeded in 741 by his two sons Pepin and Carloman, but a major aristocratic revolt convinced

them to find another Merovingian frontman. They duly promoted Childeric III, but after Carloman retired to a monastery and his own power was secure, Pepin finally procured sufficient support to take the royal title. Childeric was deposed, and Pepin promoted to kingship in 751. One of a peer group of regional aristocrats had succeeded in elbowing himself into power above his rivals.

Charlemagne and the Carolingian Empire

The dynasty was to reach new heights in the next generation. In a series of dramatic conquests, Pepin's son Charlemagne – "Charles the Great" – extended his rule over most of central and Western Europe. South of the Pyrenees, Charlemagne's reach never went much beyond Barcelona, but elsewhere his successes were astonishing. East of the Rhine, Alamannia, Thuringia, and Bavaria were quickly taken over. Further north, Saxony, too, was eventually conquered in 804, but only after 30 years of fierce resistance. South of the Alps, the entire Lombard kingdom was conquered in 774, and, in central Europe, the 200-year-old Avar Empire was dismantled in the 790s. By the year 800, Charlemagne's fiat extended from the Atlantic to the Elbe, and from the Baltic to Rome.

Not surprisingly, the king and his advisers searched for a suitable means of expressing Charlemagne's new grandeur; they also contem-plated the significance of his unprecedented success. As devout Christians who believed that God directly intervened in world affairs, they could only conclude that He was behind the victories and that God's aim was to restore the concept of empire in the West, which had been lost with the collapse of Rome. "Empire" not only indicated a scale of rule that was beyond that of a mere king, but also in the Roman imperial ideology still strongly preserved in Constantinople, carried connotations of a special relationship with God. Charlemagne and his advisers were reaching out towards the imperial title from 790 at the latest. From that point, they began to criticize parts of the Byzantines' vision of empire, accusing them of arrogance in claiming that their emperor ruled "with God". Charlemagne also set about a general reform of Christian observance. Charlemagne's decrees stated that this was the service he owed God in return for victory. Contemporary popes were hesitant about the implicit challenge to their own religious pre-eminence; however, Leo III was eventually put in the position of needing Charlemagne's support against rivals in Rome who were seeking to depose and blind him. Charlemagne came to the city in winter 800. He convened a special council on 24 December 800, which confirmed Leo in office, and was himself crowned emperor on Christmas Day.

Empire in action

The imperial title marked not so much the beginning of new stage in Charlemagne's reign, as a recognition of all that he had already achieved. Afterwards, his religious aims were strongly restated, and the running of the Empire continued much as before. What stands out are the fundamental differences between the Frankish version of empire and how the Roman model had run four centuries before. The Frankish Empire operated without a designated political capital (or capitals) and with no extensive administrative bureaucracy.

The loyalty of local landowning elites was secured by a non-stop process of travel and supervision, rather than by offering them jobs in a huge governmental machine. Charlemagne, except when old age confined him to his spa palace at Aachen, was an itinerant monarch who averaged 30km (8 miles) a day throughout his reign. This allowed local men and king reciprocal access, the king checking on their loyalty and offering them in return the chance to ask him for personal favours. A key element was the annual assembly of militarized landowners on the eve of the year's campaigning season, where they and the king could deal with pressing business. The decisions of such councils sometimes acquired written form (known as *capitularies*), but these were *aides-mémoires* reflecting an essentially oral process, rather than formal written decrees after the Roman pattern. The king had no professional army of any size separate from these landowners and their followers, and his wealth came from landholding, not developed taxation rights. In geographical scale, the Carolingian Empire matched that of the old Roman West, but in methods of government it was simply a larger version of the kind of state that had replaced the Roman Empire after its collapse, rather than an entity of an entirely different kind.

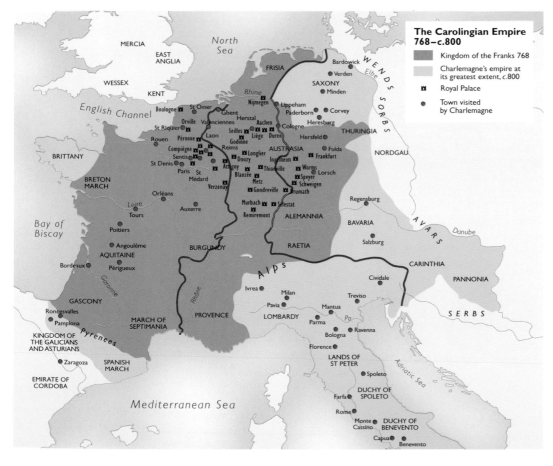

The Carolingian Empire 768–c.800

Kingdom of the Franks 768

Charlemagne's empire at its greatest extent, c.800

Royal Palace

Town visited by Charlemagne

Charlemagne's reign saw major new conquests, turning most of Western Europe into one imperial state. This empire was not governed through an administrative bureaucracy, however. Averaging 30 kilometres (8 miles) a day, Charlemagne himself travelled between a network of palaces and other stopping points to gather information, collect revenues and cow potential rebels.

Feudalism and Carolingian Decline

The Carolingian Empire was based on personal relationships among the landowning elites of Western Europe, rather than bureaucratic government. A key element was the feudal bond between unequal partners: lord and vassal. The relationship was built on defined services on the part of the vassal – military and other – in return for tenure of a piece of the lord's land and his judicial protection.

The growth of local power

These relationships were built against the backdrop of two much longer term trends that favoured the growth of local power. First, the basis of agricultural production was slowly transformed between the 7th and 11th centuries. The landed properties of the wealthy – starting with monasteries, but spreading to secular lords – were revolutionized by the growth of manorial agriculture, which placed new wealth in the hands of the lords and depressed the status of many previously free peasants. At the same time, advances in the fields of defensive armour and castle-building changed patterns of warfare – and social relations – out of all recognition. While armour rendered large but ill-equipped armies redundant, it was very expensive. Hence warfare became largely confined to the manor-holding

Under Charlemagne's grandsons, the Empire seemed undiminished. Government was increasingly bureaucratic and court culture flourished, especially under Charles the Bald, pictured here enthroned in majesty between personifications of his main territories, Franconia and Gothia. Beneath the imperial veneer, however, socio-economic change was cementing in place the dominance of more local landowners.

class and their immediate retainers. Fortifications allowed small numbers of men to tie up large numbers of opponents, so that castles were built both by kings and regional lords in large numbers after *c*.850. This, too, had important social effects. Even a small-scale local lord, if in charge of a castle, could dominate his locality and be very difficult to oust.

Feudalism and Carolingian collapse

Charlemagne had initially planned to divide the Empire between three sons, but the eldest was to be given a dominant share together with the imperial title. By the time of Charlemagne's death in 814, only Louis the Pious survived, and so he inherited everything. Louis was survived by four adult sons, who expected and extracted equal shares of land. They had even tried to take shares of power from their father in the 830s. On Louis' death in 843, the Empire was evenly divided, and his sons quickly fell out among themselves. Two in particular – Charles the Bald in the west and Louis the German in the east – survived the initial rounds of competition and rivalry. By the 850s, they were campaigning against one another and had recruited dedicated bodies of supporters for the same purpose. At the same time, Viking raids were growing in intensity, particularly in the realm of Charles the Bald, and centralized direction was far too cumbersome to fight off these raiders' unpredictable assaults. It became necessary, therefore, for the two kings both to reward their supporters in the battle for primacy and to cede local control to subordinates to run the defensive war against the Vikings.

These processes had dramatic results. The Carolingians were dependent upon military expansion to make up for a deficiency in internally derived revenues. Aggressive warfare had continued steadily from Charles Martel to Charlemagne, but came to an end in the reign of Louis the Pious. From that point, rewards for political supporters had to be made largely out of the capital stock of royal lands – itself divided between Louis' various sons – with consequences for royal power that exactly mirrored the fate of the Merovingians. The delegation of power in the western kingdom to fight the Vikings only hurried the process along. By the end of Charles the Bald's reign in 877, direct royal landholding in the west was limited only to northern areas around Paris. Elsewhere, control had passed into the hands of numerous regional and still more local lords. When Charles' immediate successor, Charles the Fat, proved an incapable war-leader against the Vikings, he was deposed and, as the contemporary Regino of Prüm put it, "each area made its own king out of its bowels".

Medieval manorial agriculture

Carolingian lords increasingly ran their estates as centrally directed productive units – ie, manors. A legally tied peasantry provided for its own needs from independent tenements in return for substantial amounts of labour that was used to farm a separate portion of the estate – the demesne. The new regime allowed landlords to introduce more productive three-crop rotations and make economies of scale in such expensive items as plough teams. As a result, the agricultural year

became a regular succession of monthly tasks that were often illustrated in calendar form. This Anglo-Saxon manuscript of *c*.1050 portrays the reaping and gathering of the August harvest.

New patterns of power

These political events intersected with the underlying trends in favour of the growth of local power to generate a variety of outcomes. East of the Rhine, in the kingdom of Louis the German, the 10th century saw considerable unity maintained for very particular reasons under the new Ottonian dynasty. In western Francia and Italy, there was greater variety. Particularly in the north, the later Carolingians (restored in the person of Louis IV d'Outremer ["from over the sea"] in 936–54), some of their trusted lieutentants in the Viking war (especially the Robertians from whom the later Capetian royal dynasty evolved), and several other dynasts, such as the Dukes of Flanders, kept control of substantial regional power blocks. They had learnt from the earlier Carolingian example and quickly adopted primogenture – succession of the first-born son – to prevent any further erosions of central power. These rulers were thus able to enjoy the fruits of manorialization themselves and keep castle-building firmly under their own control.

Elsewhere, however, power quickly devolved into the hands of local castle-holders – castellans – who became a fixed, hereditary feature of the landscape. In their own localities, the castellans quickly abrogated to themselves previously royal rights over markets, coinage, taxation, and labour dues to establish a domination which would last throughout the medieval period.

Charlemagne's Empire 114–15 ▶

The Vikings 118–19 ▶

The Ottonians 120–1 ▶

The Bonds of Society 146–7 ▶

The Vikings

In the 9th and 10th centuries, Scandinavian adventurers took to Europe's seas and rivers to make money in every possible way. From the North Sea to the Caspian, the Vikings sold furs and slaves, conducted raids, and extracted tributes. Where circumstances were right, they even settled and became new elites. The overall result of these actions was an enormous flow of wealth into Scandinavia which generated social and political revolution.

From c.800, Viking raids upon Western Europe became commonplace. The raiders targeted wealthy monasteries as well as the now well-established trading centres of the Channel. The important port of Dorestad at the mouth of the Rhine was attacked four times in the 830s alone. Around 850, the attacks grew in intensity: a process marked by Viking attackers overwintering in the West rather than going home, and by the appearance in contemporary sources of named Viking leaders. It culminated in the era of "great armies", which started in England in 865.

Previously separate raiding groups were now amalgamated into composite armies, numbering between 5000 and 10,000 men. Their increased power allowed them to conquer entire kingdoms and was probably the reason that they had banded together in the first place. Between 865 and 874, the first great army led by a coalition of kings, including the brothers Ingvar and Halfdan, conquered Northumbria, half of Mercia (roughly the region that is now the Midlands), and East Anglia. Its ravages were finally checked by Alfred the Great of Wessex at Eddington in 878. The victory prevented further conquests, but did not reverse the land seizures taking place in territories already conquered. Checked in England, the Vikings who had not won land there turned to northern France and the Low Countries, where they ravaged widely from 879–92. A further assault – again frustrated by Alfred – was made on southern England from 892–5, before the remaining unsatisfied Vikings made their return to the continent once more.

The main outcomes of this activity were twofold: large-scale transfers of western wealth to Scandinavia and the establishment of a series of Scandinavian enclaves in the West. Danelaw, comprising most of eastern England, was the largest of these, but, on the continent, there were

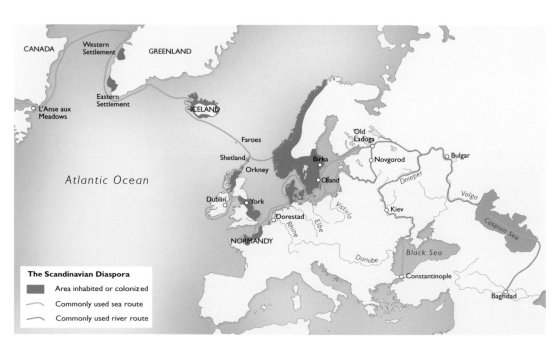

The Scandinavian Diaspora
- Area inhabited or colonized
- Commonly used sea route
- Commonly used river route

settlements at the mouths of the Seine in Normandy and the Loire, and a number of coastal communities established themselves in Ireland. Northern Scotland, Shetland, Orkney, and the western isles as far south as Man were also overrun.

Vikings of Russia

At the same time, other Scandinavians, known to the indigenous Finns as "Rus", had been making money further east, trading slaves, furs, and other products from the subarctic forest world of northern Russia. Their first permanent colony there, around Lake Ladoga, was established in *c*.750. At this stage, the extracted goods were being traded back through the Baltic to the West. Very quickly, however, the Norsemen realized that the river routes of western Russia provided access to much richer markets. South-flowing river networks, particularly those around the Dnieper and Volga, led from the subarctic north to the Black and Caspian seas and on to the rich world of medieval Islam, where the Abbasid Caliphate was at its height. By *c*.800, the first flows of Muslim silver coin – given in return for furs and slaves – were reaching the Baltic, but it was from about 880 onwards that the stream became a flood.

By this stage, the Viking merchants were no longer making the long trek south to the Caspian, but were trading with Islamic merchants in the markets of the Volga Bulgars. By *c*.900, several distinct Scandinavian settlements had established themselves in northern Russia, all under the control of the Rurikid dynasty (named after Ruric, their founder), the seat of which was established on the island fortress of Gorodische. These princes also quickly brought under their control a second set of settlements further south on the middle Dnieper, particularly at Kiev, which had begun a substantial, if secondary, trade with Constantinople.

In the later 10th and 11th centuries, as Islamic collapse rendered trade less profitable, the Rurikids developed more regular patterns of revenue generation, based on the productive capacities of surrounding Slavic tribes, and itinerant governmental structures to control them. From the extended Viking trading company of the early 9th century developed the first, Kievan, Russian state.

Viking-age Scandinavia

The Viking age also transformed Scandinavia. In the 8th century, southern Denmark was dominated by powerful chieftains capable of organizing major public works, such as the *Danewirke*, a defensive ditch and wooden wall along the

The Gokstad Ship

Excavated in the late 19th century, the beautiful 9th-century Gokstad ship, now in the Oslo Museum, provides one of the keys to the Viking age. Up to the 7th century, Scandinavian boats were oar-propelled canoes, designed for river work and the island archipelagos of the Baltic. The Gokstad ship illustrates the changes that occurred over the next century. Clinker-built spars attached to a one-piece central keel created a hull of great strength, and sails were added to drive the ships over vast distances. The advances came from the Viking's desire to participate in new trading networks that grew up in the North and Baltic Seas between 650 and 800.

southern edge of the Jutland peninsula. These political structures were far from stable and were exercised over a restricted geographical area. The flow of wealth from east and west in the Viking age completely undermined them.

The dominance of the old rulers was based on the control of purely Scandinavian resources, and they could not compete with those who returned home with overseas wealth. By 850, the old structures had collapsed and power fragmented. Larger political structures were finally re-established only from the mid-10th century when, with overseas wealth subsiding, the Jelling dynasty of Gorm and his son Harold Bluetooth united the Jutland peninsula and its adjacent islands (Sjaelland, Skåne, and Fyn). Over the next century, their successors were able to create a genuine state.

After *c*.980, no more Muslim silver flowed into the Baltic, and Svein and Canute (son and grandson of Harold) put themselves at the head of further expansionary activity in the West. Between *c*.995 and 1016, they conquered the whole of England to create a true Viking empire. The empire did not outlive Canute, its founder, but the period was used to develop stable institutions at home: the kingdom of Denmark had been born. The two centuries after the turn of the millennium saw the evolution of similarly solid structures in Norway and Sweden.

Northern Worlds 500–700   106–7 ►
The Normans   122–3 ►
The Challenge of the East   208–9 ►
Sweden, Russia,
and the Baltic   252–3 ►

The Ottonians

When the line of Louis the German – Charlemagne's grandson – ran out, the dukes of Saxony, Bavaria, Alamannia, Suebia, and Lotharingia competed for overall power. From the 920s, the Ottonian dukes of Saxony emerged to make themselves undisputed kings of East Francia and even to revive the Carolingian tradition of empire.

The rise of the Liudolfings

Liudolf (d.866) began his career as a Carolingian appointee: commander on the Elbe frontier in his native Saxony. His grandson Henry I (the Fowler: Duke of Saxony from 912 and King of East Francia from 919–36) was able to take his family's pre-eminence a stage further, primarily because of the military leadership which he provided against the Magyars. The Magyars were a nomadic grouping who had moved into the grasslands of the Hungarian Plain in the 890s. From there, they mounted a series of raids across Europe and larger campaigns into the neighbouring East Frankish kingdom, where they inflicted a series of heavy defeats on its ducal-led armies in the 900s and 910s. Henry negotiated a truce with the Magyars in 926 and used the respite to undertake military reforms. Garrisoned forts were constructed throughout the kingdom, and he turned the Saxon field army into heavy armoured cavalry. When war resumed, the forts made it impossible for the Magyars to extract easy booty, and the new Saxon army was able to inflict a first defeat upon the nomads at the battle of Riade in 933. This leadership propelled Henry to kingship over all of East Francia, although his prominence was disputed, especially by the Bavarian ducal line. Throughout his reign, Henry operated as *primus inter pares* ("first among equals"), with an ideology of *amicitia* ("friendship") towards the other dukes.

Empire

The dynasty acquired imperial status under Henry's son Otto I (936–73). Early in his reign, Otto faced challenges from members of his own family, who often combined against him with other East Frankish Dukes. Otto overcame these revolts and even used them to cement his position, replacing the indigenous ducal line of Bavaria with his younger brother Henry in 947. His ability to do this was based on two extraordinary resources unique to Saxony, which had also sustained his father. First, the silver mines of the Harz Mountains provided the Saxon ducal line with great wealth. At the same time, colonial expansion beyond the Elbe into Slavic territories gave it large amounts of new land with which to reward followers in the marches. Exploitation of these areas reached a new peak under Otto, who also undertook the Christianization of the conquered Slavs, establishing a series of missionary bishoprics under the rule of a new Archbishopric at Magdeburg. With a ready supply of new rewards, he could secure the loyalty of old magnates and attract new supporters. His consequent military strength allowed him to defeat internal challenges and administer a final coup de grâce to Magyar expansionism in 955 at the battle of the Lech. Thereafter, the Magyars quickly converted to Christianity and joined the club of Western Christendom. Otto's successes also opened up the path to Italy, where he again conquered much new territory and intervened in the Papal State. Otto steadily replaced local Italians with churchmen from northern Europe interested in continuing the Carolingian projects of reform. The policy bore fruit in 962 when Otto was crowned emperor in Rome by Pope John XII.

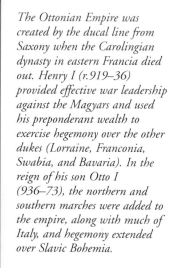

The Ottonian Empire was created by the ducal line from Saxony when the Carolingian dynasty in eastern Francia died out. Henry I (r.919–36) provided effective war leadership against the Magyars and used his preponderant wealth to exercise hegemony over the other dukes (Lorraine, Franconia, Swabia, and Bavaria). In the reign of his son Otto I (936–73), the northern and southern marches were added to the empire, along with much of Italy, and hegemony extended over Slavic Bohemia.

The Ottonian Empire 936–72
- Ottonian Empire 936
- Additions to Ottonian Empire by 972

Like the Carolingians before them, the Ottonians used classicizing pictorial models to express their imperial power. Here, from his magnificently illustrated Coronation Gospels, *the power of Otto II is represented by female personifications of dependent territories bringing him free offerings of their agricultural produce as tribute.*

The golden age

Otto's coronation heralded a new golden age. His son Otto II married a Byzantine princess, Theophanou, and their court was celebrated for its magnificent culture. Writing blossomed, splendid metalwork was created, and a series of beautiful illuminated manuscripts was produced. Into the orbit of this imperial greatness were drawn the new, largely Slavic, monarchies of central and Eastern Europe: Poland, Bohemia, and Russia. Each of these states had been built around a core territory of dense settlement ringed with royal castles. From these core areas, the new monarchies dismantled old tribal structures in their immediate surroundings and squabbled with their peers. Their political history is marked, therefore, by great rises and falls, as the strong man from first one of the monarchies, then another, temporarily added vast tracts of Eastern Europe to his core powerbase. In cultural terms, Russia moved partly in a Byzantine orbit, but Poland, Bohemia, the new Magyar monarchy, and the territories in between became part of a larger Ottonian hegemony. The great symbolic moment came in AD 1000, when Otto III (king from 983; emperor 996–1002), grandson of Otto I, made an imperial progress to Poland, inaugurating the independent Christian province of Poland under its own archbishop at Gniezno.

The limits of the Ottonian Empire

Like its Carolingian predecessor, the Ottonian Empire had limitations. Within East Francia, powerful ducal structures remained, and imperial landholding and travel were largely limited to Saxony itself. The Ottonians' ability to dominate this constellation of dukes was based on its unique access to extraordinary sources of wealth, and, in the later 10th century, this was cut off. Muslim forces inflicted a huge defeat on the Emperor Otto II at Cap Colonne in 982. This setback, closely followed by Otto's relatively early death, provided the Elbe Slavs with the opportunity to throw off colonial domination. A huge, co-ordinated revolt throughout the marchlands in 983 re-established Slavic independence and was marked by a rejection of Christianity. Otto III also failed to produce an heir, so that the imperial title passed at this point to the Salians, descendants of Otto I's younger brother Henry, whom he had installed in Bavaria. By this time, the power sources that had made Otto so dominant were ebbing away, and the Holy Roman Empire, the state he created, began its evolution from imperial power to electoral commonwealth.

The Normans

Normandy had its origins in a licensed settlement of Vikings on the Upper Seine in 911. By the end of the century, it had become a powerful, autonomous duchy. The new state preserved Viking expansionary traditions. Both its dukes and lesser nobility were ready to seize every available opportunity, so that, by 1100, Normans were running much of the British Isles and large parts of France and southern Italy.

From settlement to duchy

The career details of the first leader of the Rouen Vikings, Rollo, are lost in the mists of time. Defeated by the Franks at Chartres in 910, he was baptized and settled on the Upper Seine to guard the region against other Vikings. This was one of several such settlements at the time – with others occurring in Brittany and the Loire – and was probably part of the fall-out from the second great army repulsed from England in the mid-890s. The power of the Rouen settlement and its leaders grew in stages. In the 930s, William Longsword, Rollo's son, started to play a more prominent role in the political rivalries of the great magnates of north-western Francia: Carolingian kings, Capetian lords, and counts of Flanders. For his troubles, he was granted further lands west of Rouen, but paid for them with his life: in 942, Count Arnulf of Flanders, one of his main opponents, organized his assassination. Under William's son, Richard I (Count of Rouen 945–96), more land came under the dynasty's control, its remit now stretching west to Bayeux and the Cotentin and south to Evreux. Much of this success was based on the great wealth deriving from Rouen's position as one of the great trading centres of northern Europe, which came to the dynasty in taxes and tolls. From Richard I's time, the rulers of Normandy thus maintained a substantial coinage, and many coin hoards have been found, the largest a spectacular 8586 coins at Fecamp. The rise of Normandy within Francia reached its apogee under Richard II. Shortly before he entertained the Frankish king at Fecamp in 1006, he began to use the title *dux* (duke) and to appoint a series of counts to the territories within his domains. This grand title reflected the greater expanse of territory under his control and his ability to extract recognition from his contemporaries.

The conquest of England

The size and position of the new duchy gave it an important role in international affairs. In the early 11th century, the Vikings returned to England, and Ethelred ("the Unready") wanted to prevent the raiders from using Normandy as a base. Richard II's daughter Emma became his queen, and, when his dynasty was ousted from England by Canute in 1016, his surviving children sought refuge in Normandy. After 1042, when Canute's line gave out, Ethelred's grandson, Edward the Confessor, returned to England, but retained close connections with his adopted homeland. He occupied a very difficult political situation, facing over-mighty subjects in the family of the Earl of Wessex: Godwin and his son Harold. Having no children, Edward sought to protect his position by making an outsider his heir; he could not have chosen a Godwin, or they would have sidelined him completely. He naturally turned to Normandy and Richard II's bastard son William. He kept some independence, but, in the longer term, the result could only be war. The Godwins would never accept a Norman ruler, and the Normans could not tolerate them. When Edward died in 1066, therefore, Harold seized the throne and William invaded. In the great showdown just outside Hastings, Harold and his brothers were killed: the Norman ducal line had now become a royal one. William proceeded to reward the supporters who had

The Domesday Book of 1086 contains an astonishingly detailed survey of the English town and countryside. The annual income of each unit of production was valued in monetary terms, and many assets (labour force, ploughs, etc) were individually listed. The results, organized by landowner, provide a clear account of exactly who gained what from the Norman Conquest.

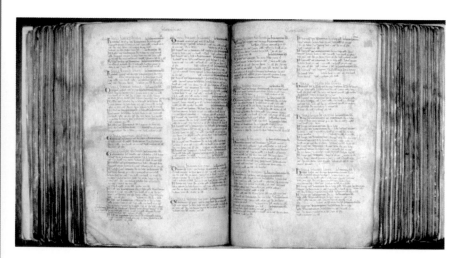

backed him so effectively. By 1086, as recorded in the Domesday Book, the landowning class of Anglo-Saxon England had been almost entirely replaced by Normans (for example, only 6 out of 180 chief landowners were Anglo-Saxons).

This new state, spanning the English Channel, was one of the richest in Europe, and, in the first generations, its rulers retained their Norman orientation. William the Conqueror and his sons divided their time two-thirds to one-third between Normandy and England, and essentially used the wealth of England to further their continental political ambitions, in particular to fend off the power of their notional overlords, the kings of France.

Wider horizons

From their continental and later English bases, individual Norman magnates quickly moved into Wales and Scotland in the 11th century, and Ireland in the 12th century The most dramatic example of Norman magnate-led expansion occurred, however, in southern Italy. In the early 11th century the region was politically fragmented. The Lombard princes of Benevento, Salerno, and Capua were fighting among themselves and against Byzantine overlordship. The need for mercenaries was strong, and Norman warlords and their men found employment in ever-increasing numbers. In 1030, the erstwhile employees began the process of turning themselves into masters. They seized the Calabrian town of Aversa; Melfi followed in 1041, then attacks were made on the Byzantines in Apulia and Calabria, who turned to the papacy for assistance. At the battle of Civitate in 1053, Pope Leo IX was captured by the Normans, and a great realignment followed. The papacy switched its backing to the Normans, formally granting their leaders lands they had not yet conquered in the Investiture of Melfi on 2 March 1059 and which still belonged to the Byzantines and Muslims. Richard of Aversa was proclaimed the legitimate ruler of Capua; Robert Guiscard that of Calabria, Apulia, and Sicily. Guiscard quickly turned theory into practice, conquering Calabria in 1060 and Apulia in 1071. Meanwhile, his brother Roger turned his attention to Muslim-held Sicily. The invasion began in 1061, and slow but steady progress was made. Palermo was captured in 1072, and final victory eventually followed in 1092. The Norman domination of Sicily inaugurated a period of peaceful prosperity, marked by artistic and cultural patronage of the highest order, particularly under King Roger II. The greatest surviving monuments from the period are the vast and richly decorated Cathedral and Palace of Palermo and the cathedrals of Monreale and Cefiti.

Edward the Confessor, king of England 1042–66, used his Norman connections to protect himself from the Godwin family. They were as wealthy as he was himself, and he named William of Normandy as his heir to bolster his own position. In the longer term, however, it gave William a claim to the English throne.

THE NORMANS   123

An ivory panel from the 6th-century throne of Bishop Maximian of Ravenna. The upper panel contains the Chi-Rho of Christ flanked by deer and peacocks, symbols of heavenly paradise. This was the central Christian message of hope proclaimed by John the Baptist (centre) and the four evangelists, pictured in the central panel below.

CHRISTIANITY AND SOCIETY

The conversion of Constantine brought wealth, converts, and greater unity to the Christian religion, which had previously consisted of largely autonomous communities dotted around the Mediterranean rim. These transformations had turned the Church into a substantial but by no means monolithic entity by AD 500. The countryside was far from fully Christianized, and few missions had been mounted beyond the old Roman frontiers.

Between 500 and 1000, further missionary work, the development of more regular religious provision, and the transformation of its structures of authority combined to make Christianity the dominant religion of Europe.

Huge efforts were put into spreading the word, both into the countryside and more generally into non-Roman Europe. The populations of Ireland and Scotland embraced the Christian message in the 5th and 6th centuries; the Anglo-Saxons did so in the 7th; continental Germany up to the Elbe was converted in the 8th; the Slavs in the 9th and 10th centuries; and Scandinavia in the 10th and 11th centuries. Some points of resistance remained, particularly among the Elbe Slavs; however, by the start of the second Christian millennium the new religion was a dominating force across the map of Europe. The fundamental problem now facing Christian leaders was how to ensure adequate Christian provision across this huge expanse of territory. Missionary work was conducted by relatively small groups of priests and monks, and many individual missionaries, in order to minimize hostility among potential converts, incorporated as much as possible of pre-Christian religious beliefs and practice into their message. The result of this combination of toleration and a shortage of priests tended to be syncretism: local mixtures of pre- and Christian belief and practice. The situation only really began to be addressed in the Carolingian Renaissance. At that time, on the back of Charlemagne's power and prestige, the Christian scholars gathered at his court defined a core of necessary Christian learning and, through it, established for the first time general standards of piety and practice for monks, priests, and laymen. Trained manpower on a very large scale – many thousands per kingdom – was required to bring the reform programme to fruition, which was not achieved before the end of the millennium.

At the same time, Church structures and patterns of authority had been transformed beyond all recognition. Early medieval kings and emperors saw themselves as divinely appointed rulers. On this basis, they exercised power over Church institutions and resources, often with good intentions, but with an in-built tendency to fragment the Church by making its structures operate on a kingdom-by-kingdom basis. As the successors of St Peter, popes had long been acknowledged as the most senior of Western bishops. Between the 9th and the 11th centuries, however, the papacy reinvented itself, partly on the back of the central role Charlemagne had given it in the Carolingian Renaissance, to become a unifying force within Western Christendom. Ideological acceptance of its authority combined with the emergence of a Rome-centred canon law gave the Western Church a unity that, to a significant extent, operated independently of political boundaries. The price, however, was high. Popes had effectively claimed the kind of religious authority which Byzantine emperors considered their sole preserve. The resulting friction culminated in a definitive split between Greek East and Latin West in the Great Schism of 1054, when the Western Church definitively rejected Byzantine pretensions to hegemony over all Christians.

Christian Microcosms

Early medieval Christians believed they belonged to one religion. In practice, however, the fall of the Roman Empire halted the processes which had begun to generate real unity of practice, belief, and discipline, all of which depended upon the legal authority and financial support of the emperors. In fact, the early medieval Church was a loose association of regional units, despite continued papal claims to universal authority.

Structures of authority

Roman imperial collapse returned some early medieval Churches to the isolated position characteristic of early Christian communities under Roman persecution. The British Church, in particular, was left to itself, with very little contact with the continent from the mid-5th century. As a result, it and the Irish Church which developed from it preserved many of the practices and doctrines of the Church in c.400 in fossilized form, while the rest of the Church continued to develop. When these Churches came back into contact with the Western mainstream in the late 6th century, their lack of hierarchically organized bishops and deviant views on the date of Easter caused serious problems.

The rest of the former Roman West was divided between successor kingdoms, the borders of which sometimes failed to correspond to those of the Church. In the early 500s, successive metropolitan

The 6th-century manual of John Climakos saw monks as climbing a long and narrow ladder to heaven, from which demons attempted to pull them back to earth. This image quickly took visual form, as in this 12th-century example from St Catherine's monastery on Mt Sinai.

bishops of Arles, located in Visigothic and then Ostrogothic territory, had suffragan bishops in the Burgundian kingdom. As a result of the cross-border contacts they maintained, they attracted accusations of disloyalty. In practice, Christianity largely functioned on a kingdom-by-kingdom basis, as kings appointed bishops and were unwilling to allow too much contact with other Churches in a world where political frontiers were still very fluid. The vigour of these functionally separate Churches varied. In 6th-century Gaul and 7th-century Spain, traditions were established of regular kingdom-wide ecclesiastical councils of bishops, called to deal with all kinds of issues: doctrinal, ceremonial, and organizational. The gathered bishops were aware of ancient Church practice and the previous decisions of their own councils, and coherent traditions of ecclesiastical evolution were established. These gatherings relied upon kings to call the councils and to help enforce their decisions, so that, as royal power grew and waned in effectiveness, such regional Church traditions rose and fell. As the kingdom of the Merovingian Franks collapsed in the 7th century, so did the coherence of the Frankish Church.

The papacy

The role of the papacy in the post-Roman period was extremely limited. In preceding centuries, the papacy had established its reputation as a bastion of orthodoxy, but the ability of individual popes to intervene in a set of events depended upon their location. In central and southern Italy, Sicily, and Sardinia, popes enjoyed full metropolitan powers. More than metropolitan bishops elsewhere, they could influence episcopal appointments and were also responsible for calling councils of subordinates and overseeing all doctrinal matters. Elsewhere, popes had no direct powers of appointment and little active influence. Because of the Roman See's prestige, some kings liked their leading bishop to receive the papal *pallium*, a woollen sash marking out the recipient as a special

papal representative; however, popes could demand little in return. Popes also remained a potential court of final appeal for difficult cases involving churchmen, but the costs of travel and unwillingness of kings to allow issues to pass outside their borders meant that few appeals were made. The one region of the West with a closer relationship to the papacy was Anglo-Saxon England. Much of the evangelization of this country was conducted by the Roman mission sent by Pope Gregory I in 597, and close ties continued. Popes occasionally even supplied Archbishops of Canterbury, of whom the most significant was Theodore of Tarsus (archbishop from 668–90). Within his episcopate, the entire English Church was reorganized and its standards brought into line with the best of current continental practice.

Monasticism

Monastic endeavour during this period was also characterized by similarly fragmented patterns. Monasticism originally emerged as a response to the conversion of Roman emperors, which caused the Church to grow hugely in wealth and brought to an end martyrdom as a route for Christians to show particular devotion to their faith. Monasticism – often referred to as a "living martyrdom"– emerged as a replacement, for the most part originally in the form of individual asceticism and to satisfy those who felt that standards were slipping within the Church. This early period was characterized by extraordinary feats of endurance, such as those of St Antony, who lived in the Egyptian desert for 40 years or St Symeon the Stylite, who lived on top of a pillar in Syria. By definition, therefore, early monasticism stood outside the mainstream Church and was sometimes overtly critical of it, even if bishops periodically attempted to assert their authority over the phenomenon.

In the 5th to 7th centuries, in the central areas of the West – Italy, France, and Spain – bishops to an extent brought the monastic movement under control. In particular, because of the dangers of excess and the arrogance of self-appointed authority inherent in individual asceticism, they worked to establish a communal form of monasticism. Under the new norms, the authority of a community's leader – the abbot – was strongly emphasized, monks were not allowed to move around as they pleased, and the pattern of life became generally moderate, involving reasonable amounts of food and a mixed day of labour, study, and prayer. By the 6th century, these norms were reflected, in different variants, in a cluster of rules related to the running of monastic life, such as *The Rule of the Master* and *The Rule of St Benedict*. Even so, bishops were not generally able to interfere in the daily workings of these institutions, and monastic founders were able to control life as they chose. This allowed many local variations. In northern Europe, for instance, among the Franks and Anglo-Saxons, kings granted monastic land considerable tax relief. Local aristocrats quickly established family monasteries in response: these were effectively tax shelters where one could store surplus relatives who might otherwise have claimed a share of family land. In western Britain and Ireland, cut off after 400, older, more individual ascetic traditions prevailed; when the two worlds came back into contact in the late 6th century, continental churchmen were suddenly confronted with great individual ascetics such as the Irish saint Columbanus. This determined ascetic made a huge impression, and he established abbeys in France and Italy, and a stringently austere set of rules. Not only did the regional Churches of individual kingdoms function in largely separate fashion in the early Middle Ages, therefore, but so, too, did the monasteries.

St Symeon the Stylite's self-denial of all material comforts and even human companionship won huge admiration from the flocks of pilgrims who came to Qu'alat Siman in Syria both during his lifetime and after his death. The remains of the pilgrim hostels, three huge pilgrimage churches, and even the bottom portion of his pillar can still be seen there today.

The Christianization of Europe

Roman imperial power spread the Christian religion as far north as Hadrian's Wall in the north of England, and up to the rivers Rhine and Danube by the end of the 5th century. Over the next 500 years, missionary heroes would spread Christianity to the Arctic Circle and as far east as the river Volga.

Northern Europe

Early medieval sources preserve the names of many individual missionaries of the period. One of the first victories for the Christian faith came in Ireland, where, from the early 5th century, St Patrick made many converts. Much of the missionary work in Ireland was carried out by British missionaries, their efforts supplemented by missionaries from Roman Gaul such as Palladius. The Irish Church, through individual ascetics such as Columba and Ninian, was then responsible for spreading Christianity into Scotland. In 597, Pope Gregory I sent a Roman mission under St Augustine of Canterbury to Anglo-Saxon England, where Aethelbert, king of Kent and overlord of much of southern England, had married a Christian Frankish princess. His conversion made him the first Anglo-Saxon king. This papal initiative was supplemented by the efforts again of Irish missionaries, such as the brothers Cedd and Chad, who in the early 6th century moved from Scotland into England. The last pagan Anglo-Saxon realm, on the Isle of Wight, was converted by armed intervention in 682.

Missionary work in the Low Countries and northern Germany began in the 8th century. The Anglo-Saxon missionary Boniface was instrumental, particularly in Frisia, until his martyrdom in 754; however, it was the Carolingians who carried the work to fruition. Between 772 and 804, Charlemagne imposed Christianity upon the pagan Saxons, and his son Louis was responsible for the first attempts to convert Scandinavia through St Anskar in 830 and 845. It was not until the mid-10th century, however – with King Harold Bluetooth – that large-scale success followed.

The conversion of the Slavs

Much of the conversion of the Slavs to Christianity was accomplished by Western missionaries. Successive Archbishops of Salzburg in the south, receiving considerable financial and military assistance from Frankish kings, organized the 9th-century conversions of Bohemia and Moravia. Further north, Otto I established a series of bishoprics east of the Elbe under control of a new archbishopric at Magdeburg in the 10th century, and his grandson Otto III set in place a separate Polish Church under its own archbishop at Gniezno. For the Elbe Slavs, however, the association with imperial domination was too strong. They rejected Christianity in the great rebellion of 983 and did not return to it until the 12th century. These Western efforts were periodically supplemented by Byzantine missions. In the 860s, the Moravians requested missionaries from the Byzantine Empire because they again perceived Frankish Christianity as an instrument of Carolingian domination. This led two brothers, Cyril and Methodius, with papal blessing, to journey north, where they famously created the first written version of a Slavic tongue – Glagolithic – into which they translated the Gospels and other religious texts. Frankish pressure caused the expulsion of Methodius after Cyril's death in 869, but their legacy flourished in Macedonia, from where the Bulgarian Empire was converted in the 880s. In the next century, the Kievan Rus were also converted under Byzantine influence, when

This 12th-century illustration to the Chronicle of John Scylitzes *portrays the epoch-making moment when an embassy from King Vladimir of Kiev arrived in Constantinople to receive formal instruction in Christianity from the Patriarch. The king's conversion was quickly followed by that of the Russian elites and marked the birth of Orthodox Holy Russia.*

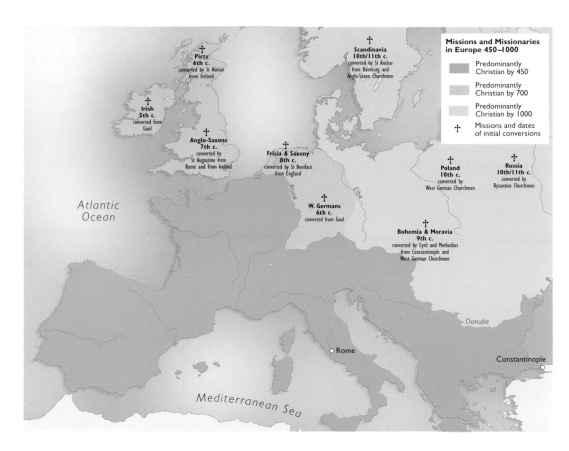

Picts
6th c.
converted by St Ninian from Ireland

Scandinavia
10th/11th c.
converted by St Anskar from Hamburg and Anglo-Saxon Churchmen

Irish
5th c.
converted from Gaul

Anglo-Saxons
7th c.
converted by St Augustine from Rome and from Ireland

Frisia & Saxony
8th c.
converted by St Boniface from England

Poland
10th c.
converted by West German Churchmen

Russia
10th/11th c.
converted by Byzantine Churchmen

Atlantic Ocean

Rhine

Elbe

W. Germans
6th c.
converted from Gaul

Bohemia & Moravia
9th c.
converted by Cyril and Methodius from Constantinople and West German Churchmen

Danube

○ Rome

Constantinople ○

Mediterranean Sea

By c.450, Christianity had spread to the imperial frontiers, even if it was still a substantially urban phenomenon. This map shows the subsequent spread of Christianity northwards and eastwards during the rest of the millennium, from the British Isles by c.700, to Poland, Scandinavia, and Russia by c.1050. These dates mark the formal conversion of the elite, and a long process of Christianization was to follow before the religion was established in all strata of the European population.

first Olga and then her son Prince Vladimir accepted the faith. With this conversion, the majority of Slavic-speaking Europe had become nominally Christian.

Christianity and the countryside

The Christianization of Europe was not accomplished merely by converting royal houses and baptizing their subjects. Such acts only declared an intention. Church leaders also needed to bring notionally converted populations to a fuller Christian observance, spreading knowledge of the faith and providing the priests and churches that would make it possible for populations to lead fully Christian lives. Until that happened, the missionary situation characteristically generated syncretism: local mixtures of new Christian and old pagan practice and belief. In some places, too – as was famously recommended by Pope Gregory I to Abbot Mellitus on the latter's journey to Anglo-Saxon England in 597 – churchmen deliberately retained what they could of pagan cultic practice to minimize any hostility to their new religion.

The challenge of converting the north required substantial structural changes to a religion that had grown up in the urban Mediterranean. Early Christianity had customarily limited preaching to bishops only, to preserve purity of teaching. This worked in the Mediterranean where the majority of the population lived in towns and could gather in one place. In the larger, rural dioceses of the north, however, this meant that few people could hear a sermon at any one time. Hence Bishop Caesarius of Arles began to license priests to preach in the 520s, and the new custom was generally adopted over the next two generations. Northern bishops also began to create rural chapels in their dioceses. By the 590s, there were 40 such rural chapels in the diocese of Tours alone, and, in areas such as these, Christianity was evolving a parish system, with a priest and church in every rural community. At this stage, as has been well documented in Anglo-Saxon England, rural priests probably lived at one central place and worked in teams, visiting the communities in their charge only periodically. By such means, Christianity began to adapt to the challenges of the north, but much remained to be done. The quality of Christian observance depended ultimately on the quality of the priesthood charged with transmitting the religion, and here, as late as the 8th century, matters varied greatly. As well as leading the mission to Frisia, Boniface also encountered Frankish bishops with very dubious beliefs. It was only in the Carolingian period that higher general standards of religious observance began to be set for the clergy, and, through them, to reach the population at large.

Northern Worlds 500–700   106–7 ▶

The Rise of the Slavs   108–9 ▶

Christian Microcosms   126–7 ▶

The Carolingian Renaissance   130–1 ▶

The Carolingian Renaissance

The Carolingian Renaissance witnessed a general revival in the teaching of Latin in Western Europe, but only as a means to an end. Firmly believing that his victories were the result of God's favour, Charlemagne was determined to reform the Church. He was particularly concerned that the clergy's poor Latin had led to the corruption of Biblical texts and service books, so that incorrect doctrines were being taught.

Learning

Charlemagne was also concerned that, without adequate Latin, religious services were losing their efficacy. This thinking was ritualistic, in that only "correct" religious performance would have the desired effect with God. To address the problem, Charlemagne gathered at his court the leading scholars of his day and the best late Roman teaching texts, such as the grammars of Donatus and Priscian. Their texts on Latin grammar had been written centuries before and were the standard texts throughout the Middle Ages. Men and texts combined to re-create a tradition, and from *c*.800, classical Latin became the standard language of educated churchmen. Charlemagne also set his scholars to produce "correct" texts of all the vital religious works. Pope Hadrian was approached for the best available copies of holy books, which

Carolingian kings recycled wealth in vast quantities to their flagship monastic foundations, in thanks for the victories that they ascribed to divine intervention. A characteristic feature of the great monastic cathedrals was their imposing western façades. That of Corvey in Germany (built between 873 and 886) is one of the few to survive largely intact.

provided the starting point. Among others, Alcuin from Northumbria set to work to reconstruct the "true" text of the Bible from the four Latin traditions currently in circulation, and Paul the Deacon, from Italy, worked to produce a standard service book. Others concentrated upon canon law. The new set texts – with an apparatus of Latin grammars and literature, Biblical commentary, and wider theological reflection – became part of a new standard collection of materials necessary for any educated churchman. With the emperor's backing, this new stock library of Latin Christianity was disseminated to all the major monasteries within Charlemagne's domains – such as St Riquier, Gall, Lorsch, and Tours – and established the basic curriculum of medieval learning. In the process, much classical literature, considered useful for learning Latin or for the information it contained, was preserved, but much also was lost. Few pre-Carolingian manuscripts survive; anything the Carolingians did not find useful was thrown away forever. At heart, then, the Carolingian intellectual effort was preservative rather than creative, although, even in its first generation, the assembled scholars competed with each other to attract Charlemagne's favour through a very vigorous court poetry. In subsequent generations, however, more creative work followed in every field: history, theology, and astronomy, among many others.

Christian observance

Charlemagne always intended his intellectuals to contribute to a wider reform of Christian observance. Characteristic of his reign were general statements, such as the *Admonitio Generalis* of 789, which combined general urgings for a holier life for everyone with long lists of more precise measures. To turn big words into practical action, the emperor organized reforming synods throughout his domains in the 800s. These were impressively practical occasions, with reforming bishops setting targets for improvement for the local clergy that reflected their current situations. A much simpler set of improvements was laid out east in Metz, for instance, than in the old Christian centre of Orléans. A similar approach to monasticism was also taken under Louis the Pious. Between 817 and 820, further reforming councils defined a standard form of monasticism, based on the *Rule of St Benedict* as revised by Benedict of Aniane in the late 8th century, and urged it upon all existing monastic houses. The new standard demanded a complete separation of monasteries from secular influence, the centralized direction of all their landed assets, and a life devoted to prayer and study.

The effects of all this are hard to judge. Few monasteries immediately adopted the new reform, and it was to be centuries before even Western clergymen generally conformed to the new standards set for them, let alone their parishioners. For the first time, however, efforts had been made to enforce a definition of the levels of Christian piety appropriate to laymen, monks, and clergy throughout Western Christendom. As the Carolingians lost power in the later 9th century, so, too, was lost their ability to turn ambition into practice; however, an overall vision had been established that would later be brought to fruition by the medieval papacy.

Art and architecture

Charlemagne's astonishing victories brought a huge amount of wealth into his hands, and substantial sums were recycled for artistic endeavour of all kinds. In painting, as reflected in manuscript illumination, there was a decisive shift back towards classical models. The richly coloured pictures of the *Coronation Gospels* of Charlemagne's own time and the narrative pen and ink drawings of the *Utrecht Psalter* (*c*.830) both rejected the abstract, and they seem to have drawn directly on now lost classical exemplars. Although other works were not quite as classical in style, there was no continuation of the abstract Hiberno-Saxon style seen in post-Roman Britain.

Exquisite work was also done in fields such as ivory and metalwork. The most impressive body of surviving evidence, however, relates to architecture: palace complexes and, particularly, churches. Here, as Charlemagne's surviving palatine chapel at Aachen shows, there was some experimentation with Byzantine-style domed structures, but the basilica became the basic form of Carolingian architecture. The great monastery church at Fulda was based on the basilica of Old St Peter's in Rome, which also influenced other great constructions such as the churches built at St Riquier and advocated in the Plan of St Gall. The latter was not actually built, but the plan itself was highly influential. This design for an idealized monastery was created in accordance with the rules for monastic life as laid out by St Benedict. It illustrates a great three-aisled basilica with apses at both the western and the traditional eastern end – a Carolingian innovation – and six towers, placed three at each end. Although the decline of the Carolingians reduced the amount of wealth available for grand building programmes in the second half of the 9th century, nonetheless the first, crucial steps towards Romanesque architecture were taken in the elaborate basilicas constructed under their aegis.

The Carolingian Renaissance extended into most fields of artistic endeavour. This ivory book cover, carved in realistic high relief, portrays the Archangel Michael slaying the dragon described in the Book of Revelation. *It was produced in the Rhineland in the early 9th century.*

Redefining the Papacy

Early popes claimed to be the successors of St Peter, but enjoyed little real power. The Emperor Charlemagne, however, regularly sought papal rulings on religious disputes, bringing the papacy a new centrality in the Latin Church by the early 9th century. Over the next two centuries, papal authority over canon law, and the prestige derived from its sponsorship of monastic reform, turned old ideological claims into practical power.

Popes and Carolingians

From the mid-8th century, popes turned to the Carolingian rulers of Francia, first as kings then as emperors, for temporal support as Byzantine power in Italy ebbed away and Lombard power increased. A series of armed Frankish interventions first halted Lombard acquisitions of papal territory, and, when Charlemagne finally conquered the Lombard kingdom in 774, he gave Pope Hadrian full temporal control of a designated body of lands: the Papal States. For their part, the popes provided political and religious legitimacy to the new imperial house of the West. The first Carolingian king Pepin I's acquisition of monarchical power was formally approved by Pope Zacharias in 751, and Charlemagne's imperial coronation was conducted by Pope Leo in Rome. More generally, Charlemagne always sought advice and uncorrupted sacred texts from the papal see in attempting his Church reforms.

Canon law

The Carolingians' use of the papacy established the general custom among Western churchmen of turning to Rome for advice on non-doctrinal matters. Also from the 9th century, new developments in canon law greatly developed papal authority. Canon law had been built up slowly from a variety of sources: Old and New Testament extracts, the writings of church fathers, and collected decisions of church councils. In the late and post-Roman periods, the church council was the main mechanism for amplifying old rulings and dealing with new problems, but this had tended to generate fragmentation when the successor states' churches largely operated as separate conciliar bodies. Papal letters had always been considered a possible source of canon law; however, because of the Carolingian's use of the papacy, they became, from the 9th century, the only generally acknowledged source of authoritative new rulings. Old materials were retained, but new problems – doctrinal and practical – were increasingly referred to the papacy, and papal letters increasingly dominated canon law collections. Strikingly, papal letters had become, by c.850, the key documents to forge. The greatest canon law forgery was the *Pseudo-Isidorean Decretals*, which was compiled in later 9th-century Francia to protect the rights of suffragan bishops against the interference of their metropolitans and proclaimed the rights of popes over all secular rulers. It contained the forged Donation of Constantine, purporting that Constantine had left his throne to the pope. All its important forgeries took the form of supposed papal letters.

Monastic reform

Ideological acceptance of this general increase in papal authority was generated by the role popes played in continuing monastic reform. Moves to de-secularize Western monasteries began under the Carolingians, with their imperial power used to override local interests. With the collapse of the dynasty, this strategy lost impetus, but interest in its reformed Benedictine observance remained strong among Western clerics. The necessary support to override local secular interests was obtained, therefore, by a new route: negotiating simultaneously with the regional secular lords who replaced Carolingian emperors and with popes. Papal protection thus became a characteristic mark of the new reformed monastic federations. The most famous of these grew up around Cluny in Burgundy, but there were others: in the Rhineland around the monastery of Gorze, in Rome itself, and in other centres further north, such as the foundations of William of Volpiano in Flanders. The whole ideology of Benedictine reform centred on the separation of the Church from secular interests, and this ideology became increasingly influential as monks from the reformed houses were promoted to the episcopate by regional rulers who accepted the legitimacy of this new vision of Christianity. Over time, this again promoted the papal profile, as the upper echelons of the different regional sections of the Western Church were increasingly populated by men who considered that the Church ought to be a more separate entity than had their forbears of previous centuries and who saw the pope as the champion and practical head of this independent body.

The creation of Western Christendom

Further impetus was added to the general reforming ideology centring on the papacy by the Ottonians, who consistently appointed reform-minded churchmen from northern Europe to Italian positions in the 10th century. In the 11th century, this bore unexpected fruit in the doctrines of papal monarchy developed in the circles of Pope Leo IX and Gregory VII. From monastic reform, they took the idea that Church and State should be separate. Secular rulers did not have the right to appoint men to high positions in the Church, whose head was really the pope. Canon law, now to be updated only by papal decision

thanks to the Carolingian legacy, provided the practical vehicle by which that headship could be expressed. Journeys to Rome remained expensive, and the Church controlled too much landed wealth for kings ever to be willing to lose all control over its senior appointments. The practical everyday involvement of the pope in the affairs of regional Churches everywhere from Scotland to Poland was nonetheless accomplished by other means. Papal authority was brought to the regions, not via the pope in person, but in the form of collected and carefully edited editions of papal decisions – manuals of canon law – the strictures of which were applied by local judges whose courts got their authority from papal appointment. This mechanism required several centuries for its full evolution, and regional Churches were never fully extracted from the interference of their kings, but the foundations of the medieval and modern papacy were securely laid.

Charlemagne considered that God had made him emperor to reform the Christian Church, and that the papacy existed to assist him. The papal view, that the emperor was in fact their subordinate, eventually prevailed, however. The stock image become one of Leo III crowning a submissive Charlemagne, as here. This difference pointed the way towards the ideological claims of the Papal monarchs of the high Middle Ages.

Iconoclasm and the East–West Divide

In the late Roman period, Greek churchmen, operating through the Patriarchate of Constantinople, had largely set the agenda defining the evolution of Christianity. For the first time, however, Western churchmen threw off this domination in the iconoclast dispute of the 8th century. Over the next two centuries, the papacy's refusal to toe an Eastern line eventually generated a formal split between Rome and Constantinople.

The iconoclast dispute

Byzantine state ideology held that the Empire had been created by God and that emperors were chosen by God to rule with Him on earth. Such an ideology created respect for the imperial office, but meant that disasters, such as the 7th-century Arab conquests, were bound to result in religious self-examination. Why was God punishing his chosen people? In the early 8th century, Byzantine emperors and churchmen concluded that icons – pictures of saints, the Virgin, and Christ – were the problem. In c.725, Leo III decreed that they broke the Second Commandment and were leading the people into idolatry: the reason for God's manifest anger. Icons were a natural scapegoat because, in

the late 680s, the Emperor Justinian II, for the first time ever, used an actual image of Christ on his coinage and, at the same moment, reopened the war against Islam. The Islamic world reacted by definitively rejecting all forms of figurative art (the change, to judge by Islamic coins, coming precisely in the 690s), and Justinian lost heavily. God had made His position on icons clear.

The destruction of icons aroused some hostility within Byzantium, particularly among monks, who used them in their devotions. For believers, icons captured the essence of the holy men and women they pictured. They opened a "window into heaven" and could induce the saint to use his or her power on the petitioner's behalf. They varied in size from great wall paintings to small handheld medallions, and were used to cure everything from life-threatening diseases to illiteracy. Leo's choice seemed to be justified, however, by the return of stability to the Islamic front. In the 740s, the Abbasids overthrew the Umayyads, and the capital moved from Syria to Baghdad in Iraq, shifting the centre of gravity of the Islamic world. This reduced Byzantium to a very peripheral concern and eased the military pressure exerted upon it. The First Iconoclasm came to an end, therefore, only late in the 8th century, when the Empress Irene called the second Council of Nicaea in 787, which duly lifted the ban on figurative religious art. But more military disasters followed, this time administered by the Bulgurs under their Khagan Krum, who killed the Emperor Nicephorus I in 811. Because of this, iconoclasm was restored under Leo V in 815; however, this time, its association with victory was broken by further disasters, especially the loss of the key fortress of Amorium to Muslim forces. In 843, in the Restoration of Orthodoxy – a formal ceremony on the first Sunday of Lent held in the cathedral of Hagia Sophia in Constantinople – iconoclasm was definitively rejected by the Greek Church.

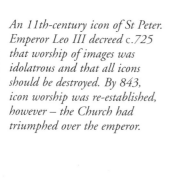

An 11th-century icon of St Peter. Emperor Leo III decreed c.725 that worship of images was idolatrous and that all icons should be destroyed. By 843, icon worship was re-established, however – the Church had triumphed over the emperor.

Within Christendom as a whole, iconoclasm had some very broad ramifications. Its initial adoption was condemned by churchmen from Syria to Ireland, and its failure to win over wider Christian opinion was one reason why Irene rescinded it in 787. By this stage, however, a triumphant Charlemagne already had his eyes on the imperial title and was ready to use even the restoration of images as an occasion to criticize Byzantine pretensions to Christian leadership. Where Pope Hadrian accepted the decrees of the second Council of Nicaea with enthusiasm, Charlemagne's Frankish Church in the Synod of Frankfurt of 794 argued that Byzantine policy on images was still erroneous, as they were placing them too much at the heart of worship. This was part of a general attack on Byzantine pretensions that their emperor ruled "with God".

Filioque and the Great Schism

Once Charlemagne had secured his imperial title and Byzantine recognition – granted by Michael I in 812 – Carolingian religious criticism of Byzantium

subsided. By the middle of the 9th century, however, an alternative and rising religious power in the West, the papacy, was becoming self-assertive enough to engage in outright criticism of the Byzantine Church for its own purposes. None of the issues was insoluble in itself, but, when the general context demanded it, they together formed the basis of a periodically fierce hostility. In the 860s, Pope Nicholas I took the Patriarch Photius of Constantinople to task on three points. The pope had sponsored a Latin mission to Bulgaria, but Photius maintained that the Bulgarians "belonged" to the Greek East. Nicholas was also personally critical of Photius as a political appointee of the Byzantine Emperor Michael III. Thirdly, East and West disagreed over the wording of the Creed. In the West, from the third Council of Toledo in 589, the custom had developed of adding the words "and the Son" (*filioque*) to the standard Creed of Nicaea-Constantinople, where it talked about the "procession" of the Holy Spirit. In the Carolingian period, as part of Charlemagne's reform of Christian observance, it became customary for the Creed to be chanted during the Mass, which generalized the habit. The Eastern Church maintained the original wording of the Creed, which talked of procession only from the Father.

Such hostilities were not consistently maintained, and, in the 10th century, with the rise of the Ottonians and their influence over the papacy, some of the heat went out of the disputes. Otto II married a Byzantine princess, and all the Ottos respected Byzantine interests in Italy, so that relations between East and West were generally good. From the early 11th century, as reforming Western churchmen developed ever stronger ideas of papal leadership, however, hostilities began again on a series of fronts. Politically, in the early 1050s, the papacy switched its backing from the Byzantines to the intrusive Normans in southern Italy. *Filioque* remained an issue, and, as part of their general rejection of the claims of kings and emperors to have control over the Church, popes were ready to act aggressively towards the imperially appointed Eastern Patriarchs. When Michael Cerularius sent letters on his accession demanding recognition as "oecumenical [general or senior] Patriarch", Leo IX responded by demanding that the Roman see be recognized as "head and mother of the Church" ("*caput et mater ecclesiarum*"). Mutual excommunications followed in 1054, and the Great Schism was born. Within it, various doctrinal and disciplinary issues were significant, but, at heart, it was the product of Western self-assertion against Eastern pretensions to religious hegemony, in an era when secular control of the Church was being rejected.

The extinction of Carolingians freed the Papacy from the rival religious claims of a Western imperial dynasty, but the Patriarchate of Constantinople remained under the control of Byzantine emperors, who claimed to be the heads of Christendom. This underlying rivalry expressed itself in a range of disputes, and came to a head in Leo IX's excommunication of Michael Keroularios, here pictured in a 15th-century Greek manuscript, which inaugurated the Great Schism.

THE MIDDLE AGES

1000–1400

POLITICS AND GOVERNMENT

1095–9 First Crusade launched by Pope Urban II at Clermont in November 1095. It recaptures Jerusalem at a terrible cost. Crusader states are established at Jerusalem, Antioch, and Tripoli.

1066 William Duke of Normandy defeats Harold of Wessex, the last Anglo-Saxon king, at the Battle of Hastings.

1209–26 The Albigensian Crusades attempt to stamp out the Cathar heresy in the Languedoc.

1201–4 Fourth Crusade, culminating in the sack of Constantinople by Western forces.

1190–2 Third Crusade is a qualified success for Westerners.

1183 The Peace of Constance. The Lombard League recognizes imperial overlordship.

1167 The towns of northern Italy form the Lombard League in defiance of Frederick Barbarossa's imperial claims.

1146–8 Second Crusade fails to recapture Edessa from Zengi, Atabeg of Mosul.

| 1000 | 1062 | 1125 | 1187 |

1049 At the Council of Rheims Pope Leo IX condemns priests and bishops who have paid for their appointments, beginning a high-profile programme of reform focusing on lay interference in ecclesiastical matters.

1054 Schism between Western and Eastern Churches, triggered by a dispute over the precise wording of the Creed.

1073 Popular acclaim in Rome sweeps Cardinal Hildebrand to the papal throne as Gregory VII.

1098 Robert of Molesmes founds a monastery at Citeaux. It becomes the home of the new Cistercian order.

1119 Foundation of the Knights Templar in Jerusalem.

SOCIETY AND CULTURE

1137–51 Abbot Suger begins a massive rebuilding of the Abbey Church of St Denis in a new, light, ambitious style later derided as Gothic.

1194 Beginning of the rebuilding of Chartres Cathedral.

1200 Grant of charter to the University of Paris by Philip I.

1215 Magna Carta. The charter confirms the liberties of the English Church and sets out the barons' feudal duties to the monarch.

1357 Start of the peasant revolts across Europe. The most notable are in France and and England. Known as the *jacqueries* in France, the rebels burnt and pillaged castles massacring the inhabitants. The rebellion was put down violently. The peasants revolt starting in 1381 in England claims to champion the rights of the rural poor.

1307–14 Trial of the Knights Templar results in their abolition and the public burning of their grand master.

1337–1453 The Hundred Years War, a convenient label for protracted hostilities resulting from the rival claims of England and France. Both countries are forced to revolutionize their taxation and administration systems.

| 1312 | 1375 | 1400 |

1274 Death of St Thomas Aquinas. His *Summa Theologica* was the most influential work of Christian philosophy of the Middle Ages.

1321 Death of Dante Alighieri. His *Divine Comedy* offers the single most complete snapshot of life and thought in 13th and 14th century Europe.

1309 Clement V takes the papacy into exile at Avignon.

1348–9 Black Death ravages Europe, killing at least one fifth of the population.

1351 Boccacio completes *The Decameron*, a tale of 10 travellers taking refuge from the Black Death.

1377 Return of the papacy to Rome under Gregory IX. Later in the year two rival claimants are acclaimed as pope beginning almost 40 years of schism. The schism will finally come to an end in 1514 with the Council of Constance.

c.1260 The Polo family begin their travels in the Mongol Empire. Beginning of paper manufacture at Fabriano.

1252 Florence and Genoa strike their own gold florins.

The 14th-century Siennese painter
Duccio here depicts the temptation
of Christ on the mountain. He
draws upon a common medieval
theme, the snares of worldly power.
Perhaps appropriately, he was
working in one of the greatest
commercial cities of his age.

THE SHAPE OF MEDIEVAL EUROPE

The authors of the chronicles, letters and treaties that shape our perception of medieval Europe were almost always untypical; their works may be as misleading as they are evocative. Far fewer people believed that the world was flat than we might imagine, yet the period remains a strange landscape in which the familiar is surrounded by the alien.

The cathedrals and mosques, mosaics and minarets that map out today's tourist trail are the legacy of a political geography a millennium old. From the early 8th century onwards, the western and southern shores of the Mediterranean belonged to the Islamic Empire. Byzantium and Islam had contested its eastern shores since the 7th century, while its northern shores were divided between Byzantium and the West. By the 10th century, Islam was no longer an empire but a series of caliphates. It is easy, however, to exaggerate its fragmentation: more than one of the pieces were larger than the empire of Charlemagne. From the 9th to the 13th centuries, the Russian princes of the "Rus" dynasty ruled a great empire covering most of Russia in Europe. Between Russia and Germany lay the Baltic peoples, still pagan and relatively independent of German or Christian influence. The 10th century had been the heyday of Scandinavian influence. For a time in the 11th century, one Viking, Cnut, had ruled in Denmark, England, Norway, and parts of Sweden.

Between Islam, Byzantium, Russia, and Scandinavia, the shape of Western Europe was defined. In the 9th century, the empire of Charlemagne had fragmented into three: the western fragment corresponded roughly to France; the eastern roughly to Germany. The middle comprised Lorraine, Provence, Burgundy, and much of Italy. In 1000, it was a collection of kingdoms and principalities; those to the south were often subject to anarchy or violent takeover bids; those to the north were usually part of Germany. In 1100, the corners of Christendom were all held by Normans: England, Sicily, southern Italy, and parts of Spain and Byzantium. The Norman kings of England could claim lordship over the duchy of Normandy in France. Their successors, the Angevins, claimed an even wider lordship extending to Anjou and Aquitaine. In this period, the Baltic, which divided lowland Germany and Denmark, was far more of a frontier than the English channel.

Three large linguistic groups dominated Europe then as now: the western and southern Romance languages, descendants of Latin; the Germanic languages of the north; and the Slavonic languages of the east. A wealth of distinct tongues can be identified within each of these groups, not to mention many local dialects. It is very difficult to know precisely which languages and dialects were mutually intelligible. As is suggested by the 25 or more sub-dialects of modern Basque, for instance, it is likely that static societies produced quite isolated dialects that would sound alien even to the ears of a visitor from just over the horizon.

The Shape of Medieval Europe c.AD 1000

The Two Roman Empires

In AD 1000, the imperial mantle of Rome was claimed by two empires – Byzantium and the Holy Roman Empire. Although culturally and spiritually divorced, they shared many formative experiences. Both had been and continued to be shaped by forces outside Christendom – Vikings, Magyars, Mongols, and Turks – and both faced similar challenges to imperial authority from within their own borders.

Built on a site holy to all three monotheistic religions, the Dome of the Rock in Jerusalem was the meeting point of empires. Jerusalem had been transferred from Christian to Muslim hands in 638. This seismic event, more than any other, shaped the political geography of medieval Europe.

In the period between the accession of Basil I in 867 and the death of Basil II in 1025, Byzantium reached its zenith. In 880, Basil I retook lands in southern Italy. In the 10th century, successive campaigns recovered Syria, Cyprus, Crete, Cilicia, and parts of Mesopotamia and brought the Bulgars to terms. By the time of the death of Alexius I Comnenus in 1118, much in the east had been lost to Islam.

The Holy Roman Empire

In 962, the king of Germany, Otto the Great, was crowned Holy Roman emperor by the pope. The empire of Charlemagne was long gone, and the frontier between what is now known as France and Germany was on the way to becoming the most conspicuous political boundary within Western Christendom. The imperial title had no precise political significance, although it did carry great prestige. The German emperors saw themselves as, variously, the apex of Christian society, the heirs of Charlemagne, and rulers of the Kingdom of Burgundy and of the Italian peninsula. In the early part of this period, they defended their right to be crowned in Rome and thus determine the holder of the papacy. Yet despite all of these claims and pretensions, the duchies that made up the kingdom were based on traditional and deep-rooted divisions between peoples, and they were reluctant to accept a higher level of authority.

Frederick Barbarossa

The career of Emperor Frederick Barbarossa demonstrates the peculiar dynamic that dominated medieval German politics. The nephew of the previous emperor, Conrad III (1137–52), he was elected by the German nobles in preference to Conrad's son, largely because he was directly descended from both of the two great warring family factions of German politics. In 1155, he marched into northern Italy, retrieving Ancona and Spoletto from their Norman conquerors, and, despite opposition, Frederick was crowned emperor by Pope Hadrian IV. The next year he married Beatrice, heir to the throne of Burgundy, and was acclaimed "father of his country". By 1157, however, an old argument had been rekindled: Hadrian claimed to have conferred the Empire on Frederick, whereas Barbarossa maintained that it had never been his to give. When Hadrian died in 1159, two claimants to the papacy

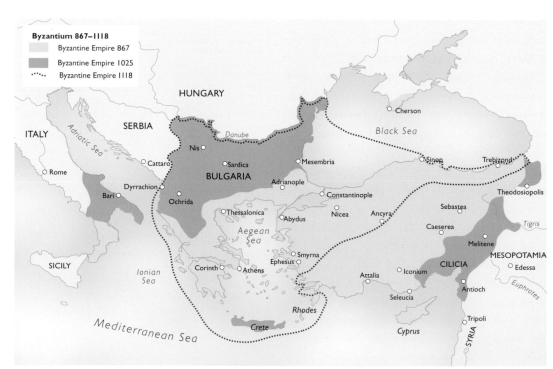

Byzantium 867–1118

- Byzantine Empire 867
- Byzantine Empire 1025
- Byzantine Empire 1118

arose: Alexander III was proclaimed pope in Rome, while Frederick, whether in ignorance, guile, or earnest, proclaimed his own "imperialist" candidate, the anti-pope Victor IV. This provided a pretext for certain German princes to voice their discontent, and from then on Frederick could not rely on unanimous support for his Italian ventures. The towns of northern Italy seized upon the papal cause as justification for denying Frederick's claims of overlordship. In 1168, the newly united towns built a city at the junction of the Tanaro and Bormida to keep Frederick on his side of the Alps; they called it Alessandria, after Alexander III.

Although the ensuing 20 years were beset by defeat, victory, and compromise, Frederick only saw his role as that of emperor. The kingdoms of Burgundy and Italy were not "foreign"; the journeys to Rome were not merely for display; the settlements with German nobles were not "concessions". All three fell within his orbit of imperial power. It is perhaps fitting that Frederick died on crusade – those sorry expeditions epitomized the universalist aspirations of Christendom and the huge difficulties faced by those who sought to realize them.

The Byzantine Empire

In 1204, Constantinople fell to the Fourth Crusade. This single, shattering event colours all too easily the way in which we view Byzantine society in the first two centuries of the second millennium. It should be remembered that this Eastern Roman Empire survived the Western by a thousand years to become the longest-lived human empire after those of the Chinese and Egyptians. At the time of the death of Emperor Basil II (963–1025), Byzantium was the greatest power in the Mediterranean and Near East, and its capital the most glittering city. Its culture and learning were at the forefront of the European experience, but the history of Byzantine politics is characterized by senseless intrigue. Several dynasties vied for the throne, and Byzantium's political life was dominated by two powerful groups: the military aristocracy and the court officials. Basil II had kept both under control, but, when he died, the warlords proceeded to gather more and more of the Empire into their own hands. To compound problems, disputes over a minor technicality of doctrine led to a breakdown in ecclesiastical relations between East and West such that, in 1054, the pope excommunicated the spiritual leader of the Orthodox Church, the patriarch of Constantinople.

Alexius I Comnenus

It is telling that 13 emperors held office in the half-century following the death of Basil II in 1025. The

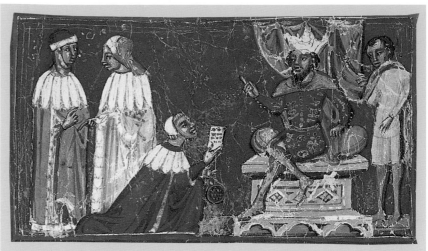

Frederick Barbarossa

The most striking example of Frederick Barbarossa's understanding of imperial authority was his elevation of Duke Vladislav II of Bohemia to the rank of king in 1158. Creating a king, and therefore a kingdom, where there had not been one before was a serious business. Previously, when Pepin the Short had sought to become first king of the Franks in the mid-8th century, he had secured the pope's aid in advance. Pope Hadrian IV had equally strong views on the extent and limits of imperial power, and in 1155 had refused to crown Frederick emperor until he had shown due reverence and held the pope's bridle as though a vassal of the Holy Father. Hadrian would have recalled that Charlemagne himself received the title Roman Emperor from Pope Leo III, but Frederick knew that Charlemagne had then turned his back on Rome. Here, Frederick is shown receiving a papal legate. We can imagine that the exchange was heated.

coup and subsequent accession of Alexius I Comnenus (1081–1118) introduced a new dynasty to the throne and a new vigour to Byzantine military and diplomatic activity. His life is celebrated in one of the most enjoyable of medieval biographies, the *Alexiad*, written by his daughter, Anna Comnena. For all her enthusiastic eulogizing of her father, Anna really did have something to boast about.

In the early 1080s, Alexius' most formidable enemy was the Norman Robert Guiscard, overlord by conquest of southern Italy and Sicily, and an opportunist of genius whose European ambitions seemingly knew no limit. Alexius, short of soldiers and cash, allied himself with Venice and brought to a halt Guiscard's eastern forays. Next, Alexius was threatened by the Patzinaks, a semi-barbarian horde settled to his north-east whom he eventually defeated in 1091. By 1095, he had succeeded in restoring the frontiers of the Empire in Europe to the Danube and the Adriatic. He then looked eastwards to Anatolia and the distant Euphrates. It was at this juncture that Alexius inadvertently precipitated a new and alarming crisis by appealing to the West for military aid. Unbeknownst to him, he had set in motion the avalanche of the Crusades.

Charlemagne's Empire 114–15 ▶

The New Papacy 144–5 ▶

The Crusades for the Holy Land 180–1 ▶

The Great Schism 184–5 ▶

The New Papacy

The second half of the 11th century was the heroic age of papal history. Reforming popes and their followers sought to purify the Church of what was seen as the taint of lay corruption and to establish the superiority of spiritual power over the secular. Above all, this came to mean a struggle with the German emperors, who, from the 10th-century Ottonians onwards, considered themselves the heirs of Charlemagne.

The origins of papal reform

The intellectual position of the reforming papacy of the 11th century was essentially that set out by Leo the Great and Gelasius I in the 5th century, that in all spiritual matters the pope superseded any king; however, at the turn of the first millennium, kings and emperors continued to treat bishoprics and abbeys as part of their royal domain. In the mid-11th century, four-fifths of the 140 monasteries attached to the monastery of Gorze in Lorraine were subject to a king. Little wonder: they were profitable and practical as instruments of government. The first great stand against this had been taken by Duke William "the Pious" of Aquitaine. In 910, he pronounced a curse on any layman who sought to interfere with Cluny Abbey, his vast new foundation in Burgundy. Over the next century and a half, this spirit of reform gained momentum, engendering both debate and pamphlet wars, as intellectuals and propagandists alike turned their thoughts to the dangers of purchasing clerical office (known as simony), the wrongs of selling pardons and indulgences, and the political dimensions of religious orthodoxy. In 1048, the matter was still open: Pope Leo IX was nominated and invested with the ring and staff of his office by the German king Henry III. A year later, the same Leo stood before the relics of St Remigius at the Council of Rheims, where he asked in a deceptively innocent voice which of those bishops present had paid for their office. Most, including the Archbishop himself, had. Leo's reaction was so extreme that some bishops fled, some were censured, and the council was brought to a close with rigorous decrees. Christendom had received a shock from which it was not to to recover.

Pope Gregory VII and King Henry IV

Leo died in 1054, Henry in 1056. While the papal court was filled with ardent reformers, the German throne was left to an infant, Henry IV, and for 20 years the papal star was in the ascendant. The most zealous of the reformers was Cardinal Humbert of Silva Candida, who in his *Book against Simoniacs* launched a coruscating attack on the entire relationship of seculars to the Church, in particular imperial investiture of bishops. Humbert objected profoundly to the fact that bishops were seen to receive their authority from laymen. His arguments found favour with Pope Alexander II (1061–73) and, most famously, Pope Gregory VII (1073–85). At this time, the principal weapon of the papacy was excommunication: total exclusion from Christian society and loss of all hope of salvation. Early in 1073, Alexander unleashed this weapon against five councillors of Henry IV who were seeking to influence the appointment of a new Archbishop of Milan. Alexander then died, leaving the new pope, Gregory, over-extended.

In 1076, a number of German bishops met at Worms and declared Gregory deposed, no doubt preferring the patronage of an emperor to the interference of a pope. Gregory responded in kind, excommunicating both the bishops and the emperor who had encouraged them. For those

A late 15th-century version of the St Albans Chronicle *depicts the 9th-century king of Wessex, Aethelwulf, kneeling before the pope and his cardinals. Although Aethelwulf probably had been to Rome, the first cardinals were not appointed until 200 years after his death. This picture is more about symbolism in the 15th century than history in the 9th.*

The Cleansing of the Temple

The greatest aim of the reforming papacy was to ensure that secular powers had no authority in Church matters. One of the justifications for the papacy's occasional militancy in enforcing this was Christ's cleansing of the Temple (depicted here by Giotto). Images of moneylenders and traders being driven out were used as shorthand for this belief by papalist patrons of art, particularly those like Gregory VII and Cardinal Humbert, who believed that simony was tantamount to selling the divine office. By his time, it had gained an added significance – the excesses of wealth and profits of banking among the elite of the Italian cities lay many snares for the faithful.

German princes who resented Henry's rule, this was too good an opportunity to miss – if God's vicar did not support Henry, how could they? In the autumn of 1076, they sat in judgement on their emperor and declared that, if he had not received papal absolution by the following February, he would be deposed. Just in case he tried to seek this in person, they closed the passes through the Alps. Henry received his absolution at the eleventh hour, only after he had crossed the Alps on foot and in secret and prostrated himself before the pope at Canossa, Italy, for four days. The humiliation was grave, but politically Henry emerged the winner.

Gregory died an exile from his beloved Rome, having been kidnapped by the very Norman forces he had hoped would protect him from political threats, but his voice is one of only a very few that echo down through the centuries. His struggles with Henry, often termed the investiture contest, were not simply about power, as his 11th- and 21st-century critics claim, but born of a world view in which the correct ordering of a divinely ordained Christian society was paramount. "Righteousness" was his constant refrain. He cursed those who "kept back their sword from blood, that is kept back their tongues from condemning wrong". As a "soldier of Christ", he revelled in military metaphors and mined deeply the Old Testament prophets, particularly Elijah and Jeremiah. His argument was not just that the spiritual should always take precedence over the secular whenever the two came into contact; it was also that the papacy itself lay at the heart of spiritual authority on earth. A saying of Leo the Great declared that, while other bishops have pastoral care attributed to them, the papacy alone has plenitude of power. If Gregory had adhered less closely to this precept, he might have found more support for his reforms elsewhere in the Church. But Gregory was never a politician; he was Christ's vicar and St Peter's heir.

The legacy of conflict

The papal reform movement is often given Gregory's name; however, when he died in 1085, it had a long history ahead of it, not least because of cogent imperial opposition. It was indeed true that Charlemagne had intervened in the affairs of the Church, sat in judgement on a pope, and dictated doctrinal issues. Henry IV never forgot that his father had deposed three popes and appointed three more. The imperial crown, the symbol of the emperors' temporal power, was made deliberately high so that a cloth mitre, the symbol of ecclesiastical authority, could be worn underneath it. This same crown was worn by Emperor Frederick Barbarossa during his conflicts with Pope Alexander III a century later. At an ideological level (perhaps not always the level at which kings and popes thought), this crown stood at the crux of the issue: emperors believed that they, too, had a religious function, one that was divinely ordained. The most powerful imperial tract directed against Gregory VII was called *On the Unity of the Church*; it argued that Gregory was disrupting God's order and that the consequences of this disruption might be dire. This argument held good in political circles for much of the rest of the Middle Ages. In the mid-14th century, English kings were prohibited appeal to the papal court in any matter concerning English Benefices. This statute, *Praemunire*, was to become one of Henry VIII of England's most powerful weapons in enforcing his split from Rome 150 years later.

The Bonds of Society

Traditional medieval wisdom divided society into three estates: the clergy, who prayed and looked to society's spiritual wellbeing; the warriors, who defended the land and people; and the labourers, whose toil supported the other two orders. Just as the reforming popes were concerned with the correct ordering of society on a European scale, so on a local scale each person had to perform his allotted duty.

A 14th-century Swiss illustration of the Dominican Eberhard of Sax praying before the altar of the Virgin Mary. The idea that the spiritual battles of monks were as important, if not more so, than the physical battles of soldiers grew in strength in the Middle Ages.

The ties that bound

In the 11th century, a few small independent proprietors still existed, but most arable land was exploited according to the manorial system. Generally speaking, a manor comprised a handful of neighbouring villages all dependent on and bound to a single lord's residence; its component fields were organized as a single agricultural endeavour. Peasants were granted smallholdings on an outlying portion of a manor in exchange for tending the inner core, the lord's demesne (lands). The servile nature of their tenure meant that they were legally unfree. They owed a heavy burden of agricultural services throughout the year, perhaps two or three days a week of ploughing, sowing, or carting, with additional duties at harvest. They might also owe more personal duties, which were often attached to specific tenancies within the manor, such as assisting on hunts, tending the lord's dogs, fencing game enclosures, or repairing the lord's hall. Duties were excused on holy days, and communities were always keen to venerate new saints; but for every saint's day the village priest was pressurized into recognizing, a day of "voluntary" service was introduced by the lord.

There was some differentiation between classes of peasants according to how much land they held and what they owed, but most villages had no real economic hierarchy. Only the reeves – the supervisors of the manor – stood out. These men performed administrative functions on behalf of their lord and often did very well out of their positions. If a peasant did not render to his lord his due, it was the reeve and his bailiffs who came to exact it, and court records are full of accusations that reeves lined their own pockets in the process. Similar accusations were levelled occasionally at parish priests, who were entitled to a tithe – one-tenth – of all produce for the maintenance of the church and its offices. For all the attempts at reform by popes from Leo IX onwards, many parish priests took wives, bore weapons, and charged for the favours their position allowed like any layman.

Many minor crimes and some major ones were tried in the lord's manorial court. The records of one monastic court in the 13th century tell of men and women who were fined for petty theft, failing to turn up for jury service, illegal brewing, failing to ensure that they were members of a

Medieval justice

Medieval kings and emperors prided themselves on their ability to dispense justice. Imprisonment was rarer then than it is today; generally, punishments were fines and forfeits, or mutilation and execution. The most gruesome deaths were saved for traitors, counterfeiters, and, later, heretics. In much of Europe justice was private and seigneurial – nobles long defended their right to try and punish criminals – but in Carolingian France and Anglo-Saxon England, justice was public. This image shows a trial and execution before the witan, representatives of the English shire.

tithing (by which, in theory, unfree men in formerly Carolingian and Anglo-Saxon areas were associated in groups of 10 or 12 so that each would be responsible for the others' behaviour), and even allowing their cattle to trample the vicar's peas. Fines for evasion of labour dues were among the most common. Matters were even worse for peasants living in areas designated as forest land. Forest land was preserved for hunting, and French and English kings famously maintained huge tracts in which deer and boar were protected and encroachment was forbidden. Court records bear witness to the tensions forest law created among rural communities.

Changing priorities

Money was more important than labour to some lords, and on certain manors peasants held their land wholly or partially by rent. As the Middle Ages wore on and the labour pool grew as the population increased, this system became more and more common until often the demesne itself was let out. In addition to their rent, many peasants now provided their lord with a series of payments at births, deaths, and marriages that marked their continued servile status. During the late 12th and 13th centuries, it became common for serfs, either individually or in groups, to buy their legal freedom for a lump sum, changing their status to that of rent-paying tenants. In theory, this should also have allowed a greater degree of economic freedom; often, rent-paying tenants sought to bring areas of wasteland and woodland into profitable cultivation

for themselves without their lord's knowledge. In practice, for many, this increased productivity did not necessarily counterbalance increased rent, and they were left with nothing but their labour to sell.

The single greatest stimulus to any regional economy was proximity to a growing, prosperous town, and urbanization and changes to the manorial system are closely linked. In northern Italy, the most urbanized part of medieval Europe, the old manors were breaking up, and leases replaced labour dues. By the late 12th century, the landlord was often not a noble at all, but a city-based merchant. By contrast, southern Italy was much less urbanized, and here the great manors endured, with most peasants remaining serfs. A similar pattern can be seen in the Low Countries. Around the recently developed industrial and commercial cities of Flanders, 12th-century peasants were gaining their freedom and pursuing their own goals, while in the more economically depressed areas of Namur and Luxembourg, most peasants remained serfs until the end of the Middle Ages. But the trend was not uniform: in places, the late 13th century saw a reaction to this by lords, who began to retrieve their labour services and take their lands back into direct cultivation. Many ecclesiastical estates had been reluctant to forego their services in the first place, as large communities of monks depended on the produce of their estates for their sustenance. Despite their periodic support for freeing serfs as a pious act, popes continued to legislate for the preserved integrity of ecclesiastical estates.

THE BONDS OF SOCIETY   **147**

Knighthood

Towards the end of the 11th century, a new idea began to gain currency, the notion of the warrior as "the soldier of Christ". It came to focus on the ceremony in which a man was dubbed a knight. Here, in supposed opposition to the aristocratic violence that was almost endemic in northern Europe, the aspiring knight dedicated his sword to the altar and made a profession of vows to the service of the Church.

Ever since St Odo of Cluny wrote The Life of Gerald, *his pen-portrait of the perfect Christian knight, images in which Christ and his knights together vanquished evil were popular. Often, this was juxtaposed with images of tyrants in league with devils.*

THE MIDDLE AGES | 1000–1400

A 15th-century French interpretation of The Romance of King Arthur and the Knights of the Round Table *by the 12th-century writer Chrétien de Troyes. By the later Middle Ages, "Arthurian" tournaments were a regular feature of noble life and a means of uniting martial combat with social display. Even the merchants of London were staging their own jousts by this time.*

The origins of knighthood

In the mid-12th century, the scholar Peter Abelard cautioned Abbess Héloïse against choosing a noble-born woman as prioress: "such a woman tends to be presumptuous and arrogant because of her birth". Although the word "noble" designated neither title nor office, there was something in the bloodline of certain families that meant that they and their contemporaries considered themselves such, and it was a quality that could not be bought or lost. Those seeking to include themselves in this class, and exclude others, compiled lengthy genealogies and controlled inheritance and marriages with paranoid care. The various medieval words for "knight", on the other hand, all have their origin in the profession of mounted warriors, with only occasional reference to descent. At the beginning of this period, some knights were simply employees of nobles, paid to do their fighting, while others were the younger sons of nobles and their cousins roving across the continent seeking to make a name for themselves. These young men often looked more like minor war bands than anything else, and medieval writers, especially churchmen, came to regard them as a public menace. A public relations war developed.

In the 10th century, St Odo of Cluny had written of his ideal knight, Gerald of Aurillac, a man so pious that he fought only with the flat of his sword. Cluny was also behind the formation of certain principles that limited aristocratic violence to certain activities and certain times. In the 11th century, this idea was given its fullest expression by Popes Gregory VII and Urban II: knights, as soldiers of Christ, waged a war against the worldly agents of the Devil, just as monks fought their spiritual counterparts. In the 12th century, a further step was taken by the influential Cistercian abbot, Bernard of Clairvaux, who promoted an institutional form of religious knighthood by encouraging men to join the new military order of the Templars. Its members undertook both ordinary monastic vows and the defence of Jerusalem from the infidel. It was said that he preached his cause so persuasively that mothers locked up their sons for fear he would spirit them away.

Chivalry

The notion that there might be both heavenly and worldly honour in the profession of arms was an attractive one for young (and old) men seeking to assure or better their status. The nebulous collection of ideas that has developed around this notion is known as chivalry, from *chevalier*, the French word for knight. Books were written telling knights how to conduct themselves in every last regard, epics were composed to hold forth shining examples of excellence, and tournaments were fought to apply those examples to real life. Just how far chivalric ideals applied to reality is extremely

Becoming a knight

The ritual of dubbing was fundamental to the concept of knighthood. The squire, pictured here receiving his sword and spurs from his lord and attendants, would have undergone lengthy preparations and been expected to undertake certain challenges. The ceremony began with a bath, recalling baptism. Next, he put on brown stockings to signify the earth to which his body would return. A white belt represented chastity. Spurs were to show him that he must always be as swift to follow God's commandments as a charger, and the two sharp edges of his sword indicated that justice and loyalty must go together.

uncertain. The chivalric epic poems known as *chansons de geste* ("songs of great deeds") show little interest in how noble actions impacted upon the rest of society, and, for all the prominence of the new literary notion of courtly love, noblewomen were still abducted and forced into marriages as much as they had ever been.

The German poet Gottfried von Strassburg engaged these double standards in his epic *Tristan*, written in the early 13th century. In his tale, the young Tristan studied literature, languages, music, wrestling, fencing, and hunting to become the perfect Arthurian knight, a physical and intellectual paradigm. After many adventures, he arrived at the court of King Mark, revealed as his uncle, who knighted him for his many past and anticipated virtues. Having woven his mythic tapestry so skilfully, however, Gottfried then tears it apart. Tristan lusts after the king's bride, Isolde, and together they deceive the king and plan the murder of the only witness to their crime. Tristan is forced into combat with Mark's champion, whom he strikes down in an orgy of gushing blood and shattered bone. Tristan, our hero, mocks the broken champion before hacking off his head. For Gottfried, often praised as a great chivalric writer, the reality of knighthood was all too evident.

Warfare

Perhaps the most vivid and extended descriptions of warfare in the Middle Ages are the various chronicles of the crusades. Many were based on first-hand experience, and all have a common theme: hardship. One author describes the crusaders' march south from Acre, pursued by the Turks, shortly after the city fell in 1191: "Arrows and spears flew and hissed through the air. Even the brightness of the sun was darkened by the multitude of missiles, as though by the wintry density of hail or snow … The points of darts and arrows covered the ground so that if anyone wished to collect them, a single snatch would provide him with least twenty."

Combat waged with blades, horses, and fire was always a horrifically bloody business, and wherever possible hunger and fear were the preferred weapons. An invading army needed to keep its supply lines open above all else, and so would often besiege castles or towns that otherwise might attack its train of carts. In the 1050s, Duke William of Normandy, the future conqueror of England, sought to avoid open combat in northern France by mutilating prisoners as a means of persuading the citizens of recalcitrant towns to surrender. Despite this, the Normans were the most famous and feared knights in medieval Europe; their equipment and formations were recognized from England to Sicily, from Cordoba to Constantinople. Both are illustrated clearly in the depiction in the Bayeux Tapestry of the Battle of Hastings of 1066. The Normans fought on horseback – unlike the English, who fought on foot – and their cavalry employed a series of co-ordinated feints and outflanking manoeuvres. They wore heavy, knee-length mail coats, carried kite-shaped shields, and fought with sword, throwing spear, and couched lance (which went on to become the famous weapon of the joust). Perhaps most important of all, they developed a quick and ready base of operations, a timber tower on top of a huge earth mound within a fortified compound. These structures came to be known as motte and bailey castles; they were the tool by which much of England was subjugated.

In the early Middle Ages, the
ports of the Rhone delta had all
carried a considerable volume of
trade. By the end of the period,
however, natural silting had
reduced all but Marseilles to
very minor operations. Marseilles
exercised a corresponding
influence, and, by the 14th
century, its merchants were able
to demand favourable treatment
in the Italian ports.

KINGDOMS AND COMMUNITIES

Medieval narrative sources often focus on kings and their nobles; lords and their peasants; popes and their priests. It is easy to think that social groups were always defined in terms of those above and those below. This is true in part, but it is potentially misleading and certainly depressing. Membership of a village, town, province, guild, and, above all, kingdom were equally powerful, and in these ways community was at least as important as hierarchy.

The term "feudalism" is today used to refer to almost any oppressive or hierarchical system. When applied to the Middle Ages, the most common analogy is a pyramid: the king or emperor is at the very top with high-ranking nobles below him. They in turn are on top of a larger number of petty nobles and bureaucrats, all resting on a huge mass of impoverished peasants. Feudalism is sometimes used in the more specific sense of relations between nobles: one man might become the vassal of another by paying homage to him, swearing fidelity, and undertaking to provide him with soldiers if needed, in exchange for a piece of land (known as a "fief") and promises of good lordship. This constituted a feudal relationship and could only exist between freemen. Feudalism is sometimes extended to governmental systems: in Norman England, all land was held ultimately by the king, who granted it to his nobles on condition that they contribute a designated number of soldiers to the feudal host. These nobles might in turn grant a portion of their lands to their own men under a similar arrangement. It is easy to see how this concept can be used to explain the social structure of medieval Europe.

The reality was less clear cut, and there was a number of less formal relations in which men and women might enter into. The words "vassal" and "fief" are less common in medieval documents than might be expected, and, even when they do appear, they probably conceal a variety of different relationships: ruler and subject; patron and client; landlord and tenant; employer and employee; general and soldier; bully and victim. How one stood in relation to one's peers was far more important than how one stood in relation to distant social inferiors or superiors. Concepts of nobility and freedom were not concrete. Among the most highly respected knights of the German kings were the *minisiteriales*. These skilled warriors and bureaucrats held considerable lands of the king, but they were not freemen in the eyes of the law. The case of the *ministeriales* is instructive. They formed part of a movement in which, as collective activity became more organized, bureaucracy developed. Literacy increased the range and power of propaganda, governments came to rely less on direct interpersonal relations, and feudal stereotypes become less applicable.

Law

In early medieval Europe, it was only kings who could legislate, but the bedrock of law throughout the West was unwritten custom. Even the "Roman law" in which parts of Italy took pride can be seen as not much more than another variety of custom. Customary law was enacted in formally constituted courts. Regular occasions of collective judgement did much to foster not only a sense of community, but also a readiness and ability on the part of those communities to act on their own account. During the 12th and 13th centuries, the strengthening of government began to transform law by emphasizing one source of its authority and enforcement above all others. More and more crimes came to incur formal penalties, but responsibility for the maintenance of law and order depended throughout on collective self-policing. It is a fact of medieval European state-building that the more central authority was enforced, the more the foundations upon which it rested were strengthened.

Nation-States

An individual's horizons might close around a small village or extend beyond Christendom, but medieval writers almost always thought of the kingdom as the highest of all secular communities. Some kingdoms, such as those of northern Spain, appeared less united than some smaller units of government, such as Brittany, but throughout the Middle Ages kingdoms were normally perceived as the ideal type of political unit.

The community of the realm

A kingdom was more than the geographical area within which a king ruled. Just as the Church, although united in universal faith, varied its customs according to local tradition, so a kingdom comprised and was to be identified with a "people", a natural and inherited community of tradition and descent. From at least the 10th century, writers combined biblical and classical elements to concoct myths of the origin and descent of their peoples. From the 12th century these myths were copied in vernacular poems and stories intended for popular audiences. By the 13th they were even creeping into political documents. But common descent and law alone did not make a kingdom. One of the most important political developments of this period was that in many areas the loyalties of kingship formulated in the first millennium after Rome came to coincide with solidarities of supposed common descent and law. In part, this was due to the increasing role of representation and consultation in medieval government. It would be wrong to view medieval councils and parliaments as striving towards modern representative government: direct election was almost unknown in the Middle Ages, but the idea that the leading men of a community might represent it to its king, and vice versa, was perfectly natural. The development of a nexus that bound local communities into the community of the realm was fundamental to the building of medieval states.

England

The expression "community of the realm" is particularly associated with England. The various English kingdoms were not united under a single king until the late 9th century, but they had long shared a common identity as a single people with a single name, language, and Church. It was an accommodating identity: in the 10th century, there was a clear distinction drawn between Danish invaders on the one hand and Englishmen and women who happened to be of Danish descent on the other. The Norman Conquest of 1066 did not

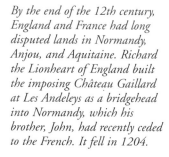

By the end of the 12th century, England and France had long disputed lands in Normandy, Anjou, and Aquitaine. Richard the Lionheart of England built the imposing Château Gaillard at Les Andeleys as a bridgehead into Normandy, which his brother, John, had recently ceded to the French. It fell in 1204.

The Hundred Years War

For the greater part of the period 1338–1453, England and France were formally at war. Since the 19th century, historians have called this time of trouble the Hundred Years War. The name is misleading. Famous campaigns such as Poitiers (1356) and Agincourt (1415) were separated by long periods, sometimes decades, of inactivity. The crux of the issue was England's claim to parts of northern and central France, at times even the throne. In theory, France should have proved the stronger, but English naval power protected the island from all but France's allies in the north, the Scots, who often proved England's most dangerous and immediate foe. By the mid-15th century, England had ceded almost all of its possessions in France, but neither country really emerged the winner. Each had had their bureaucratic fiscal machinery placed on a war footing, each had had their national identities forcibly reassessed, and each had lost many lives and much money for little tangible political gain.

create a new kingdom, and, by the 12th century, Anglo-Norman historians were lauding the patriotic principles enjoyed by "we English". William the Conqueror occupied the English throne for 21 years; he owed much of his ongoing success to the fact that, although a foreigner, he sat at the hub of a sophisticated governmental system that frustrated anything other than very localized resistance.

The following century saw prolonged civil war, and much of this cohesion was lost. In large part it was regained by the demands that late 12th-century kings made for men and money in order to fight their wars in France. Conflict with the French kings over Normandy and other northern French lands was the single greatest legacy of the Norman Conquest. Opposition to these demands was in itself a powerful unifying force. In the 13th century, the expression "community of the realm" was invoked against excessive royal demands, but royal government did not foster unity simply by its oppression. The 12th-century extension of royal justice sent judges on regular circuits of the country, administering increasingly uniform procedures. When there were complaints, they were about corruption, not about the principle of royal control. It is significant that, when King John was brought to task by rebel barons in 1215, it was not less royal justice that they wanted, but more.

France

In the early 10th century, the division of the Frankish kingdom into two halves was still very recent, and, although both were occasionally called

the kingdom of the Franks, it is unlikely that either had very much regnal solidarity. When Hugh Capet, the founder of the line of Capetian kings, made himself king in 987, most of his kingdom took little notice of him. But the Capetians had remarkable staying power, if only because they were very fortunate in producing male heirs at the right times and confined their political objectives to the area immediately around Paris. Beyond that, French nobles were able to administer their territories as princes and occupy their castles with impunity. It is telling that Abbot Suger of St Denis thought that the co-operation of French nobles against the German emperor's invasion of 1124 was unusual enough to be Francia's finest hour.

Wars with England over Normandy did as much to strengthen national solidarity in France as they did across the Channel. The re-conquest of English-held Normandy and Anjou by the French king Philip II, most notably at the Battle of Bovines which frustrated King John of England's claims in France followed closely by the French-led Albigensian crusade against the Cathar heretics in the south of the country transformed the position of the early 13th-century French monarchy. It is no coincidence that references to the Trojan descent of the Franks first appear at this time. Initially at least, notions of the French kingdom faltered on the language barrier of *oïl* and *oc*, and sometimes "Francia" was taken to apply only to the north. Nonetheless, contemporaries were coming to think in terms of a common law that applied to the entire kingdom and of the king as having ultimate jurisdiction over it.

Towns and Communes

The growth of towns reflects the curve of medieval economic history, but it also heralded the rediscovery of a lost way of living. At a time when much of the rural population was bound to the soil by servile obligations, the townsman was free to move about as he wished, change occupation, and even take orders in the Church without the approval of any lord. This freedom fostered greater political ambitions.

THE MIDDLE AGES   1000–1400

The Italian city-states

Cities had been important in Roman Italy, but their administrative and cultural identity were shattered by the Lombardic invasions of the 6th century. Three hundred years later, the Carolingians still had no effective control of this part of their empire, and local counts were able to do more or less as they wished. The Ottonian emperors sought to use bishops (whose appointment they could manipulate) as a means of exerting influence, but the picture remained confused. Meanwhile, opportunities offered by the expansion of the Mediterranean economy reinvigorated certain north Italian towns as trade centres and encouraged the growth of a middle class. In these uncertain times, members of the old comitial families and new merchants formed sworn associations in large cities and small communities alike, seeking to establish their

A page of the 15th-century Guild Book of the Barber Surgeons of York. *Guilds were a common feature of medieval urban life. Sworn fraternities of trade or craft, they managed their affairs and protected their members in similar ways to modern unions and golf clubs. Unlike lofty physicians or lowly apothecaries, the barber surgeons cut hair, knocked out teeth, and amputated fingers.*

power – sometimes in conflict with the bishop, sometimes in alliance. These associations often made claims to be representatives of the "people" in an appeal to historic precedent, but they were never public bodies in origin.

The struggles with the reforming popes did much to shake imperial rule in northern Italy from the late 11th century onwards. Emperors soon granted concessions to the leading men of certain cities in exchange for their nominal support. The development of town consulates (connected to the Roman institution of the same name by nostalgia alone) followed soon after. To balance the claims of rival civic factions that often erupted into street fights, many cities appointed professional administrators from outside their walls to serve as head, or *podesta*, for a fixed term, on condition that they abstain from all trade and commerce.

Each city had its own army and often navy that fought other cities for commercial advantage: to capture a rival city's standard was a great triumph. The accession of Frederick Barbarossa in 1152, however, saw in an emperor determined to regain his traditional rights and began a century of political struggle in which old differences between the city-states were temporarily set aside. In 1167, the towns of Lombardy formed the Lombard League, renewing their alliance in 1226 on the accession of the ambitious Frederick II. The cities of Tuscany were slower to organize themselves, but they, too, formed an alliance in 1198. Barbarossa was defeated roundly by the Lombard cities at Legnano in 1176. In the treaty of the Peace of Constance of 1183, he accepted the right of the cities to elect their own consuls, build fortifications, and govern their hinterlands.

Venice

Venice was unlike all other Italian city-states. The earliest settlements around its lagoons had been dependent on Byzantium; however, in the Middle Ages Venetians cultivated the idea that their city had always been an independent republic under

began to develop a political aspect in the 11th and 12th centuries. Market law is referred to in both France and Germany in the 11th century, and if grants of rights to hold markets and gather tolls were more common for the towns of Germany and Flanders than France, that was probably because royal authority in France was too weak to make royal charters worth having. The tolls townsmen paid or from which they were exempt consolidated their common interests. Common funds are suggested by the fact that at least two English towns had paid a lump sum for their local mint by 1086.

The late 11th and 12th centuries saw many old northern towns acquire a more complete independence, often by fairly unsystematic means. In 1070, the citizens of Le Mans cast off the control of their bishop and proclaimed themselves to be a commune. Worms, Cologne, and other Rhineland cities soon followed suit. In the ensuing two centuries of conflict, the cities generally held their own against the bishops, largely because of the support of the German emperors, who found the new communes to be powerful allies against the Church. Most of the larger German towns came to be designated "imperial cities", dependent only on the emperor.

As imperial power diminished over the period, so the cities' autonomy increased, and in time many banded together as leagues against those princes who still sought to exert their authority upon them. Certain Swiss cities (then under German imperial rule), including Zug, Zurich, and Bern, entered the Swiss confederation as individual cantons. As in Italy, the apparent absence of a closed governing class in the towns of northern Europe does not mean that there were no discontents; however, the rulers of these towns were more closely supervised from outside than were those in Italy, and so serious conflicts do not seem to have come to a head so quickly. When they did, they were often expressed through craft associations. The cloth city of Flanders saw the most fierce conflicts of economic interest because the range and complexity of the cloth trade made it easier for its wealthier merchants to abuse their position by excluding weavers and fullers from the town franchise.

In France and England, the communal movement never really gained momentum, despite the best efforts of London. In both countries relations between the crown and the cities remained largely good, however, not least because the new commercial classes of the cities provided the crown with a useful ally against the nobility. In the 13th century, English cities became integrated into a system of parliamentary representation.

At various times, more than 200 cities belonged to the Hanseatic League, a far-flung confederation of "free cities of the sea" stretching from the Atlantic to the Gulf of Finland. The English word "sterling" derives from "Easterling", an epithet commonly applied to Hansa merchants.

the patronage of St Mark. At its head was the doge, elected by the General Assembly, which comprised representatives of a relatively small number of leading families, some of which claimed Roman descent. Despite occasional accusations of nepotism, culminating in the assassination of Doge Vital II in 1172, this system appears to have been far more stable than that of *podesta* practised elsewhere: although only 150 families were implicated in rule in a population of 120,000, Venice was relatively untroubled by faction. It had no hinterland to speak of and so was entirely dependent on sea trade and its colonies, both of which were hugely boosted by the Crusades. Venetians wangled preferential trading rights in Constantinople, tenders to transport Crusaders to the Holy Land, and lending contracts to bankroll the whole enterprise. To all intents and purposes, they engineered the Fourth Crusade of 1204.

Northern European towns

Canterbury, the first and most important cathedral town of England, could claim no more continuity with its Roman origins than the towns of northern Italy; however, by the 9th century its inhabitants were calling themselves "portmen" from the Latin *portus*, meaning trading place. Archaeological finds in German towns suggest that they, too, were on the rise economically, long before town identity

Architecture and Urbanism 84–5 ▶
Trade, Industry and Agriculture 158–9 ▶
Architecture 168–9 ▶
Cities and Education 194–5 ▶

Magna Carta

In 1215, rebel English barons, tired of what they perceived to be autocratic and incompetent rule, forced King John to sign a great charter of rights and liberties. Although tentative steps had been taken elsewhere, England became the first country in Europe to have a written constitutional check on the king's power. It was to become one of the most famous documents in the English-speaking world.

The royal seal of Henry II of England. The royal seal was often attached to documents issued by the chancery. It served both as a readily identifiable means of authentication and a powerful and widely circulated image of the king in majesty, enthroned and crowned with orb and sword.

The background to Magna Carta

By the 13th century, England had a long history of participatory government. Anglo-Saxon kings consulted local representatives on many matters and wrote to their subjects promising good lordship. In 1100, Henry I, youngest son of William the Conqueror, issued his celebrated Coronation Charter, in which he promised a more settled and less savage regime than that of his predecessor and brother, William Rufus. Addressed to the entire country, it was intended to win back the much-needed support of alienated barons. The tide, however, was against reconciliation. In the following century, expanding royal government saw the rise of non-noble officials, the overburdening of already cumbersome judicial procedure, and increasing disregard for the property rights and dignities of the aristocracy. The murder of Thomas à Becket under Henry II in 1170 provided a further pretext for dissent. The situation became more tense in the first decade of the 13th century when King John lost a succession of disputed lands in northern France to the French king, Philip Augustus. Henry's Coronation Charter became a rallying point for disaffected nobles and churchmen. In 1206, a dispute arose over King John's unwillingness to appoint as Archbishop of Canterbury Stephen Langton, a leading intellectual light and the pope's preferred candidate, providing the excuse for open rebellion. A tentative peace was reached in 1213, but the situation remained hostile. Faced with military threat and the combined weight of his barons and bishops, John was forced to set his seal to the rebel barons' demands enshrined in the Magna Carta. on 15 June 1215. To add insult to injury, Langton officiated over the proceedings.

The clauses

Although the Magna Carta contains at least one shining expression of principle – "no freeman shall be arrested, imprisoned, dispossessed, outlawed, exiled, or in any way ruined except by judgement of his peers or by the law of the land" (clause 39) – most of its more than 60 clauses are concerned with administrative or legal details. Some were aimed at dismantling John's machinery of control: the expulsion of foreign mercenaries; the remission of huge fines; and the dismissal of certain named royal officials. Others attacked certain economic restrictions: fish weirs were to be removed from specified rivers; foreign merchants were to be treated reasonably in all things; and all restrictions relating to royal forest law were to be lifted. One clause, heavy with future significance, stated that the taxes known as "scutage" and "aid" would not be levied without "the common counsel of the kingdom". In an odd paradox, the rebels did not want less royal justice, but more, and the law of the land was trumpeted in opposition to the king's mere will. Many of the clauses sought to make the machinery of justice more regular, equitable, and accessible. The most remarkable innovation came in clause 61. This established a committee of 25 barons before whom any complaints of infringements by the

Orford Castle, Norfolk, England was built by Henry II between 1165 and 1173 as a check on the Earl of Norfolk. It cost more than £1,400 to erect. The design is unusual in that it is cylindrical inside and polygonal outside, with three projecting towers.

The murder of Thomas à Becket

Thomas à Becket was Chancellor of England (1155–62), then Archbishop of Canterbury (1162–70) under Henry II. Although initially a staunch supporter of the king, he became increasingly interested in the cause of the established Church and so became a thorn in Henry's side. In 1170, a small group of knights broke into Canterbury Cathedral and murdered Thomas on the altar, perhaps acting on the king's instructions. European public opinion was such that the next year the king appeared in sackcloth and ashes before the cathedral clergy. Thomas was quickly venerated as a saint, and images of his martyrdom proliferated across Europe.

king were to be brought. If these barons judged that the king had not made good within 40 days, the 25 were permitted to seize his castles, lands, and other royal properties until such time as he did so. A general oath was sworn stating that the 25 were to be supported by "the commune of the whole land".

Magna Carta's legacy

The charter is renowned throughout the English-speaking world; however, this fame is due more to the use made of it by 17th-century parliamentarians in their struggles with the Stuart kings, and the subsequent export of this newly fostered myth to New England, than to its intrinsic merits. At the end of 1215, it was a failure. Magna Carta was intended to bring peace, but instead provoked war. It was legally valid for no more than three months, during which time it was never properly executed. However, between the death of King John in 1216 and the majority of his son and heir, Henry III, in 1225, it was reissued three times with minor and major revisions. The fourth and final version was eventually confirmed in Parliament. Three of its clauses still stand on the English Statute Book, and others have only recently departed (the clause referring to fish weirs was only removed in 1970). The animating principles of consent to taxation, due process, and the rule of law are all present in Magna Carta.

Magna Carta was intimately connected with developing political theories in the 12th century – in his *Policraticus*, the scholar John of Salisbury had written of the justification of tyrannicide – and these theories bore some relation to reality. In 1183, Frederick Barbarossa had conceded practical independence of imperial rule to the Lombard cities. In 1188, King Alfonso IX of Léon promulgated ordinances conferring important privileges on his nobles. In 1205, King Peter II of Aragon drew up similar ordinances for his subjects in Catalonia, although they were never enacted. King Andrew II of Hungary granted his subjects a collection of rights under the Golden Bull of 1222. The English charter was part, albeit the most detailed example, of a Europe-wide movement towards a recognition of the constitutional rights of the community of the realm. Of course, there were problems. Just as the American Declaration of Independence ignored slaves, so, too, Magna Carta made no mention of the unfree, and in effect the "judgement by peers" was intended to ensure that barons looked after their own. But even though Magna Carta was only an active piece of legislation during the ten years of Henry III's minority, it has lived on as a powerful myth for centuries.

Trade, Industry, and Agriculture

In much of Western Europe, the most important economic developments that took place before the modern industrial revolution were during the High Middle Ages. Beginning in the 10th century in some parts of Europe, an economic boom lasted until the first decades of the 14th century.

Although the Middle Ages saw a great commercial expansion, many people maintained an ambiguous or even wholly damning view of money and its temptations. This early engraving depicts a three-horned devil with tail and goat's legs pouring money into the fire.

Trade

By the end of the first millennium, steady population growth had encouraged the exploitation of new land, the increase of food production, and improvements in communications; much energy was devoted to draining marshland, clearing forests, and building bridges, roads, and docks. These developments, together with the ending of the Viking and Magyar threats, created conditions in which merchants with contacts in the East (and there had always been some willing to take their chances throughout even the most dangerous periods) could do very well for themselves. Ships docked initially in Venice, Amalfi, Pisa, and Genoa laden with silks and spices from Byzantium and the Muslim empires, and returned eastward weighed down with timber, iron, and cloth. The Crusades provided a great impetus to expansion in the south, and, by the 14th century, the Mediterranean cities were trading in almost any commodity from figs to firs, indigo to ivory. There was an ever more lucrative east–west trade in slaves (it betrays a grim truth that the word has a common origin with Slav). The growth of the Mongol empire in the 13th century offered yet more opportunities in the Far East, first exploited by Venetian merchants and, in particular, a family called Polo: their travels from 1271–92 are famously recorded by the younger son, Marco. Even bolder were the Vivaldi brothers of Genoa, who, 200 years before Columbus, set out to find the Indies via a westerly route. They never returned.

Trade in the north of Europe did not have the same level of risk as Italian trade. It was less dominated by high-value, low-volume goods, less was invested in each individual shipment, and so correspondingly the whole business was less precarious. Bremen, Hamburg, Elbe, and Lübeck were the northern counterparts of the four main Italian centres of trade. Associations of merchants known as *hansas* handled grain, fish, timber, metals, salt, honey, firs, and the other raw materials of the north. They formed a powerful economic mesh incorporating England, the Low Countries, Poland, Russia, Hungary, and Scandinavia, with northern Germany at the centre.

Industry

Growth was not confined to the Mediterranean and Baltic. The Low Countries saw great economic expansion, much of which was centred on Bruges. The city owed its prominence to cloth; after agriculture, textile manufacture was the single greatest industry of the Middle Ages. Flemish commercial links with England and Germany were established in the early 9th century and held fast up to the end of the 13th century. Early successes owed much to the ready availability of raw materials such as wool, hemp, dyes, flax, teasels, and fullers' earth (used as a detergent), together with a growing urban workforce. As the industry expanded, imports of wool from England and Spain, exotic dyes from the East, and alum (mineral salts used for cleansing cloth and fixing dyes) played an ever greater part. The great Flemish merchants of the first half of this period maintained a stranglehold on the cities' weavers and fullers to generate vast profits; however, by the later 13th century a series of urban revolts had rocked the merchant associations, and the industry entered a steady decline. By the early 14th century, rivals in England, Italy, and Aragon had taken over much of their business.

Most 18th-century industries were already developed in the 13th century: coal was mined, metal ores extracted, iron smelted, silk spun, and leather worked. With these pursuits came increasing mechanization, of which the best example is the mill. Water mills of various descriptions had been common across medieval Europe from at least the late 11th century. The Domesday Book (1086) lists more than 5000 in England, and by the late 12th century few rural communities would have been without one. Windmills soon followed, and, in the 13th century, the development of the water-powered fulling mill (which thickened and

The development of money

In the course of the Middle Ages, money increasingly became the favoured means of exchange. It had the obvious advantages over barter and goods in that it was portable and measurable, but that does not mean it was accepted everywhere – merchants sometimes preferred spices. Nonetheless, more and more peasants paid their taxes in coins, and such was the success of the small currency that the number of grams of silver to the pound-tale (i.e. 240 pennies) in France fell from 80 to 22 between 1250 and 1500. Gold was particularly associated with the great trading and banking centres of Italy. This Genoese coin also makes a political point – it was minted by the imperialist Ghibeline party.

felted cloth) dragged much industry out of the towns and into the countryside. There the mills worked wool, ground corn, tanned leather, beat metal, and even made paper, first manufactured in Fabriano at the end of the 13th century.

Agriculture

Much of medieval Europe enjoyed highly specialized farming arrangements best illustrated by the wide variety of wines available. Throughout the Middle Ages, however, cereal production was the basis of farming; even animal husbandry played little part in most lives. Wheat and rye were sown in the autumn and reaped between June and August. The medieval varieties did not grow well on poor soil and succumbed quickly to harsh winters, but their grains could easily be threshed free of their husks and ground to a fine flour which could be baked into bread. Oats and barley cropped rather better on poorer soils and because sown in the spring were less subject to bad weather. These grains produced only a low-grade flour that would not rise, so most oats were served as a porridge or fed to animals, while barley was malted to produce beer, the staple drink of medieval Europe.

For the most part, these crops were combined in a three-field rotational system comprising an autumn-sown crop, a spring-sown crop, and a fallow. Despite this system, most soil was over-used and under-manured, and so yields declined over the years. Improvements in ploughing techniques after the introduction of asymmetrical metal shares helped, and the incorporation of legumes into the system, especially peas and beans, not only benefited the medieval diet, but also reintroduced nitrogen into the depleted soil. Nonetheless, there was little concerted effort to improve soil fertility, and the growing population was provided for mostly by bringing new land into cultivation.

Most trade in the Indian Ocean was in high-value, low-volume goods; these boats are laden with bales and barrels, probably containing spices and oils. This was one of the reasons why a safe westerly route was so important: loss of a single ship could mean economic ruin for a merchant.

The Black Death

The Black Death was the most devastating epidemic to strike Europe. Many contemporaries viewed it as the end of the world; many modern historians as the end of an era. Cathedrals begun before its onset remained unfinished into modern times, while the great quadrangles of Oxford University exist only because the city beneath them was laid waste by the plague. Its economic consequences are sometimes difficult to see, but its social and emotional consequences are all too clear.

Medieval churches and churchyards were full of grisly images of Death personified. From the middle of the 14th century, plague was a familiar feature of the European experience and representations of Death as king became more and more common. This one comes from a 15th-century French book of hours by René d'Anjou, King of Sicily.

One of the more ghoulish side effects of the Black Death of 1348–9 was the increasing popularity of the danse macabre, *or dance of death, and of illustrations of it. This anonymous engraving calls to mind the effigies of cadavers often featured on later medieval tombs beneath a truer effigy of the deceased.*

The onset

The Black Death was brought to Europe from Asia. In the mid-1340s, a group of Tartar warriors on campaign in China became infected. By 1346, they had brought the disease to their home in the Crimea, where it killed around 100,000 people. In the resulting pandemonium, Christian merchants, an unpopular minority, were made scapegoats for this apocalyptic horror, and, towards the end of the year, the Genoese trading outpost Caffa, now Feodosia on the Crimean coast, was besieged by a Tartar army. The army quickly succumbed to the plague, but as a parting shot catapulted infected corpses over the Italians' walls. As soon as the siege was lifted, the Genoese merchants fled the city, but they were not nearly quick enough to escape contagion; the disease appeared wherever their galleys touched shore. Sicily, Calabria, and the port cities of Genoa and Marseilles were all infected by the end of 1347. By the end of 1348, the plague had spread across much of Western Europe. By 1349, it had reached most of Germany and the British Isles and even made inroads into Scandinavia. By 1351, it was all but gone, although sporadic outbreaks blighted the remainder of the Middle Ages.

The Black Death was an inexplicable horror; it did not even receive its name until the 17th century. Today we know it to have been a deadly cocktail of three diseases. The primary component was bubonic plague, a disease carried in the blood of infected rats and spread by fleas, which causes its victims to break out in great tumours or buboes. It kills more than two-thirds of those infected in less than a week. It combined with pneumonic plague, an altogether more virulent disease that attacks the lungs. Spread by coughing, it is lethal in under two days. The third and rarest component was septicaemic plague, a disease that swamps the bloodstream with bacilli in less than two hours; it kills long before buboes have time to appear.

Population

Population in medieval Europe is very difficult to estimate because the necessary records do not exist. It may have peaked at the very beginning of the 14th century, then in places begun a gradual decline. What is certain is that the Black Death caused a massive dislocation. The parish register of Givry, in Burgundy, survives to tell a grim tale. Before the onset of the plague, it recorded an average of almost 40 deaths a year, suggesting a population of about one thousand. In 1348, the death toll jumped to 649, of which 630 occurred between July and November. This horrific record is far from exceptional; it is mirrored in such records as there are for taxation, burials, and census. Infants accounted for a high proportion of deaths, and each outbreak must have led to several generations of diminished birth rate until its effects had been exhausted. Each locality suffered its own individual fate – some escaped entirely – and generalizations are almost impossible; however, at least one-fifth of Europe's population died in 1348–9.

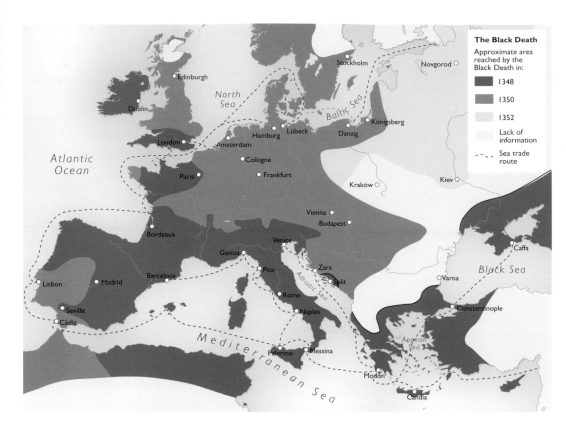

The Black Death spread across Europe with alarming speed. Broadly, coastal areas were affected earlier than inland areas, and those coastal areas that were hit first were connected to each other by sea trade routes. It easy to see how so few ships could spread the plague across the continent.

The Black Death

Approximate area reached by the Black Death in:

- 1348
- 1350
- 1352
- Lack of information
- - - Sea trade route

Economic consequences

Fields went unploughed and crops unharvested. Immediate shortages led to panic buying, and prices rose. Many better-off families fled cities where infection appeared to be worse. (In 1351, Boccaccio wrote *The Decameron,* the story of ten noblemen and women who fled the plague in Florence and whiled away their time in telling tales; although fiction, it mirrors reality.) But these were all short-term consequences. Within three or four years, they had passed, and Europe was left to face more serious consequences.

In the first decade of the 14th century when population was at its peak, good agricultural land was scarce, and much marginal land was bought into cultivation. Peasant labour, meanwhile, was abundant, and so land values were high and wages were low. The Black Death reversed this relationship. The reduction of the labour force by at least one-fifth made it a relatively scarce commodity. Whereas once manorial courts had been inundated with peasants bidding against each other for land, surviving peasants were now able to dictate their own terms. Landlords resisted and attempted to reimpose servile obligations, leading to a bitter and often successful peasant backlash across Europe, of which the best-known examples are the French peasant uprising of 1357 (the Jacquerie) and the English Peasants Revolt in 1381. At the same time, total demand for produce was reduced, and so

village communities could focus their attentions on farming better soils. Survivors and the subsequent generations enjoyed a better quality of life.

Social consequences

More land could never make up for the loss of loved ones. For medieval writers, the plague was a cataclysm; as one English monk described it, "it is uncertain whether any of Adam's race will survive to tell this tale". Images of death and decaying corpses began to feature more prominently in painting, literature, and sculpture, and the morbid dance of death became a regular feature of village life.

In Germany, notions that the plague was a form of divine retribution for man's sinfulness gave rise to two peculiar and unpleasant phenomena. The Brotherhood of Flagellants had their origin in the more or less widely accepted belief that mortification of the flesh might assist the remission of sins. Highly organized and, initially, very well respected bands of men and women travelled from town to town, beating themselves viciously in public ceremonies of expiation. Others directed their anger and fear outwards. Between 1348 and 1351, thousands of Jews were massacred in organized pogroms across Germany and into the neighbouring countries. Like the Christians at Coffa, they were seen as outsiders whose "perversions" had brought down this dreadful punishment and whose blood might buy salvation.

For many members of the upper
ranks of society, hunting was the
focus of their cultural and social
life. Often their tenants were
required to turn out to act as
beaters for the hunt.

CULTURAL LIFE

Thinkers of the Renaissance looked back on this period as "a middle age" in which nothing of importance was achieved. The term has stuck, but looking back we can see a constant flow of artistic and intellectual creativity running throughout history. Cathedrals and illuminated manuscripts seize the imagination because the lost timber-framed houses and unrecorded songs cannot. Magnificent though it is, our view of medieval cultural life could in fact be a very distorted one.

The difficulties of understanding medieval culture are best appreciated through its music. Secular music was rarely given written notation before the 13th century, nor were its lyrics set down in ink. The English "Sumer is icumen in" ("Summer has come") is a rare exception, but we can have no idea of whether or not it is a typical composition of its time. Certainly it must have been one among an innumerable many. Manuscript illustrations depict musicians at every turn plucking harps, bowing viols, strumming gitterns (a guitar-like instrument), hammering dulcimers, and blowing bagpipes. Nor was all of this necessarily "low culture". For example, the minstrels on campaign with Henry V at Agincourt were paid 12 pence a day, twice what an archer earned and as much as a master surgeon. Certain medieval theorists even believed that music and medicine were mutually complimentary.

Music was part of the curriculum of medieval scholastic study and was inextricably bound up with the Church, so it inevitably became the subject of theological and intellectual debate. The greatest legacy of medieval church music is the wholly choral plainchant and polyphony of the daily services, but at the time it was a hotly debated issue. What was an appropriate degree of ornamentation for divine worship? At what point did a monk begin to take more pleasure in the music than in his worship of God? How might music best reflect the wonder of creation? These types of question make it tempting to view music-making as an academic exercise. Was function ultimately more important than aesthetics in church music? It only takes a sympathetic ear a

moment to decide that this was not the case, but these are the types of difficulty that thinkers and artists of the Middle Ages sought to overcome. The struggle is an unfamiliar one to us, and, while we might agree to take medieval culture on its own terms, identifying the terms themselves is not always easy.

What is certain about music in the Middle Ages is its universality. Similarly, grand architecture would have touched the lives of many – when the monasteries were torn down during the Reformation, it left ugly scars on the psyches of many small 16th-century communities. Literature, however, remained far more selective throughout the Middle Ages. The interests of most medieval literary works were either courtly or ecclesiastical, and many were composed for a particular wealthy patron, although they may have had a wider audience through performance. That is not to say that medieval Europe was largely illiterate. Many commercial activities required a relatively high degree of practical literacy and numeracy, and from at least the 13th century, manuals were written for almost every small business imaginable. In the urban schools of Italy, at the forefront of commerce, writing, calculation, and vernacular languages were taught to the exclusion of the classics. In Florence in 1338, out of a population of about 90,000, approximately 10,000 children were being taught the rudiments of reading and writing. In England, it is estimated that 30 per cent of the 15th-century population could read. These statistics compare favourably with the literacy level during the Industrial Revolution.

Education and Learning

Most Christian scholarship at the beginning of this period was rooted deeply in the work of the pagan philosophers, Aristotle and Plato, as preserved and interpreted by the Church Fathers and scholars of the late Roman Empire. But the early 12th century saw reason applied to many old problems with new vigour, heralding an intellectual revolution.

The Middle Ages, in particular the 14th century, saw a proliferation of places of learning, many with reputations for certain specializations. The finest Roman lawyers sought Bologna, the finest canon lawyers Paris. There was a good deal of cross-fertilization between the different types of institution. The oldest universities generally have their origins in the private schools of well-known teachers, who might themselves have been taught in a cathedral or monastery.

Scholastic humanism

In the 11th and 12th centuries, most learning and intellectual debate took place in cathedral schools such as the one presided over by St Bernard at Chartres. There students studied and masters debated the seven liberal arts of antiquity – the *quadrivium* of arithmetic, geometry, astronomy, and musical theory, and the *trivium* of logic, grammar, and rhetoric. It had long been held that the sciences of the ancient pagan world had their proper place in a Christian curriculum, as they played a part in the huge task of interpreting the Bible (albeit in ways that may seem odd or forced to us today); however, scholarship had vested little confidence in the potential of human beings. From the late 11th century, however, scholars such as Bernard of Clairvaux, Guibert of Nogent, and Peter Abelard turned their attention to the problems of the inner self. The 12th century saw an influx of hitherto unknown pagan works of science and philosophy from Byzantium and the Muslim East,

most importantly new contributions from Aristotle, which demanded a rethinking of the relationship between the laws which governed the material and the spiritual worlds. By the mid-12th century, a new, vibrant tradition of thought had gained momentum – scholastic humanism. This early humanism had nothing to do with the materialist humanism of the Renaissance three centuries later. Instead, it involved a deep intellectual concern with the role of people as individuals within an ordered universe, created by a God who himself became flesh so that he might experience and redeem the human condition. It became the driving force behind the century's intellectual, artistic, and literary endeavours.

Peter Abelard

Peter Abelard's fame today is due largely to a long autobiographical letter in which he laments his treatment at the hands of orthodox scholars and recounts his rather seedy love affair with a young noblewoman, Héloïse, as a result of which he was mutilated by her relatives and retired into a monastery in disgrace. But his fame in the early 12th century as a maverick teacher and writer of firecracker theology did much to establish Paris, where he was based, as the wellspring of intellectual renaissance. As a young man, he renounced the military career that his father had planned for him and travelled from cathedral to cathedral first to learn from then to debate publicly with some of the most renowned theologians of the time. By his own account, he bested them all and struck out on his own. His *Treatise on the Unity and Trinity of God* of 1121 turned this sparring into official Church condemnation. The work engaged the nature of universals, or what was truly real at a philosophical level, which had provoked debate between the contemporary Realist (Platonic) and Nominalist (Aristotelian) schools. Plato believed that only ideal forms were truly real, whereas Aristotle held that only individual things were fully real. Abelard sought to reconcile the two, but many Church officials considered the work overly

Intellectual and Religious Centres of Learning

- 📖 Universities evolving from pre-13th century schools
- 📖 Universities founded in the 14th century
- 📖 Universities founded in the 13th century
- † Cathedral school
- ■ Monastery school

North Sea

†Durham
■ Rievaulx
Hereford †
📖 Cambridge
Exeter † Oxford 📖
Canterbury †
Tournai †
■ Deutz
Le Bec ■ Paris 📖 ■ Cologne 📖 Erfurt
St-Evroult ■ †Reims ■ Heidelberg
†Chartres
Angers † † Orléans ■ Morimond
Tours 📖 Kraków
• Cluny
Atlantic Ocean
📖 Vienna
📖 Buda
Cahors 📖
Grenoble Vicenza 📖 Treviso 📖 Pécs
Palencia 📖 Toulouse 📖 Orange 📖 Padua
Valladolid Huesca Avignon Bologna
Coimbra Salamanca Montpellier Pisa 📖 Florence
■ Lisbon Lerida Siena 📖 Perugia
† Toledo ■ Rome
■ Monte Cassino
■ Seville †Salerno
Mediterranean Sea

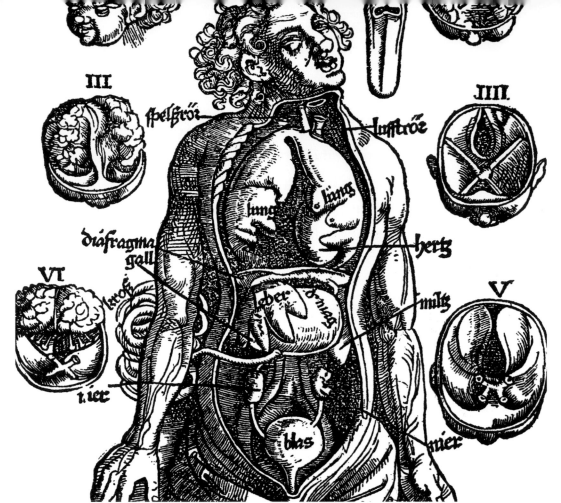

Medicine and anatomy were developing sciences during this period, but dissection retained a certain taboo. For the most part, only those who had died at the hands of an executioner were handed over to anatomists, a practice that continued into the 19th century.

dependent on pagan thought, and it was publicly burned. In another work, *Sic et Non* (literally, *Yes and No*), Abelard set down 158 questions on theological problems alongside selections from Christian and pagan writers both for and against the proposition, as an invitation to apply logical thought to theology. Even at the end of his life, as an exiled monk, he retained his enthusiasm for this dialectical method and a suspicion of orthodoxy. The title of his final work says it all: *Dialogue between a Philosopher, a Pagan and a Jew.*

Universities

Abelard's approach was refined and developed by the greatest theologian of the Middle Ages, a 13th-century Dominican professor at the University of Paris called Thomas Aquinas. His *Summa Theologiae* represents the pinnacle of medieval humanism. But the fact that St Thomas had a logical tradition to develop, or a university at which to be a professor, owed much to the advances, struggles, and downright hubris of Abelard. His name did much for the reputation of 12th-century Paris as a font of learning and hotbed of new ideas at a time when advanced education was a disparate affair. The schools of particular towns might be known for particular specializations, but there was no coherent standard. As with so much else, these were thrown into sharp relief by the struggles between empire and papacy. As early as 1158, Frederick Barbarossa had conferred his protection upon the scholars of Bologna, "by whose knowledge [of Roman law] the world is illuminated in obedience to God and us, his ministers, and the life of his subjects is shaped" – i.e. a thick veneer of political theory would do the Empire no harm at all. The reforming papacy, with its stress on a literate priesthood and its grounding in canon law, needed its own proponents and turned increasingly to the cathedral schools of Paris. King Philip Augustus had granted a charter to the nascent university in 1200, but Pope Innocent III went further to grant its scholars the right to elect their own officials in 1215, freeing them from clerical control. Governments, too, needed ever increasing numbers of trained officials, and this tripartite fostering of education brought the schools of various towns together, in an organic and unsystematic manner, as universities (the word then meant something similar to guild). Over the 12th century, the student seeking education as a path to riches became a favourite target of satirists. The idea that academia was a trade in itself, which produced a valuable commodity, learning, did not gain much momentum until the next century. By the 14th century, the idea had caught on such that rival German dynasties sought to outdo each other in the foundation of universities at Prague, Vienna, and elsewhere.

Literature

The spoken, written, and sung word were closely related in the Middle Ages. All three overlapped and intertwined in legal, church, courtly, and learned circles. Just as many theological treatises had their origin in public debates, so also much chivalric literature was born of heroic folk tales. It is telling that the most famous literary epic of the period is known as a song – the _Chanson de Roland._

Taverns and courts

About 100 troubadours are known by name from the century after 1150, including some 20 women. They were heirs of a rich tradition of story-telling and composition. Certain chansons from Spain combine Arabic and Hebrew elements with an early Spanish dialect. The majority draw upon the romantic doctrines of the Angevin courts, English nostalgia for the past, and Celtic mythology. In time, an increasing self-consciousness on the part of educated noble patrons created an environment in which different strands of tales and songs were woven together into courtly romances (the word means simply that they were composed in a vernacular Romance language). About 100 survive from the century after 1150, of which the most famous and accomplished were by Marie de France, Chrétien de Troyes, and Gautier d'Arras. The so-called "Matter of Britain", the body of stories about King Arthur, Lancelot, Perceval, and the Grail, was the favoured topic and Chrétien its master. His epics _Erec, Perceval, Yvain_, and others are sweeping canvases intended to excite, educate, and, to an extent, rehabilitate the aristocracy.

The other great epic tradition of the Middle Ages, of similarly rich and organic heritage, came from further north and east. The Scandinavian sagas were centuries old when they were first written down in the 13th century by the historian Snorri Sturlson and others. Filled with a deep, unsentimental pessimism in which man, the gods, and nature are all cruel, they tell of the wars of gods among themselves, giants and dragons, and the appalling sacrifices made by Odin, father of the gods, in his search for ultimate knowledge. By turns macabre, funny, and moving, they provide an impressive self-portrait of a people generally marginalized in studies of European culture and prefigure much visionary and apocalyptic literature of the later medieval West. The _Nibelungenlied_, the great Germanic heroic epic that inspired Wagner's _Ring_ cycle, tells a similarly bleak tale of a lost people and broken pantheon doomed by a

woman's hatred. If in Western Europe even mythical literary epics had deep Christian overtones, further east they were more scarce, if not absent.

Dante

Dante Alighieri was born in Florence in 1265. Like most Florentine nobles, his family were supporters of the Guelf party, a papal faction in origin, although by this time local concerns carried more weight. He married, but subsequently fell in love with another young noblewoman, Beatrice.

Although she died in 1290, he idealized her as a model of virtue and courtesy for the rest of his life. In 1300, the Guelf party split in two, and Dante found himself on the wrong side of political power. In 1302, he was convicted on trumped-up charges of embezzlement and anti-papalism and exiled from his beloved Florence. His magnificent *Divine Comedy* was forged in these fires of love and hatred.

The Divine Comedy centres on one pilgrim's journey, Dante's own, to God, through hell, purgatory, and finally paradise, drawn on by the agency of Beatrice. The reader is intended to understand that the pilgrim's journey is that of Everyman and that God will aid Everyman as he has the pilgrim, but Dante's vision of redemption is by turns apocalyptic and damning. He is just as concerned with those who are not redeemed as those who are. Of the 79 named people Dante encounters in his hell, 32 were Florentines. Only four made it as far as purgatory and only two to paradise. Popes and emperors fared no better than the common person. In Dante's heaven, there are outbursts against Pope Clement V and the Curial Church. The Knights Templar, recently suppressed, receive a staunch defence, as do the Franciscan friars, much persecuted for their overt poverty. Thomas Aquinas sits in heaven, but he sings the praises of the almost heretical Siger of Brabant, a scourge of recent orthodoxy. There are few heretical ideas that Dante does not incorporate in this deeply symbolic work of poetry. As much as *The Divine Comedy* is an elaborate vision of a new heaven and a new earth, it is also a celebration of Dante's native language. Language is not secondary to meaning, and, through Dante's, Italian achieved a depth and articulation unparalleled in the Middle Ages.

Carmina Burana

Carmina Burana was the name given to a 13th-century manuscript containing 300 or so poems and lyrics, unearthed in a Benedictine library at Beuron, near Munich, by its first editor in 1847. Today the name is best known through Carl Orff's exuberant settings of some 20 of the poems for choir and orchestra, but its importance extends further: it is the largest and most varied surviving anthology of medieval Latin poetry written by the last poets to use that language as fluently as they did their native tongues. Within a few generations, their themes – love, drinking, gaming, adventure, and satire – were to be written almost exclusively in the vernacular. No subject is too high or too low for the *Carmina*. The best known, both because of Orff's famous opening and countless medieval illuminations, concerns Dame Fortune turning her

Geoffrey Chaucer

Born around 1343, the son of a London vintner, Geoffrey Chaucer led a colourful life. He was a prisoner of war in France, controller of customs in London, Knight of the Shire for Kent, and a deputy forester in Somerset. He was also the most prolific and versatile writer of his time. He produced plays, the standard treatise on the astrolabe, and a translation of Boethius' *Consolation of Philosophy*, but is best known for *The Canterbury Tales*. These sharp and often irreverent caricatures of a group of pilgrims en route to the shrine of Thomas à Becket at Canterbury are full of unparalleled insights into medieval life, both grand and mundane.

wheel, "O how Fortune ... apes the moon's inconstancy: waxing, waning, losing, gaining ... Life treats us detestably." Others, less contemplative, list the noises made by all known animals or the erotic speculations of men in taverns.

The Paston library

Even at the close of the Middle Ages, printing was rare and expensive, and the circulation of books necessarily constrained. Nonetheless, the library catalogues of noble households suggest that much epic, romance, and history was read. The library of one Sir John Paston gives some indication of what a 15th-century English gentleman's library might contain. He had Chaucer's *Troilus and Criseyde*, a chronicle of England to the reign of Edward III, Cicero's *On Friendship* and *On Old Age*, a book of knighthood, a book of heraldry, and a book on the death of Arthur, among many other titles. The number of books a man possessed is no real guide to the range of his reading, as many items might be gathered together in a single volume. Paston referred to his "Great Book", a compendium so similar to others known in later medieval England as to suggest that it was a standard collection readily available at any stationers for a reasonable price. Medieval Europe had its coffee table books, sumptuous illuminated Grail romances and so forth, but it also had its budget paperbacks.

Architecture

Grand architecture in the Middle Ages was a result of conflicting forces. Medieval cathedrals stand as supreme acts of praise – we can only imagine what went through the mind of a mason embarking on his stupendous task with only chisels, pulleys, and scaffolding. But those same cathedrals are also symbols of hubris. Conquering kings left magnificent cathedrals in their wakes – a clear message for all to read.

The Torre del Mangio, completed by 1341, dominates Siena, outstripping even the cathedral in height. It forms part of the town hall complex of the central piazza, the Campo, which housed the communal government known as the Noveschi (the Nine). It was situated so as not to favour any one district of the city.

Romanesque churches were drenched with colour and detail. Altars, screens, fonts, columns, and archways commonly featured decorative or allegorical designs and images. Decorated capitals are particularly intriguing: despite their inconspicuous situation, they were as richly worked as any stone in the church. This example comes from the Cathedral at Pamplona in Spain.

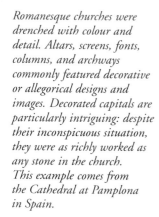

From Romanesque to Gothic

The beginning of this period saw a great architectural expansion both in the number and the scale of buildings. Magnificent though Charlemagne's palatine chapel at Aachen was (built *c*.805), it was dwarfed by the churches built by kings and emperors in the 10th and 11th centuries. Most came to adopt an almost classical style now known as Romanesque. Almost always cross-shaped, and generally having an apse at the east end, their naves and roofs were supported by comparatively plain, round-headed arches. Windows were few and small, but engravings and paintings were many and rich. Grand examples are the cathedrals of St Martin of Tours and Santiago de Compostela. Uniquely, in Germany, cathedrals of the time often had two choirs, perhaps referring to the twin powers of Church and state united under imperial patronage. The best examples are the three imperial cathedrals, Speyer, Worms, and Mainz. Elsewhere, many small local churches still bear the characteristic decorative motifs of interlocking beaked heads and a zigzag design around their doors and windows. But as scholarly interest in the divine mechanics of the universe increased in the 12th century, so architects began to experiment, albeit often piecemeal, with a new style that reached for the heavens and gathered in the stars. Gothic architecture, as it was disparagingly termed by artists of the classicizing Renaissance, adopted intricate vaults of the type first seen in Durham Cathedral in 1104 and tall, pointed arches, typical of church architecture in Burgundy, to raise roofs high above the congregation and clear the way for soaring windows, creating cathedrals of light. The combination of artistry and trigonometric ingenuity that was so much part of the Gothic movement is encapsulated in its most typical feature, the flying buttress, which allowed higher, more delicate walls and greater apertures than ever before. The best examples today are Notre Dame Cathedral, Chartres Cathedral and the monastic church of Mont St Michel. The first complete Gothic church was that of the Cathedral of St-Etienne in Sens, the

archbishop of which, Henri Sanglier (1122–42), has a strong claim to be numbered among the great architectural innovators of the Middle Ages, but the Gothic style will forever be associated with Abbot Suger of St Denis.

Architecture and society

From the late 1130s, Abbot Suger began an extensive programme of rebuilding the ancient church of the Abbey of St Denis, near Paris in a new, invigorating style. He wrote two very influential and widely circulated books that explained his architectural agenda and justified his endeavours. There is no doubting Suger's godliness, but nor is there any doubting his worldliness. St Denis was the patron saint of the relatively lowly Capetian kings of France. Suger was an influential royal adviser. Can it be a coincidence that the rebuilding of the abbey church was conceived immediately after the Capetian king Louis VI had brought the French nobility together with unprecedented success to face down the German Emperor Henry V? In Suger's account, St Denis himself miraculously aided the construction work, thus sealing the project with a holy approval that would have given much credibility to the Capetian dynasty. A complex political reality underlay the architectural advances of this relatively unimportant suburb, and the association of the steady expansion of Capetian power beyond the Ile de France and the expansion of Gothic architecture is striking.

Not everyone approved of lavish construction work. St Bernard of Clairvaux railed against those, especially the Cluniacs, who devoted money and energy to excessive projects, which were hardly in keeping with the simplicity of the monastic lifestyle. The grandeur of the church at Cluny suggests that he had a point. Bernard's own order, the Cistercians, developed a distinctive, restrained architectural style that, for a few decades at least, was uniform throughout its houses, from Fountains in England to Fontenay in France. Elsewhere, architecture sought to give far more explicit instruction. The bas-relief at Amiens Cathedral shows a noblewoman kicking a servant in the belly. A huge stone ox stands high on the towers of Laon Cathedral as a tribute to the nobility of the animal world, appreciated more by humanists than ever before. Monks appear in the guise of voracious wolves devouring sheep, Jews are shown as pigs, and women appear in all forms from Queen of Heaven to devils suckling toads.

Architecture and the state

The use of architecture as a means of propaganda reached its apogee in the Italian city-states, of

The construction of the cathedral at Chartres, begun in 1194, signalled the beginning of the elaborate style known as High Gothic. Architectural patronage was very important. The statues and windows of the south portal, pictured here, were paid for by Peter of Dreux, Count of Brittany.

which Siena is the most powerful example. There, the whole city was subordinated to a grand design for communal living by the detailed planning regulations of the *Noveschi*, the communal government. Fortified towers built by the various leading families were subject to height limits, and, from 1297, all buildings on the central square were forced to conform to a certain design: columns were mandatory, but balconies forbidden. An elaborate scheme of city-wide public fountains was begun the next year. Siena's principal public building, the Palazzo Publico, itself housed the most overtly political piece of art in any of the city-states: Ambroglio Lorenzetti's frescoes on the themes of good and bad government in the government's meeting room contained allegories on justice, the common good, and tyranny.

It was not (quite) all politics in the Italian city-states. The best known and most influential architectural artist of the communes was Giotto. Born of peasant background at the end of the 13th century, his work contains not only anti-imperial imagery (seen in the frescoes in the Scrovegni Chapel, Padua), but also narratives of the lives of two famous ascetics, St Francis and St John the Baptist (the Church of Santa Croce, Padua). Perhaps Giotto was commissioned to rub out the taint of money which successful patrons of art in the city-states inevitably acquired.

The Roots of Renaissance

The Renaissance is generally thought to have begun around 1450, but it is easier to identify what its characteristics were not, than what they were. It was not just a renewed interest in classical art and scholarship, nor a sudden rejection of medieval views, values, and beliefs. Almost any aspect of the Renaissance can be prefigured in medieval Europe.

A 14th-century manuscript of Dante's Divine Comedy *picturing the Florentine poet together with Virgil, his guide, in hell with the damned. In his thinking on the relationships between religion, philosophy, and art, and his celebration of the learning of the classical world, Dante prefigured much that is generally associated with the 15th-century Renaissance.*

Learning

The new learning of the 15th century possessed three more or less novel features, all related. First, it cultivated many classical authors well known today, but almost ignored by scholars of the Middle Ages, particularly Cicero and Homer. Secondly, ancient Greek played an increasingly prominent role in scholarship, parallel with Latin. Thirdly, biblical scholarship moved away from the extremes of symbolic interpretation to concentrate on linguistic studies of the original Hebrew and Greek texts. At the forefront of this new learning was a Dutchman called Gerhard Gerhards, better known by his Latin and Greek pen names, Desiderius and Erasmus. A regular visitor to London and Cambridge, he did more than any other to unite scientific study of the classics and scripture with the Catholic tradition of the medieval church. His heyday coincided with the dawn of widespread printing and his *In Praise of Folly* ran to 43 editions in his lifetime.

Anti-clericalism

Though the Renaissance was not an abandonment of Catholic Christianity, it was a rejection of many of its trappings. In answer to his own question, "What would happen if the pope imitated Christ in his poverty?", Erasmus said "thousands of scribes, sycophants and pimps would go out of business". Similar denunciations had been uttered earlier in the Middle Ages by such "heretical" groups as the Waldensians; however, in the 15th century, increasing emphasis on the direct relationship between the individual and God without the need for a priest as intercessor or confessor – what was to become Protestantism – brought much clerical ritual under attack. At times this erupted into acts of iconoclasm, but for the most part it meant that the power of the Church was gradually limited to its religious concerns. Pope Gregory VII's 400-year-old dreams of a papal monarchy were slowly consigned to oblivion, and religion increasingly became a matter for private conscience.

Calumny of Appelles, *Botticelli. Sandro Botticelli was the most individual and perhaps most influential artist in Florence at the end of the 15th century. It is likely that he had a member of the ruling Medici family as his patron. It is generally felt that the classical gods and heroes in his work are not carefree Olympians, but symbolic embodiments of some deep moral or metaphysical truth.*

Florence is still defined by its late medieval skyline. Its towers, now much admired for their architectural splendour, then housed warring factions of the sort that Dante found himself caught up in. It is an odd phenomenon that Florence produced so many renowned artists whereas the neighbouring Siena, equally prosperous, produced so few.

Science and society

As a result of the Church's diminishing authority over the secular world, scientists and philosophers were able to explore new ideas with less fear of censure. It was felt at this time that the secrets of the universe could be revealed by God-given ingenuity. In some senses, this is not so very far from the advances made by 12th- and 13th-century scholars such as Abelard, John of Salisbury, and Thomas Aquinas, but their interest was in what the divine in man could reveal through introspection and logical thought rather than in what the intellect could prise open.

The foremost quality of the Renaissance has been seen as independence of mind, and none possessed it as abundantly as Leonardo da Vinci. Born in 1452, he is best known for his paintings, particularly the *Mona Lisa* and the *Last Supper*. Painting was only ever a hobby; his principal interests were science and mechanics. Among the many unrealized designs in his notebooks were the machine gun, helicopter, and submarine.

World view

The Renaissance will always be thought of in terms of its great scientific thinkers – Leonardo, Galileo, Copernicus, and Bacon – but as with any great intellectual revolution, their thoughts hardly accorded with prevailing ideas about the world. This was still the age of astrology, alchemy, and magic. Nonetheless, the idea that humanity was capable of mastering the world in which it lived was growing, and the importance of Providence waning. The chains of sin weighed less heavily upon Renaissance thinkers than many of their predecessors, and in large part their achievement was not the conquest of new territory, but the overcoming of old fears.

One indication of this shift is the increasing reference to Europe, rather than Christendom. Of course, medieval scholars had known that they lived on a continent called Europe by classical geographers, but for many their knowledge of the world beyond their own locality came from tales of martyrs, pilgrims, and crusaders. During the course of the Middle Ages, the idea that Christendom was a common fold for the peoples of Europe had suffered many erosions. Princes had bought off popes. An ecumenical conference of 1439 in Florence allowed the Catholic and Greek Orthodox Churches to take a good look at each other and realize just how different they were. The "Christendom of Europe", as one priest put it in 1572, was being pushed ever westwards. The Ottoman conquests of the East prevented it from ever returning.

THE ROOTS OF RENAISSANCE   **171**

The Ebstorf map (c.1283). Not all medieval maps were created for practical purposes. Often they were intended to show the symbolic importance of Jerusalem as the centre of a flat world and Christ as its ruler. That is not to say that there was no such skill as cartography – many Medieval maps of Europe could guide a fairly tolerant traveller today.

THE CHURCH AND BELIEF

Looking back at the Middle Ages today, we can see far more of the broad trends than contemporaries ever could, but almost nothing of personal life. For the most part, belief can only be traced through its institution, the Church. Seen in that distant mirror, belief drove people to seek the earthly Jerusalem on pilgrimage and crusade, and it gave popes the authority to meld a monarchy out of the bishopric of Rome.

Heaven and hell

Medieval art produced many striking images of heaven and hell. For most people a painting above a church altar of the Devil, horned, winged, and bathed in fire, was far more immediate than any words of scripture a priest might read beneath it. The physical torments of Dante's *Inferno* were as imminent as the physical blessings of his *Paradise*, so much so that the 12th-century German bishop Otto of Freising reminded his readers that descriptions of the afterlife in scripture were not necessarily to be taken literally. From the late 12th century, the geography of the otherworld gained a new continent. The idea that there might be a state between salvation and damnation had been considered likely by the Church fathers, but it was not until after 1170 that purgatory was recognized as a place where venial sins were punished between death and the Last Judgement. In *The Divine Comedy,* although its torments are no less horrendous, purgatory is a happier place than hell because it has hope of eventual redemption. The notion of purgatory brought with it huge spiritual motivation, not just to be faithful, but also to be obedient. In the course of the Middle Ages, a fourth region emerged. Unbaptized children and worthy souls who had never known Christ because they lived before His time or where His teaching had not yet reached were consigned to limbo, a state without punishment, but with no possibility of redemption. There Dante finds Homer, Plato, and Aristotle as well as the Muslim general Saladin.

Jerusalem as the centre of the world

More often than not, medieval maps did not have any practical agenda. Instead, they sought to show the fundamental importance of Jerusalem, both literally and symbolically, by placing it at the centre of the world. The literal and symbolic were united in 1099 when the city was recaptured from Islam during the First Crusade. The author of one chronicle describes the tomb of Christ as "the navel of the world".

The range of belief

The Middle Ages are generally spoken of as "an age of faith", but perhaps things were not so clear cut. First impressions are of the incredible wealth of the Church, the grandeur of its buildings, and the nature of surviving documents. But the ecclesiastical writers who shape our conception of the medieval world were not just writing for us, they were also writing for their contemporaries who might very well have needed cajoling with pious imprecations and a few plainly stated examples. Architects and their patrons knew perfectly well that magnificent churches reinforced the majesty of God, as well as reflecting it. A cynic might note how many more representations of judgement there are in medieval church art than of salvation. Genuine faith shaped belief, but so did politics, varying interpretations of scripture, convenience, vice, and doubt. As a consequence, the medieval Church was far more accommodating than usually assumed. King Henry I of England acknowledged more than 20 illegitimate children, but after his death chroniclers remembered his reign as a peaceful one blessed by God. His brother, William Rufus, was remembered in no such terms, but then he took little trouble to hide his total contempt for matters of the Church. There is a place for religious scepticism in our thinking about the Middle Ages.

The Monastic Orders

Economic and political concerns could easily intrude upon the contemplative life. As a result, many monastic houses looked to strict regulations to preserve their way of life. The most influential was Benedict's Rule, drawn up by St Benedict of Nursia for the monastery of Monte Cassino in the early 6th century. Three hundred years later, St Benedict of Aniane fostered its implementation across Christendom.

Benedictine monasticism

The guiding principle of Benedict's Rule was humility in all things. The particulars of humility, in terms of food, drink, sleep, and duties, were spelled out in detail. Implicit in Benedict's concept of humility was total obedience to one's superior; in the case of a monk, his abbot. Should the abbot demand an impossible act, the monk was to explain, meekly, why this was so, but if the abbot insisted, then the monk was to trust in God and obey. Humility was also to be learnt by daily toil in the fields, between the many hours of meticulously timetabled prayer and worship. Above all, the Rule was a sensible one for communal living. It ordained that monks should sleep in separate beds within a dormitory; bedclothes varied according to a monk's age and health. Instructions were given for the care of the sick. Food was to be frugal but adequate, and monks were to prepare it each in turn.

Benedict's Rule was profoundly important, but its focus was inwards. Monasteries remained part of the world, often dependent on some form of secular sponsorship or support, or falling under the sway of a local bishop who might himself have a political agenda. An awareness of this led to a period of intensive and radical monastic reform in the 10th century. The Burgundian monastery of Cluny, founded in 909, was placed beyond the interference of any but the pope by its founder, William of Aquitaine. Through it, and its ever increasing number of dependent houses, the idea that outside interference was undesirable gained currency not just among monks but among lay men as well. No wonder that for the century or so following 1050 Cluny and the reforming papacy enjoyed such good relations.

The new orders

Cluny's successes were overt. It gathered about itself an almost feudal network of nearly 1500 dependent smaller monasteries across Germany, Spain, Italy, and France, and encouraged wealthy

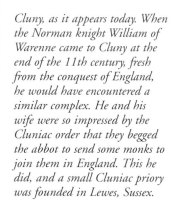

Cluny, as it appears today. When the Norman knight William of Warenne came to Cluny at the end of the 11th century, fresh from the conquest of England, he would have encountered a similar complex. He and his wife were so impressed by the Cluniac order that they begged the abbot to send some monks to join them in England. This he did, and a small Cluniac priory was founded in Lewes, Sussex.

This 15th-century illumination shows St Bernard teaching in a Dominican house. This event could never have occurred – St Bernard died half a century before the Dominican movement got underway – but it shows the close association that came to be perceived between the intellectual rigour for which St Bernard was famed and the Dominican Order, which increasingly sunk its roots in the universities.

sinners to repent by donating their goods to its houses. It emphasized pilgrimage as a means of penitence and placed its authority behind a number of high-profile schemes to limit aristocratic warmongering – including the Peace and Truce of God – which restricted knightly violence to certain activities and certain times. Consequently it became very much part of the pious noble's way of life. It even encouraged "lay brothers" to join its ranks and tend its fields as a partial commitment to a monastic life. For all its many merits, by the early 12th century, Cluny had become far more wordly than its early abbots had ever intended.

Towards the end of the 11th century, Bruno of Cologne, a former master of theology at Rheims, established a rule and community of monks at La Chartreuse, high in the Alps. Their houses were rough and ready, their diet intensely meagre, their shirts often woven of hair. In fact, their only extravagance was a rich library. Such was the withdrawal from the world of what was to become the Carthusian order that its monks met with each other only a few times each week, and water was piped to each monk's cell to limit accidental encounters. Elsewhere, at Citeaux in Burgundy, a disenchanted Cluniac monk, Robert of Molesme, had established a house according to his own austere principles at Citeaux in France. Robert himself returned to the Cluniacs, but his foundation prospered to become the home of the Cistercian order. Seeking to return to the letter of St Benedict's Rule, the community devoted a fixed part of each day to manual labour. It is a fitting irony that, as the Middle Ages wore on, the Cistercian order gained a reputation for large-scale cultivation and land management.

Bernard of Clairvaux

The Cistercians came to be more widespread and influential than any other order. Preferring remote sites where they could be alone and self-sufficient – such as Fountains, Rievaulx, and Tintern in England – they became masters of civil engineering in desolate river valleys. They were fortunate in having a series of dynamic abbots. The third abbot, Stephen Harding, compared Cistercian copies of scripture with those housed elsewhere and, in consultation with native speakers of Hebrew, sought to produce an authoritative version. Most important, however, because of his many influential and widespread writings, was St Bernard of Clairvaux. He joined the Cistercians in 1113 and founded his famous house at Clairvaux in 1115. By the time of his death in 1153, it had 65 daughter houses.

On reading some of the many surviving letters of St Bernard, one could be forgiven for thinking that he wanted to turn the whole world into Citeaux, as seen in his exchanges with his friend William of St Thierry concerning Cluniac architecture or his attacks on the pomp of Peter Abelard. But in –addition to his constant engagement with the key spiritual questions of the time, his great ability was in finding a path for those who could not submit wholly to the cloistered life. He encouraged his friend St Norbert in his establishment of the Premonstratensian Canons, who were to be partly monastic, partly active, and partly apostolic. He was also a staunch supporter of the new military orders formed in Jerusalem in the 12th century for the defence of the kingdom. For all the wrong reasons, the Knights Templar and Knights Hospitaller are better known today than any other monastic order.

Christian Microcosms   126–7 ▶
Redefining the Papacy   132–3 ▶
Heretics, Mystics, and Friars   176–7 ▶
The Council of Trent   214–15 ▶

Heretics, Mystics, and Friars

The monastic ideal was a simple life of spiritual toil, lived out in a community which offered support, provided structure, and limited excess. For some this did not go far enough – the monastery brought its own temptations. Others found certain teachings of the Catholic Church unacceptable. This was as much a time of charismatic dissenters as it was of orthodox teachers. The friction between them was a seismic force.

Asceticism

In the Middle Ages, an obvious means of asserting one's holy credentials was in great acts of physical privation and spiritual resolution. In the first few centuries of Christianity, feats of endurance had become almost a spiritual industry. St Macarius of Alexandria, for example, could not bear to be outdone and would seek to better any act of self-denial. He never matched the performance of St Symeon the Stylite, who stood unprotected on top of a pillar for 33 years. St Daniel was made of yet sterner stuff and bested him by three months. For many, this ostentatious withdrawal from the world of the flesh, in its milder forms at least, had a more obvious spiritual currency than popes on their thrones and bishops in their palaces. Not only did it offer inspiration to souls searching spiritual solace, but it also provided a ready weapon with which protesters could attack the perceived errors and excesses of the established Church.

Heresy

In the medieval Church, those who followed a religion other than Christianity were pitied or derided as schismatics. Heresy, however, was in the eye of the beholder. Over the centuries, certain sects had indeed placed themselves in clear opposition to the central precepts of Christianity, but many preachers, who perhaps saw themselves in the mould of Elijah or John the Baptist, found their teaching branded heretical by popes who felt them too close, or too far, for comfort. It was an easy trap to fall into, and it caught many who did little more than rock a bishop's boat. In the early 12th century, Arnold of Brescia, a man of educated and noble background, preached a return to apostolic simplicity and was condemned by Pope Innocent II for his troubles. Later in the 12th century, a merchant from Lyons called Peter Waldo chose to do as St Matthew advised and sold his goods to give to the poor. He embarked on a life of preaching, translating the scriptures into the vernacular to aid him in his task. As a broadly anti-clerical layman, teaching and interpreting the Word, he and his followers, the Waldensians, a movement practising extreme humility, teetered on the edge of condemnation for many years.

Most damaging to the medieval Church was the Cathar movement. The Cathar answer to why there was evil in a world created by a good God was a simple but drastic extension of Christian belief: a Light God reigned over the spiritual world, but a Dark God presided over the physical. Such a belief came very close to denying the incarnation of God and the possibility of His redeeming the world, but its simple answers to questions of injustice and the human condition appealed to many who felt little affinity with bejewelled bishops and mercenary monks. Cathar preachers roamed the countryside in pairs, dissociating themselves from the physical world by ever greater degrees of deprivation and gaining ever more converts, especially among the villages and lesser nobility of southern France. Perhaps the greatest catalyst to its success was that it welcomed women as active participants.

Friars

The medieval Church had little answer to these attacks. Many popular movements for poverty such as the Waldensians overtly practised what

A grisly illustration of the Knights Templar being burned at the stake following their condemnation by Philip IV of France between 1307 and 1314. The illustration comes from a 14th-century manuscript of the World Chronicle *by Bernard Guy, the most infamous of the Dominican inquisitors.*

Giotto's fresco of St Francis of Assisi preaching to the birds from the Upper Church at Assisi, Italy. The fresco cycle at Assisi portrays the establishment view of St Francis and the friars. Following the papal line, it very much underplays the extent to which Francis felt unease at the increasingly institutional nature of the order.

they preached. Some had become intertwined with those parts of society with which the Church had little contact, particularly the urban poor. It was perhaps in recognition of this fact that Pope Innocent III and in particular Cardinal Ugolino, the future Pope Gregory IX, were so keen to foster and encourage the activities of a young merchant from Assisi who, at the beginning of the 13th century, renounced all worldly goods to preach and care for the sick.

St Francis of Assisi is one of the best-known and most charismatic figures of the Middle Ages, which is just how his official biographers wanted it. Within a few years of his revelation, he had acquired a small group of followers, the *fratres minor* (little brothers), or friars, and written a simple Rule for their lives. At the heart of their existence was poverty. The friars were to be homeless, begging for the smallest amount necessary to keep body and soul together. Although Francis met with the most powerful men of his time, even trying to convert the Egyptian sultan al-Kamil, he never accepted that any good could come of money. He wished to die a hermit, but his example was too useful a one to be allowed to pass unnoticed. When Ugolino became pope, he ordained that the Franciscan order could hold property and buildings by means of a third party to aid in its

organization and propagation. Step by step, the papacy remodelled the original order into a spiritual powerhouse from which St Francis would have recoiled.

Francis considered knowledge to be a form of property, which was not a view shared by his contemporary Dominic of Guzman. St Dominic was also of a wealthy background, and, having acquired a first-rate education, he, too, renounced his material wealth. During the first two decades of the 13th century, he wandered the Midi region of France as a pauper, preaching in particular to Cathars. Where others had failed, his poverty and austerity allowed him to succeed. He and his small group of followers came to the attention of Innocent III, who recognized the potential of educated but unworldly preachers and supported Dominic in his establishment of the order that bears his name. By 1219, he had set up houses in Paris, Bologna, Rome, Madrid, and Seville. Two years later, Dominic himself succumbed to the rigours of his self-imposed lifestyle. Fifty years after that there were 450 Dominican priories across Europe. The Dominicans became prominent in the universities and were often called upon to provide official theologians; because of this they were to become the order in charge of the Inquisition.

HERETICS, MYSTICS, AND FRIARS   177

Pilgrimage

In 1026, Duke Richard II of Normandy together with Abbot Richard of St Vanne set out for the Holy Land. A six-month journey brought them to Jerusalem on Palm Sunday 1027. Holy Week was spent visiting the sites of Christ's Passion, culminating at Calvary where, according to the abbot's biographer, many tears were shed. It is easy to think of this as an elaborate public relations exercise, but for many the tears were genuine. Pilgrimage had become an integral part of the religious life.

Pilgrimage is founded in the idea that there is something special about proximity to holy places and in particular holy relics. Consequently, individuals and communities went to great lengths to safeguard and venerate those in their possession. This 8th-century reliquary from Lombardy, which would once have housed the bone of a saint, is richly worked in silver and gilt.

Given the right sort of encouragement, pilgrimage sites could develop very quickly, as was the case with the shrine of Thomas à Becket at Canterbury. It was already exerting a powerful attraction within a few years of the archbishop's death, and by the 14th century, it was the primary pilgrimage destination in England.

Relics

A pilgrimage to Jerusalem would have seemed infinitely remote to most people, but the physical remains of saints, together with items connected with the life and death of Christ, held a fundamental place in the fabric of medieval life. They could be found on altars to invoke blessing, in courts of law to guarantee oaths, and on the battlefield to confer protection. For many ordinary people, they were the main conduits of supernatural power. Particularly powerful were the relics of martyrs, the healing properties of which often bore a grisly relationship to the martyr's demises: the relics of a decapitated saint, for example, were held to be very good for headaches.

For religious communities, relics ensured both a sympathetic ear in heaven along with considerable prestige on earth, so much so that monks plundered tombs, raided other churches, and made dubious deals in the hope of acquiring a holy finger or toe. Not surprisingly, selling holy relics could be a lucrative business, and there was a good deal of deliberate fraud. The Pardoner in Chaucer's *Canterbury Tales* did rather well for himself selling pig's bones to the faithful, and Protestant reformers took great delight in counting how many fingers of St Peter were in circulation, for example, or speculating as to how large a galleon could be built from the fragments of the True Cross.

Penitence

Why would a pilgrim travel to see relics if St Peter's fingers were to be found throughout Europe? Certainly the relics of more highly placed saints were believed to possess a greater potency than their lesser brethren, and the closer a saint had been to Christ the greater their appeal. Thus Rome, which could claim St Peter and St Paul in addition to countless Christian martyrs, was second only to Jerusalem as a pilgrimage destination.

There was also a threefold penitential aspect to pilgrimage. First, journeys beyond the horizon were generally uncommon, and so pilgrimage was an arduous business that could stand simply as punishment for venial sins. Secondly, as this idea gained momentum, certain pilgrimages brought with them official Church indulgences – set amounts of time off purgatory for good behaviour – and different destinations could be rated against each other: three pilgrimages to Canterbury were "worth" one to Rome, which itself had to be visited twice to match Jerusalem. Thirdly, a saint might intercede with God, according to his or her own rank, to remit yet more sin. The great 12th-century church at Conques in France housed the (stolen) relics of a Roman martyr, Faith. A tympanum over the west door showed wonderfully horrific scenes of the Last Judgement, reminding the pilgrim that the intercession of St Faith was worth having. With that in mind, they might very well dig a little deeper in their pockets.

Santiago de Compostela

One element in the great success of the cult of St Faith, in all other respects a rather minor saint, was that Conques was on the Camino de Santiago (the Way of St James) – the great pilgrim road running from Le Puy in northern France to Compostela in north-west Spain. In the early 9th century, Bishop Diego of Compostela announced that he had uncovered the body of St James in his cathedral's foundations. The discovery was a happy one. St James was an apostle, the only member of Christ's inner circle whose relics were not known to reside anywhere else, and since the 7th century it was believed that St James had visited Spain. A steady trickle of pilgrims came to the shrine, which grew in importance in the 10th and 11th centuries. By the 12th century, Santiago de Compostela exerted a greater pull for pilgrims than anywhere other than Jerusalem and Rome. St James's cockle shell became a great mark of prestige and spiritual succour worn by successful pilgrims (or those who wished to appear so) for centuries to come. Compostela no longer had bishops; it had archbishops.

Bardsey Island

Bardsey Island, just off the tip of the Lleyn Peninsula in Wales, was known in the Middle Ages as the Isle of 20,000 Saints, after the number of saints believed to be buried there. A prescribed pilgrimage route ran down the north coast of the peninsula from church to church, most of which housed their own relics. Almost unknown now, during the Middle Ages it was a site of national importance. Two pilgrimages to the island were the equivalent of one to Canterbury. In a wonderfully typical piece of medieval circularity, burial on Bardsey guaranteed that one became a saint.

Santiago was closely associated with Cluny. The Burgundian house established dependent priories and hostels along the Way of St James to put up weary pilgrims, many of which acquired their own relics and developed their own cults until the Way became almost a package tour. Cluny also seems to have encouraged northern knights to travel to Spain to aid the border kingdoms of Navarre and Léon-Castile in their battles with Muslims who had annexed large parts of central and southern Spain in the 8th century. These knights bore the standard of St James.

Pilgrimage and crusade

When medieval writers referred to the events now known as the Crusades, they spoke only of armed pilgrimages. Crusaders, like pilgrims, received spiritual privileges – indulgences – which in the popular mind at least meant that those who died on crusade were guaranteed an immediate place in Heaven, their sins wiped clean. The idea of long, arduous penitential journeys was a necessary precursor to the preaching of any crusading ideas. More important still was the understanding that there was something of special and immediate importance about the Holy Land, even a millennium or more after Christ's ascension. Relics, too, played an important part in the development of a crusading ideology. In 1098, the Crusaders were besieged at Antioch by the army of Karbuqa, emir of Mosul. The situation was desperate until a group of soldiers from Provence were guided by a vision to discover in the Church of St Peter the lance that had pierced the side of the crucified Christ. The effect on morale was miraculous – what greater divine endorsement? – and three days later the Turkish army was routed.

The Crusades for the Holy Land

In early 1095, representatives of the Byzantine emperor Alexius I Comnenus appealed to Pope Urban II for military aid against the incursions of the Seljuk Turks into Asia Minor. In November, in a stage-managed showcase in Clermont in the Auvergne, Urban called Western Christendom to arms to reunite the Eastern and Western Churches.

A late 12th-century portrait of Saladin I, sultan of Egypt, from the Fatamid school of painting. Though "the enemy", Saladin was much admired in Western Christendom for his martial valour and personal nobility. In his Divine Comedy, *Dante placed him not in Hell, but in purgatory together with Virgil, Homer, and other virtuous non-Christians.*

The origins of the crusading idea

The Crusades were responsible for fundamental changes in Western Europe. Not only did the movement of tens of thousands of men, women, horses, and their provisions to and from Palestine and the East necessitate a revolution in transport, finance, and government, but the Crusades also brought the world beyond the borders of Western Christendom more sharply into focus than ever before. Their effects are far easier to identify than their causes. Certainly once under way, any large-scale military endeavour gathers its own momentum, but what initially inspired so very many people across Europe to answer the pope's call?

The events of 1095 were not wholly unexpected. Gregory VII had thought he might lead his own expedition in 1074, and Western knights had been fighting the Arab world under the banner of the cross in southern Spain for many decades. The

idea of a just or holy war had been gaining intellectual ground since the time of St Augustine, but it is unlikely to have penetrated popular consciousness. More influential was the long-established tradition of pilgrimage and veneration of the Holy Land, together with the popular movement known as the Peace and Truce of God. The Peace and Truce sought to place limits on knightly violence, forbidding it outright on certain holy days and under certain circumstances, offering a manageable compromise to many nobles who might otherwise have fallen under outright condemnation. In time, the Peace and Truce became the badge of honour of the knight of God. Urban melded these ideas together to form a weapon and offered as added inducement remission of penances imposed by the Church in this lifetime to those who "took the cross". Fairly quickly this developed into the idea that those

Crusaders answered the call of Urban II from across Christendom, although most knights seem to have come from France, the Western Empire, and the Norman lands. The pope expected a single army to march, but in the event four almost independent professional armies formed, together with a fifth popular movement, each of which followed their own routes to Constantinople. They converged in the spring of 1097.

Christianity and Islam 1095–1099

- Latin Christendom
- Byzantine Empire 1097 (Greek Orthodox Christians)
- Byzantine frontier 1070
- Muslim states
- Byzantine Christians under Muslim rule

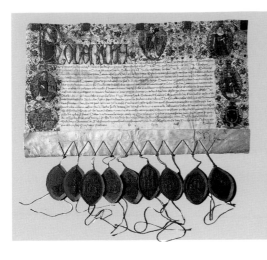

Indulgences

Indulgences, official written grants which remitted penances or even bought off time in purgatory, were one of the principal rewards of pilgrims and crusaders, as was the case with this 15th-century German example. But many more were sold for profit by popes, bishops, and lesser scoundrels than ever rewarded the faithful. Pope Nicholas IV (1288–92) paid for most of his new church of Santa Maria Maggiore at Colonna, including elaborate mosaics, out of indulgence income, while pardoners, who sold fake indulgences to line their own pockets, were the butt of much medieval satire.

who died on crusade went directly to heaven. In addition to this spiritual reward, there was the chance for unlimited plunder.

The First Crusade

Within a year of Urban's sermon at Clermont, expeditions were being prepared by some of the great lords of Europe, including Hugh, brother of King Philip I of France; Robert, Duke of Normandy; and Stephen, Count of Blois. They were joined by one of the most dynamic military leaders in Christendom, the Norman Bohemund, fresh from conquests in southern Italy. The first contingents reached Constantinople in November 1096, though huge numbers had been lost en route. By April 1097, the various crusading armies were camped outside Constantinople and starting to fight among themselves. Alexius sought to extract oaths of loyalty from these increasingly unwelcome guests, but ultimately the Crusades were more disastrous for Byzantium than the Muslim world.

Two years after they had gathered at Constantinople, in July 1099, the crusaders captured Jerusalem. It had taken two major battles at Dorylaeum and Antioch, and three long sieges at Nicaea, Antioch, and Jerusalem to bring them there, and they had suffered terrible losses. The expedition had done nothing to reunite the Eastern and Western Churches – if anything, it had fostered mutual distrust between Greece and Rome – but it had returned a large part of Asia Minor to Byzantium, and Westerners had carved out four states for themselves in the East: Edessa, Antioch, Jerusalem, and Tripoli. In the words of the chronicler Fulcher of Chartres, many poor people became extremely wealthy.

The Crusades to 1204

The establishment of the Crusader States committed Westerners to crusading for some time. The Second Crusade, launched in 1146, was a response to the conquest of Edessa by Zengi, Atabeg of Mosul, at Christmas 1144. Pope Eugenius III and King Louis VII of France sought to muster a response, but to no real avail. It took a lengthy preaching campaign by Bernard of Clairvaux to get the enterprise off the ground, rallying French, German, Spanish, and English leaders. Perhaps because it was initially so dependent on one man's charisma, once under way the Second Crusade was less able to withstand the horrors of war, and it suffered major defeats at Dorylaeum and Laodecia, almost collapsing in confusion. Only the discipline and determination of the Knights Templar saved the army from total defeat in the winter of 1147–8. Bernard was blamed for the failure of the Second Crusade, somewhat unjustly, but the real losers were the Franks settled and increasingly isolated in the Crusader States. By 1187, the brilliant sultan of Egypt, Saladin, had captured Jerusalem and Tripoli.

The Third Crusade, launched to recapture Jerusalem in 1190, was under the command of three kings, Richard the Lionheart of England, Philip II of France, and Frederick Barbarossa of Germany. None trusted the others, and so each planned meticulously for his own safety. Following some modest successes, Richard, by then the effective leader, made a three-year truce with Saladin in 1192. Hostilities were resumed under Pope Innocent III in 1198, and the Crusades were placed on an altogether more commercial footing. Venice financed the expedition on unfavourable terms, leaving the pope and Crusaders in debt. When the deposed Byzantine emperor Alexius Angelus offered the West vast sums of money to help him regain his throne, the possibilities of financial gain finally outstripped religious and even political motivation. On 13 April 1204, the crusaders breached the walls of Constantinople. The next three days were spent pillaging the richest city in the world.

The Other Crusades

In the late 11th century, Islam had been seen to present a threat on two fronts, both in the east and in the Iberian Peninsula. Pagan Slavs were targeted by the Second Crusade. The campaigns of Henry the Lion, Duke of Saxony, against the pagan Wends of the Baltic were granted crusade status by Pope Eugenius III in 1147. In 1209, Innocent III inaugurated the Albigensian Crusade against the Cathar heretics.

Spain

Not until 1113 did campaigning against Islam in the Iberian Peninsula earn the same indulgences as campaigning in the Holy Land, even though it had a far longer history. After the collapse of the Caliphate of Cordoba in 1002, Muslim Spain had broken up into a number of small emirates. The Christian kingdoms in the north were just as fragmentary, but, as they were poorer, they were less cultured and more militant than their neighbours. The first to take any action against Islam was Ferdinand I of Léon-Castile, conquering much of what was to become Portugal. After his death, his sons Sancho and Alfonso fought for the throne. Alfonso eventually emerged as ruler. He had as his general one of the best-known and most revered military leaders of Christendom, Rodrigo Diaz, known as El Cid, who carved out a principality for himself at Valencia and combined diplomacy and brilliant military tactics to limit Muslim re-conquest. Alfonso captured Toledo in 1085, a great success, but after the death of El Cid in 1099 was unable to hold back the vast African army of the Almoravid prophet-general Yusuf. The Christian initiative

passed to Aragon, and, by the 1170s, the Christian kingdoms had regained some of their former strength. In the wake of setbacks in the East, the papacy took a renewed interest in the Iberian Peninsula. Under the sponsorship of the tireless and implacable Innocent III, the united forces of Navarre, Castile, and Aragon, supported by some French knights, inflicted a massive defeat on the Almohad Muslims under al-Nasir at Las Navas in 1206. This battle has traditionally been seen as the great watershed of Spanish medieval history.

The Albigensian Crusade

The initial response of the papacy to the growth of the Cathar heresy was one of preaching followed by excommunication, but its appeal was too great and too entrenched and the failings of many orthodox priests too obvious for this to have any long-term effect. Innocent III sent regular missions to Languedoc, the Cathar heartland, but clearly felt the frustration of a century and a half of reforming popes before him and became ever more militant in his language. He appealed initially to the French king, Philip II, then to the foremost French

An illustration of a battle between Christians and Muslims from the 14th-century Romance of Geoffrey of Bouillon. *Such conflicts were the single greatest formative influence upon the Iberian Peninsula in the Middle Ages, determining its territorial and political structure and cultural and religious outlooks for centuries to come.*

Montsegur in southern France, constructed as a Cathar stronghold at the beginning of the 13th century. Understandably, it was thought impregnable. When the castle finally fell to royalist forces in 1244, four generations of its lord's family were found there. As the Inquisition was to discover, Catharism was often a family affair with widely spread roots.

lords to back his words with force of arms, but it took the murder of a papal legate in Languedoc in 1208 to spur the French nobility into action.

In 1209, a crusade of troops from France and its neighbours swept down the Rhone to capture several Cathar strongholds; however, many, having completed the term for which they had signed up and got their time off Purgatory, returned home. A new leader was chosen, the efficient and brutal Simon de Montfort, who managed to make enemies of most of the rulers of southern France. He killed in battle Peter II of Aragon, an orthodox ruler seeking only to defend his interests north of the Pyrenees. De Montfort himself was killed besieging Toulouse in 1218, and over the next six years the enterprise was beaten back. King Louis VIII of France led a second invasion in 1226, and three years later the south surrendered. The crusade had been as horrific as any of the Eastern ventures. The motto of one of its leaders is indicative of the crusaders' brutality: "kill them all, let God sort them out".

The Albigensian Crusade, named after the Cathar stronghold Albi, was unlike all others because it was directed against an internal enemy. As with the early Crusades, however, it highlighted the extent to which such undertakings were dependent on the abilities and charisma of their rulers and subject to those rulers pursuing their own interests. The lessons learnt in the early years of the Crusades led the Fourth Lateran council of 1215 to lay down ordinances requiring the co-operation of secular powers in the fight against heresy. It also made provision for the Inquisition.

The Inquisition

The Inquisition was created by Pope Gregory IX in the early 13th century to seek out heretics and either bring them back within the fold of orthodoxy or punish their obstinacy. Inquisitors, for the most part Dominican friars because of their impeccable spiritual credentials and skills in doctrinal debate, followed set circuits in pairs. Upon arrival in a new region, they demanded that heretics be denounced or themselves come forwards. The fear which will forever be associated with the Inquisition arose out of the fact that witnesses made their denunciations in private: communities could be destroyed quickly. A person denounced as a heretic had no legal defence, no knowledge of his accuser, and only a vague idea of what evidence had been brought against him. Torture came to play an increasing part in proceedings. For most, innocent or guilty, the only option was confession in the hope that the penance imposed would be bearable. Those who refused to admit guilt were deemed obdurate and handed over to the secular authorities for punishment. In some famous cases, they were burned alive. In the vast majority of cases, punishments were less brutal, and the accused lived to repent, in public at least. Nonetheless, for most individuals and communities, a visit from the Inquisition could mean only horror, suspicion, and pain.

The Great Schism

Boniface VIII (1294–1303) possessed all the characteristics of a medieval pope in abundance. He was very active in politics and was responsible for a significant contribution to the corpus of canon law and the Bull *Unam Sanctam*, an extreme assertion of papal supremacy. In 1303, he was kidnapped by an agent of the French king Philip IV and died in captivity. French pressure mounted, and six years later the papacy went into exile.

A contemporary illustration of a battle between Hussites and crusaders from the so-called Jena Codex. *Hus' followers were so enraged by his excommunication that they launched what was in effect a national uprising. In 1419, the pope announced a general crusade against them, but their popular base was too strong. Year after year, waves of German crusaders were defeated.*

The Great Schism of 1378–1417 divided Europe along political lines defined almost directly by the relationship of a particular country with France. Scotland, for instance, was often an ally of France in its conflicts with England, and hence threw such weight as it had behind the Avignon pope. England, on the other hand, preferred Rome for the same reason.

Exile

Thanks to the efforts of the French faction in Rome, Pope Clement V took the papacy into exile at Avignon in 1309. It finally returned to Rome under Gregory IX in 1377. Avignon itself was an independent papal enclave, but, whatever half-hearted notions of escaping politics were held, French influence was felt all around. All seven Avignon popes were Frenchmen elected by a French-dominated college of cardinals. Unsurprisingly, many of its decisions were made with French interests in mind. Most notorious was the trial and dissolution of the Knights Templar (1307–14), culminating in the public burning of the Grand Master, Jacques de Molai, pursued largely because of the vendetta of Philippe le Bel, grandson of King Louis IX.

Many countries were ambivalent in their attitude towards the Avignon papacy and its spiritual authority lost much credibility. Despite the threat of the Inquisition, ever more unorthodox sects sprang up across Europe, often following the model of the friars. The Franciscan Spirituals (Fraticelli), Beguines, and Friends of God all rejected property and the trappings of clerical religion, emphasizing instead mysticism and personal communion with God. Particularly influential were the teachings of the Czech John Hus and Englishman John Wycliffe. Wycliffe, an Oxford academic, denounced wealth, papal supremacy, and the doctrine of transubstantiation. His followers, the Lollards, formed the most widespread popular religious movement in medieval England. After his death, Wycliffe's body was exhumed and burnt for heresy. Hus, once head of the University of Prague, developed Wycliffe's ideas in Bohemia and became the focus for Czech resentment of the German hierarchy.

Schism

On its return to Rome in 1377, the College of Cardinals was politically riven and immediately managed to elect two men as pope simultaneously, Urban VI and Clement VII. There had been anti-popes in the past, but never before had the papacy so obviously brought such a scandal down on its own head. Over the next 30 years, neither man was moved to compromise, and both were given to atrocious reprisals against their opponents. Finally, in 1409 a third pope was elected by the increasingly desperate and terrified College of Cardinals. This situation persisted until 1414, when the German king Sigismund, with the support of the despairing Parisian professors, summoned all cardinals, bishops, abbots, friars, princes, and teachers to Constance to settle the matter. Eighteen thousand answered his call.

The Council of Constance lasted three years. It brought the schism to an end by setting aside all three popes and electing unanimously in their place Cardinal Odo Colonna as Martin V (1417–31). The council sought to limit the power of the papacy over secular institutions, but it also burned John Hus as a destabilizing heretic. A further council to

The Great Schism 1378–1417
- Areas recognizing Rome-based pope
- Areas recognizing Avignon-based pope
- Centre of Hussite activity
- Centre of Lollard activity

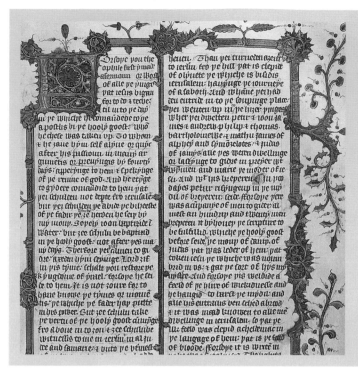

Wycliffe's Bible

For much of the Middle Ages, the Bible was only ever available in the Vulgate, ie Latin, version. To John Wycliffe, religious reformer, this created an unbridgeable chasm between lay people and their personal relationship with God, perpetuating the distance between the clergy and the people. He and his followers, known as the Lollards, set about translating the whole of scripture into English. It was a massive task, condemned as heretical, but thanks to the efforts of a network of sympathetic nobles, the English Bible spread across the country. In this way, as in many others, the Lollard movement was a Reformation before its time.

consider the relationship of Church and State was instituted, eventually taking place under the protection of the Duke of Savoy in 1431. It came into conflict with the then pope, Eugene IV, over the old problems and ended with the Duke himself being elected as anti-pope. For all its original intentions, in the long run, the conciliar movement reinforced the claims of those who wanted a strong papacy.

The end of the medieval church

It is easy to look back on medieval churchmen and decide that they failed because they were corrupt. After all, even St Thomas Aquinas struggled with the problem of Christian poverty when so many of its exponents seemed to possess an excess of spiritual pride. Reforming popes believed it morally right that, as St Peter's heirs, they should direct secular governments towards the protection of the Church, both at times of military crisis and on a day-to-day institutional level. Medieval Europe was never a theocracy, but there were those who thought it should have been. Urban II and Innocent III came closest to being able to wield secular power as though it was their own – perhaps that was much of the point of the First and Fourth Crusades. But the Church was only one nation whose citizens permitted its leaders to rule, and it was a nation that sprawled over many others.

Wycliffe and Hus were the immediate forerunners of Protestantism, although the name had not then been claimed. Many of their teachings – criticism of the papacy, indulgences, monks, and bish-

ops – made sense to the wholly orthodox. Chaucer had mocked the parson in his *Canterbury Tales* in terms more comic but no less scathing than had Gregory VII the illiterate priest, while humanist thinkers of the 12th and 13th centuries had explored the special relationship between the individual and God, and had found in it divine grace. Over the course of the Middle Ages, however, a growing religious literacy across Europe allowed such ideas to be extended to their logical conclusions. Wycliffe's precept "justification by faith", later Martin Luther's, might not seem so very radical, but it brought with it a rejection of all that was seen to be extraneous or diverting: confession and absolution before a priest, the intercession of saints, the penance of pilgrimage, and above all the authority of popes to bind and loose the sins of men either on earth or in heaven.

By the middle of the 16th century, Martin Luther had nailed 95 refutations of the practice of indulgences to a church door and Jean Calvin had denounced transubstantiation as "conjury". But if the tide was on the turn, it still had a long way to come in. Wycliffe had denounced what he called the magic of the medieval church, in particular exorcisms and hallowing, but we should not be too quick to bid medieval mysticism farewell. It is worth remembering that the sign of the cross, oaths on the Bible in court, faith healing, blessing with holy water and pilgrimage have all survived both the Reformation and the scientific revolution as parts of both Catholic and Protestant spirituality.

Iconoclasm and the
East–West Divide 134–5 ▶
Heretics, Mystics, and Friars 176–7 ▶
The Rise of Protestantism 202–3 ▶
The Council of Trent 214–15 ▶

THE DAWN OF MODERN EUROPE

1400–1599

POLITICS AND GOVERNMENT

1493 Pope Alexander VI publishes a bull dividing the new world between Spain and Portugal.

1492 Subjugation of Granada. Ferdinand and Isabella end Moorish presence in Spanish peninsula and unite kingdoms of Castile and Aragon.

1485 Accession of Henry VII of England after the Battle of Bosworth ends the Wars of the Roses.

1477 Battle of Nancy. Defeat and death of Charles the Bold breaks power of Burgundy.

1431 Joan of Arc is executed by the English

1400   1425   1450   1475

SOCIETY AND CULTURE

1415 Jan Hus, Bohemian Protestant martyr burnt at the stake in Prague.

1450 Johannes Gutenberg develops moveable type for printing. The Gutenberg Bible, the first printed book, is printed in 1453.

1492 Columbus sets sail on *Santa Maria*. He arrives in the Bahamas in October.

1500

1550

1524 Peasants Revolt in Germany.

1530 The Diet of Augsburg. Protestant movement in Germany takes institutional form.

1533 Henry VIII is excommunicated by Pope Clement VIII. Henry becomes head of the newly formed Church of England in 1534.

1519 Election of Charles V as Holy Roman Emperor. Spanish conquistador Cortes completes his conquest of Mexico.

1571 Defeat of the Ottoman fleet at Lepanto by the Holy League of Spain, Venice, and Rome.

1572 St Bartholomew's Day Massacre. Over 3000 Huguenots die in Paris following the order of the massacre by Charles IX under the influence of his mother Catherine de'Medici.

1555 Peace of Augsburg brings settlement of religious question in Germany.

1598 Edict of Nantes brings end to religious war in France. Death of Philip II of Spain.

1568–1609 The Dutch revolt against Spanish rule in the Netherlands.

1587 Execution of the Catholic Mary Queen of Scots by Elizabeth I of England.

1558 Accession of Elizabeth I in England tilts strategic balance in Western Europe towards Protestantism.

1576 Sack of Antwerp by the Spanish.

1588 Defeat of the Spanish Armada by the English fleet.

---

00   1525   1550   1575   1600

1513 Machiavelli writes *The Prince* (published in 1532).

1508–20 Raphael is at work on the papal palace in Rome.

1519–21 Portuguese explorer Ferdinand Megallan starts his circumnavigation of the globe. In 1521 he reaches the East Indies (the Philippines) where he is killed. One ship returns to Spain to complete the circumnavigation of the globe.

1516 Publication of asmus' *New Testament* Thomas More's *Utopia.*

1517 Luther's protest against indulgences ignites the Reformation.

1556 Ignatius Loyola dies. He was the founder of the Jesuit Order.

1568–80 Montaigne writes his *Essais,* which launch a new literary form.

1582 Italy, Spain, France, and Portugal adopt the Gregorian calender.

1594–6 Shakespeare writes first major plays for London theatre.

1599 Globe Theatre is built in London.

1532–4 Publication of Rabelais' *Pantagruel* and *Gargantua.*

1532–43 Holbein is active at the court of Henry VIII.

1547–64 Michelangelo paints the Sistine Chapel in the Vatican.

1500

1550

*The spectacular victory of the
Holy Alliance of Spain, Venice,
and the pope over the Ottoman
navy at the Battle of Lepanto
in 1571 was a rare example of
successful co-operation between
European states against a
common enemy. More often,
competition would drive them
into enmity and conflict.*

MODERN MONARCHIES AND STATES

At the dawn of the 16th century, the political map of modern Europe began to take shape. As the feudal regime crumbled, a new administrative apparatus emerged as kingship became more confident and government more ambitious and wide-ranging.

The dawn of a new era brought important changes to the political map of Europe. France, a hundred years before, almost submerged beneath the challenge of England and Burgundy, emerged triumphant from the tribulation of the Hundred Years War. Suppression of the last independent apanages of Britanny and Bourbon early in the 16th century consolidated a rich and densely populated territory. Meanwhile, in the south, the unification of Castile and Aragon heralded the rise of Spain. When the Catholic monarchs, Ferdinand of Aragon and Isabella of Castile, applied the combined resources of their kingdoms to the subjugation of the Moorish kingdom of Granada in 1492, the last vestige of Muslim power in the peninsula was removed. At first the union of crowns was personal only, a consequence of their marriage: the full unification of the kingdoms was achieved only with the accession of their grandson, Charles of Ghent, also the heir to the rich Burgundian lands of the Netherlands. When, through his other grandfather Maximilian I, Charles was also able to make good his claim to the imperial crown in Germany, the Holy Roman Empire, a formidable new power, had emerged. Conflict with the other great continental power, France, was virtually assured.

Meanwhile, to the north and east, other new monarchies took shape. In England, the new Tudor dynasty emerged from the chaos of the Wars of the Roses eager to assert itself on the European stage. In Scandinavia, Sweden broke away from the Danish crown, to which it had been united for three centuries, beginning a bitter rivalry that would dominate the affairs of the Baltic for the rest of the century. All of these developments had two consequences of fundamental importance: the centre of gravity of European affairs moved north and westwards, and the moral ascendancy of the Italian city-states, during the medieval period both economic powerhouses and admired models of government, was effectively past.

The emergence of these new states had profound consequences for European society. Inveterate competitiveness bred a culture of display with rulers vying for the most sophisticated courts, the best music, and the most lively scholars and artists. This was Renaissance monarchy: costly, ostentatious, and elegant. The ambition to build territory brought a large increase of diplomatic activity as rulers sought to create alliances. Then, as states fell inevitably into war, the need to raise troops brought an increasing need for higher taxation.

As states were changing, so, too, was warfare. The growing influence of firepower and artillery made the cavalry, the mainstay of medieval feudalism, far less potent. Instead, states raised ever larger armies of relatively untrained infantry. Sieges, rather than battles, increasingly defined the outcome of a conflict.

With the need for more taxes came the need for a more sophisticated feudal state to raise and spend the money. More and more, the crown aspired to direct rule over the furthest territories, rather than relying on the authority of the local magnate nobles as its representative. The institutional effect of these changes varied. In some parts of Europe representative assemblies became true partners in government, such as the Estates of Eastern Europe. Elsewhere, the king ruled through officials alone, and representative assemblies, such as the French Estates General, diminished in importance.

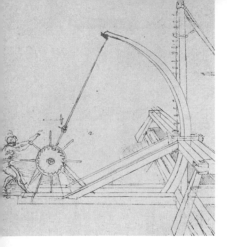

Science and Technology

The great advances of the 16th century would not have been possible without technical innovation, but most of the major technical advances were gradual and incremental, building on a body of knowledge inherited from the medieval period. Only with printing did the period witness genuine technological breakthrough.

Leonardo da Vinci, catapult – sketch. The technical advances of the Renaissance involved a restless quest for knowledge in all fields. In this respect, Leonardo da Vinci was the archetypal Renaissance polymath: a man for whom scientific observation and artistic endeavor were two sides of an all-encompassing search for new knowledge.

1400–1599

THE DAWN OF MODERN EUROPE

A page from the Gutenberg Bible. Printing represented the most staggering technical advance of the age, offering literally boundless growth in the capacities of the book to reach an ever expanding audience. In the first age, however, purchasers still expected luxury artifacts, and many of the first books closely resemble the highly illustrated manuscripts they would gradually replace.

When it comes to the field of technological change it would be misleading to make too radical a distinction between the medieval world and the era that followed. Most of the truly transforming technological innovations arose out of the needs of medieval craft societies and through the patient application of trial and error. This was true both of printing – the triumph of medieval guild technology – and of the improvements in ship design that made possible long-distance voyages of discovery. Only new departures in the field of cartography illustrate a truly new world view at work, and here, ironically, the voyages of exploration were stimulated as much by the mapmakers' errors as by their successes.

Exploration

The voyages of discovery depended in almost equal degree on the new imaginative renderings of space created by cartographers. The seaman of the 15th century made more progress than the more scientifically inclined cartographers. In the world of cartography, much was made of the rediscovery of the work of the 2nd-century Greek mapmaker Ptolemy. From Ptolemy, Columbus and his contemporaries learned that the earth was a perfect sphere (an inaccurate observation, but universally believed at the time), and that the inhabited world extended in a continuous land mass from Europe to the easternmost limit of Asia. But the conclusions drawn from Ptolemy illustrate the dangers of this alluring but only partially accurate knowledge. If Ptolemy were right, sailing west across the ocean offered a plausible route to Asia's riches.

The spatial sense of the 15th century was only partially created from the visual images of maps. While Columbus revered Ptolemy, he was also inspired by prose classics that explored in more colourful ways the exotic glories of the East, such as the travels of Marco Polo and the fictitious work of John de Mandeville, a hugely popular travelogue later revealed as a complete fabrication.

Ignorance and misunderstanding thus played as critical a role in stimulating exploration as true knowledge and technological progress. The

seafarers of the age built on far surer foundations with improvements in navigational techniques and ship design. By the 15th century, great strides had been made in the development of astronomical navigation. By the end of this century, the best Portuguese navigators could calculate their position at sea fairly accurately by a combination of observed latitude and dead reckoning.

The same process of trial and error brought notable steps forward in ship design and rigging. Following the introduction of the square-rigged sail on the main-mast in the 13th century, sailors gradually evolved the full-rigged ship of three masts. All of this permitted a gradual increase in the size of vessels. At the beginning of the 14th century, the normal size of a Hanseatic ship was about 75 tons. By the 16th century, 400 tons had become a normal size for most cogs, and there were numerous Venetians carracks of 600–700 tons. Ships in Europe did not grow much above this size until after 1800. Incremental change of

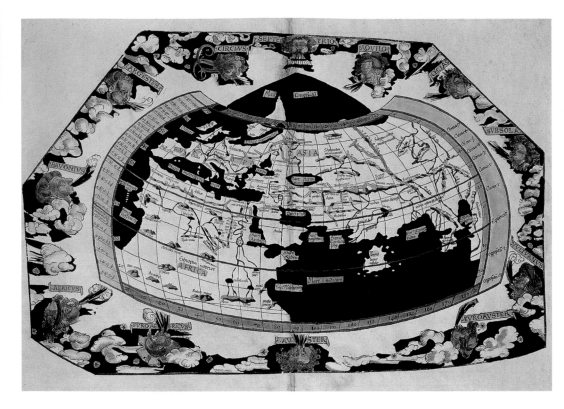

Ptolemy's Map of the World. These rare, brilliant, and evocative cartographical creations illustrate the extent of the geographical knowledge of the ancients (reasonably accurate for Europe and the Levant), but also the frightening degree of ignorance of what lay beyond Europe.

the sort described here is impossible to identify with a particular date or period. The most dramatic technological change of the age – the invention of printing – can be far more accurately dated.

Advances in printing

Between 1440 and 1460, a small number of dedicated and inspired entrepreneurs tackled and solved the problem that unlocked the potential of the vast appetite for books which already existed in medieval society. The technical vision was in its day breathtaking, involving as it did the casting in metal of many thousands of individual letters of uniform size and style, to be used to ink an impression on paper or vellum (cured animal skin), before these could be dried, printed on the reverse, gathered, and folded to form a book. It was an extraordinarily complex, expensive, and daring endeavour, and it was the skills and technologies of the medieval guild society that made this possible, not least of which was the capitalization of such an ambitious project.

In the first years of printing, fortunes were lost amid acrimonious quarrels between inventor and investors. But the book soon outgrew its tentative beginnings and became an independent artefact in its own right. The first printed books appeared in Mainz, Germany, around 1455, yet within 30 years the new technology was generalized around much of Western Europe. By 1480, printing had

been established in at least 30 cities. By the first years of the 16th century, there were presses in over 100 locations, and certain European cities, such as Venice, Paris, Rome, and Antwerp, had already established reputations as major centres of book production.

By this time, the book, until recently the most experimental of technologies, was also attaining its mature form. In the larger, better financed houses, printers had successfully experimented with the use of more sophisticated specialized types such as Hebrew and Greek fonts. The initial slavish imitation of the appearance of manuscripts through a uniform body of text in one font size had given way to more ambitious compositions, using varying types, marginalia, decorative initial letters, and, in the most sophisticated books, woodcut text illustrations. As the publishing industry became established in this way, there sprung up around it a range of associated specialist trades: the bookbinders, type-founders, and merchants who specialized exclusively in the distribution and sale of books. The vastly increased demand for paper had spawned a huge increase in the number and quality of local paper mills. Most of all, printers had by now mastered the techniques for producing reliable texts at relatively modest prices, and this in turn had begun to transform the market for books. The age of mass literacy was now technically possible.

SCIENCE AND TECHNOLOGY   193

Cities and Education

Pre-modern society was rural and local. Ninety per cent of Europe's population lived in the countryside and depended on agriculture for its livelihood. Despite much patient attention to improving the productivity of their fields, agriculture remained overwhelmingly dependent on fickle circumstances outside human control: incidence of war, crop disease, and above all, the weather.

In the ceaseless search for improved farming methods, some progress was made in understanding the benefits of fertilization and use of fallow crops such as turnips for crop rotation. But large improvements in crop yields remained in the future. That is not to deny that the rich could enjoy a wide and varied diet if they chose. Eager merchants would bring to the tables of noble households a vast variety of meat, fish, and game – though this did not necessarily make for variety diet. Because they could afford it, many from society's higher echelons ate far too much meat and suffered in consequence agonies from ulcers and vitamin B deficiency. For those nearer the margins of subsistence, diet remained monotonous and low in quality. Bread, often made up of inferior grains and heavily adulterated, made up 80 per cent of the diet of the poor, eked out by milk and dairy products. In times of poor harvest, starvation loomed.

Such was life in the countryside, and it was no wonder that many from peasant families, particularly those who did not stand to inherit land, chose to make for the cities. But towns and cities could be perilous places. With so many people packed close together in unsanitary conditions, cities were busy, stinking places, with no source of clean water, and there was no real understanding of the need for efficient disposal of human waste. They could be deadly places: epidemic disease periodically ravaged their populations, and other natural disasters – fire and flood – were frequent visitors. In consequence, mortality was severe: no early modern cities could renew their population naturally and instead depended on steady inward migration to compensate for the high death rate.

Cities and trade

Nevertheless, people with ambition were increasingly prepared to take their chances in the cities, for these were the real motors of economic growth in pre-modern society. The large concentrations of people with disposable wealth created a ready market for luxury products, either home-made or imported. Cities were the crucial points in a trade route that, by the 16th century, stretched through the whole of Europe and beyond. The growth of international trade created its own specialized industries, catering for the international market, such as banking and insurance. By the beginning of the 16th century, the established splendour of the Italian cities was rivalled by the new giants in

A view of Antwerp from the sea. This delicate, naturalistic view of northern Europe's rising entrepôt illustrates the importance of seaborne trade, much carried, as here, on tiny coasting vessels. Antwerp would enjoy a period of spectacular growth during this time as a centre of regional and international trade, before the vagaries of war brought decline.

Holbein's portrait of Erasmus

Scholar, philologist, political thinker, above all author and entrepreneur: Erasmus of Rotterdam was one of the most multi-faceted intellectuals of the 16th century and the first man ever to make a fortune from the craft of writing. His scholarly reputation was built on a seminal translation of the New Testament, and it was this that attracted both the admiration of Europe's scholars and the eager patronage of its crowned heads. Erasmus was not afraid to write also in a lighter vein, however, and it was these works, the *Adages*, satires, and correspondence, that made his fortune. Erasmus was courted by all who aspired to the company of scholars, including men such as the painter Hans Holbein, who created this delicate portrait.

northern Europe: Paris, Antwerp, Nuremberg, and Augsburg.

For all that, economic growth depended on the established structures of medieval guild and trading societies. This was a craft-based rather than an industrial society. Indeed, the domination of the conservatively minded craft guilds, defending the rights and expertise of local masters, tended to militate against ambitious economic ventures. As a consequence, large-scale industrial enterprise tended to be concentrated in the countryside: this was true both of the established industries, such as coal- and silver-mining, and of newly developed techniques for the refining of iron and glass. Industries situated near towns were disadvantaged by the increasing scarcity of local supplies of wood or because their pollution of the city's water supplies aroused the ire of inhabitants.

Education and humanism

Cities were also major centres of information exchange and education. By the 15th century, almost all towns of any size had a Latin school, and many boasted a university. This was an age that witnessed a vast growth in demand for reading and writing skills among the laity and a wish to free professional educational services from the traditional domination of the clergy. Later, in Protestant Europe, this movement received additional propulsion from the confiscation of Church property, although less of this was turned over to educational purposes than was originally intended. Throughout Europe, the new educational agenda was powerfully enhanced by the spreading influence of humanism.

Humanism was a multifaceted phenomenon: an intellectual movement, an aspiration of educational renewal, and, at a much more humdrum level, an educational curriculum. Taken at its most basic, humanism was the pursuit of a classical education, the study of the literature and languages of Ancient Greece and Rome. The study of the classics had a particular end in mind. Humanists were firmly convinced of the relevance of classical learning to modern life. The Renaissance desire to study classical culture was partly aimed at recovering the achievements of that age. The core activity of the Renaissance scholar was the hunt for classical texts and, when they were discovered, the discernment of an authentic text by critical comparison of surviving manuscripts.

Humanism involved not only a new educational agenda, but also a new rhetoric. In an age that normally revered the past, humanism gloried in the denigration of earlier traditions of scholarship such as scholasticism. In bitter exchanges, the humanists would carry the day because their extraordinary self-confidence was combined with serious scholarly achievement. The rediscovery of classical texts and their diffusion in print led to the techniques of textual criticism that were among the enduring achievements of the Renaissance.

These achievements were personified by the career of Desiderius Erasmus. A scholar of unquestionable ability and a rampant self-publicist, he published work of enduring scholarly value, epitomized by his *Novum Instrumentum*, the groundbreaking translation of the New Testament from the original Greek. At the same time, through his more ephemeral satire and polemic, Erasmus came to personify the wider characteristics of humanism: arrogant, scathing, and unashamedly elitist. In the process, he was courted and idolized by Europe's rulers and made himself a fortune.

Exploration and Empires

The voyages of discovery paved the way for one of the most fundamental developments of world history: the domination of non-European cultures by the West. But the origins of this colonization lay in a mass of disparate and speculative ventures: perilous and foolhardy expeditions into the unknown by tough and reckless men.

This portrait of a Peruvian Indian, which exploits the Renaissance interest in the human form in a classic evocation of the "noble savage", demonstrates the collision of two conflicting visions of people who were the subject of both curiosity and suspicion.

Portugal and Spain led world exploration in the 16th century. Portuguese ships found routes through the Atlantic and Indian oceans to India. The Spanish headed westwards and discovered the Carribbean islands and the Americas. Magellan's circumnavigation of the globe uncovered a western route across the Pacific Ocean.

The eastern voyages

In opening up worlds beyond the Atlantic coasts, the peoples of Europe would owe an incalculable debt to the seafarers of Portugal. The Iberian kingdom, with its rugged extended coastline and lush coastal habitat, to a large extent already lived from the sea, and in the 15th century, the Portuguese had made steady progress in expanding the coastal and island regions known to Europeans. In 1415, a Portuguese army captured Ceuta in Morocco, and with this embarked on a progressive discovery of the West African coast. Ships driven off this coast chanced upon the important Atlantic islands, and these were progressively explored and colonized: Madeira, the Azores, and the Cape Verde Islands. By the 1460s, the Portuguese had reached the Gulf of Africa and Sierra Leone. As they pressed south, they learned that the Indian Ocean was accessible from the sea: a momentous discovery confirmed by the audacious voyage of Bartholomeu Dias, who in 1488 rounded the Cape of Good Hope. In the last years of the 15th century, Vasco da Gama at last confirmed the hope of this optimistic name by pressing on around the Cape to reach India. A decade later, the Portuguese were in China.

In 1519, the Portuguese explorer Ferdinand Magellan set off for what became the first circumnavigation of the globe. Having fallen from favour at the Portuguese court, he accepted a commission from Charles I of Spain to sail west to the spice islands of the Moluccas to ascertain that they were within Spanish territory. To reach his destination, Magellan navigated the southern tip of America and discovered the straits which bear his name. Returning, he took the unprecedented decision to head home by sailing westwards. Magellan was killed in 1521 in a battle with the natives of the Philippines. His journey was completed by his deputy, Sebastian del Cano.

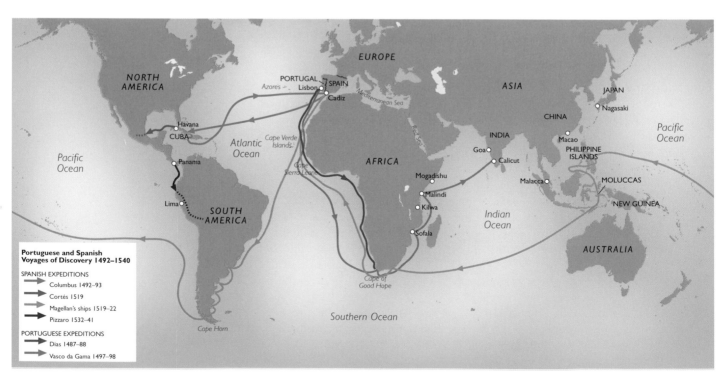

Portuguese and Spanish
Voyages of Discovery 1492–1540

SPANISH EXPEDITIONS
→ Columbus 1492–93
→ Cortés 1519
→ Magellan's ships 1519–22
→ Pizzaro 1532–41

PORTUGUESE EXPEDITIONS
→ Dias 1487–88
→ Vasco da Gama 1497–98

The rapid and astonishing success of these voyages reveals the intelligent sense of direction and purpose that lay behind them. The major expeditions were sponsored by the crown; their clear and unclouded intention was to appropriate a large part of the rich Eastern trade. In the second decade of the 16th century, another brilliant seaman and royal servant, Afonso de Albuquerque, laid the basis of empire, taking Goa in India (1510), as well as the vital Malacca (1511) and Hormuz on the horn of Arabia (1515). These conquests set the tone for the Portuguese settlements, which would become a network of strategic trading ports, rather than colonies. The Portuguese had neither the men nor the resources to establish a colonial empire.

The western voyages

The character of the explorations to the East differed markedly from the rhythm of the westward enterprises. With voyages to the Indies, Europeans were dealing with familiar civilizations and known opportunities. The westward voyages were of an entirely different character. Here, what was to be experienced beyond the newly discovered Atlantic islands was a genuine mystery. The scanty scientific evidence available of this new world was simultaneously enticing and wholly misleading.

The motives of the first voyages mixed curiosity and greed in almost equal measure. But once the first conquistadors had subdued the rich indigenous civilizations, the gains to be had were all too obvious. In the 16th century, these went mainly to Spain, the first, and in this age the greatest, of the European imperial powers.

Colonization and exploitation

The cost to the indigenous peoples was very high. The campaigns of the first subjugation were swift and bloody, but it was the long process of exploitation that followed that took the greatest toll on lives. By the end of the century, the indigenous populations were devastated and the face of the continent changed for ever. Warfare, mistreatment, and harsh, unfamiliar labour all took a toll: most deadly of all were European diseases, against which native peoples had no immunity. The figures make terrible reading. The indigenous population of central Mexico, estimated at 25 million in 1521, fell to 16 million by 1532 and a pitiful 2.6 million in 1568. Comparable trends apply to many of the island settlements and the rest of Central America. In Peru, the decline was less severe, but still marked: from 3.3 million in 1520 to 1.3 million in 1570. In all regions, but particularly in the Caribbean islands, the maintenance of a functioning

economy soon demanded large numbers of Africans as slave labour.

Even among these much reduced native populations, the new settlers were thinly spread. It is estimated that something short of a quarter of a million people of European origin emigrated to the Spanish New World dominions in the first 80 years after Columbus. In a survey of 1570, they represented little more than one per cent of the total population of the Spanish colonies. The new settlers were in the main landowners, engineers, and soldiers. From an early stage, too, missionaries were among their number, for the Spaniards proved almost as eager to save the souls of the indigenous populations as they were to exploit their wealth. In the first generation, the search for gold proved an unpredictable and frustrating business. But, from 1545, the Spaniards made a series of major strikes, all of silver: first at Potosí in Peru, then at Guanajuato and Pachuca in Mexico in the 1550s.

The Spanish silver mines soon came to have an almost mythical place in the European consciousness. The Spanish government developed an elaborate administration to protect the *Carrera de Indias*, a convoy system that linked Spain and the Indies. No wonder, for other European powers could not observe the extraordinary wealth that flowed from the Spanish and Portuguese overseas possessions without wishing to have their part.

The fabulous wealth revealed by the subjugation of the Aztec and Inca civilizations was a confirmation of hopes of wealth that fuelled the explorers' ardour from the time of the first voyages. In due course, plunder gave way to the search for new deposits; when the Spanish found silver, they opened up a new source of wealth that would shape European perceptions of the New World throughout the period.

Spanish Exploration

The new Spanish kingdom would be the principal beneficiary of the first great age of exploration. The bold incursions of the first explorers would create an empire of such wealth and grandeur that Europe's other powers feared the consequences for their own independence in the light of Spain's success.

Christopher Columbus's vision of westward expansion was built on a long history of frustrated initiative in many fields. As a seafarer, merchant, and keen but limited amateur cartographer, Columbus seemed destined to achieve little; however, it was the combination of these eclectic interests that allowed him to carry off his extraordinary and world-changing voyages.

The Inca Emperor Atahualpa as prisoner of the Spaniards at Cajamarca. The brutality with which the Spaniards dealt with their most illustrious captives demonstrated that the chivalric values which infused the knightly warrior code were not always adhered to in the new territories. Both Atahualpa and Montezuma were done to death after their safety had been assured.

Columbus

It was therefore something of an irony that the first significant force in Spanish voyaging was not Castilian, but the Genoese Christopher Columbus. Columbus's early career was that of many ambitious citizens of the Italian republics. What marked him out was a precocious interest in cartography and a determination to pursue exploration beyond the contours of the Atlantic islands. In other respects, Columbus would show the strengths and failings of his age. His appreciation of the world's continents was sketchy in the extreme, formed as much by fictional travel narratives as any exact knowledge. He also left something to be desired as a seaman: although he prided himself on his navigational skill, Columbus never mastered the art of measuring latitude. But he had discerned enough of the likely demand of long-distance ocean sailing to have the sense to re-rig the smallest vessel of his tiny first fleet, the *Niña*, from triangular lateen sails to a square rig. The little ship triumphantly stood the test of the voyage.

In August 1492, Columbus set sail from Palos with three small ships, the *Pinta*, the *Niña*, and the *Santa Maria*. After 33 days of anxious sailing, land was sighted in the Bahamas. In three months of pleasant cruising round the islands, Columbus alighted on Hispaniola and, at last, found gold, before the loss of his flagship, the *Santa Maria*, necessitated a rapid return home.

On arrival in Spain, Columbus hastened to the royal court at Barcelona with natives and gold trinkets to convince his royal patrons that discoveries of significance had been made. In 1493, Columbus sailed again with a vastly larger fleet of 17 assorted caravels and pinnaces manned by some 1200 men. A swift voyage brought the fleet to San Domingo and thence to Hispaniola, where Columbus established a settlement, Isabella. Although Columbus was an explorer of genius and insight, as a colonial governor his skills never matched his gradiose ambitions. His new colony was poorly sited and badly led. By the time Columbus returned to Spain in 1496, it had effectively failed. Despite the fact that he had

nothing to show for their sizeable investment in this second voyage, Columbus still had enough credit with the Spanish monarchs to win support for a new expedition in 1498, during which he discovered the vast continent of South America; however, the collapse of the colony of Hispaniola led to his removal and return to Spain in disgrace. A succession of tough-minded agents of the crown now began the settlement of the Caribbean islands in earnest. From these secure bases, other Spanish voyagers discovered and prospected the isthmus of Central America. In 1513, Vasco Núñez de Balboa led an expedition through the tropical forests of Panama to gaze, for the first time, on the Pacific.

The first encounter between Columbus and the Indians, as imagined by the 16th century Dutch painter and engraver Theodore De Bry. This image perfectly encapsulates the belief of the Europeans that they were bringing a superior way of life to heathen peoples. In a Biblical allusion, the Indians present Columbus with gifts of gold, frankincense, and myrrh.

The conquest of America

Of all the great histories of European expansion, nothing is as extraordinary as the destruction of the great empires of Mexico and South America. The Mexican empire of the Aztecs and the Inca dominion of Peru were two of the world's great civilizations, as even those who destroyed them recognized. From their base in the valley of Mexico, the Aztecs had, by 1500, created a well-settled dominion that stretched from the Pacific to the Caribbean. A population of around 20 million was divided between prosperous villages and great cities such as the capital Tenochtitlán (now Mexico City), a marvel that amazed all who saw it. Their carefully organized territories were unified by networks of roads and imperial institutions as sophisticated as anything then evident in Europe.

The conquest of the Aztec Empire was the work of Hernán Cortés, an experienced warrior who had made his reputation in the conquest of Cuba. His tiny force consisted of 11 ships, 600 men, and some 16 horses. Advancing into the interior, Cortés quickly grasped the Aztecs' unpopularity with their subject peoples, and hence their vulnerability. When Cortés completed the long march to Tenochtitlán, he acted decisively to seize the Aztec king, Montezuma and, through him, the city. This victory marked the end of the Aztec Empire.

Cortés was named as Governor General of the new territories, but a disastrous expedition into Honduras dissipated much of his political capital, and a commission of enquiry despatched from Spain threatened ruin. Although a personal appeal to the king initially rescued the situation, following the appointment of a new viceroy, Cortés abandoned his new lands to spend the rest of his days in Spain, abandoned by the court.

The conqueror of Mexico – Francisco Pizarro was the archetypal adventurer, an illegitimate, illiterate son of a soldier. Like Cortés, Pizarro had committed himself to the New World and by the time of his expedition to Peru, he was the veteran of several campaigns and had carved out a position of wealth and influence in the new town of Panama.

His expeditionary force was small: a mere 180 men and 27 horses. But his return to Peru coincided with the last stages of a debilitating civil war in the Inca kingdoms. Profiting from the confusion, Pizarro pressed inland to Cajamarca, where, under cover of a parlay, he treacherously captured the Inca king Atahualpa. Reinforced with a further 600 men, Pizarro was able to extract a huge ransom from Atahualpa, who was then put to death. The Inca army melted away, and the capital, Cuzco, surrendered. Peru was conquered, and Pizarro and his companions settled there to enjoy the spoils.

The real benefits, however, would be reaped by those who came after. The leaders of the Pizarro expedition almost all died violent deaths, as the greed and ambition that had fuelled their courage led to feuding. The consolidation of Spanish power required the presence of sober, experienced administrators: this was achieved with the establishment of viceroys in both Mexico (1535) and Peru (1543). Gradually the new men were able to impose a new sense of order on the conquered territories.

The Clash of Empires

As the full majesty of the Spanish discoveries became clear, Europe's other seafarers could not be expected to stand by idly. The assault on the Iberian monopoly of the New World began almost as soon as news of the discoveries began to circulate around the courts and seafaring communities of Europe. Despite this, Spanish power in the New World was not seriously threatened until the last quarter of the century.

Spain and Portugal

In the first phase of exploration, the dangerous potential clash between Spain and Portugal was carefully avoided. Portugal had spurned Columbus's initial advances; however, a landfall at Lisbon on his return from his first voyage had alerted the shrewd Portuguese king to what might be accomplished by westward expansion. With two major powers now strongly committed to exploration, the necessity of agreed lines of demarcation was apparent. The result was the Treaty of Tordesillas of 1494, agreed with the help of a complaisant Spanish pope, Alexander VI, and intended to separate a Portuguese zone of influence in Africa eastwards from the Spanish westward explorations. At the last moment, the Portuguese succeeded in pushing the line of demarcation 275 leagues westward, on the grounds that their ships were often forced to sail far out into the Atlantic to catch favourable winds for the southern voyage. Although they did not know it at the time, this would ultimately give them rights to the as yet undiscovered territories of Brazil.

France and England

In truth, Portugal was now fully occupied with the valuable Eastern spice trade and the less certain potential of Brazil. But other nations were quick to sense the profit in challenging the Spanish monopoly. As early as 1504, French privateers began raiding Spanish transatlantic shipping on the final stages of the voyage towards home waters. In 1523, one Jean Fleury even succeeded in detaching two vessels, bringing the wealth of the Mexican conquests back to Charles V. This spectacular treasure galvanized French seafarers into making a concerted assault on Spanish shipping, a campaign legitimized by the sporadic state of war between Emperor Charles V and the French king, Francis I. From the 1530s, the French corsairs extended their marauding into the Caribbean.

The French fared less well as colonists. Plans to settle in Brazil and Florida were easily repulsed by the Portuguese and Spanish, respectively. The collapse of these early colonizing ventures, and the subsequent preoccupation of the French Wars of Religion in the latter half of the century, left the way open for a new, and ultimately more formidable, interloper. English encroachment, always an irritant to the Spanish, grew ever more damaging, leading ultimately to a total rupture between the two nations. The English ventures flourished partly because the objectives of the voyages, left largely in the hands of hard-nosed seafaring captains, remained pragmatic and focussed on critical economic objectives. John Hawkins had visited the French colony at Florida only days before its final destruction, and he had seen the pitiful rabble to which it had been reduced. It was a hard lesson that small, undercapitalized colonial missions had little chance of success. Rather, the English would flourish by forcing an entry into the Spanish monopoly at its most vulnerable point – the

English colonists arrive at Roanoke Island, Virginia, first settled by Sir Walter Raleigh in 1585. The first Roanoke colony lasted a total of ten months. The colonists were ill prepared and were forced to rely on the local Indians for food.

The ships of the United East India Company arrive back in Amsterdam in 1604 after travelling to Indonesia to obtain spices. The United East Company could be considered the world's first modern company, with shares and shareholders, or subscribers.

lucrative trade in African slaves – and, as tension grew into open hostility, by blatant assaults on Spanish cargoes.

These expeditions, indignantly opposed by the Spanish authorities and surreptitiously financed by the English elite, gradually brought relations between the two powers to the point of collapse. But the English were less successful in this period as colonists. Even the charismatic leadership of Sir Walter Raleigh could not save the Virginian colony established on the river Roanoke. Determinedly and expensively reinforced from England, it enjoyed a fitful existence until 1590, when the latest fleet found the fort abandoned and the colonists disappeared. Raleigh returned to privateering; the Virginia colony was not revived until 1607.

The Dutch

The last decade of the century witnessed an intensification of the sea war and the first emergence of a power that would enjoy a great colonial future: the Dutch. The war against Spain had already taught the Dutch the profits to be made in preying on enemy shipping, and the emergence of a free northern state after 1585 set the Dutch on the road to more ambitious ventures. The final crucial element in this new venturing was the incorporation, since 1580, of the Portuguese crown in the dominions of the Spanish Philip II. In the short term, this made available to Philip the formidable Portuguese ocean-going fleet for the Enterprise of England. The damaging

long-term consequence, however, was that all Portuguese possessions had now become a legitimate target for the enemies of Spain.

The Dutch were not slow to take advantage. The great expansion of Dutch enterprise in the last years of the century touched all aspects of Europe's most lucrative trading activities: the Baltic, Mediterranean, and Levant, the Africa trade, and the Caribbean. It was only in the final years of the century that the potential of the Indies trade was fully realized. At this point, in Amsterdam Dutch intervention came with the establishment of the *"Compagnie van verre"* (literally, the "Long Distance Company") by a consortium of nine rich businessmen. They pooled a capital of 290,000 guilders, enough to buy the equivalent of 60 or 70 large houses in Amsterdam. The fleet they sent out to the East Indies returned in 1597, and, although depleted and much diminished by the hardship of the voyage, the success of the venture ignited the imagination of the Dutch mercantile world. Other companies were founded to exploit the new opportunities, and, by the end of 1601, no fewer than 65 ships had sailed. The danger of competition between rivals spoiling the trade spurred the states of Holland to step in. In 1602, after months of negotiations, the United East India Company was duly founded. By this time, too, the English had realized the promise of the East. The English version of the East India Company was first constituted, with a list of 101 subscribing merchants, in 1599. One of the great rivalries of the first imperial age was set to begin.

Biblia/das ist/ die gantze Heilige Schrifft Deudsch.

Mart. Luth.

Wittemberg.

Begnadet mit Kür-furstlicher zu Sachsen freiheit.

Gedruckt durch Hans Lufft.

M. D. XXXIIII.

The title page of an early Wittenberg edition of Luther's German Bible. The German Bible was Luther's most enduring literary achievement, but for Protestantism it was only part of a torrent of print with which the evangelical leadership pressed its case. Luther wrote ceaselessly for an insatiable market; printers and publishers grew rich on the proceeds.

THE RISE OF PROTESTANTISM

Throughout the Middle Ages, calls for reform had been a constant part of the institutional life of the Church. It was not immediately clear why an obscure clerical quarrel emanating from Germany should pose so much more substantial a threat or why it should have created a movement – Protestantism – that permanently divided the Western Church.

In the last part of the 15th century, the Western Church seemed at last to have entered a period of calm after centuries of upheaval. The great and fundamental questions raised by the conciliar movement had finally been resolved, to the benefit of papal authority. After centuries in which prelates, scholars, and monarchs had disputed the claims of the papacy to theological authority within the Church, the popes had finally triumphed. The papacy was restored to Rome, and the dark days of the Schism, when rival popes ruled in Avignon, were banished for ever.

A series of dynamic patron popes threw themselves into re-modelling Rome as a capital fit for the Church and for the new age of the Renaissance. It was, ironically, an aspect of this rebuilding that would spark off what would become the Protestant Reformation. To finance the rebuilding of St Peter's Cathedral, Pope Julius II proclaimed a new indulgence: this device, already a major source of income for the late medieval Church, was to be exploited for a European fundraising effort. Indulgences were already controversial for reform-minded Catholics, as they coupled the suggestion of mercy in the afterlife with financial contributions: technically, they offered remission of pains in purgatory. But the pope, now Julius's successor Leo X, was clearly wholly unprepared for the storm provoked when a previously obscure German friar, Martin Luther, spoke out against the fundraising campaign.

The initially laconic reaction to Luther in Rome is not surprising, but the challenge of Protestantism proved more threatening than medieval criticism for three main reasons. First, among the educated elite, the Church had to face the new challenge of humanism. In the first years, Luther's criticism struck a chord because, all over Europe, humanists had voiced similar concerns about clerical discipline, standards of education, and the abuse of papal power. Secondly, the humanist agenda coalesced with a more general sense of rising expectations among the laity, linked with a rise in literacy. They invested large amounts of money in the decoration of their churches and in employing more priests to say masses for their souls. Especially in Europe's confident urban communities, they expected high standards in return; where their clergy fell short, they gave Luther a hearing. Finally, the message of the reformers could reach a far wider audience than ever before through the recent invention of printing. This, most of all, explains why Luther's movement became an international one.

Building from their criticism of indulgences, Luther and his supporters would in due course pose a formidable challenge to Catholic orthodoxy. In the first years, most powerful – and most shocking – was the denunciation of the Church hierarchy. Once the papacy had failed to heed the call for reform, Luther was quick to identify it as the seat of the Antichrist; many would eventually accept his repudiation of papal authority without necessarily condoning the violence of his language. This courageous attack was fuelled by Luther's profound sense of calling. Here, Luther's theological basis was a reworking of the Augustinian doctrine of Grace that laid unusual stress on God's redemptive power, unassisted by the efforts of the individual fallen Christian (justification by faith). In the early years of the Reformation, this was all the more powerful because it was by no means clear to Catholics that this understanding of justification was heretical. By the time the Church had found its voice, the damage had already been done.

Martin Luther and John Calvin

In the early years of the German evangelical movement, Martin Luther was a towering presence: a personality of iron will and a preacher and writer of rare talent. His personality dominated the German reform movement. But it was left to others, notably the French lawyer John Calvin, to create the Church structures that would make Protestantism a permanent force in much of northern and western Europe.

This portrait of John Calvin captures well the steely restraint that contemporaries found so difficult to penetrate. A study in contrasts with the more gregarious and voluble Luther, the lawyerly Genevan helped to bring order and system to the Reformation after the first generation of more explosive and volatile change.

Luther, Calvin, and their fellow reformers. This idealized portrait gallery was one of the most popular and widely reproduced images of the Bible. It provided an image of scholarly unity that was in marked contrast to the reality of bitter doctrinal disputes that divided many of those portrayed.

Martin Luther

Of all the provinces of the Western Church, the territories of the Holy Roman Empire, particularly the German core, were potentially the most troublesome for Rome. The rich city-states and rural territories (many ruled directly by their bishops) offered lucrative tax revenues and patronage, but Germans frequently expressed their frustrations at the lack of local accountability. These grievances were periodically presented to the imperial Diets – meetings of the princes and city representatives – as a formal catalogue or petition – *Gravamina*. The young Martin Luther was, however, an unlikely spokesman for this movement. From the time that he entered the Augustinian order, Luther achieved rapid promotion, then gained a Chair in theology at the new university of Wittenberg. His career, until the indulgences controversy of 1517, was a monument to what could be achieved within the Catholic Church. But Luther had also embarked on a theological journey, one that led to a fundamentally new understanding of the concept of Grace and salvation. Man, he believed, was saved by God's free gift alone, not by any works. Initially orthodox, in the context of a debate over the fundamentals of papal authority, this would prove explosive.

Luther's criticisms of indulgences attracted immediate public interest. In April 1518, he attended a meeting of his own Augustinian order in Heidelberg and won many friends: to many, the early stages of the Reformation appeared a squabble between two religious orders, as the Dominicans supplied many of Luther's earliest opponents. Initially, the Church fought back by conventional means. Luther was summoned to meet the papal legate in Germany, and only when he refused to submit were his views condemned, in the Papal Bull *Exsurge Domine* of 1520. Outraged,

'tLicht is op den   kandelaer gestelt

Luther denounced the papacy as the agency of the Devil and repudiated its authority. Now Luther argued that only Scripture could be the ultimate authority in a reformed Church. Luther was also shrewd enough to exploit the public sympathy for his treatment by adopting the larger criticisms of the clergy and Church affairs in Germany which touched the lives of the many thousands engaged by the indulgences controversy, but unable to understand the wider theological issues. The result, expressed in a torrent of pamphlets from Luther, was that Luther's cause and that of German reform became one. When the Emperor Charles V met Luther at the Diet of Worms to confirm the pope's condemnation in 1521, the order proved unenforceable. Within a few years, numerous German cities and territories had adopted the Reformation, and the Protestant movement was born.

Luther's movement did not carry all before it. Erasmus remained loyal to the pope, as did other notable figures such as the Frenchman Jacques Lefèvre d'Etaples, who criticized the Church, but believed that reform should come from within. Nearer to home, the German Peasants' War of 1524–5 showed the limits of the social and political aspirations that could be accommodated within Luther's magisterial reform. The peasants saw Luther's attack on the Church as proof of divine support for their economic grievances, but Luther condemned the revolt, which added to its defeat. After the slaughter of the peasant armies, the remnant of the movement drifted into the radical fringes of Anabaptism, denounced by Luther. The Anabaptist movement reached its climax with the seizure of the north German city of Münster in 1534. Proclaimed the New Jerusalem in anticipation of the imminent end of time, Münster and its experimental Anabaptist government attracted many thousands of followers from all over northern Europe, before the increasingly erratic behaviour of its self-styled king, John of Leiden, brought the whole experiment into disrepute. Münster was put down with great ferocity in 1535, but the movement lived on, always on the fringes of society, but tenacious and brave.

The extremes of Münster were a propaganda gift for Catholic critics of the Reformation and effectively destroyed the early hopes of consensual evangelical renewal. Most damaging of all in this regard was the quarrel between Luther and Huldreich Zwingli, the leader of the Reformation in the Swiss Confederation. Zwingli, originally an admirer of Luther, had orchestrated the conversion of Zurich, the largest of the Swiss city-states, at an early date. But he nurtured an interpretation of the reform agenda more radical in several respects,

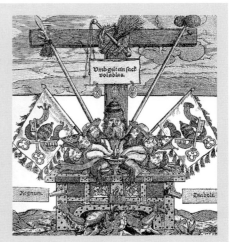

The Reformation Broadsheet

This famous image was one of the most widely circulated of the polemical images of the Reformation. It skilfully combines the burning issue of the first years of the conflict (Luther's protest against indulgences) with his fierce denunciation of papal power: here the pope is identified with the seven-headed dragon of the Apocalypse. Such images were widely disseminated in the first decades of the evangelical protest and did much to build identification with the evangelical cause.

practical and doctrinal, than Luther would allow. Luther was repelled by the visual austerity of Zurich worship, where in contrast to Wittenberg all images and statues had been removed as unacceptable. He also found Zwingli's austere Eucharistic theology unpalatable. The two men were tempted to express their differences in print, and a damaging pamphlet war ensued. An attempt to reconcile the two leaders at the Colloquy of Marburg in 1529 achieved nothing, and, when Zwingli was killed two years later leading Zurich's troops against the armies of the Catholic cantons of the Confederation, Luther could not disguise his satisfaction.

For a decade or more, the two Reformations went their separate ways. The initial rapid progress of the movement flagged. Although in Germany the work of church-building continued, in France, the Netherlands, and elsewhere, official repression stifled the initially vibrant evangelical movements.

John Calvin

The Reformation needed a second wind, and it found it through the work of the French evangelical John Calvin. A fugitive from the clampdown on evangelicals in Paris in the mid-1530s, Calvin found a new home in the small French-speaking city of Geneva, on the periphery of the Swiss Confederation. Under his tutelage, Geneva was transformed into a model of the Reformed Christian community. Meanwhile Calvin articulated, most notably in his *Institutes of the Christian Religion* of 1536, the systematic theology that the movement had thus far lacked. Calvin's system was remarkable both for its clarity and its comprehensiveness, drawing on the best of both the German and Swiss theological traditions in a masterful evocation of the new Christian vision of God, the Church, and society. It was the secure rock on which to build the second great age of Protestant expansion.

Henry VIII and Elizabeth I

At the beginning of the 16th century, England lay at the very periphery of European affairs. A century later, its position was transformed: the emerging kingdom was now the lynchpin of European diplomacy. Presiding over this English Renaissance were two outstanding monarchs: the monstrous egomaniac Henry VIII and his wilful, enigmatic daughter, Elizabeth I.

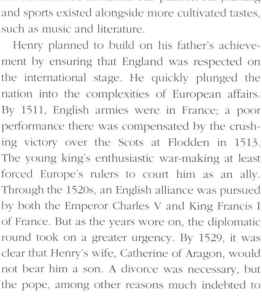

The opulence and pomp of this formal portrait of Henry VIII by Hans Holbein does not disguise the iron will of a man determined that his word would be law. By turn capricious and brutal, cultured, and intelligent, Henry was by and large admired by subjects desperate for security after decades of dynastic insecurity.

The accession of the Tudor dynasty in 1485 followed a period of profound instability in English affairs. The Wars of the Roses (1450–85) had seen the crown of England change hands seven times over the course of 40 years of brutal fighting among nobles. The fortuitous triumph of Henry Tudor, the distant Welsh heir to the Lancastrian claim, was only possible because of the elimination of so many other leading figures. But the new king, Henry VII, showed an instinct for rule that made light of his previous inexperience. Former Yorkist opponents were either pacified or cowed into obedience and the depleted royal finances restored through capable husbandry. The birth of two sons, Arthur and Henry, raised the prospect of the peaceful, uncontested succession for which all of England yearned. When the much-loved Arthur died prematurely in 1502, it was Henry who stepped forwards to claim the kingdom on his father's death in 1509.

The young Henry VIII was all that Europe expected in a king. Tall, handsome, and vigorous, Henry combined the traditional passions of the aristocracy with the new cultivated tastes of the Renaissance monarch. His passion for jousting and sports existed alongside more cultivated tastes, such as music and literature.

Henry planned to build on his father's achievement by ensuring that England was respected on the international stage. He quickly plunged the nation into the complexities of European affairs. By 1511, English armies were in France; a poor performance there was compensated by the crushing victory over the Scots at Flodden in 1513. The young king's enthusiastic war-making at least forced Europe's rulers to court him as an ally. Through the 1520s, an English alliance was pursued by both the Emperor Charles V and King Francis I of France. But as the years wore on, the diplomatic round took on a greater urgency. By 1529, it was clear that Henry's wife, Catherine of Aragon, would not bear him a son. A divorce was necessary, but the pope, among other reasons much indebted to

the emperor (Catherine's nephew), could not oblige. Failure to solve this diplomatic conundrum brought disgrace to Henry's faithful minister, Cardinal Wolsey, the architect of his military campaigns. Now, new men emerged to propose more radical solutions to "the King's Great Matter".

In 1532, the frustrated king took a new love, Ann Boleyn, and a solution could not be long delayed. Henry repudiated both his wife and the authority of the pope. An obedient Parliament enacted legislation that both confirmed English independence from Rome and established the king's royal supremacy over the Church. This was not Protestantism – Henry never shifted from the theological orthodoxy of his youth – and those Protestants who moved too fast did so at their peril. But in practical terms the changes introduced in Henry's new Church differed little from the reforms of continental Protestant princes. By 1540, England had a vernacular Bible, and Parliament had abolished purgatory, shrines, and pilgrimages. Most important, the dissolution of the monasteries had stripped the Church of much of its land and one of its most important institutions.

The crisis of mid-century

Henry's death in 1547 ushered in difficult years. Only Henry's third wife, Jane Seymour, had borne Henry the long-wished-for son, who now succeeded as Edward VI at the age of nine. His youth demanded a minority administration: power was exercised by his maternal uncle, the Duke of Somerset. Somerset was removed by his fellow councillors in 1549, but the new chief minister, the Duke of Northumberland, continued his policies, and, by 1553, England had a full Protestant Church settlement. When Edward died in 1553, on the verge of active kingship, all of this was thrown into question. The rightful queen, Mary, the daughter of Catherine of Aragon, was a firm Catholic, and the failed attempt to divert the succession to Lady Jane Grey only confirmed her determination to reintroduce the Catholic faith. Marriage to Philip of Spain (later Philip II) further cemented this decisive reorientation of policy.

But Mary, too, was destined for disappointment. The marriage with Philip drew England inexorably into Spain's quarrels abroad, but did not produce the heir that would have secured the Catholic succession. So when Mary died in 1558, childless and disappointed, the bruised kingdom fell to Elizabeth, the last of Henry's children and the last hope of the Tudor line.

The Elizabethan age

The new queen acted quickly to reverse both the Spanish friendship and her sister's religious priorities. A new Church settlement established Protestantism once and for all as the religion of England. Although Protestants schooled in the continental Churches of Geneva and Germany would regret that Elizabeth would not adopt their

precepts in all things, this new Anglican Church still firmly aligned England with Europe's Protestant powers. Puritan criticism of Elizabeth's Church grew gradually less strident as the reign wore on. By the last critical decade, all but a few unreconciled separatists identified strongly with the new Protestant state.

Abroad, England emerged as the most formidable opponent of Spanish power. The voyages of Hawkins, Drake, and Raleigh exposed the vulnerability of the Spanish Empire, and England's help to Protestant rebels abroad finally provoked Philip II beyond endurance. When the Spanish Armada set sail in 1588, the peril was great – English armies were inexperienced and unprepared, and only the Channel stood in the way of Philip's invading army. Elizabeth's luck held, however, and the destruction of the Spanish fleet tipped the balance of the conflict decisively in England's favour.

At home, too, this was a period of great achievement. Elizabeth was blessed with a generation of fine ministers, and the frequent meetings of Parliament to raise taxes and enact religious change had confirmed its role in the government of the kingdom. Most of all, this was a golden age for English culture. The work of Shakespeare and his contemporaries transformed English literature and enabled the English language finally to shed its dependency on more confident continental cultures. When Elizabeth died in 1603, England was poised for its emergence as one of Europe's greatest powers.

*The Battle of Mohàcs, 1526.
The most decisive battle of
the 16th century decimated the
Hungarian nobility, extinguished
the Jagiello dynasty, and left
central Europe exposed to Turkish
conquest. Only the Habsburgs
could successfully fill such a void.*

THE CHALLENGE OF THE EAST

In the 16th century, many of Europe's rising nation-states, and most eye-catching events, were congregated on its Atlantic fringe. But no one underestimated the importance of events further east: the steadily growing Habsburg Empire and the looming power of the Ottoman Turks.

One of the most significant, if hardly known, battles of the 16th century took place on the plains of Hungary near the town of Mohács, on 29 August 1526. On this fateful day, the young King of Hungary, Louis Jagiello, led his army against the Ottoman host. By nightfall, the Hungarian army was shattered: the king and the cream of his nobility lay dead on the field.

With the death of Louis, the Jagiello dynasty was extinguished, and a dangerous power vacuum opened up in one of Europe's most critical regions. Fifteenth-century Bohemia was one of the richest and most prized kingdoms of the Holy Roman Empire. Both Hungary and Bohemia were closely connected with the economic and cultural life of Germany, as, to a lesser extent, was Poland to the north. In all of these lands, humanism and the Renaissance had made a deep impact, leaving a fine legacy of scholarship, libraries, and buildings.

These, then, were the proud and rich cultures that seemed in 1526 to lie prostrate before the Ottoman advance. The thankless task of defending Christendom's vulnerable eastern flank fell to Ferdinand of Habsburg, brother of Emperor Charles V. Ferdinand exploited the marriage connection between the Habsburg and Jagiello dynasties to claim the Hungarian throne – but a portion of the Hungarian nobility preferred the local magnate John Zápolya, and a damaging civil war threatened to undermine the necessary defensive conflict against the Ottomans.

Gradually, Ferdinand asserted his authority and stabilized the front. The Habsburg presence in Eastern Europe, established in these unpropitious circumstances, would become a permanent feature on the European political landscape. Thus was born the Austro-Hungarian Empire – one of Europe's most enduring, if troubled, great powers.

The confrontation of the Habsburg and Ottoman empires was one of Eastern Europe's most significant geopolitical conflicts; the other was the struggle for supremacy in the Baltic. In the far north lay Denmark and Sweden, until the early years of the 16th century part of the united kingdom of Scandinavia. In 1521, Sweden claimed independence, but bitterness lingered between the two, to be reignited later in the century in the Great Northern War. These quarrels inevitably drew in Poland, the great sprawling kingdom along the southern Baltic shore. Poland-Lithuania played an important part in the politics of the era, both through its strategic location and through a growing reputation as a haven of toleration for refugees from the period's religious conflicts. In the second half of the 16th century, Poland was a multi-confessional state, presided over by benign monarchs and an enlightened nobility. In the last decades, the failure of the Jagiello dynasty brought difficulties, particularly as the Polish tradition of elective monarchy offered little continuity, and those elected often proved shallow in their commitment to Polish interests. The eventual victory in this contest of the Swedish Vasas dragged Poland inexorably into Scandinavian quarrels.

Looming further to the east was the vast brooding power of Muscovy. For much of the century, during the long minority of Tsar Ivan, Muscovy was consumed by internal troubles, but as Ivan grew to maturity the sleeping giant stirred. In the late 16th century, Ivan – aptly named the Terrible – was a turbulent and malign presence in European politics. He returned to haunt the Poles at frequent intervals, proposing himself as king when the crown fell vacant in 1572 and taking advantage of Poland's internal preoccupations to pounce on Livonia in 1558 to increase access to the Baltic. Many breathed a sigh of relief when, on 18 March 1584 and exactly as predicted by his 60 astrologers, Ivan suddenly expired.

The Ottoman Empire

The Ottoman advance through Europe struck terror through the hearts of Europe's citizens. As the Turks continued their march through the remnant of Byzantium, what few could perceive was that Western Christendom was encountering a rich and subtle civilization, and one from which European society had much to learn.

A miniature showing the parade of the Ottoman army before the walls of Tiflis after the fall of the city during the Ottoman war against the Persians. The soldiers recruited among the subject European peoples of the Balkans played an essential role in the Ottoman expansion eastward.

By 1500, the Ottoman Empire covered the lands to the south and west of the Black Sea. As the century progressed, the Ottomans focused on Europe, advancing first into Moldavia, then Hungary after the Battle of Mohács in 1526. Their unsuccessful attempt to lay siege to Vienna in 1529 marked the limit of their progression west, but they continued to apply pressure to the border of the Habsburg Empire for the rest of the century.

The Ottoman threat

By the end of the 15th century, a considerable portion of the European land mass lay in Turkish hands. The fall of Constantinople in 1453 falls near the mid point of the two centuries of steady Ottoman progress through the Balkans towards Latin Europe. In the hundred years before they took Constantinople, the Ottomans had already invested and colonized much of the Byzantine hinterland, including Thrace, Bulgaria, and Macedonia. Two campaigns in 1454 and 1455 smashed the Serbs, in territorial terms the largest geographical buffer between the Ottoman Empire and the West; the fall of Nova Brno also gave them control of its important silver and gold mines. In the following decade, the Turkish advance enveloped the rest of the Greek peninsula (1458–61), followed by Herzegovina (absorbed 1483) and Albania (1468–78). Meanwhile, Venice was progressively driven back in the struggle for the Aegean Islands and the Dalmatian (Adriatic) coast. In 1520, the Ottoman host seized Belgrade, the southern key to Hungary; the triumph of Mohács then allowed the progressive occupation of much of Hungary. In 1529, they advanced to threaten Vienna: Western Europe lay open, and apparently defenceless before their conquering army. The Turkish threat was finally defeated by the Holy Roman Emperor Charles V who lifted the siege of Vienna in 1529.

The Ottoman advance towards the heart of Christian Europe, and particularly the collapse of the kingdom of Hungary, had a profound impact on the European psyche. For Martin Luther in Wittenberg, not so very far away, the victory of the Turkish horde was a sure sign of the imminent end time. Several times during his career he had addressed the issue of the infidel threat to Christian society, and even as his life drew to an end he still gave anxious thought to the Turkish advance. In 1543, he wrote to the Saxon elector declining a personal exemption from the Turkish war tax. "I want," he declared, "to fight the Turk with my poor man's penny, alongside the next fellow; and who knows whether my little free-will offering, like the widow's mite, may not do more than all the rich compulsory taxes."

Luther's fears were allayed by the formation of the Holy League of Spain, Venice, and Rome, which defeated the Turkish fleet at Lepanto, at the entrance to the Gulf of Corinth, in October 1571. The battle was celebrated throughout Europe as a decisive victory for Christendom against the Islamic threat.

Life under Ottoman rule

But for all the scholarly writings and pamphlets devoted to the Turkish threat, one senses the Western European public actually knew very little

The Frontier of the Ottoman Empire 1500–1606
- Ottoman Empire 1500
- Ottoman Empire 1606
- Ottoman vassal states 1606
- Temporary Ottoman conquests
- Habsburg possessions 1606
- Major battles

Majolica charger showing Eastern horseman

Fascination with the Eastern civilizations was by no means confined to those who lived directly along the threatened borders. News of the Turkish wars provided healthy profits for enterprising publishers in all of Western Europe, often in little books of two or more sheets that drew on a small array of stock illustrations and formed part of the popular sensation literature of the day. Such tales did little to build real knowledge of Ottoman civilization, but among Europe's elites there was a growing recognition of the qualities of a civilization that was more than merely a potent military power.

of life under Turkish rule. In particular, they had little sense of what Ottoman rule must have meant for the approximately 5 million Christian peoples settled in the Turkish provinces within Europe. Fed a diet that repeatedly harked on the ruthless cruelty of the sultan and the pitiless ferocity of his soldiery, the realities of the situation might well have surprised them.

The Ottomans, for instance, never attempted any forced or large-scale Islamicization of the Balkans. To exploit the new lands, they continued most of the existing tax regime, overlaid with their own new system for the extraction of a steady tribute from agricultural areas. Certain local taxes and dues were reserved for the sultan, others allocated to support the local administration of the appointed Turkish officials. The cornerstone of Ottoman rural administration was the *tinar* system – grants of rights of exploitation to selected *sipalvi*, originally trusted servants who had played their part in the conquest. Revenue was raised through a modest levy of peasant labour service (three days a year, much as had been customary under Christian rule) and a more substantial tithe on the annual harvest.

The Ottoman system also relied heavily on these captured Christian provinces for recruits to man their armies, which could then be deployed to face Muslim rivals in Anatolia (southern Turkey) and the Arab world. Most famous and notorious were the janissaries: Christian children forcibly removed from their homes to be brought up to serve the sultan. The youths were given new Muslim names and obliged to adopt the Islamic faith; those who refused faced death.

The human suffering that underpinned such a system is obvious, but for those who came through the strict training, the life of a janissary offered considerable career opportunities. A substantial number from the ethnic subject peoples in due course rose to become some of the most privileged and powerful soldier administrators in the Empire. Of the 49 grand vezirs who served the sultan between 1453 and 1623, a clear majority was of Christian European origin, including at least 11 Slavs, 11 Albanians, and six Greeks; only five were of Turkish extraction. The Balkan peoples were an essential agent of the expansion of Ottoman influence throughout the Arab world.

The conquerors also made no attempt to suppress the Eastern Orthodox Church. For most Orthodox Christians, life under Ottoman rule was not oppressive. The Church retained extensive jurisdiction in civil and family matters such as marriage and inheritance, where Ottoman law was not easily applicable. In return, the local clergy took a conspicuous role in local administration, even acting as assessors and collectors for taxes levied by the Ottoman state apparatus.

What then can be said, in summary, of the impact of the Ottoman Empire in Europe? Certainly there was a certain curiosity about Arabic culture, shared by even so trenchant a critic as Luther. In 1537, he published with a new preface an edition of a 15th-century account of captivity under the Ottomans. Five years later, he published a free translation of the exposition on the Koran by the 13th-century Dominican Ricoldus. When the first tide of eschatological fear receded, there were many in Western Europe who were prepared to recognize the Ottoman Empire for what it certainly was: an ordered society and a great civilization. But this perception was based on the experience of merchants and of diplomats at the Ottoman court, rather than any real sense of what life entailed for the Christian peoples under Ottoman rule. Theirs was essentially a hidden experience.

The Arab Conquests 100–1 ▶
The Conquests for the Holy Land 180–1 ▶
Martin Luther and John Calvin 204–5 ▶
The Challenge of the East 208–9 ▶
The Ottoman Empire 254–5 ▶

Sala del Capitolo of the Scuola Grande di St Rocco in Venice. Decorated by Tintoretto, the opulent magnificence of this Baroque chamber demonstrates the growing self-confidence of a Catholic culture gradually emerging from the shadow of relentless Protestant criticism.

THE COUNTER-REFORMATION

In the longer term, the rise of Protestantism would stimulate Europe's Catholics to undertake a wholesale re-evaluation of their beliefs and practice. But that, inevitably, took time: in the first critical decades, the most effective defenders of the old faith would be princes and rulers of a traditional cast of mind, men like Emperor Charles V and Philip II of Spain.

The growth of Protestantism set the Catholic Church some difficult problems. Although Rome was quick to condemn Luther's heresies, many within the Old Church acknowledged that his beliefs were built on a sound tradition of Catholic teaching – it could hardly be otherwise given his background and training. Reform-minded Catholics could also hardly deny the urgency of reform, and many shared his low estimation of the capacity of the popes to provide the impetus.

The first two decades after the beginnings of the German Reformation were exceptionally difficult times for Catholicism. From the first days, the teachings of Luther and his allies were vehemently opposed by those who recognized early on the full implications of his rejection of papal authority. Most of all, it remained uncertain precisely what was being defended. In France, the question of how far Catholicism could accommodate reform – and what reform – was hotly debated for more than two decades. In Germany, conferences between Protestants and Catholics aimed at the reconciliation of theological differences continued with some hopes of success until the Colloquy of Regensburg in 1541. Even after this, powerful forces within the Catholic establishment in Italy continued to explore theological formulations that were by no means incompatible with the Protestant understanding of justification by faith. When this failed, there were further high-profile defections to Protestantism.

In these circumstances, with the Church itself so uncertain, in the first half of the 16th century the more effective defence of Catholicism thus came from those who had been the leading stakeholders in the pre-Reformation Church: Europe's Catholic rulers. There was enough resistance among them to ensure that the Reformation outside Germany would suffer some notable reverses. Francis I punctured the optimism of those who hoped for reform in France through the executions of Louis de Berquin in 1529 and Etienne Dolet in 1546. However, the defence of the faith by these methods had distinct limitations. The Church was always vulnerable to a personal volte-face by the monarch, or a change of ruler. The same Henry VIII who burned the Protestants John Lambert and Robert Barnes also decided that theological conservatism could be consistent with repudiation of the pope.

It was for these reasons that the defence of the old faith became so closely associated with the personal crusade of the Habsburgs. There was never a real chance that the young Emperor Charles V would tolerate Protestantism. Although he was brought up at the sophisticated Burgundian Court, his personal faith had more in common with the Spanish core of his dominions. Here, the Catholic Church was perceived in a more positive light, respected and revered for its part in the reconquest of the Spanish peninsula. Charles manifested a similarly straightforward allegiance to the faith of his fathers. In the Holy Roman Empire, his first instinct was to condemn Luther unseen, and their meeting at the Diet of Worms concluded with a forthright declaration against Luther. In 1523 Charles's hereditary dominions, the Netherlands, saw the first executions for Protestant beliefs anywhere in Europe.

The 16th century would be the Habsburg century, and therein lay the Church's salvation. As Charles V passed the core of his massive dominions to his son Philip II, the tradition of Catholic loyalty would continue undiminished. But by then the Church had finally found its voice: the Counter-Reformation was in full swing.

The Council of Trent

The deliberations of the Council of Trent decisively set the limits of acceptable theological belief in the 16th century. The Council had been a long time in preparation, and the council's deliberations took over 20 years, but its eventual achievement was considerable, providing the solid theological and institutional core for the long-desired movement of Catholic renewal.

Francis Xavier, Jesuit saint and apostle to Asia. The Jesuits embodied the commitment and fervour needed to combat the insidious spread of Protestantism in Europe and to carry forth the missionary effort to the newly discovered lands of Asia and the Americas.

Emperor Charles V favoured a meeting under his influence in Germany, but successive popes were determined on an Italian location. Trent (now Trento), within the borders of the Holy Roman Empire, but in the Italian-speaking enclave south of the Alps, eventually satisfied both parties.

When the council finally met the pomp of the opening procession on 13 December 1545 only barely disguised a disappointing turn-out. But the assembled Church fathers persevered, through long discussions and, at times, heated argument. By the time the council closed some 20 years later, they had achieved that comprehensive definition of Catholic belief that the Church so badly needed.

The first substantive decision of the Council of Trent was to affirm the validity of the Latin Vulgate: a peremptory repudiation of years of Protestant (and humanist) criticism of the venerable received text of the Bible. The following year, the Council adopted a decree on justification equally unequivocal in its forthright rejection of Luther's perception of justification by faith alone, and went on to affirm the canonicity of the seven sacraments (Protestants recognized only two). The fathers also affirmed the continuing value of tradition alongside the authority of Scripture. The second period, 1551–2, produced a landmark declaration affirming transubstantiation. These doctrinal debates dominated the early sessions. It was only in the last sessions of 1561–3 that the bishops were able finally to conclude the decrees on Church reform that would shape the Church's approach to internal renewal over the following centuries: strengthening the authority of bishops over chapters and colleges, ordering episcopal visitations, and reform of religious orders and clerical discipline.

The Jesuits and new orders

In the history of the Counter-Reformation, a special place is always reserved for the new religious orders and, first and foremost, the Jesuits. The vision that lay behind the foundation of the Jesuits was that of a Basque nobleman, Ignatius Loyola. Loyola had dedicated his life to the Church after an early career as a soldier. When, in 1528, he settled in Paris to pursue his theological studies, he soon collected around him a small company of like-minded individuals, among them his fellow Basque, Francis Xavier. Together the group practised the rigorous programme of worship and self-examination devised by Ignatius immortalized as his *Spiritual Exercises*. Ordained priests in 1537, in 1540 Ignatius and his followers were formally constituted as the Society of Jesus, dedicated to an active life of preaching and ministry and acknowledging absolute and direct obedience to the pope. The principles embodied by Loyola – meticulous preparation and training, unwavering obedience, and a religious life of active service outside the cloister – proved an inspiration and lifeline to an embattled Church. Loyola's fame ensured a steady stream of new adepts. By the time of his death in 1556, the original group of ten members had grown to 1500, and this number would increase tenfold by the end of the century. All novices who joined the order would be

This artistic representation of the concluding session of the Council of Trent in 1564 is found in a 17th-century painting. After an uncertain and sparcely attended opening, the glittering closing ceremony was a tangible symbol of the council's success. Three sessions spread over 20 years had rearmed Catholicism for the struggle against heresy.

Peter Paul Rubens, The Miracle of Ignatius Loyola. *This baroque representation was a far cry from the austerity preached by the first Jesuits and epitomized in the career and writings of their founder, Ignatius Loyola. The search for new saints, however, was an essential part of the repudiation of Protestant values and the ornate splendour of the Baroque its visual manifestation.*

required to follow the full course of the *Spiritual Exercises.* The training was hard, and many did not last the course, but those who did emerged fully committed to the order's primary goals of preaching, teaching, and conversion. Jesuits eschewed the parochial ministry for service in schools, hospitals, and the mission field, and also at court, for the order soon counted a number of Europe's crowned heads among their most fervent admirers.

The efforts of the Jesuits were seconded by other new orders that emerged from this era of turbulence and self-examination within Catholicism. The Capuchins began as an offshoot of the Italian Observant movement, and they spread rapidly through the peninsula during the 1530s. The order made its name in works of charity and in preaching. The Theatrines, founded in Rome in 1524, dedicated themselves to ministry and liturgical reform. The re-examination of the vocation of the female religious life also led to significant new initiatives, notably the foundation in 1532 of the Company of St Ursula (the Ursulines). It is significant that so many of these new initiatives emanated from Italy, and there can be little doubt

that this active revivalism played an important role in deflecting the movement of evangelical reform within the peninsula from a more profound engagement with Protestantism.

It was in the field of education that the Jesuits left their most profound mark. There were seven Jesuit colleges in existence by 1544; by 1565, there were 30 colleges in Italy alone, and new foundations were carrying the Jesuitism towards places like Prague and Poland. In the first generation, the most important role of the new religious orders was providing a model of inspirational service: of sacrifice, if necessary unto death. To Europe's Catholics, desperate for clear guidance in a world where the familiar was under threat, the new orders offered patient certainties and unflinching resistance to the Church's foes. Further afield, inspiration was provided by men like Francis Xavier, who in 1542 embarked on the first of his missions to the non-Christian world: India, from where he established Goa as a base for Jesuit operations in Asia, and latterly in Japan. Missionary successes provided some compensation for the losses suffered to Protestantism nearer to home.

Redefining the Papacy   134–5 ►
The Monastic Orders   174–5 ►
Martin Luther and John Calvin   204–5 ►
The Counter-Reformation   212–13 ►

The Wars of Religion

The second half of the 16th century brought a new and murderous intensity to the religious conflicts of the age. The rise of Calvinism and the emergence of Counter-Reformation Catholicism brought two strong, self-confident and mutually incompatible faiths into conflict. The result was to plunge Northern and Western Europe into 40 years of turmoil, culminating in the infamous massacres of Paris and Antwerp, before peace was restored.

France

The first country to feel the effects of new developments was Calvin's own homeland, France. Calvin had left France in 1536; however, as his ministry in Geneva became more firmly established, he never forgot the suffering evangelicals of his homeland. By 1555, the steady infiltration of Calvinist ideas was beginning to have its effect in France. Churches were established in many of France's largest cities. Despite continuing persecution by the Catholic authorities, these churches grew steadily in size and self-confidence, urged on by Calvin's encouragement and more tangible help in the form of ministers dispatched from Geneva to lead them.

Then, in a few months in 1558–9, the prospects of the movement changed dramatically. In England, the Catholic queen Mary died, to be replaced by the Protestant Elizabeth. This shift in the geopolitical balance was confirmed when Henry II of France was fatally wounded at a tournament to celebrate the peace with Spain. The succession of his 15-year-old son Francis II unleashed a power struggle at court that bitterly exacerbated existing religious tensions. For the first time, leading nobles openly associated themselves with calls for religious toleration.

When Francis II in turn died unexpectedly (of an ear abscess, in December 1560), a new government, led by the Queen Mother, Catherine de Medici, attempted to pacify the new Calvinist Church, since 1555 grown to a mass movement of over 1,000 congregations and one million members. It was not to be. The Colloquy of Poissy of 1561, a meeting of Catholic bishops and Calvinist pastors aimed at providing for a settlement, broke up without agreement. When Catherine went ahead and proclaimed limited toleration anyway, outraged Catholics took to arms. The massacre of a Protestant congregation at Vassy in March 1562 gave the signal for a general conflict.

The wars unleashed in 1562 would last for 36 years. During this time, the fighting was far from continuous. There would be seven bursts of military activity, none lasting more than two years. Once the fighting had commenced, however, it proved almost impossible to rebuild any sense of trust. The well-meaning peace settlements concluded after each conflict collapsed under the pressure of events. For this was, from the beginning, an international conflict.

Scotland

After France, the first to feel the consequence of the new political constellation was Scotland, where the accession of a Protestant regime in England emboldened a small group of dissident Scottish nobles, urged on by John Knox, to establish Protestant worship. By the end of the year, evangelicals had seized churches in several Scottish burghs and forced the French regent Mary of Guise to take refuge in Edinburgh castle. When

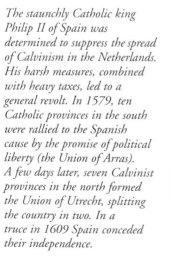

The staunchly Catholic king Philip II of Spain was determined to suppress the spread of Calvinism in the Netherlands. His harsh measures, combined with heavy taxes, led to a general revolt. In 1579, ten Catholic provinces in the south were rallied to the Spanish cause by the promise of political liberty (the Union of Arras). A few days later, seven Calvinist provinces in the north formed the Union of Utrecht, splitting the country in two. In a truce in 1609 Spain conceded their independence.

The Dutch Revolt 1568-1609

- Extent of Spanish Netherlands 1568
- Union of Arras 1579
- Joined Union of Utrecht 1579 and 1581
- Limit of Spanish advance 1589
- Netherlands in terms of 1609 truce
- Boundary of Holy Roman Empire 1568

English troops intervened on the Protestant side, victory was assured, and the Scottish revolution had created an unlikely triumph for the Reformation.

Revolt in the Netherlands

All of these events could only make difficulties for Philip II, whose northern territories in the Netherlands now looked dangerously exposed. In 1559 Philip abandoned his northern domains and returned to Spain. He left behind a land nursing an increasing sense of grievance at foreign, Spanish rule.

The Low Countries, too, were beginning to be unsettled by the spreading Calvinist heresy. Many of its inhabitants (particularly in the southern Walloon provinces where French was the predominant language) had friends and relatives in France, and reports of the violence and disruption there spread quickly across the frontier. Soon Calvinist cells were active in all of the major towns of Flanders and Brabant, encouraged by ministers who moved easily back and forth across the Channel to safe havens in England.

The dissidents' pleas for toleration were increasingly echoed by members of the nobility, led by William of Orange, who were happy to use the religious question as a stick with which to beat

Philip's unfortunate regent, Margaret of Parma. When Philip, in Spain, firmly rejected her recommendation to exhibit more moderation in his pursuit of heresy, the nobility staged a mass demonstration of defiance, riding armed into Margaret's chamber in Brussels.

Margaret had little choice but to give way, and, in April 1566, she ordered a temporary suspension of the heresy laws. The Calvinists thought their hour had come. Hurrying back from their exile in towns abroad to join the growing congregations, in the summer of 1566 they staged a series of mass open-air sermons – the so-called "hedge-preaching". In August, they went a step further. Sensing the opportunity to force the issue, small bands were sent into the churches to strip them of their Catholic statues and images, and cleanse them for Protestant worship.

The controlled violence of the iconoclasm initially achieved its objective: cowed town councils hastened to make available buildings for the Protestant congregations. But it also destroyed the loose opposition coalition that joined the nobility and the ministers. Shocked by the radicalism of what had occurred, the nobles drew back and assisted Margaret of Parma in putting down the Calvinist insurrection by force. By 1567, the churches were shut up and the Calvinists forced back into exile.

If Philip now felt that the problem of rebellion in the Netherlands had been solved, his hopes were premature. He took a decisive and fatal step when he dispatched to the Netherlands his most distinguished general, the Duke of Alva, to replace the exhausted Margaret as regent. Alva interpreted his instructions to punish the guilty with a severity that made thousands of new converts to the cause.

The Calvinists, secure in their exile strongholds, were able to make effective war on Alva through a campaign of privateering that preyed on the vital seaborne trade of the Netherlands. Soon the Netherlands was plunged into an economic crisis rendered more severe by the taxes Alva demanded to pay for the occupying army.

When, in 1572, a small group of rebel troops descended on the coast of Holland, most towns in the northern province soon opened their gates. Alva was compelled to subjugate them by force, but a brutal campaign of sieges failed to dislodge them. The valiant resistance of Leiden, inspired by the leadership of William of Orange, finally broke the spirit of the Spanish troops. Unpaid and mutinous, thousands mutinied in 1576 and descended on Antwerp in search of loot. The richest city of the Netherlands was plundered in three days of lawless violence that left thousands

Philip II *by Titian, an allegory of the Battle of Lepanto. To Philip of Spain fell the responsibility to defend the Catholic faith on several fronts: against Protestant heresy in the north and west, against the Ottomans in the Mediterranean. The victory of Lepanto in 1571 was his finest hour, celebrated throughout Europe as a decisive blow in the defence of Christendom.*

dead in the Sack of Antwerp. The outraged Dutch now banded together in an alliance – the Pacification of Ghent – dedicated to expelling the Spaniards once and for all.

The Catholic retaliation

In France, the first religious war had ended after a year of inconclusive fighting. The prospects for reconciliation looked relatively good. An optimistic Catherine de' Medici concluded the Peace of Amboise in 1560, promising limited toleration for the Protestant Huguenots, and immediately embarked on a two-year tour of France to introduce the young Charles IX to his people.

But in too many parts of France, the Catholics and Huguenots now hated each other with a passion, and the smallest incident could set off violence once more. In the event, the spark for renewed fighting came from outside the kingdom. The passage of the Duke of Alva's army to the Netherlands raised fears among Protestants everywhere. In France, the jittery Huguenot nobles once more took to arms, in two further bursts of fighting, in 1567–8 and 1568–70, ended by a new peace with the Treaty of St Germain in 1570.

Once again, Catherine attempted to construct a coalition for peace, now to be sealed by the marriage of Charles IX's sister Margaret de Valois to the titular head of the Huguenot movement, the young Henry of Navarre (later Henry IV). But events again conspired to thwart these good intentions. The struggle of the Dutch Calvinists had engaged the loyalty of many Huguenots, and now their most distinguished commander, Admiral Coligny, urged Charles IX to intervene in the Netherlands on the Protestant side. Catholics recoiled in horror, and Catherine, alarmed at Coligny's influence over the young Charles IX, was persuaded to take action to avoid an entanglement that would have meant certain war against Spain. A bungled assassination attempt against Coligny led to the fatal order for a pre-emptive strike against the Huguenot leaders gathered in Paris for the royal wedding. The attack, enthusiastically supported by the fanatically Catholic population of Paris, turned into an indiscriminate slaughter that became one of the most notorious crimes of the century: the St Bartholomew's Day Massacre, in which thousands of Huguenots were killed in Paris.

The events in Paris devastated the Huguenot leadership and accelerated a decline for French Protestantism that had begun with the Huguenot failure to win the first war. But the Church survived, secure in strongholds in the south of France, far from royal power. However, for all the bold words of Huguenot resistance theory, the fate of the movement was essentially decided: French Protestantism would survive, but as a minority movement. The opportunity for the conversion of France was gone.

In the Netherlands, too, these years brought an improvement of Catholic prospects. Chastened by the calamities of 1576, Philip's representatives adopted a more conciliatory tone, and this soon began to erode the fragile unity of the revolt. In 1579, a group of the southern provinces was persuaded to renew their loyalty to Spain in the Union of Arras. When the northern rebel provinces responded with their own Union of Utrecht, the future division of the Netherlands into a free north – the United Provinces or Dutch Republic – and a Spanish south – in modern-day Belgium – emerged.

Only military action could resolve the situation, and in the Duke of Parma the Spaniards had the finest general of the age. When Philip of Spain at last committed the necessary resources, the Spanish armies won some significant victories. Successive campaigning seasons brought the capitulation of most of the major cities of the southern plains, culminating in 1585 with the fall of Antwerp.

The resolution of the Reformation conflict

The assassination of William of Orange in 1584 and the fall of Antwerp plunged the Dutch Revolt into

Portrait of Henry II, King of France, and his wife, Catherine of Medici. The death of Henry II in 1559 would plunge France into crisis. His widow, Catherine, would remain a figure of political influence through the reign of three sons and three decades of religious warfare.

THE DAWN OF MODERN EUROPE   1400–1599

The Massacre of the Innocents

Brueghel lived through the turbulent events of the Dutch Revolt, and this darkly moving picture is often thought to be a veiled commentary on that period. Brueghel takes the well-known Nativity tale of the massacre of the first-born ordered by Herod and reinterpets it as a winter landscape. But here the tranquil beauty of the town is destroyed by murderous and pillaging soldiers, watched by a black-armoured commander, sometimes taken to be the Duke of Alva. Events like this were a frequent feature of the Dutch Revolt, and hatred of the Spanish soldiers eventually led the provinces to unite and throw off Spanish rule.

crisis. To sustain the revolt, Elizabeth I of England finally pledged military aid: the long-delayed showdown with Philip of Spain drew ever closer. English troops in the Netherlands did enough to persuade Philip that the final defeat of the Netherlands would occur only if England were subdued first.

This was the genesis of the famous Armada campaign of 1588: in effect, an attempt to solve the whole complex of problems of Northern Europe. In France, Philip could be assured of the support of the resurgent Guise family, now united in their hostility to the succession of a Huguenot king, Henry of Navarre, heir since the death of the last Valois brother, the Duke of Anjou, in 1584. In the Netherlands, the Duke of Parma was ordered to suspend his campaign and to prepare to embark his battle-hardened troops for England.

The strategic ambition was impressive, but the consequence of failure calamitous. As the Armada limped home, scattered by English fire-ships and adverse weather, Philip's entire position began to unravel. In France, King Henry III, emboldened by Philip's humiliation, made one last effort to free himself from the powerful Guise family. In

December 1588, he summoned the Duke of Guise and his brother the Cardinal and had them assassinated. When Henry was himself murdered by an avenging member of the Catholic League

Henry of Navarre became Henry IV.

It would take Henry a further five years finally to quell the League and make good his claim to the throne. Philip made frantic efforts to prevent his victory, twice ordering the Duke of Parma to march his army south from the Netherlands to assist the League. But this merely afforded the hard-pressed Dutch breathing space, and, by 1594, the survival of an independent Dutch state was assured.

In France, Henry IV's victory came at a cost. A realist, he recognized that he could not govern without taking the religion of the majority of his subjects, and, in 1593, he converted to Catholicism. The settlement with his former Huguenot allies in 1598, the Edict of Nantes, allowing freedom of worship, brought the French civil wars to an end. The conflicts in France, the Netherlands, and Britain had brought war and hardship for more than a generation, but they had effectively settled the religious map of Western Europe for the next three centuries.

THE WARS OF RELIGION   **219**

The High Renaissance

In the early Renaissance, Italy had no rival as the cultural centre of Europe. Europe's rulers vied for the service of Italy's best-known artists and architects. Gradually, however, the influence of Italian culture spread through the continent; by the end of the 16th century, German, French, and Dutch artists could equal the best that Italy had to offer.

The last three decades of the 15th century were a wondrous time in the history of the arts. In these years, the culture of the Italian city-states reached its apogee: the proud cities of Florence, Venice, and Milan vied for supremacy, and the wealth o their leading citizens was poured out in an extravagant rebuilding and redecoration of the urban environment. These were great years for artists and architects. In Florence, the distinctive style of Sandro Botticelli gave way to that of Filippo and Filippino Lippi. Waiting in the wings was the prodigious genius of the young Raphael.

By the end of the century, the power of Florence declined as successive French invasions exposed the vulnerability of the smaller independent states. But the eager cultural patronage of a succession of ambitious popes ensured a new source of lucrative commissions in Rome. Raphael and Michelangelo were both employed on the redecoration of the new Papal Palace and St Peter's Cathedral, with Michelangelo devoting the last 20 years of his life to his master work, the Sistine Chapel.

The Northern Renaissance

Artistic visitors to Italy ensured that the new discoveries of the Renaissance – the mastery of perspective and the realistic rendering of the human form – did not remain confined to the peninsula. One of the first to carry the techniques back to a northern context was the precocious German artist Albrecht Dürer. Dürer brought the lessons of Italian technique to bear on the naturalistic German tradition of painting with its deeply felt interest in land-

Hans Holbein, The Ambassadors. *In the 16th century, the lessons of the Renaissance gradually made their way from Italy across the Alps, and thence to Northern Europe. Hans Holbein, a German trained in Basel, provided the vital link with England, where his portraits of the court were an artistic sensation.*

scape – known as the Danube school. Dürer was a genuine innovator. He excelled not only in the conventional modes of panel painting, but also in the new forms of woodcut and metal engraving.

The woodcut, an illustrative form capable of mass production, was German art's distinctive contribution to the Renaissance. The darkly brooding intensity of the late Gothic masters, epitomized by the work of Matthias Grünewald, gave way to a host of artist entrepreneurs, whose work was characterized by an enormous variety of modes and styles – among them Albrecht Altdorfer of Regensburg and Lucas Cranach at Wittenberg. None grasped the new potential of the marketplace better than the multi-talented Hans Holbein the Younger. Holbein settled first in Basle, then, when the Reformation threatened the market in Church art, in England. Here he became court painter to Henry VIII, producing a series of portraits of nobles and courtiers in a modern style previously unknown in England. Typically for a Renaissance court artist, Holbein's work for Henry included eclectic commissions such as the decoration of furniture, designs for precious vases, and book illustration. The concept of the artist as master of an individual style – rather than the talented artisan working to order – emerged only gradually.

The Renaissance in France

The development of the northern Renaissance in no way submerged the admiration of things Italian. The French armies that descended on the peninsula left a disreputable trail of plunder and ransacked buildings, but their kings and generals maintained a profound respect for Italian art and craftsmanship. Louis XII and Francis I continued to look to Italy for cultural models, and many of Italy's leading artists were tempted north by their offer of salaries and lucrative commissions. Andrea del Sarto and Benvenuto Cellini were among those who worked for Francis I, and Leonardo da Vinci was able to trade his reputation for a comfortable and affluent retirement in France.

For all the eager imitation of all things Italian, the most enduring legacy of this French Renaissance would be the distinctive style of architecture. France's kings lavished enormous energy on the rebuilding of their castles and residences, evolving in the process a unique style that merged classical Italian principles with those of the northern tradition. The châteaux of the Loire exuded the confidence of a new monarchy that no longer required their places of residence to be fortified for defence. It was a style of architectural statement that was in turn widely imitated throughout Europe.

Michelangelo's David. *Created to epitomize the values of a proud city-state, Michelangelo's exuberant celebration of the human form formed a massive and tangible expression of the values of both the humanist movement and the Renaissance.*

The Renaissance in Italy

In Italy itself, the second half of the century brought new opportunities. The challenge of Protestantism reinforced the importance of the papacy as the focus of the Catholic Church. The growing confidence of Catholic renewal after the Council of Trent brought the development of new, self-consciously opulent forms of devotional art. In Italy, this was the age of the High Renaissance and Mannerism, epitomized by the dominance of the Venetian school. Its best-known figure, Titian, was an artist of truly international reputation. He travelled widely, fulfilling commissions for both Charles V and Philip II, as well as successive popes. In contrast, the best of Tintoretto's work was for local patrons, including the remarkable series of decorative paintings for the Scuola di San Rocco that occupied him for almost 20 years from 1565. Paolo Veronese, meanwhile, was occupied on a similarly grandiose scheme in the ducal palace. In Venice, Veronese's deep interest in the architectural structure of painting had occasioned charges that religious themes were not sufficiently respected and even, in 1573, a summons from the Venetian Inquisition: an early indication of the problems that would later dog the free-wheeling genius Caravaggio. More representative of the new religiosity was El Greco, born in Crete but active mostly in Spain. The tormented spirituality of his figures attracted the admiration of Philip II of Spain. With the growth of new capitals in Vienna and Prague, the Habsburgs would therefore end the century as they had begun: as the most significant artistic patrons of the age.

The Carolingian Renaissance   130–1 ▶
The Roots of Renaissance   170–1 ▶
The Counter-Reformation   212–13 ▶
Technological and
Intellectual Progress   222–3 ▶

Technological and Intellectual Progress

The 16th century was not a period of startling technological change: none of the transforming scientific inventions or discoveries can be dated to this period. It did witness a steady advance in the sophistication of scientific enquiry, however, as men of learning turned enquiring minds towards the natural world, the human body, and the heavens.

Scientific enquiry in the 16th century could broadly be said to fall within three traditions: the organic, or science of observation, based on analogies drawn from the natural world; the magical, which cast God as the interpreter of nature; and the mechanistic, based on the notion of the universe as machine, working within a framework of regularity, permanence, and predictability. Although each made its contribution to the advancement of knowledge, these approaches were not equally conducive to the growth of modern science.

Anatomy and botany

Significant progress was made in the 16th century in the science of observation, notably in the fields of anatomy and botany. The opening up of new continents further stimulated an already acute interest in the workings of the human body and the animal world. Especially influential was the work of the great German botanist Leonard Fuchs. In France, Pierre Belon published an influential series of studies, cast as travel narratives, based on close observation of the plant and animal kingdoms of Europe and Asia. Belon, like Fuchs, was deeply indebted to the illustrative woodcut, which reached its full potential in these works of scientific description. The woodcut, in fact, made a powerful and often underestimated contribution to the development of the scientific book.

In the field of anatomy, the crucial figure was Andreas Vesalius (1514–1564), professor of surgery and anatomy at Padua. Vesalius's famous anatomical treatise *De Humanis Corporis fabrica* of 1543 was based on studies of cadavers, but the

Nicolaus Copernicus' 1543 map of the universe, showing his theory of the earth, the planets, and the zodiac circling the sun. Martin Luther was among those who rejected Copernicus' ideas, stating: "I believe in the Holy Scripture, since Joshua ordered the Sun, not the Earth, to stand still."

observation – and glorification – of the human form remained within the framework of an essentially moralistic world view. The science of anatomy led to few significant breakthroughs in the treatment of illness and disease. The wonderfully gifted German physician Paracelsus remained a maverick and an outsider. Paracelsus's criticism of the accepted orthodoxy of the 2nd-century Greek anatomist Galen to some extent anticipated a more modern school of organic treatment, moving beyond the Greek tradition that the roots of disease were to be found in a disordered balance of the four humours: phlegm, choler, melancholy, and blood. But his insistence on chemical remedies and faith in the Jewish cabbala plotted no clear route forward. Medical science advanced dramatically only with William Harvey's discovery of the circulation of the blood in the following century.

Science and religion

Other scientific investigators concentrated on three main fields: mathematics, astrology, and alchemy. All had strongly theological agendas. The science of numbers also had strong links with the cabbala, a connection embodied in the career of the Elizabethan scientist-magician John Dee. Dee epitomized the strangely ambiguous world of 16th-century science, combining a profound fascination with the wisdom of the ancients and an acute interest in observation and experiments. Thus the critical experiment of Galileo – his analysis of the acceleration of falling bodies – was to some extent anticipated by 16th-century figures, such as the Dutch mathematician and engineer Simon Stevin. Much of the most profound and intense interest was devoted to the observation of the heavens and celestial bodies. The 16th century saw the first radical criticism of the geocentric theory of the universe inherited from Aristotle and Ptolemy. The Polish astronomer Nicolaus Copernicus revolutionized the traditional Ptolemaic cosmology by placing the sun at the centre of the universe, with the earth moving round it in an annual revolution. He also argued that the earth rotated on its axis every 24 hours.

These were extraordinary discoveries, but in his own day Copernicus was spurned, not least by the Protestant reformers Luther and Melanchthon, who preferred a science firmly grounded in the Bible. This is one of the many reasons why the scientific discoveries of the 16th century remained more potential than real. This was an age caught between conflicting and mutually contradictory impulses. The wisdom of the ancients was simultaneously revered – by the humanists of the Renaissance – and distrusted. Many did not believe

Sixteenth-century medicine

The system of the veins, a woodcut from Andreas Vesalis' *De Humani Corporis fabrica* (1543). Sixteenth-century medicine continued to be dominated by the conflicting theoretical systems of the ancients and remained too remote and academic to make much real improvement in the field of healthcare. But the ground was prepared for future breakthroughs by an increased interest in the observation of nature, here epitomized by the science of anatomy. Scholarly enquiry of this sort was indebted to the development of the woodcut, which provided the opportunity for the precise rendering of scientific observation.

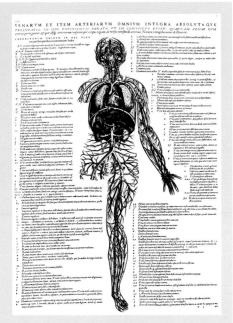

that God would have revealed the secrets of the universe to heathens. Much scientific energy was poured into alchemy, the search to transform base metal into gold. This deluded search at least built on the genuine, incremental technical advances in the manufacture of kilns and foundries, two of the real technological successes of the age. There was also increasing scientific interest in the arts of war, notably ballistics. Most of all, however, the 16th century had as yet no place for a godless science – a science of observation made only halting progress against a world view based on spiritual and theoretical principles.

Political thought

More concrete were the achievements in political thought. The political developments of a turbulent age stimulated men already attuned to fundamental questions of social organization by the acute observations of the ancients. Now talented thinkers applied these lessons to important contemporary developments, especially the rise of the State and the class of rival religious systems. The result was some notable theoretical writing, ranging from the broadly monarchist views of Claude de Seyssel and Jean Bodin, to the radical speculations of those who argued for a right of resistance to State power in defence of true religion. In the 17th century, it would be the former that narrowly triumphed, with the onward march of royal absolutism. But the articulation of a sense of the independence and nobility of the human spirit, evident in writers as diverse as Erasmus and Montaigne, also put down enduring roots.

ABSOLUTISM AND ENLIGHTENMENT

1600–1789

POLITICS AND GOVERNMENT

1642 Outbreak of the English Civil War between King Charles I and Members of Parliament. The war ends in 1645 with the Royalist defeat at the Battle of Naseby. Charles is eventually tried and executed in 1649.

1635 France declares war on Spain, beginning the decline of Spain as a European power and its supersession by France.

1618–48 The Defenestration of Prague begins the Thirty Years War, involving almost every European power. The war ends with the Peace of Westphalia in 1648.

1630 Gustavus II Adolphus, King of Sweden, lands in Pomerania with his army to defend the Protestant cause.

1689 Peter the Great assumes the throne in Russia, initially sharing power with his brother Ivan, who dies in 1696.

1688–9 Glorious Revolution in England. James II deposed and replaced by Protestants William III and his wife Mary.

1683 Siege of Vienna by the Turks is relieved, ending the threat of Turkish forces in central Europe.

1652 Fronde revolt finally ends in France, paving the way for the assumption of absolute power under Louis XIV.

1653 Cromwell becomes Lord Protector in Britain. Following his death in 1658, his son becomes Lord Protector, but the threat of renewed civil war leads to the restoration of Charles I's son, Charles II, in 1660.

1672 Louis XIV begins attempt to conquer the Netherlands and is opposed by William of Orange (William III).

1600 | **1625** | **1650** | **1675**

SOCIETY AND CULTURE

1619 William Harvey lectures on the circulation of the blood at St Bartholomew's Hospital, London.

1633 Astronomer Galileo Galilei is tried by the Roman Inquisition for championing the Copernican view of the universe. He is forced to recant these beliefs.

1635 Académie Française is set up through the initiative of Cardinal Richelieu.

1687 Isaac Newton publishes *Principia Mathematica* (*The Principles of Mathematics*), introducing the concept of gravity.

1664–73 Molière writes and performs his greatest plays including *Le Misanthrope* (1666); *L'Avare* (1668), and *Le Malade Imaginaire* (1673).

1644 Descartes publishes his *Principia Philosophica*, discussing the laws of motion.

1607 Monteverdi composes *L'Orfeo* – generally considered the first opera.

1602 Dutch East India Company formed from amalgamation of smaller Dutch companies and ejects the Portuguese from the spice trade.

1651 Thomas Hobbes publishes his *Leviathan*, urging the creation of a sovereign power to avoid anarchy and disorder.

1697 Peter the Great sets out on a journey to learn the technology of the West; he brings back hundreds of artisans to Russia.

1701 Outbreak of War of Spanish Succession, plunging Europe into 12 years of warfare to curb Louis XIV's ambition to control the crown of Spain.

1748 Treaty of Aix-la-Chapelle ends first round of warfare over Silesia.

1756 Outbreak of Seven Years War.

1762 Catherine the Great becomes Tsarina of Russia.

1740 Frederick the Great of Prussia seizes Silesia in defiance of the Pragmatic Sanction, precipitating a generation of conflict in Central Europe.

1733–5 War of Polish Succession weakens Polish state and foreshadows the intervention of other powers in Polish affairs.

1763 Peace of Paris ends Seven Years War. Britain gains control of most of North America and India.

1772 First Partition of Poland between Austria, Prussia, and Russia.

1709 Peter the Great secures a decisive victory at Pultava over Charles XII of Sweden, destroying Swedish power in the Baltic.

1776 American Declaration of Independence adopted by representatives of the 13 North American colonies.

1713–14 Treaties of Utrecht, Rastadt, and Baden conclude the War of Spanish Succession.

1715 Jacobite rising fails in Great Britain; the House of Hanover is secured on the throne.

1787 Assembly of Notables meets in France but rejects reform proposals, precipitating the final crisis of the French government.

1725   **1750**   **1775**   **1800**

1762 Publication of Rousseau's *Emile*, and *The Social Contract*.

1789 Lavoisier's *Treatise on Chemistry* founds modern science of chemistry.

1720–1 Vico outlines his Universal Law connecting the philosophy of law with general philosophy.

1748 Montesquieu produces *L'Esprit des lois* (*The Spirit of Laws*), examining the relationship between a society's laws and its character.

1751–77 Diderot and d'Alembert edit and publish the multi-volumed *Encyclopédie ou dictionnaire raisonné des métiers par une société de gens de lettres*, which accounts for all the new ideas of the time and starts the Enlightenment.

1786 Mozart composes the *Marriage of Figaro*. Some of his finest works include the operas *Don Giovanni* (1787); *The Magic Flute* (1791).

1726 Jonathan Swift publishes *Gulliver's Travels*.

1729 Bach composes *St Matthew's Passion*.

1776 Adam Smith's *Wealth of Nations* published, advocating free trade and examining the role of the market.

1702 The *Daily Courant*, the first European daily newspaper, is founded in England.

1700 Academy of Science founded in Berlin under the influence of Leibnitz.

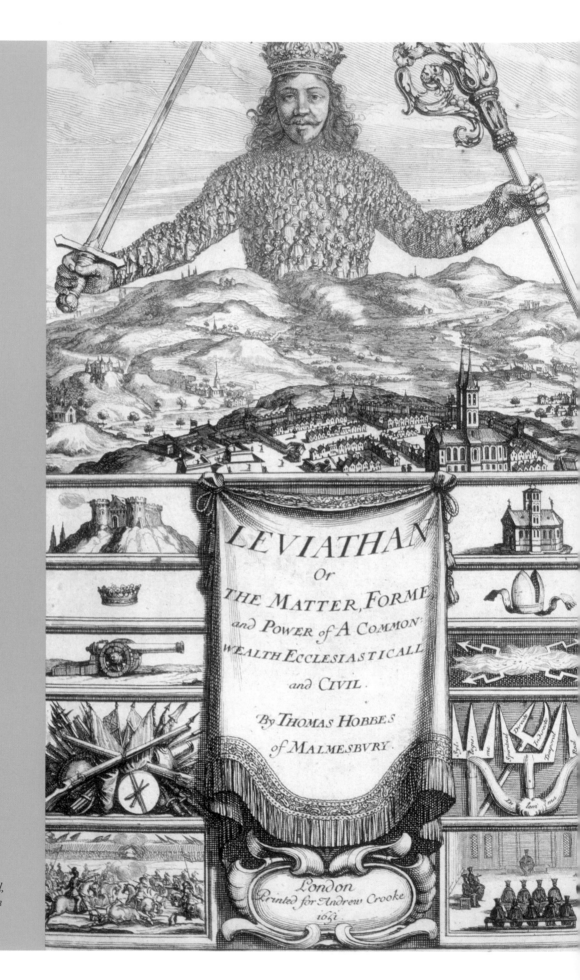

Thomas Hobbes, like many of his contemporaries, was obsessed with the sociopolitical disorder of the age and the apparent collapse of traditional political authority. In Leviathan *(1651)* he called for the creation of all-powerful states possessing the power to force their subjects to live in harmony; this, he stated, was the best hope of the restoration of civil order in Europe.

THE SEARCH FOR ORDER AND HARMONY

National and international conflicts in the 16th century had demonstrated the fragility of the forces of order and harmony, but, although a measure of stability had been achieved across much of Europe by 1600, sociopolitical tensions soon manifested themselves again and plunged Europe back into war.

Religious differences made their contribution to renewed conflict, yet in a way that was paradoxical. Churches overcame doctrinal divisions within their ranks, but this internal unity increased their tendency to confront each other. Thus, the Council of Trent equipped the Catholic Church with a clearly defined doctrine and organizational discipline with which to conduct a Counter-Reformation to recover lands and people lost to Protestantism. On their side, the Lutherans resolved their theological differences through the Formula of Concord and presented a united front to the Counter-Reformation. Meanwhile, Calvinism flourished in Switzerland, the Dutch Republic, Scotland, parts of Germany, and France. Relations between Calvinism and Lutheranism were little better than with Catholicism.

Rulers responded to the challenge of governing multi-confessional societies by adhering to a principle adopted at the Peace of Augsburg: *cuius regio, eius religio* ("whose the region, his the religion"). That is to say, in each state or territory, the religion of the ruler should be that of the subjects. For those who refused to comply, it was up to the ruler to decide whether to force them into obedience, impose discriminatory legislation, or extend toleration to them; but this was a matter for the ruler alone. This principle suffered many infractions, but it was the most effective response in Europe to the question of how to deal with multi-confessional societies.

Another source of continuing sociopolitical division was what might be termed "constitutional" tensions. Rulers wielded considerable powers, but also acknowledged the "rights" of their subjects. Little agreement existed, however, as to the boundaries between powers and rights. Bodies such as Parliament in England, provincial Estates in France, and the various Cortes in Spain laid claim to rights regarding, for example, the passage of legislation or consent to taxation; on their side, monarchs often argued that these "rights" usurped their powers. Many of the rebellions and civil wars of the 17th century revolved around such questions.

When monarchs did suppress the "rights" of legally constituted bodies, they sought to justify their actions by two principal explanations which, when taken together, provided theoretical foundations of absolutism. One was the theory of the Divine Right of Kings. Catholic and Protestant monarchs alike stressed the divine foundations of their legitimacy. They proclaimed that they had been chosen by God and that their policies fulfilled the divine purpose; because of this, there were no circumstances under which subjects legitimately might resist the ruler. The second was the theory of *raison d'état*. This contended that, should circumstances arise in which the very existence of the state was placed in jeopardy, there were no limits as to what the ruler might do to save the state. Expressed in such simple terms, the theory carried much force, provided that it referred to temporary arrangements that would be abandoned once the crisis was over. However, in a Europe where warfare was endemic for long periods, governments, in the name of *raison d'état*, resorted to measures that looked like becoming permanent, but which diminished the "rights" of their subjects. Were rulers tending towards despotism, and, if so, how far should they be resisted?

Economic Stagnation and the Growth of Trade

The 17th century is usually depicted by economic historians as a period of "pause" between the more dynamic 16th and 18th centuries. The period saw two main changes. The price inflation of the preceding century came to an end, and prices thereafter remained stable, while the volume of economic activity in Europe failed to continue expanding at the same rate as in the 1500s. Relative economic stagnation set in.

The commercial revolution of the 17th century owed much to advances in financial services. Stock exchanges, such as that in Amsterdam as shown here, opened up companies to investors, and enabled international capital to find the best markets and highest returns. Behind the dealing and exchanges were some of the finest financial minds of the age. The Amsterdam bourse was a leader in its field and made an important contribution to the prosperity of the Dutch Republic.

The "little ice age"

This unfavourable context owed much to harsh climatic conditions. The 17th century was the climax of the "little ice age" which lasted from about 1400 to the mid-1700s. Average temperatures were lower than they are today – summers were cooler and shorter, and autumn, winter, and spring longer, wetter, and colder. The worst winter of the period was that of 1708–9, when extensive areas of Europe were frozen for several months, and much economic activity ceased. In France, for example, the autumn of 1708 was already unusually cold; in January 1709 temperatures plummeted, reaching -20 degrees Celsius (-4 degrees Fahrenheit) even in Montpellier and Marseilles. Stretches of the Seine, Garonne, and Rhône froze; in the countryside, fruit trees, and root and seed crops were ruined, and livestock and wildlife died. Within the human population, the death rate among the old, poor, and weak accelerated. The crisis lasted through February and most of March, with catastrophic consequences for harvests later in the year. The experience of France was repeated across northern and central Europe, and even south into the Mediterranean region. The winter of 1708–9 may have been exceptional, but it demonstrated the vulnerability of economic activity of the period to meteorological variation.

Agriculture was by far the most important sector of the economy, and its inability to augment the food supply to any appreciable extent is one of the chief factors in the relative stagnation of the period. Crops and livestock continued to be managed in traditional ways – open fields, crop rotation, fallow periods, the grazing of livestock between crops and on common ground – and it was only by opening up new territory, as happened, for example, in the Ukraine, that production could be increased significantly. It was not until the 18th century that the "New

Agriculture", associated with names such as Arthur Young, attempted to transform traditional practices by the application of scientific principles and techniques. In the 17th century, most agriculture remained at subsistence level or slightly above, with produce consumed locally. One important exception to this was Poland, which had large surpluses of grain available for export.

These factors had demographic consequences. Although reliable population figures for the 17th

The coldest winter during the last phase of the "little ice age" was that of 1708–9. Temperatures dropped rapidly in January 1709 and remained low (as much as -20 degrees Celsius) throughout much of February. The whole of Europe was affected, resulting in such rare spectacles as people skating on the ice in Venice.

century are extremely difficult to establish, the total population of Europe west of Russia seems to have been about 70 million in the 1680s, compared with about 60 million in the 1560s. Yet both of these figures were inferior to that of 80 million in 1340. In other words, Europe was still recovering from the demographic effects of the Black Death, and it was only by the 1730s that the population once again attained the levels of the Middle Ages. In part, this slow recovery was deliberate. Conscious of the precarious nature of the food supply and the frequency of subsistence crises, Europeans married late and had relatively small families (four or five children on average). In France, England, and elsewhere, most men were over 25 and most women in their early twenties when they married. Also, about 10 per cent of the population remained celibate, either for religious or economic reasons. The birth rate was on average 30–38 per thousand, while the death rate was about 28–35 per thousand. Although these figures indicate a slowly growing population, subsistence crises interrupted the process and prevented a sustained rise. Death rates were especially high among children. On average, a quarter, or even more, could die within two years of birth, and only half reached the age of 20. The slow expansion of the population was both a product of, and a contributor to, agricultural stagnation.

Commerce and trade

If agriculture remained relatively stagnant, commerce proved to be dynamic. The main European seaways and river systems continued to sustain commercial enterprise, while Mediterranean ports maintained links with Asian markets via centres such as Constantinople and Cairo. However, in the 16th century, a commercial revolution had begun that at first affected only the western seaboard of Europe, but eventually touched the lives of most Europeans. This revolution derived from the creation of European colonies in the Americas. Those colonies provided primary materials in abundance: precious metals, timber, sugar, tobacco, and their associated products. European manufactured goods and African slaves were transported to the colonies. The Atlantic trade, like many other facets of European long-distance commerce, was protected by home governments, and conducted by trading companies that enjoyed monopolies. The profits were immense, and transformed Western Europe from an economic backwater into an economic frontier.

The Americas also helped to augment the European food supply to the point that, in the 18th century, surpluses allowed the population to increase more rapidly. The key was found in crops from the Americas that flourished in Europe. Two were of revolutionary importance: the potato and maize. They were both easy to grow and highly nutritious; by the early 1700s, they were sufficiently widespread to enhance the diet of most Europeans significantly. As an approximate guide, north of a line drawn from Bordeaux across the continent, the potato flourished, and, south of the line maize did. By the mid-1700s, for the first time in its history, Europe had the capacity to feed itself comfortably.

Social Order and Social Strife

Although European societies were hierarchical, the nature of those hierarchies varied. Noble and ecclesiastical titles generally held the key to gradations among the elites, but, among commoners, rank could be determined by other factors, including wealth. Social stratification was seen as the most effective means of binding together people of diverse power, and wealth, so that all might co-operate for the good of society.

The worst excesses of social distress were combated by charitable organizations, both ecclesiastical and lay. These respectable-looking women governors of the alms-houses in Haarlem, the Netherlands, are representative of the kinds of socially aware people whose organizational skills and voluntary endeavour were crucial to alleviating the suffering of the destitute.

To enforce social order, central governments and provincial and municipal authorities possessed formal apparatus of legislation, law courts, militias, and, in the last resort, the army. However, these came into operation only when order had broken down; social order itself was preserved mainly through institutional and moral forces. The former category included the established Churches, whether Catholic, Protestant, or Orthodox, which preached obedience to legally established authorities and the virtues of a given social system. Schools, colleges, and universities likewise sought to instil habits of obedience and respect for authority. Religious confraternities, trade guilds, associations of merchants, and other bodies contributed to the spiritual and economic ordering of society. In many parts of rural Europe, village communities regulated local affairs, providing a forum for resolving disputes or tensions.

Social order

These institutions were backed by traditional social assumptions. People of lower status displayed deference towards those of higher rank; they admitted the right of those above to exert authority over those below. Family structures reinforced such values. The authority of the paternal head was paramount: he exerted control over every facet of the lives of the members of the household. Children were brought up to believe that a well-ordered family, in which authority was respected, was a model for society at large; the imperatives that underpinned domestic tranquillity also held society together.

Social protest and conflict lay just below the surface of peasant life in many parts of Europe. When subsistence crises occurred, peasants often resorted to violent protest. They also had to protect their scarce resources from bands of marauding soldiers. Skirmishes between peasants and raiders were common, with little mercy shown by either side.

Pride in one's village, town, or province also helped to preserve social order. This was especially true of Italian city-states, Swiss cantons, and towns and provinces of the decentralized Dutch Republic, but was a feature of Europe as a whole. Local loyalties were intense, and provided a vigorous sense of unity within communities. From the point of view of governments, some of the most dangerous manifestations of rebellion were those in which the "vertical" ties of a hierarchical society combined with provincial sentiment in a movement of resistance. This happened, for example, in France in 1639 when almost the whole of Normandy, including nobles, priests, and peasants, rose against the fiscal policies of the crown.

Social breakdown

When social order did break down, it usually began as protest triggered by grievances, or conflict between social groups. If the disorder lasted more than a week or two, protest and conflict could become enmeshed. Protest was usually directed by lower groups against their superiors – peasants against landlords, employees against employers – or by an entire community against external pressures, especially the fiscal demands of governments. Social protest often had economic roots and was common at times of subsistence crises when food prices rose, but governments still increased the tax burden. Europeans were also notoriously xenophobic, and much protest was directed at outsiders deemed to be a menace. In 1620, when word arrived in Marseilles that a local ship had been taken by Algerian pirates and the crew killed, a mob demonstrated against Turkish merchants in the town, resulting in the massacre of more than 50 of the Turkish community.

Social conflict remained equally problematic. Religious antagonisms could turn violent and unleash intercommunal fury; noble factions fought against each other (much sociopolitical disorder in Poland in the second half of the century arose out of wars between nobles); towns and villages could find themselves at odds with their neighbours; and, within large towns, guilds or other organizations were frequently in conflict. Town councils and other local authorities generally feared social conflict, not least because it disrupted the local economy and resulted in serious material damage. The attitudes of central governments were more ambivalent: when faced with united protest in the provinces, governments could undermine it through judicious concessions to certain groups, so dividing the opposition and turning an original protest against government into a conflict between social groups.

Peasants' Meal by Louis le Nain

The works of Louis Le Nain (c.1600–48) include scenes from peasant life, a theme much in vogue in the Netherlands, but less so in France, where allegorical or classical scenes were more usual. Le Nain is credited with introducing genre painting to France, depicting rural life with the classical elements typical of historical painting. He treated his subjects with dignity, avoiding sentimentality or mockery. This painting of a family at table is geometrically composed, with the figures arranged as in a classical frieze against a plain, dark background. The atmosphere is one of calm and sobriety.

Social strife remained endemic, but, although much of it was brief and of local significance, there were periods when it fused into clusters of revolt indicating widespread social problems. This was the case from the late 1630s to the early 1660s. During that period, scarcely any part of Europe avoided revolt, rebellion, or civil war. To many historians, these decades were the climax of a "general crisis" affecting European civilization. Some historians saw this "crisis" as having an economic cause: primitive capitalism, as represented mainly by commercial entrepreneurship, was undermining older economic structures, and a rising bourgeoisie was beginning to challenge the sociopolitical dominance of the noble elite. Others found the key in the growth of the modern state. The intervention of the state in the lives of its subjects (justified in monarchic Europe by appeal to the Divine Right of Kings or *raison d'état*) had reached such a pitch that a movement of resistance swelled up from Ireland to the Ukraine and from Sweden to Sicily. Whatever the merits of such all-embracing analyses of the "general crisis", there is no denying that social disorder could translate from the local to the international arena.

The Arts and Architecture

This period saw a flourishing of the visual and performing arts, with innovations in all artistic spheres. The exuberance of the baroque style included painting, architecture, and music, and was to develop into the stylized artifice of the rococo style. New markets began to appear for paintings, with the prosperous middle classes buying portraits and still lifes to decorate their homes.

Baroque sculpture emphasized the grotesque, the contorted, and the exaggerated. It employed elaborate and detailed decoration, and sought to impress the observer by the exorbitance, not to say the excess, of its treatment of its subjects. Baroque sculpture was not "comfortable": it provoked, excited, and disturbed.

The subject matter of most paintings of the period can be divided into four categories. First, there were great historical, including biblical and mythological, themes, as may be seen in works by Rubens. A second category was genre painting, including landscapes, interiors, and scenes of urban and rural life. Artists such as Claude Lorraine, Vermeer, and Steen raised genre painting to exceptional heights. Portraits constituted the third category. Rembrandt, Velázquez, and Van Dyck, among others, expanded its conventions and left a magnificent heritage. The final category was still life.

Although artists preserved stylistic diversity, some ideas acquired international currency. The innovations of Caravaggio were taken up throughout Europe. Reacting against the formality and emotional restraint of 16th-century art, he injected tension and violence into his paintings by choosing dramatic subjects, introducing extreme contrasts between light and shade (known as *chiaroscuro*), and depicting his human figures with extravagant gestures, as seen in *The Martyrdom of St Matthew*. Few artists escaped his influence, and he stands as the radical giant of the age who transformed painting.

The baroque style

In architecture, Rome was unrivalled, not only for the number and quality of its classical buildings, but as the city that pioneered the new baroque style of architecture as well. Baroque buildings were constructed according to principles that reinterpreted and even broke the rules of classical architecture, to create a sense of shock and wonder in the viewer. In place of classical harmony and balance, grandeur, exuberance, and ornamentation characterized baroque buildings. The chief masters of Roman baroque architecture were Cortona, Bernini, and Borromini. Borromini's church of San Carlo alle Quatro Fontane epitomized the baroque style, with its undulating walls and unusual internal perspectives. St Peter's Basilica and its Piazza Obliqua, completed by

Bernini, proclaimed the triumph of baroque as conceived on a grand scale.

Baroque architecture spread throughout Europe, including England, where Blenheim Palace in Oxfordshire, designed by Sir John Vanburgh, stands as a fine example. The baroque style inspired much Catholic church-building, to the extent that some have seen it as the architectural embodiment of the Counter-Reformation. It was equally adaptable to secular purposes, and found some of its most sumptuous achievements in the reconstruction of Vienna after the siege of 1683. Fischer von Erlach, Lukas von Hildebrandt, and Prandtauer were the Viennese equivalents of Cortona, Bernini, and Borromini, and, with such buildings as the Clam-Gallas Palace and the Winter Palace of Eugene of Savoy, made Vienna an architectural rival of Rome.

A shift from restraint to exuberance also occurred in music. Composers employed devices such as varieties of tempo or volume, or followed solo passages with combined choral and instrumental sections, to achieve "baroque" effects. They broke pieces up into contrasting movements, and learned how to resolve the ends of movements by harmonic progressions. This philosophy of composition, in which the emphasis was on variety, antithesis, and the unexpected, came to be known as *concertante* (ie based on contrast). Both religious and secular music conformed to the new style. Music aimed to stir the emotions and excite the passions; to that end, composers employed techniques that were the counterpart of those in painting and architecture.

Monteverdi was probably the first to compose consistently in the baroque style. Indeed, for long periods, Italy dominated the musical and visual arts, for Monteverdi had distinguished successors in Cavalli, Cesti, and Frescobaldi. As early as 1610, Monteverdi published church vespers in the new style; he also helped to develop opera, in which instrumental and vocal music came together with dance and theatre to create spectacles of extraordinary emotional power. His first opera, *L'Orfeo* (1607), was revolutionary in its drama. In northern Europe, Monteverdi had his nearest counterpart in Schütz, whose opera *Dafne* was first performed in 1627. In keyboard music, Buxtehude rivalled anything by Frescobaldi. As the century progressed, all of the great centres of musical activity contributed to the new styles and forms – London with Purcell, Paris with Lully – and offered new outlets for musical activity. When an opera house was built in Venice in 1637, this inspired other cities to follow suit. The first opera house in Germany was built in Hamburg in 1678.

Literature

It is difficult to view the literature of the 17th century through one overarching trend because of national and regional variations of subject matter and style. However, certain general features were apparent. The trend towards literature in vernacular languages, which had gathered pace during the 16th century, continued. John Milton, for example, might still write in Latin, but he composed even more poetry and prose in English. In Russia, the Archpriest Avvakum, caught up in the events of the Great Schism, composed his life story – often considered the first great work of Russian literature – in his native language. Grimmelshausen left a vivid account, in German, of the horrors of the Thirty Years War in his novel *Simplicius Simplicissimus* (1668). The very triumph of European literature in vernacular languages posed problems of linguistic standardization and required moves towards the precise definitions of words and the acceptance of common rules of grammar

and spelling in the various languages. The foundation of the Académie Française (1635) was an acknowledgement of this imperative.

Although books were usually published in small numbers (rarely above 1000), popular works went through many editions. Literary tastes crossed social and gender boundaries; it not possible to speak of "noble" tastes being different from, say, "bourgeois", or those of men from women. Indeed, women made outstanding contributions to the literature of the period, whether as novelists, such as Madame de La Fayette, author of *La Princesse de Clèves*, or as memoirists.

The rise of the rococo style

The age of baroque exuberance spilled over from the 17th to the 18th century and was to develop into the sumptuous, elaborate style known as rococo, which was followed by a reaction in favour of the formal values of the neoclassical style. By the end of the century, this had led to early examples of the Romantic movement.

Rococo developed from the baroque as an elegant, decorative style of ornamentation, often deriving its inspiration from nature and natural forms. Playful and witty, it often adopted as its motifs plants, animals, and the fauna of the seashore. Classical and oriental motifs were also incorporated in an almost riotous exuberance. In painting, the work of Watteau, Chardin, and Boucher exemplified the charm and informality of the rococo style. Fragonard, a pupil of Boucher, provided one of the best examples of the style with his painting *The Swing*. More serious examples of the rococo style were to be found in

The French artist Nicolas Poussin spent many years studying in Rome and learning the "Roman" style. In this painting, he tackles a subject of exceptional violence: the mass rape of the Sabine women by Romans. It is a fine example of "history" painting, in which the artist was required to display his full powers of design, use of colour and light, and representation of the human figure in a variety of postures.

THE ARTS AND ARCHITECTURE 235

the work of the Venetian artist Giambattista Tiepolo, who painted frescos and paintings for church interiors in an increasingly free style.

While the wit and gaiety of rococo painting flourished in France, British painting became widely recognized for its fine portraiture, as practised by such artists as Sir Joshua Reynolds and Thomas Gainsborough. Although art retained considerable diversity across Europe, the influence of the classical world was never far removed. Prints of ancient Rome by the great architectural engraver Giambattista Piranesi decorated the houses of gentlemen who had visited Italy on the "Grand Tour" and many who had not. By the middle of the century, the critical ideas of Johann Joachim Winckelmann were having an influence on German art. His *On the Imitation of Greek Works* (1755) urged a return to the "simplicity and grandeur" of classical models. Classical works, particularly Roman models, were attractive to the wealthy classes whose education since Renaissance times had been orientated around the classics. Antique statuary, artefacts, and coins became part of a collecting mania. Where antique statuary was not directly available, contemporary sculptors such as John Flaxman and Antonio Canova self-consciously adopted the style in their own works.

Architecture in the 18th century
The rococo style was best suited to elegant and elaborate interiors. At its most sumptuous, it could be seen in the state apartments created for Louis XIV in the palace of Versailles, and, at its most dazzling, in the Hall of Mirrors in the Amalienburg, the pavilion built for the Elector of Bavaria near Munich in 1734–9. In the latter, decorative floral motifs in gilt climb up the walls between mirrors to spread out across the ceiling. But from the middle of the century the straight, simple lines of the neoclassical style were increasingly in favour. The first major French building to display the style was the Pantheon in Paris built in 1755–6. Popularized in Britain by Lord Burlington and transmitted via the work of the Renaissance architect Andrea Palladio, "Palladianism" became the most widely adopted form of neoclassical architecture in Britain, seen in the country houses of the period.

Music in the 18th century
The musical life of early 18th-century Europe was still dominated by court and Church, although some of the larger and more prosperous cities were already supporting public concerts and opera performances. Bach and Handel were the two most significant figures spanning the baroque and classical eras. Both took music to new levels of grandeur and sophistication, drawing on the rich choral and orchestral traditions of northern Europe. Bach was born at Eisenach into a musical family. While studying in Saxony, he came into contact with the church music of Hamburg and French court music at Hanover. After a period as court organist and director of chamber music at Cothen, Bach settled in Leipzig in 1723 as musical director of St Thomas's Church and School. Much of Bach's vast corpus of works was not published until after his death. His huge instrumental and chamber output, including the *Brandenburg Concertos* (1719), *The Art of the Fugue* (1749), *The Well-Tempered Clavier*, and the six cello suites only subsequently achieved a wider audience. In contrast, Handel worked in the more commercial

In the 18th century, opera became more restrained and formal than in the 17th. Handel composed about 40 operas, consisting almost entirely of alternating recitatives and arias. Their purpose was to allow the beauties of the human voice to be displayed, rather than dramatic action exhibited. His Flavio *(pictured here) was first performed in 1723; the cast included the famous castrato Bernardino Senesino and the soprano Francesca Cuzzoni.*

environment of Hanoverian England, leaving a post as *kapellmeister* to the Elector of Hanover for a position at the English court. As well as suites for royal occasions such as *The Water Music* (1715) and *Music for the Royal Fireworks* (1749), Handel was an impresario in his own right, staging Italian-style operas in London, of which he wrote 46. When his opera company was dissolved, Handel continued to attempt to present opera for another 13 years. When these proved unsuccessful, he turned to the composition of oratorios for public performance, including the famous *Messiah*, first performed in 1741. The towering reputations of these two transitional figures between the baroque and classical eras relegate to the sidelines important composers such as Telemann, Bach's predecessor at St Thomas's in Leipzig, who wrote 40 operas and 46 oratorios. Italian music was represented by Vivaldi, a priest who spent much of his life as the music teacher at a girls' orphanage in Venice. Vivaldi composed nearly 250 string concertos and 40 operas, his best-known work being *The Four Seasons* (1723).

One of the major composers to emerge from the late 18th-century milieu of court and commercial music was Hadyn. For more than 30 years *kapellmeister* to the Esterhazy household in Austria, he was lionized on his visits to London in 1791 and 1794. A writer of oratorios, masses, and chamber works, he was of major importance in fashioning the new symphonic style, which was to have a great influence on later composers, including Beethoven. The astonishing genius of the classical era, Mozart, was a direct heir of Haydn's legacy. The son of a professional musician at the archbishop's court in Salzburg, Mozart started composing at the age of five and was exhibited as a child prodigy in London, Paris, and Munich. His prolific career ended just before his 36th birthday, but included more than 40 symphonies and 27 piano concertos, as well as chamber works and church music. It was as an opera composer, however, that he was to achieve lasting fame, with *The Marriage of Figaro* (1786), *Don Giovanni* (1787), and *The Magic Flute* (1791) achieving permanent places in the opera repertoire.

Literature in the 18th century

The 18th century witnessed an explosion of print. In Britain, the effective ending of press censorship with the expiry of the Licensing Act of 1695 led to a huge expansion of newspapers, periodicals, and literature. Periodicals such as *Tatler* (1709–11) and *The Spectator* (1711–12) set the tone of civilized, urbane reading for the middle classes of London and other cities, later taken up by monthly

Jean-Baptiste Poquelin known as "Molière", wrote comic plays and comédie-ballets which won him patronage at the highest levels of French society, including that of Louis XIV himself. Many of his plays were social satires, and if some, such as Les Précieuses Ridicules *(1659),* were farces, others, notably Tartuffe *(1669), provoked an outcry and brought Molière powerful enemies. This portrait shows Molière playing Julius Caesar in Pierre Corneille's play* La Mort de Pompee (The Death of Pompey) *(1642).*

publications such as the *Gentleman's Magazine* (1736) and the *Annual Register* (1757). Daniel Defoe is often considered to have written the first English novel with *Robinson Crusoe* (1719), followed by *Moll Flanders* (1722). With Samuel Richardson's *Pamela* (1740), Henry Fielding's *Tom Jones* (1749), the inimitable Laurence Sterne's *The Life and Opinions of Tristram Shandy, Gentleman* (1760–7), and Tobias Smollett's *Roderick Random* (1748) and *Humphrey Clinker* (1771), the English novel was becoming a major literary form. Many English writers drew their inspiration from Cervantes' 17th-century comic masterpiece, *Don Quixote*, which was also an influence on the French novel, notably Alain le Sage's *Gil Blas*. The new culture of sensibility was represented by women writers such as Fanny Burney with *Evalina* (1778) and, in the last decade of the century, the first novels of Jane Austen. An important fresh development came with the stimulus of the imagination offered by "Gothic" novels such as Horace Walpole's *The Castle of Otranto* (1764) and Mrs Radcliffe's *The Mysteries of Udolpho* (1794). Voltaire became the talk of France with *Candide* (1759), *L'Ingenu* (1767), and *La Princesse de Babylone* (1768), using his novels to convey his philosophical ideas.

By the end of the 18th century, the literary world had expanded enormously to include a wide reading public served by novels, poetry, plays, periodicals, and newspapers. Although circulation of literary works remained relatively small and expensive, a growing audience for these and for newspapers laid the foundations for the mass readership of the 19th century.

Architecture and Urbanism   84–5 ▶
Architecture   168–9 ▶
The High Renaissance   220–1 ▶
Romanticism and the Arts   308–11▶

The Scientific Revolution

The 17th century is often described as the period of "Scientific Revolution", a phrase signifying fundamental shifts in both the content of scientific knowledge and the methods by which it was acquired. Francis Bacon was a key figure in this latter respect. In such works as the *Advancement of Learning* (1605) and *The Novum Organum* (1620) he rejected knowledge based on the authority of ancient Greeks, and advocated a method of learning rooted in experiment and observation.

The clock-making industry was well established in the 17th century and produced instruments of remarkable complexity and reliability. The precision mechanics required to make accurate clocks were transferred to other branches of scientific instrument making.

In France, René Descartes expressed similar dissatisfaction with traditional learning and, in the *Discours de la Méthode* (*Discourse on Method*) (1637) and other writings, developed a method of acquiring knowledge based on rationalism.

Mathematics

The importance of mathematics to the Scientific Revolution was considerable. Not only were new branches of mathematics developed, such as infinitesimal calculus by Leibnitz and Newton, but also mathematics was seen as revealing physical reality. If, for example, the motions of a planet appear to correspond to a mathematical formula, then the planet physically reveals what the formula says. This proposition was especially controversial in astronomy. For centuries, the universe had been understood according to the model propounded chiefly by Aristotle: the universe was composed of a series of concentric spheres containing the stars and planets, and the spheres carried celestial bodies in circular orbits around the static earth at the centre. This theory was so deeply integrated into European philosophy and theology that challenges to the

theory were bound to have philosophical and theological implications. Such a challenge came in 1543 when Nicolaus Copernicus published *De Revolutionibus Orbium Coelestium* (*On the Motions of the Heavenly Spheres*). Using a mathematical demonstration, he contended that the sun, not the earth, was the centre of the universe, and that the earth was not static, but moved. It was on such a mathematical foundation that Johannes Kepler, in his *Astronomia Nova* (*New Astronomy*) (1609), went beyond Copernicus by maintaining that planetary orbits were elliptical, not circular, and that planets did not maintain constant velocity.

Astronomy

Copernicanism won many adherents, including Galileo Galilei. Galileo's work in physics and mechanics earned him international renown, but it was his work in astronomy that made him a controversial figure. Already known for his Copernican views, in 1609 he transformed the practice of astronomy by adapting the recently invented telescope to astronomical observation (which, up until then, had been conducted with

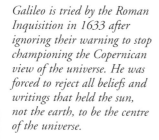

Galileo is tried by the Roman Inquisition in 1633 after ignoring their warning to stop championing the Copernican view of the universe. He was forced to reject all beliefs and writings that held the sun, not the earth, to be the centre of the universe.

Royal Observatory, Greenwich

Charles II established the Royal Observatory on the site of a medieval tower at Greenwich, England. In 1675 the tower was dismantled and the observatory, designed by Sir Christopher Wren, built in its place. It contained no instruments, and the newly appointed Astronomer Royal, John Flamsteed, had to provide them himself. The purpose of the observatory was to advance knowledge of astronomy and navigation. Flamsteed's strategy was to determine the positions of stars, the sun, and the planets, but especially to track the motions of the moon. In 1725, his catalogue of almost 3000 stars was published, surpassing all other catalogues in the accuracy of its data.

the naked eye). He announced his discoveries in *Siderius Nuncius* (*The Starry Messenger*) (1610): millions of previously unseen stars, mountains on the moon, moons around Jupiter, and other phenomena. Many of these observations were incompatible with the Aristotelian universe, but could be accommodated within the Copernican. In 1616, Galileo met a commission of the Roman Inquisition. After discussing his views, the commission instructed him not to teach Copernicanism. In 1632, however, he published his *Dialogo* (*Dialogues*), in which he championed the Copernican against the Aristotelian universe. He was tried by the Roman Inquisition, who feared that theological orthodoxy would be undermined by the *Dialogo* and forced him to retract his views.

The Mechanical Philosophy

Equally contentious issues arose in the physical sciences. Figures such as Descartes, Gassendi, and Boyle came to think of matter as composed of tiny, indivisible particles ("atoms"). The differences in size and shape of these "atoms" determined the structure and motions of terrestrial matter. This was the basis of the Mechanical Philosophy, according to which all matter and motion are subject to deterministic laws arising out of the atomic structure of the material concerned. The Mechanical Philosophy raised key philosophical and theological issues: in so far as human beings are material creatures, is there such a thing as free will, or are they governed by forces beyond their control? What is the role of God in a "mechanical" universe? Is God anything more than the Creator who leaves the universe to run according to mechanistic laws?

The concept of a Scientific Revolution also rests on changes in the organization of scientific activity. Scientific societies were founded in Italy, London, and Paris. Scientific societies supported the individual research of their members, organized collaborative projects and overseas expeditions, acted as channels through which science was placed at the service of the state, and helped to disseminate and popularize scientific knowledge. This last purpose was aided by journals such as *Philosophical Transactions*, published from 1665, and books popularizing scientific subjects, which became bestsellers.

The works of British scientist Isaac Newton are often seen as the culmination of the Scientific Revolution; however, while there is no denying his genius, or the fact that his *Principia Mathematica* (*The Principles of Mathematics*) (1687) is one of the seminal texts of modern science, it would be too simplistic to view him simply as a "modern" scientist whose work utterly invalidated "ancient" scientific learning. He remained interested in alchemy and the deciphering of biblical prophecies, and to some contemporaries the *Principia* turned back the scientific clock when Newton claimed that all motion is governed by a non-material, attractive force called "gravity". To a generation brought up on the Mechanical Philosophy, this looked like a revival of discredited ideas of the occult. The Newton of the *Principia* is but one facet of an extraordinarily complex figure; although *philosophes* of the Enlightenment revered him as a forerunner of their rationalist world, some aspects of his theories would not have surprised a medieval philosopher.

Science and Medicine 40–1 ►
Technological Advances 192–3 ►
Intellectual Progress 222–3 ►
The Advance of Science 370–1 ►

After declaring war on the Dutch Republic on 6 April 1672, Louis XIV led an invasion through its eastern frontier. The French crossed the Rhine and rapidly took Utrecht. However, Louis failed to force the Dutch into surrender. Allies came to the assistance of the Dutch and a major European war developed.

ABSOLUTISM AND INTERNATIONAL RELATIONS

Absolutism is associated with particular kinds of monarchy, and can best be understood as a response both to the internal sociopolitical unrest that proliferated in Europe, and to the fiscal and social pressures created by war. The term "absolutism" should not be equated with despotism or tyranny. Strictly speaking, it meant a form of government in which a single person held sovereignty.

Although some monarchies avowedly were absolute – France and Denmark (after a royal coup in 1665) fell into this category – others were ambiguous over the question: it was unclear, for example, whether the kings of Spain or the Stuart kings of England shared sovereignty with the Cortes and Parliament, or whether those assemblies were only advisory. Unlike Russian autocracy, in which there were no theoretical limits on the tsar, absolutist monarchs acknowledged that they exercised their powers within certain constraints. They were bound by the fundamental, "constitutional" laws of the kingdom; they claimed to respect the rights and privileges of their subjects; and, as Christian rulers, were subject to the law of God. Nevertheless, by appealing to the twin arguments of the Divine Right of Kings and *raison d'état*, they claimed that domestic unrest and international warfare sometimes left them with no option but to expand their powers even beyond traditional limits.

Warfare was an almost permanent feature in the 17th century. Between 1600 and 1720, Europe experienced only about five years of peace. Yet even the most aggressive governments came to recognize that they could not sustain war indefinitely; it was necessary to find alternative means of regulating international disputes. In 1625, the Dutch jurist Hugo Grotius made such a call. His *De Jure Belli ac Pacis* (*On the Law of War and Peace*) (1625) appealed for the mitigation of warfare through the observance by states of a "natural law" governing their relations.

Practical attempts to regulate international relations came through peace congresses. The first great international congress of the century was held in Westphalia from 1643–8. Although cumbersome in its procedures, it brought peace to much of Europe after the Thirty Years War.

Governments also developed more sustained diplomatic contacts in their search for orderly international relations. Diplomacy was pursued with greater vigour and permanent ambassadors became the norm, and the major governments of Europe expanded their ministries of foreign affairs in order to manage international relations in a more consistent manner.

The emergence of the idea of a European "balance of power" in place of the preponderance of one state also aimed to stabilize Europe. The phrase itself appeared by the 1680s, even though its meaning was not precisely defined. However, the principal international peace treaties of the late 1600s and early 1700s indicate that "balance of power" implied that no state would enjoy hegemony, agreed frontiers would be created by peace treaties, and post-treaty alliances would be created to guarantee their terms.

The effects of such measures were considerable. Certainly, wars were fought between 1721 and the outbreak of the French Revolutionary Wars in 1792, but they were fewer and shorter than in the preceding century. The turbulence that characterized international relations in the 17th century gradually abated in favour of the prospect of order.

The Thirty Years War

In 1618, Europe relapsed into a phase of war that lasted until 1660. It began with the Thirty Years War (1618–48), leading to all-out war between Catholics and Protestants, and involving almost every European power. It was prolonged by wars between the Dutch Republic and Spain, France and Spain, and between the Baltic powers.

In 1618 the Habsburg dynasty exerted immense influence across much of central, southern and Western Europe. France, still recovering from the Wars of Religion, felt endangered by Habsburg "encirclement", and the self-styled Dutch Republic likewise felt threatened. Religious and political tensions in the Holy Roman Empire had been mounting since the beginning of the century, and in 1618 dragged Europe into the Thirty Years War.

The origins of the war

The Thirty Years War began as a rebellion in Bohemia led by Protestant nobles. They resisted the Counter-Reformation policies in religion and the centralization of government pursued by ministers of the king, Matthias. Matthias, a member of the Habsburg family, was also Holy Roman Emperor. He died in 1619, but his successor, Ferdinand, who also became Emperor Ferdinand II, was "deposed" by the rebels, who conferred the Bohemian crown on a German Protestant prince, Frederick V of the Palatinate. Ferdinand prepared a counter-attack, and was promised help from Spain and the Catholic League (an association of Catholic princes of the Holy Roman Empire). In 1620, Ferdinand crushed the Bohemian rising, and the Spanish occupied the Palatinate. They did so, not only because of solidarity with Ferdinand, but also because the truce that they had signed with the Dutch Republic in 1609 was to expire in 1621. They anticipated a new war against the Dutch; control of the Palatinate, part of which dominated a crucial stretch of the Rhine, served their military plans. In Bohemia, the triumphant Ferdinand set about eliminating Protestantism and transferring

land from Protestant to Catholic owners. In 1627 he declared the crown, hitherto elective, a hereditary possession of the Habsburgs. Meanwhile, in 1621, a new Spanish–Dutch war began. The early stages went in favour of Spain, which also enjoyed success in Italy by securing de facto control of the Valtelline, a territory through which Spanish troops passed to the Netherlands.

The victories of the Austrian and Spanish Habsburgs alarmed other governments, and, in 1624, Christian IV of Denmark, who was also a prince of the Holy Roman Empire, intervened, with the backing of the English and Dutch, to defend Protestant territories in the empire. The episode was a disaster. The armies of Ferdinand II, led by Wallenstein, occupied most of northern Germany and invaded Denmark, which surrendered in 1629. Ferdinand II had imperial Germany at his mercy, and issued the Edict of Restitution also in 1629: all lands which had become Protestant since 1552 were to be restored to Catholicism. Protestantism in Germany was threatened with annihilation, and Ferdinand was poised to diminish the autonomy of the princes of the Holy Roman Empire.

Protestant German princes looked abroad for help. They found it in Gustavus II Adolphus of Sweden. This Protestant king had an excellent army and had just ended a war against Poland. In 1630, he entered Germany, proclaiming that his mission was to save Protestantism. Backed by French subsidies, he drew several princes into alliance and, in a series of remarkable campaigns, overwhelmed Ferdinand's forces. Within 18 months, he had liberated northern Germany and had penetrated deep into the south. Ferdinand recalled Wallenstein, whom he had dismissed in 1630. The general fought Gustavus at Lützen in 1632, but, although the Swedish army carried the day, Gustavus was killed. Military stalemate led to peace talks between Ferdinand and German Protestant princes. By the Peace of Prague (1635), Ferdinand rescinded the Edict of Restitution.

A more general settlement looked possible, but in 1635 France stepped in by declaring war on

Europe c.1618

◼ Areas Ruled by Spanish Habsburgs

— Boundaries of the Holy Roman Empire

North Sea

ENGLAND

London

DUTCH REPUBLIC

Antwerp
SPANISH NETHERLANDS

Atlantic Ocean

Paris

HOLY ROMAN EMPIRE

AUSTRIA

FRANCE

FRANCHE COMTÉ

Milan

HUNGARY

Corunna

Genoa

Venice

SPAIN

Madrid

Florence

PAPAL STATES

Barcelona

Rome

SARDINIA

Ceuta

Mediterranean Sea

Melilla

Algiers

SICILY

Tunis

The Defenestration of Prague

The Defenestration of Prague, 23 May 1618, began the Thirty Years War. The king of Bohemia, Matthias, resided in Vienna, leaving the government of Bohemia to a council of regents. The regents pursued a policy of Counter-Reformation and centralization. In 1618, an assembly of Protestant nobles met in Prague and called on the regents to desist. Representatives of the Protestants met two of the regents – Slavata and Martinitz – at the Hradschin castle, but the meeting ended in deadlock. The nobles flung the regents with their secretary from a window. Although none of the victims was hurt, this was a clear symbol of rebellion, for it was by such a defenestration that the Hussite risings began in 1419.

Spain. France, whose main objective was to end the preponderance of Spain in Western Europe, had supported the Swedes financially and had undertaken military engagements against the Spanish in Italy. The war between the Dutch Republic and Spain was still being fought, and Cardinal Richelieu, the French principal minister, judged that Spanish resources were sufficiently stretched for France to make a direct challenge. Fearing that Ferdinand would release troops to assist Spain if the Peace of Prague held, Richelieu persuaded Sweden to continue war against him.

The Peace of Westphalia

The Thirty Years War entered its most destructive phase as armies crisscrossed Germany, causing havoc. War extended to the Low Countries, Italy, and the Franco-Spanish border. By 1643, peace talks were imminent, and preliminary discussions began in Westphalia. A full international congress gathered in 1645. After long negotiations, treaties were signed in 1648, bringing peace to most of Europe, with the major exception of France and Spain, who remained at war. By the terms of the Peace of Westphalia, Ferdinand confirmed the rights of the princes and relinquished any hope of restoring the Holy Roman Empire fully to Catholicism. Peace between the Dutch Republic and Spain was settled, and Sweden acquired territory on the Baltic coast and in north-west Germany. The Peace of Westphalia marks a major

juncture in international relations, not just because of the content of the treaties, but also because it signified a concerted attempt to create conditions for long-term peace in central Europe.

Continuing conflict

Two more conflicts took place during the 1650s. One was the continuing Franco-Spanish war, which ended with the Peace of the Pyrenees (1659). Although this peace included territorial concessions by Spain to France, its chief significance lies in the fact that thereafter Spain was on defensive terms with its neighbour. The "Spanish preponderance" had ended, and the main danger facing Europe now was that it might be replaced by a French preponderance. The other conflict was in the Baltic. In the early 1650s, Russia and Poland were at war. Charles X of Sweden exploited this opportunity to seize more coastal lands from Poland and, in 1655, invaded. Other powers became involved – Ferdinand II, Denmark, Brandenburg, the Dutch Republic – and their combined efforts led to two peace treaties in 1660: that of Oliva, by which Sweden was conceded more Baltic territory, and that of Copenhagen, which ended war between Sweden and Denmark. In 1660, Sweden was the paramount power in the Baltic. Whereas the Peace of Westphalia aimed to stabilize Germany and central Europe, Oliva and Copenhagen were only pauses in a longer Baltic struggle.

The Low Countries in the 17th Century

In 1609, Spain, which had been at war with its seven rebel provinces in the northern Netherlands since the 1560s, signed a 12-year truce with the self-styled Dutch Republic. Spain did not recognize the Republic, whose reconquest remained a central aim of policy. Now that the borders between the Spanish Netherlands and the Republic were open, economic links were renewed and the movement of people resumed.

This Dutch market scene, which is dominated in the foreground by a meat stall at which beef is displayed prominently, testifies to a degree of prosperity among the shoppers. That beef (instead of cheaper cuts of pork or chicken) could be bought by these ordinarily dressed housewives indicates a relatively high standard of living.

The economic prosperity of the Dutch Republic owed much to the predominance of its shipping in the trade of the Mediterranean, Baltic, and North seas. Dutch ships were also prominent in transatlantic commerce and along the sea-lanes to the Far East. Technically, the Dutch ship-building industry was the most advanced in Europe, and inspired much rivalry from France and England.

For several years, urban growth and economic recovery were the chief priorities throughout the Low Countries; however, as 1621 approached, Spain prepared to resume war. It built up its military installations in the Spanish Netherlands and, early in the Thirty Years War, it occupied the Lower Palatinate at the behest of Emperor Ferdinand II: control of this territory enhanced Spanish power along an important stretch of the Rhine and helped to protect the land route taken by Spanish troops moving between northern Italy and the Netherlands. In 1621, war between Spain and the Dutch Republic duly reopened, but, in spite of early victories, the Spanish were still incapable of defeating the Dutch. Hampered by their failure to establish control of the Channel and North Sea, they had to divert forces to conflicts in Italy, mostly against interventions by France; and, when the Austrian Habsburg cause collapsed in the early 1630s and the Dutch recaptured towns such as Venloo and Maastricht, there was talk of another truce. Dutch confidence further increased when France declared war on Spain in 1635. The Dutch enjoyed a spectacular naval victory over the Spanish at the Battle of the Downs in 1639. Moves towards a general European settlement in the 1640s involved the Spanish and Dutch. The Peace of Westphalia included a settlement whereby Spain finally recognized the Republic.

The Dutch Republic

The Dutch Republic was admired throughout Europe. This small country of just over one million people had fought the Spanish for some 80 years, and had even managed to subsidize allies during the Thirty Years War. Moreover, in an age that tended to assume that absolutist techniques of government offered the most effective means of harnessing national resources, there had evolved in the Dutch Republic the most decentralized system of government in Europe. Although federal affairs were the responsibility of an Estates General, political power lay with the provincial Estates and, within them, with the representatives of the towns. The Republic flourished economically, demonstrating that absolutism was not a precondition of prosperity. The Dutch economy was based mainly on overseas commerce. Dutch ships dominated the trade of the Baltic and North seas, and were prominent along the Mediterranean and Atlantic seaways. The Republic had its own overseas possessions, above all in Asia; their wealth was exploited by trading companies such as the United East India Company .

The Republic was, by contemporary standards, highly urbanized and well educated. It had five universities and excellent schools. Dutch theologians, such as Arminius, made distinguished contributions to Calvinist theology. Scientists such as Leeuwenhoek, Swammerdam, and Huygens were at the forefront of their disciplines, while Dutch navigational and scientific instrument makers were renowned throughout Europe. In

The Estates General of the Dutch Republic was composed of delegates from the seven provinces comprising the Republic. Delegates voiced provincial, not their own, opinions, and voted according to instructions from the provinces. Decisions normally required a unanimous vote, although under certain circumstances – whether to declare war or peace, for example – a majority vote was sufficient.

the visual arts, Rembrandt, Vermeer, Hals, Van Goyen, and others contributed to the "Golden Age" of Dutch painting and left a detailed visual record of the Republic. The modern observer possesses a wonderful pictorial resource with which to study the communities and activities that made up the life within it.

The French threat

After 1648, a new threat emerged in the France of Louis XIV. Commercial, political, and ideological antagonisms grew between the two states, and, in 1672, Louis XIV launched an invasion. The unprepared Dutch Republic collapsed as the French took one town after another. Amsterdam only saved itself by opening dykes, flooding the surrounding countryside, and turning itself into an island. Mass rioting spread across the Republic and swept William III of Orange into power, who became *stadholder* (chief executive officer of the Republic) and commander of the armed forces. He imposed his political authority throughout the Republic, formed an international anti-French coalition and drove the French out of the country. In the Peace of Nijmegen (1678), William III secured advantageous terms for the Republic, including a commercial treaty with France.

In the 1680s, Dutch leaders concentrated on economic recovery, but developments involving French seizures of territory in the Rhineland brought Europe to the brink of war by 1688. The Republic's international standing was enhanced by an unexpected event in England: a political crisis led to the overthrow of James II and the accession of William III of Orange and his Stuart wife, Mary. William co-ordinated the policies and resources of England and the Dutch Republic in a war against France that lasted until 1697. Relations with France improved temporarily, but the War of the Spanish Succession (1702–13) saw the Republic siding again with England against France and Spain.

England

The Republic bore an enormous military and financial burden, but, after William III's death in 1702, was eclipsed by England at the head of the coalition against France and Spain. As the war drew to its close, England abandoned its Dutch ally and signed a peace with France; by the terms of the Peace of Utrecht (1713), England secured territorial and commercial concessions from Spain. The Republic prevented the Spanish Netherlands from passing into French possession (they went to the Austrian Habsburgs), but achieved little else. In 1713, the Low Countries were in a weaker position than a century before: the southern provinces were Austrian possessions, while the Dutch Republic was facing decline in its economy and in its influence upon international relations.

THE LOW COUNTRIES IN THE 17TH CENTURY

Civil Wars and Constitutional Monarchy in Britain

In 1621, the House of Commons issued "the Great Protestation", a statement of parliamentary rights. This controversial theme of the respective rights of crown and Parliament was to run through to 1691.

The year 1649 was one of turbulence in England. Monarchy was abolished, but the Scottish government refused to accept the decision. Ireland was controlled by the Catholic Confederation. Political and social radicals were active, and two regiments in the army mutinied. Cromwell and Thomas Fairfax (the commander in chief of the army) reacted with force; they suppressed the mutiny and had the ringleaders executed.

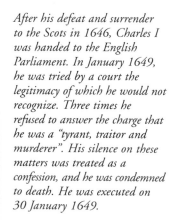

After his defeat and surrender to the Scots in 1646, Charles I was handed to the English Parliament. In January 1649, he was tried by a court the legitimacy of which he would not recognize. Three times he refused to answer the charge that he was a "tyrant, traitor and murderer". His silence on these matters was treated as a confession, and he was condemned to death. He was executed on 30 January 1649.

Charles I succeeded to the throne in 1625. He signed an alliance with the Dutch and French, and, in 1627, sent a fleet to France in support of Protestant rebels. To finance these enterprises, Charles employed fiscal measures the legality of which was challenged in the Commons. Critics blamed his favourite, the Duke of Buckingham. When Buckingham was assassinated in 1628, it seemed that relations between the king and Parliament might improve, but he dissolved the assembly in 1629, and, for 11 years, ruled without it.

Charles compounded his "offence" against Parliament with a religious policy that alienated many of his subjects in England, Scotland, and Ireland. In collaboration with William Laud, Archbishop of Canterbury, he attempted to impose High Church liturgy throughout his three kingdoms. He encountered widespread resistance, especially among Scottish Presbyterians. In 1638, his Scottish opponents launched the National Covenant in defence of Presbyterianism. Charles denounced the Covenanters as rebels and gathered an army to crush them. He failed, and, in 1640, recalled the English Parliament to vote subsidies for another campaign. Parliament refused and as a result was dissolved by the king in three weeks.

Civil war

Charles raised another army from his own resources, but was defeated again by the Covenanters, who invaded England and forced peace on him at Ripon in 1640. He called Parliament for the second time in 1640, but the Commons demanded that royal financial policy must have parliamentary consent and that Parliament must meet at least every three years. In 1641, news arrived of a Catholic uprising in Ireland and Charles faced the collapse of his authority in all three kingdoms. Relations between Charles and Parliament fully broke down when the latter drew up the Grand Remonstrance in 1641, a comprehensive attack upon Charles's rule. The king left London and established his base at York. Fearing an attack, Parliament raised an army. Through the Nineteen Propositions in 1642 it made its last offer to Charles of the conditions under which it would co-operate with him. When he rejected the Propositions, Parliament announced that he was unfit to be king. Civil war began.

Although Charles won early victories such as Edgehill in 1642, the New Model Army, which Parliament authorized, gradually wore him down. In 1643, Parliament entered into league with the

Scots Covenanters, whose price was the adoption throughout England of Presbyterian faith and worship. These and other developments strained the unity of Parliament's cause. The New Model Army, commanded by Oliver Cromwell, contained religious and political radicals who, because many were officers, exercised a disproportionate influence. As the war progressed, the question of how far Parliament could trust the army became increasingly urgent.

In 1646, Charles I surrendered and was held by Parliament. He secretly contacted supporters in Scotland, who raised a force and invaded England in 1648. Cromwell defeated them, after which a General Council of Army demanded that Charles be tried. Most Parliamentarians were reluctant: monarchy was their preferred form of government, provided that it respected their rights. The army purged Parliament of "moderates", leaving a radical "Rump" which oversaw the trial and execution of the king in 1649.

The war was not finished. In 1649, Cromwell led an expedition to Ireland and, in 1650, went on a similar mission to Scotland, where Charles II – hitherto a refugee in France – had arrived and mustered an army. Charles evaded Cromwell and entered England. Cromwell caught and defeated him at Worcester in 1651, but Charles escaped back to France. General Monck completed the conquest of Scotland. The Scottish Parliament was dissolved. Scottish members henceforth sat in Parliament in England. "Britain" was a constitutional reality, with the title of "Commonwealth".

Restoration of the monarchy

It proved impossible to establish a republican government that commanded general consent. In 1654, the Commonwealth became a Protectorate under Cromwell. After his death in 1658, the system threatened to collapse under the weight of military and parliamentary intrigue, and General Monck stepped in. In 1660, he occupied London, restored the pre-Rump Parliament and, with its co-operation, invited Charles II to return. Charles was restored to the throne amidst public jubilation.

Charles II strove to avoid quarrels with Parliament, but relations were often tense. In previous years, Parliament had enacted anti-Catholic and anti-Dissenter legislation. Charles moderated its application by issuing Declarations of Indulgence, which exempted selected people from its provisions. Some Members of Parliament regarded such Declarations as attacks by the crown on Parliament. In 1661, a crisis occurred over the Exclusion Bill: Charles's brother and successor, James, was Catholic and there was a move in the Commons to have

The English Civil War

✗ Major battles
Situation on 1 May 1643
▨ Held by Parliament
☐ Held by the king

Much of England was affected by the military campaigns and battles of the Civil War. The success of Parliament owed much to its control of London. Charles I's failure to capture the capital after having advanced on London after his victory at Edgehill (1642) was a major blow to his prospects. The defeats of the Royalist armies at Marston Moor (1644) and Naseby (1645) fatally weakened Charles's position. He surrendered in 1646.

James excluded from the succession. The proposal was rejected by the House of Lords, but, had it passed, a conflict between Parliament and the crown would have been inescapable.

When James II came to the throne in 1685, he was unequivocal about his Catholicism and the primacy of the royal will. He dispensed with Parliament, absolved all Catholics and Dissenters from the penal laws, and promoted Catholics at court and in the army. He might have survived had his successor remained his Protestant daughter Mary, wife of William III of Orange, but, in 1688, he had a son, James, who was baptised a Catholic. Given the prospect of a Catholic succession, a group of nobles invited William III to come to the aid of Protestantism in England. William arrived with troops, but James II put up little resistance and retreated to France. A special Parliament declared that he had abdicated and that William III and Mary were joint monarchs. Parliament followed this with the Declaration of Rights in 1689, which defined the functions and powers of monarchy. England acquired a "constitutional" monarchy as a result of the unexpected contingencies of 1688. James II attempted to recover the throne via a campaign in Ireland. In 1689, with French help, he landed in Ireland where volunteers joined him. He occupied Dublin, but doubts over his leadership rose when he failed to capture Londonderry after a siege. In 1690, William III fought James at the Battle of the Boyne. James was defeated and fled to France. The remaining Jacobite forces surrendered at Limerick in 1691. William and Mary were now secure rulers of the three kingdoms, although on terms laid down by Parliament.

Magna Carta 156–7 ▶
The French Revolution 286–7 ▶
Reform in Britain,
Autocracy in Russia 298–9 ▶
The Russian Revolution 400–1 ▶

Louis XIV's France

Louis XIV was an absolute monarch buttressed by a rich tradition of political thought, as well as history. Since at least the late 16th century, French political thinkers had advocated absolute monarchy as the form of government most appropriate to France. It was the largest and most populous country in Western Europe. With a population of around 22 million, it outstripped its main rival Spain (8 million), and dwarfed such states as the Dutch Republic or Britain and Ireland.

Henri IV ended the French Wars of Religion by the Edict of Nantes (1598), which conferred on French Protestants (Huguenots) liberty of conscience, freedom of worship in designated parts of the country, and guarantees of security. Louis XIV's persecution of the Huguenots culminated in his revoking the Edict in 1685.

Louis XIV embodied the ideal of absolute monarchy, with its emphases on authority, glory, service, and achievement. Towards the end of his reign, which involved France in several costly and destructive wars, voices of criticism were being heard, and even Louis himself was having difficulty in justifying the principles by which he had ruled.

The task of governing such large numbers of people was difficult in itself, but was made even more problematic by the fact that sociopolitical breakdown was a constant possibility. Rebellions had occurred throughout the 1620s and 1630s, and, when Louis XIV was still a boy, he and his mother, Anne of Austria, the regent, faced further widespread insurrection from 1648–53, known as the Fronde. In later years, it confirmed his belief that civil war and rebellion flourished when monarchy was weak. The corollary was self-evident: France would prosper and be stable only when absolute monarchy exercised its powers in full.

Louis was only four years old when his father, Louis XIII, died in 1643. During her regency, which lasted until 1651, Anne of Austria relied heavily on her Italian-born principal minister, Cardinal Mazarin. It was Mazarin who prepared the young king for government. When Mazarin died in 1661, Louis XIV dispensed with a principal minister and ruled personally. He devoted many hours each day to meetings with ministerial councils, the study of governmental papers, and all the complex demands of administration. Whatever his other failings, Louis XIV could not be criticized for lethargy: he was one of the most hard-working monarchs in the history of Europe.

Domestic policy

In the formulation of policy, he turned for guidance to only a handful of advisers. Most came from the Colbert, Le Tellier, and Phélypeaux families who, with their own followers, formed what at times resembled an oligarchic system of government. They discussed policy with the king in secret council, but decisions rested with Louis alone. Other councils administered policy, but had to do so by working through a host of municipal and provincial assemblies whose co-operation, or lack of it, could determine whether or not policy

actually worked. This was undoubtedly one of the most severe limitations on royal authority: provincial Estates, law courts, town councils, and other bodies could frustrate policies with which they disagreed by resorting to procrastination or appeals to the minutiae of legal precedent. If necessary, Louis imposed his will by force, but refused to do so as a matter of course. He placed royal representatives, *Intendants*, in the provinces, to oversee the execution of policy. They, too, employed force only as a last resort. More often they used negotiation, even bribery, to cajole provincial

Versailles was expanded by Louis XIV into an immense palace to which the court and government moved in 1682. The principal architects were Le Vau and Mansart, the main cycles of decorative painting were by Lebrun, and the gardens were planned by Le Nôtre. In conception and design, Versailles became the inspiration for palaces throughout Europe.

bodies into implementing the king's will, for confrontation risked provoking rebellion.

Further risings did occur. In the mid-1670s, for example, when the cost of war forced Louis to impose higher fiscal demands, a tide of rebellion swept across Brittany. If, on the other hand, Louis judged that the majority of his subjects backed him in a particular policy, he did not hesitate to impose it ruthlessly. This applied especially in the sphere of religion. He regarded Protestantism as a stain on the honour of France, and subjected his Protestant (Huguenot) subjects to unremitting persecution, forcing many thousands to convert, while others fled the country. In 1685, this policy culminated in his revocation of the Edict of Nantes of 1598, which had conferred legal recognition on Huguenots. All but a stubborn minority of remaining Huguenots formally joined the Catholic Church, although the authenticity of their conversion was doubtful. Louis was equally zealous in his pursuit of Jansenism, a branch of Catholicism whose orthodoxy was suspect. Jansenists, too, were subjected to fierce oppression and made to conform to theological orthodoxy.

Conscious of his obligation to ameliorate the material condition of his subjects, in the 1660s, he authorized Jean Baptiste Colbert, one of his chief ministers, to introduce financial and economic reforms. Had they been pursued consistently, they might have had an appreciable effect. However, in 1672, Louis invaded the Dutch Republic. He anticipated a short campaign, but bungled the

invasion. He found himself caught up in a war that not only pitted him against an array of enemies, but proved to be the first of a series of major conflicts which ran almost uninterrupted until the end of his reign. The tension between domestic reform and foreign war was resolved in favour of the latter; any final verdict on Louis XIV must conclude that his attempts to *soulager le peuple* ("comfort the people") as he put it, ended in failure.

The court of the Sun King

One realm in which Louis XIV unquestionably was master was the royal court which, in 1682, settled at Versailles. Court society was rigidly stratified and its activities highly orchestrated, the purpose being to create a model of France in which the king's will was supreme and his glory and majesty acknowledged. The very architecture and decoration of the palace and gardens (which then, as now, were open to the public) proclaimed the principles according to which absolute monarchy functioned; the palace was designed to impress upon the visitor the virtues and achievements of Louis XIV – known as the Sun King – and to propagate the vision of France which inspired the king himself. In a sense, Louis XIV ruled two Frances: the actual kingdom with all of its problems and blemishes, and the idealized France created at Versailles. The latter was the basis of a cult of Louis XIV which inspired not only his contemporaries, but also early historians such as Voltaire and many French scholars down to the present day.

The War of the Spanish Succession

In 1600, the king of Spain also ruled Portugal, much of Italy, the Spanish Netherlands, and the Franche-Comté in France, as well as the Spanish and Portuguese overseas colonies. When Emperor Charles V (Charles I of Spain) divided his succession in 1556, these lands, with the exception of Portugal, constituted the portion that went to his son Philip II.

The Duke of Marlborough, with Prince Eugene of Savoy, was commander of the allied forces against the French and Spanish in the War of the Spanish Succession. After victory at Oudenaarde (11 July 1708) they went on to besiege Lille, which held out for three months before surrendering on 9 December 1708.

The hegemony in western and southern Europe that Spain had enjoyed at the beginning of the 17th century gradually disappeared after the Thirty Years War. After conceding the independence of the Dutch Republic (1648) and Portugal (1668), Spain also abandoned territory to France (1678). The War of the Spanish Succession proved disastrous: by 1714, all the Spanish possessions in Italy and the Mediterranean had been lost.

Philip inherited Portugal in 1578 on the reported death of its king, Sebastian (who disappeared while on campaign in Morocco). Philip's Habsburg successors – Philip III, Philip IV, and Charles II – retained most of the succession, the major losses being the northern provinces of the Netherlands, Portugal, and the Franche-Comté. It was the first Bourbon king, Philip V, who lost Italy and the rest of the Netherlands. The association between Spain and these other territories was a result of dynastic accident, not strategic accumulation. The losses adversely affected the prestige of the ruling house, but not necessarily the wellbeing of Spain itself.

Strictly speaking, there was no such person as the king of Spain. Spain was a compound of three kingdoms: Castile, Aragon, and Navarre, each with its own assembly (Cortes), laws, and institutions. The king of Spain (this title of convenience was used), ruling from Madrid in Castile, treated his other kingdoms as autonomous entities. Organs of government for the whole of Spain did exist, but they were few and cumbersome. Castile was the backbone of Spain. It was the most populous of the kingdoms, paid more in taxes than the rest combined, supplied most of the soldiers in the army, and administered the American colonies.

Warfare and rebellion

Given the extent of the territories they ruled and the complexity of the problems they faced, the kings of Spain were drawn into decades of warfare, which wrecked public finances and led to state bankruptcies in 1607, 1627, 1647, and 1666. Apart from the periods 1609–21 and 1659–67, Spain was at war almost permanently from the late 1560s to 1713, and it was Castile that bore the brunt of the financial and human cost. In 1624, Philip IV's chief minister, Olivares, tried to rectify this imbalance through reforms aimed at bringing the political,

judicial, and administrative institutions of the rest of Spain into line with those of Castile. In 1625, Olivares announced the Union of Arms, an ambitious and far-reaching programme whereby all the king's European possessions would contribute men to the armed forces. Such policies generated a tide of resistance that resulted in two great rebellions in 1640: those of Catalonia and Portugal.

The Catalan rising was triggered by the billeting of Castilian troops defending the frontier against the French. The rebels repudiated their allegiance to Philip IV, accepted Louis XIII as their prince, and admitted French troops into Barcelona. Philip IV's commitments in the Thirty Years War, which kept a high proportion of his forces in northern Europe, prevented him from retaking Catalonia immediately, but when peace was signed with the Dutch Republic in 1648, troops became available. In 1652, Barcelona fell to Philip IV; it was now only a matter of time before the rest of the province surrendered, and, in 1653, he was restored throughout Catalonia .

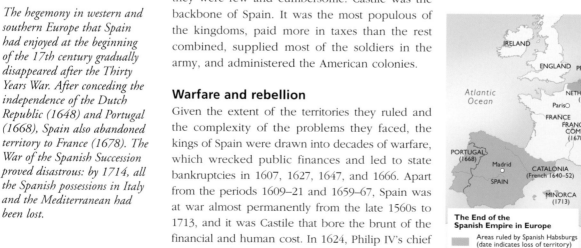

The End of the Spanish Empire in Europe

☐ Areas ruled by Spanish Habsburgs (date indicates loss of territory)

■ Areas ruled by Austrian Habsburgs

The financial and military demands emanating
from Madrid also provoked Portugal into
rebellion. Anti-fiscal riots occurred in the 1620s
and 1630s, and there was widespread resistance
to the Union of Arms. Anti-Spanish sentiment was
channelled through "Sebastianism", a belief that
Sebastian had not died in 1578, and either was
alive or had his authentic successor in John
of Braganza, a leading Portuguese aristocrat. In
1640, a group of Portuguese nobles proclaimed
Braganza "King John IV". A long war with Spain
ensued; however, in spite of numerous attempts,
the Spanish were unable to reconquer Portugal.
In 1668, they conceded its independence. Other
risings against Philip IV occurred in Sicily
and Naples in 1647, and although they were
crushed, they drained essential military and
financial resources.

After the Peace of the Pyrenees in 1659, Spain
experienced modest social and economic revival
as the population rose and commerce with
the colonies increased. There were occasional
outbursts of unrest, notably in Catalonia in 1688–9
and Valencia in 1693, but not on the scale of the
1640s. Even so, the wars in which Spain fought
from the late 1660s to 1697 maintained financial
pressure on the government, and hindered the
process of socioeconomic recovery.

The War of the Spanish Succession

By the late 1690s, the main political problem
concerned a successor to Charles II, who had no
children. Louis XIV claimed the succession for his
son through Louis's deceased wife, Maria Teresa,
a sister of Charles II. She had renounced her
claim to the throne of Spain when she married,
but Louis XIV regarded the renunciation as
invalid. The other claimant was Emperor
Leopold I, who wanted Spain for his son Charles.
Charles II's priority was to preserve the Spanish
Succession intact (the English and Dutch had
proposed partitioning the Spanish Empire). When
he died in 1700, he bequeathed Spain and all of
its territories to a grandson of Louis XIV, who
took the title Philip V. The affair might have
ended there had Louis XIV not taken a number of
actions that convinced other governments
that he might unite Spain and France. In 1702,
Leopold I, England, the Dutch Republic, and
others formed a Grand Alliance and declared war
on France and Spain.

The effects of the war on Spain were
paradoxical. In one sense, they were disastrous.
Spain was invaded by England and the Dutch
Republic (in 1706, Madrid fell to the allies), and
Catalonia, Aragon, and Valencia rose against
Philip V. Gibraltar fell to the English, and Italy
and the Spanish Netherlands eventually were
lost. On the other hand, within Spain itself,
Philip V retook Madrid and gradually overcame his
opponents in Aragon, Valencia, and Catalonia. As
he did so, he curtailed the autonomy of these
regions, abolished internal customs duties, and
standardized taxes. In short, although the Treaty
of Utrecht of 1713 deprived Philip V of Spain's
possessions elsewhere in Europe, he created a
kingdom that was united politically, financially,
and economically. The decline of Spain on
the international stage was counterbalanced by
fundamental changes at home.

The Wars of Religion 216–17 ▶
The Thirty Years War 242–3 ▶
The Low Countries
in the 17th Century 244–5 ▶
Louis XIV's France 248–9 ▶

Sweden, Russia, and the Baltic

The dominant themes of Baltic history are the creation of Swedish hegemony up to 1660, and the challenges presented by rival states thereafter. The Swedish king Gustavus II Adolphus was a warrior who profited from his conquests along the Polish and German Baltic coasts.

Charles XII of Sweden proved a daring young military commander. Coming to the throne aged 15, within three years he was involved in the Great Northern War. He successfully defended Sweden from being overwhelmed by a Franco-Danish-Russian alliance, but his failed invasion of Russia and disastrous defeat at Poltava in 1709 witnessed the end of Swedish supremacy in the Baltic.

Swedish hegemony was created in the Baltic region chiefly by conquest. Gustavus II Adolphus and his successors fought victorious and profitable wars which, by 1660, gave Sweden control not only of much of the Baltic coastline, but of the mouths of some of the principal rivers. Swedish territory also extended into north-west Germany, giving Sweden a base on the North Sea coast.

then Charles X continued his policy until, by 1660 when the Peace of Oliva was signed, extensive tracts of the Baltic region were in Swedish hands. Russia, by contrast, was struggling to recover from the anarchy of the Time of Troubles of 1598–1613, when various claims were made on the Russian throne. A resolute start was made by tsars Michael Romanov and Alexis, but although they repaired the worst of the socioeconomic damage, internal unrest was a constant threat. In 1648, riots spread across the country and, in the 1650s, the Orthodox Church was split by the Great Schism, a crisis accompanied by further social unrest. From 1667–71, Alexis faced the rising of the Volga Cossacks, who were eventually defeated. Internal disorder did not debar Alexis from a foreign policy of expansionism. In the 1650s, he intervened in Poland and the Ukraine, and by the Peace of Andrusovo in 1667 secured lands east of the Dnieper, including Smolensk and Kiev. Despite this, Russia still had no outlet on the Baltic.

Meanwhile, the preservation of its Baltic possessions was problematic for Sweden. Heavily dependent on French subsidies, it was drawn into

France's war against the Dutch Republic and the Republic's allies in 1672–8. It suffered a heavy defeat by the army of Brandenburg at Fehrbellin in 1675, and lost several ports and islands to Denmark and Brandenburg during the war. It was only at French insistence that these losses were restored to Sweden in the Peace of Nijmegen of 1678. Sweden remained neutral during the next war involving France, that of the League of Augsburg of 1688–97. From 1697, however, it faced a mounting challenge to its Baltic supremacy

By this time, Russia had a new tsar in Peter I ("the Great"). For many years, he had ruled jointly with his half-brother, Ivan V, but Ivan died in 1696. After fighting the Turks in the Black Sea region, Peter aimed to secure for Russia part of the Baltic coastline, but for this he needed allies. In 1697, he travelled across Western Europe, where he met the Elector of Brandenburg to plan joint action and, in 1699, Poland and Denmark signed an alliance with Peter. Their plan was to partition the Swedish "empire" and create a Baltic region within which no single power exerted hegemony. The moment seemed right: Sweden had a young king, Charles XII, who, when he succeeded in 1697, was only 15 years old. In 1700, the coalition opened the Great Northern War against Sweden.

The Great Northern War

The Great Northern War (1700–21) was fought in parallel with the conflict at the heart of Europe known as the War of Spanish Succession. Although attracting less attention, it decided control of the Baltic. The war saw the defeat of Sweden and its decline as a great power. In its place, Russia was to emerge as the dominant power in Eastern Europe.

The characters of the two monarchs formed a significant contrast. Literally a giant (2m/7ft tall), Peter I of Russia was violent and unstable, but in matters of state pursued a course to modernize Russia and bring it into line with the West. He fashioned an up-to-date army and navy, equipped with the latest weaponry. He overcame the power of the nobility and brought the Church under his

The Swedish Empire 1610–60

Swedish territory at the Peace of Oliva (1660)

control. Reforms were instituted throughout society, including the prohibition of traditional dress and beards. The founding of St Petersburg in 1703 on the Gulf of Finland as a "window on the West" was a symbol of Peter's determination to bring Russia into contact with Western Europe.

Charles XII of Sweden was less colourful than Peter. Almost unconcerned with domestic issues, he was thrust into a turbulent military environment in which he quickly proved himself an outstanding leader. Faced with a combined assault by Russia and Denmark seeking to exploit his inexperience, he responded with vigour. A lightning assault on Denmark, threatening Copenhagen, forced the Danes to conclude a peace in August 1700. In November 1700, he secured a crushing victory over the Russians at Narva. The following year, the Saxons were defeated at Riga, and Charles invaded Poland and took Warsaw. Marching on Saxony, he secured his candidate on the throne of Poland by the Peace of Altranstadt in 1706. Charles's series of brilliant victories now tempted him to invade Russia. After overwintering in Saxony in 1706–7, he marched his army east, but found his approach to Moscow cut off by the scorched-earth policies of his enemies. Crossing the Dnieper River in 1708, he was lured into the Ukraine in the hope of catching Peter's main army, besieging the town of Pultava. Peter hastened to lift the siege, but with a better trained and equipped army than he had possessed at Narva. The depleted and exhausted Swedes were defeated in the ensuing battle of Pultava, fought on 8 July 1708. Charles's veteran army was smashed,

much of it falling captive, and Charles himself was forced to seek refuge in Turkey. Peter secured his grip on Sweden's former Baltic provinces of Livonia and Estonia by 1710, and occupied Finland in 1714. Other former Swedish lands fell into Prussian and Danish hands. In 1715, Peter brought his army west and established a base at Mecklenburg, hoping to find allies for an attack from the south. He failed and returned to Russia to consolidate the victory achieved at Pultava.

The end of Swedish power

Swedish power was broken. Charles's death at the siege of Frederickshald on 11 December 1718 signalled the final act of Swedish power. The treaty of Nystadt in 1721 ceded most of Sweden's former territories on the southern and eastern shores of the Baltic to Russia. Other treaties returned to Denmark territories lost earlier to Sweden.

The clearest outcome of the Northern War was the end of Swedish power in the Baltic region and its replacement by Russia. Although still viewed with distaste as an alien barbarian by the Western courts, Peter's domestic reforms and victory over Sweden had established Russia decisively as one of the great powers. With the country's huge reserves of manpower and rich natural resources, Russia had the capacity, under capable leadership, to compete effectively with the West. Unlike the decaying empires of the Ottomans and Moguls, Russia was to emerge after Peter's death in 1725 as a major player in the power struggles of the *ancien régime* and an arbiter of the fate of Poland.

Following Peter the Great's journey across Western Europe, he returned with thousands of artisans and in 1703 began to create St Petersburg as Russia's "window on the West". Sited on the Gulf of Finland with access to the Baltic and ultimately the Atlantic it was a symbol of Russia's entry into the ranks of the major European powers. Built by thousands of serfs and embellished with great palaces and churches by Peter and his successors, an unpromising, swampy site was turned into the "Venice of the North".

The Challenge of the East 208–9 ▶

Austria, Russia and Poland 270–1 ▶

Reform in Britain,
Autocracy in Russia 298–9 ▶

Reforms in Russia 1855–81 318–19 ▶

The Ottoman Empire

The Ottoman Empire dwarfed most European states. From its capital in Constantinople, it extended to the frontier with Persia, down through the Levant to Egypt and along the coast of North Africa, up through the Balkans and most of Hungary to the borders of Poland, and across to the Black Sea.

This multi-ethnic, multi-linguistic and multi-religious empire had been created by military conquest, and in the last resort was held together by force. The army enjoyed the highest possible esteem in the Empire. The army also exercised political influence, and was capable of making or breaking sultans. The Ottoman Empire did not demand conformity to Islam from its subjects, but it did exact obedience. Rebellion was crushed mercilessly. Constantinople, residence of the sultans, was one of the most imposing cities in Europe: it was a political capital, a centre of commerce, and a focus of religious significance. The sultan had scores of wives and several hundred children. When he died, his successor emerged from this large brood of sons, or perhaps from among his brothers, often after bloody intrigue. The theory was that Ottoman succession rested on the will of God. It was God who chose the new sultan, although the method might be sanguinary.

In the government of the Empire the sultan discussed affairs with a general council (*divan*), but he also relied on individual advisers, of whom the most important was the Grand Vizier. In 1656, Sultan Mehmed IV appointed as Grand Vizier a figure of remarkable political gifts: Mehmed Köprölu. He came to office at a difficult time: the Venetians had recently destroyed a Turkish fleet in the Dardanelles, the army was in revolt, and Constantinople had erupted into riot. Over the next five years (he died in 1661), Köprölu hammered the rebels into submission through mass executions (more than 36,000), or imprisonments. He strengthened the defences of the Empire by the construction of castles at the mouths of the Don and Dnieper, and at either side of the Dardanelles.

Köprölu's years in office also marked a new phase of Ottoman expansionism in central Europe. Since the beginning of the century, the Turks had been content to hold the line there, but, by the mid-1650s, they were contemplating war again. Their wars against Persia had ended in 1639, and Köprölu had restored political stability in Constantinople. Furthermore, as the Peace of Westphalia had

At its height, the Ottoman Empire encompassed an extraordinary diversity of peoples, languages, and religions. Its existence ultimately depended on military force, and its frontiers fluctuated according to the fortunes of war. In 1683, the Turks attempted to consolidate their position in central Europe by seizing Vienna. Their failure marked the beginning of their territorial retreat.

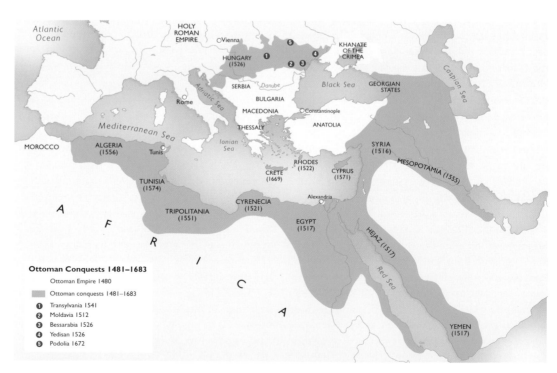

Ottoman Conquests 1481–1683

  Ottoman Empire 1480

  Ottoman conquests 1481–1683

1 Transylvania 1541
2 Moldavia 1512
3 Bessarabia 1526
4 Yedisan 1526
5 Podolia 1672

In spite of territorial losses in the late 17th century, the Ottoman Empire remained a powerful force. The splendours of Constantinople and of the sultan's palace, the Topkapi, equalled anything that Europe had to offer. Monarchs from both East and West sent embassies to cultivate relations with the sultans, who still enjoyed considerable prestige among their fellow rulers.

released Emperor Leopold I, who was also King of Hungary, from his German wars, he may have been tempted to turn against Turkish Hungary. The question of Transylvania initiated Turkish moves. This province enjoyed semi-autonomous status under Turkish suzerainty, but, by the mid-1650s, its prince, George Rákóczy, was acting independently and threatened to break away from the Ottoman Empire. The Turks invaded Transylvania and defeated and killed Rákóczy in 1660.

They also decided to pre-empt any attempts by Leopold I to recover Hungary by declaring war on him in 1663. They invaded Royal Hungary (that remnant of Hungary still under Habsburg control) and entered Austria, forcing Leopold to appeal for international help. In 1664, forces from Germany, France, and elsewhere came to his aid and, at the battle of St Gotthard, defeated the Turks. Leopold signed the Peace of Vasvar in 1664 with the Ottoman Empire, ceding all the territory which the Turks had taken. Vasvar marks the territorial height of the Ottoman Empire in Europe.

The Ottoman Empire in central Europe

The peace was signed for 20 years, during which time the Turks consolidated their power in central Europe. Leopold faced sustained rebellion in Royal Hungary throughout the 1670s into the 1680s, and, as the expiry of the Peace of Vasvar approached, the Turks concluded that circumstances were right for another army of conquest at Leopold's expense. The Grand Vizier, Kara Mustafa, approached the

Hungarian rebel leadership and offered to set it up at the head of a semi-independent region under Turkish protection. The offer was accepted, and, in 1683, Kara Mustafa led an army that conquered most of Royal Hungary and invaded Austria. Kara Mustafa decided to besiege Vienna. An international relief force broke the siege after two months, and the Turks were driven into retreat.

In 1684, Pope Innocent XI formed the Holy League, the principal members of which were Austria, Hungary, and Venice; its aim was to drive the Turks from Christendom. The league was joined by Russia in 1687. It fought the Turks for 15 years. In the first phase, to 1689, most of the victories went to the league. The Venetians seized control of the Adriatic and Ionian seas; Austro-Hungarian troops occupied most of Hungary, Transylvania, and Croatia. Belgrade was taken in 1688. Over the next few years, the Turks revived. They retook Belgrade in 1690 and invaded Hungary in 1691; they also restored their presence in the Adriatic and Ionian seas. The Russians, however, had taken strong points on the Black Sea, and, from the mid-1690s, the Turks were driven back on all fronts. Peace was agreed at Carlowitz in 1699. Most of Hungary and Transylvania was ceded to Leopold, and Dalmatia to Venice. They signed a separate peace with Russia at Constantinople in 1700 and surrendered Azov. The Ottoman Empire remained a major European power, but it had lost its pre-eminence in central Europe and never again attained the territorial expansion reached in 1664.

The Habsburg Monarchy

The Habsburgs were a remarkable dynasty. From minor noble origins, they rose to become the pre-eminent ruling house of Christendom. In the early 17th century, the head of the Austrian branch was Grand Duke of Austria, King of Bohemia, King of Hungary, and Holy Roman Emperor. The Spanish branch ruled Spain and its possessions in Europe and overseas.

From 1618–48, the Austrian Habsburgs were preoccupied with the Thirty Years War. While they succeeded in confirming their authority throughout Austria and Bohemia, their attempts to diminish the autonomy of the territories that comprised the Holy Roman Empire and to restore the Empire to Catholicism failed. The end of the war allowed them to concentrate again on their patrimonial lands. Ferdinand III (r.1637–57) took measures to revive the economy of Austria, but his successor Leopold I (r.1657–1705) had to confront the most problematic issue of all – Hungary.

Hungarian rebellion

Most of Hungary had been Turkish since 1526, with the Habsburgs retaining only a narrow segment – "Royal Hungary" – bordering Austria. They regarded the recovery of Hungary as an abiding objective, but the Turkish invasion of 1663 and Leopold's humiliation in the Peace of Vasvar confirmed how unlikely this was in the near future. Leopold's incompetence drove powerful Hungarian aristocrats into rebellion in 1664. He defeated them

in 1670, and proceeded to impose Catholicism throughout Royal Hungary and confiscate the estates of Protestant nobles. Thereby he provoked a more dangerous movement of rebellion: the Kuruc, the aim of which was to replace Leopold with a French or Polish prince. In 1681, admitting the failure of his policy, Leopold revoked much of his anti-Protestant legislation.

It was into this context that the Turks burst dramatically in 1683, laying seige to Vienna. However, the relief of Vienna by an international force not only marked the point from which the Turkish position in Hungary declined, but also signalled the beginning of Leopold's revival. The Holy League, of which he was a member, drove back the Turks and enabled him to quell the remnant of the Kuruc rebellion. With international assistance, he realized the long-held Habsburg ambition of reconquering Hungary, including Transylvania. The Peace of Carlowitz marked his triumph in central Europe.

The other principal conflict in which Leopold was involved was the War of the Spanish

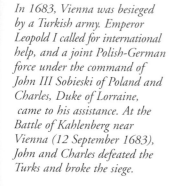

In 1683, Vienna was besieged by a Turkish army. Emperor Leopold I called for international help, and a joint Polish-German force under the command of John III Sobieski of Poland and Charles, Duke of Lorraine, came to his assistance. At the Battle of Kahlenberg near Vienna (12 September 1683), John and Charles defeated the Turks and broke the siege.

Succession. When Charles II of Spain died in 1700 and left the entire succession to a French prince instead of an Austrian Habsburg, Leopold was prepared to fight, but could only do so with English and Dutch support. Hesitant at first, they were provoked into war by Louis XIV. The Grand Alliance, which they and Leopold formed, fought through to the Peace of Utrecht of 1713, by which time Leopold's younger son Charles was emperor. Under the peace settlement, the crown of Spain remained with the Bourbon Philip V, but the Austrian Habsburgs secured compensation: Spanish lands in Italy and the Spanish Netherlands. In 1713, the power and prestige of the Austrian Habsburgs stood higher than at any time since the early 1500s.

The making of the Habsburg monarchy

Under Charles VI, the Habsburg monarchy remained one of the great powers of Europe, but vulnerable to the rise of Russia and Prussia as great powers. Following the Great Northern War, Russia represented a new rival for territories in Eastern Europe, but also a potential ally against the Ottomans. The rise of Prussia under the Great Elector, Frederick William, then under the brilliant leadership of Frederick the Great, also posed a threat to Austrian power. This was soon revealed by Frederick's seizure of the province of Silesia in 1740 and the series of wars that ensued when Austria attempted to recapture it. Fortunately for Habsburg power, the Ottoman Empire no longer posed a threat to the very existence of the dynasty, although it was still capable of successful military operations against its neighbours. For the Habsburgs, the recovery of Hungary marked a decisive turning point. Thereafter Habsburg attention would be primarily directed towards the struggle for dominance between the European nation-states.

Charles VI was without male heirs, and so he sought to secure the Habsburg lands from division after his death. He established an order of succession under the "Pragmatic Sanction". This decreed that the lands belonging to the Austrian Empire should be indivisible, and, in the case of no male heirs, the Habsburg lands should devolve upon Charles's daughters, the eldest of whom was Maria Theresa. Provision was also made for the daughters of his brother to inherit the realm if his own daughters failed to succeed him. In order to secure the inheritance, numerous diplomatic negotiations were required. An alliance was struck between Austria and Spain in 1725, but this proved short-lived. Participation in the war of Polish Succession from 1733–8 led to the loss of lands in Italy, but secured French support for the Pragmatic Sanction.

Prince Eugene of Savoy

Prince Eugene of Savoy (1663–1736) was one of the foremost generals of Europe and a key figure in maintaining the House of Austria as a major power. He entered the service of Leopòld II in 1683. The defeat of the Turks at Zenta in 1697 was followed by his famous partnership with the Duke of Marlborough in the War of Spanish Succession, defeating the French at Blenheim in 1704 and at Malplaquet in 1709. Following peace between Austria and France in 1714, he fought against the Ottoman Empire in 1716–17. He last took up command at the age of 70, in the War of Polish Succession in 1733.

The War of Austrian Succession

On Charles's death in 1740, several claimants for the Austrian crown emerged alongside the heir under the Pragmatic Sanction, Maria Theresa. Charles Albert, the Elector of Bavaria; Philip V of Spain; and Augustus III of Saxony all advanced claims. The first to act, however, was Frederick the Great of Prussia. Claiming legal title to part of the Habsburg territory of Silesia, Frederick offered to support Maria Theresa against other claimants if his claim in Silesia was recognized. When it was refused, he opened the first Silesian War, or War of Austrian Succession by seizing the whole of the province of Silesia.

Dismemberment of the Austrian lands looked likely as France, Bavaria, Spain, Saxony, and Prussia joined forces in 1741. Maria Theresa retreated into Hungary, where she regrouped her forces. An alliance was concluded with Britain, and Austria retook Bavaria and laid siege to Prague. Seeking to buy off her most dangerous opponent, Maria Theresa conceded Silesia to Frederick at the Peace of Breslau in 1742. Frederick, fearing a rise of Austrian power, renewed the war. Peace was secured in 1748 at Aix-la-Chapelle, and Maria Theresa was confirmed on the throne of Austria, but the loss of Silesia to Prussia was ratified.

Maria Theresa ruled the Habsburg lands for the next 40 years with an eye to consolidation and prudent reform. The lands she ruled had had no formal definition before the Pragmatic Sanction. Linguistic, ethnic, and geographical diversity were to remain the hallmark of the Austrian state. However, reforms created a reasonably efficient administration, and the Austrian state was able to achieve financial stability and support a large army. Habsburg was to remain one of the great powers throughout the 18th century and beyond.

The Thirty Years War 242–3 ▶
The Wars of the
Spanish Succession 250–1 ▶
The Ottoman Empire 254–5 ▶
The Habsburg Empire 348–9 ▶

Vaccination against smallpox was one of the triumphs of 18th-century science. Inoculation using smallpox had proved effective in some instances, but some patients contracted the disease and died. The use of the relatively harmless cowpox as a vaccine reduced deaths from one of the great killers of the early modern period.

IMPROVING THE HUMAN CONDITION

The 18th century saw Europe reach levels of civilization not seen since the classical Greek world so much admired by the intellectuals of the period. The ending of the religious strife of the previous century brought a new stability to European affairs. The emergence of a group of more prosperous and stable nation-states increasingly allowed Europeans to pursue intellectual advance and social improvement.

The Scientific Revolution of the 17th century and the exhaustion of religious passions brought about by the Thirty Years War marked the beginning of a more humane and civilized era in European affairs. The watchwords were improvement and toleration. Science was now an accepted part of the way in which the educated classes of Europe thought about the world in which they lived. Significantly, witchcraft – once taken seriously as a threat – was now dismissed as ignorant superstition. Intellectual exploration was increasingly free from the restraints imposed in the past by religious bigotry. Early scientific advances into areas such as the laws of motion by Isaac Newton and the circulation of the blood by William Harvey in 1619 demonstrated that key aspects of the natural world could be properly investigated and studied. Astronomy was making considerable advances so that it was now impossible to deny that the earth was part of a solar system and that the earth rotated around the sun. By the early 18th century, six planets, including the earth were known, and the greatly improved telescope of William Herschel revealed a seventh, Uranus, in 1781.

Exploration was reaching new parts of the world through the invention of a marine chronometer by John Harrison in 1761–2. This revolutionized maritime navigation in the 18th century, facilitating both exploration and trade. Captain James Cook undertook three voyages of exploration between 1768 and 1776, charting vast new areas of the Pacific, including New Zealand and the islands of Tahiti and Samoa.

In the natural sciences, discoveries proceeded apace with the investigation into the properties of heat by the Glasgow scientist Joseph Black. Electricity was becoming a subject of investigation through the work of Luigi Galvani, who discovered electrical current in 1786, and Alessandro Volta, who invented the "voltaic pile", the first electrical battery, in 1800. Experiment with electricity attracted figures as diverse as Benjamin Franklin and John Wesley during the 18th century, the latter seeing it as a potential cure for many diseases. In botany, the great Swedish botanist Carolus Linnaeus founded the modern classification of plants with his *Systema Naturae* (1735). In chemistry, the English dissenter Joseph Priestley and the French chemist Antoine Lavoisier laid the basis for the understanding of chemical reactions and the discovery of oxygen.

Advances in the scientific world appeared to offer an ever expanding universe of knowledge and the ability to improve the lot of mankind. Although detailed knowledge of germ theory and the spread of infection was lacking, important advances were made in the conquest of diseases such as bubonic plague by improvements to sanitation and housing. The last major outbreak of bubonic plague in Western Europe was in Marseilles in 1720. A major medical breakthrough came with the introduction of inoculation against smallpox in the early 18th century, followed by the safer vaccination pioneered by Edward Jenner in 1796. It prevented a disease that had become almost as big a scourge as plague in the period before 1700.

The Enlightenment

The Enlightenment was a literary and philosophical movement, with its origins in the scientific movement of the 17th century. In the course of the 18th century, it had a profound effect upon the way in which rulers saw their duty towards their subjects and, ultimately, the way in which subjects saw themselves and their rights within society.

1600–1789

ABSOLUTISM AND ENLIGHTENMENT

The Encyclopédie of Denis Diderot and Jean d'Alembert was the most famous intellectual product of the 18th century. Its 28 volumes, including 11 of plates, published between 1751 and 1777, attempted a universal compendium of knowledge. It was, however, pervaded by the sceptical and anti-clerical tone of the Enlightenment, and was banned in many countries. The term encyclopédiste became attached to those who held liberal opinions.

The intellectual pedigree of the Enlightenment could be traced as far back as the Renaissance, but its more immediate precursors lay in the scientific movement that had discovered the basic physical laws of the universe and undermined the necessity for religious belief in order to explain it. Attributed to writers such as Thomas Hobbes and John Locke was the belief in rational enquiry and an orderly series of rights and duties in the political world. Locke's An *Essay Concerning Human Understanding* suggested that men could become masters of their world through the exercise of reason, which was the feature that distinguished all mankind from brute creation. Man could free himself from ignorance through the application of reason. In theory, it offered mankind the possibility of improvement in all aspects of human affairs.

At its most benign, the Enlightenment simply offered an extension of the scientific and philosophical enquiries of the previous century, but it was their application to political, religious, economic, and social affairs that was to have the most widespread consequences. Every institution could now be subject to the critique of reason, its existence questioned for its utility and rationality. Everything from monarchy to capital punishment could be examined, including the most fundamental aspects of human society.

Where scientific enquiry introduced a fresh perspective on the human condition, foreign travel and literature about contemporary society provided a climate in which it was possible to criticize existing conditions. Contacts with powerful, well-regulated states such as the Mogul and Chinese empires suggested that effective rule was possible without Christianity, and revealed a range of new ideas and customs. Contact with the South Sea Islanders and Native Americans lent credence to the idea of the "noble savage" – both an innocent untainted existing society and a *tabula rasa* on which a new beginning might be inscribed. Defoe's *Robinson Crusoe* (1719), Montesquieu's *Persian Letters* (1721), and Voltaire's *Zaire* (1732) were examples of the use of the "noble savage"

and foreign locations to expose some of the features of contemporary society. Probably the most influential book of the early 18th-century Enlightenment was Montesquieu's *L'Esprit des Lois* (*The Spirit of Laws*) (1748). Reprinted 22 times in two years, it categorized existing governments into despotic and balanced. In the former, the power of the ruler was unrestricted; in the latter, separation of powers and the rule of law prevailed. As a model of the rational criticism of political institutions, it represented an enormous step towards the "scientific" analysis of contemporary society.

The *Encylopédie*

In 1751, the first volume appeared of the *Encyclopédie* by Denis Diderot and Jean-le-Rond d'Alembert. Published between 1751 and 1777, it represented an attempt to provide a universal compendium of current knowledge, with essays on individual subjects. With almost 4000 subscribers, the work had the initial support of the official censor. Its basic premise was that by collating and disseminating information, the general improvement of society would follow. Much of the work was devoted to the skills of artisans, for as well as considering the great issues of political constitutions, the existence of a supreme being, and the nature of the world about them, the enlightened thinkers were interested in the wellbeing of the common people. A major strand of enlightened thought was economic. The physiocratic movement in France was concerned with improving agriculture, seen as the source of all wealth and national wellbeing. Interest in technical processes and improvements also formed part of the agenda. Adam Smith's *Wealth of Nations* (1776) brought the tone of rational enquiry into the realms of the economy and the workings of the market. The plea for free trade was to become one of the features of the reforms called for by enlightened thinkers.

The largest impact, however, was felt in the widening sphere of political enquiry. The burgeoning world of print and literature in Europe conveyed the ideas of the Enlightenment far and wide. Novels such as Voltaire's *Candide* (1759) brought the world of sceptical enquiry into middle-class and even artisan homes. In France, the salon – gatherings of *philosophes*, artists, and fashionable society – provided a focus for the discussion of ideas. Elsewhere, literary, philosophical, and scientific societies, such as the Lunar Society in Birmingham, were forums where the latest ideas could be discussed. In Scotland, Edinburgh and Glasgow became centres of the "Scottish Enlightenment" focussed around their universities and gaining a worldwide reputation. Thinkers such as the philosopher David Hume, the economist Adam Smith, the poet Robert Burns, and the inventor James Watt represented a high point in Scottish intellectual life. *The Encyclopedia Britannica*, edited by William Smellie as "a dictionary of the arts and sciences", began to emerge in weekly instalments in 1768, in England and the first edition was published in three volumes in 1771.

The diffusion of enlightened ideas was not confined to the upper classes. In many areas, these ideas filtered down to the world of the shopkeeper, craftsman, and artisan. Cheap editions, particularly of scurrilous and critical works, found a popular audience in what has been called the "Grub Street Enlightenment". In France, printers and authors such as Nicolas-Edme Restif de la Bretonne produced a chaotic mixture of social criticism,

Cesare Beccaria

Cesare Beccaria (1738–94) was the most prominent figure of the Italian Enlightenment. Influenced by Montesquieu to investigate philosophical and social problems, his *Dei Delitte e Delle Pene* (*Treatise on Crimes and Punishments*), published at Leghorn in 1764, was an immense success, pioneering liberal penal reform. His argument that brutal retribution should be replaced by more systematic and measured punishments in order to reform the criminal attracted attention from many of the enlightened absolutists, such as Catherine the Great and Joseph II, who implemented Beccaria's ideas by reducing or abolishing capital punishment.

fantasy, and pornography. Thomas Paine came from a similarly poor environment, working as a corset-maker and customs official before becoming famous as a journalist for his advocacy of the cause of American independence in *Common Sense* (1776), and his later *Rights of Man* (1791).

Enlightenment and reform

By the close of the 18th century, the Enlightenment had produced a climate of criticism, which implied the need for reform of existing institutions. An agreed agenda of reforms included such issues as religious toleration, economic liberalism, uniform law codes and rational administration, humane penal systems, and an end to censorship. Much of this agenda was adopted by the so-called "enlightened despots". Where previously rulers had merely assumed that their dynastic inheritance or divine sanction was sufficient to justify their authority, a new generation of rulers sought to justify themselves promoting the welfare of their subjects. The sentiment of the monarch as "the first servant of the state" was one that was adopted by rulers such as Frederick the Great of Prussia, Catherine the Great of Russia, Charles III of Spain, and Joseph II of Austria. Although widely divergent in their policies, they all professed themselves to be supporters of enlightened principles. In practice, many rulers were to absorb the rationalizing and centralizing features of the Enlightenment at the expense of its more "liberal" implications of political rights and wider citizien participation. The wide diffusion of enlightened ideas, however, was to ensure that concepts of representative democracy and constitutionalism became a central feature of the revolutionary aspirations of the last quarter of the century.

Cosmopolitanism and Public Life

The 18th century was notable for the development of its enlightened approach to human affairs. The spirit of rational enquiry, optimism, and improvement was felt generally across Europe, both at the courts and in public forums, but in differing degrees according to the nature of the states themselves and their level of development.

An English gentleman, William Perry, painted on the "Grand Tour" with the Colosseum of Rome in the background. The Grand Tour of Italy became almost obligatory as part of the education of wealthy gentlemen from northern Europe, where they could experience directly the remains of classical antiquity, often bringing artefacts home with them.

Coffee houses became important centres for commerce, sociability, and entertainment during the 18th century. London had more than 500 by 1739, with Paris, Berlin, and other important cities emulating the fashion. Newspapers and pamphlets were available in these coffee houses, as well as cartoons and caricatures on issues of the day, contributing to the rise of a broad "public opinion".

Cosmopolitanism

By the end of the 18th century, enlightened ideas were having an effect across virtually the whole of Europe to a greater or lesser extent. They had even reached as far afield as the European colonies in North America, Latin America, and the West Indies, where they were to bear fruit in revolt and rebellion. Initially, however, the early Enlightenment of the Scientific Revolution and the first writings of the *philosophes* such as Montesquieu and Voltaire was largely confined to north-western Europe – to the British Isles, France, and the Low Countries. There were also important outposts of the Enlightenment in southern Italy and Sweden. From the middle of the 18th century, however, enlightened ideals spread across Europe through their influence on the so-called "enlightened despots". Enlightened rulers, such as Catherine the Great of Russia and Frederick the Great of Prussia not only communicated with the great intellectuals of the day, but also sought to put enlightened reforms into effect, involving the bureaucrats,

nobles and educated classes of the countries with programmes of reform.

It was one of the most famous *philosophes*, Jean-Jacques Rousseau, who declared, "there is no longer a France, a Germany, a Spain, not even England, there are only Europeans. All have the same tastes, same passions, same way of life". Although an exaggeration, there was an extent to which Rousseau was reflecting an important truth. Few countries escaped the influence of the new ideas. In the Iberian peninsula, so long the bastion of Catholic reaction and Counter-Reformation, the spirit of Enlightenment was beginning to be evident. In Portugal, the Marquis of Pombal rebuilt Lisbon on model lines after the disastrous earthquake of 1755, and set about a programme of economic and educational reform on behalf of the monarch, Joseph I. In Spain, Charles III also instituted a programme of reform in order to restore Spain's position as a great power. The main thrust of Spanish reform was administrative efficiency from the "top down", carried out at the behest of the

Entitled A Reading from Molière, *this painting captures the atmosphere of the salons that became fashionable meeting places in 18th-century France. Usually centred on an aristocratic hostess, they provided a gathering place for intellectuals, artists, and members of the aristocracy away from the court, and an opportunity for the discussion of new ideas.*

established authorities. In both cases, there were powerful vested interests in the nobility and the Church who opposed any fundamental change. In Italy, too, some enlightened rulers began a programme of administrative rationalization, notably in the Tuscany of Leopold II. In Naples, Cesare Beccaria wrote one of the most influential works of the Enlightenment with his *Treatise on Crimes and Punishments* of 1764, advocating a humane system of criminal justice. Again, it was the urge for effective reform that caused even conservative-minded rulers to adopt elements of the new ideas. The concept of the "well-ordered police state" in which absolute rulers adopted only those aspects of the Enlightenment that suited their purpose, also had relevance in the German and Austrian lands. A tradition of legal education in the German Protestant universities produced the "Cameralist" administrators of the German states who ensured that states were professionally governed. This sometimes lead to genuinely "liberal" measures, such as the toleration extended to religious minorities or migrants who were deemed useful to rulers, the promotion of education, and economic innovation. In most cases, however, they were states in which the ecclesiastical or princely authorities remained in control. One of the most significant examples of "partial enlightenment" was Maria Theresa's rule in Austria-Hungary, with her concentration on reforms that would enhance the efficiency of the state while retaining its Catholic and authoritarian nature.

Polite society and public life

There was also a spread of enlightened ideas among the educated elite and the growing middle classes of the more economically developed parts of Europe. Enlightened ideas became a subject for debate among "polite society". In addition to court circles that could be influenced by enlightened rulers, there were an increasing number of venues at which the new ideas could be discussed. In some cases, universities such as those at Edinburgh and Glasgow in Scotland provided the focus for intellectual movements, but elsewhere, educated classes were able to meet and widen public debate through the medium of salons, coffee houses, and societies. Court society everywhere spoke French, the language of the *philosophes*, and French and English were the principal languages of enlightened thought. An increasing number of books, journals, and newspapers broadcast the new ideas. The first European daily newspaper, the *Daily Courant* was founded in England in 1702. The works of the leading figures of the European Enlightenment – Voltaire, Montesquieu, Hume, Beccaria, and Rousseau – were available in translations across Europe. Increasingly, educated men and women shared a common language of ideas and culture.

Tourism and the Grand Tour

Even before the use of the railway, writers, artists, and intellectuals engaged in extensive travel, reinforcing the cosmopolitanism of enlightened culture. Even the Atlantic was regularly crossed by figures such as Benjamin Franklin, providing the New World with the ideas of Europe. European colonists in the West Indies and Latin America imported the ideas of the Enlightenment to their societies. Within Europe, the popularity of travel, especially the "Grand Tour" to view the remains of antiquity in Italy, provided a common point of reference for the educated classes of Europe. Ideals of imperial grandeur, of Republican virtue, of empire and democracy, would affect the intellectual climate of the late 18th century and influence both the American and French revolutions.

Economic Growth and Colonial Expansion

The growth of Europe's population and economy in the 18th century stimulated colonial expansion. Agriculture was more productive, trade was increasing, and, by the late 18th century, Britain was becoming the first industrial nation. Trading opportunities beyond Europe took European merchants all over the world, establishing new colonies in the Americas and forging trade links with Africa, India, and the Far East.

A plate from Diderot and d'Alambert's Encyclopédie *of 1762 shows work on the land. In spite of the growth of trade and industry, agriculture remained the basis of the European economy in the 18th century. Its improvement and prosperity lay at the heart of early enlightened ideas about economic growth and social progress. Groups such as the physiocrats advocated free trade in agricultural produce, and improved agricultural techniques attracted much attention.*

Ports in Europe had been steadily expanding in the 16th and 17th centuries with the rise of overseas and colonial trade. During the 18th century, there was further, huge expansion, especially in the ports serving the booming Atlantic trade. This demanded larger vessels as well as improved docks and other facilities.

Population growth

An underlying feature of European expansion and economic growth in the 18th century was a rise in population. Even before the Industrial Revolution, Europe witnessed steady growth in the number of its inhabitants. A number of factors were at work. The gradual decline of plague as a major killer and the conquest of smallpox through inoculation and vaccination reduced the overall death rate. As important was the gradual elimination of the devastating "crises of subsistence" or killing famines, which had periodically affected Europe as a result of bad harvests. Improved agricultural techniques were raising productivity and creating a more regular surplus of food. New crops were also being cultivated such as maize and rice in Southern Europe and the potato in Northern Europe, which produced cheap substitutes for traditional cereals and could be used in times of harvest failure. Better transport by sea, road, and, later, canal also permitted greater flexibility of supply. Although periods of shortage and high prices could still occur as a result of bad harvests, as in the years immediately prior to the French Revolution, the effect of famine upon population growth was reduced. Moreover, the first half of the 18th century saw a long run of favourable harvests and relatively benign climatic conditions.

The results were also being felt of minor improvements in such areas as housing, cheap, washable clothing, the availability of soap, and nutrition. The consequence was a general downward trend in death rates throughout almost all European countries, with populations rising even in countries that had experienced little mercantile or industrial expansion such as Ireland, Austria-Hungary, and Russia. Where trade and industry flourished, however, further impetus was given to population growth. Opportunities in commerce and manufacturing, particularly in the growing towns and cities, allowed people to marry earlier than was the norm in agricultural employment and to have children earlier. In the most advanced economies, such as in Britain and the Low Countries, population growth was at its fastest because birth rates were rising while death rates were falling.

Economic expansion

Trade and manufacturing flourished in this expanding environment. Growing population and increasing wealth stimulated the demand for a wide range of manufactured goods, including textiles, metalware, pottery, and foodstuffs.

Domestic industry, small workshops, and hand-working remained the key means of production. Even in Britain, the domestic system and hand-working remained the principal method of producing most manufactured goods during the 18th century, and water power remained the most widely used source of energy in the textile industry. It was not until the end of the century that steam power began to be used by some sectors of industry. There was some concentration of production; early "factories" grouped workers together under one roof, but often still utilizing traditional techniques of manufacture and water power.

Colonial expansion

International trade played a major role in the economic growth of Europe. The early colonial empires of Spain, Portugal, and Holland provided a ready market for traders and merchants from Britain and France. The establishment of colonies in North America and the West Indies, and their continued development in the 18th century, provided a major stimulus to trade. Manufactured goods could be exported from Europe to the colonies, with colonial produce being brought back in return for direct sale or for processing and re-export. In the larger port cities, such as London, Amsterdam, and Antwerp, some of the largest enterprises were involved in refining and processing colonial goods, producing sugar, rum, tobacco, and other commodities for direct consumption or re-export. Most of Europe's most fashionable products such as tea, coffee, and tobacco were the result of extensive networks of trade.

A particularly grim aspect of the expansion in trade was the trade in humans – the slave trade. Although in existence for centuries, the Atlantic slave trade grew into a huge business as an estimated 10 million African slaves were transported by European slavers to work the plantations of the Americas and the West Indies. Usually sold on by African or Arab slavers to European shippers, African labour was felt necessary for heavy work in the tropics or the colonial plantations of North America. Hundreds of thousands perished from the sufferings of the "middle passage" across the Atlantic or from disease, cruelty, and overwork. This trade brought unheard-of prosperity to the Atlantic ports of Europe and North America, laying the foundations for the prosperity of ports such as Liverpool, Bristol, Bordeaux, and Le Havre.

Wars of colonial rivalry were now being fought by France and Britain to secure part of the trade of the declining empires of Spain and Portugal. In 1713, British merchants obtained the Asiento Treaty with Spain to deliver up to 4800 slaves annually to

François Quesnay

François Quesnay (1694–1774) was a leading French physician and political economist, one of the founders of the "physiocrats" and a contributor to the *Encyclopédie* on agricultural topics. The physiocrats saw agriculture as the main producer of wealth and supported free trade and free labour in order to improve output. Along with other writers such as Mirabeau and Mercier de la Rivière, Quesnay argued for the removal of controls over the grain trade, policies adopted in countries such as Spain under the enlightened Charles III. Their fundamental belief was that, if agriculture were free of controls and restrictions, the laws of nature would lead to increasing wealth. Along with their near contemporary, Adam Smith, whose *Wealth of Nations* was published in 1776, enlightened economic thinkers sought the promotion of economic freedom, as well as a less restricted political order.

the Spanish colonies and to send one ship a year to trade with Panama. But Spain was unable to provide its colonies with sufficient slaves or manufactured goods, leading to constant friction as British merchants attempted to trade illegally with the Spanish colonies. Initially, the Dutch in the Far East had taken over from the Portuguese, establishing trading stations in Ceylon, the East Indies, and as far as Japan. The Dutch East India Company, founded in 1602, was based on Batavia in Java and was one of the most powerful commercial organizations of the 18th century. It was soon rivalled, however, by the British East India Company, whose trading posts in India in Bombay, Bengal, and Madras provided the basis for British control of the lucrative trade in spices, tea, and precious stones. Rival French trading bases in India, such as Pondicherry, were undermined by British successes in the Seven Years War (1756–63). Similarly, the strong French position in Canada, including Quebec and Montreal, was broken by British military victories in the same conflict, forcing the surrender of the whole of Canada to Britain. Although both Britain and France retained colonies in the important sugar-producing islands of the West Indies, by the late 18th century, Britain had emerged as the dominant colonial power. Britain's mercantile involvement was worldwide, reaching as far afield as the Pacific, India, the West Coast of Africa, and the Americas. Even after the loss of 13 American colonies, Britain found its trade with America increasing under the influence of free-trade ideas. One of the most lucrative trades was in cotton from the southern states, fuelling the rise of Britain's cotton textile industry.

Maria Theresa succeeded as ruler of the Austrian lands in 1740. She was forced to fight protracted and, ultimately, unsuccessful wars to retain the province of Silesia, seized by Frederick the Great on her accession. Her administrative reforms strengthened the Austrian state, although her conservative, Catholic outlook inhibited the more liberal reforms advocated by her son during her lifetime.

THE EASTERN POWERS AND ENLIGHTENED ABSOLUTISM

It was in central and Eastern Europe that the full consequences and contradictions of enlightened despotism were realized. Three rulers, Frederick the Great, Catherine the Great, and Joseph II, showed a genuine commitment to enlightened ideals that went beyond mere lip service. At the same time, they demonstrated a lack of scruple in international relations that saw Poland dismembered and extinguished.

The conditions in which the Enlightenment developed were different in the East than in Western Europe. The states of Prussia, Austria-Hungary, and Russia were still primarily agricultural and scarcely affected by the growth of trade and industry that was transforming parts of Western Europe. In central and Eastern Europe, towns were generally smaller and the mercantile and professional elite were less numerous and more dependent upon established structures of authority. Socially, institutions such as serfdom were still maintained across much of Europe east of the Elbe. The theory of absolute power was virtually unmitigated in Russia and Austria-Hungary, and scarcely less so in Prussia. The position of the nobles, however, was a powerful, latent force that could obstruct the actions of the enlightened despots and curtail their freedom of action. In Austria-Hungary and Russia, the power of the great nobles was only partially kept in check. The institution of serfdom and labour service was untouched by Maria Theresa, but was one of the causes that would upset Joseph II's enlightened regime. A similar balance of forces operated in Russia where the power of the nobility was too great to allow Catherine the Great the opportunity to abolish serfdom even if she had genuinely wished to.

Nonetheless, Frederick the Great, Joseph II, and Catherine the Great form the most thoroughgoing examples of enlightened despotism in action. In spite of the practical limitations of their positions, they conferred with enlightened thinkers and publicly espoused enlightened principles. Frederick the Great took Prussia from the ranks of a second-class power to one of the most admired countries in Europe. Catherine the Great greatly expanded Russia's borders, creating the largest territorial power in Europe. Joseph II's reign witnessed the most determined attempt by any ruler to implement a thoroughly reformed regime. He was, however, unable to overcome the vested interests and suspicions of his subjects and the powerful ruling elite in his far-flung and disunited empire.

The contradictions in the behaviour of the enlightened despots of central and Eastern Europe became most apparent in the sphere of international politics. However enlightened their ideals, they existed in an international system that was dangerous for vulnerable states. The need to maintain absolute control meant that few concessions were made to the political involvement of the wider ranks of society. Internally, Catherine the Great faced a major challenge to her authority in the Pugachev Rising of 1773, and the Austrian state faced a major peasant revolt in 1765.

Above all, the enlightened rulers of Eastern Europe were predatory upon each other and upon neighbouring states. Frederick the Great's seizure of Silesia in 1740 was to be followed by years of bitter warfare, culminating in the Seven Years War. Thereafter the enlightened powers turned their attention towards a more vulnerable target – Poland – erasing it from the map of Europe in one of the most ruthless acts of international *realpolitik* ever witnessed.

The Rise of Prussia

The rise of Prussia to the status of a great power was primarily the work of Frederick the Great, king from 1740–86. Building on the work of his father, Frederick William I, he established the most feared army in Europe, triumphing in the Seven Years War of 1756–63. His reputation also extended to his work as an enlightened despot, creating one of the most efficient and well-governed European states.

Prussia was relatively weak at the beginning of the 18th century. When Frederick William I came to the throne in 1713, he inherited from his grandfather, Frederick William, the Great Elector, a state with no obvious natural frontiers and 2.5 million inhabitants. However, he had also inherited an efficient administration and a financial regime that allowed him to maintain a standing army. On his accession, Frederick William I set about reforming the court to eliminate any extravagance, devoting generous resources to the army. During his reign, its size increased from 40,000 to 80,000 men, and it was trained to the highest standards. But by keeping Prussia at peace, Frederick William built up a financial surplus and handed over to his son a full treasury and the most professional army in Europe.

Frederick II (1712–86) – Frederick the Great – was a man of a very different character from his father. Whereas Frederick William preferred the simple life of a soldier, showing no interest in the arts and treating his son with extraordinary harshness, Frederick the Great was receptive to new currents of thought. An accomplished musician and friend of Voltaire, he set out to make his reign one of dedicated service to the state. His famous

dictum that he was "the first servant of the state" was combined with his belief that rulers should learn from the *philosophes* the best principles of government. Shortly before his accession, he wrote: "Philosophers should be the teachers of the world and the teachers of princes."

Frederick the Great established from the outset a strict regime of hard work for himself and his officials. Among the first of his principles was religious toleration, allowing useful immigrants of any religion to settle in his lands. He placed a high priority on law reform, instituting a Ministry of Justice in Berlin and salaried judges. Torture was abolished and capital punishment reduced. He regarded the codification of Prussian law as one of his greatest ambitions, although this was only completed in 1791 after his death. Agriculture was encouraged and tens of thousands of colonists attracted with grants of land and credit facilities.

The Prussian administration was closely linked to the military administration, often staffed by ex-officers and NCOs. The Directory was the central governing body, with provincial chambers to administer the component regions of the state. New departments were added to deal with the

An engraving shows the various forms of military punishment that could be employed to discipline Prussian soldiers. The Prussian army became legendary under Frederick the Great and his father for its meticulous drill and fierce discipline, laying the foundation for its fearsome reputation in the 18th century. Under Frederick the Great it became the most professional and highly trained army in Europe.

economy and the maintenance of the army. In order to maintain an efficient financial system, he used French experts to advise on the remodelling of his excise taxes. Reform of the Directory came in the 1760s under Ludwig von Hagen. A State Bank was organized, professional training and examinations for the bureaucracy introduced, and specialized sub-departments instituted. In the localities, Frederick accepted a compromise with the *Junkers* (aristocrats) over the selection of the main local official, the *Landrat*, selecting the candidates from a list nominated by the *Junkers*.

Frederick's domestic policies were not entirely consistent with enlightened principles. His economic policy sought to increase the revenues of the Prussian state and protect its industries and agriculture, if necessary at the expense of the free trade advocated by Adam Smith. His dependence on the nobility to staff the officer corps and higher ranks of the bureaucracy did not encourage social mobility. Moreover, while Frederick offered the peasants the protection of the royal courts, he drew back from interfering with the institution of serfdom. Although the atmosphere of the state was not overly oppressive, with public criticism and satire accepted, there was no attempt to liberalize the constitution of Prussia, which remained firmly monarchical and authoritarian.

On the field of battle, Frederick blazed a course across European affairs. Widely admired for his reforming zeal, he was hated and admired in equal measure for his military conquests. Building upon the work of his predecessors, Frederick built up an army that was soon the envy of Europe. From the beginning of his reign, he sought to expand Prussia's territories, with the rationale that attack was the only form of defence for a small state with vulnerable borders. His response on his accession to the throne was one of outright aggression. Prussia had accepted the Pragmatic Sanction created by Charles VI of Austria to ensure that his daughter Maria Theresa would inherit all the Habsburg lands unopposed. On Charles' death in 1740, Frederick only consented to uphold the agreement if the Austrian territory of Silesia was ceded to him, and he occupied the territory with his army. The successful battle of Mollwitz on 10 April 1741 allowed him to make a favourable peace with Austria at Breslau, but it was only temporary. Frederick's aggression in Silesia committed him to a further war, the Second Silesian War of 1744–5. After initial failure when he invaded Bohemia, his victories on the battlefield in 1745 brought the war to a successful conclusion. Silesia was secured by the Treaty of Dresden and Frederick's military reputation was established.

The Seven Years War

The Seven Years War made Frederick one of the most renowned generals of the century. Deeply resentful at the loss of Silesia, Austria acted to bring an overwhelming coalition of forces against Prussia, forming alliances with France and Russia. Frederick made his own preparations and, with financial assistance from France's enemy, Britain, he made a pre-emptive strike by occupying Saxony. Its revenues provided him with much-needed resources and fresh recruits, but it also committed him to an attritional struggle that saw defeats and victories over the next seven years. Brilliant victories at Rossbach and Leuthen in 1757 raised Frederick's military reputation to new heights, but Berlin was occupied by the Russians in 1760, and at Kolin (1757), and Kunersdorf (1759), he suffered serious reverses. The staying power of the Prussian state proved decisive as Frederick fought his more numerous opponents to a standstill and secured the Peace of Hubertusberg in February 1763.

Frederick was now able to deploy his energies almost exclusively on domestic reform. Because of the reputation he had acquired, he participated as an equal partner in the partitions of Poland. Attempts by Austria to lay claim to Bavaria were forestalled in the War of Bavarian Succession in 1778–9, in which Frederick occupied Bohemia. The Peace of Teschen in 1779 ended the conflict with little serious fighting having occurred.

By the time of his death in 1786, Frederick had established Prussia as a first-rank state with an army and bureaucracy the envy of Europe and a ruler known universally as "the Great".

Unlike many other European states, Frederick the Great's Prussia practised religious toleration for almost all groups, including the Jews (shown here being welcomed into a town). Frederick espoused this policy not only because it fitted in with his enlightened views, but also to promote the immigration of useful subjects to stimulate the economy and replenish the enormous losses caused by his wars.

Austria, Russia, Poland 266–7 ▶
The Effects of the
French Revolution onEurope 288–9 ▶
The Revolutions of 1848–9 302–3 ▶
The Prussian Wars 326–7 ▶

Austria, Russia, and Poland

The great empires of the east, Austria-Hungary and Russia, represented some of the greatest problems of government in 18th-century Europe. Large, primarily rural, diverse in religion and language, the Austro-Hungarian lands comprised a hotchpotch of territories brought together under Habsburg rule. Russia was even more economically backward and also faced huge problems of size and diversity. In both cases, their enlightened rulers sought to reform their states from above, while maintaining a ruthless policy towards their vulnerable neighbours.

Catherine the Great c.1770. Under her rule Russia became accepted as a leading European power, participating in the partitions of Poland and forming close links with Prussia and Austria. In her domestic policy, her enlightened interest in reform clashed with her determination to maintain absolute power.

Catherine the Great

The dominant figure to govern Russia after Peter the Great was Catherine II. A German princess, the daughter of the prince of Anhalt-Zerbst, the governor of Stettin and a Prussian Field Marshal, she married Peter, the nephew of the reigning Empress Elizabeth of Russia. Succeeding to the Russian throne, Peter III reigned for only a few months before he was murdered by a group of nobles, one of whom was Catherine's lover. Although she disclaimed any involvement, it appears likely that she instigated or connived at the murder. Taking the throne herself, she soon proved to be a formidable ruler with strong inclinations to enlightened rule. Like Frederick the Great, she corresponded with leading *philosophes*, including Voltaire, and assisted the publication of the later volumes of Diderot and d'Alembert's *Encyclopédie*. In 1765, she appointed a Legislative Commission to investigate the reform of Russian society. Few practical reforms ensued, largely because Catherine was unwilling to surrender significant power, arguing that Russia's vastness required a single, absolute sovereign. It was also the case that reforms that she favoured, such as the emancipation of the serfs, would have been bitterly opposed by the nobles upon whose support and acquiescence she relied. This dependence was reinforced by the Pugachev rising of 1773, led by a Cossack chief, Emelyan Pugachev, who claimed to be the dead Peter III. The revolt was suppressed after considerable effort, forcing Catherine to recognize her vulnerability. As a result, in 1785, her reign saw the Charter of the Nobility, which defined the nobles' status as an "inalienable right". Serfdom remained in place and even increased as Catherine gave grants of land and serfs to her favourites. On her own lands, some emancipation occurred, while in other areas of Russian life she was able to introduce reform. Censorship was abolished and foreign books translated. The law was codified and both torture and capital punishment reduced. Religious toleration was extended, not only to other non-Orthodox Christians, but also to Jews and Muslims. Administrative reforms sought the modernization of the provincial administration, raising the number of salaried officials from 12,000 to 27,000. The last years of her reign saw a more reactionary phase, caused in part by the outbreak of the French Revolution and Catherine's realization that further reform might undermine the fragile political balance she had achieved.

In foreign policy, Catherine had already shown her ruthlessness, consolidating her empire and enlarging its frontiers at the expense of Poland in the three partitions that followed after 1772. Wars with Turkey in 1768–74 and again in 1787–92, and with Sweden in 1788–90, extended Russian territory and influence to its greatest extent.

Austria-Hungary

The legacy of Maria Theresa was a reformed and capable Habsburg state, but one that was still dominated by the conservative and Catholic influences she had favoured. Bureaucratically, the state was not as efficient as Prussia, nor as ostensibly liberal in many matters as Catherine the Great's Russia. Joseph II, Maria Theresa's son, had fully absorbed the ideas of the Enlightenment. But, as co-regent from 1765, he found his reforming ideas frustrated at every turn by her conservatism. With her death in 1780, he set about reform at breakneck speed, proving himself the most determined of the enlightened rulers. He sought to reform almost every aspect of society, and 6206 reforming edicts were published in nine years. The Church was brought under state control and religious toleration was introduced, including the removal of most of the disabilities on the Jewish community. Educational reforms were introduced and the

Europe c.1740

~ Boundary of
The Holy
Roman Empire

This map shows the major European states by the middle of the 18th century. France, Austria, Prussia, and Russia dominated continental diplomacy. Sweden and Spain were in decline, while Great Britain was emerging as a major maritime power. The large Kingdom of Poland lay vulnerable to its neighbours in eastern Europe.

labour services on the serfs and peasantry reduced. Censorship was virtually abolished, the death penalty removed from almost all offences, heresy and witchcraft taken out of the area of criminal jurisdiction, and the law codified.

Joseph II's attempt to relax labour services and to create a centralized administration proved steps too far. By the time of his death in 1790, Hungary was on the brink of revolt, and the Austrian Netherlands were witnessing an armed uprising. Almost everywhere, it seemed, Joseph's reform plans had proved too advanced for even some of their proposed beneficiaries – the peasants and serfs – to appreciate what was being done for them. Vested interests such as the nobility were unwilling to bend to his will, facing him with the prospect of armed rebellion. On his deathbed, Joseph II is reported to have said: "Here lies a prince whose intentions were pure, but who had the misfortune to see all his plans collapse."

The partition of Poland

Whatever the principles of enlightenment practised by Frederick the Great, Catherine the Great, and the rulers of the Habsburg lands, they showed little mercy in international affairs. The three powers co-operated to partition Poland in three stages in 1772, 1793, and 1795, through a combination of stealth and ruthlessness. It was an act almost without precedent, deliberately destroying one of Europe's oldest and largest states. Poland's problem was its internal weakness with an elective, not hereditary,

monarchy. As a result, the monarchy had become a pawn in international diplomacy. The Polish Diet, or *Sejm*, was crippled by the practice of the *liberum veto* – the right of any member to terminate its proceedings by expressing discontent. Although populous, with a population of 11 million people, there was only a tiny army and no central treasury. When the king of Poland died in 1763, Catherine the Great pushed her former lover, Stanislaus Poniatowski, onto the throne. Catherine's attempts to enforce religious toleration in Poland provoked a conspiracy against Russian influence, the Confederation of Bar. In order to quell the opposition, the first partition of Poland was agreed between the three powers. Poland lost about a third of its territory, with Russian troops forcing the Polish Diet to accept the partition. However, the situation was not all loss for Poland, as Stanislaus was allowed to develop a modernization programme. The solution lasted only 20 years, until further attempts were made by the Polish Diet to initiate meaningful reform, including a modern army of 100,000 men. A second partition was agreed between Russia and Prussia, implemented in 1793, when the Polish Diet was compelled to accept reduction to a small state of four million people. This humiliation provoked a national uprising in spring 1794 led by Kosciuzko, which was finally defeated by the end of the year. The three powers decided to put a final end to Polish independence in 1795. Poland had been expunged from the map of Europe, not to return for more than a hundred years.

Engrav'd Printed & Sold by PAUL REVERE BOSTON

The Boston Massacre on 5 March 1770 was a violent clash between the inhabitants of Boston and British troops sent to keep the peace during anti-government riots. Five people were killed in an episode whose propaganda value was quickly utilized by the more radical colonists to inflame opinion against British rule.

THE DEMAND FOR REPRESENTATION

Criticism of the prevailing political institutions was one of the most prominent and universal features of the Enlightenment. Systems of government were examined for their utility, and the rationale for the exercise of authority was questioned. Out of this examination grew the justification for wider representation, shaped by the particular forces at work in Britain, France, and North America.

Traditional views of monarchy and other institutions such as feudalism were now subjects for discussion as, where possible, enlightened thinkers sought to put government and society on a more rational footing. Belief in the divine right of kings was difficult to sustain in the face of enlightened distrust of religion. Experience of the wars of religion in the 16th and 17th centuries bred scepticism about the religious basis of political authority. It was now felt that rulers should instead be judged on whether they governed for the general good of their subjects. Examples of religious intolerance interfering with the effective government of states were among the first targets of writers such as Voltaire. In his history of Louis XIV's reign, he condemned the Revocation of the Edict of Nantes in 1685. The pursuit of personal glory and dynastic ambition through war was also condemned as detrimental by enlightened writers.

As a result, a rational critique of government developed, which saw the duty of government as being to pursue the improvement of the lives of their citizens. Enlightened thinkers were not, initially, opposed to monarchy, provided it operated on enlightened principles. Steeped in classical learning, many writers of the 18th century professed admiration for rulers in antiquity who combined enlightened rule with absolute power.

Accordingly, Voltaire, Diderot, and other *philosophes* were often prepared to serve the cause of enlightened rulers such as Frederick the Great and Catherine the Great, corresponding with them and even staying at their courts. In turn, such rulers were happy to bask in the approbation their relationship offered and genuinely saw themselves as ruling in a new spirit. Rulers were no longer seen to be above the law, but preferably exercising power within a codified and written framework of laws.

But a rational critique of government could also imply larger changes. In *The Spirit of Law* of 1748, Montesquieu investigated absolute and "balanced" forms of government across many countries. Particularly impressed by his experience in England, he advocated what he believed operated in Hanoverian Britain: a constitutional equilibrium based on a separation of powers between executive, legislature, and judiciary. The call for political representation was taken further by Rousseau, who argued that the only justification for the exercise of political power lay in the "general will" of the whole people.

The so-called "age of the democratic revolution" saw various strands of thought coming together. The Enlightenment provided a rational basis on which to question existing institutions. Wider notions of democratic rights were being enunciated on the continent by men such as Rousseau, but also by British writers such as Major John Cartwright in the 1770s, drawing on ideas of "Anglo-Saxon liberty" to argue that universal suffrage and more frequent parliaments had existed before the imposition of the "Norman Yoke" in 1066. From whatever source, a claim for representation and for "rights" would emerge in the latter half of the 18th century with enormous impact in France, North America, and Britain.

18th-Century Britain

The "Glorious Revolution" of 1688–9 set Britain on the course of parliamentary monarchy. Burgeoning trade and agriculture allowed the Hanoverian succession to occur peacefully. Under Sir Robert Walpole, Britain became a stable and wealthy society. Under Pitt the Elder, the first of the British Empire was established in India, North America, and the Caribbean. The electoral corruption that had underpinned the system, however, came under challenge from the 1760s.

The replacement of James II by William and Mary in 1688–9 saw the introduction of an era of political stability after the upheavals of the 17th century. The assurance of a Protestant succession to the throne, confirmed in the Act of Settlement of 1701, and the regular meeting of Parliament to vote financial supplies to the crown produced an underlying stability that was belied by the so-called "rage of party" in the reign of Queen Anne (r.1702–14). Although deeply resented by many Anglicans, the Toleration Act of 1689 gave the nonconformists or "dissenters" freedom of worship. In spite of some remaining disabilities, effective religious toleration had been achieved. The end of the War of Spanish Succession in 1713 under the Treaty of Utrecht quieted the major disagreements that had emerged over the conduct of foreign policy. A by-product of war, however, had been the development of new financial instruments such as the Bank of England in 1694 and the National Debt, which had provided finance for the war. The National Debt, a system of perpetual debt in which the government paid annual interest to its creditors, established a vested interest in the regime. As a result, the accession of George I of Hanover passed off relatively peacefully. An unsuccessful Jacobite rising in 1715 confirmed the Whigs in power as the firmest supporters of the Hanoverian and Protestant succession.

The rise of Walpole

Sir Robert Walpole emerged as a leading figure among the Whigs. Walpole was renowned for his industry, professionalism, and financial ability. The South Sea Bubble of 1720–1 rocked the Hanoverian regime and made Walpole's reputation. Frantic speculation in the stock of the South Seas Company was com-

pounded by the government's encouragement of stockholders in the National Debt to swap their government stock for shares in the company. When the bubble burst, thousands were ruined, including many government stockholders. Walpole, not directly involved in the scandal, salvaged the situation and re-established confidence in the government. He was then able to secure himself in office. The basis of Walpole's power lay in the control he exercised over the House of Commons and the confidence he enjoyed at court, becoming, in effect, the king's "first" or "prime" Minister. Walpole deployed the patronage available to him to secure an unprecedented rule of more than 20 years. His tenure of power was assisted by the Septennial Act of 1716, which meant that elections needed only to be called every seven years (as opposed to three under the Triennial Act of 1694). Boroughs with small electorates, the so-called "pocket" or "rotten" boroughs, were exploited to preserve his hold on power.

The "Robinocracy" seemed secure, but Walpole overreached himself in his attempt to raise taxes via an excise scheme in 1733. The resulting outcry forced him to back down. Moreover, his habitual peace policy, which was intended to secure the loyalty of backbenchers by keeping taxation low, was outflanked by the rise of bellicose patriotism. Led by the merchants who wished to adopt a more aggressive approach to trade with the Spanish colonies, the calls for war with Spain reached a crescendo with the affair of "Captain Jenkins' Ear", allegedly torn off by Spanish coastguards. Faced with the clamour for war, Walpole conceded, but proved a reluctant war leader, and this allowed his enemies to gather "the patriots" to aid in his downfall. In 1742, after successive

A medal commemorating the birth of James III, the "Old Pretender". The deposition of James II by William and Mary in 1688–9 left the Jacobite line as rival claimants to the throne. The failure to prevent Hanoverian succession in 1714 led to the failed Jacobite rebellions of 1715 and 1745–6.

defeats, Walpole was forced to resign. His fall demonstrated that the key to political power now lay in the House of Commons. The seeds of parliamentary government had now been firmly laid.

Jacobitism

The displaced Jacobite line had attempted to recapture the throne in 1715 when the Earl of Mar sought to raise support for James II's son, James Edward Stuart, the "Old Pretender". Although the rising – known as "the 15" – had support in the Highlands, it failed to generate enough of a following in England to pose a serious threat. After 1715, Jacobitism failed to combine the necessary ingredients for a successful seizure of power. Foreign support was lacking at the crucial moments when Hanoverian rule appeared weakest, and, as years went by, the Hanoverian regime seemed increasingly secure. Walpole's fall and the War of Austrian Succession provided a fresh opportunity for the Jacobites. The promise of French support led Charles Edward Stuart, the "Young Pretender", to make a second attempt on the throne. Landing in the Highlands in August 1745, he proclaimed his father king and raised the highland clans in the rebellion known as "the 45". Charles proceeded to occupy Edinburgh and defeat an army sent against him at Prestonpans, but the rising had only a minority following even from the highland clans. Hoping for greater support in England, Charles marched south, reaching Derby, but a large Hanoverian army between him and London forced him to retreat. In April 1746, Charles's army of 5000 exhausted and weakened Highlanders was crushed at Culloden Moor by an army commanded by the Duke of Cumberland. Although Charles escaped to France, a ruthless campaign in the Highlands – the notorious Clearances – broke the power of the clans forever.

Pitt the Elder

The War of Austrian Succession was concluded in 1748, but Britain's colonial rivalry with France broke out into warfare in North America in 1756. Pitt the Elder had made his reputation opposing Walpole's reluctant war policy in 1739–42. He became secretary of state, effectively prime minister, in 1757. His vigour and skill in choosing personnel was to turn the war around, culminating in the victories at Quebec and Plessey in 1759, which gave Britain mastery of Canada as well as India. Forced from office by the new king, George III, in 1761, Pitt had nonetheless established opportunities for trade and further conquest.

Reform

The accession of George III provoked a crisis in political affairs. The attempt by the inexperienced young king to to force out the powerful figures of Pitt and Newcastle led to demands for reform of Parliament. The metropolitan-based radical Jonathan Wilkes attacked George III's government in his newspaper, the *North Briton*. His arrest made "Wilkes and Liberty" the popular cry in London. Elected Member of Parliament but denied his seat on a technicality, Wilkes roused the "mob" in support and was eventually admitted to Parliament. During the American War of Independence, discontent with the political system was also shown by Christopher Wyvill's Yorkshire Association in 1779, which demanded an end to the corruption of Parliament. Bills for modest parliamentary reform were introduced in the early 1780s, and more radical ideas, such as universal suffrage, were supported by bodies such as the Westminster Association. The ending of the American War of Independence in 1783 took the urgency out of the issue, but the French Revolution would bring it back to the fore.

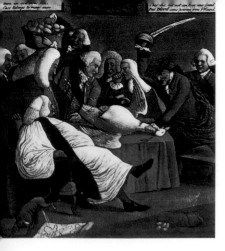

The American Revolution

The American Revolution saw many of the ideas of the European Enlightenment and British constitutional tradition fused together in rebellion against colonial rule. What began as a tax revolt turned into a general war and the creation of a new nation, expressing many of the most advanced political ideas of the era.

A cartoon shows the fat American goose about to be sacrificed by avaricious British politicians. American resentment at being taxed to pay for imperial defence underlay the growing sense of distance and separation from Britain. The cry of "No Taxation without Representation" would eventually lead to all-out rebellion.

North America after the British victory over France in the Seven Years War. Although Britain was now the dominant power, the 13 colonies were hemmed in along the Atlantic seaboard by the Proclamation Line declared at the end of the war in 1763. The Proclamation Line irritated the colonists, who were denied access to the vast hinterland of North America because Britain was wary of conflict with Native Americans and other European powers.

By the 1760s, the colonization of North America was well over a century old. Spanish, French, and British colonies occupied parts of what would eventually become the United States. Spanish influence extended into Texas, New Mexico, California, and Florida. France occupied a vast area that hemmed in the English colonies of the Atlantic seaboard. The original 13 colonies founded from the 17th century had grown and prospered by the mid-18th century to a population of over two million. Increasingly assertive, they found themselves in conflict with a British government that had seen its empire grow in an almost unprecedented way through the successes of the Seven Years War.

The "Boston Tea Party"

The Treaty of Paris of 1763 brought to an end almost 70 years of conflict between Britain and France in North America. France surrendered all its North American possessions east of the Mississippi, giving Britain control over the whole of Canada. But Britain had incurred huge debts and was fearful of a resurgence of French power. An attempt to set up a buffer zone between the British colonies and

the French and Native Americans of the interior led to the creation of the Proclamation Line of 1763 just west of the Alleghenies, forbidding the further expansion of the colonies beyond that point. From the point of view of the colonists, however, the defeat of the French offered more, not less, opportunities for expansion, fuelling unrest. Conflict came to a head over taxation to assist the British government to pay the cost of the wars. A series of acts were passed to tighten control over American trade and to exact revenue. The hated Stamp Act of 1765 imposed a duty on legal documents, antagonizing the professional and merchant classes of New England. Resistance to the Stamp Act led to demonstrations and riots, and began to forge a solidarity hitherto unknown among the separate colonies. In 1765, nine colonies sent representatives to a Stamp Act Congress in New York. The following year, the Stamp Act was repealed, but the British government also passed the Declaratory Act, insisting on its right to tax the colonies if it so wished. This right was enforced with new duties on goods such as paper, glass, and tea, leading to violent clashes between protesters and British troops in the Boston Massacre of March 1770, in which five of the crowd were killed. Boston remained the centre of bitter opposition to the government in London. It demonstrated its hostility towards attempts to offload cheap tea in North America to help the East India Company with the "Boston Tea Party" of December 1773 when a group of Bostonians dressed as Native Americans boarded tea ships and dumped the tea in the harbour. The government reaction in closing the port of Boston and suspending normal colonial government sparked general resistance. The result was the meeting of the First Continental Congress in Philadelphia on 5 September 1774, attended by representatives of 12 of the colonies and, later, by the remaining state, Georgia. There was little talk of independence, but they voted to embargo trade with Britain and called on their fellow colonists to raise troops.

The British government regarded the colonies as having moved into a state of rebellion. Attempts to disarm the colonists and secure strong-points led

Map

HUDSON'S BAY COMPANY

NOVA SCOTIA

PROVINCE OF QUÉBEC

MAINE

Mississippi

Missouri

Ohio

LOUISIANA

Saratoga 1777

Lexington 1775

Atlantic Ocean

NATIVE AMERICAN RESERVE

Yorktown 1781

British North America 1763–75

The Thirteen Colonies

Proclamation Line of 1763

Boundary of the Thirteen Colonies, 1756

Boundary of Québec, 1774

Major battle (date)

WEST FLORIDA

EAST FLORIDA

Gulf of Mexico

1 Massachusetts
2 New Hampshire
3 Rhode Island
4 Connecticut
5 New York
6 New Jersey
7 Pennsylvania
8 Delaware
9 Maryland
10 Virginia
11 N. Carolina
12 S. Carolina
13 Georgia

to the first clashes when Massachusetts militiamen opened fire on British troops at Lexington and Concord on 19 April 1775. British reinforcements poured in to bolster the defence of Boston, leading to the first major battle at Bunker Hill on 17 June. The British were successful, but at heavy cost. The Americans now appointed George Washington as commander of their army, who launched an attack on Canada. After initial success in capturing Montreal, the American forces were beaten back from Quebec on New Year's Eve 1775.

The Declaration of Independence

Hopes of reconciliation were now long past, and, on 4 July 1776, the Congress formalized the break with Britain by passing the Declaration of Independence. The Declaration exuded the spirit of the radical Enlightenment, establishing first principles of government. Among its instigators was Thomas Paine, an Englishman who had emigrated to Philadelphia from England in 1774 and whose pamphlet *Common Sense* had done much to encourage a radical approach to the situation. In effect, what had begun as a revolt over tax and trade had become the first demonstration of how to construct a model society on the basis of philosophical ideas. Drafted by Thomas Jefferson, the Declaration contained a list of grievances, including taxation without consent and other arbitrary acts, but its opening words struck a different note to all earlier documents in the Anglo-Saxon world: "We hold these truths to be self-evident, that all men are created equal, that they are endowed by their Creator with certain inalienable Rights...".

Although the Declaration, signed by members of the Congress on 2 August, was a great rallying cry for the American cause, it did little immediately to assist the colonists. American independence had more to do with the failure of British arms than the rhetoric of the Declaration. The British forces captured Long Island and New York in autumn 1776, but Washington was able to keep his army together and mount local counter-attacks in the winter of 1776–7. A grand British strategy aimed to bring the rebellion to an end with a two-pronged attack, with an army under General Burgoyne marching down from Canada to meet one from General Howe marching up the Hudson River. A delay to Howe's forces led to disaster for Burgoyne, who was forced to surrender at Saratoga on 17 October 1777. This defeat marked a turning point, as it encouraged the French to join the war against Britain in July 1778 and bring much-needed assistance to the colonists. French troops landed under the command of volunteers such as the Marquis de Lafayette, later to play a prominent part in the

The Declaration of Independence

The Declaration of Independence was primarily the work of one man, Thomas Jefferson, a Virginian planter. Chairing the committee that drew up the Declaration, he was largely responsible for its phrasing; one of his abettors, John Adams, referred to his "happy talent of composition". Combining lofty sentiments with specific grievances against George III for his treatment of the colonists, the first draft was completed as early as 28 June 1776. After several days of debate in Congress it was ready for signing by the evening of 4 July. All present signed, with the exception of John Dickinson of Pennsylvania, making the 13 former colonies independent states.

French Revolution. In 1779, Spain joined the war, and Britain was soon faced with an "Armed Neutrality" of Baltic powers and the entry of the Dutch into hostilities. Britain faced war on an almost unprecedented scale. American and French privateers preyed on British shipping around the British coast, while the war in America proved more difficult by the day as neutrals and would-be loyalists deserted to the American cause. In Britain itself, the war was increasingly unpopular. Sympathy with the colonists was widespread among the opponents of the government and George III. When the war proved unsuccessful, this opposition began to threaten its survival. The surrender of General Cornwallis to George Washington's forces on 19 October 1781 finally broke British determination to continue the war. The defeat of Lord North's government in May 1782 was symptomatic of the mood in Britain – the government must go, and the war must end.

Peace was eventually signed in September 1783, with Britain relinquishing control over the 13 colonies at the Treaty of Versailles. The colonies drew up a federal constitution in 1787, which became effective in 1789, with Washington as first President of the United States. The success of the American Revolution was an encouragement to democratic ideals elsewhere, particularly in France where returning volunteers spread the gospel of liberty in a country now virtually bankrupted by the assistance it had given to the colonists.

The Struggle against Despotism in France

France, the home of the *philosophes*, was an absolute monarchy, but already one showing signs of weakness by the middle of the 18th century. The state built by Louis XIV as the greatest power in Europe was beset by a complex political, financial, and social crisis to which the new enlightened ideas offered criticism but few constructive solutions, short of a wholesale remodelling of France and its government.

Louis XVI inherited all the theoretically absolute powers of the French monarchy, but was increasingly presiding over a state where the power of the monarch was insufficient to circumvent the opposition of privileged groups such as the nobility. The political impasse was broken by the calling of the Estates General in 1789 in an attempt to solve the crown's financial problems.

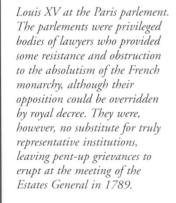

Louis XV at the Paris parlement. The parlements were privileged bodies of lawyers who provided some resistance and obstruction to the absolutism of the French monarchy, although their opposition could be overridden by royal decree. They were, however, no substitute for truly representative institutions, leaving pent-up grievances to erupt at the meeting of the Estates General in 1789.

The distribution of power

Under Louis XIV, political power had become heavily concentrated on the royal court at Versailles. France had no effective representative institutions, the Estates General having been last called in 1614. Legal bodies, the *parlements,* had some say over legislation, but they were primarily privileged bodies of lawyers without even the representative functions of the British Parliament. France was still a society of privileged ranks. Stripped very largely of their political power, the nobility served at court and in the higher echelons of the army and the Church. They had also secured exemption from taxation. Many could still call on feudal dues and obligations from the peasantry, although, apart from in parts of eastern France, serfdom had been largely abolished. The Church still occupied a privileged position as an arm of the state. The expulsion of many Huguenots following the Revocation of the Edict of Nantes in 1685 had ended any real pretence of official toleration. The Church occupied a key position in relation to censorship and charges of blasphemy, frequently bringing it into conflict with the writers and thinkers of the Enlightenment.

Deprived of an effective say in government, the middle classes sought to establish themselves as office-holders and, if possible, to purchase titles. Privileged positions were built up in the administration, financial system, and judiciary, which were to prove major obstacles to reform.

Under Louis XV, the political and financial system ossified. Costly wars and a huge standing army drained the treasury. The court at Versailles was a source of magnificent extravagance. The fiscal system was in disarray, dependent on tax-farmers who had bought their positions in return for a large "cut" of the taxes gathered. France's credit rating with bankers was poor, forcing the government to pay heavy rates of interest on any debts. Compared with the relatively efficient tax-gathering systems of Prussia and Britain, France was a creaking giant, still formidable, but badly in need of reform.

During the Seven Years War, France gained nothing in Europe and lost most of its overseas possessions. France was exhausted by the "double effort" of carrying on both a continental war against Frederick the Great and a colonial war against its great overseas rival, Great Britain. On his death in 1774, Louis XV was reported to have uttered the phrase, "After me, the deluge." His successor, Louis XVI, was scarcely the determined monarch France required. Aware of the need for reform, he was handicapped by his own blinkered approach to his role and the growing unpopularity of his Austrian wife, Marie Antoinette, daughter of Maria Theresa. She was, quite unjustly, blamed for the financial extravagance of the court and made into a scapegoat. Her reputation plunged to new depths with the "the diamond necklace affair", a fraudulent scheme to purchase a piece of jewellery in which the conspirators impersonated the queen. Although blameless, her name was dragged through almost nine months of proceedings.

Attempts at reform

Attempts to reform the economic position by Finance Minister Turgot in 1774–6 met with such intense opposition from privileged groups that they were abandoned and Turgot dismissed. His successor was Necker, who superintended finance from 1777–81. His efforts, however, were destroyed by the combination of French support for the American colonists, which bankrupted the government, and the opposition of factions at court to his reform programme. His resignation left others, notably Calonne and Brienne, to attempt to resolve the intractable problems of the fiscal system, notably the exemption of more than a quarter of a million of the wealthiest subjects – nobles, clergy, and officials – from taxation. The result was a crushing burden placed on the rest of society, including even the poorest, who had to find excise duties on items such as salt and pay the poll tax. Local customs duties raised the price of corn, while many peasants were forced to meet feudal dues and labour obligations.

The failure of fundamental financial reform made the French monarchy vulnerable to calls for change at a time when the *philosophes* were offering a wide range of political options for the future. The radical ideas sketched out by the likes of Rousseau in his novels *Émile* (1762) and *The Social Contract* (1762) were being disseminated among the "polite society" of late 18th-century France. Criticism of the status quo was axiomatic among the intellectual classes, while scurrilous comment on the establishment was the stock-in-trade of Grub Street printers and cartoonists.

The diamond necklace affair
In 1785, the court jeweller of France was defrauded of a diamond necklace that he had previously offered to Marie Antoinette. An adventuress, the Countess de la Motte, forged the queen's signature and persuaded the Cardinal de Rohen to purchase the necklace. De la Motte then obtained the necklace for herself, but was discovered. Although she was found guilty, her trial brought unfavourable publicity to the queen's allegedly lavish tastes. This hostility contributed to the general dissatisfaction with Louis XVI's reign, which was soon to explode in revolution.

Moreover, the example of America was fresh in people's minds. Here was a "model" declaration of first principles of government, offering republican government without the weaknesses of hereditary monarchy.

The Estates General

The privileged orders in the *parlements* obstructed reforming efforts at every turn. The *parlement* of Paris in 1787 refused to register a new land tax for the wealthy, and the measure had to be forced through and the *parlement* exiled. Hoping for a more efficient reform programme, the finance minister Brienne proposed replacing all of the *parlements* with a single body. The strong reaction to this proposal forced Louis XVI to cancel the measure and accept Brienne's resignation. With reform blocked, the decision was taken amidst mounting unrest to break the deadlock by convoking the Estates General, which had not met for 173 years. The suggestion had come from Lafayette, veteran of the American War of Independence, and was seen by many as the only way to resolve the political and financial bankruptcy of the Bourbon monarchy.

The Estates General consisted of representatives of the three orders of society – nobles, clergy, and Commons, or Third Estate. Unsure of the mode of election, Louis XVI allowed a double representation for the Third Estate, from 300 to 600, in order to balance the other two, perhaps foreshadowing a united body. But, following the inaugural proceeding of the first sittings on 4 and 5 May 1789, it became apparent that the nobles and clergy intended to keep themselves separate. The Third Estate took matters into its own hands and, on 17 June, declared itself the National Assembly of France. The French Revolution had begun.

THE AGE OF REVOLUTION

1789–1848

POLITICS AND GOVERNMENT

1792 Outbreak of the Revolutionary Wars; Prussia and Austria declare war on France.

1793–4 The Reign of Terror: The Jacobins under Robespierre execute the king and much of the aristocracy, and eliminate their political opponents, eventually being executed themselves.

1789 Fall of the Bastille heralds the beginning of the French Revolution. National Assembly publishes Declaration of the Rights of Man and begins drawing up a new constitution.

1799 Coup d'état by Napoleon makes him ruler of France.

1815 "The Hundred Days". Defeat of Napoleon at Waterloo and his exile to St Helena. Congress of Vienna redraws the map of Europe.

1814 Napoleon's first abdication and exile to Elba. Monarchy restored to France.

1812 Napoleon's invasion of Russia and retreat from Moscow begin his decline.

1803 Breakdown of the Treaty of Amiens begins second phase of hostilities between France and the rest of Europe – the Napoleonic Wars.

1780

1800

SOCIETY AND CULTURE

1792 Johann Wolfgang von Goethe becomes Director of Theatre at Weimar; beginning of the Weimar era of German Romamticism.

1798 William Wordsworth and Samuel Taylor Coleridge publish the *Lyrical Ballads*, giving impetus to the Romantic movement in Britain. Napoleon's Egyptian expedition opens up Egyptology to European scholars.

1808 Publication of Part I of Goethe's *Faust*.

1813 Sir Walter Scott begins publication of the "Waverley" novels.

1804 The Code Napoleon is brought into force. It and other codes introduced by Napoleon serve as a model for law codes elsewhere.

1803 Ludwig van Beethoven's *Fidelio* first performed.

1801 French Republic introduces the metric system.

1825 Decembrist revolt suppressed in Russia. Stern autocrat Nicholas I is unflinching in opposition to reform.

1830 A cholera outbreak kills nearly 30 million people in Russia.

1830–2 Revolution in France; reactionary Charles X replaced by Louis Philippe. Belgian revolt succeeds. Greece becomes independent. Great Reform Bill is passed in Britain. Polish revolt is crushed.

1848–9 'Year of Revolutions'. Widespread revolution in France, Germany, the Habsburg lands, and Italy.

820 Revolts in aples and Spain il to dislodge estored overnments and re crushed.

20   1840   1860

1831 Aleksander Pushkin's Eugene Onegin inaugurates the great era of Russian literature.

1848 Karl Marx and Frederich Engels The Communist Manifesto is first published.
Chopin gives his last performance at the Guildhall, London.

1828–48 Honoré de Balzac ublishes his series La Comédie Humaine, through which he develops a new type of Realism. The series included Eugénie Grandet (1833), and Cousin Bette (1846).

1836 Charles Dickens achieves success with his novel The Pickwick Papers.

1830 First European regular passenger service opened between Manchester and Liverpool. Delacroix paints Liberty Leading the People.

Présenté par le S[.] [...] lun des Vainqueur de la Bastille

The bad harvests and high prices
of 1788–9 sharpened popular
discontent with the monarchy in
France. On 14 July 1789 a mob
of Parisian workmen stormed
the Bastille, an ancient state
prison, hated as the symbol of
royal absolutism. The revolution
had begun in earnest.

REVOLUTION IN EUROPE

The French Revolution precipitated more than two decades of political upheaval and war. Not until Napoleon's final defeat at Waterloo in 1815 would Europe finally achieve peace. Moreover, the consequences of the revolution would reach well beyond France and its immediate neighbours. The effects would ultimately be felt as far away as the steppes of Russia, the west coast of Ireland, and the valley of the Nile.

At the outset, the French Revolution appeared benign. The initial response to it was often favourable, especially among artists and intellectuals who saw in France the fulfilment of enlightened ideas prefigured in the American Revolution. But events in France were greeted with growing concern by politicians, increasingly alarmed by the revolutionaries' radical tone. Hopes for the emergence of a constitutional monarchy ended with the rise of the radical Jacobins in 1793 and the execution of Louis XVI in the following year. By 1793, with Britain joining Prussia and Austria in the war against France, much of Europe was embroiled in war. The conservative powers looked on with growing alarm and incredulity as the aristocracy and the political opponents of the regime perished in the Terror. But even with the fall of Robespierre and the ending of the Terror, there was no lasting peace. The revolution had awakened demands for reform, and a war of ideas developed between the exponents of the principles generated by the French Revolution and the defence of the established order by conservatives. Moreover, in international affairs, the successes of the revolutionary armies in the Low Countries and Italy destabilized the existing balance of power in Europe, committing the continent to almost a quarter of a century of warfare.

Britain was to prove France's most enduring opponent until France was defeated in 1815. Increasingly, the struggle became one between the growing maritime and commercial might of Great Britain and Napoleonic France. The rise of Napoleon Bonaparte set events on a new course. His coup d'état and triumphant campaign in Italy in 1801 brought the first phase of the Revolutionary Wars to an end. From 1801 Napoleon secured his hold on France, beginning its reconstruction on the basis of the changes brought about by the revolution. Increasingly centralized and efficient, France was now dominated by a military genius who, crowning himself emperor in 1804, sought to bring the whole of Europe under his control.

Renewal of war with Britain in 1803 set the scene for the long struggle of Napoleon against the rest of Europe. Yet however often Napoleon defeated his continental opponents, he proved unable to knock Britain out of the war. In so far as any conflict could be seen as such before the 20th century, the Napoleonic Wars represented a "total war" involving mass mobilization, the use of economic warfare, and the development of propaganda in the war of ideas between the revolutionaries and the established powers. Eventually Napoleon overreached himself with his invasion of Russia and increasingly faced popular resistance to his imperial and dynastic ambitions. Forced to abdicate, he was exiled to Elba in 1814. But even as the European powers sought to reassemble the old order, Napoleon escaped and, in the whirlwind "Hundred Days" in 1815, attempted to restore his fortunes. Finally defeated at Waterloo, his exile to St Helena brought the Napoleonic Wars to a close.

At Vienna in 1815, the victorious powers attempted to find a lasting solution to the consequences of the years of war. A revival of French power was to be prevented and the pre-revolutionary status quo restored. While territories proved easy enough to allocate, however, Europe was left with a legacy of revolutionary ideas that would prove more difficult to contain.

The French Revolution

Between the calling of the Estates General in June 1789 and Napoleon proclaiming himself emperor in 1804, France underwent an almost bewildering upheaval. The political crisis of 1788–9 forced reforms on the French monarchy, but attempts to create a constitutional monarchy were swept aside by the momentum created, leading to the Terror and Napoleonic dictatorship.

The dashing young general Napoleon Bonaparte, here pictured crossing the St Bernard Pass in May 1800 on his way to crush the Austrian armies in Italy. Napoleon became the symbol of the energy and enthusiasm of the French Revolution, bringing the prospect of freedom from arbitrary rule and centuries-old despotism. Soon, however, such hopes would be disappointed by Napoleon's imperial ambitions.

By the end of the 18th century, the absolute monarchy of France was in serious difficulties. State finances were in a ruinous condition, with huge debts and a poor yield from taxation. Reform was blocked by the nobility and clergy, who wished to cling on to their privileges of exemption from ordinary taxation. The growing middle class was still largely excluded from political power. Poverty was widespread among the peasantry and urban workers, the majority of whom depended upon a good harvest to ensure a basis subsistence. Peasants also resented feudal dues and obligations, which had to be paid in goods or services to the aristocracy.

The coming of revolution

French participation in America's struggle for independence had highlighted the possibilities of creating a written constitution and guaranteed rights for every citizen. Now, the financial crisis put reform in France on the agenda. When attempts to tax the privileged classes failed and an economic downturn and poor harvests caused widespread popular unrest, Louis XVI had no alternative but to call the Estates General, not summoned since 1614. It was given the opportunity to draw up lists of grievances, the *cahiers*, many of which were complaints about feudal obligations to the aristocracy. When the Estates General met in 1789, the middle classes of the Third Estate, frustrated by the obstruction of the clergy and aristocracy, proclaimed themselves a National Assembly and drew up a constitution for a limited monarchy.

From revolution to terror

The poor harvests and subsequent high prices of 1788–9 provoked a vengeful atmosphere of suspicion – the so-called "Great Fear" – with stories circulating of an aristocratic plot to massacre the people. Peasant mobs ransacked châteaux, often burning the manorial records of feudal obligations, while, in the towns, food riots become widespread.

Many urban workers hoped that reform might bring some relief. The dismissal of the popular finance minister, Jacques Necker, produced widespread anger. On 14 July 1789, a mob of Parisian workmen stormed the Bastille, an ancient state prison, hated as the symbol of royal absolutism. Responding to the demands for a fresh beginning, the National Assembly abolished feudal rights and privileges. On 26 August, the Declaration of the Rights of Man and of Citizens proclaimed the equality of all citizens before the law. By 1791, the National Assembly had produced a "model" constitution for a limited monarchy and a legislative assembly, but its careful checks and balances were swept away by the radicalization of events. The royal family's attempt to flee Paris in June 1791, halted at Varennes, demonstrated the king's lack of commitment to the revolution. Moderate constitutionalists increasingly found themselves outflanked by the growing radicalism of the Parisian populace, the sans-culottes. The collapse of the paper currency and continuing food shortages also produced a volatile situation. The preparations of Austria and Prussia to invade in 1792, assisted by émigré royalists at the French border, brought matters to a head. In August 1792, the Parisian mob invaded the Tuileries, seizing the royal family. On 21 September a republic was proclaimed. In practice dominated by the Parisian electoral districts and the radical Jacobins led by Robespierre, the new republic improvised an army by mass conscription to defend the frontiers in the autumn of 1792. Counter-revolutionary risings were suppressed, and, in January 1793, Louis XVI was put on trial and executed.

The crisis of the war deepened in March 1793 with the defection of the republic's commander, General Dumouriez, to the Austrians. The Convention devolved draconian powers on a Revolutionary Tribunal and a Committee of Public Safety. The Committee held the power of life and death, the signature of only three of its members sufficient to make a decree law. The moderate Girondins were purged from the Convention in June. A futile rising by them was quickly crushed at Caen, the only resistance coming when Charlotte Corday stabbed the prominent radical Jean Paul Marat in his bath on 13 July 1793. With Robespierre leading the Committee of Public Safety, the Revolutionary Tribunal executed more than 2700 people in Paris alone during the Terror, which lasted from the summer of 1793 until July 1794. The most spectacular trials were of the great rival to Robespierre, Georges Jacques Danton, and his followers, and of the extreme radical followers of Jacques René Hébert. Some 18,000 people fell victim to the guillotine, and up to another 25,000 were killed by other means. Amidst the Terror, the Jacobins crushed the counter-revolutions, checked the pace of inflation, and organized the armies so that, on 26 June 1794, the defeat of the Austrians at Fleurus finally drove the invading armies from French soil. But Robespierre fell victim to the revolutionary climate he had encouraged. On 4 June 1794, he had been elected President of the Convention by a record majority. Six weeks later, fearing a dictatorship, a group of deputies arranged for the arrest of Robespierre and his closest associates on 9 Thermidor (27 July 1794). He and another 115 supporters were executed the following day. The Thermidorean reaction marked a consolidation of the republic. The execution of the Jacobins was followed by the suppression of the Jacobin club, the end of the Revolutionary Tribunal and Committee of Public Safety, and a higher tax threshold for electors. From this period of more conservative government, a five-man Directory was formed in October 1795. This Directory appointed the young

general Napoleon Bonaparte to command its Army of Italy. His brilliant successes there, followed by his Egyptian expedition of 1798–9, made him a glamorous figure compared to the lacklustre leaders of the Directory. Leading a successful coup d'état on 2 November 1799, Napoleon overthrew the Directory.

The making of Napoleonic France

Initially, Napoleon ruled as First Consul, appointed for ten years, with two other consuls, who only had a consultative role. The new constitution of the Year VIII (1799), effectively created a dictatorship under the appearance of a republic. A Senate, Tribunate, and Legislative Chamber were created, but with little effective power. Any remnant of democracy was removed by a system of selective election in which only local notables were likely to reach the legislative bodies, while the Senate consisted of 80 well-paid senators, appointed for life. Moreover, the administration of France was reorganized in February 1800 to recreate a centralized system of government under the Prefects for the administration of the Departments, the new local government units set up shortly after the revolution. The tax system was reorganised on the basis of the new system and conscription regularized. Higher education was reformed and Napoleon commenced the codification of the laws, finalized in 1810 as the Code Napoleon. A Concordat with the Papacy in 1802 re-established the Roman Catholic hierarchy in France further stabilizing the regime. Made First Consul for life in 1802, Napoleon's military achievements abroad and his centralizing reforms at home paved the way for his assumption of the title of Emperor in May 1804.

The flight to Varennes

Hopes that a constitutional monarchy could be established in France were undermined by Louis XVI's wavering support for the new order. Even as a new constitution was being drafted by the constituent assembly, there were fears that the king would seek to re-establish his power with the assistance of foreign intervention and royalist émigrés gathered on France's eastern border. Louis, anxious for the safety of his family now virtually held as captives in the Tuileries palace, decided to seek refuge in a strongly royalist area close to the border with Luxembourg. Escaping in disguise on the night of 20–21 June 1791, the royal party was discovered and arrested at Varennes, only a few miles short of the frontier. The flight fatally compromised the king's position. Brought back to Paris in disgrace, his eventual acceptance of the new constitution could not prevent the royal family from being seen as enemies of the revolution, leading ultimately to the king's trial and execution.

The Effects of the French Revolution on Europe

Alarm soon spread at the threat of the principles of the French Revolution spreading beyond France. As well as undergoing a battle of ideas, Europe was soon engulfed by war as the established powers sought to contain the forces unleashed by revolution.

An anti-Jacobin cartoon by James Gillray caricatures "Tommy Paine, the little American tailor, taking the measure of the crown for a new pair of revolution Breeches." Thomas Paine (1737–1809) was one of the most powerful political pamphleteers of the revolutionary era.

This map shows the internal and external challenges faced by the early French revolutionary regime in 1792–3. The armies of Prussia and Austria, in league with French émigrés, threatened France from the east, while Britain offered support to counter-revolutionary risings around the French coast.

The initial response

The political turmoil in France was at first looked on benignly by Europe's rulers, as they hoped to see France preoccupied with its own affairs. However, the early events of the French Revolution captured the imagination of writers, artists, and intellectuals who saw in the abolition of feudalism, the creation of a constitutional monarchy, and the rationalization of French institutions an enactment of the best principles of the Enlightenment. In Britain, writers such as the veteran of the American War of Independence, Thomas Paine, translated the ideas of the French Revolution into his widely read *The Rights of Man* (1791–2), promoting universal suffrage, a republican constitution, and a basic form of welfare state. Soon, reform-minded societies were being founded across Europe. In Geneva and the Dutch Republic, the reformers who had been defeated during the 1780s took fresh heart. Belgian and Dutch exiles from the failed "Patriot" revolt of 1787 called on the French to assist them, though these pleas were initially ignored. In Hungary, the lesser nobility, resentful of Joseph II's "Austrian" reforms and of the greater nobles, demanded more autonomy for Hungary. In Britain, bodies such as the London Corresponding Society organized regular meetings to discuss radical literature and prepare petitions for reform. In Scotland, the unenfranchised inhabitants of Perth, Dundee, and Edinburgh joined together to plant "Liberty trees" and celebrate events in France. Even distant Russia was affected, stimulating criticism of existing conditions and leading to a fierce reaction from Catherine the Great.

Counter-revolution

Quickly, however, the heady enthusiasm for the French Revolution began to dissipate. An early warning was given by Edmund Burke. His *Reflections on the Revolution in France*, published in 1790, prophesied chaos and military despotism.

These fears seemed justified when the Jacobins took power in France and declared a republic, threatening the safety of the royal family. By August 1792, both Prussia and Austria were at war with revolutionary France. Their initial campaigns against France proved a failure: the Prussians were repulsed at Valmy in September and the Austrians defeated at Jemappes in November. The élan of the revolutionary armies, strengthened by regulars from the old royalist armies, proved more than a match for their cumbersome opponents. As the French revolutionary armies moved into the Low Countries, Britain could not remain out of the conflict for long. The execution of the king in January 1793 led to war the following month.

The Revolutionary Wars

The failure of the armies of Austria and Prussia to extinguish the revolution quickly committed

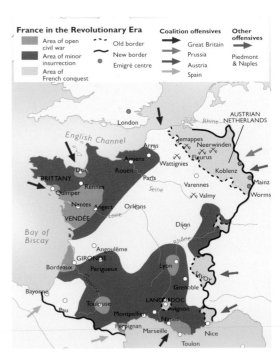

France in the Revolutionary Era

	Coalition offensives	Other offensives
Area of open civil war	Old border / Great Britain	
Area of minor insurrection	New border / Prussia	Piedmont & Naples
Area of French conquest	Emigré centre / Austria	
	Spain	

Europe to a generation of warfare. Britain's powerful fleet, extensive commerce, and financial strength enabled it to act as the organizer of successive coalitions against France, but it could not defeat France alone. Throughout the 1790s, France proved able to defeat the coalitions mobilized against it, but, equally, was unable to overcome British sea power. By 1795, Prussia was knocked out of the war, ceding territory to France on the left bank of the Rhine. The French armies conquered Holland and then invaded northern Italy, led by the dashing young Napoleon Bonaparte. By 1797, at the Treaty of Camp Formio, Austria was forced to accept the creation of the Cisalpine and Ligurian republics in northern Italy and the ceding of Belgium, Nice, and Savoy to France. British naval victories in 1794 and 1797 assured its safety from invasion, but no more. France's attempts to open Britain's "back door", Ireland, by assisting potential Irish rebels proved a failure. Although Britain faced a large-scale Irish rebellion which was suppressed only with great loss of life in 1798, French troops did not land until after it was defeated.

The war also had an ideological character which was different from earlier ones. The French Jacobins had issued a Declaration of Fraternity in November 1792, offering to assist subject peoples to throw off their rulers. The French revolutionary armies carried French principles to Holland, the Rhineland, and Italy, while Irish rebels sought French assistance against British rule. The established powers, in turn, suppressed discontent at home. The "enlightened" Catherine the Great condemned the Revolution and the British prime minister William Pitt drove Paine into exile and put radical leaders on trial for high treason. The French were denounced as conquerors and atheists.

War without end?

In February 1798, French forces occupied Rome, capturing Pope Pious VI and setting up a Roman Republic. In April, the Swiss Confederation was reorganized under French protection, and the Kingdom of Naples was overturned and a Parthenopean Republic proclaimed by the French revolutionary army. Increasingly, France appeared as an expansionist power, ruthlessly annexing territory and setting up puppet states with little popular support. Britain remained undefeated, thwarting Napoleon's ambitions for an Eastern empire in the Egyptian campaign. The wholesale destruction of his fleet at the Nile in August 1798 turned French ambitions once more to Europe.

Napoleon's virtual dictatorship after the coup d'etat of 2 November 1799 allowed him to turn his attention to destroying the coalition of forces still

The Egyptian expedition

Napoleon's successes in Italy encouraged him to mount one of the most audacious campaigns of the period, the invasion of Egypt, with the intention of cutting Britain's communications with its colonial possessions in India and establishing a French empire in the East. In May 1798, an expeditionary force of 55,000 was dispatched across the Mediterranean to Egypt, consisting not only of soldiers and sailors, but also of scholars and scientists who would make the first serious study of the remains of ancient Egypt. Napoleon landed successfully, defeating the local forces at the Battle of the Pyramids in July and capturing

Cairo. Plans for long-term conquest, however, were compromised by Nelson's complete destruction of the French fleet in Aboukir Bay on 1 August. Undaunted, Napoleon marched northwards to attack Syria, but his progress was frustrated by the failure to capture Acre, defended by Sir Sidney Smith and a Turkish garrison. Forced under appalling hardships to retreat to Egypt, Napoleon abandoned his command to General Kleber, returning to France to capitalize upon his still untarnished reputation and to participate in the overthrow of the Directory. The remaining French forces in Egypt finally surrendered in August 1801.

ranged against France. In 1800, a double campaign against Austria saw Napoleon fighting in Italy and General Moreau in Germany. In May, Napoleon forced the passage of the Great St Bernard Pass and restored the Cisalpine Republic, then inflicted a major defeat on the Austrians at Marengo on 14 June, forcing them into a truce. In Germany, the Austrian armies were also forced back and defeated at Hohenlinden in December 1800. By early 1801, Austria was forced to sue for peace, signing the Treaty of Luneville in February, which confirmed the existence of the new republics established by France in Italy (the Cisapline and Ligurian), in Holland (the Batavian), and in Switzerland (the Helvetic). Austria also conceded to France all territory west of the Rhine, including Belgium and Luxembourg. Russia also ceased hostilities against France, forcing Britain to accept that immediate prospects of success against Napoleon were fruitless. Preliminaries of peace were signed between Britain and France at Amiens in October 1801. Britain conceded virtually all her colonial gains. Though welcomed as a break from almost a decade of war, neither Britain nor Austria could remain permanently reconciled to the ascendency of Napoleonic France.

The Napoleonic Wars

The position of dominance Napoleon had achieved by 1801 unsettled his European rivals and made lasting peace impossible. Britain supplied the basis for fresh coalitions against France, and Napoleon's ambitions drove him to attempt to extend his power to every corner of Europe. Napoleon's disastrous invasion of Russia in 1812 marked the beginning of his ultimate defeat in 1815.

At the Battle of Trafalgar on 21 October 1805, Admiral Nelson defeated the Franco-Spanish fleet commanded by Admiral Villeneuve, ending any immediate French hopes of a successful invasion of Britain. Nelson was mortally wounded at the height of the battle, immortalizing him as Britain's greatest naval hero.

The Napoleonic Empire at its height in 1812. Apart from Great Britain and Russia, almost all of Europe was under either Napoleon's direct control or his influence. The map of Germany and Italy had been redrawn and a client Polish state created in the Grand Duchy of Warsaw.

The outbreak of war

Napoleon's peace with Britain, agreed in 1801 and ratified in 1802 as the Treaty of Amiens, and the Treaty of Luneville with Austria in 1801 were regarded as little more than an armed truce. Napoleon's extension of power into Italy, the Low Countries, and Germany could not be accepted permanently. British refusal to evacuate Malta under the terms of the Treaty of Amiens led to renewed hostilities in 1803. Napoleon assembled an army of invasion at Boulogne, awaiting the chance to cross the Channel when the English fleet was either defeated or diverted. In Britain, an army of volunteers was raised and preparations made for the evacuation of the royal family from London. Admiral Horatio Nelson's victory over the combined Franco-Spanish fleet at Trafalgar on 21 October 1805 secured Britain from the immediate threat of invasion.

Napoleonic Europe by 1812

- French Empire
- Dependent states
- French allies

Napoleon's zenith

Even before Trafalgar, the camp at Boulogne had been broken up, as Napoleon marched east to meet a new threat from Austria and Russia, acting in coalition with Britain. In a brilliant campaign, Napoleon forced one Austrian army to surrender at Ulm on the day before Trafalgar, and went on to defeat a combined Austrian and Russian army on 2 December 1805. In a fresh round of gains for France, Austria was compelled to give up the last of its Italian possessions and accept Napoleon's reorganization of the German states into a Confederation of the Rhine under French "protection". The confederation withdrew from the historic Holy Roman Empire, which had been dominated by Austria for centuries, effectively bringing it to an end and, with it, Austrian influence over the German states. Alarmed by this extension of French power into Germany, Frederick William of Prussia demanded that Napoleon withdraw his troops to the west of the Rhine. Napoleon's reaction was the destruction of the Prussian armies at the twin battles of Jena and Auerstädt in October 1806. Berlin was occupied, and, after two more battles at Eylau and Friedland in 1807, Prussia was forced into a humiliating peace. Peace was signed at Tilsit, where Napoleon met with Tsar Alexander I on a raft on the river Niemen. Russia recognized French reorganization of Germany and agreed to the creation of a Grand Duchy of Warsaw in Poland. Russia also agreed to support Napoleon's economic campaign against Britain, the Continental System (see below). Prussia lost territory, had its army limited to 42,000 men, had to support an army of occupation, and had to pay a war indemnity.

The downfall of Napoleon

At Tilsit, Napoleon had secured victory rather than peace. At the zenith of his power, Britain remained undefeated and his former enemies vengeful. Increasingly, too, the struggle against Napoleon took on a new character. Once hailed as liberators, the French armies were seen now as oppressors. France appeared expansionist and Napoleon's ambitions openly dynastic as he placed members of his family on the thrones of Europe. One brother, Joseph, was King of Naples; another, Jerome, King of Westphalia; a third, Louis Napoleon, was King of Holland. French exaction of indemnities, levies of troops, and supplies aroused popular resentment. National and patriotic sentiment in Britain, Germany, Russia, Spain, and elsewhere was now turned against Napoleon. Additional hardships in Europe were brought about by Napoleon's attempt to force Britain to the conference table by throttling its trade. The Continental System established by the Berlin Decrees of 1806 and the Milan Decrees of the following year banned British trade with the continent of Europe. Britain retaliated with the Orders in Council, blockading France and preventing neutral ships trading with it. Although British trade was harmed, smuggling and the diversion of trade elsewhere allowed Britain to survive commercially. More importantly, Napoleon's attempts to enforce the Continental System led to wider, and fatal, involvement in the Iberian Peninsula and Russia. Intervention in Portugal to enforce the trade war with Britain, and then in Spain, embroiled France in a bitter guerrilla war, as well as regular battles with the Duke of Wellington's army of the peninsula and his Iberian allies. Over a million men were lost by 1813, and Wellington's army was poised to invade France from Spain. By then, however, Napoleon had been the architect of his own defeat through his decision to invade Russia. Invasion by a massive army of over half a million men failed to bring Alexander I to terms

Spain witnessed a series of British and French attempts to secure control of the Iberian peninsula. Britain's advantage lay in its command of the sea, which allowed it to reinforce or evacuate its armies at will. The French, meanwhile, were involved in bitter guerrilla warfare with the Spanish population.

even after the capture of Moscow. Forced into a dreadful retreat, most of Napoleon's army perished, along with his reputation for invincibility. In 1814, defeat by a coalition of almost all the European powers at the battle of Leipzig in October sealed Napoleon's fate. With armies invading from the south and the east, Napoleon was forced to abdicate on 11 April 1814. But, even as peacemaking was in progress, in March 1815, Napoleon made one last throw of the dice. Escaping from exile on the island of Elba and raising an army, he began the "Hundred Days" which culminated in his defeat at Waterloo on 18 June 1815 by Wellington's army and General Blücher's Prussian cavalry. His final exile to the island of St Helena, where he died in 1821, brought the Napoleonic Wars to an end.

Guerrilla war

The war against Napoleon in Spain gave a new word to the military vocabulary – guerrilla. France's occupation of Spain aroused the wrath of the populace, who supported resistance rather than surrender. A popular uprising in support of Ferdinand VII, the legitimate heir to the throne who had been replaced by Joseph Bonaparte, was crushed by the French in May 1808; however, risings organized by provincial *juntas* (councils) trapped the French forces into a protracted guerrilla war. Occasional successes by the Spanish regular forces, as at Baylen on 20 July 1808, encouraged fanatical resistance such as at the seven-week siege of Saragossa in January–February 1809, when men, women, and clergy defended their city house-to-house, eventually surrendering a half-ruined shell to the French. In the countryside, Spanish guerrillas cut off stragglers and drained French resources in a country of which it was said "small armies are defeated and large armies starve". By the time Wellington defeated the French forces in October 1813, Spain had become a byword for the cruelties and savagery of irregular warfare.

The French Revolution 286–7 ▶
The Effects of the French Revolution on Europe 288–9 ▶
The Congress of Vienna and the Concert of Europe 292–3 ▶

The Congress of Vienna and the Concert of Europe

At the Congress of Vienna, the great powers sought to limit the power of France and to restore as much as possible of the old order disrupted by the upheavals of the Revolutionary and Napoleonic wars. But a lasting settlement had to contend with revolutionary ideas, as well as changes in boundaries and territories.

Klemens von Metternich, Austrian statesman and diplomat, was the principal architect of the Vienna Settlement.

The Congress of Vienna

After Napoleon's first abdication in 1814, it was decided to hold a congress at Vienna to settle the affairs of the continent. Attended by monarchs and rulers, as well as their advisers and representatives, business was conducted by a series of committees and, informally, at social events and balls laid on for the distinguished guests. Amidst this glittering scene, the map of Europe was redrawn in a fashion that would last in some cases up to World War I and even beyond. A pioneering attempt was also made to set up a regular series of meetings or congresses in the future, the "Concert of Europe", which would settle problems as they arose. The overriding aim of the participants was to ensure that France would not become dominant again and to restore the balance of power upset by Napoleon's conquests. The major coalition powers against Napoleon, acting as the "great powers" – a phrase first used in 1815 – felt free to dispose of lesser territories and weaker powers as they saw fit. Wherever possible, "legitimacy" was upheld and the status quo restored. Broadly speaking, states that had opposed Napoleon were rewarded and those that had supported him were penalized.

To secure the French frontier, states adjacent to France were strengthened to act as "buffer states" to French expansion. An enlarged Kingdom of the Netherlands was formed from the former Dutch Republic and the Austrian Netherlands (the area that is roughly modern Belgium). The patchwork of German states reorganized by Napoleon into the Confederation of the Rhine and dominated by France was consolidated into a German Confederation, loosely joined together under Austrian leadership. Similarly, the kingdom of Piedmont on France's south-eastern frontier was also strengthened. Restoration was the order of the day, and Austria regained its Italian territories, but now including the former Venetian Republic, which had been extinguished by Napoleon. The Grand Duchy of Warsaw was carved up between the Eastern powers, with Russia taking the largest share in a fourth partition of Poland. The former rulers were restored in Spain, the Papal States, and the Kingdom of Naples, as well as in France. Britain, the most implacable of France's opponents over more than 20 years, obtained significant colonial gains from France and Holland, including the Cape of Good Hope, Malta, and islands in the West Indies.

Initially, at the first Treaty of Paris in May 1814, France was treated generously, retaining larger boundaries than at the outbreak of the Revolution and put under no financial penalty. Undoubtedly, a

France was flanked by the enlarged buffer states of the United Netherlands and Savoy. The German states and Italy were put back under legitimist rule and the majority of Poles forced to return to Russian rule.

Europe after the Congress of Vienna 1814–15

- Area of expansion
- Border of German Confederation 1815
- **Newly created states and confederations**
- United Netherlands 1815–30
- Switzerland 1815
- Grand Duchy of Luxembourg 1815
- Republic of Kraków 1815–46
- Union of Norway and Sweden 1815–1905

desire to secure Louis XVIII's restoration played a part. The second Treaty of Paris, after the "Hundred Days", was less lenient: France's borders were returned to those of 1789; an army of occupation was installed, to be removed only when an indemnity had been paid; and art treasures plundered from Europe were restored to their former owners.

The Metternich System

The implications of the settlement went beyond mere boundary changes. When the major powers pledged themselves at the Agreement of Chaumont in March 1814 to co-operate until Napoleon was defeated, a de facto Concert of Europe came into being. Austria, Britain, Prussia, and Russia had renewed their co-operation when Napoleon returned from exile in 1815, committing themselves to raise an army of some 180,000 men to defeat him.

The four powers formed the Quadruple Alliance to maintain the settlement, pledging to uphold it by military force if necessary. Meetings or "congresses" were to be held at regular intervals to deal with pressing issues. Tsar Alexander of Russia was responsible for another agreement, the "Holy Alliance", signed by virtually all of Europe's rulers, in which they undertook to conduct diplomacy on Christian principles, rather than by force.

Largely conservative and legitimist, the representatives of the great powers saw it as their duty to counteract the revolutionary principles spread by the French Revolution. The Austrian chancellor Klemens von Metternich gave his name to the "Metternich system", in which the Holy Alliance was invoked to prevent any destabilization of what had been achieved in the long struggle to defeat Napoleon and restore the status quo. In practice, the "system" worked along traditional lines of late 18th-century diplomacy, in which the larger states acted in their own interests to restrain any disruptive forces, but which were now identified with liberalism and nationalism. It was combined internally with repression in the Austrian lands and throughout Germany and Italy aimed at suppressing any manifestation of dissent from intellectuals, students, and nationalists. A cynical policy of playing off rival groups and ethnic minorities against each other also helped to maintain an equilibrium within the Austro-Hungarian emipre, threatened by disruptive national sentiments.

However, the co-operation agreed in 1815 did not survive beyond the four congresses held between 1815 and 1822. The Eastern powers, Austria and Russia, invoked the Holy Alliance to restrain liberalism and nationalism wherever it appeared, while Britain showed sympathy for some of the movements that arose in Greece and southern Europe. Although the diplomats at Vienna were later criticized for failing to recognize and accept the new forces, the history of Europe for the next 50 years was dominated by the framework they had set.

The Effects of the
French Revolution on Europe   288–9 ▶
The Napoleonic Wars   290–1 ▶
International Relations   352–3 ▶
The Paris Peace Conference   402–3 ▶

The fall of the ancient Parisian fortress and state prison of the Bastille on 14 July 1789 became a symbol of the revolutionary period. The attack on one of the institutions of absolute power by the artisans and workmen of the surrounding districts of Paris testified to a new era in politics in which the people would play a part.

SOCIAL AND POLITICAL CHANGE

The war against the French Revolution and Napoleon was a war of ideas, as well as a war of armies and battles. In 1815, the great powers were mindful of the need not only to restore the frontiers of Europe, but also to secure the rule of legitimate monarchs deposed in the revolutionary upheavals of the previous era. The clock could not be stopped entirely, however: new ideas had been generated and broadcast across Europe.

The slogan "Liberty, Equality, Fraternity" continued to be an inspiration. Programmes of liberal reform, the concept of nationhood, and the first socialist ideas would become major issues of contention over the next century. To these ideological and political forces were added the economic and social dislocations of urbanization and the beginnings of the Industrial Revolution. The massing of increasing numbers of the middle classes and workers into an urban environment was to create a volatile situation in which the cities became centres of discontent. Moreover, an acceptance that change, turmoil, and strife were part of the human condition underlay aspects of the Romantic era in art and literature. Individual striving and the passionate involvement of artists and intellectuals in the world around them became a hallmark of the revolutionary era.

The Declaration of the Rights of Man at the outset of the French Revolution had proclaimed the individual worth of each citizen. Building on the example of the American Revolution, the declaration implied just and fair treatment of all individuals and, most politically explosive of all, the right to a say in their government. Out of these propositions evolved the demands from 19th-century liberals for a constitution, representative institutions, wider voting rights, equality before the law, careers open to talent, freedom of expression, and liberty of conscience. From the idea that the only legitimate form of government was one supported by the whole people came the concept of "the sovereignty of the people" and the idea of nationhood. Increasingly, national leaders sought to justify a claim for self-government through the traits of language,

religion, custom, and folklore that defined a people and a nation. Liberalism and nationalism often worked hand in hand, seeking to overturn a restored old order that failed to recognize the rights of citizens and the aspirations for nationhood. Even more radical in their implications were the first socialist ideas, seeking an end to economic exploitation and a genuine realization of the brotherhood of man. Linked to a progressive view of history, socialist ideas developed from the early ideals of co-operation and utopian communities to the "scientific socialism" of Marx and Engels. Against the backdrop of industrialization and the growth of great cities, demands for greater recognition of the economic plight of the toiling masses gave rise to trade unionism and the first socialist movements. The intellectual and cultural atmosphere was one that encouraged engagement in the political struggle, with artists and writers committing themselves to the attempts to change the order restored in 1815.

The era of Romanticism in the arts rejected the stately world of 18th-century rationalism and order for the passion and dynamism of the individual artist and also, by implication, the strivings of oppressed groups and nations. Art and culture would often express the political and social demands of the groups still excluded from power after the Revolutionary and Napoleonic wars.

These forces were to make the era after 1815 one of challenge and revolt, as the ideological forces released by the French Revolution were combined with the social and economic discontents of early industrialization. Europe was to be shaken by a succession of upheavals in 1820 and 1830–2, culminating in the great revolutionary upsurge of 1848–9.

The Revolutions of 1830

The 1815 settlement at Vienna quickly faced challenge from the forces of liberalism and nationalism in Spain, Italy, and Greece, but with differing results. Revolts in Spain and Italy were suppressed, while the cause of Greek independence was supported by liberal nationalists throughout Europe. Meanwhile, the restored monarchy in France proved unable to adjust to the new climate, leading to the revolution of 1830.

Charles X, king of France from 1824–30. The brother of Louis XVIII, he led the right-wing "Ultras" after 1815. His accession to the throne aroused opposition as a result of his support of the reactionary "Ordinances", provoking the revolution of 1830 and his replacement by the more liberal Louis Philippe.

1789–1848

THE AGE OF REVOLUTION

The Polish Prometheus graphically depicts the defeat of the Polish revolution of 1830–1. In Greek mythology, Prometheus was chained to a rock and condemned to have his liver perpetually devoured by an eagle – here the Romanov eagle of Russia preys on the prostrate Poland.

Restoration under challenge

At the first meeting under the Congress System held at Aix-la-Chapelle in 1818, France was admitted to the Quadruple Alliance as one of the great powers. Britain was already suspicious of the readiness of the Holy Alliance to justify interference in the internal affairs of other countries. By the time of the next meeting at Troppau in 1820, the issue had become pressing. A revolt had broken out in Spain against the repressive rule of Ferdinand VII, calling for the recognition of the liberal constitution drawn up by the Spanish Cortes in 1812 at the height of the patriotic war against Napoleon. The revolutionary mood had also spread to Naples, supported by the secret society of the *Carbonari*. Fearing the spread of revolutionary discontent throughout Italy and into central Europe, Metternich, the reactionary Austrian chancellor, obtained the approval of the Eastern powers for intervention. The Congress of

Laibach in 1821 authorized Austria to suppress the revolt in Naples, and an Austrian army also put down a liberal revolt in Piedmont in Northern Italy. Following the Congress of Verona in 1822, a French army was dispatched to put down the Spanish revolt, originally started in 1820. Ferdinand VII was restored to the throne, and carried out savage reprisals against his opponents. Even in places where open revolt had not occurred, Metternich was repressive. Meanwhile, in Germany, pro-nationalist and liberal demonstrations by students at the Festival of Wartburg in 1817 led to the Carlsbad Decrees of 1819, censoring the press and introducing police surveillance at the universities.

The spread of revolt

The spirit of revolt was not entirely repressed. The Latin American colonies of Spain and Portugal seized the opportunity provided by the distractions

The Parisian insurgents of July 1830 consisted of a mixture of the middle classes, former members of the National Guard, students, and artisans. Throwing up barricades, they quickly seized control of the centre of Paris and forced the abdication of Charles X. Once again, the streets of Paris determined the political fate of France.

of their European rulers to launch wars of independence. Supported by Britain and the USA, most of the Latin American states had secured independence from European rule by 1830, offering an example to the oppressed peoples of Europe. The position of the Greeks provided the most emotive cause of the era. Ruled for centuries by the Turks as part of the Ottoman Empire, Greece was the focus for the romantic nationalism of the "phil-hellenes", classically educated Europeans who saw Greece as the cradle of civilization and a symbol of liberty. When the Greeks rose in revolt against Turkish rule in 1821, volunteers such as the poet Lord Byron flocked to its support. The Greek cause became that of liberals and nationalists everywhere. In a long struggle, marked by atrocities on both sides, the intervention of some of the great powers on the side of Greece proved decisive. In 1827, a combined British, French, and Russian fleet destroyed the Turkish fleet at the battle of Navarino. Greek independence was granted by the Treaty of Adrianople in September 1829 and subsequently confirmed in London when Prince Otto of Bavaria became the first king of Greece.

Another part of the Vienna settlement was set aside in Belgium. Separated by culture and tradition, the Austrian Netherlands had been yoked to the Dutch Republic to create a large buffer state on France's northern frontier. In 1830, demonstrations for separation in Brussels led to the formation of a National Congress and a declaration of independence. Dutch forces were driven from Brussels, but still occupied Antwerp. After British mediation, the Dutch were persuaded to leave in December

1832. The Belgian crown was offered to Leopold of Saxe-Coburg, creating an independent Belgium. Poland was less successful: although it enjoyed a degree of autonomy, dreams of independence led to a rising against Russian rule in November 1830. After initial success, the revolt was brutally put down and the country brought more firmly under Russian administration by 1830.

The French Revolution of 1830

In France, Louis XVIII's restoration by the allied powers initially seemed secure. After a short period of reaction which saw former Bonapartists, such as Marshal Ney, executed, the new regime benefited from the reforms in taxation and administration brought about by the revolution. However, the assassination of the Duc de Berry in February 1820, by a fanatic aiming to destroy the Bourbon line, pushed the country in a more reactionary direction. Press censorship was introduced, and an already strongly pro-royalist Chamber was further restricted in its franchise. The accession of Charles X in 1824 brought further reaction, with pro-clerical policies, tighter press censorship, and the disbanding of the Parisian National Guard. A new ultra-royalist ministry formed under Polignac in August 1829 was faced with demands for liberalization. The ministry's proposal instead for a new set of reactionary "Ordinances" provoked an uprising in Paris in July 1830 in which over 6000 people were killed. Charles was forced to abdicate, and the liberal Duc d'Orléans, Louis Philippe, was offered the crown. He was to bring a few years of stability to a France torn between monarchy and republicanism.

Reform in Britain, Autocracy in Russia

Great Britain and Russia represented the opposite poles of reform and repression in the age of revolution. Britain, the most economically advanced country, yielded limited reform to ward off revolution. Russia, the most backward state, turned to repression in order to avoid reform.

The path to reform

Demands for reform in Britain had surfaced in the early years of the reign of George III during the 1760s. The movements headed by John Wilkes and Christopher Wyvill aimed at reducing "corruption", principally the manipulation of the electoral system by the government of the day to perpetuate itself and frustrate opposition. During the American Revolution, demands for "economical reform", reducing the amount of patronage available to the government, became widespread, as well as more radical proposals to extend the franchise, shorten the duration of parliaments, and transfer seats from the "rotten boroughs" to the counties and growing towns. The fall of Lord North and the ending of the war in America had deprived reform of much of its

momentum, only to be revived under the stimulus of events in France. The French Revolution introduced more radical ideas in writings such as Thomas Paine's *The Rights of Man*, which reached an unprecedentedly wide audience and stimulated the formation of artisan reform societies in places such as London, Norwich, and Sheffield. By the mid-1790s, there were several hundred reform societies, mostly peaceable, with many of them calling for universal suffrage and annual parliaments. Middle-class reformers soon felt threatened by the excesses of the French Revolution and the fear of radical reform at home. Government repression and loyalism in the face of invasion threats also undermined popular radicalism. It re-emerged, however, at the end of the Napoleonic

Peterloo Massacre

Following the end of the Napoleonic wars, the Tory Government of Lord Liverpool in Britain resisted popular pressure for radical parliamentary reform. The Home Secretary, Lord Sidmouth, forced radical journalists such as William Cobbett into temporary exile and muzzled the press with new laws and prosecutions. Although the government was faced with some small insurrectionary movements such as the Spa Fields Rising in December 1816 and the

Pentridge Rising in Derbyshire in 1817, its overreaction to legitimate agitation for reform blackened its reputation. The break-up by troops of a peaceful reform meeting at St Peter's Fields in Manchester in August 1819 in a bungled attempt to arrest the popular orator Henry Hunt, causing 11 deaths and 400 injuries among a peaceful, unarmed crowd, converted many to the cause of reform. Dubbed "Peterloo" in ironic reference to the great victory earned four years earlier, it became the symbol of postwar repression of reform.

Wars, with growing social discontent and anger at government corruption. Journalists such as William Cobbett in his *Political Register* urged the poor to turn to reform rather than violence to redress their grievances, while the growing middle class in cities such as Leeds, Birmingham, and Manchester demanded representation. But repression continued after 1815 as the Tory government acted against even legitimate reform activity, including peaceful meetings such as that at St Peter's Fields, Manchester, in the "Peterloo" Massacre.

The Great Reform Act

The break-up of Lord Liverpool's Tory government after 1827 gave the opportunity for reform. Political unions were formed in the unrepresented cities, often combining middle- and lower-class agitation for change. The Whigs introduced a Reform Bill in 1831; its rejection by the House of Lords was met by rioting in Derby, Nottingham, and Bristol. The tense "May Days" were the outcome of the political struggle for reform. For a few days, the country was without a government, waiting to see whether William IV would create a sufficient number of new peers to force the Bill through the House of Lords. In the end, the Lords' resistance crumbled and the Reform Act was passed in 1832. The Act swept away "rotten boroughs", gave representation to the unrepresented commercial and manufacturing towns such as Manchester and Liverpool, and regularized the franchise qualifications on the basis of property ownership. It was conservative in only raising the total electorate to about 650,000, a small fraction of even the male population. Dissatisfaction with the Act led popular radicals to agitate for radical reform in the "People's Charter" after 1832. Despite this dissatisfaction, the most corrupt elements of the old system had been removed and the way opened for progressive extension of the franchise in 1867, 1884, and 1918.

Russia resists reform

Russia remained the most autocratic of all European states. Although Tsar Alexander I had hinted at liberalization early in his reign, he became increasingly religious and conservative. The Holy Alliance was created on his initiative, and, after 1815, acted to repress liberal and national movements across Europe. At his death in December 1825, sections of the nobility and the Palace Guard demonstrated in favour of the accession of the more liberal Constantine and the granting of a constitution. The resulting Decembrist Rising was quickly put down by the chosen heir, Alexander's brother Nicholas I, a stern autocrat who was to rule Russia with unflinching conservatism until his death in 1855. Nicholas's watchwords were "autocracy, orthodoxy, and nationalism", and he sought to make a virtue of Russia's distinctiveness from Western Europe. Russia's trade and industry were less developed than almost any other part of Europe, providing fewer middle-class supporters for reform and liberal ideas, while the majority of the general population were serfs tied to the land. Nicholas tightened his grip at any sign of discontent. The Polish revolt of 1830–2 was crushed, rigid press censorship maintained, foreign books largely banned, and a secret police set up to infiltrate liberal groups. Russian opposition was largely silenced at home. Intellectuals could only voice discontent discreetly through literature or escape by exile. By the mid-19th century, some of the most important Russian thinkers had fled Russia, beginning a tradition of an intelligentsia in exile that would continue into the next century.

When Europe blazed into revolution in 1848, Russia remained inert, its armies used to suppress revolts in central Europe. But Russia could not resist reform for ever: the Crimean War exposed the backwardness of the Russian army and state system. Calls for modernization under Nicholas's successor, Alexander II, would lead to demands for wider reform.

Nicholas I of Russia was tsar from 1825. He crushed the constitutionalist Decembrist Rising at his accession and suppressed the Polish revolt of 1830–1. He ruled Russia with unflinching authoritarianism, creating a new secret police, restricting the press and education, and assisting neighbouring Austria to suppress the liberal revolts of 1848–9.

Labour Movements and the Rise of Socialism

The 19th- and 20th-century socialist movement saw the coming together of two developments – the need for workers to organize to defend their interests during industrialization and the growing demand for economic equality in the new social order springing up around them. New social movements rose up to meet these demands.

Robert Owen pioneered the idea of co-operation at his model factory of New Lanark in Scotland. His New View of Society *(1813) offered a Utopian prospect of moral reform and national education. He greatly influenced the attempts to set up a general union of all workmen in the 1830s, also devoting much of his time to setting up Owenite communities in Britain and the USA.*

1789–1848

THE AGE OF REVOLUTION

The rise of the unions

Craft organizations and guilds had existed for centuries among the skilled workers of Europe to supervise apprenticeship and regulate specific trades. The growth of towns and industry put craft organizations under pressure, with competition from unskilled labour, from new machines, and from a climate that favoured deregulation and laissez-faire. In the most advanced economy, Britain, trade groups had moved beyond the medieval guild organization by the late 18th century to form trade societies, in effect early trade unions, which were especially strong in places such as London, Norwich, and the textile and mining districts in the north and the west of England. "Combinations", or strikes, became so frequent that in 1799–1800 the British government passed the Combination Acts, prohibiting workmen from combining to raise wages or alter their working conditions. Many survived, however, disguised as friendly societies or benefit clubs, and others operated clandestinely, protected by secret oaths.

Workers fought a protracted battle through negotiation, strikes, violence, and threats to protect their position. In the Luddite outbreaks in the north and Midlands in 1810–12, textile workers smashed hundreds of machines, which they believed were undermining their livelihood. Suppressed by the mobilization of more than 10,000 troops and a spate of executions, an undercurrent of "collective bargaining by riot" remained a feature of early trade unionism, breaking out again in 1816 and 1826.

In France, the Le Chapelier Law of 1791 forbade associations of workers, although the Jacobins temporarily regulated prices and wages in the Law of the Maximum in 1793–4. Their fall saw workmen coming under pressures similar to those in Britain. The 1810 penal code and a law of April 1834 demonstrated government determination to repress labour organizations. Benefit clubs, often organized around workshops and cafés, provided a rudimentary organization that mobilized workers to participate in the Paris insurrections of 1789, 1830, and 1848. In the great silk-weaving centre of Lyons, two uprisings in the early 1830s saw the silk workers defending their craft privileges. Under the slogan "live working or die fighting", thousands of them were killed in the insurrection of 1834. The French government remained fearful of such unrest, and trade unions were not fully legalized until 1864.

In Britain, the Combination Acts were repealed in 1824, but unions were still obliged to operate cautiously. In 1834, six Dorsetshire agricultural labourers were sentenced to transportation for taking illegal oaths. After widespread protests, the "Tolpuddle Martyrs" were eventually released. Many workers remained ununionized and instead swelled the ranks of the Chartist movement, which derived its name from the People's Charter of 1838, demanding a six-point agenda of radical reform, including universal suffrage, annual parliaments, and secret ballots. Three mass petitions to Parliament in 1839, 1842, and 1848 failed to win parliamentary approval. Many elite craft groups were reluctant to align themselves with a mass movement sometimes tainted with violence and disorder, but declining craft groups such as the handloom weavers saw in it their only hope for change. By mid-century, the former were able to form "model unions" such as the Amalgamated Society of Engineers, with 12,000 members in 1851.

Owenite socialism

The philanthropic industrialist, Robert Owen, pioneered "co-operation" through his model factory and community at New Lanark, near Glasgow. His *New View of Society* (1813) was widely read and a number of Owenite model communities were established in Britain and the USA. Owenite ideas also lay behind the attempts to set up a "general union of the trades", resulting in the short-lived Grand National Consolidated Trade Union in 1834.

Co-operative endeavour also lay behind the Chartist Land Plan, set up in 1845, and attempting to resettle industrial workers on communally owned agricultural holdings. Although several estates were set up, the scheme had collapsed by 1851. More successful was the co-operative retail movement started in Rochdale in 1844, which flourished as a non-profitmaking concern. In France, the egalitarian ideas of Claude St Simon, François Fourier, and Pierre Proudhon also offered a vision of a socialist future where the exploitation of workers and peasants would cease. Louis Blanc produced in 1840 *L'Organisation du travail*, an indictment of the child labour and exploitation he saw about him in contemporary France; he argued the need for a form of state socialism in which the state would buy out private enterprises, creating 'national workshops' which would destroy the competition from private, capitalist enterprise, and operating a kind of workers' communism. Political activists such as Auguste Blanqui urged workers to seek in a republic the end of the "state of war between rich and poor" which he argued existed under the Orleanist monarchy, leading many to join the insurrection that brought about its end in 1848.

The Communist Manifesto

Poor trade and bad harvests made the 1840s a catalyst for early socialist ideas, many of them based on a straightforward analysis of existing inequalities. The desire for a new social order and the experience of the transformation wrought by industrialization was brought together by Karl Marx and Friedrich Engels. Interpreting the whole of past history as representing the struggle between capital and labour, seen in the social division between "bourgeoisie" and "proletariat" in his own day, Marx put socialism on what he perceived to be a "scientific" basis, predicting the collapse of bourgeois society in revolution and the creation of an egalitarian world of social harmony or "communism". *The Communist Manifesto* of 1848 was the key statement of Marxist principles that were to be so influential in the future. At this early stage, Marx had few followers and his pamphlet little influence. Such socialist societies as existed were politically of little significance and few yet looked to Marx as their prophet. In time, however, the rapid development of industrialization and labour movements would lead many workers and intellectuals, especially on the continent, to look to Marxism as a convincing interpretation of the world about them.

The conviction and sentencing of six Dorsetshire agricultural labourers to transportation to Australia for trade union activities in 1834 aroused a tremendous outcry and demonstrations in their support. Although trade unions had been made legal in 1824 with the Repeal of the Combination Acts, swearing oaths and other actions were still punishable by law. The outcry saw the men substantially vindicated.

LABOUR MOVEMENTS AND THE RISE OF SOCIALISM   **301**

The Revolutions of 1848–9

The pent-up discontent of the revolutionary era burst out in the unprecedented "year of revolutions" in 1848. Although governments were overturned and the cause of liberalism and nationalism briefly triumphed, much of the old order proved too resilient to be dislodged.

Karl Marx was the father of "scientific socialism", or Marxism, distinguishing himself from "Utopian" socialists such as Owen and Fourier. Marx based his political views upon his interpretation of the economic laws of history, promulgated in The Communist Manifesto *and demonstrated in his* Das Kapital, *the first volume of which was published in 1867. After his expulsion from Germany for participation in the revolts of 1848, he settled in London.*

The uprisings in the revolutions of 1848 were very widespread. Many of Europe's major cities erupted into violence, especially in Italy, Germany, and Austria-Hungary. Only Russia and Britain were unaffected.

The tide of revolt

Underlying the revolts of 1848–9 were the ideas of liberalism and nationalism inspired by the French Revolution and which had flared up sporadically since 1815. However reactionary the autocratic powers of central and Eastern Europe, population growth and urbanization were producing ever larger numbers of people excluded from political power. Calls for a written constitution, the end of arbitrary government, representative assemblies, freedom of expression, and a wider franchise became popular causes among the urban middle and artisan classes. National feeling, too, had been stimulated by the national revolts in Greece, Begium, Poland, and Latin America. Intellectuals and artists increasingly identified with national sentiment, providing support and justification for revolt against oppressive rulers. Discontent was fuelled by the authoritarian policies of Metternich and Nicholas I. Under these rulers, any sign of dissent was suppressed, offering apparently no prospect of piecemeal reform as had occurred in Britain and France by the 1840s.

To these discontents were added the stresses and strains of population growth, urbanization, and the early Industrial Revolution. The growth of the cities and large towns massed hordes of impoverished workers at the centres of government and administration. The power of the mob had already been seen in the Paris revolts of 1789 and 1830. By the 1840s, the lessons of Paris were to be learned across Europe. The middle years of the decade proved troubled ones: trade depression, harvest failures, potato blight, and cholera marked the years 1845–7, creating conditions in which revolt only needed a trigger. What was to be striking in 1848–9 was the widespread character of the revolt. The spark was provided by revolution in Paris and southern Italy, spreading quickly to Germany, central Europe and central and northern Italy. Britain and Russia were the only countries untouched. Almost everywhere, the cities were centres of discontent; the rural masses remained largely inert until the later stages of the risings, if at all.

The course of revolt

In France, the experiment with republicanism by the Jacobins in the 1790s had left a legacy of dissatisfaction with the restored monarchy of 1815 and the compromise Orleanist monarchy of 1830. A series of reform banquets in Paris, supported by the liberal opposition in the Chamber, called for an extension of the franchise. When the government attempted to suppress the banquets in January 1848, radical and republican journalists organized a series of demonstrations, forcing Louis Philippe to dismiss his government. Far from subsiding, discontent grew. Following clashes with the Municipal Guard, crowds armed themselves and threw up barricades. By 24 February, an estimated 100,000 Parisians were on the streets, precipitating Louis's abdication and the proclamation of a republic based on universal suffrage. Briefly, Paris witnessed a replay of the mid-1790s, as radical leaders sought to inaugurate a genuinely republican government, providing "National Workshops" for the unemployed and using the mob to dictate to the National Assembly. Increasingly, the middle classes became

The 1848 Revolutions
- ✱ Main centres of revolution
- ✱ Other centres of revolution
- ⌒ Boundary of German Confederation

DENMARK
SCHLESWIG-HOLSTEIN
Berlin
RUSSIAN EMPIRE
PRUSSIA
Paris
Frankfurt
Prague
FRANCE
Vienna
AUSTRO-HUNGARIAN EMPIRE
Milan
Budapest
SARDINIA (PIEDMONT)
VENETIA
Venice
LOMBARDY
PAPAL STATES
Rome
OTTOMAN EMPIRE
SARDINIA
Mediterranean Sea
KINGDOM OF THE TWO SICILIES
Palermo

The Austrians attack Venice with balloons armed with bombs during the final days of the revolution of 1848–9. Daniele Manin led a revolt in March 1848 that threw off the Austrian yoke and set up a Venetian Republic. Gradually, the Austrian armies reasserted control over the Italian states. Venice was the last city to succumb; cannonaded by the Austrians and ravaged by cholera within, it surrendered on 25 August 1849.

alarmed at the radical direction of events. When an attempt was made to close down the National Workshops in June, the workers mounted an insurrection. Under government direction, the army under General Cavaignac was called in to put down the revolt. In the bloody "June Days", more than 2000 workers were killed and over 4000 imprisoned or exiled. The republic survived precariously.

Revolt spread across Europe. Even before the rising in Paris, there was a rising in the Kingdom of Naples demanding the constitution of 1812, which Metternich had undertaken to suppress. Initially successful, the revolt spread to Tuscany, the Papal States, Milan, and Venice, where Daniele Manin proclaimed a republic. In Prussia, a rising in Berlin forced King Frederick William IV to grant a constitution. On 31 March, the Vorparlament met at Frankfurt, recasting itself as a German National Assembly. On 18 May, it offered Frederick William IV the crown as "Emperor of the Germans". His refusal dismayed the revolutionaries, leaving the Assembly as little more than a futile talking shop. Throughout the Austro-Hungarian Empire, revolts broke out. Uprisings occurred in Prague and Vienna, forcing Metternich's resignation and the granting of a constitution. In Hungary, Kossuth led a Magyar revolt securing separation from the weakened government in Vienna. Feudal obligations were abolished, bringing an end to serfdom in Austrian lands.

The successes of the revolts outside France were short-lived. Several rulers had been forced to make concessions, but reneged on their promises once they had escaped immediate danger. The revolutionaries themselves proved weak and divided in their objectives, ill equipped to turn their insurrections into stable and effective government. Liberals quarrelled with nationalists, and nationalists quarrelled with each other, as in Hungary where Kossuth's policy of Magyarization alienated other nationalities. Elsewhere, the idea of nationalism was still barely understood outside the cities and intellectual circles. Finally, however brave and committed, poorly armed and inadequately trained insurrectionaries were no match for the regular armies that were eventually mobilized against them. By 1849, revolt after revolt was crushed and the leaders dead, imprisoned, or scattered.

The old order had proved remarkably durable, but there were some gains. The Bourbon monarchy in France no longer existed. In Prussia and Piedmont, the seeds of constitutionalism had been planted. Serfdom, once abolished, could not be reimposed in the Austro-Hungarian Empire. Although unrealized in 1848, German and Italian unification had been advanced. Everywhere, the situation in the cities was now considered anxiously, with schemes for social reform and urban improvement implemented to prevent uprisings in the future.

The French Revolution   286–7 ▶
The Revolutions of 1830   296–7 ▶
The Third Republic   332–3 ▶
Gorbachev and the
End of Communism, 1989   464–5 ▶

The Early Industrial Revolution

From the late 18th century, Britain pioneered economic developments that would transform Europe over the course of the next two centuries. A growing population, flourishing agriculture, and thriving commerce combined to stimulate technical inventions and new forms of production that would create the first Industrial Revolution.

The context of change

The growth of Britain's population from the mid-18th century was not directly caused by industrialization. A run of good harvests in the first half of the century and consequent low food prices, the decline of the plague as a major killer, and a number of minor improvements in health all combined to lower death rates and produce a rise in population. By the end of the 18th century, birth rates also began to rise as general prosperity in trade and early manufacturing allowed people to marry earlier and to have more children. Unlike the situation in Ireland and some other European countries where population growth led to impoverishment and famine, Britain's commercial and agricultural prosperity contributed to increased demand for products of every kind, stimulating innovation and increasing output.

Previously, periods of economic expansion had been ended by runs of poor harvests and a general downturn of the economy. By the middle of the 18th century, a thriving domestic economy and overseas trade enabled landowners to borrow money to invest in agricultural expansion. The Enclosure Movement allowed individual land-holdings to be consolidated rather than held in scattered strips in the medieval open fields. The commons and wastes were similarly split up, creating larger, efficient farms, in which more productive techniques could be employed, such as improved animal husbandry, new root crops and crop rotations, and the application of fertilizers and the first agricultural machines. Enclosure

Acts, secured through Parliament, had affected about a fifth of the acreage of England by 1845, including some of its most productive agricultural land. Enclosure favoured the larger farmers, who could afford to make use of the new techniques, driving many smallholders to give up their holdings as unviable without access to the commons and wastes. Contrary to common myth, enclosure in the 18th and 19th centuries did not necessarily depopulate the countryside, but often required more labour. The rising rural population was, however, often forced to seek employment in the towns. Above all, agricultural output rose, allowing the population to increase and the demand for manufactured goods to expand.

Foreign trade was also growing, providing an incentive for increased production. One of the first industries to feel this increased demand was mining, as the need for more domestic fuel grew. Output increased fourfold in the 18th century, assisted by and stimulating the development of more efficient steam engines that could pump water from mines and permit deeper mining. Coal-fired steam engines of the type patented by James Watt in the 1770s provided an immensely efficient new source of power. Machines also demanded cheap iron. The small output based on the use of charcoal was transformed in the 18th century by the coke-smelting techniques pioneered by Abraham Darby at his works in Coalbrookdale, Shropshire, enabling iron to become a widely used material for making machines and iron structures such as bridges.

The machine age

With the development of steam power and abundant cheap iron, the most important innovation of the Industrial Revolution was the introduction of labour-saving machinery. This occurred most dramatically in the cotton industry, which witnessed a succession of technical breakthroughs that revolutionized the entire process of manufacture from spinning to weaving, allowing the concentration of production under one roof in which steam-driven machines worked night and day. Other industries developed in a more piecemeal way: the woollen industry still relied heavily on water power, and many other industries, such as pottery and metal-working, saw concentration of production in larger concerns only, rather than the wholesale adoption of machinery.

Concentration of production required both capital and cheap transport. By 1800, 400 country banks, although subject to panics and failures, provided a basic financial network, often issuing their own notes. They began to be superseded by

Canals in Britain c.1837

- ⌇ Canals
- ⌇ Navigable rivers
- ① Leeds & Liverpool
- ② Huddersfield
- ③ Chesterfield
- ④ Grand Trunk
- ⑤ Birmingham & Liverpool
- ⑥ Grand Union
- ⑦ Worcester & Birmingham
- ⑧ Thames & Severn
- ⑨ Kennet & Avon

As a result of the "canal mania" of the late 18th century, Britain achieved a network of canals linking the major ports with the inland manufacturing areas, such as the Potteries and the Black Country. The network had reached its fullest extent just as the first railways were being constructed.

"joint stock" banks after 1826. In 1844, the Bank Charter Act secured the role of the Bank of England as the note-issuing authority and guarantor of the system.

Land transport remained slow and expensive for goods traffic in spite of improvements brought about by the turnpike system of toll roads that reduced journey times for mail and passenger traffic. Water transport was much cheaper than land, and the development of canals grew apace from the mid-18th century. The Duke of Bridgewater's canal, built in 1757 to transport coal to Manchester cut costs dramatically and was quickly copied throughout the country. A frantic speculation in canal building – "canal mania" – gave Britain a network of trunk canals by the early 19th century, linking the major ports to the centres of manufacture. The development of the railways after the opening of the Stockton and Darlington Railway in 1825 gave a major boost to the economy, making it possible to move bulky goods ever more cheaply. Production could be concentrated even more, swelling the size of the industrial conurbations based upon the coalfields of Britain. During the British railway boom of the 1840s, pioneers such as George Stephenson, Isambard Kingdom Brunel, George Hudson, and Thomas Brassey laid down the first extensive railway network in the world.

By 1850, Britain had pioneered all the major elements of the world's first Industrial Revolution, and its effects were beginning to be felt across the continent of Europe. With the promise of massive increases in production also came the social consequences of industrial growth.

The Scientific Revolution 238–9 ▶
Labour Movements and the Rise of Socialism 300–1 ▶
The Effects of Industrialization 306–7 ▶
Industrial Developments 366–7 ▶

The Effects of Industrialization

By 1850, Britain had become the first industrial nation due to its pioneering of steam power, new machinery, and factory production. The new techniques soon spread to favoured parts of the continent – those with good communications and access to coal and iron – where the rest of Europe began to experience the economic and social consequences of industrial development.

Le Creusot developed as one of the major industrial centres of France during the late 18th and early 19th centuries. The presence of coal and iron provided the classic combination to develop a major metalworking industry, one of the first on the continent of Europe. Coal, however, was not as plentiful in France as it was in Britain or Belgium, a factor which delayed French industrial growth in the 19th century.

The first 50 years of the 19th century saw an unprecedented level of economic development across Europe, with Britain playing the leading role in European industrialization. The new technologies pioneered by the end of the 18th century created the basis for an industrial society. Population growth and urban development accompanied the growth of industry and trade. Steam power was applied to transport, creating the first European railway network by the middle of the 19th century. The problems caused by industrialization for urban life led Britain to develop much of the municipal and social infrastructure that was to become standard as the Industrial Revolution spread across Europe.

Britain's lead

British economic growth in the half century after 1815 was dramatic, even compared with the earlier phase of industrialization. Between 1815 and 1850, coal output trebled, iron production rose fourfold, and cotton output grew eight times. Being first in the field meant that Britain maintained and increased its lead over other countries through continued advances in mechanization and factory production. Britain supplied more than 50 per cent of the world's trade in manufactured goods by 1850, stimulated by policies of free trade.

Industrialization on the continent

The techniques and processes of industrialization quickly spread to favoured parts of France, Belgium, and Germany. Belgium was the most advanced by 1850, based upon its long-established tradition as a textile manufacturing centre and its ample supplies of coal and iron. France, too, had existing manufacturing industries based around the great ironworking and armaments centre of St Etienne and the silk-weaving district around Lyons. Both expanded rapidly after 1815. By 1850, it was estimated that there were more than 50,000 people working in the Lyons silk industry, many of them operating the newly invented loom of Joseph-Marie Jacquard, allowing elaborate designs to be woven into silk fabrics. St Etienne developed into a sprawling complex of mines, ironworks, and

The impressive power of the new heavy machinery made possible by the use of iron and, later, steel is demonstrated by this scene in a copper foundry at Toulon, France.

workshops, and new industrial areas opened up in the north and Pas de Calais based on the local coalfields and access to raw materials imported from Britain. The number of steam engines employed in France rose from 2000 in 1842 to over 5000 in 1850 as France entered the new industrial era. German coal production, though still dwarfed by that of Britain, increased tenfold between 1815 and 1850. Over the next 20 years, German industry would develop by leaps and bounds in coal, iron, and engineering. British expertise was imported to develop the European railway system, with rails, steam engines, and a workforce, as well as capital, being used to connect the major cities. France had over 320 kilometres (200 miles) of railway track by the time of the 1848 revolution, and the basic network linking Europe's capital cities and ports would be in place by 1870.

The social consequences

Early industry had sometimes occupied rural locations, using water power or isolated sources of raw materials and fuel. Over the century from 1789, the face of Europe was to be transformed by the growth of large cities and towns – many of them the products of industrialization – and sprawling industrial conurbations. Britain was the prime example, but this pattern was soon repeated elsewhere. By the middle of the 19th century, there were more than 70 towns in Britain with populations of more than 10,000, eight with more than 100,000, and four with over 250,000. By 1851, more than half the population lived in urban areas, compared with about a sixth in 1700. The total population had risen threefold in a little over a century to more than 20 million in 1851. The rest of Europe followed a similar pattern: in 1801, there were only 14 European cities and towns with more than 100,000 inhabitants; by 1870, however, there were more than 100. In 1851, Paris was double the size it had been in 1789, reaching over a million people, while the new capital of Belgium, Brussels, increased four times to reach over a quarter of a million. In mining, textile, and metalworking areas, small villages became towns ,as workers flocked in search of employment. Many industrial recruits travelled only a short distance from the local countryside, but others came from further afield. Scottish and Irish workers, southern Italians, and German peasants were often obliged to migrate long distances to find work.

The urban world

Conditions in the early industrial towns were often cramped and insanitary. Rapid expansion meant that families crowded into cheap lodging, cellars,

Cholera

Cholera, arriving in Europe from the East in the early 1830s and causing epidemics into the 1840s and beyond, highlighted the desperately poor state of sanitation and public health in the growing towns and cities of industrializing Europe. A waterborne disease, it was found to be concentrated where people used communal facilities and highlighted the need for clean water and adequate reservoirs. Other diseases, such as typhoid, resulted from the contamination of water supplies with sewage. Disease was no respecter of social class, forcing a huge effort to improve water supply, sewerage arrangements, and housing. In Britain, Royal Commissions led in the 1840s to the establishment of a Board of Health and a Medical Officer of Health in 1848. Sewers emptied directly into the Thames as late as the 1860s, giving the river a grim reputation for its effects on the health of the population.

and courtyards. Piped water supplies and sanitary services were often totally inadequate, resulting in very high mortality rates, especially among young children. In 1842, the average life expectancy for children of labouring families in Manchester was 17 years, compared to 38 in the countryside. Cholera epidemics in 1831–3 and 1847–8 focussed attention upon the need to improve sanitary conditions. Britain saw its first Public Health Act in 1848 and pioneered many of the advances of municipal services, such as water supply and sewers. Although many factory owners built houses for their workers, they were often of the cheapest kind, leaving a backlog of slum housing in many industrial cities. Little thought was given to the effects of pollution. Only later would it become apparent that a wholesale transformation had occurred in the lives of the inhabitants of the new industrial world. Workers were now massed together and would begin to bargain for their rights. The urban middle classes were to be at the forefront of demands for political rights and the reform of their new urban world.

Romanticism and the Arts

The era of revolutionary upheaval saw major changes in the cultural climate of Europe. The Romantic movement rejected the rationalism of the Enlightenment for emotion and individual expression. Literature and poetry were the most characteristic vehicles of Romanticism, but the new mood was soon reflected in all areas of thought.

The rise of the Romantic

By the late 18th century, classical forms in literature and the other arts were giving way to new currents. Interest in historical and exotic locations other than the classical past were reflected in the growing interest in Scandinavian and Celtic mythology and a passion for the medieval period. The "Gothic" novel, pioneered in Horace Walpole's *The Castle of Otranto* (1765), was soon copied widely, reaching its most dramatic expression in Mary Shelley's *Frankenstein* (1817). A passion for historical locations was reflected in the immense popularity of Sir Walter Scott's novels, which drew on the Scottish past. In Germany, the desire for greater emotional intensity was expressed in the *Sturm und Drang* (Storm and Stress) movement promulgated by Johann Herder in the 1770s. His influence was felt by the greatest German poet and dramatist of the Romantic era, Johann Wolfgang von Goethe, whose *The Sufferings of Young Werther* (1774) depicted the intensity of feeling induced by young love. Goethe's depiction of the great moral dilemmas of temptation and self-knowledge in his celebrated *Faust* is one of the most famous examples of Romantic literature.

By this time, the ideals of the French Revolution had begun to influence a new generation of writers. The English "Lake poets", especially William Wordsworth and Samuel Taylor Coleridge, were noted for their lyric poetry, publishing the *Lyrical Ballads* in 1798, which included Coleridge's "Rime of the Ancient Mariner". A fresh generation of poets, Percy Bysshe Shelley and Lord Byron among them, picked up the gauntlet of opposition

Poet and dramatist Johann Wolfgang von Goethe was the towering figure of the German Romantic movement. A foremost figure in the Sturm und Drang movement, he reacted against French and classical influence, seeking to put away all that was artificial to return to "nature" and "reality". His later work, however, moved back towards the Greek ideals of calm and harmony.

William Hutchinson's Guide to the Lakes of 1774, with ten editions by 1812, established the English Lake District as a prime "romantic" landscape for tourists. It also provided inspiration for the "Lake poets", Wordsworth and Coleridge, who sought inspiration in the countryside and closeness to nature. In turn, Wordsworth's lifelong sojourn in the Lake District at Dove Cottage, near Grasmere, made the Lakes a centre of literary and artistic pilgrimage.

to the repressive government of the time. Shelley was to achieve immortality as a lyric poet, dying young in a boating accident in Italy. Byron was to be lauded Europe-wide as a Romantic poet and for his support for the cause of Greek independence. After volunteering to fight for the Greeks, he died of fever at Missolonghi in 1824.

The Romantic movement spread throughout Europe. The Italian writer Alessandro Manzoni's *The Betrothed* (1840–2) was strongly influenced by Scott, and Byron's influence was felt in the work of Alexander Pushkin, the first major and greatest Russian poet. His *Eugene Onegin* (1831) centred on a Romantic, Byronic hero. Byron's influence was also seen in the work of the first Russian novelist, Mikhail Lermontov, author of *A Hero of Our Time* (1835). In France, the new movement found its expression in the novels and dramas of Victor Hugo, several of which were set in the medieval past. Significantly, the first performance of his play *Hernani* (1830) provoked riots for its abandonment of the classical rules of theatre. The novels of George Sand and the historical romances of Alexandre Dumas also reflected the new mood.

The focus on history proved particularly attractive to those seeking to fashion national identity from folklore and tradition. Scott's Scottish ballads were mirrored in the folk tales collected by the brothers Grimm in Germany and the compilation of the Finnish folk-epic, *The Kalevala*, by Elias Lönnrot, first published in 1835.

Social issues were increasingly a subject for literature, particularly in the novels of Hugo and the writings of Honoré de Balzac in his series of novels and stories, *La Comédie humaine*. Charles

Dickens's novels also took issue with many of the evils of the day, including poverty, the treatment of debtors and orphans, the poor law, and the squalor of urban life. By mid-century, the passionate expression of individual feeling was giving way to a more generalized social commentary, focussing on urban and provincial life.

Culture and philosophy

The profound cultural transition from the emphasis on the guiding light of reason to the cult of individual feeling and identity was felt in both political philosophy and in the writing of history. The French Revolution seemed to many to express the "madness of reason" in its excesses. Edmund Burke had raised the issue of the limits of reason in his *Reflections on the Revolution in France* (1790), which appealed to an organic conception of society. Burke argued that human society was too fragile and complicated to be reconstructed on the abstract designs of the *philosophes*, predicting disaster as a result of their efforts and the risk of military dictatorship. When, indeed, such disasters appeared to befall France in the rise of the sansculottes and then the rule of Napoleon, Burke's text became the bible of counter-revolution. His emphasis upon the value of history, tradition, and religion offered a political defence of the status quo, provided it made "conservative" and prudent adjustments to the forces of change. Taken up by writers such as the aristocratic émigré François René Chateaubriand in his *The Genius of Christianity* (1802), and by political writers such as De Maistre and Bonald, the age of Romanticism saw an apologia for tradition and religion in the

Ludwig van Beethoven, here pictured with the manuscript of his Missa Solemnis, *translated the Romantic ideals of individual feeling and artistic integrity into his musical compositions. Although forced to work for patrons, his dynamic energies burst the bounds of contemporary musical conventions, earning him an enduring place in the history of culture.*

wave of reaction that dominated Europe after the Vienna Settlement of 1815. Christian revival was felt in the evangelical movement in Britain and religious renewal in Germany. In the latter, however, "idealism" became the prevailing philosophy, stimulated by the work of the philosophers Immanuel Kant, Johann Fichte, and Friedrich Schelling. They instilled an optimistic temper, welcoming artistic interpretation of the world about them and believing in the higher meaning of nature. The greatest German philosopher of the Romantic era, Georg Wilhelm Hegel, was an important influence on Marx through his dynamic view of history as a process. History could now be seen in terms of progress, stimulated by the epochal changes of the French Revolution and, later, the economic forces unleashed by industrialization.

Music

The Romantic era in music reflected not only changes in styles, but also intellectual, social, and technological developments. Music saw a growing emphasis on the individual artist and on self-expression and virtuoso performance. It also changed its audience and the means of making music. Music-making in the 18th century had been largely dominated by the patronage of courts and the Church, although a tradition of concert-going had developed in large cities. Following the French Revolution, there was a reduction in court and Church patronage, yet at the same time, the

growing towns provided a larger audience for musical performance. New, larger auditoria were created, which demanded larger orchestras and concert-length works. New instruments such as the grand piano supplanted the harpsichord, just as the symphony orchestra displaced the smaller string ensembles of court music. Great religious choral works for public performance, after the manner of Mendelssohn's *Oratorios*, became the most widely appreciated forms of religious music. Although not originating in the 19th century, opera underwent a popular revival, tapping into a public demand for elaborate spectacle and exotic locations. The works of Rossini were particularly popular and played an important part in this revival.

The Romantic era saw the composer rise from the rank of mere craftsmen to the status of artist, with almost god-like powers to express the deeper longings and sentiments of mankind. Ludwig van Beethoven was perhaps the most potent exponent of this transition. His turbulent temperament and pioneering of new musical forms provided the prototype for the 19th-century artist-genius. His work expressed the Romantic themes of struggle against tyranny, seen in his Third Symphony, *Eroica*, of 1803, his opera *Fidelio*, and his setting of Schiller's "Ode to Joy" in the choral movement of his Ninth Symphony. Beethoven's deafness and the lack of appreciation of his more complex chamber works added to his mystique.

Even less appreciated in his own time was Franz Schubert, much of whose work was not performed until after his death. Between them, Beethoven and Schubert transformed the symphony and the concerto. Beethoven's intense chamber works and Schubert's song cycles were a world away from the decorous "wallpaper" of court music, and were conceived self-consciously as "art". But popular acclaim was to be had, too, as attested by the success of the piano concerts and operas of Carl Maria von Weber.

Many musicians consciously drew on Romantic literature: Hector Berlioz based orchestral and operatic pieces on the works of Byron, Scott, and Goethe. Musicianship itself was attracting a Romantic following. By the time of Berlioz's *Symphonie Fantastique* (1830), vast orchestras of standardized instruments were controlled by a single conductor. Virtuosi performers such as Niccolò Paganini made reputations from their instrumental skills. The Polish-born Frédéric Chopin combined Romantic artist and virtuoso performer. Exiled from his native land, his brilliant, sensitive musicianship, cut short by an early death from consumption, left the world an enduring reputation. As with many mid-19th-century artists, his work was influenced by "national" music – Polish folk songs and mazurkas.

Painting

Painting evolved less dramatically, but its subject matter did alter. Jacques-Louis David celebrated the revolutionary spirit with his portraits of the young Napoleon. Eugène Delacroix exploited colour and movement to the full in his vast canvasses, such as *The Death of Sardanapalus* (1827) taken from an oriental verse play by Byron.

Francisco de Goya spanned a wide range of themes and approaches, from traditional court paintings to work which touched on the irrational and nightmarish, most graphically in his depictions of the horrors of the guerrilla war in Spain. Similar forces were seen in the works of English artists such as Henry Fuseli and William Blake. Blake's etchings depict an imaginary, visionary world, while Fuseli, an admirer of Blake's work, created an often grotesque world in works such as *Nightmare* (1782). Such turbulent forces even lurked in the pastoral painting of John Constable, whose deceptively calm, rural scenes disguise great vigour and movement in their cloudscapes. These qualities were taken even further in the works of J.M.W. Turner, whose later paintings lose virtually all attempt at representation in a haze of light and colour. In the hands of the German painters Caspar David Friedrich and Philipp Otto Runge, landscape could be seen to reflect the state of mind of the figure depicted within it.

Fingal's Cave

An intrinsic part of the Romantic movement was a feeling for wild and desolate landscapes, including those rich in Scandinavian and Celtic mythology. Dr Johnson explored the wild Hebrides in the company of his biographer James Boswell and the late 18th and early 19th centuries provided a ready market for works of literature and music that evoked these associations. The island of Staffa off the west coast of Mull, with its dramatic rock formations and mythological associations,

provided inspiration for the 20-year-old Felix Mendelssohn on his visit in 1829. His concert overture *The Hebrides*, also known as *Fingal's Cave*, attempted to convey his impression of its majesty. First performed in London in 1832, it was typical of Romantic compositions that attempted to describe scenery or literary subjects.

By the 1840s, painting, like literature, was beginning to enter a realist phase and was more influenced by social themes, as seen in the work of British painters such as David Wilkie and William Frith and French artist Gustave Courbet, whose slogan was that "the artist must be of his own time". The court was increasingly left behind.

Eugène Delacroix was the leading French painter of the Romantic movement. Favouring exotic historical themes, marked by their violence, frenzy, and drama, he brought an emotional force to his paintings far removed from the neoclassicism of the pre-revolutionary era. The Death of Sardanapalus (1827) conjures up a world of oriental eroticism and violence, a favoured theme of Romantic writers, who often placed extremities of action and feeling in a mythologized "oriental" setting.

The High Renaissance 220–1 ▶

The Enlightenment 260–1 ▶

Literature, Music, and Photography 378–9 ▶

Interwar Culture 420–3 ▶

Counterculture and Mass Culture 470–1 ▶

NATION-STATE AND EMPIRE

1849–1914

POLITICS AND GOVERNMENT

1859–61 France and Piedmont defeat Austria in war. Revolutions in central Italy and Garibaldi's victory in the south lead to King Victor Emmanuel II proclaimed king of Italy.

1867 Austro-Hungarian compromise creates dual monarchy. Austria-Hungary receives a federal structure. Magyars dominate the east; Germans dominate the west.

1870–1 Franco-Prussian War: France is defeated, Napoleon III captured. German Empire proclaimed at Versailles, with William I as Emperor. Paris Commune is crushed.

1879 Germany and Austria-Hungary sign Dual Alliance as Bismarck tries to bind Austria-Hungary to the new German order.

1866 Habsburgs defeated by Prussia at Sadowa; North German Confederation created. Italy gains Venice.

1856 Peace of Paris ends the Crimean War. The Holy Alliance is broken, and the Italian Question is opened.

1878 Congress of Berlin. Bismarck tries to stabilize the new Europe, and Russia is thwarted in the Near East.

1840   **1850**   **1860**   **1870**

SOCIETY AND CULTURE

1850 Cross-Channel telegraph cable laid, part of communications revolution that brings Europe closer together.

1873 Financial crisis in Europe precipitates the Great Depression, which lasts until 1896, providing much impetus for socialism across Europe.

1861 Tsar Alexander II of Russia abolishes serfdom.

1874 First Impressionist exhibition in Paris.

THE LION OF THE SEASON.

1859 Charles Darwin publishes *On the Origin of the Species*, leading to a radical shift in the way humans are perceived in relation to nature and one another.

1867 Manet paints *The Execution of Emperor Maximilian*, a critical appraisal of Napoleon III's foreign policy in Mexico.

1876 Richard Wagner's *Der Ring des Nibelungen* fir performed. Predicts catastrophic results from th pursuit of capitalism. Alexander Graham Bell invents the telephone.

314

1898 Fashoda incident in Sudan between Britain and France effectively ends French hopes of re-establishing its influence in Egypt.

1904 Entente cordiale signed between Britain and France ends colonial disputes and paves the way for military co-operation.

1882 Germany, Austria-Hungary, and Italy sign the Triple Alliance, as Bismarck seeks to keep Europe secure and reassure Austria-Hungary.

1897 Germany begins to build a major battle fleet with the aim of challenging Britain's naval supremacy and its empire; this creates tension between Britain and Germany.

1905 Bloody Sunday massacre in St Petersburg begins the 1905 Revolution. The tsar is shaken and grants a constitution and parliament.

1893 Alliance between France and Russia in common desire to preserve peace.

1914 Assassination of Archduke Franz Ferdinand begins Europe's slide into World War I. Serbia rejects some of Austria-Hungary's demands as the great powers declare war on one another.

1890   1900   1910   1920

1895 Guglielmo Marconi invents the wireless radio, easing communications. Lumière brothers invent motion picture camera in France. Continental Europe pushes ahead of Britain in the age of new discovery.

1909 Louis Blériot makes the first flight across the Channel in a plane. The age of aviation has reached Europe.

1885 Gottlieb Daimler invents internal combustion engine and Karl Benz builds single-cylinder engine for the car. Germany dominates invention towards the end of the century.

1898 The novelist Zola writes a famous defence of Captain Dreyfus, unjustly accused of being a traitor, in a French national newspaper.

1907 The Hague Convention formulates much of the law governing the conduct of international warfare.

1903 Women's Social and Political Union established in Britain to campaign for female suffrage and advocates increasingly violent means.

1884 Charles Parsons builds first usable steam engine, making deep-shaft mining easier and fuelling industrial development, especially in Germany.

1901 Completion of Trans-Siberian Railway. Russia is able to push its influence into the Far East; transport within Russia is eased.

The Crimean War

The Crimean War of 1854–6 was born of a Franco-Russian quarrel over the rights of Catholic and Orthodox priests in the Ottoman Empire. The British and French were also concerned with supporting the Ottoman Empire, control of access to the Black Sea, and growing Russian power. The war was bitter and bloody, and ended in Russian defeat.

Tsar Nicholas I, Tsar of all the Russias. The tsar's intransigence and determination to protect the rights of Orthodox monks in the Ottoman Empire helped precipitate the Crimean war. The accession of Alexander II paved the way for peace amongst the exhausted protagonists, but defeat during the war was to weaken severely Russian military credibility.

By the 1850s, conflict was growing between Russia and the other powers of Europe, principally as a result of the attempts by Russia to encroach upon the Turkish Empire, dubbed by Tsar Nicholas I of Russia the "sick man" of Europe. Russia sought to increase its influence over the Christian Slav peoples of the Balkans and, if possible, annex territory. Moreover, Russia's exclusive claims to protect the rights of Christians in the "Holy Places" of Palestine had led to a diplomatic conflict with France, in which the French emperor Napoleon III sided with the Turks against the Russians and was prepared to protect Turkey against any acts of Russian aggression.

Russia was confident it could defeat France if the other great powers – Britain, Prussia, and the Habsburg Empire – remained neutral. Once France was defeated, Russian power at the court of the Ottomans would be reasserted. However, the other powers were far from neutral: Britain and France were equally determined to prop up the Ottomans as an independent power. Only a stable Ottoman

Empire, with its Turkish heartland secure, would bar Russia from threatening their interests in the Near East and Britain's position in India.

In July 1853, Russian troops crossed into the Ottomans' Danubian Principalities in order to threaten Turkey. The resulting rounds of diplomacy saw the Habsburgs decide to stay neutral, fearing the Russian threat to their own territories in the Danube and the French threat to Italy. Napoleon III had long been obsessed with helping the cause of Italian nationalism, and the Habsburgs rightly feared that, should they join with Russia in the Near East, Napoleon III might support an Italian bid to expel Austria from Italy. Prussia also stayed neutral. The Prussians had no interest in the Near East except to ensure that Russia did not overrun the Habsburg Empire. Furthermore, Prussia would never side against Russia, on whom it was dependent to keep the nationalist Poles in check in Prussia.

As the Russian threat grew in the Near East, Britain and France, fearing a Russian assault on

British Nurse Florence Nightingale can be seen here tending the wounded following the Battle of Alma in September 1854, when the allies defeated the Russians during the Crimean War. Conditions for servicemen on both sides were notoriously poor, and far more died as a result of disease or poor living conditions than from combat. Criticism of medical facilities by journalists such as W.H. Russell of The Times *prompted the government to allow Nightingale to take nurses to the Crimea.*

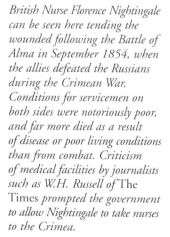

The charge of the Light Brigade on 25 October 1854 during the Battle of Balaklava was immortalized through the poetry of Lord Alfred Tennyson. Balaklava was a victory for the British, French, and Turkish forces; however, the action of the Light Brigade in charging the Russian artillery and the subsequent heavy losses came to be seen as a terrible military blunder.

Turkey, sent their fleets to Constantinople. Napoleon III was an arch-adventurer and with the Napoleonic legacy of his uncle ever present; he was desperate to overthrow the conservative system that had held Europe in its grip since 1815. By securing a victory against Russia, Napoleon believed that he would make steps towards breaking the stranglehold the great powers had imposed on France at Vienna. He also hoped to establish his own reputation for glorious endeavour with the French public, while simultaneously making an ally of Britain. The British simply wanted to keep Turkey intact as a buffer state.

War declared

In March 1854, Britain and France declared war on Russia. In April, they made a formal alliance and sent their forces to protect Constantinople and shortly after, to invade the Crimea. Britain's greatest military asset was its navy, and the Royal Navy could only be used to check the tsar in an area accessible by sea. The Crimea was the obvious choice. The British and French secured benevolent neutrality from Austria. The Habsburgs feared the presence of the Russian army in the Balkans, where Austrian rule was precarious. Consequently, the Habsburg emperor agreed four "points" as war aims to which the tsar must agree. The most important of these was a revision of the Straits Convention of 1841, in which France and Britain had joined forces to prevent Russian control of the area. The British, French, and Austrians now intended to bar Russia from the Black Sea.

The war in the Crimea reached a bloody stalemate. For the allies, the French provided the majority of the soldiers and Britain the naval support. On each side, the armies were beset with poor leadership, lack of supplies, and inadequate medical conditions. The Western allies besieged the Russian fortress of Sebastopol from November 1854, but faced dogged Russian resistance. The Austrians agreed to mobilize their Balkan armies to keep the Russians pinned down in the Danube area in an attempt to force the Russians to negotiate. In January 1855, Piedmont also joined in the coalition against the tsar. After the death of Nicholas I and under mounting international pressure, Russia agreed to negotiate. The resulting peace conference in Vienna failed, and the allies went back to war in the Crimea. When Sebastopol fell in September 1855, Britain and France were at a loss as to what should be their next move.

With Russia exhausted and Britain fearing a continental backlash against it, the warring sides eventually turned to peace in 1856. The war had cost over 500,000 lives, two-thirds from disease.

The aftermath

The Paris Peace Treaty of 30 March 1856 could never really bolster the faltering Turks or change the balance of power in the Black Sea once Britain and France left. The real results were in central Europe, where the myth of Russian military power was destroyed until 1945. Moreover, the Holy Alliance of Austria, Prussia, and Russia had broken down irretrievably. When Russia was threatened, Austria had assumed armed neutrality, and Prussia refused to be drawn into a struggle where it had nothing to gain and everything to lose. Europe was left open to the ambitions of Napoleon III, heir to the revolutionary tradition. The Crimean War completed the work of 1848 in ending the system with which Metternich had hoped to keep Europe stable. The Russians were to spend much of the rest of the century trying to revise the restrictions imposed on them in the Black Sea.

The Ottoman Empire   254–5 ▶

The Napoleonic Wars   290–1 ▶

Reforms in Russia 1855–81   318–19▶

A Changing Empire   350–1 ▶

Reforms in Russia: 1855–81

The Crimean War had been an enormous strain on Russia and provided massive impetus to reform what was essentially a very backward society. Poor health and shortages of equipment had been the scourge of the tsar's army. There was also widespread concern about the practical and moral implications of the existence of serfdom in Russia. In 1858, Tsar Alexander II became committed to emancipating the serfs, which was to be the first of many steps on the road to bringing tsarist Russia into the industrial age – or at least the same century as Western Europe.

The Russian Empire was by far the biggest in Europe, but its size and climate created socio-economic constraints on development faced by no other power. Russia's vast natural resources of coal, iron, oil, and gold were often inaccessible, and it encompassed a huge range of nationalities, cultures, and languages, including more than half the world's Jews. Governing such an enormous empire would never be easy.

Russia's government and social structure reflected its military foundations. Politically, the tsar was the sole ruler ordained by God under the "Fundamental Laws", which gave him unlimited autocratic power. Theoretically, the "Tsar of all the Russias" had the allegiance of the nobility, army, bureaucracy, and the Orthodox Church. He certainly needed all these just to govern effectively.

The emancipation of the serfs

Tsar Alexander II attempted to implement substantial changes in the country's social and political system. In 1861, the serfs were emancipated. Serfs were labourers who could not be removed from their lord's land and who were transferred with that land when it passed to another owner. Their emancipation meant that all peasants in Russia were freed from their former masters. The freedom was purchased by tax, which also paid for them to have a share in the village land. The peasants then became members of the village commune or *mir*, which would allocate land on a collective basis and was responsible for paying taxes and redemption dues on behalf of the individual. In 1864, local government was introduced in the form of local assemblies, or *zemstvas*. The army and

This contemporary painting by Alexej Karsuchin of a Russian peasant scene helps to show the rudimentary nature of family life. Most Russians were peasants in the 19th century and were used to a life of domestic hardships and backbreaking toil.

the judicial system were also reformed. This programme of change created political opposition, but also great optimism.

In 1870, municipal government was reformed. Limited autonomy had already been extended to Moscow and Odessa in 1862–3. After 1870, voting rights allowed all-estate representation in the municipal council, or *duma*, although this was qualified on the basis of tax and property ownership. The duma could manage city finances and a broad range of responsibilities, although the budgetary powers of these councils were weak. The city councils aroused little enthusiasm from the nobility and were dominated by representatives of trade and industry. The sense of class identity that evolved as a consequence was to have more serious repercussions once Russia became more industrialized. The conflicts between municipal government and central administration that followed led to an emergence of radicals, political consciousness, and a sense of identity that fostered a readiness to oppose the tsarist regime.

A rural economy

The social structure of 19th-century Russia was overwhelmingly rural with perhaps only 10 per cent of the population living in urban areas. Agriculture was central to the Russian way of life, and the majority of both rich and poor made their living from the land. The landowning nobles dominated rural Russia, and the loss of serfdom made it much harder for them to manage their estates. The poor climate and communications made it difficult to attract migrant rural labour, and there was limited

technology and expertise to develop the land. Between 1861 and 1905, the quantity of land held by nobles fell by one-third. Emancipation created great anxiety on the part of the nobles. In their attempts to maintain control of the peasantry, they combined with the government keep peasants isolated and under strict local authority. In addition, their failure to update traditional farming techniques led to relative rural economic decline, which further undermined the role of the nobility itself. The landowners were usually staunchly loyal to the government, but their power was ebbing.

Before emancipation, the serfs had been subject to taxes, long military service, travel restrictions, and corporal punishment. Yet the reality of emancipation was a great disappointment. Peasants were expected to pay for their freedom in redemption payments to the government over 49 years. As the rural population grew, land became scarcer. The mir now took decisions formerly taken by landowners. Most labour was done by hand, and productivity remained between one-third and half that of Western Europe.

The 1866 attempt on Alexander II's life and his assassination in 1881 seemed to realize the fears of those who opposed reform. Yet without further reform Russia would be left isolated as a second-rate power at the mercy of the industrialized states, particularly Germany, Britain, and, increasingly, the USA. Russia had been defeated by two industrialized powers in the Crimea and was trying to contest control of Central Asia with Britain. After 1870 Russia faced the threat of the newly united German Empire.

Sweden, Russia, and the Baltic 252–3 ►
The 1905 Revolution 346–7 ►
The Russian Revolution 402–3 ►
Lenin and the Russian Civil War 414–15►

Italian Unification

After the defeat of the 1848 revolutions in Italy, the liberals and nationalists seemed to be in retreat. The established order had won the day, and the dreams of the revolutionaries for an Italian state lay in ruins. Yet, within 22 years, the Italians – with help from neighbouring states – had made an Italian state a reality.

In 1848, the liberals and nationalists had been crushed resoundingly. Only Piedmont, where Victor Emmanuel II had retained a limited constitution, had any semblance of revolutionary activity. Yet there were signs that the restored regimes were shaken, and the rise of Napoleon III in France, with his deep sympathy for Italian nationalism, offered some promise of better times to come.

A combination of factors was to transform the fate of nationalism on the Italian peninsula. Pressure from the nationalist movement helped to shape and define the march towards a nation-state. The leadership of established states married their ambition to those of the nationalists, while states in decline made concessions to nationalism or were simply too weak to resist. In addition,

other great powers were prepared to use force to overcome the many obstacles in the path to the creation of a unified Italy. War and diplomacy made Italy.

The events of 1848 seemed to show the nationalists that they needed force to achieve their dreams. The hopes of all Italian nationalists began to unite, with republican, liberal, federal, and democratic nationalists focussing their hopes on the one liberal, independent Italian monarchy – Piedmont. Vincenzo Gioberti renounced his plans for a papal federation, Daniele Manin gave up his dreams of a federal republic, and even Giuseppe Garibaldi, the hero of 1848, saw Victor Emmanuel as the possible future king of Italy.

There was also a perceptible change in the nature of nationalism throughout the course of Italian unification. Nationalists grew more realistic after the disappointments of 1848–9. Parochial and ideological differences were put to one side as Piedmontese leadership was accepted more and more in the pursuit of the national goal. The links between nationalism and liberalism were loosened, and national identity began to be promoted to reinforce loyalty to the state, not as a threat to the establishment. Nationalism was becoming conservative, middle class, and respectable. Similar trends could be detected across the whole of Europe from Britain to Germany after the 1850s: established states invested in nationalism and the nationalists bought into the establishment. But with Austria re-established in the north and the pope firmly set against liberalism and nationalism, the idea of a unified state appeared as far away as ever.

Piedmontese power

Victor Emmanuel II, king of Piedmont, began to see the merits of extending Piedmontese (and his own) power through the popular appeal of nationalism. Victor Emmanuel was one of the new breed of politicians who sought revolutionary aims without revolutionary means. With Cavour as premier, Piedmontese military spending increased, trade trebled, and 1800 kilometres (1125 miles) of railway was laid. Cavour almost certainly had no clear plan to establish Italian unification. He simply saw that to extend Piedmontese influence he had to expel Austria from Italy, which could not be done without assistance from a great power, in this case France. Italy could not make itself – it needed to be made by France. The Crimean War had shattered the Holy Alliance, which meant that Austria could no longer rely on Russian aid in quashing its insurgencies. Prussia demanded that, in exchange

Camillo di Cavour
Before 1848 Cavour was a moderate liberal nationalist and editor of *il Risorgimento* newspaper. But he was utterly loyal to the Piedmontese monarchy and rejected revolution and democracy. From 1852 he was premier of Piedmont and sought to promote Piedmont as the leader of Italy, encouraging both military and economic development.

for helping Austria, it expected Austrian recognition of Prussian dominance in Germany as the price. Austria was not prepared to pay – swapping Germany for Italy was not a fair bargain, and it ended up with neither. Britain also would not intervene: the Tory government disliked Napoleon III, but the British public disliked Austria far more, and Italian nationalism had long been one of the most fashionable and popular causes in British politics. Cavour was prepared to exploit the international situation to further his ambitions for Piedmont. With Austria isolated, it was time to strike.

French intervention

Before 1860, the key figure in Italy was Napoleon III. The legacy of Napoleon I's victories in the peninsula had filled Napoleon III with a strong desire to "do something for Italy". Napoleon thought that, if he could overthrow the Viennese settlement in Italy, it might crumble across Europe without recourse to a revolutionary war.

In 1858, Felice Orsini, an Italian nationalist, had tried to assassinate Napoleon. At his trial, Orsini appealed to Napoleon to help his country. Although Orsini was eventually executed, Napoleon did respond to his appeal by making the secret Treaty Plombières with Cavour in 1858. The two sides agreed that a war with Austria must be engineered in Italy, but engineering a war would not be so easy. Nevertheless, with Piedmontese help, the French agreed to drive the enfeebled Austrians out of Lombardy and Venetia in return for Savoy and Nice. The French sought to replace Austrian influence in Italy with a weak Italian state subservient to France. Napoleon wanted to help Piedmont create a Kingdom of North Italy at

Austria's expense, establish a Kingdom of the Central Italian States under French patronage, and ensure papal leadership of Italy. The French army became indispensable in the establishment of the Italian nation.

The War of 1859

The Plombières meeting in July 1858 was crucial to the unification of Italy. Napoleon III and Camillo de Cavour, now a leading proponent of unification, agreed four points: that Prince Jerome of France would marry Victor Emmanuel's daughter; that Piedmont and France would join in a war with Austria; that Italy would be a federation under the pope (to please Napoleon's Catholic public in France); and that Piedmont would surrender Savoy to Napoleon, thus restoring the "natural frontiers" of France and satisfying his people's desire for *la gloire*. Cavour's duty was to find a non-revolutionary pretext for war with Austria, while Napoleon ensured that the Habsburgs were diplomatically isolated. As Austria was already isolated, it certainly seemed Cavour had the harder task. Unfortunately for him, Austria had done nothing to give grounds for conflict. The Austrian presence in Italy was entirely in accordance with internationally recognized agreements signed at Vienna.

Yet Austria ultimately came to Cavour's rescue. The Habsburgs were emboldened by what they perceived as Prussian and British sympathy, and they wanted to teach Cavour a lesson. The Austrians believed that Napoleon would hesitate rather than face war and hoped to lure Britain onto their side. In April 1859, Austria demanded Piedmont be disarmed before the two sides could negotiate the future of Italy. Cavour rejected the demand, and, on 29 April, Austrian troops invaded Piedmont. Next, on 3 May, Napoleon announced that France would defend the Piedmontese. Through impatience and rashness, Austria had opened the way for the reconstruction of Europe and the breaking of the 1815 mould.

The war was truly unique in that, to avoid blame, Napoleon and Cavour were dependent on Austria attacking – the Austrians duly obliged. In trying to remake Italy, the Piedmontese and French were acting contrary to all law and yet they enjoyed widespread support.

In June, Austria suffered two major defeats: 4 June saw the country defeated at Magenta and driven from Lombardy; and, on 24 June, the Habsburgs attempted to break out of their fortresses in the Quadrilateral and were defeated at Solferino. Yet the Austrian armies were still intact and indeed entrenched in the heavily fortified Quadrilateral. More fighting would be required to expel them from the whole of Italy.

On 24 June, the Prussians mobilized their army, seeking to intimidate France into an armed mediation. Napoleon III was terrified of a Prussian attack and had been sickened by his own experience of the fighting, while the Austrians began to fear that the other powers would unite against them and impose a harsh settlement. Therefore, on 12 July, a peace settlement between France and Austria was signed at Villafranca, according to which Austria ceded Milan to France. To Cavour's chagrin, the Austrians were still firmly in place in Venetia.

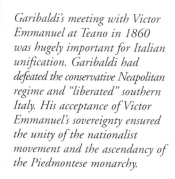

Garibaldi's meeting with Victor Emmanuel at Teano in 1860 was hugely important for Italian unification. Garibaldi had defeated the conservative Neapolitan regime and "liberated" southern Italy. His acceptance of Victor Emmanuel's sovereignty ensured the unity of the nationalist movement and the ascendancy of the Piedmontese monarchy.

Towards an Italian state

Unforeseen by Napoleon, the war in the north had sparked off events elsewhere in Italy, with a series of revolts in the central Italian states. The Italian National Society in the central states had established committees across Italy as a link between Cavour and the radicals. In the central states, 20,000 volunteers joined the revolts. The nationalists in the centre wanted to join with Piedmont. Cavour agreed with Napoleon that plebiscites in the central states would be held, along with plebiscites in Nice and Savoy. France was given Nice and Savoy, and Piedmont received the Italian states.

To Cavour's further dismay, a revolt in Sicily against Francis II, king of the Two Sicilies, flared up in April 1860. Garibaldi took 1000 men, the Red Shirts, from Piedmont to aid the revolutionaries. Improbably, he conquered Sicily and crossed into mainland Naples, where he defeated the Neapolitan armies in September 1860.

Garibaldi's success was a threat to Cavour, however, as Garibaldi sought a democratic Italy centred on Rome, which would mean expelling the French army there. Cavour and Victor Emmanuel had to outbid Garibaldi for domination of the peninsula. Cavour gambled and invaded the Papal States, but avoided Rome. Although many of the inhabitants wanted southern Italy as a republic, with Garibaldi its leader, Garibaldi's loyalties lay with Victor Emmanuel, recognizing him as king of Italy when he met Victor Emanuel's army in 1860. Piedmont and Garibaldi had conquered Italy. In March 1861, a parliament from all of Italy except Venetia and Rome announced that Victor Emmanuel was king of Italy, and Italy was made

Venetia and Rome still remained outside the Italian state. It would take foreign wars and not nationalism, to unify the rest of Italy. In 1866, Italy supported Bismarck's Prussia against Austria and received Venetia, excluding South Tyrol and Istria, when Prussia won. Once again, the Austrians would not trade hegemony in Germany for their presence in Italy, and once again they lost both.

Irredentism

In 1870, when the French were at war with Prussia, the French army in Rome was recalled to fight Bismarck. The Italians simply occupied Rome, and the new Italy was almost complete. But it was not the Italy dreamt of by idealistic Italian republicans prior to 1848. Only 2 per cent of the populace could vote and only a similar number could speak Italian.

The Unification of Italy
1848–71

■ Kingdom of Piedmont-Sardinia, 1815 (with Nice and Savoy)

▨ Gained by Piedmont, 1859

▨ Gained by Piedmont, 1860

▨ Ceded to France, 1860

▨ Gained by Piedmont, 1860

■ Gained by Italy after Austro-Prussian War, 1866

▨ Gained by Italy after Franco-Prussian War, 1870

➤ Garibaldi's advance, 1860

This map shows the very different events that unified Italy. French soldiers helped gain Lombardy for Piedmont. The central states threw off their rulers to join Piedmont. Garibaldi conquered the Two Sicilies. Prussian victories against Austria and France delivered Venetia and then Rome to Italy.

Irredentism – the desire to recover outstanding Italian lands – still remained in Italy. There was a strong sense of inferiority to the established states accompanied by a desire to "create" an Italian character and incorporate the remaining Italian peoples in Trentino, Trieste, and elsewhere into the new state. Massimo d'Azeglio, the premier and author, had said as early as 1861 that "We have made Italy, now we must make Italians". This theme was to reoccur later in Italian history.

The Italians believed that colonies and military conquest would establish a feeling of national identity among the people. Despite Italy's defeat in Abyssinia in 1896, its conquest of Libya in 1912 was seen as proof of its national strength and the prowess of its people. Journals such as *l'Idea Nazionale*, along with the Nationalist Party established in 1910, espoused the importance of completing the work of Cavour and conquering the Italian lands still under foreign yoke.

With the enormous importance attached to military prowess, Italy's entry into World War I was guaranteed; neutrality was not an option. It remained to be seen whose side it would join. The promise of the complete unification of Italy made joining the allies a certainty. In 1918, Italy acquired South Tyrol, having suffered terrible losses.

The Napoleonic Wars 290–1 ▶
The Revolutions of 1848–9 302–3 ▶
Nationalism and Empire 358–9 ▶
Italy: 1918–39 412–13 ▶

Bismarck and German Unification

In 1871, the Germans had a unified state and the Reichstag had universal suffrage. Even with the Prussian king Wilhelm I as emperor, it was a distinctly German empire. It appeared that the aspirations of 1848 had been realized, yet it took three wars and years of Bismarckian diplomacy to create Germany.

The German Burschenshaften, *student societies, were powerful vehicles for nationalism during the conservative years after 1848. With organized duelling and other festivals, students celebrated their culture and spread their ideas away from the sight of the authorities. A new generation of Germans grew up steeped in the desire to unify their land.*

Germany was not unified by a sudden act or revolution, but by hard diplomacy and warfare over a period of several years. The German Empire which emerged in 1871 was not the Grossdeutschland *many had hoped for. Instead the new Germany excluded Austria altogether. Prussia was very definitely the dominant power.*

After 1848, the question of a united Germany was placed firmly on the political agenda. Bismarck wanted a Germany unified under Prussian leadership. He sought to exclude the liberals as far as possible and keep the monarchy independent (except of himself). The Italian unification of 1859 revived German nationalism, leading to the establishment of a *Nationalverein* (National Association) in Hanover in 1859. The Nationalverein was liberal and middle class, and sought Prussian leadership with the hope that Prussia could be the "the German Piedmont". The *Burschenschaften* (student clubs) in the universities became vehicles of underground nationalist expression. Fear of

Napoleon III on the Rhine also spurred German nationalists, particularly after the French annexed Nice and Savoy. Following the failure of the Frankfurt Parliament, the new German nationalists admired power more than ideology. Only Prussia had the power to unify Germany.

At the end of the 1850s, Prussia's king Wilhelm I was seen as the defender of Germany against France. In Prussia in 1862, the liberal-dominated *Landtag* (legislative assembly) clashed with the king over army reforms. When Bismarck was appointed prime minister, he resolved the crisis by dissolving the Landtag and passing the army reforms. Bismarck chose to ignore the liberals, and

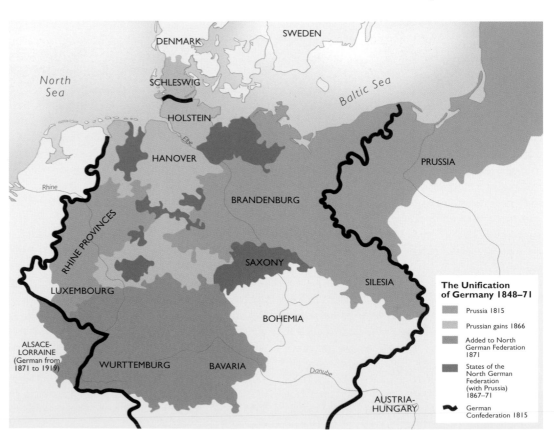

The Unification of Germany 1848–71

- Prussia 1815
- Prussian gains 1866
- Added to North German Federation 1871
- States of the North German Federation (with Prussia) 1867–71
- German Confederation 1815

1849–1914

the hopes of a liberal nationalism subsided to be replaced with a more pragmatic approach.

Bismarck excluded Austria from the German customs union, or *Zollverein*, in 1865; the Zollverein included most of the German states, and to many it seemed the precursor of a united Germany. Despite this, the majority of the Zollverein did not join with Prussia against Austria in 1866; it was not the Zollverein that created Germany. The Prussian economy had boomed during the 1850s, making Prussia even more powerful within the German Confederation and giving Bismarck the strength to challenge Austria.

Liberal nationalists in Prussia saw Bismarck as a dangerous reactionary, a view that was reinforced by Bismarck's actions over Schleswig-Holstein. In 1864, when faced with the question of succession in Schleswig-Holstein, Prussia and Austria fought briefly against Denmark over the annexing of Schleswig, and they decided to frame the future of the two duchies between themselves – this was to be the pretext for the Austro-Prussian War. Bismarck circumvented the German Confederation's attempts to resolve the issue on a national basis and dealt directly with the problem himself, pursuing Prussian policies ahead of German ones In 1866, he did this again to gain Holstein from Austria and expel the Habsburgs from northern Germany.

When Bismarck's policy led to war with Austria in 1866, he appealed to nationalist sentiment in Germany. The nationalists ignored him. Prussia was seen as playing old-fashioned power politics, while Austria had the support of Saxony, Hanover, Bavaria, Württemburg, and Baden. Prussia had succeeded in provoking a civil war, not a war of national liberation. This changed after the Prussian victory at Sadowa in 1866, when Bismarck created the North German Confederation. The nationalists were intoxicated by the realization of their *Kleindeutschland* dream, and their opposition to Bismarck ebbed away. Bismarck was creating a national, although not a liberal, Germany.

Liberal opposition to Bismarck was similarly shelved. Many liberals were willing to accept Bismarck, as he was the only man capable of uniting Germany – a long-cherished dream – even if it meant sacrificing some of their liberal aspirations. The Prussian chancellor was now under pressure from the nationalists to include the south German states in the new Germany. Bismarck himself thought his position against France and Austria would be strengthened by union with the southern states. The Prussians were constrained, however, by fear of creating a national and liberal state, which might limit the power of the Prussian king and chancellor. Bismarck was also wary of the

Otto von Bismarck was recalled from his post as ambassador to Russia in 1862 and offered the position of Prussian chancellor. He soon dissolved the Landtag, overruling its opposition to army reforms. His mastery of diplomacy helped him to unify Germany, and he became German chancellor in 1871, an office he held until dismissed in 1890.

accession of the predominantly Catholic south to his new Germany. As Bismarck waited, nationalists grew more restless.

Bismarck exploited an international dispute over succession to the Spanish throne to provoke a war with France. He orchestrated the situation, resulting in a wave of patriotic fervour throughout Germany, including the southern states. The Prussian victory against France at Sedan led to enormous popular pressure for unification, which Bismarck encouraged. The German Empire, which was declared in the Hall of Mirrors in Versailles in January 1871, included some recognition of the south German princes. The constitution made reference to the national legitimacy of the new state.

Nationalism in 1862–71 had not played a direct role in the unification of Germany, but it did shape Bismarck's policies for Prussia. A German identity was at the heart of the new empire. Bismarck was a politician of realpolitik – the politics of pragmatism, rather than ideology. He had ridden the wave of popular sentiment to secure Prussian dominance in Germany, the dominance of the kaiser (emperor) in the new state, and his influence over the kaiser. His greatest creation was the transformation of the German Confederation from a loose group of states into the German Empire, with the complete exclusion of Austria. He then had to spend much of the remainder of his career propping up Austria as an independent state to justify its exclusion from Germany and secure his southern flank. Maintaining a balance of power in the Europe he had created was a hugely taxing job for any statesman, but as the wars of 1866 and 1870 showed, he was a true master of the diplomatic arts.

The Prussian Wars

Bismarck was unparalleled in the arts of diplomacy and outmanoeuvred a number of opponents. He recognized that the world had changed since 1848 and that the old order and the international system were lost. He was driven by consistent aims to enhance Prussian power in Germany, and remodelled Germany and Europe to Prussia's advantage. First he had to exclude Austria from Germany and overcome the ever-present threat of France.

Von Moltke in Versailles. Von Moltke was in command of the Prussian armies, and masterminded the emphatic defeats of both the Habsburg and the French armies between 1866 and 1871. The new and highly professional Prussian and German armies he created became models for the rest of Europe.

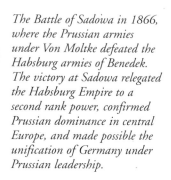

The Battle of Sadowa in 1866, where the Prussian armies under Von Moltke defeated the Habsburg armies of Benedek. The victory at Sadowa relegated the Habsburg Empire to a second rank power, confirmed Prussian dominance in central Europe, and made possible the unification of Germany under Prussian leadership.

Prussia's first international drama under Bismarck occurred in 1864. In 1863, the Danish had attempted to incorporate the duchies of Schleswig and Holstein more completely into Denmark. German nationalists opposed these moves and hoped the German Confederation would endorse the claim of the Duke of Augustenburg to the Schleswig-Holstein throne. Bismarck ignored this and planned for Prussia to annex the duchies. He made a pact with Austria to divide Schleswig and Holstein between Prussia and Austria, on condition that the German Confederation and its Federal Diet would not be involved. After a short war against Denmark, Prussia and Austria occupied Schleswig and Holstein, respectively. In his dealing with the affair, Bismarck claimed to be acting on rights laid down in the Treaty of London of 1852. When the Austrians violated their pact with Prussia over the fate of the duchies, Bismarck was able to ensure that Prussia's rise to power would not be hijacked by a nationalist campaign. In 1864, Austria began to press for the Duke of Augustenburg to be recognized as ruler of the duchies. When Bismarck insisted that the duke would have to be totally dependent on Prussia, the German Diet sided with Austria. Although an agreement was reached, tension continued to mount between Prussia and Austria. In October 1865, Bismarck met Napoleon at Biarritz to ensure French neutrality in the event of an Austro-Prussian war. Bismarck made an alliance with Italy, granting the latter Venetia in a war with Austria. Napoleon III was now certain to remain neutral because Bismarck had offered him a chance to help unify Italy, his long-standing dream. Bismarck had succeeded in isolating Austria and, in 1866, challenged Austria, risking war.

The Austro-Prussian War

The issue was now one of strength, and Prussia had been growing stronger than Austria since the

In 1870 the French under Napoleon III were comprehensively beaten and surrendered to the North German Confederation at Sedan. Napoleon was captured, and France became a republic once more. The French defeat signalled the arrival of Germany as the hegemonic power on the continent and created a friction between the two countries which did not ease until Germany's total defeat in 1945.

1850s. The Austrians needed eight weeks to mobilize, whereas Prussia, because of its far superior railways, needed only three. It was crucial, then, that Austria move first. Fearing Italian attack, the Austrians mobilized in April 1866, thus making Bismarck appear the victim of Austrian aggression. On 1 June, Austria referred the duchies question to the Federal Diet, infringing its agreement with Prussia. In response, Bismarck occupied Holstein. On 14 June, an Austrian motion for a Federal mobilization was passed, and Prussia declared the end of the German Confederation and invaded Saxony. Austria had been tormented beyond endurance by Bismarck and had provoked war.

The Austro-Prussian War was extremely brief. The Prussian railways allowed the commander, von Moltke, to place a superior army in the field before Austria. On 3 July 1866 the Austrians were routed at Sadowa and Austrian hegemony in Germany was ended. Austria was excluded from German affairs, Prussia had military hegemony north of the river Main, the southern states were independent, and the German Confederation was dissolved. The balance of power in Europe had been altered at a stroke.

The Franco-Prussian War

The French realized that their neutrality had been bought in order for Prussia to dominate Germany and that Napoleon had gained very little from this agreement. Napoleon now demanded some form of compensation in the form of French aggrandisement in Belgium and Luxembourg. French public opinion became fervently in favour of territorial expansion. In 1867, the king of Holland publicly announced that he had made an agreement with France over Luxembourg; German public sentiment was outraged, as Luxembourg had a German garrison.

Faced with a growing crisis, Napoleon found himself without an ally. Britain made a pact with Bismarck to defend Luxembourg, and Russia would not ally with France because of lingering disputes in the Near East and fear of the Germans arousing Polish rebellion. Austria would only ally with France if it had French support in the Near East against Russia, but the French were more concerned with central than Eastern Europe. The French government backed down, but the French public was seething.

It was the dispute between Prussia and France over the succession to the Spanish throne that precipitated the crisis. When Prussia gave way, Napoleon demanded humiliating concessions from the kaiser, intent on war for its own sake. Bismarck saw that war could be waged on national terms, and he could thereby unite the southern states into Germany under loyalty to his kaiser.

Napoleon III's belief in his military strength and his ability to gain allies were unfounded. The southern German states joined the northern ones against France, and the Prussian army routed the French at Sedan on 2 September 1870, capturing Napoleon. To emphasize the humiliation, Italy invaded Rome in September 1870.

Sedan marked the end of French dominance and confirmed German hegemony, which had been won at Sadowa. The German Empire was constituted in January 1871 including all the southern states. A peace treaty was signed between France and Germany in Frankfurt on 10 May 1871. German ascendancy was proven, and French anger was ensured, particularly by the resulting annexation of Alsace and Lorraine by Germany.

The Origins of World War I   362–3 ▶

A Changing Empire   350–1 ▶

The Second Empire
and Napoleon III   330–1 ▶

Bismarck and
German Unification   324–5 ▶

The Third Republic, which
followed the collapse of the
Second Empire in France in 1870,
was deeply divided. The Paris
Commune, a revolutionary
government elected in Paris in
1871, was brutally suppressed
by government troops from
Versailles. Here, a member of
the Commune poses in front
of barricades just before the
conflict begins.

FRANCE: 1851–1914

France had been the military powerhouse of Europe for at least 100 years. The age of Napoleon Bonaparte had seen French armies and French influence dominate the European continent from Moscow to Madrid, spreading revolutionary fervour and unseating the old regime. Only a coalition of all the European powers had managed to keep France in check, and post-1815 Europe ran on a system designed to maintain this.

In 1851 a new Napoleon, Charles Louis Napoleon Bonaparte, became president and then Emperor of France as Napoleon III. He was devoted to overturning the Vienna settlement. Napoleon's great causes were Italian and Polish nationalism, the spread of the revolution, the establishment of France as Europe's greatest power, and the quest for *la gloire*. In truth, Napoleon III's obsession with Italy was an admission of French weakness, for France was not strong enough to reshape central Europe on its own.

Napoleon III sought to strengthen France, which was falling behind its industrialized neighbour Britain. During eight years of dictatorial rule, he encouraged material progress, building railways, investing in cities, and authorizing investment banks. Abroad, Napoleon tried to remake Europe as safely as he could. He made an ally of Britain and defeated Russia in the Crimean War. The subsequent Treaty of Paris in 1856 was meant to show that France was once again the mightiest power in Europe, yet the defeat of Austria in the Italian war of 1859 proved less popular at home. Moreover, Napoleon had drawn the wrath of the Roman Catholic Church because many Italian nationalists wanted Rome as the capital of their newly united Italy, threatening the pope's temporal domain.

To restore credibility, Napoleon tried to launch a more liberal domestic policy combined with imperialism outside Europe. The liberal policy proved successful, but also gave room for greater criticism of the Empire. The French attempt to rival Britain as a global power was also undermined by its structural weakness. Despite many foreign triumphs, Napoleon's world policy was forever marred by the defeat in Mexico and the assassination of Emperor Maximilian in 1866. In Europe, France had lost its dominant role. The defeat at Sedan and Napoleon's capture in the Franco-Prussian War showed the world that the real force was now Germany.

The Third Republic followed the fall of Napoleon III. The Republic was born in defeat, national humiliation, and the painful loss of Alsace-Lorraine to Germany. Adolphe Thiers, its president in 1871, said that the Republic was "the government which divided Frenchmen least". With absolute and constitutional monarchy, republicanism, and empire all discredited in the previous 100 years; it was no surprise that France contained many factions who sought alternative ways to govern the state. Racked by crisis and scandal, the Third Republic had 60 governments between 1871 and 1914.

Within France, the Third Republic saw social and political division. Externally, France lagged further behind its neighbours: Germany enjoyed a boom after 1871 and was clearly intent on playing a global role commensurate with its power, Britain maintained the world's largest navy and empire, and Russia was seeking influence in China. Consequently, French governments found themselves with limited room for diplomatic manoeuvre, and France seemed to encounter rivalry at every turn. Yet, although torn by division and corruption, the Third Republic helped France make significant economic advancements. The era 1871–1914 is also known as *la belle époque*, when France led Europe in painting, sculpture, music, literature, science, and philosophy. Moreover, when war came in 1914, France was not alone. It had powerful allies and an impressive empire.

The Second Empire and Napoleon III

The Second Empire was born of a coup d'état by Napoleon III. His ambitions were central to its history, as he was determined to live up to the Bonaparte name. He sought to create a centralized France dependent on its authority while challenging the international order. France's internal problems and relative weakness doomed him to failure.

This painting, The Execution of Maximilian, *by Édouard Manet, was a damning commentary on a disastrous foreign policy adventure for Napoleon III. Manet represents the executioners in French military uniform, making it clear that he places the blame for Maximilian's death at France's feet.*

The building of the ironclad warship La Gloire *in 1860 was a triumph for Napoleon III.* La Gloire *had iron armour outside its wooden hull, giving it greater protection. At a stroke, France had stolen a naval lead on Britain, winning Napoleon great prestige. The British navy was prompted to modernize, as tension mounted between the two powers.*

The creation of the Second Empire

Following the 1848 revolution in France, Charles Louis Napoleon Bonaparte galvanized support to become elected president of the Second Republic on 10 December 1848. He immediately set to work on securing his position. He appeased the Roman Catholic Church by sending French forces into Rome in July 1849 to restore the papacy after Pius IX had been expelled by revolutionaries. His 1850 education bill restored Church influence on schooling. With the support of the army, Louis Napoleon launched a coup d'état in December 1851. He dissolved the legislative chamber and called a plebiscite on a new constitution. He won with 92 per cent of the vote and secured for himself a 10-year presidential term and a reduced role for the legislature. In December 1852, a new plebiscite elected Louis Napoleon as Emperor Napoleon III and a Second Empire was proclaimed.

Authoritarian Empire

Napoleon embarked on a mission to make his own authority absolutely secure and to safeguard the Empire. In February 1852, he introduced laws restricting the press. He also targeted workers' societies, schoolteachers, and the republican leadership. In the government of the Empire, ministers had no contact with the legislative body, and appointment of ministers was left solely to Napoleon. In the Senate, the vast majority of members could be appointed for life by the emperor. The Senate itself could only be convened by Napoleon and its measures subjected to his approval. Similarly, the emperor appointed and dismissed the president and vice-president. Sessions of the legislative body were limited to three months annually, and deputies in the legislature had limited powers.

Napoleon was also involved in appointing local prefects, whose powers were increased. Moreover, French tax revenues were distributed by the central government, which meant that a region was very unlikely to receive financial subsidy if local politicians opposed the emperor. The vast majority of Napoleon's officials came from the upper echelons of French military, aristocratic, or professional life. But because Napoleon's ideology was a heterogenous collection of ideas, he never truly accrued a distinct power base and was to rely on the previously established elite of French society.

Restrictions eased

The repressive nature of Napoleon's first eight years in office had begun to have an adverse effect. By 1858, republicans had gained seven of

the ten Paris constituencies, and, fearing a backlash, Napoleon began to liberalize his regime. In 1860, he allowed greater direct contact between the Senate and the legislative body, accompanied by a lifting of press restrictions. In 1861, the legislature was given control of the budget. Nevertheless, there was growing criticism within France, exacerbated by the newly freed press. New industrialists condemned his economic policy for not being protectionist enough. In the 1863 elections, opposition candidates carried nearly all the major towns.

A series of foreign policy problems gave renewed impetus to the opposition. The worst were the Mexican adventures of 1861–7 in support of Emperor Maximilian, Archduke of Austria, who was made emperor of Mexico after Napoleon sought to extend French imperial power by invading that country. Napoleon was undermined when, in the face of international pressure, he withdrew his support for Maximilian, who was then overthrown and executed by firing squad in 1867. Napoleon responded by granting the Senate and legislature far more rights and by lifting the final restrictions on the press. However, many of the new measures simply weakened confidence in him. Ministers were still not responsible to parliament, and the new papers were even more free to criticize Napoleon's leadership.

Napoleon III

Charles Louis Napoleon Bonaparte – Napoleon III – was the nephew of Napoleon I. He was driven by liberalism and Bonapartism, and took part in the 1830–1 revolutions in Italy. When he attempted revolution in 1840, he was imprisoned in Ham in France until his escape in 1846. Napoleon III could never escape his uncle's legacy and sought a role for France that could not be achieved. He was motivated by a desire to help the Italian, Polish, and German nationalists, all of whom caused him problems. He was finally defeated by the more able statesman Bismarck and died in exile in 1873.

Domestic issues also galvanized opposition to the government. A banking crisis of 1866–7 led to the collapse of the Crédit Mobilier bank, the textile industry was in decline, and agriculture needed reform. A new generation of capitalists whose vast wealth was based on joint-stock companies was seeking a greater say in government. All of these factors were accompanied by the social problems brought about by the Industrial Revolution.

In the 1869 elections, pro-government candidates lost nearly one million votes and 116 deputies subsequently called for ministerial responsibility. In June, there was a wave of strikes across France and vicious press attacks on the regime. Napoleon was forced to amend the constitution and share power with his legislature and Senate. These reforms were endorsed by a majority in a plebiscite of 1870.

The Second Empire was characterized by internal frictions. Napoleon's authoritarian rule heightened opposition to him from liberal elements. When he attempted to liberalize the Empire, his failure to build a power base was to undermine him gravely. Moreover, France under the Second Empire was being overtaken as a great power, both economically and militarily. By 1860, the manufacturing output of not only Britain but also Germany exceeded that of France. British naval and Germany military construction had copied and then improved on French designs, and France was caught between a stronger maritime and a stronger continental power. In 1870, Napoleon was defeated by Bismarck, and it was his capture in the Franco-Prussian War that condemned the Second Empire to far more than internal pressures.

The Third Republic 332–3 ▶
The Revolutions of 1848–9 302–3 ▶
The Revolutions of 1830 296–7 ▶
The Effects of Industrialization 306–7 ▶

The Third Republic

The Third Republic grew from the defeat of France and its humiliating loss of Alsace-Lorraine to Germany. It was divided between monarchists, republicans, and socialists. Socially, it was equally heterogeneous, with all the strains associated with the Industrial Revolution. The period was one of internal conflict, yet it was peaceful – although France had a dangerous new neighbour across the Rhine.

The bloodshed which accompanied the Paris Commune and Thiers's attempts to crush it shocked France. The revolutionary traditions of the city, which had led many Parisians to man the barricades in defence of the Commune, came to be seen as the unacceptable face of left-wing politics.

The Third Republic was proclaimed after the German defeat of France in 1870. Adolphe Thiers became its first president, even though he was a monarchist – one of many contradictions of the Republic. In the 1871 election 400 monarchists took seats in an assembly of 645. Yet France had a strong left-wing contingent. For communists and monarchists alike, the Third Republic had limited appeal.

French society

France was comprised of many different traditions and economies during this era. There were the landowning notables, who were largely monarchist and against universal suffrage. Provincial France turned to the notables after 1870 to offer paternalistic rule working with the Catholic Church. By 1870, 67.5 per cent of the population lived in the country and were largely conservative. The small urban working class were heirs of the revolutionary tradi-

tion and were often republican. The rich middle classes or "barony of bankers" had enjoyed much power under Napoleon III; their numbers grew from 1870–1900 as France became more industrialized.

Republicans espoused radicalism, a belief in citizens' rights, and the duty of the individual, rejecting the idea of class conflict. Rationalism and secularism were central to the republicans, who were strongly anti-clerical and shared the faith in progress held by so many in the 19th century.

The Paris Commune

During the German siege of Paris during the Franco-Prussian War, the National Guard had run the city. Thiers was suspicious of Parisian radicalism, and, in March, he sent in the troops to disarm the National Guard. The army was repelled and all government forces and bureaucrats left the city. The Committee of the National Guard was now free to act as it chose. Elections were held and a new independent government for Paris was established: the Paris Commune. Thiers saw his authority challenged and his capital in the hands of a revolutionary government and, in May 1871, sent in more troops to destroy the Commune. There followed widespread class warfare, with 20,000 people massacred. The Communards were finally defeated and the terrible bloodshed discredited the left-wing for many years.

In 1873, Thiers resigned, and Marshall MacMahon became president, promising a moral, Catholic society. MacMahon was a monarchist, although not leader of the monarchist faction. The monarchists were plagued by infighting, which undermined their credibility. Their leader, the Duc de Broglie, was not accepted by all monarchists, and his refusal to accept the Tricolour as the national flag left them open to ridicule. With the monarchists discredited, the republicans gained ground.

16 May 1877

In the 1876 elections, the republicans gained two-thirds of the representative seats on universal suffrage and a power struggle with MacMahon

1849–1914

NATION-STATE AND EMPIRE

The French considered Alsace-Lorraine as within their natural frontiers, and the provinces were secured even after the defeat of 1815. In 1871, the victorious Prussians took Alsace-Lorraine for Germany. For France to accept the loss was a humiliation, but to regain the land required the military defeat of Germany.

The Rhine Frontier 1814–71

- French territory in 1814
- French territory in 1815
- French territory after 1871
- Other borders

North Sea

HOLLAND

BELGIUM

Liège

Cologne

LUXEMBOURG
Luxembourg

Mainz

PRUSSIA

Metz

ALSACE-LORRAINE

BADEN

FRANCE

Strasbourg

Rhine

ensued On 16 May 1877, MacMahon dismissed his republican ministers and asked the Duc de Broglie to form a government. When the republican Assembly refused to work with the duke, new elections were called, which the republicans won. The republicans also won the 1879 Senate elections, and MacMahon resigned. He was succeeded by the republican Jules Grèvy.

Republican reforms

The aim of the republicans was to create a new France. The *Marseillaise* – written during the French Revolution – was adopted as the national anthem. In 1881, freedom of the press and of gatherings was declared. In 1882 and 1884, the notables' control was broken when mayors and local councils were elected. In 1884, trade unions were legalized. In 1878, the Freycinet Plan was introduced, an ambitious scheme to build transport routes throughout the country. Huge construction of railways, ports, and canals followed.

Education was of vital importance to the republicans, and they sought to replace the traditional clerical education with a rational, scientific one. Jules Ferry introduced widespread reforms to make teaching more available and more secular. In 1882, free primary education was compulsory, state secondary schools for girls were established, and universities became free from religious influence.

Tariffs were introduced to protect peasants from foreign trade. The republicans were sensible enough not to pursue the recovery of Alsace-Lorraine and instead spent their energy building an empire in Africa and South-East Asia.

The divided opposition

The Right was seriously weakened by the affair of 16 May 1877. The main opposition came from the Left, which was itself discredited after the Paris Commune massacres. There were few trade unionists to provide a bedrock of support, and the socialists were divided between many parties. Throughout the 1890s, therefore, the republicans were relatively secure in power. The major shock to the republican regime was the Panama Canal scandal when, in 1892, it emerged that the now-bankrupt company that had built the canal had done so by bribing many right-wing politicians. The weakness of the opposition precluded them from exploiting the affair to bring about the fall of the republicans.

The Dreyfus affair

In 1894, Captain Dreyfus, a Jewish captain in the French army, was convicted of spying. Despite evidence pointing to Dreyfus' innocence, the army refused to reopen the case. It later transpired that documents had been faked to prove Dreyfus's guilt. The author Emile Zola wrote an open letter, *J'accuse*, charging the government and army with anti-Semitism and corruption. The Dreyfus affair divided the country. The Right supported the army, while the Left was furious with its institutionalized religious intolerance and corruption. The republican movement split, and Dreyfus was eventually cleared and reinstated in 1906.

The Left gained strength from the Dreyfus affair, and the republicans became split between left and right. In 1902, a new left-leaning ministry took office. Meanwhile, the trade unions gathered strength, and, throughout the 1900s, there were major strikes. The Clemenceau government of 1906–9 broke the strikes with military force and arrested the union leaders. Nevertheless, before 1914 successor governments had introduced old-age pensions and income tax as a step towards fulfilling a radical programme.

After the 1890s, significant industrial growthhad taken place, but much of France was still rural. France's quest for an empire was reduced to regaining Alsace-Lorraine, and France was too weak for that. Despite this, the Third Republic achieved constitutional stability and oversaw a gradual modernization in France.

The cartoon shows Dreyfus as a treacherous snake, typifying the fierce passions aroused in French society by the Dreyfus affair. The conservative right sought to defend the army, viciously accusing Dreyfus of being a Jewish traitor. The left, on the other hand, portrayed the army and the establishment as deeply corrupt, morally bankrupt, and anti-Semitic.

The Great Exhibition at Crystal
Palace in 1851 was intended
as a celebration of Victorian
Britain's pre-eminent place in
the world. Many thousands of
visitors flocked to admire the
exhibits, which demonstrated
Britain's industrial and commercial
prowess. At the same time, the
exhibits from far away lands
were testimony to the extent of
Britain's influence across the globe.

VICTORIAN BRITAIN

During the reign of Queen Victoria (1837–1901), Britain was arguably the most powerful nation in the world. Its economic, industrial, and naval might reached its zenith around 1870. From then on, European powers and the USA began to catch up and overtake Britain in every sphere, save financial services. Britain's imperial might went hand in hand with a sense of social responsibility on the part of many British leaders.

Mid-Victorian Liberalism was the most dominant force in 19th-century British politics. The period 1850–74 saw almost uninterrupted rule by the new Liberal Party. With a deep sense of moral purpose and reforming zeal, the great Liberals of the day ruled the country during an "Age of Equipoise", with Liberal policies focussing on free trade, retrenchment, meritocracy, social reform, and individual responsibility. From the late 1860s until 1894, the greatest Liberal prime minister of all, William Gladstone, bestrode the national stage. The Liberal Party established an economic orthodoxy of the day based on Adam Smith's principles of free trade and laissez-faire government. The Liberals concerned themselves with all the great political issues: international relations, electoral reform, civil service reform, religious reform, temperance, the "Social Question", and the "Irish Question". The repeal of the Corn Laws, which had removed protective tariffs on the import of food and had bitterly divided the Tory Party, had given way to an unprecedented consensus about the benefits of free trade and a free society.

Yet Liberalism itself was deeply divided inside and outside the parliamentary party. The limited franchise meant that the industrial classes in the most industrialized nation in the world never fully set the agenda, and consequently it is difficult to establish just how accurately mid-Victorian Liberalism represented the nation.

Certainly, from 1874 onwards the Conservative Party was to be renewed as a force in politics. The Conservatives appeared more able to master the mass electorate. Benjamin Disraeli seemed to have made the party relevant again with the Second Reform Act in 1867, which gave the vote to many urban working-class men for the first time and doubled the electorate. A sudden burst of social legislation suggested that the Conservatives, too, had answers for the issues of the day. Middle-class Britain, which after 1885 was firmly within the political sphere, appeared eager to be accepted into mainstream society. Conservative Party organization became highly effective and appealed to the public's innate conservatism. The Primrose League became a vehicle for persuading British men and women of their duty to follow Conservative principles. Electoral reform created a strange landscape in which the Grand Old Men of British politics, representing the elite and the privileged, were feeling their way among a new massed and largely urban electorate. Before the 1867 Reform Act, Disraeli had said that he was "shooting Niagara", meaning that he did not know what the consequences of his actions would be. Politicians, businessmen, and religious leaders faced an array of new problems and choices, and met them in different ways.

The Liberals broke under the pressure of the issues of the day. The more radical Liberals were unhappy with laissez-faire government, and the issue of Irish Home Rule tore the party apart. From 1885, it seemed as if the Conservatives, with their appeal to nation, empire, "Tory Democracy", and a less sanctimonious approach to politics, were the natural party of government.

Underneath the outward stability, Britain was a nation going through great turmoil. For a highly industrialized nation at the height of its power, undergoing unprecedented democratic, demographic, and social change, there were myriad concerns to divide or unite the people.

Political and Social Reform

Victorian Britain saw itself as being at the vanguard of an age of progress. As the leading industrial nation, it led the rest of Europe in manufacturing and was the first truly modern industrial society. Within a stable constitutional monarchy, Liberals, Conservatives, and radicals fought for the allegiance of an expanding electorate. Only Ireland's poverty and discontent marred the political and social advance.

William Gladstone was one of the towering political figures of the 19th century. His belief in personal responsibility, the rule of law, economic retrenchment, imperial restraint, and liberal social reform made him the embodiment of the mid-Victorian Liberal Party.

The Irish Potato Famine was a result of potato blight which struck in 1845. With around half the Irish population dependent on the potato, the resulting misery was appalling. The suffering the blight caused created bitter resentment in Ireland at British misrule.

Liberal hegemony

Adhering to the principles of free trade, the Liberal Party symbolized a nation whose entrepreneurial flair had made it the industrial giant of the world. Gladstone's Liberal budgets of 1853–5 and 1859–65 slashed restrictive tariffs. Free trade became a moral imperative because as government stood back, it allowed individuals to manage their own businesses, fostering self-respect.

The Liberal Party fulfilled its moral duties by disestablishing the Church of Ireland, reforming entry procedure for the civil service and the army, and pursuing electoral reform. Reforming the franchise was one of the most important and difficult tasks of the government. In 1865, Gladstone and Lord John Russell attempted to introduce a moderate reform bill, but it was defeated, and the Liberal ministry broke up. Disraeli and the Earl of Derby formed a minority Conservative government, which in 1867 passed a much more radical bill giving household suffrage in the boroughs. Disraeli wanted to keep open an issue that was splitting the Liberal Party and to pass a major bill to assert Conservative authority. It is possible that he did not fear working-class voters, sensing that they could be made into Conservatives. The Gladstone government of 1868–74 saw the culmination of Liberal reforms, including education reform, Irish Land reform, and licensing laws. These last were to cost the Liberals: Gladstone himself felt that he had lost the 1874 election "borne down by a torrent of gin and beer".

The Conservative revival

In 1874, the Conservatives won their first majority since 1846. In 1867 and 1870, Conservative organization improved, and they began adapting to mass politics by targeting the boroughs. Disraeli's government introduced several social reforms, which helped to create the idea of a Conservative Party that cared for the public. After 1881, the Conservatives began to dominate politics by linking themselves to the aspirations of the urban middle classes. Disraeli's Lancashire and Crystal Palace speeches in 1872 shaped his party as one of patriotism and property.

Gladstone's Midlothian campaign helped to win him the 1880 election. He had remarkable public appeal, but the government was beset with division. The public was alienated by disasters such as the death of General Gordon, killed in Khartoum after being sent by the government to put down an uprising in Sudan. The electoral reform of 1884, which extended household suffrage to the

counties, was undermined when the Conservative House of Lords redistributed the seats to their advantage. The Liberals then became dependent on Irish MPs to pass measures in the House of Commons.

The "Irish Question"

The Irish Land Question was becoming an issue of increasing importance to the British government and referred to policies of land ownership under British rule. Centuries of absentee Scottish and English landlords had resulted in a population with limited land rights and poor living conditions, and who were paid far less than the English. The Potato Famine of 1845–9 eclipsed all other issues on the agenda. Ireland's peasants were dependent on potatoes rather than corn for sustenance. When the crops failed due to blight, an estimated one million died from starvation and disease; a further one million emigrated, mainly to the USA. An embittered populace remained, desperate for reform.

Fenian (pro-republican) violence alarmed Gladstone. Despite disestablishment of the Irish Church and the Irish Land Act of 1870, which increased the rights of tenants, Irish emotions were running high. Irish nationalism employed physical force and moral appeals. In 1882, the

Free trade

Free trade was based on the principles of the 18th-century economist Adam Smith. Its premise was that if people could trade with one another under the rule of a just legal system, then the influence of shared self-interest would lead to prosperity for all. The state should stand aside and let the people run their affairs. By dividing labour, each society could produce more and make more money, and the consumer would benefit from lower costs. Trade would make nations interdependent and war impossible. In Britain, the principles of free trade grew into a religion and to disagree was considered heresy.

brutal murder of the Irish Secretary in Dublin astonished the English.

In 1885, Gladstone converted to Home Rule, attempting to establish a separate Irish legislature. In any case, he needed the support of Irish MPs in Westminster. The 1886 Home Rule Bill split the Liberal Party, and 93 Liberal Unionists defected to the Conservatives. Gladstone controlled the rump of the party and accepted a radical agenda, but their continued support for Home Rule kept the Liberals out of power until 1892. A new bill could not pass the House of Lords in 1894, and the Liberals lost the next two elections.

The Monarchy

The monarchy and aristocracy changed least of all the classes in 19th-century Britain. The aristocracy absorbed new wealth and retained considerable power and prestige. Queen Victoria and her consort, Prince Albert, re-established the monarchy's popularity by adopting a responsible attitude to their duties and espousing a settled family life matching the middle-class ideals of many of their subjects. However, Victoria's long mourning and seclusion after the death of Albert in 1861 was deeply unpopular and fed a strong republican movement. Nevertheless, Victoria's sheer longevity gave a sense of coherence to a time of great change and the Jubilee celebrations of 1887 and 1897 seemed to vindicate British achievements and power.

18th-Century Britain   274–5 ▶

Reform in Britain,
Autocracy in Russia   298–9 ▶

Labour Movements
and the Rise of Socialism   300–1 ▶

The Social Question   338–9 ▶

The Social Question

The social changes in Britain during the 19th century were radical, exhilarating, and frightening. The Industrial Revolution offered hopes of creating wealth on an unprecedented scale, yet it also seemed to threaten the fabric of society. The age of improvement was haunted by the "Social Question".

The Great Exhibition of 1851, staged in London's Hyde Park, was a monument to Britain's liberalism and progress. More than six million visitors attended to see exhibits from all over the world. The amicable crowds of people from all social backgrounds seemed to suggest a country at ease with itself. Yet the 1851 census revealed that Britain had become the first country in the world where more people lived in towns than in the country and that Britain was increasingly secular. Nineteenth-century British society was more fragmented than many had thought.

The structure of society

Fear of conflict between society's haves and have-nots permeated the century. Industrial change overthrew the old regime, and class distinctions became less clear. A labourer might define himself along lines of ethnic group, gender, or linguistic group rather than by class. With a new material base operating alongside the old allegiances, society became increasingly uncertain.

In Britain, a tiny proportion of the populace owned over 50 per cent of the land, creating many issues for the landless, such as franchise reform (the vote was based on house ownership after 1867) or, in Ireland, nationality. Workers lived by factories, roads, canals, and railways in conditions that were noisy and unhygienic. The conditions in the towns were awful: sanitation was poor, the air was polluted, crime was high, and alcoholism was rife. Even when the well-off tried to improve conditions by forming commissions to provide water, sewerage, and lighting, efforts were piecemeal and dependent on local initiatives.

Living in towns could be very expensive; a tolerable house might cost a quarter of a skilled man's weekly income to rent, and few could afford this. Slums multiplied in the old inner cities, and cellar dwellings abounded in London, Manchester, and Liverpool. Indeed, specific slums were newly created by speculative builders, such as the back-to-back houses in Yorkshire.

Health reform

Health was not just an issue of class: the wealthy became vulnerable to the diseases of poverty as they were carried by tradesmen or domestic servants. An 1848 Act gave municipalities the power to set up local boards of health subject to three public health commissioners. With the civil service still recruiting by patronage until Gladstone's reforms, it remained inept, and it was often only individuals who could help the poor. Many philanthropists such as the future Earl of Shaftesbury took it upon themselves to change the lot of the poor, and they helped labourers to improve their slum dwellings and standard of living. By 1854, the appointment of medical officers of health was made compulsory in major

John Bright was one of the most influential of the radical liberals of the 19th century. Bright campaigned heavily for religious reform and an end to social inequality, and he was one of the chief agitators for electoral reform. Bright was a powerful force behind the 1867 Reform Act, which extended the franchise to skilled urban artisans.

Joseph Chamberlain was a strident advocate for social reform in the later 19th century. He undertook much philanthropic work in his native Birmingham and became a powerful figure in the Liberal and later the Conservative parties. A talented politician, he built a significant power base on the strength of the appeal of his reforming policies.

cities and was a critical factor in promoting the use of drainage, clearing slum houses, and enforcing building regulations.

The urban worker

Rural Britain was in sharp decline, particularly after the 1860s, when cheap grain from the USA, Australia, and Argentina could be imported and much of Europe raised its protective tariffs. Britain was easily Europe's most urbanized country in the mid-Victorian era, and rural workers migrated to the cities on a huge scale. Once they were living in the city, workers often lost all social bonds such as Church and family, contributing to a sense of dislocation and a society of the dispossessed.

Despite the "great depression" of the 1870s, workers' conditions slowly improved as a result of rising wages and a falling birth rate. Most chose to spend their extra money on small luxuries or leisure activities. Workers began to take holidays, previously unheard of, and excursions to seaside resorts such as Blackpool and Southend became annual trips. The urban worker began to play a greater role in the economy and thus the nation.

Politicians' response

While the lot of many urban workers gradually improved, the conditions in many inner cities remained appalling. From the 1870s, politicians became increasingly aware of the need to do some-thing about the "Social Question". The Conservative government responded by introducing a raft of social legislation. Much of it was pushed through by the Home Secretary, R.A. Cross. Nonetheless, in the 1874–80 government, Disraeli passed acts on artisans' dwellings, public health, river pollution, trade unionism, licensing, and education. Although most of the legislation was not compulsory, it seemed that laissez-faire government was not standing aloof from social issues.

Radical Liberals such as Joseph Chamberlain took an active interest in helping the poor, and he in particular did much to improve conditions in Birmingham. When Gladstone accepted a more radical platform from the National Liberal Association in Newcastle in 1891, the Liberal Party decided to take a more interventionist position. As well as strongly advocating land reform, Liberals proposed direct taxation as a means of redistributing wealth for the benefit of the poor. To this end, the 1892–5 Liberal government introduced death duties (a tax paid on the capital value of assets owned by a person at his or her death).

The deep changes within society, the economy, and the demography of Britain produced huge challenges for the whole nation. The unprecedented nature, speed, and scale of the changes meant that Victorian politicians were only partly successful in implementing radical improvements in the social conditions of Britain.

Kaiser Wilhelm II regarded himself as the strong man of Germany. He adored being in military uniform, as seen in the picture, and was fascinated by military and naval issues. The kaiser's desire to assert Germany's interests in foreign affairs helped to destroy the delicate system Bismarck had created to safeguard Germany from its neighbours.

IMPERIAL GERMANY: 1870–1914

Bismarck had transformed the German Confederation into a Prussian-dominated German empire. The new Germany was to undergo a period of phenomenal industrial expansion, which gave rise to socialist forces seeking a democratic state or more radical solutions. Bismarck's overriding aims were to consolidate and expand Prussian power within Germany, the kaiser's position within the German state, and Germany's position in Europe. He was to spend the rest of his career trying to secure the nation he had built.

Bismarck sought to defeat the modest demands of the Prussian liberals by turning their own weapons against them. The new Germany satisfied the liberals' desire for a strong and unified national state; the Germans also had universal male suffrage, although the Reichstag had limited powers. Bismarck made these gestures to liberalism even though they aroused the suspicion of the conservative kaiser. At the same time, he could never truly become reconciled to the liberals and always treated the Social Democratic Party as revolutionary long after it had become respectable. They in turn distrusted Bismarck's Junker conservative instincts.

Bismarck had to exploit the balance of power between new and established forces in Germany. He sought to bind the people to his new nation while suppressing dissent and had to negotiate the kaiser, Reichstag, and courtly officials. Abroad, he was to build an elaborate web of alliances within the great power framework, all intended to stabilize Europe and protect the German Empire. Imperial expansion beyond Europe was sought as a means of playing the great powers off against one another and appeasing opposition at home. While Bismarck was able to achieve his aims and manage to ensure stability in Europe, his successors found the task beyond them.

After unification, Germany's industrial and economic expansion went ahead at a breathtaking pace. Germany rivalled Britain's industrial supremacy, overtaking its output of steel by 1900 and forging ahead in new industries such as

chemicals and industrial goods. The German army became a model for the rest of Europe, and its navy aimed to supersede Britain's.

Those who succeeded Bismarck in 1890, however, could not translate this prowess into world power or European domination. Instead, in 1914 Germany found itself facing domestic radicalism and encirclement in foreign affairs. The Social Democratic Party was the biggest in the Reichstag, and Britain, France, and Russia were allied against it. Germany's colonies were dwarfed by the British Empire, and the High Seas Fleet was no match for the Royal Navy.

Germany's strength was at the root of its problems. It could never challenge the British Empire abroad unless it had security in Europe, but this was impossible because France and Russia remained independent great powers. France could never forget the humiliation of losing Alsace-Lorraine, and Russia would always stand by France rather than see Germany unconstrained and powerful at its western border. If Germany were to attain what it believed to be its rightful place, Europe would have to be settled on German terms, which meant conquest.

Domestically, the nation Bismarck had built was ultra-conservative. Bismarck's Germany rested on the power of the landowners and the aristocracy. German industrialization, literacy, and national fervour created a highly politicized class, which was always likely to challenge the established order based on nobility and agriculture. These domestic and foreign conflicts coincided in 1914.

Bismarck and Kaiser Wilhelm II

The German Empire was proclaimed in the Hall of Mirrors at Versailles in January 1871. The North German Confederation had been extended to Bavaria, Baden, Hesse, Württemburg, and now Alsace-Lorraine. Kaiser Wilhelm I of Prussia was proclaimed German emperor, and Bismarck was made chancellor.

The Dreadnought-class battleship dramatically changed the nature of naval strategy. Previous ships became almost obsolete. Britain and Germany began a naval race to build more Dreadnoughts, during which costs and tensions spiralled, prompting a political crisis in Britain.

In theory, Germany was a constitutional monarchy based on a federal structure in which local rulers retained a high degree of power. In practice, it was highly autocratic, dominated by the Prussian bureaucracy and military. The Reichstag was elected on universal male suffrage, but its powers were very limited, with neither the government nor chancellor answerable to it. However, although the Reichstag had little actual power, it did become an important arena for ideas to be discussed and criticisms voiced. Still, the new Germany was governed from above and had its foundations in force.

Domestic policies

Germany was a divided state. More than 10 per cent of the population was Danish, Polish, or French, and there were large numbers of Catholics in the south. The north-west was becoming industrial and urban, whereas the south and east remained rural and agricultural. The unification and industrialization of Germany were catalysts in creating socialist and democratic forces, which threatened Bismarck's state. Any minority group – but particularly Catholics and socialists – which might jeopardize Bismarck's plans were declared enemies of the state, or *Reichsfeinde*.

Bismarck feared the Catholics and their allegiance with the pope and the Poles. The Catholic Church was strong in southern Germany, and the Catholic Centre Party became the second largest political party in the country. After the Vatican declared the Doctrine of Papal Infallibility

Kaiser Wilhelm II inspects German troops during an exercise. Regular training ensured high professionalism in the German army, which the Kaiser was keen to use to secure a dominant position in world affairs.

in 1870, Bismarck declared a cultural war on Catholicism – *Kulturkampf*. A protracted struggle ensued. The chancellor passed many anti-Catholic measures with the aim of forcing Catholics to assimilate into the new German Empire. Ultimately, the *Kulturkampf* failed due to strong Catholic resistance and the Catholic Centre Party grew in power. The period from 1879–82 saw the repeal of many of the anti-Catholic measures.

Bismarck had feared the spectre of socialism since 1848. The rapid industrialization of Germany had created a new working class receptive to socialist ideas. In 1878, Bismarck passed his anti-socialist laws. The Socialist Workers Party (SWP) could operate at a national level, but at local level members were arrested or activities restricted. However, the SWP was resilient and gained in popularity. The anti-socialist laws were discontinued in 1890, and by 1914, the renamed Social Democratic Party had one million members.

Bismarck attempted to reduce the appeal of socialism through his own social legislation, such as introducing sickness insurance in 1883. Other effective ways of binding the masses to the state included encouraging the teaching of German history in schools and introducing conscription.

Foreign policy

Bismarck feared being surrounded by hostile European neighbours, especially after the rapid French recovery following 1871. He sought to keep France happy and to turn its attentions to Africa. To maintain the new order, the chancellor created an intricate web of alliances. In 1872, he founded the *Dreikaiserbund*, or Three Emperor's League, with Russia and Austria-Hungary, with the aim of maintaining a peaceful status quo in Europe. The Dreikaiserbund failed because Russia and Austria faced growing tensions in the Near East. Bismarck concluded the Dual Alliance with Austria-Hungary in 1879 to provide security for both countries in the event of an attack by Russia. In 1887, Germany, Austria-Hungary, and Italy made an alliance to maintain the status quo in the Mediterranean. In 1887, Bismarck concluded a Reinsurance Treaty with Russia, aiming to gain Russia as an ally after the breakdown of the Dreikaiserbund. When he left office in 1890, Bismarck had secured his objectives of isolating France and preventing German encirclement, but the 1879 agreement with Austria would one day drag Germany into a war with Russia.

Kaiser Wilhelm II

Two years before Bismarck fell, Kaiser Wilhelm II came to power in 1888. Germany was in new hands. The new kaiser saw himself as divinely

The naval race

In 1898, Germany passed its first Naval Law allowing Admiral Tirpitz, with the kaiser's approval, to begin building a fleet to challenge the Royal Navy. Tirpitz planned that Germany should stay on good terms with Britain until the German fleet was large enough to force imperial concessions from it. The Royal Navy would not be able to defend the Empire and protect Britain. The plan failed because naval power was far more important to Britain than it was to Germany. The Royal Navy simply outbuilt the German Navy and the Germans only succeeded in antagonizing Britain.

appointed, but he lacked focus and did not command universal respect. Wilhelm hated the Reichstag, but had a strong interest in the military and Prussian heritage.

Despite the weakness and unpopularity of Wilhelm II, from 1890 the German economy expanded faster than any other European state and by 1914, had overtaken Britain. Germany developed strong armed forces, a highly educated populace, a large urban society, and a formidable industrial base. The industrial growth gave rise to social unrest. In 1912, there were nearly 3000 strikes due to long hours and poor pay. The rise of the Social Democratic Party alarmed the kaiser.

Foreign expansion

Germany's leaders stoked national sentiment and a vigorous foreign policy as a way of counteracting the socialists. They adopted *Weltpolitik*, a policy of making Germany a world power, and sought an empire. The biggest obstacle appeared to be Britain and the Royal Navy. Wilhelm believed that he must match British naval might and attempted this by building his own huge fleet. Although the policy failed, Britain was so alarmed by the German Navy that it made an entente cordiale with France in 1904 and the Triple Entente with France and Russia in 1907. Wilhelm's failure to renew the Reinsurance Treaty with Russia had already provoked a Franco-Russian defensive alliance.

From 1911, German leaders began to grow desperate at their isolation. Germany's ally Austria-Hungary was being threatened in the Balkans, and pre-emptive war began to seem the only way out of the stranglehold.

The magnificent spectacle of
Tsar Nicholas II's coronation in
Moscow on 26 May 1896.
The tsar's position was strengthened
by the loyalty of the Russian
Orthodox Church. Russian
peasants were often devoutly
religious, and the Church helped
to underline their fidelity to
the royal family.

IMPERIAL RUSSIA: 1881–1914

Following the assassination of Alexander II in 1881, Alexander III became tsar. The final years of tsarist rule can be divided into two parts. The first period involved an impressive state-driven economic expansion brought about by the sudden realization that Russia was falling behind its rivals. The second period was one of internal strife and revolution. The 1905 revolution almost brought about collapse, but gave a last chance for reform to work in Russia.

When Alexander III became tsar, Russia had yet to restore its position in the Black Sea and was facing the mighty challenge of an advanced Germany to the west. In 1892, Count Sergei Witte became finance minister and immediately took steps to modernize Russia's economy.

Witte expanded on the railway-building programme of the 1880s and planned the Trans-Siberian Railway. In order for these developments to take place, Russia needed a stable rouble, and, in 1897, Witte took Russia onto the gold standard. To keep a healthy balance of trade, the government forced peasants to sell grain for export. The results were impressive: the value of Russian industry doubled in 10 years, with centres developing for textiles, coal, chemicals, and iron ore, and its railway network was second only to the USA.

This rapid industrialization had powerful socioeconomic repercussions. Most of the country went hungry, and infant mortality was the worst in Europe. Peasants who were recruited for the factories faced low pay and poor working conditions. There was little urban housing, and poor sanitation led to cholera epidemics. Unions and strikes were fiercely suppressed.

Nicholas, tsar in 1894, reacted harshly to calls for change, seeing it as his duty to protect the monarchy. When industrial growth began to slow, he forced Witte to resign. Facing industrial turmoil, the government encouraged the persecution of the Jews to alleviate the pressure of social unrest. When the pogroms failed, the tsar went to war against Japan to divert attention away from the home front. Mobilization and defeat fuelled the flames of unrest. By 1903, the discontent of the tsar's subjects was obvious. Peasants were

demanding more land while workers were asking for better pay and conditions. Nobles and the professional classes wanted an assembly.

In 1902, there had been major peasant uprisings in the Ukraine; in 1905, the army suppressed 3000 peasant disturbances. Strikes in 1902 were violently suppressed, and employers and even the police began to question the government's approach. Despite the regime's fierce reactions, it was not able to repress the growing agitation.

In 1905, the disastrous war against Japan unified the opposition against the regime. The terrible defeats, the loss of the fleet, and the mobilization convinced many Russians that the time had come to rebel against their rulers.

Stimulated by Witte's reforms, Russia underwent rapid industrial advancement before World War I. Although it was gradually catching up with its competitors, the map below shows just how scattered Russia's centres of economic development were in the years before 1914. Nevertheless, industrialization in Moscow and St Petersburg unleashed social upheaval in Russia's centres of power.

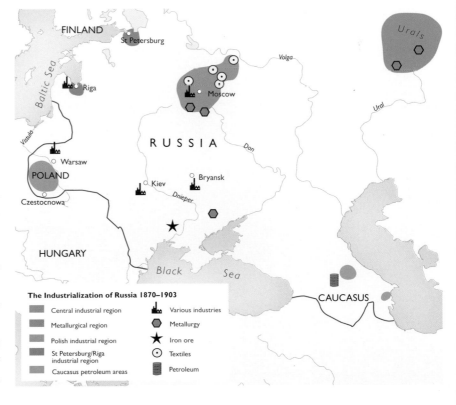

The Industrialization of Russia 1870–1903

- Central industrial region
- Metallurgical region
- Polish industrial region
- St Petersburg/Riga industrial region
- Caucasus petroleum areas
- 🏭 Various industries
- ⬡ Metallurgy
- ★ Iron ore
- ⊙ Textiles
- ▤ Petroleum

The 1905 Revolution

The Russo-Japanese War influenced the combustible mix of social and political grievances in the Russian Empire. Before the war, Russian peasants, industrial workers, ethnic minorities, liberals, radicals, and nobles had all begun to seek changes. The defeats in the Far East finally forced the disillusioned men and women of Russia into action.

The war against Japan caused great hardships for ordinary Russians. It had caused a marked rise in government expenditure, which was met by the populace. The war also disrupted Russia's communications systems, making it difficult to transport commodities, which led to a rise in food prices. The harsh winter of 1904–5 added an edge to dissenters' complaints. In January 1905, a massive strike closed St Petersburg's factories. On 22 January, a 200,000-strong procession marched through the city, protesting to the government. The tsar fled and Cossack soldiers opened fire on the protesters, killing many. The incident became known as Bloody Sunday and caused considerable damage to the tsar's prestige.

Revolutionary activity

Before the conflict, there had already been calls for reform. Educated noblemen had demanded a greater hand in running government, and support grew for the Union of Liberation, established in 1904. The union, made up of nobles, professionals, and liberals active in zemstvas, aimed to remove the tsar and replace him with a democracy. The Social Revolutionary Party had been established in 1901 and sought direct action to overthrow the government, promote workers' rights, and give more land to the peasants. The Marxists found a voice in the Social Democratic Worker's Party, which believed that the Industrial Revolution would lead the workers and peasants to rebel. After Bloody Sunday, the revolutionaries grew more impatient.

In February 1905, the tsar promised to summon a consultative assembly. Yet this failed to appease the country: there were more radical demands and revolts by Poles, Finns, and Georgians. Peasants seized land, causing the government to cancel redemption dues. The All-Russian Peasants' Union was formed and called for a constituent assembly.

Mutinies followed on the battleship *Potemkin*, at Kronstadt, and in the Far East. Despite crushing the

Imperial Russian soldiers guard the Winter Palace, home of tsar and tsarina, during the 1905 Revolution. Unrest and revolution in the capital, St Petersburg, and other major cities in Russia helped to force the Tsar to promise to grant a constitution.

The tsar and tsarina are seen
in 17th-century costume as they
attend a court ball in 1903.
Nicholas II was one of the richest
men in the world and was
absolute ruler of Russia with its
vast impoverished population.
The extremely privileged lifestyle
of the royal family and the
tremendous disparity in wealth
within Russia helped contribute
towards the unrest during
Nicholas's reign.

mutinies, the regime was shaken. In September, more strikes followed, as the workers became more militant. To facilitate political action, workers' councils, known as soviets, appeared in Russia and plotted revolution, published journals, and forged links with other soviets. The tsar crushed the uprisings but the crisis was not over.

Nicholas II recalled Witte, who urged him to grant a constitution. Nicholas agreed to this, and, on 17 October, a manifesto was issued guaranteeing civil liberties and promising a national assembly elected on a broad franchise. Ordinary Russians were generally in favour of working within the existing framework and supported the constitution, leaving the radicals isolated and crushed by the armies returning from the war. By December, the Revolution was over.

The aftermath

It seemed that Russia was on the path to becoming a liberal modern state. Nicholas II had granted the October Constitution under extreme pressure and would never accept a position as a constitutional monarch. In 1906, the "Fundamental Laws" declared that the supreme autocratic power belonged to the tsar. Under the terms of the constitution, the tsar had granted a *duma*, a representative body established by suffrage. No laws could be passed without the consent of the duma, yet it could have its bills vetoed by the state council, it had limited financial authority, and its ministers were responsible solely to the tsar, who was accountable to God. The duma was a sham, and when it appeared to show signs of legitimate opposition, the tsar dissolved it.

The tsar continued to respond to unrest with force. By 1911, 600 political parties and unions had been shut down. Political prisoners were jailed and 2500 peasant leaders executed between 1906 and 1909. Although the peasants could vote and the duma was a permanent institution, the reforms in Russia seemed superficial at best. The autocratic tsar and his family grew ever more isolated from the nation, which was rapidly losing confidence in him.

In rural areas after 1906, the tsar's chief minister Stolypin tried to reform agrarian society. In 1906 a decree permitted all peasants to apply for property ownership and scattered land was consolidated. The Peasant Land Bank, which enabled peasants to borrow money for purchasing land, had its resources increased, and the government aided resettlement schemes. The aim was to create a more prosperous and stable peasant class. Redemption dues were also cancelled in 1907, fulfilling the earlier promise of 1905. The reforms were a progressive move, but many peasants simply did not know how to farm away from the commune – the village community that regulated much of peasant life – and those who did created resentment among poorer peasants. Stolypin's measures were not met with universal approval: he was assassinated in 1911. By 1914, the reforms had had little effect – the peasantry was still too numerous and too backward.

The conditions of the tsar's working-class subjects remained poor. In 1912, sickness benefit funds and accident insurance were introduced, but they were barely adequate, and strikes were widespread in 1912. The workers had no involvement in government, revolutionary leaders were exiled, and the police repressed unrest with violence. The government once again resorted to encouraging attacks on Jews to air dissatisfaction, and the tsar's minority races faced a campaign of "Russification" in which non-Russians were subjected to linguistic and religious colonization. This was aimed particularly at Finland, which inflamed radical opinion.

Russia enjoyed strong industrial growth in 1909–13 and harvests were good. The number of schools increased by 85 per cent. But per capita income was still only one-third of its competitors, literacy remained poor, and living conditions were often terrible. If the reforms introduced after 1905 were to have worked at all, they required a flexible tsar and a long period of sustained peace. Russia had neither. After three years of total war, tsarist Russia completely collapsed.

A street scene from mid-19th-century Vienna, the prosperous seat of the Habsburg rulers. Despite the tensions that were tearing the Habsburg Empire apart, Vienna flourished as a cultural centre, at the cutting edge in music, painting, and architecture,

THE HABSBURG EMPIRE

The Habsburg Empire was a diverse collection of lands spread across central and southern Europe, which had been accrued over centuries. After 1878, the Habsburg Empire also included the former Ottoman colony of Bosnia-Herzegovina. Unlike the other great patchwork empire, Russia, in the Habsburg Empire there was no single dominating nationality. Germans, Magyars, Poles, Czechs, Italians, Ruthenes, Slovenes, Slovaks, Romanians, Croats, and Jews all lived under the rule of the Habsburg dynasty.

The 1848 revolutions had rocked the Empire to its foundations. The Russians had to be called in to help suppress the Magyars, a sign that the Habsburgs were losing grip of their multifarious peoples. The Habsburg Empire had faced revolt from almost all its peoples for a plethora of reasons and grievances. Divided by language, geography, tradition, culture, prosperity, educational standards, religion, power, and many other factors, the people of the Habsburg lands were growing increasingly difficult to govern. Paramount among the Empire's domestic worries was the sheer force of Magyar nationalism. Encouraged by the success of Kossuth, who had led their revolution in 1848, the Magyars, the Habsburgs' second most powerful race, were set on a course to change the Empire. There was a growing Magyar nationalist movement, which sought recognition of parity with Austria inside the Habsburg Empire; indeed, many saw this as the first step to complete independence.

The Habsburg Empire also faced new challenges from without. Growing Italian nationalism threatened its provinces in the peninsula. Pan-Slavic nationalism encouraged its Slavic races to look to Russia for allegiance and salvation and the former ally was now hostile after Austria's armed neutrality in the Crimean War. The Russian threat to the Habsburgs' lifeline – the Danube – remained ever present over the next 70 years. To the west, the new French Empire under Napoleon III seemed like the realization of Metternich's nightmares: the new Napoleon could overturn Europe in a renewed bid for mastery in which the

Habsburgs had most to lose. To the north, Germany was suddenly a threat. Prussia was growing in strength and soon would be able to challenge the Austrians, Bismarck was intent on expelling Austria from north Germany, and growing nationalism in the German race questioned the Habsburgs' very foundations.

The Habsburg lands were also undergoing rapid social and economic change. The traditional pattern of rural, subsistence agriculture was being overhauled by the Industrial Revolution. Workers migrated to the great cities, where they found new allegiances and grew susceptible to new ideas. Increasing education and the growing diversity of city life often brought their own challenges to the old order.

Overall, the Habsburg Empire, which had stood for centuries, was suddenly looking perilous. Under attack from within and without, and subject to profound social, political, and economic transformation, the Habsburgs were facing grave times. How could an empire that was dependent on eschewing the nationalist principle in favour of loyalty to an archduke, survive in an age of nationalism and liberalism?

And yet the Empire did not suddenly crumble – it took another 70 years before Habsburg rule was banished from central Europe. It withstood crises at home and abroad, and outlived the Russian Empire. Only a war of unprecedented ferocity against Britain, Russia, France, Italy, Serbia, and later the USA could bring it down. But in order to survive in such tumultuous times, the Habsburgs were obliged to change.

A Changing Empire

The growing pressure on their empire forced the Habsburgs into sweeping changes in the second half of the 19th century. Facing difficulties in both domestic and foreign spheres, and the consequences of the Industrial Revolution, a series of responses, including the *Augsleich*, marked the Habsburg reaction to the modern times.

The nationalist challenge

The Austrian defeat in Italy in 1859 sparked a constitutional crisis, and a limited constitutional government was introduced in 1860–1. The constitution was strictly under Viennese control, thereby failing to appease nationalist sentiment. The Hungarians in particular wanted autonomy from the Empire, and, in 1865, Vienna reinstated the Hungarian assembly.

After the Habsburg defeat at Sadowa, the Hungarians exploited Austrian weakness to push for further recognition of Magyar equality with Austria. The *Augsleich*, or compromise, of 1867 was the result and led to the creation of the Dual Monarchy: the Habsburg Empire became the Austro-Hungarian Empire. Austria included Bohemia, Moravia, and Galicia. Hungary included Croatia, Transylvania, and Slovenia. Each half had its own parliament and administration responsible for internal matters, and unity was maintained by having joint ministries for defence, foreign policy, and finance, while the armed forces remained as one. There was a strong Catholic influence on the new state, embodied in Emperor Franz Josef I.

The two halves grew into separate units. Austria was dominated by the Germans, particularly as the vote was restricted to the wealthiest – mostly German – people. This did not prevent fractious relations between the nationalities, and even the powerful Germans were not truly appeased. In Hungary, the Magyars entrenched their supremacy and the landowners dominated an increasingly nationalist state. The minority nationalities in each half were ignored. The *Augsleich* was effectively an Austro-Hungarian alliance against the Slavs. The Austrians saw this as an essential compromise; the Magyars saw it as a step towards independence.

Austrian national issues

Different national agendas caused tensions within the Empire. With 10 million German speakers and most of the vote, Germans dominated culturally and politically, but they were not a majority in the Austrian half of the Empire. There were over six million Czechs, who were growing increasingly hostile to the power enjoyed by the neighbouring Magyars. Czech nationalism grew, creating national societies and a Czech bank, and the Czechs began to demand autonomy. Although there were five million Poles, with Poland facing Austrian, German, and Russian opposition, there was little chance of a Polish state. The Poles concentrated on limiting German and Czech power. The peasant Ruthenes began to look to the Ukraine for national succour, and, after 1900, the 750,000 Italians in the South Tyrol increasingly demanded unification with Italy.

As nationalist agitation grew, competing Austrian groups paralysed politics, and there was little consensus on how to remake Austria. In 1907, universal male suffrage was introduced in an attempt to placate the masses. The result was national fragmentation as the first parliament saw 17 different sizable national parties. Only strong ministerial rule overcame parliamentary deadlock. Moreover, Austria saw the growth of the most virulent right-wing nationalism before World War I, with Austrians looking to the German Empire to protect them from their Slavic neighbours and Jewish immigrants.

Hungarian national issues

The Magyars constituted nearly half the Hungarian population, with other races small, divided, and

Austria-Hungary, sandwiched between Italy, Germany, Serbia, and Russia, was a ramshackle empire. With so many different nationalities, religions, languages, ethnic groups, cultures, and loyalties, it was extremely difficult for the emperor to foster national cohesion in the face of external threat and internal challenge.

Peoples of the Austro-Hungarian Empire 1867–1914

- Germans
- Magyars
- Slavs
- Romanians
- Italians

Emperor Franz Josef

Franz Josef I was born near Vienna in 1830 and became Habsburg emperor in 1848. He believed in a strong central government without political parties. He allied his monarchy firmly to the Catholic Church, much to the annoyance of his Orthodox subjects and neighbours in Serbia. His 68-year rule was over a period of tremendous strife for the Austro-Hungarian Empire, and his death in 1916 came just two years before the end of the empire he had ruled.

rural. Hungary became an unashamedly national state, with Magyars dominating state posts and the professions. The three million Romanians looked to Romania for assistance; Slovaks looked to the Czechs to counter the Magyars; and Croats and Serbs allied in a South Slav bloc.

Despite this, Hungary refused to lose its grip on power. The 1868 Nationalities Law ensured that the Magyar language was used at all important levels and excluded non-Magyars from top government. The 1870s saw the Hungarians attempt to suppress Slavic nationalism and resist universal male suffrage – in the last Hungarian elections before 1918, Magyars had 450 seats and non-Magyars only eight.

The Industrial Revolution

The substantial economic growth that took place after 1867 was unevenly spread throughout Austria-Hungary. The advance in industry led to a 5 per cent annual increase in output from 1873 to 1913, but the growth per capita was small, reflecting the growing separation between rural and urban regions. Economic growth in the Austrian half of the Empire followed a regular pattern, centred on urban areas or industries such as textiles, which had grown since the Industrial Revolution. Economic growth in the Hungarian half was concentrated on agricultural industries such as brewing, reinforcing the dominance of the landowners.

Budapest and Vienna in particular saw the arrival of immigrants, either seeking work or fleeing pogroms, but society was still dominated by aristocrats and landowners, heightening social tension. In the backward regions of the Empire, emigration was rife and five million left between 1876 and 1914, leaving a dislocated, depressed society.

The other "sick man of Europe"?

The Habsburg Empire was subject to immense strains in the years before 1914. A truly multi-national empire, its very integrity was endangered by the rise of nationalist movements among its consituent peoples. Most threatening of all were the successes achieved by the Serbian and Bulgarian nationalists in setting up nation-states by the 1870s, an example that might well be emulated by other nationalities. Moreover, Slav nationalists had a ready supporter in Russia, which sought to establish itself as protector to the cluster of small Slav states in the Balkans and thereby control the area. These possibilities fired the imagination of all Slavs in the Austro-Hungarian Empire, but especially the Croats, Slovenes, and Serbs still living within its borders. Many of them, encouraged by Serbian groups, formed revolutionary societies, which carried out a wave of assassinations of Austro-Hungarian officials prior to 1914.

Redoubling its efforts to control the rising tide of nationalism, Austria-Hungary's annexation of Bosnia-Herzegovina in 1908 was the result, attempting to forestall south Slav nationalism by bringing the disputed area within the Empire. The hope proved false, as the continued operations of the revolutionary societies showed.

In spite of its many problems, however, Austria-Hungary remained a vital, dynamic society – its very diversity providing it with an artistic and intellectual life of brilliant achievement in the years before 1914. In music, painting, and architecture, Vienna was at the cutting edge of the avant-garde. But the fateful attempt to solve its political problems by war was to bring the dissolution it had fought so long to prevent.

The Origins of World War I 362–3 ▶
The Prussian Wars 326–7 ▶
A New European Order 406–7 ▶
The Balkans 484–5 ▶

*The 1878 Congress of Berlin
brought dignitaries from across
Europe together to discuss the
Eastern Question. Bismarck
can be seen greeting delegates;
the German Chancellor's role
as host reflected Germany's
pre-eminent position in
European power politics.*

INTERNATIONAL RELATIONS

Between 1871 and 1914, the balance of power in Europe was essentially stable, despite what contemporaries thought. The great powers of 1871 were still great powers in 1914; however, tension lay beneath the surface. The continental powers built huge armies for a coming war, and only a careful balancing of interests kept the peace.

French resentment at losing Alsace-Lorraine ran extremely deep. There were many who sought immediate reconquest of the two lost states. France sought allies to offset Germany, but Austria now accepted Germany's position as guarantor of its security against Russia. Neither Britain nor Russia had immediate fears about Germany, leaving France isolated. When France quarrelled with Germany in 1875, both Britain and Russia acquiesced to the German settlement on the Rhine, and the French defeat was complete.

In July 1875, another crisis arose when Bosnia-Herzegovina revolted against Turkish rule. Russia and Austria had key interests. Russia could not let its fellow Slavs fail, and Austria could not afford to let them win and threaten its Danubian empire. Attempts by the great powers to solve the issue failed. In 1877, Russia entered the war, arousing fierce hostility in Britain. Under British pressure, Russia eventually agreed to peace at the Congress of Berlin in 1878. Russian aims were defeated at the congress, and, under Bismarck's guidance, the great powers had turned away from war.

Bismarck was desperate to maintain the balance of power and so persuaded Austria-Hungary to join him in a permanent alliance in 1879. Bismarck then had to stave off the effects of the alliance by convincing Russia that it was not a threat. The result was the *Dreikaiserbund* of 1881, signed with Russia and Austria to reassure the tsar he was not in danger.

In 1882, Germany and Austria made the Triple Alliance with Italy. Bismarck gained the security that his Austrian ally would not be attacked by Italy if there were a war between Austria and Russia. Bismarck's system was complex: the Triple Alliance assumed Austro-Russian conflict; the Dreikaiserbund assumed Austro-Russian co-operation. His attempt to control his allies and neighbours was not successful because France and Russia were still independent and powerful, and, if they ever allied, Germany would face danger.

In the late 1880s, Britain and France were involved in a dispute over Egypt, and French economic links drew it closer to Russia. Germany, meanwhile, was growing friendlier with Britain, alarming France and the tsar. In 1891, an entente was formed between France and Russia, but the threat of being caught in a Russo-British conflict encouraged France to make better terms with Britain. In 1904, France and Britain signed an agreement over their colonial disputes in Egypt and Morocco, and the entente began.

In 1905, with Russia in revolution and the French armed forces in disrepair, Germany saw a chance to dominate Europe. The Germans made an alliance with Russia. This renewed German threat forced Britain and France to work together in preparation for a war against Germany, strengthening the entente. Britain and Russia settled their colonial disputes in 1907 and formed an alliance.

In 1908, news of two new German shipbuilding contracts outraged Britain. Britain felt that Germany was bidding for naval supremacy and continued to expand its own navy. If Britain feared German hegemony, Germany feared encirclement by France, Russia, and Britain. Europe now had a system intended to guarantee peace, which saw Britain, France, and Russia on one side and Germany and Austria-Hungary on the other, with Italy yet to decide. The stage was set for war.

The New Imperialism

Between 1870 and 1910, the European empires grew by over 26 million square kilometres (10 million square miles) and encompassed 150 million new subjects. By 1914, Europe and the USA had acquired over 17 per cent of the world's surface.

Europe had long had an influence across the world. The Spanish and Portuguese had built large South American empires. France and Britain had won and lost North American empires, and Britain had established itself in the Indian subcontinent, Australia, and elsewhere. Russia had already colonized much of Central Asia, and Holland had acquired the Dutch East Indies (now Indonesia). But, by the end of the 19th century, Europeans had formally colonized much more of the world. France had conquered north-west Africa and much of South-East Asia, plus many islands in the Pacific and Atlantic. Portugal acquired Angola and Mozambique. Italy took Libya. Germany acquired German South-West Africa, Kaiser Wilhelmland, German East Africa, Cameroon, and Togo. Britain took South Africa, Bechuanaland, Northern and Southern Rhodesia, Egypt, Sudan, British East Africa, Nigeria, and other areas of Africa. The British Empire also included India, Canada, Australia, New Zealand, the West Indies, Hong Kong, and many other territories.

The causes of the new imperialism

Was the "new imperialism" of the late 19th and early 20th centuries a continuation of established patterns of international behaviour, or was it connected with industrialized economies? Many believe it was an example of Western "economic" imperialism and was the result of a search for new markets and raw materials. Some historians believe that the significance of the age of imperialism was merely to postpone World War I. Was this colonial expansion then, a matter of European powers engaging in a trial of strength away from home? Many have claimed that the nationalist fervour that gripped much of Europe from 1870 to 1914 was simply transferred to new arenas, suggesting that imperial expansion was an accident that happened when trading interests could not be left to the local powers already in place.

The impact of new technology

The superiority of European weaponry and other technologies accounts for colonial success: there

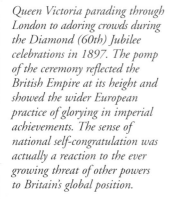

Queen Victoria parading through London to adoring crowds during the Diamond (60th) Jubilee celebrations in 1897. The pomp of the ceremony reflected the British Empire at its height and showed the wider European practice of glorying in imperial achievements. The sense of national self-congratulation was actually a reaction to the ever growing threat of other powers to Britain's global position.

was no way in which the Europeans could have subjugated 620,000 square kilometres (240,000 square miles) a year if they had not been better armed than their foes. The native peoples of North America and Australasia, however brave, stood little chance against the well-equipped European settlers. The Russian expansion into the emirates of Central Asia was facilitated by its overwhelming firepower. At the Battle of Omdurman in the Sudan, the British force killed 11,000 Dervishes for the loss of a handful of men. Better-armed enemies such as those in India proved much harder to quell.

Overland and sea expansion was made possible with new technology. The steamship enabled nations to keep their missions, industries, armies, and settlers well supplied. Moreover, those going abroad drew morale from the knowledge that they were not entirely separated from their homeland. Contemporary historians noted that the rise to great-power status was now unthinkable without a mighty navy and overseas colonies.

The railway was equally significant. In its battle with the Japanese for control of the Far East, Russia was able to keep an army of 750,000 men in the field at around 11,000 kilometres (7000 miles) distance. Germany wanted to extend its influence in the Near East through a Berlin–Baghdad railway and Cecil Rhodes speculated on a railway from Cairo to Cape Town. Wherever Europeans were faced with inhospitable terrain, they could use the railway to keep their forces well supplied. Once a territory was subdued, the railway could open up previously impassable land to commercial exploitation. The railway's ability to gain access to

the interior of a state to mine or for trade provided a purpose for imperialism as well as a means.

The telegraph aided a communications revolution as significant as that of the late 20th century. Commanders of armies could receive orders or intelligence from distant headquarters, and the fact that one was still in touch with one's home nation gave succour to those who left for distant lands.

Advances in medicinal science also played their part: new medicines such as quinine were able to assist Europeans in overcoming tropical diseases and establish permanent settlements.

Social beliefs

Samuel Smiles's book *Self-Help* of 1859 stated that "life is a struggle in which every individual must be prepared to engage on his own". These views were reinforced by Darwin's *On the Origin of the Species*. Social Darwinists believed that Darwin had shown that competition for survival was absolutely necessary, if not desirable. These theories were used to bolster the notion that Europeans, with their superior technology, were a superior society. It was believed to be the duty of Christian civilizations – "the white man's burden" – to conquer and civilize the peoples of less developed societies.

If a nation were to stay among the first ranks of European states, then it had to have an empire, good ports and coaling stations, and a large land mass. Italy and Germany were determined to carve out empires as a means of proving their status. Russia and France could not expand into Europe because Germany blocked the way, and so they turned to far afield lands to restore their pride.

This British telegraph centre from the 1882 war in Egypt shows how technological superiority enabled European armies to maintain and control large numbers of troops in inhospitable colonial environments. Through such measures, small European expeditions could subdue large native forces.

The Scramble for Africa

The phenomenon known as the Scramble for Africa began around 1876. There had already been European influence in Africa in previous centuries, but, in the last quarter of the 19th century, the European powers engaged in a spree of formal colonization of their interests in Africa. By 1914, almost all of Africa was under European rule.

By 1914, almost the whole of Africa was under European rule. Bar Austria-Hungary and Russia, all the major European powers were present in the continent. Germany, the strongest nation in Europe, had one of the smallest overseas empires, much to her chagrin. France, driven from Europe, sought imperial splendour in Africa, while Britain had formalized its vast informal empire.

The origins

It was, surprisingly, the leader of a small nation, Leopold II, king of the Belgians, who started the age of "New Imperialism". In 1876, Leopold II formed the International Association of the Congo as a capitalist venture, intending to acquire territory in the Congo as his own private land, rather than as a Belgian colony. De Brazza, the French explorer, decided to enter the competition on the north side of the Congo, claiming territories for France. Keen not be left out, in 1884, Britain recognized an old Portuguese claim to the mouth of the Congo; Britain hoped that this would thwart both Leopold and France in expanding further. When

Britain and France disagreed over claims to the Congo, Bismarck proposed a League of Neutrals in 1884, designed to hinder British expansion. Bismarck saw German colonialism in Africa as a means of driving a wedge between Britain and France, and, in June 1884, Britain recognized German settlement of South-West Africa. Later in the same year, the West African Congress was called in Berlin, devised to partition much of sub-Saharan Africa among Europe and the USA. Not one representative from a single African country was present. This set the pattern for the colonization of the rest of Africa.

The reasons for the Scramble

For France, the Scramble for Africa had a variety of causes. Unable to recapture Alsace-Lorraine, the French sought glory by establishing an empire. There was a widely shared belief that great-power status in the coming century would be held by those states that could accrue a large industrial base, which meant people, resources, and industry. With the French population growing more slowly than its rivals, it needed foreign acquisitions to compete. France was to develop through its dynamic foreign policy. During the Third Republic, there was a consistent and influential imperial lobby that the rapidly changing governments were unable to curb, even had they wanted to do so.

Germany saw in Africa a chance for a glorious empire that would symbolize and entrench its new place as a first-ranked power. The Germans saw that their main rivals had already acquired much overseas territory by 1870 and felt that they had to make up for lost ground. As it was at the centre of Europe, Germany could expand neither east nor west, and therefore expansion outside of Europe was its way of avoiding encirclement. Encouraged by the German Navy League and the Pan-German League, Kaiser Wilhelm II was determined to stake his claim. Foreign expansion also provided a means of easing domestic strife by giving the populace a cause behind which to unite.

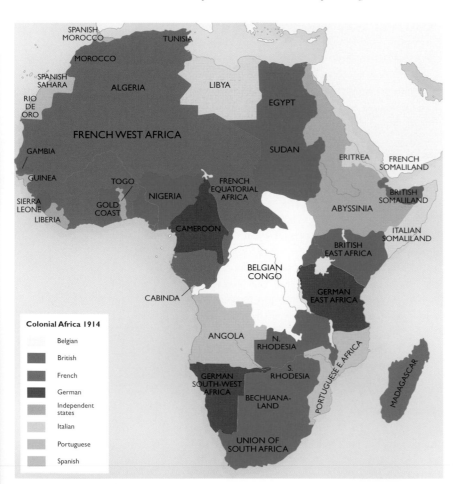

Colonial Africa 1914

- Belgian
- British
- French
- German
- Independent states
- Italian
- Portuguese
- Spanish

SPANISH MOROCCO
TUNISIA
MOROCCO
SPANISH SAHARA
ALGERIA
LIBYA
RIO DE ORO
EGYPT
FRENCH WEST AFRICA
GAMBIA
SUDAN
ERITREA
FRENCH SOMALILAND
GUINEA
TOGO
FRENCH EQUATORIAL AFRICA
SIERRA LEONE
NIGERIA
GOLD COAST
BRITISH SOMALILAND
ABYSSINIA
LIBERIA
CAMEROON
ITALIAN SOMALILAND
BRITISH EAST AFRICA
BELGIAN CONGO
CABINDA
GERMAN EAST AFRICA
ANGOLA
N. RHODESIA
PORTUGUESE E. AFRICA
S. RHODESIA
MADAGASCAR
GERMAN SOUTH-WEST AFRICA
BECHUANA-LAND
UNION OF SOUTH AFRICA

Belgian King Leopold II is depicted carrying bags stuffed with money. His decision to carve out his own piece of territory from the Congo for personal profit was typical of many Westerners' rapacious attitude to empire building. Leopold's actions inadvertently sparked an energetic European "scramble" to create large colonies in Africa.

For Britain, the real interest in Africa was protecting the Suez and Cape routes to India. By acquiring large areas of East Africa such as Kenya and areas bordering Egypt, Britain was forestalling threats to its older empire.

The term "scramble" is a misnomer, but it was symptomatic of the popular hysteria among banks, politicians, and the public. Most of Africa was divided by dialogue, not force. During the Scramble, Britain achieved the lion's share because of its already predominant interests in the continent. With its extensive presence in Africa and the power of the Royal Navy, Britain was able to curtail the expansion of its rivals. If Britain had felt really under threat from the new European powers such as Italy and Germany, it could have used the power of the Royal Navy to crush their influence. It seems that a willingness to compromise and share the spoils in Africa is a more accurate description than a "scramble".

While European rivalries were important, confrontations between the Europeans and the Africans were also significant. Egyptian and Afrikaner nationalism drew Britain into its most significant adventures. The instability of Morocco under Sultan Abdul Aziz was highly influential in France's intervention there, as French business interests worried about profits under a crumbling regime. The rise of the Mahdi, a muslim leader, in the Sudan, temporarily reducing British influence, encouraged Italy to begin its African adventure in the Nile Valley.

Trade

The theory that capitalism led to the exploitation of Africa is a weak one. French, German, and British trading efforts were focussed mainly in Europe, Latin America, and Asia. Return on investment was higher in South America than Africa. While there was a degree of economic exploitation, in particular in forcing cash crops on locals, African imperialism was marked by very low levels of systematic economic activity. African trade represented a tiny percentage of overall European figures. Britain's African trade declined in the 1890s, and Germany's ability to cope once its African colonies had been occupied in World War I shows how insignificant their value was.

By the beginning of the 20th century Europe had acquired a huge African empire, but had yet to decide what to do with it. Within only a few years of carving up the continent, the reasons for doing so had become less relevant, and the territories were to be neglected for half a century then, ultimately relinquished.

For Italy, an empire was an important way of bringing cohesion to a nation that had little. Italy was divided geographically, culturally, and economically, so many Italians had little attachment to the new state. By seizing an empire, Italy could bring its people together as well as confirm its status as a great power.

Britain's involvement in the partition of Africa was based less on real needs than an attempt to make up for its growing insecurity in the face of economic and military competition from the continent. Britain found it much harder to control its empire informally under foreign competition, and the official partition protected its colonies. Africa was the subject of most European diplomatic and military activity in the last years of the century, and Britain was concerned about its rivals' influence.

Nationalism and Empire

While Social Darwinism was important in shaping European attitudes towards imperialism, so was its bedfellow, nationalism. Nationalism had been the great cause of the 19th century, and in the new "national" states, as well as the old established states, imperialism was employed as a way of binding the masses to the establishment.

The rise of nationalism

The newly industrialized society had created large conurbations where people lived, worked, and socialized in close proximity to one another. With the increase in primary education across Europe and the corresponding rise of the popular press, it became easy to spread nationalist fervour into the dense cities. The press in Germany enthused the public with the idea of a Berlin–Baghdad railway to spread German influence into the Middle East. Winston Churchill's stories of capture and escape in the Boer War made him a national hero. Organizations such as the Union Coloniale in France and the Pan-German League helped to instil in the public a patriotic love of empire. Statesmen like Francesco Crispi, the Italian prime minister, saw an empire as a way of binding the newly enfranchised masses to the conservative order. By serving in the imperial forces, the youth of the nation could be taught the virtues of nationalism.

For France, imperialism was a way of alleviating the stress of the loss of Alsace-Lorraine without fighting Germany. In addition, while soldiers were away in the tropics, they would not be under the dangerous political influences at home, which might have upset the conservative order. Trapped between Germany's great land empire and Britain's great maritime empire, it was imperative for French pride that it carve out its own territories. The loss of Egypt to Britain in 1882 was a terrible blow to prestige, one which took the gaining of Morocco to soothe.

The new German and Italian states were born of warfare, and they needed to prove their martial virtue on the colonial battlefield to feel as powerful as their neighbours. Germany was encircled by its neighbours and wanted a "place in the sun" of its own to show its strength. Russia's rebuffs in the Near East turned it to the Far East.

For smaller countries, too, establishing an empire was a means of achieving greatness. Belgium created its empire on the Congo, and Portugal made an empire in west and east Africa.

The small countries could thereby play at being great powers without ever challenging a true great power and inviting destruction.

Those states that were defeated by "backward nations" suffered terrible humiliation. Italy's loss at Abyssinia deeply wounded Italian pride, which was only partly assuaged by its conquest of Libya. Russia's defeat at Japanese hands in 1905 led to revolution, and France's ejection from Mexico severely wounded Napoleon III's prestige. Largely, however, empires allowed European states to bask in their superiority over others.

The race for empire

When Germany entered the colonial race in 1884–5, it was primarily a manoeuvre to split the

In 1896, the Italian prime minister, Francesco Crispi, attempted to seize Abyssinia (modern-day Ethiopia) to satisfy Italian nationalists' desire for an empire. Italy's defeat at Adowa in was an unprecedented and humiliating reversal for a European army in Africa. A wounded Crispi is shown here limping alongside his troops.

British and French. Bismarck believed that, by Germany acquiring its own empire it could force Britain into colonial aggression, pushing France and Germany closer together and isolating Britain. If that happened, Britain's alternative might have been to seek an alliance with Austria-Hungary, which would have removed the burden for the latter's defence from Germany. This greatly intensified the struggle for conquest. The West African Congress in Berlin in 1884–5 led to a spate of pre-emptive acquisitions. States thought that they needed to claim their empire before an international congress could take it from them. The popular franchise in the Reichstag also allowed public pressure to force Germany into empire-building. Kaiser Wilhelm II needed no encouragement to create overseas colonies. After 1890, Germany sought directly to challenge the British Empire. Under Alfred von Tirpitz, Germany built a great fleet and pushed for colonial concessions from Britain. Britain sensed that Germany's challenge was a very real threat, and it poured vast resources into outbuilding the German navy.

Britain's empire had always been an informal one, based on trading interests. If pressure were needed to secure British interests, it could be applied through gunboats or financial inducements – this was the model by which India had been accrued. The sudden burst of fresh colonial acquisitions in Africa and Asia was a reflection of its growing weakness. Other countries were matching Britain's industrialization and its power. Britain could not protect its informal empire and required overt demarcation of its territory. Britain's weakness in sub-Saharan Africa was made all too clear to Bismarck when it agreed to the West African Congress on colonial issues. Similarly, Britain controlled 70 per cent of trade with China, but was unable to prevent France, Germany, and Japan acquiring territory, dividing the country into spheres of influence, and establishing their own commerical relations and diplomatic legations in Peking. Other states annexed territories close to Britain's and then imposed tariffs on British goods, threatening its trade supremacy.

The decline of maritime power

The imperial fervour that swept Britain from 1870 was a recognition that the nation's greatness was threatened. Most important of all, Britain's naval powers were in decline. Other states were now able to build large navies that, combined, could challenge the Royal Navy. Britain's alliances with

The Fashoda Incident

The capacity of colonial rivalry to bring national feelings to fever pitch and even the brink of war is shown by the Fashoda Incident of 1898, when France and Britain squared up in the Sudan. General Jean Marchand led a small French expedition from the Congo to the Nile, which reached Fashoda, south of Khartoum, on 10 July 1898. But to the north lay a vastly superior force under General Kitchener, who asserted Britain's claim to the country. The French and British newspapers played up the affair into a crisis. But in practice neither country wanted a war, and France eventually ordered Marchand to withdraw.

Japan were acknowledgement that it had to relinquish primacy in some spheres in order to maintain it elsewhere. Even worse, naval power was declining in relative importance to land power. Once expanding railway networks opened up the vast interior resources of Asia and North America, there was no way a maritime power such as Britain could compete on an international sphere unless it extended its empire further.

Colonial co-operation

However, military and commercial rivalries did not prevent Europeans from pooling resources when they were faced with a common threat from their colonial subjects. This was the case during the Boxer Rising, a rebellion in China thus named because the rebels belonged to a secret society called the Fists of Righteous Harmony. The rebels opposed the Western presence in China, and between 1898 and 1900 they made attacks on imperial settlements in China, as well as laying siege to the foreign legations in Peking. A mixed European, American, and Japanese force defended the legation compound for two months, until relieved by a similarly international army of 20,000 troops. Even after re-establishing control, the imperial powers, which now included the Americans and the Japanese, held back from dismembering China, fearing conflict amongst themselves. As a result, China remained the last outpost of "informal empire".

Elsewhere, as in the Pacific, the great powers allocated to themselves virtually all the remaining islands and territories not yet claimed. Where necessary, as in Samoa and the Solomon Islands, groups of islands were divided, giving each of the great powers a share in the last spoils of empire.

Missionaries and Explorers

The 19th century was notable for the significant expansion of Christianity from its European heartland into Africa, Asia, the South Pacific, Australia, and North America. The belief in the "duty" to convert the heathen was concomitant with faith in the moral righteousness of imperialism. Others sought fulfilment through the pursuit of material wealth or simply through the exploration of the natural world.

Christian missions

At the beginning of the 19th century, the Roman Catholic Church was still suffering from the anti-clericalism of Napoleonic France. Protestantism was effervescent by comparison. The 18th-century Enlightenment had fostered an evangelical revival, which gave great vitality to the Protestant Churches of Europe. Convinced of their obligation to convert and therefore "civilize" the non-believing world, Protestant missionary societies flourished. The Baptist Missionary Society, the Wesleyan Methodist Missionary Society, and the Church Missionary Society, gave Britain the greatest number of religious foreign missionaries of any country. In continental Europe, Protestant missionary activity was similarly growing. These societies were frequently voluntary organizations, controlled by lay subscribers, and were often non-conformist. Evangelicalism was strong in Protestant organizations, which carried out much missionary work in

deprived areas of Europe. The evangelicals pressed for social reform such as public health improvements, while helping to educate the masses through Sunday school and promoting Sabbath observance.

Protestant missionary activity spurred a revival of Catholicism. Protestants and Catholics often saw themselves as being in competition for new followers, and for many it was a case of trying to secure salvation for unbelievers before a rival religious group influenced them. Rivalry became fierce in certain areas, particularly in eastern Africa. The Catholic missionaries were given a boost by the re-establishment of the Congregation of the Propagation of Faith – or Propaganda – in 1817. Moreover, the Roman Catholic Church had its morale raised by its continued recovery throughout the century, and the Paris Society for Foreign Missions was revived to help convert much of the French Empire in north-west Africa. The Society

The British explorer Robert Scott and his team reach the South Pole on 17 January 1912, only to discover Norwegian Roald Amundsen's tent. Amundsen had beaten them to their goal by one month. Scott and his party died on the return trip. The race for the South Pole embodied the intrepid spirit of European exploration before World War I.

Cecil Rhodes

Born in England in 1853, Cecil Rhodes first visited South Africa in 1870. In 1871, he staked a claim in the Kimberley diamond fields, which brought him tremendous wealth. Rhodes studied at Oxford, then returned to South Africa, where he secured a charter for the British South Africa Company to operate in Matabeleland and Mashonaland in 1889. This paved the way for the extension of British power into what later became Rhodesia. An imperial visionary, Rhodes believed that the expansion of the British Empire would solve social problems at home by absorbing emigrants, and he dreamt of a vast empire in Africa stretching from "the Cape to Cairo". His political schemes included complicity in the 1895 "Jameson Raid", an attempt to seize the Transvaal from the Dutch.

for the Missionaries of Africa and the St Joseph's Society for Foreign Missions were established in Britain in the 1860s as a response to evangelical missionary work.

The publicity attached to the missions helped to reinforce the image of missionaries as heroes, and well-educated, upper-class men and women began to fill the ranks of missionary societies. In southern Africa, the deeply religious Afrikaners belonged to the Dutch Reformed Church; Dutch settlers in the Transvaal and Orange Free State often saw themselves as a chosen people with a special mission in Africa.

Like the colonialists, missionaries used the new technologies to help their cause. By employing steamships, railways, and the telegraph, contact could be maintained with the home countries more easily. The use of quinine helped protect both missionaries and native peoples against malaria. European activity often sparked fierce resistance from local people, who saw their own values being eroded, or local priests who saw their influence undermined. The India Mutiny of 1857–8 and the Boxer Rebellion in China in 1900 saw missionaries murdered by the insurgents.

Explorers

The 19th century witnessed a continuation of the exploratory zeal of the 18th century. Driven by imperial fervour, religious passion, quest for financial gain, or simply the desire to explore new places, Europeans exploited new technology and medical advances to travel deep into the heart of unexplored land masses.

Africa captured the public's imagination. Known as the "Dark Continent" because of its impenetrable heartland of jungles, swamps, deserts, diseases, and strange customs, Africa inspired Europeans to prove their mettle. From the 1850s to the 1870s, the Scottish explorer David Livingstone traced the Zambezi river, navigated the previously supposed impassable waterways between Lake Tanganyika and Lake Nyasa, and named the most spectacular waterfall he saw after his queen – Victoria Falls. Evangelical explorers such as Livingstone preached the Gospel, helped the sick, and exposed the inhumanities of the slave trade. Stanley's "rescue" of Livingstone in 1871 became one of the great adventure stories of Victorian Britain.

The great French explorer de Brazza journeyed up the Congo river and launched the bid for French territory that helped spark the Scramble for Africa. De Brazza's French and Belgian successors, with British financial backing, built a railway between the Congo, Kasai, and Oubangi rivers, linking them to the Atlantic. Jean Marchand, the French general who confronted Kitchener at Fashoda in 1898 in an attempt to prevent British preponderance in Egypt, explored much of northern and inland Africa.

The attempts to find a north-west passage to Asia continued to prove fruitless, but they did lead to the rise of polar exploration. Spurred on by the international rivalry that went hand in hand with imperialism, the great powers raced to place their flags on the North and South poles. In 1893, the Norwegian Fridtjof Nansen made it close to the North Pole, a feat successfully achieved 16 years later by the American Robert Peary. In 1911, the race to the South Pole was won by Roald Amundsen of Norway, although Robert Scott's story of heroic failure remains a tragic epic that captured the imagination of the public.

The Origins of World War I

The origins of World War I have been much debated. Austro-Russian rivalry in the Balkans combined with rash German diplomacy fanned the flames of mutual hostility. Once the conflict ignited, the alliance systems and German war plan propelled Europe on a course to total war.

Gavrilo Princip, assassin of Archduke Franz Ferdinand, is arrested. The murder, in the tense atmosphere of the Balkans, where Russian, Austrian, and Serbian nationalists were often in fierce competition, led to the outbreak of World War I. Princip spent the remainder of his life in captivity while Europe tore itself apart.

The growth of European rivalry

International rivalry permeated European thought and diplomatic practice to such an extent that many felt it natural that European nations would compete with each other. Great-power politics had always had a predatory element, and the rise of nationalism and the nation-building of the middle of the century that had created a united Germany and a united Italy had left tensions. France still resented the loss of Alsace-Lorraine, creating a Franco-German antagonism at the heart of Europe. Austria-Hungary had been shorn of its Italian possessions and was now threatened by internal nationalist movements that received encouragement from the creation of national states such as Serbia on its borders. Moreover, fashionable ideas such as Social Darwinism, the concept that the struggle between nations, as between species, was both natural and desirable, gave ammunition to

nationalists, the military, businessmen, and ideologues who promoted expansion and rivalry. Popular nationalism and militarism had burgeoned throughout the period leading up to the outbreak of hostilities. All of Europe, apart from Britain, had adopted the German scheme of creating large conscript armies, in which virtually all of the able-bodied male population received military training, providing a huge reserve of men for any future war.

However, although there was widespread belief that war might occur as a result of international tensions, it was also believed that the coming war would be quick and that the nation most ready for war would be able to achieve a decisive victory at the first engagement. The Austro-Prussian War of 1866 and the Franco-Prussian War of 1870–1 seemed to offer examples, reinforced by recent other conflicts such as the Russo-Japanese War of 1904–5 or the two Balkan Wars which preceded 1914.

1849–1914

NATION-STATE AND EMPIRE

President Poincaré of France inspects his soldiers on manoeuvres in 1913. During the rising tension of the pre-war years, most European states attempted to ready themselves and their armed forces for conflict. The increasing emphasis on military preparedness served to heighten mutual fear and animosity.

Consequently, Europe was more heavily armed and prepared for war after 1900 than it had been for many decades. Increased tension, industrial and technological development, and the growing wealth and power of the European states propelled a protracted arms race. Although imperial adventures were partly a diversion from European tensions, they could not prevent the build-up of armed forces. Germany set the pace with its large population, booming industry, and formidable military reputation. France sought to match Germany by seeking an alliance with Russia, but also by gearing up its own military potential through conscription. Russia set about updating its strategic railway network so that it could match the rapid mobilization of which Germany was capable. Germany's creation of a fleet to challenge Britain had prompted naval competition in the 1890s; however, from 1906 Britain's introduction of an all big-gun class of battleship, the Dreadnought, produced a strenuous naval race between the two countries. These arms races caused much unease in Europe and helped to create a mood of mutual antagonism that paved the way for war.

Nationalism was used as a means of binding the state's subjects to the established order. In a conservative nation such as Germany, the ruling class used aggression abroad to emasculate social unrest at home, with the result that the government was safe when it undertook warlike moves and under threat when it was passive. The growth of nationalism was very much a product of its time and had been made possible only by the innovations of the 19th century. The popular press, which proliferated during this period, could shape nation's mood, while increased literacy allowed more people to access the nationalist teachings of the newspapers.

The European alliance systems were a major cause of the war, with the Franco-Russian Entente a contributing factor in Germany adopting the Schlieffen Plan. The triple entente between Britain, Russia, and France was a product of German naval enlargement, which in turn caused Germany to feel encircled and trapped by the triple entente. The Triple Alliance between Germany, Austria-Hungary, and Italy caused the French and Russians major concerns and forced them into a closer alliance. The German belief in supporting Austria-Hungary risked dragging the whole of Europe into a Balkan war.

The rise of Balkan nationalism

The decline of Turkey in the Balkans in 1912 left a vacuum that Slav nationalists in the Balkans tried to fill. Bitter conflict between Austria-Hungary and Serbia followed, threatening stability within the

The Schlieffen Plan
In 1892, Alfred Graf von Schlieffen became chief of the German general staff. He believed that Germany would face a war on two fronts – French and Russian – and would therefore have to knock out one of its enemies quickly to concentrate on the other. Russia was too big to eliminate rapidly, and the superior French railways meant that France could mobilize more quickly than Russia. In the event of a war with Russia, Germany aimed to defeat France immediately, then turn on Russia. By 1895, the Germans had committed themselves to all-out war in Europe, even if the conflict was in the Balkans.

Austro-Hungarian Empire. Germany's refusal to back Austria-Hungary in the Balkan War meant that its neighbour faced a struggle with a Slav power allied to Russia. Indeed, Russian pan-Slavism exacerbated the conflict, ensuring that Russia would be dragged into any power struggle in the Balkans. Russia's rapid development, particularly of its railway, meant that it would be able to mobilize quickly enough to render the Schlieffen Plan useless.

Germany seemed to have only a short time left in which to fight a decisive war to break its encirclement before being overtaken by rivals. The German War Council that met in December 1912 was certainly looking for war as a pre-emptive measure. This might have been the motivation for Germany's unreserved support of Austria taking action against Serbia in 1914. Franz Ferdinand was heir to the Habsburg throne and had been killed by Serb nationalists while inspecting his troops. The Austrians were convinced that Serbia was complicit in the murder and sent an ultimatum, of which Serbia accepted most, but not all, of the points. Encouraged by Germany, Austria declared war on Serbia. There is no doubt that the events that followed the assassination overwhelmed the leaders of Europe, pitching them into frenetic military mobilization and patriotic fervour. Everyone expected a short war, a trial of strength that would either put Germany in its place or break its encirclement. The immediate cause of war was Austria's action against Serbia, which provoked Russia to mobilize, leading to a German declaration of war, followed by a French one. But the real causes of hostility went far deeper than the events of the summer of 1914.

A Changing Empire 350–1 ▶

World War I 388–9 ▶

The Eastern Front 392–3 ▶

The Balkans 484–5 ▶

The Eiffel Tower was erected in 1889 to mark the centenary of the French Revolution. Gustave Eiffel's structure was the tallest in the world until 1930. Here, the tower is illuminated for the 1900 Exposition, celebrating the triumph of modern technology in both construction and lighting.

TECHNOLOGICAL ADVANCES

The second half of the 19th century was marked by exceptional industrialization across Europe. After the growth of heavy industry came new industries such as chemical manufacture and electronics. Because of these advances the experiences of different social groups across Europe were widely divergent.

From 1830–1913 per capita GDP increased 120 per cent, which was probably more rapid than at any time before. Yet merely looking at the government statistics gives a misleading impression. The real changes did not take place within nation-states, but across sectors and regions of Europe. In certain areas and at certain times, economic growth was sluggish, while in others it was meteoric.

The cotton mills of Lancashire clothed India, and textile cities became the dynamic symbols of industrialization. The railway – the icon of the age – was designed to help transport coal, but ended up bringing prosperity to huge regions, making transportation of commodities cheaper and lowering prices. With French investment Russia increased its railway network by 57 per cent between 1898–1913, and in this period Russia had the fastest growing economy in Europe.

Trade boomed and was becoming central to the European economy. In 1913, European exports reached 14 per cent of national income, which has never been achieved since. Ports and trading houses underwent a dramatic period of growth. The means of transporting goods became dominated by a small number of large, wealthy companies such as the Nord railway line in France and the Hamburg-America shipping line.

European economic growth was partly due to an increased and improved labour supply: the population of Europe was around 275 million in 1850; in 1913, it was around 481 million. The abolition of serfdom in Russia, the weakening of restrictive guilds in Western Europe, and increased literacy and education across Europe created a flexible, well-educated, and productive labour market. In Germany, in particular, the creation of craft schools and technical colleges gave it a lead in the newer technological industries.

There was staggering investment in the transport sector. Banks such as Crédit Mobilier in France were heavily involved in financing railways and new joint-stock banks such as the Midland in Britain and Deutsche Bank in Germany evolved. The second half of the century also saw profit from investment in relatively cheap new inventions that had been pioneered in Britain, such as the steam engine. French investment in Ottoman and Russian railways helped to secure large armaments orders, boosting domestic industry.

Europe was still heavily engaged in agriculture, and farming grew more prosperous. In the east and south regions of Europe, where landowners retained their influence over the workers, farms remained relatively backward, but north-western Europe saw rapid advancement. Average European yields on wheat increased rapidly in this period, as the use of manure and nitrate-based fertilizers were pioneered. Even so, it is a reflection of the rapid pace of European industrialization that despite agricultural advancements, imports of grain rose sharply.

These economic changes and upheavals have been suggested as key contributing factors to the outbreak of World War I. The theory is that German agrarian and industrial commitments put it at odds with Britain and Russia. Moreover, the process of industrialization helped to create socialist parties, and it was governments' attempts to suppress these that led to militarism. Yet capitalism was hardly to blame. Russia, the most backward great power in 1914, was an original protagonist in the war, whereas the USA was not.

Industrial Developments

In the second half of the 19th century, new industries emerged across Europe to compliment those of the early stages of industrialization. Germany in particular was adept at manufacturing chemicals and cars. This new period of development was also accompanied by many technological breakthroughs.

After 1860, new, more expensive technologies emerged in Europe, and Germany was at the forefront. Germany's higher standard of technical education and university research was helping Germany to overtake the rest of Europe in the next stage of industrial development.

Steel, iron, and transportation

In 1861, Friedrich Siemens and Pierre and Emile Martin invented a process for open-hearth steel production. Previously, steel had been far costlier than iron; this new process meant it was more readily available. In 1884, Charles Parsons made the last great breakthrough in steam technology when he developed the steam turbine. These technologies developed through one another: steam power was used in cotton mills, which expanded the market for manufacturers of iron and steel. Steam pumps and steel machinery made deeper mineshafts possible, increasing productivity. Steam power was critical to the development of the railway, which in turn provided a very important market for the coal, iron, and steel industries, and transported their produce more efficiently.

At the end of the 19th century and beginning of the 20th century, much of continental Europe was experiencing dramatic industrial changes. German pig-iron production increased from 4.1 million tons in 1890 to 13.6 million tons in 1913. In France, leading innovators pioneered much work in engineering and transport. Firms such as Schnieder, Peugot, Michelin, and Renault were at the forefront of industrial progress.

The waterways were at least as significant as the railroad. The Danube was still Austria's lifeline and the Rhine central to Germany. The canals built by Europeans made transporting goods and communicating with far-flung empires easier. The Suez Canal was built in 1867, the Panama Canal in 1895, and the Kiel Canal in 1914.

In 1859, J.J.E. Lenoir developed the first reliable combustion engine, and by 1885, Daimler Benz developed the four-stroke internal combustion engine for use in propulsion. The use of this engine in automotive transport presented the first challenge to steam propulsion. In later years, industry would be given a huge boost by the liberation of the labour force that this allowed, as well as the

The oilfields of Russia were exploited during the late 19th and early 20th centuries. Russia was desperate to catch up with the West in industrial developments, and "new industries" such as petrochemicals were of vital importance. By employing its huge natural resources, Russia made rapid strides towards advancement.

The first ever Mercedes was constructed in 1901 by Wilhelm Maybach. Germany and France led the way in the use of the internal combustion engine and the motor car. The car was destined to transform life in Europe and, at the turn of the century, could be seen as a symbol of the new geographical mobility enjoyed by those with a high enough income.

flexibility in transporting goods. The development of the car was advanced when Emile Levassor devised the gearbox in 1891 and André Michelin invented the pneumatic tyre around the same time.

In 1900, the first Zeppelin flew in Germany. These huge airships were the invention of Ferdinand Zeppelin, and they would go on to form the world's first commercial air passenger service. Meanwhile, Louis Blériot, a French pioneer in aviation, made the first crossing of the Channel in a monoplane in 1909. Blériot was a trained engineer who had already invented a successful flapping-wing model in 1901 and one of the world's first viable monoplanes six years later. He went on to become a successful plane manufacturer.

Chemicals

In 1856 William Henry Perkin, while conducting experiments with coal tar, discovered mauve dye as an accidental by-product, making possible a whole range of synthetic colours that would not fade as natural dyes did. British industry failed to exploit his breakthrough, and it was the German company BASF that began producing chemical dyes on a large scale. By 1900, 90 per cent of the world's dye was made in Germany.

As a consequence of Germany's embracing of new industries, its exports tripled between 1800 and 1913, which in turn boosted its merchant navy to the point where it was the second largest in the world. German farmers made excellent use o fertilizers and modern farming techniques to increase their crop yields, which were far higher than any other European state.

In Russia, huge new chemical factories which employed tens of thousands of workers were opened in St Petersburg and Moscow. Progress with fertilizers and farming techniques helped even the under-developed Russian agriculture

to increase its output by 2 per cent annually during the three decades prior to World War I. The Swedish Nobel brothers and French Rothschilds helped pioneer the exploitation of oil in Russia, and by 1900, the country was producing half the world's oil. In Austria-Hungary the advances in chemicals and processes helped the heavily rural population by improving production in industries such as brewing and sugar beet.

The communications revolution

The electric telegraph had been developed as a means of passing messages between railway signalmen. Samuel Morse had developed the first working telegraph in 1837, and from then it dominated communications. Its development aided all areas of life, from industry to diplomacy and the military. From 1850, there was a cross-Channel telegraph system, and from 1865, a transatlantic one. Most important diplomatic and business communications took the form of telegraphs. During wars, the telegraph came to be dreaded, bringing the worst news to families at home. In 1850, Reuter supplied foreign news via the telegraph, providing timely information on the world at large.

Communication was further transformed by the invention of the telephone in 1876 by Alexander Graham Bell. Germany, especially, took the new invention to heart, and quickly grasped its military applications. In 1895, Guglielmo Marconi demonstrated his first radio transmission and, in 1901, sent the first transmission across the Atlantic. Marconi's work became particularly important for navies and shipping lines.

In the 19th century, there was a complete transformation in communication. In 1800, a letter would take weeks to cross Europe; in 1900, the telegraph could transmit information in an hour, and the world never looked back.

The Advance of Science

It was fashionable among 19th-century intellectuals to believe that science would replace religion as a means of answering life's fundamental questions and of binding society together. Many believed that experimental science, in particular, could be the basis of all knowledge and policy.

Marie Curie was the first woman to win the Nobel Prize. In 1903, Marie and her husband Pierre, won the Nobel Prize for chemistry for discovering radium and polonium. In 1911, Marie won the Nobel Prize for Physics for continued work on radiation.

The popularity of science

The general public viewed science with awe during the 19th century. Inventions such as Auguste and Louis Lumière's *cinématographe*, which was the forerunner of the film projector and was first demonstrated in 1895, showed the public how scientific breakthroughs could impact upon their lives. Museums of natural history soon become popular destinations for families. Journals such as the *Westminster Review* celebrated scientific advancements to the literate public, and books with scientific themes proved highly popular. Scientific discoveries were discussed by the intelligentsia along with political issues.

Institutions of science

The world of science developed an institutional network, and learned societies and organizations were founded. Periodicals were established to cover the great ideas of the time, and congresses became widespread as a means for scientists to discuss their ideas. The research laboratory became the most important setting for scientific pioneering, with teams of investigators using new technology to study the world around them. Apprentice scientists learned research techniques and theories from their mentors. Justus Liebig, the great organic chemist, established one of the first laboratories in Europe, and his students were encouraged to learn from one another. Gradually, scientific research became centred on universities, especially in Germany, which had become a model for the rest of Europe.

Biology and chemistry

By the middle of the 19th century, biology had become the most significant science, both intellectually and culturally. The second half of the century saw major advances in this field. In 1858, Rudolf Virchow sought to demonstrate that cells were the basis of all life when he published his major work, *Cellular Pathology*. The following year, Charles Darwin published *On the Origin of the Species*, which offered a biological explanation for all life on earth. It was to have a profound impact on modern thought.

Louis Pasteur's work enabled him to introduce more hygienic hospital practices, vaccinate against diseases, and develop pasteurization, a process where food is heat-treated in order to kill dangerous microbes, thereby increasing its longevity.

Darwin brought together existing strands of thought within the natural sciences. He believed the world to be far older than had previously been thought and that the species of animals and plants on earth had changed over a period of time. Darwin called this process "natural selection" as a means to describe the manner in which lifeforms evolve that are best able and equipped to compete for the limited resources on the planet. *Origin* became the most influential book of the 19th century.

The theory of natural selection appeared to contradict the belief that the world was created by God, but equally controversial was where it placed man in nature's scheme. Man was no longer set apart from nature by God, but was merely another species on the planet. Darwin's view of the world seemed to leave no place for God, and, after the publication of his book, science began to penetrate all other areas of society and human enterprise.

Further advances were made elsewhere: in Moravia, a monk named Gregor Mendel laid the foundations for modern genetics by experimenting with garden peas. Mendel asserted that the natural offspring of plant hybrids showed identical characteristics to the parents and that these characteristics appeared in ratios. Mendel complemented Darwin's theory of natural selection by showing the source of variability in living things.

The French chemist and bacteriologist Louis Pasteur became a popular figure by using science to solve practical problems. Pasteur asserted that fermentation was traceable to specific living micro-organisms, and through a process of sterilization, a product such as milk could have its life preserved. This became known as pasteurization. In an age when large numbers of people were moving to urban areas, transporting milk to the customer often took a long time. Pasteurization helped many new town-dwellers to have access to safe milk. Pasteur's work also helped to protect livestock by developing inoculations against anthrax.

Influenced by Pasteur, the English surgeon Joseph Lister developed the first use of antiseptics in medicine. Lister's research uncovered the fact that micro-organisms were also related to sepsis in wounds, and, in 1865, he used the first carbolic-acid dressings to protect surgical wounds from infection. The implementation of antiseptics greatly reduced the number of post-surgical deaths.

Physics

In the field of physics, James Clerk Maxwell pioneered electromagnetic theory, which unified

Charles Darwin

Charles Darwin was born in 1809, the son of a wealthy physician. At Cambridge University, he became noted as an amateur scientist, building on his life-long interest in the natural world. Having completed his university studies, he decided to sail with HMS *Beagle* and embarked on a three-year exploratory voyage in 1836. From 1842 until his death, he studied the materials he had found on his travels and consulted with his acquaintances from a network of societies. In 1859, *On the Origin of the Species* made Darwin famous. His book was to have profound implications on modern thought and to challenge mankind's understanding of its place in the world.

electricity and magnetism, and predicted the existence of the electromagnetic qualities of light, as well as the existence of other electromagnetic radiation. Maxwell was a founder of modern theoretical physics.

Joseph John Thompson was another pioneering physicist, who, in 1897, made the first model of the atom incorporating a negatively charged electron. Ernest Rutherford, who is regarded as the founder of modern nuclear physics, developed his work. Rutherford concluded that the positive charge of an atom is contained within its central nucleus, around which the negatively charged atoms are in orbit. He was awarded the Nobel Prize for chemistry in 1908, and his research would lead to his splitting the atom in the early 20th century.

In Germany, Wilhelm von Roentgen discovered by accident that a fluorescent screen glowed when an electric current was passed through a vacuum nearby. He called the radiation responsible "X-rays" as he did not know their source. After further investigation in 1895, he was able to photograph the bones in his wife's hand, pioneering the first medical use of the X-ray. Roentgen won the first Nobel Prize for physics in 1901 as a result of this work.

These great advances in science all contributed to a feeling that there were certain fundamental laws that underpinned the universe. It was believed that these could be ascertained by scientific progress. Many scientists hoped that scientific knowledge and research would come to supplant religion or superstition as the guiding principle in human endeavour, although for many people, such a notion was unsettling, questioning as it did age-old beliefs.

The start of the 100-metre race in the first modern Olympics in 1896. The Olympics attempted to celebrate the achievements of mankind in this progressive age and to underline the contemporary passion for physical prowess. The event also reflected increased ease of travel among the participants.

CULTURAL DEVELOPMENTS

The latter half of the 19th century saw increasing upheavals in intellectual life, popular culture, and the arts. Technological advances marched alongside revolutionary ideas in the sciences. As a new mass popular culture developed, artists experimented ever more boldly with artistic expression, laying the foundations for the modernist movement.

The 19th century saw the working out of many of the intellectual traditions of the 18th century. The optimism and rationality of the Enlightenment was carried forwards in progressive, liberal movements that sought to appeal to the positive side of human nature. Progress was still seen as the intellectual birthright of the century, with widespread faith in the ability of science and technology to overcome problems presented by nature.

Scientific knowledge produced considerable questioning about a divinely created universe. A more scientific approach to history led to detailed textual criticism of the Bible and its treatment as a historical text. By the end of the century, growing interest in the inner workings of the mind produced revolutionary works of psychoanalysis, such as Sigmund Freud's *The Interpretation of Dreams*, which questioned the role of free will in human action. Along with the work of pioneering sociologists such as Emile Durkheim and Max Weber, who began to see how individuals were conditioned by their environment, intellectual developments ranged beyond orthodox Christian thought. Political thinkers such as Marx set religion to one side in their materialist view of historical development, while philosophers such as Nietzsche stressed the need for man to supersede Christian morality and break from the restraints imposed on him.

For many Europeans, however, faith in progress and social reform based on Christian or rational values remained dominant. Wealthy patrons and municipalities sought to bring many of the benefits of civilization to the workers in the new industrial towns, opening libraries, art galleries, and museums to achieve this. Social reformers promoted philanthropic activities, including adult education and model housing, in order to offer opportunities for improvement. Humanitarianism also expressed itself in international organizations, such as the International Red Cross and the Olympic Movement. Common sentiments of humanity promoted crusades against slavery and the first Hague Conventions on the conduct of war. Socialism and the movements for women's rights also emerged, emphasizing the common bonds of men and women in contrast to the increasingly vehement nationalism that also marked the era.

More profound, for the majority of Europeans, was the experience of living in mass society and an increasingly urban environment. Secularization was bred among the new urban masses because of the failure of the Church to adjust quickly enough to the pace of European urbanization. Mass culture in the towns came increasingly under commercial influence, with the bar, café, and public house becoming the centres of social life. Enlightened employers offered their own recreational facilities, while many workers' sporting organizations grew up around their place of work. Professional sport and opportunities for leisure at parks, pleasure grounds, and the seaside became an increasingly important part of popular culture. Musical entertainment in theatres and music halls was now developing in new directions, with the proliferation of cheap musical instruments and the first gramophones. By the 1900s, cinema had been born, marking the beginning of a new popular entertainment for the 20th century.

Mass Culture

The rise of urban society during the 19th century brought about a new kind of mass society and culture. As the wealth of the Industrial Revolution began to spread more widely, there was growing provision for the general population in terms of social amenities and forms of recreation, as well as a huge explosion in forms of commercial leisure.

Popularization of culture

One of the most remarkable developments in late 19th-century Europe was the growth of popular institutions of culture such as libraries, museums, and art galleries. Music also moved away from the court or the Church towards the paying customer. Grand symphonies were designed for huge concert halls and opera houses where the public could have access to the culture of the day. The middle classes became particularly keen to enjoy cultural pursuits which had previously been the preserve of the aristocracy and the very wealthy. Music and culture became part of the accomplishments with which the middle classes sought to integrate themselves with the established elites.

Some of the earliest and most famous museums dated from the Renaissance, while the Louvre, Hermitage, and the British Museum had been founded in the 18th century. By the late 19th century, most major cities boasted museums and art galleries open to the public. Private collections in palaces and great houses were made increasingly available to visitors, too. Concert halls and opera houses had been built in most of the major capitals by 1900. In some countries, notably Italy, opera was to become a genuinely popular art form, with huge followings for particular singers; elsewhere, choral societies and bands based upon cheaply produced instruments were to provide musical culture to the population at large.

Social welfare

This access to culture was a reflection of the increased leisure time and slowly improving living conditions of the working classes. Improvements in environmental standards meant that the cities of Western Europe, at least, were becoming more salubrious and offering opportunities for people to participate in commercialized leisure. Governments faced increasing pressure to grant more rights to the socially or politically disenfranchised and to offer them the possibilities of improvement through

Children queue at a cinema in Berlin in 1910. The arrival of the cinema as a form of mass entertainment was a dramatic development in European culture. Moreover, the new media offered the potential to influence and mobilize huge numbers of people.

The enormous popularity of association football around 1900 was partly a result of the large numbers of men who had moved to the towns from rural areas to find work. With increased leisure time and money, many could attend the local football ground. Supporting the local team became a powerful expression of a community's solidarity.

mass compulsory education, sickness and accident insurance, and old-age pensions.

Educational provision was already widespread in France, Germany and Belgium by the middle of the 19th century, and was gradually followed elsewhere. By 1900, basic literacy could be assumed among the ordinary population of Western Europe, leading to an enormous increase in the demand for popular newspapers, magazines, and children's comics. Accompanying the spread of the printed word was the rise of advertising and the development of brand name products. By World War I, advertising hoardings, garishly packaged goods, and promotional stunts were becoming hallmarks of mass retailing.

Leisure activities

Leisure was increasingly provided on a mass scale. Cafés and public houses grew in size and opulence, providing a wide range of entertainment. In France, this could include music and dancing. Public houses in Britain provided an increasingly comfortable environment of plush furniture and gas lighting. Throughout Europe, the tram, railway, and river steamer enabled workers to escape their drab surroundings for a few hours. This era also saw the development of mass seaside resorts, served by the railways, with new attractions such as funfairs, piers, and illuminations. Pleasure gardens such as those at Tivoli in Copenhagen, the lakes of Berlin, the banks of the Seine in Paris, and the River Thames in London provided recreation nearer to home in some of the capital cities.

Organized and commercial sport also became a major feature of mass urban culture. Many sports had developed on a village or school basis during the 19th century, but were now codified, adapted, and popularized. Horse-racing was a long-established form of sport, with dedicated racecourses going back to the 18th century. The coming of the railways, the rise of the sporting press, and the development of gambling led to the proliferation of racecourses and a wide popularity for racing among rich and poor. The rise of professional and amateur football, cycling, rugby, and tennis also provided new opportunities for recreation outside work. Initially, many football clubs were associated with places of work, taking on their names, but soon exploded with the attraction of playing and spectating. New inventions were quickly turned into sporting occasions, with the first international motorcar race organized between Paris and Lyons in 1900. Cycling followed suit with the organization of the first Tour de France in 1903.

For many urban workers, the music café, or in big cities the music hall, was one of the most popular places of entertainment. Popular songs and melodies were reproduced in vast numbers as sheet music, where they could be played or sung at home. But the role of live music was being encroached on by new forms of technology, providing ever wider access to performers. The first recordings became available just after 1900. Even more significant was the emergence of the cinema. The Lumières' *cinématographe* was first exhibited in Paris in 1895 and rapidly took off as a form of popular entertainment. Some performers, such as Charlie Chaplin, became household names.

By 1914, mass urban culture was taking on the commercialized forms familiar in the 20th century. Sport was becoming more organized into national associations and international bodies, with a rise in professionalism in some areas. A large amateur component was often tied in with popular recreation, with golf and tennis reaching out to wider audiences and athletics becoming part of a cult of physical fitness for both men and women.

Intellectual and Political Thought

The late 19th century inherited the powerful forces of liberalism and nationalism that had exploded in the age of revolution. These forces saw their fulfilment in some European countries in the years before 1914.

During this period, the ideals of liberalism and nationalism were gradually put into practice in much of Western and central Europe, as states introduced representative institutions and yielded greater voting rights to their subjects. After the Second Empire, France instituted a republic with wide voting rights and regular elections. The German Empire of 1871, although autocratic in its structure, granted universal suffrage and set up the Reichstag with functioning political parties. Britain gradually extended its franchise through Reform Acts in 1867 and 1884, so that approximately three-fifths of men had the vote. The Low Countries and Scandinavia also introduced representative institutions and a degree of universal suffrage.

The companion idea to political liberty was the doctrine of free trade. This idea extended beyond the mere removal of trade barriers and tariffs, and its implications were still being worked out. Much of the liberal agenda of uniform legal codes, the abolition of arbitrary justice and torture, and the establishment of a degree of judicial independence was introduced in even some of the more conservative states. Battles for control of education between secular government and clerical bodies in France, Spain, Italy, and Germany also reflected the desire of liberals to free education from what they saw as the malign influence of clerical control. Anti-clerical laws in France in the 1880s and the 1900s, and Bismarck's *Kulturkampf*, demonstrated that these were still live issues.

In much of Eastern Europe, liberal principles were barely acknowledged. The Austro-Hungarian Empire, although it had some of the elements of constitutionalism, was an autocratic state held together by its monarchy and the interdependence of the two dominant races, the Germans and the Magyars. Similarly, the Russian tsars kept a firm grip on power until faced with the 1905 Revolution. Russian liberalism remained a weak force, under challenge from more radical doctrines.

Nationalism

Nationalism was still one of the most powerful forces at work. The unification of Germany and of Italy were the fulfilment of ideals that had been frustrated by the restored regimes of 1815 and the failures of the revolutions of 1848–9. With the decay of the Ottoman Empire, new Balkan states

Giuseppe Pelizza da Volpedo's painting The Human Tide *captures the atmosphere within the workers' movement that became so influential across Europe at the end of the 19th century. The campaign for workers' rights resulted in the formation of powerful trade unions and led to the rise of socialism.*

Friedrich Nietzsche

The German philosopher Friedrich Wilhelm Nietzsche (1844–1900) became the symbol of the new forces of irrationalism and violence which were beginning to work beneath the surface of European civilization in the 19th century. Appointed a professor at the age of 24, he achieved notoriety for his assertion that mankind must transcend conventional constraints to achieve true self-mastery as "superman". His views have often been seen as foreshadowing 20th-century fascism. Nietzsche's famous dictum that "God is dead" and his own insanity from 1889 have only added to his mystique.

were created in Serbia, Bulgaria, and Romania, establishing precedents for other national groups to strive for independence. Ethnic nationalism became one of the main preoccupations of intellectuals in Europe. In the Austro-Hungarian Empire, Poles, Czechs, and Slavs sought to express themselves through re-establishing their history and culture. But in many of these instances, nationalism was still contained within the embrace of larger states. Almost a third of the inhabitants of the Russian Empire, for example, were non-Russian speakers, belonging to a variety of ethnic groups.

Challenges and conflicts

Nationalism and liberalism were not always mutually compatible forces. Anti-militarism and anti-clericalism on the part of liberals led to their being distrusted by more conservative forces, who put support for the nation above all else. Ethnic nationalism often proved itself to be exclusive, intolerant, and illiberal towards other nationalities.

The pursuit of national interest also led to the questioning of the economic principle of free trade. By the 1880s, several countries had set about imposing tariffs. Agricultural competition from the USA and the colonies also led to anxieties about the need to protect agriculture. Even in Britain, the home of free trade, movements for tariff reform and protection emerged in the 1900s, although they failed to obtain a decisive following.

Socialism and Marxism

The great rival to both liberalism and nationalism was socialism. Initially, the most significant expressions of workers' solidarities were the trade union movements of France and Britain. French trade unions brought strikes to Paris in 1907. In

Germany by 1912 there had been 3000 strikes, and there were over 2.6 million trade union members. In Britain, the Trades Union Congress was formed in 1868, initially of small craft unions, but soon "new unionism" began to incorporate unskilled and semi-skilled workers. With over 4 million members by 1914, trade unions looked increasingly to their own socialist parties.

For many, the ideas of Karl Marx provided the inspiration. Although the main principles of Marxism had been laid down by the 1848 *Communist Manifesto*, Marx spent the rest of his life demonstrating the accuracy of his analysis in his writings, principally *Das Kapital*. Marx, however, left no precise prescription for the political means that should be used to encourage or bring about revolution, thus leaving it open to "revisionists" such as the German Edward Bernstein to suggest that the revolution could be brought about by parliamentary means. Similarly, in Britain, where socialism was more influenced by ethical and Christian principles than by Marxism, the prevalent socialist doctrine was that of "gradualism", espoused by the Fabian Society. Elsewhere, where possibilities of reform looked much less likely, anarchists such as Mikhail Bakunin sought to bring about the revolution by direct action, including violence. For others, such as Lenin and the Bolsheviks, the lesson of Marxism was that if revolution were to be effected in a backward country such as Russia, it would have to be carried out by a tightly organized revolutionary group, such as the Bolsheviks.

By the turn of the century, intellectual and political thought was being affected by the fashion for violence and direct action that seemed in flat contradiction to the rational, "improving" assumptions of 19th-century liberalism. Much that had once been accepted was now open to question.

Internationalism

A new social and political order was emerging in late 19th-century Europe that shared sufficient assumptions about its values and beliefs to promote international causes on a European and worldwide scale. The rise of socialism promised to unite workers in whatever country, while the movement for women's rights transcended national boundaries.

Slaves in Zanzibar during the 19th century. The campaign to abolish slavery in Africa was driven by humanitarian groups from all over the world, and came to fruition at the end of the century at the Congress of Berlin.

International socialism

Many of the great principles of the 19th century had a common international focus. Socialists looked for solidarity across national boundaries, calling on workers to unite against their common enemies. This internationalism found early expression in the congregation of many radical and socialist exiles as refugees in host countries such as Britain and Switzerland. Karl Marx was only one of the most prominent of a group of exiles who found themselves forced to make the best of their sojourn in foreign capitals. Later, Russian radicals such as Lenin would be forced to take the similar route of exile to avoid prosecution by the tsarist police. This enforced internationalism found more tangible expression in the First International established by Marx and Engels in London in 1864, but which became beset by internal quarrels between Marxists and anarchists, and was dissolved in 1876. The Second International was formed in Paris in 1889 and proved more durable. It attempted to co-ordinate socialist policies against the threat of war, although these foundered amidst the call to arms of 1914, which saw its effective demise. The aspiration to international co-operation was

expressed in the famous anthem of socialist and communist workers, *L'Internationale*, written in French in 1871 to music composed by a Belgian worker-composer, and which later became the national anthem of the USSR. In practice, the aspirations to international brotherhood failed to overcome national sentiments in the wars that affected Europe between 1848 and 1914.

International causes

Internationalism proved more successful where it harnessed existing humanitarian sentiment. The International Red Cross, set up in 1864 by the Geneva Convention, attempted to ease the sufferings of soldiers in wars. It gradually acquired respected international status, laying down certain minimum conditions for the treatment of prisoners of war. Sponsored by neutral Switzerland, the Red Cross reflected the role of some of the smaller countries, which could stand aside from great-power politics and pursue moral agendas often ignored by the major nation-states. The Red Cross was part of a trend of enlightened internationalism that sought an end to war. Peace congresses were held regularly in the years up to 1900. At the

The Geneva Convention was formed in 1864 following a Diplomatic Conference held by the Swiss government. The Convention aimed to improve conditions for soldiers wounded in conflict, and was the forerunner of contemporary humanitarian laws. This painting depicts the signing of the Convention by the 16 heads of state.

International sport

The ever growing interest in sport was reflected internationally by one of the most successful international movements begun in the 19th century. In 1894, the French aristocrat Baron Pierre de Coubertin proposed the revival of the four-yearly Olympic Games, last held in AD 393. This was an attempt to encourage the ideal of Olympic sportsmanship on an individual rather than a national basis, and to this end the first modern Olympiad was held in Athens in 1896, without overt ceremony. Elsewhere, the French football team visited Britain in the 1900s, although no regular international sporting contacts were created between European nations before World War I.

Women's rights

The movement to bring equality to women began in the French revolutionary era; however, Mary Wollstonecraft's pioneering call for women's rights in the 1790s went largely unanswered from men until John Stuart Mill advocated women's rights in Parliament in Britain in the 1860s. Some progress was made in Britain as women were allowed to vote in local elections from 1872 and were also able to stand as candidates in municipal elections. Women's educational institutions became more prominent from the middle of the 19th century, and writers such as George Sand, George Eliot, and the Brontës, prominent philanthropists such as Florence Nightingale, and scientists such as Marie Curie established the place of women in the cultural life of Europe. In the Netherlands, the first women were able to enter the medical profession by 1870 and German universities were opened to women in 1909. In France the first female lawyer was appointed in 1903. Women's colleges in British universities provided women with access to higher education, although many professions remained effectively closed apart from teaching.

By 1900, Germany had over 850 organizations campaigning for women's suffrage. Finland was the first country in Europe formally to admit women to the vote in 1906. The demand for women's suffrage took shape in Britain with the establishment of the Women's Social and Political Union in 1903. On the eve of World War I, British women had been forced to a campaign of violence in order to push the issue higher up the political agenda, with still no prospect that it would be granted. Nonetheless, the campaign for women's suffrage was an obvious example of an increasingly pan-European movement. World War I would transform the position of women in the combatant nations and bring the vote to many in the years that followed.

The Women's Social and Political Union, or Suffragette movement, was founded in Britain in 1903 by Emmeline Pankhurst. In their attempts to attract attention to their cause, the suffragettes were often prepared to use direct and militant action, such as chaining themselves to parliament buildings, and vandalizing paintings in art galleries.

Hague Conferences in 1899 and 1907, the Hague Tribunal was developed, through which international disputes could be settled by arbitration, rather than by force. Less successful attempts were made to prohibit certain weapons, although by the outbreak of World War I, the Hague Convention did provide rules for the treatment of prisoners of war.

Humanitarianism also found its outlet in the continuing campaign against slavery. A growing degree of international co-operation in the first half of the 19th century culminated in the first World Anti-Slavery Convention held in London in 1840. It included representatives of British, French, and American anti-slavery organizations. In 1884, the USA, Germany, France, Britain, and other leading powers meeting at the Congress of Berlin agreed to work actively to suppress the slave trade in Africa. The atrocities committed in the quasi-independent domain of King Leopold of the Belgians in the Congo were widely reported in 1903, and pressure was brought to bear by a Congo Reform Campaign based in Britain, with support from the United States and Belgian and French missionaries. The Belgian government was forced to take over the Congo and be responsible for what took place there.

Literature, Music, and Photography

The later 19th century and early 20th century initially witnessed the continued strength of the Romantic movement. Nationalism and humanity were celebrated through veneration of folk culture. Simultaneously, there was deep concern for those whom the industrial revolution had impoverished. The concern was to give way to fear that western civilization was in peril from new social forces.

Literature

The "Social Question" was central to much 19th-century literature. The deeply romantic novels of George Sand (real name Amandine Aurore Lucie Dupin) written in the mid-19th century depicted the struggle of women against the contemporary moral order. While in exile, Victor Hugo, the high priest of the Romantic movement, wrote his fierce satires of Napoleonic France. Fyodor Dostoevsky wrote of the corruption of the modern world during his stay in London.

Charles Dickens drew on his own experiences to highlight the suffering and great social divide brought about by the Industrial Revolution. His descriptions of social inequality and the lamentable living conditions of society's poor inspired calls for social reform. Dickens wrote of the horrors of the English workhouse in *Oliver Twist* (1838), which also covered the crime, vice, and sheer unhappiness of parts of London. Emile Zola explored the influence of heredity and environment on a working-class family in his *Rougon-Macquart* series (1871–93), of which *Germinal* (1885) brought to the public's attention the reality of coal-mining in northern France.

Nevertheless, mid-19th century literature seemed to reflect a certain order or system to life. In George Eliot's *Middlemarch* (1870–1) or Dickens's *Great Expectations* (1861), the protagonists find their place in life by triumphing over adversity. In Dostoevsky's works *Crime and Punishment* (1866) and *The Idiot* (1868), individuals are morally improved by the sufferings they have experienced.

Towards the end of the 19th century and at the beginning of the 20th, modernism challenged the notion that science and progress would solve mankind's problems. Literary figures came to believe that Western civilization was dying and was in need of vigorous revival. Writers lamented the loss of spirituality, vigour, and originality, which they believed had been caused by 19th-century rationalism. Many novelists, playwrights, and poets simply despaired of post-Industrial Revolution society. Thomas Hardy was deeply pessimistic about mankind and its suffering, sharing with Nietzsche a belief that civilization was on the road to ruin. Hardy depicted life as a struggle against unseen forces that seem destined to bring depression and frustration. James Joyce wrote, "History is a nightmare, from which I am trying to awake", reflecting a dark fascination with psychology epitomized by Sigmund Freud and a loss of faith that the scientific study of man's past would point the way to its future. Franz Kafka's works *The*

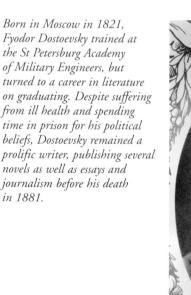

Born in Moscow in 1821, Fyodor Dostoevsky trained at the St Petersburg Academy of Military Engineers, but turned to a career in literature on graduating. Despite suffering from ill health and spending time in prison for his political beliefs, Dostoevsky remained a prolific writer, publishing several novels as well as essays and journalism before his death in 1881.

The valkyries in a performance of Wagner's Der Ring des Nibelungen in 1896. In 1876, Richard Wagner founded the Festspielhaus in Bayreuth, Bavaria, which soon became the site of the annual festival of his music.

Trial (1925) and *The Castle* (1925) are disturbing narratives of vulnerable individuals whose lives are directed by obscure and unseen forces beyond their control. An apotheosis of these sentiments is contained in Oswald Spengler's book *The Decline of the West*, written shortly before World War I. Spengler believed that the triumphs of liberal culture, prosperity, the search for ideological absolutes, and scientific discovery were evidence that the West had lost its vitality and cultural fertility. A true culture did not need this kind of reflection; people should live life instead of thinking about it.

Music

The music of the 19th century was an extremely rich reflection of the great themes of the day. Opera truly came to the public as great opera houses were built in major European cities. The Staatsoper was built in Vienna in 1869, the Paris Opera was erected in 1875, while in London the Royal Opera House was opened in 1858. In Bayreuth in 1876, Richard Wagner, with whose name it became synonymous, erected the Festspielhaus. Bayreuth was to house the annual festival in Wagner's honour.

Wagner was the greatest German composer of the later 19th century and a towering intellect. He was concerned with Germanic myth and legend, and was unhappy with much of modern life. Wagner's opera cycle *Der Ring des Nibelungen* (1853–74) can be seen as an allegory of the contemporary world, where attaining gold leads to power, but at the cost of love. *Der Ring* shows the strength of anti-modernity in the late 1800s, while simultaneously being a monumental triumph of

human spirit in its sheer intensity. Richard Strauss was another popular German composer, whose work *Die Frau Ohne Schatten* (1919) demonstrates his sharing of Wagner's interest in myth.

Myth and folk legends had been an inspiration from the 19th century, often reflecting nationalist sentiment. The Czech composers Bedrich Smetana and Leos Janácek displayed a love of folk idioms as a means of expressing Czech heroism and culture. Pyotr Tchaikovsky epitomized Romanticism in music and his veneration of Russian history can be seen in the *1812 Overture* (1880). His compatriot Modest Mussorgsky was similarly an impassioned Russian nationalist. The greatest Italian composer, Giuseppe Verdi, was an ardent nationalist. His grandest opera, *Aida*, was commissioned to celebrate the opening of the Suez Canal, celebrating a triumph of European civilization.

Photography

William Fox Talbot, the English chemist, had by 1841 pioneered a method to produce a photographic negative from which positive images could be developed. Working independently in France, in 1851, Louis Daguerre invented a method for producing photographs involving mercury vapour and an iodine-sensitive plate. This process was referred to as daguerreotype. Early photography was often employed as a means of recording events, similar to a portrait painting of a family. However, the impact of photography was soon felt on the visual arts. The Impressionist painter Degas was influenced by photography in his paintings, attempting to capture the seemingly spontaneous nature of photography in his scenes of everyday life.

Impressionism

Impressionism took art outdoors, away from the studied environment of the academy. The Impressionists tried to capture the appearance of things, literally re-creating an impression on canvas as the eye saw it. Although the artists involved did not adhere to a coherent philosophy, their work marked a seismic shift in the history of art.

Origins

In 1874, a group of artists, many of whom had had their work rejected by the Paris Salon, mounted their own exhibition in Paris. Their work was heavily criticized. Forsaking the themes and techniques of traditional academic art, they painted contemporary subject matter with a spontaneous style never seen before – many complained it looked "unfinished". One critic, Leonard Leroy, scathingly described the works as "impressionist", making reference to Claude Monet's painting *Impression: Sunrise.*

Today the term is used to describe the paintings of a group of artists working from the 1860s to the 1880s, including, among others, Claude Monet, Pierre-Auguste Renoir, Camille Pissarro, Berthe Morisot, and Alfred Sisley. Their work is characterized more by a shared attitude than a delineated set of aesthetic ideas, and, although they chose to exhibit together, they actually had very different methods of painting.

One way of understanding Impressionism is to see it as a reaction against the prevailing artistic conventions of neoclassicism and Romanticism. Impressionists sought to capture an image "scientifically", rather than emotionally, examining the effect of light and shadow on a given subject. Artists such as Monet, Sisley, and Pissarro were fascinated by the fact that light is broken up into its constituent parts of the seven colours of the spectrum when it hits an object. Thus objects reflect rays of colour to the eye, which it then combines. In trying to re-create the image received on the retina, the Impressionists became aware of subtle shades such as the blue or brown in shadows. This was to be developed later by Georges Seurat, who

Eduard Manet's The Bar at the Folies-Bergeres, *painted in 1881–2, presents a number of ambiguities for the viewer. The obscurities that lie behind the barmaid's role in life, her expression, and her surroundings highlight the uncertainty of life in Paris at the time. The Impressionists were keen to record such contemporary experiences in their paintings.*

attempted to formalize optical theory on his canvasses by creating images from a series of tiny dots of colour, a method known as pointillism.

Impressionist art

The Impressionists pioneered *plein-air* ("in the open air") painting, often working directly from the subject, rather than from preliminary drawings, as was the academic convention. They often depicted the same scene over and over again. Monet, for example, made several studies of Rouen Cathedral and of his garden at Giverny.

This devotion to the world as it is seen extended to subject matter. The Impressionists avoided the mythological and historic themes prescribed by the Académie des Beaux-Arts, and instead found inspiration in the contemporary world around them: Renoir painted scenes of Parisians at leisure, as in his celebrated *Luncheon of the Boating Party* (1881); Degas eschewed portraits of the illustrious and depicted anonymous dancers, laundresses, and ordinary workers. The teeming Paris streets, the clamour of the *café-concert*, even the factories and locomotives of the Industrial Revolution were subjects of inspiration. Édouard Manet's *Olympia* (1863) caused a scandal when it was first exhibited, as it seemed to flaunt the conventions of classical art by painting a prostitute in the pose of a classical odalisque. His *Execution of Emperor Maximilian* (1867) was officially banned from the Paris World Exhibition of the same year for its overt criticism of Napoleon III's policies in Mexico. He was to paint several versions of the scene.

The American painter James MacNeil Whistler was another important figure. Whistler took Impressionist ideas a stage further, concentrating on reproducing prominent shapes and tones, just as objects in reality are not seen equally clearly. Whistler aimed to "leave out shape and, through colour, vie with the musician who makes use of sounds". This musical analogy was made explicit through the titles of his paintings, which feature series entitled *Nocturne* and *Symphony in White*.

The influence of Impressionism

The influence of the Impressionists spread beyond painting. Sculptors were intrigued by its possibilities – in 1889, Monet exhibited with Auguste Rodin, sculptor of *The Kiss*. Rodin, too, had had many of his early works rejected by the Salon, but by the time of the joint exhibition had been commissioned to produce many public works. Monet's association with Rodin was evidence of the painter's increasing eminence.

French poets Charles Baudelaire and Stephane Mallarmé were drawn to the works of the

Optics and colour theory

From the 1850s, studies had been made in the fields of optics and colour theory. Michel Eugène Chevreul, originally a chemist, published his theories on the simultaneous perception of colours, whereby those adjacent to their complementary colour are perceived more intensely. The physicist James Clerk Maxwell had shown that the eye blends adjacent colour as though on a palette. These findings continued to have profound effects on the Impressionists and those who came afterwards, particularly Henri Matisse and the Fauves.

Impressionists. Indeed, the Paris scenes depicted in Impressionist paintings seemed to mirror the city Baudelaire evoked in his poetry, and Rodin illustrated Baudelaire's masterwork *Les Fleurs du Mal* of 1886–8. Mallarmé's poetry aimed to use words to create the equivalent of Impressionist painting, evoking moods and conjuring visual images through language.

Even music was influenced by Impressionism, with Debussy the father of its musical counterpart. Claude Debussy was reacting against the legacy of Wagner and the emotional qualities that were exhibited by Romantic music. Atmosphere and style became more important than the story being told. Debussy employed new chord combinations and innovative rhythms, and in works such as *L'Après-midi d'un faune* (1892–4) – itself inspired by the poem by Mallarmé – exhibited the idea of the musical "tone poem", which would capture the essence of the moment.

Aftermath

Impressionists were often criticized by subsequent art movements. The analytical abstraction of Cubism favoured a move away from capturing visual reality. The Italian Futurists advocated a complete break with the past and called for a celebration of speed, machinery, and the modern age.

Yet Impressionism was hugely influential within the art world. The interest in light and the technique of capturing it with paint influenced a great many successors such as Vincent Van Gogh, Henri Toulouse-Latrec, and Paul Gauguin. Today, their work is among the most instantly recognizable and best loved in the world.

Towards a Modern Art

The massive political, social, religious, and economic changes that swept Europe from 1848 to 1914 were, unsurprisingly, reflected in its art. A variety of movements emerged across literature, painting, architecture, sculpture, and other art forms, which represented reactions to the technological and cultural transformation of the European continent.

The impact of the Industrial Revolution

In the 1890s, Europe's cultural climate changed, and there was a reaction to 19th-century cultural orthodoxy across many art forms. Artists and writers began to question the assumptions that had underpinned the ideas of mid-century thinkers, and they began to take on radically new forms. The outside world no longer seemed a unified entity subject to the law of rationalism, but a fragmented and confused one. The cultural world began to accept that it was the role of the avant-garde artist to express this fragmentation.

Art nouveau

From the 1890s through to the early 1900s, art nouveau became the international artistic style in Western Europe and was applied to all spheres of art and design – from architecture and furniture to fine art, illustration, and textiles. It can be seen as both a product of and a reaction to the Industrial Revolution. With its characteristic organic shapes and sinuous, interwoven lines, art nouveau seemed to embody an absinthe-inspired dream, a wilful rejection of the reality of the industrial age.

The langorous women featured in the poster designs of the Czech artist Alponse Mucha seem to inhabit a world apart from the steam age. Yet artists and designers working within the style emphasized the importance of good-quality design and in so doing exploited the new technologies to their fullest potential. The entrances to the Paris Metro, designed by Hector Guimard in 1900, clearly demonstrate the art nouveau style and make full use of the possibilities of new materials such as cast iron.

Charles Rennie Mackintosh, the startlingly original Scottish architect, was a bridge between the world of art nouveau and the beginnings of the modern movement in Europe. His pioneering Glasgow Art School and smaller commissions in and around Glasgow attracted the attention of the Viennese Secession, the group of avant-garde artists and architects working in the art nouveau idiom in Vienna. Mackintosh was invited to exhibit with them, demonstrating the increasingly international character of artistic experimentation.

Although the visual style of art nouveau had fallen out of favour by the outbreak of World War

The Bathers by Paul Cézanne was one of a group of paintings dubbed "post-Impressionist" at the start of the 20th century. These artists reacted against the lack of structure in Impressionist compositions, and intended to make their art into something more solid.

I, its emphasis on the quality of design and craftsmanship would influence later 20th-century movements, such as the Bauhaus in the 1920s.

Aesthetic movement

As the birthplace of the Industrial Revolution, Britain felt its effects keenly, and from the 1870s to the 1890s, saw the rise of the aesthetic movement. Its exponents rejected all that industrial society had to offer and proclaimed art's sole purpose was to express beauty. The aesthetics' rallying cry, "art for art's sake", was unambiguous: art did not have a moral or political agenda. The critic John Ruskin and the group of artists known as the Pre-Raphaelites sought to recapture the innocence and beauty of a pre-industrial age. The movement gained a reputation for decadence, personified by the writer, aesthete, and wit Oscar Wilde, whose flamboyant conduct and dress sense made him the talk of London.

The aesthetics' affectations were lampooned in the press, yet the movement was to have a wider significance. The rejection of industry and what was perceived as the shoddiness of machine-made goods inspired William Morris's arts and crafts movement, which emphasized the importance of skilled craftsmanship and design.

Fauvism

The Fauves ("wild beasts") were a short-lived art movement based in Paris from 1905. Influenced by the increasingly "primitive" styles of post-Impressionist painters such as Paul Cézanne, Paul Gauguin, and Vincent Van Gogh, the Fauves' work was characterized by intense colour, applied directly onto the canvas without mixing. Chief among the Fauves was Henri Matisse, whose experiments with colour and compelling personality drew artists such as Raoul Dufy and André Derain to the movement. Fauvist paintings were raw and vibrant, characterized by vidid colours, strong brushwork, and a flattened sense of space as a means of expressing emotions.

For many of the Fauves, the movement was a period of transition and experiment. Matisse alone would pursue the path that he had developed and would exert a strong influence on 20th-century art. Georges Braque's Fauvist work of this period foreshadowed the direction that would ultimately lead to cubism.

Expressionism

The expressionist movement took place in Germany as a reaction against German academic art. It was influenced by the rawness and spatial

Art Nouveau was established as the first new decorative style of the 20th century at the 1900 World's Fair in Paris. One of many examples of the form can be seen in the Paris Metro network; the entrances to the stations are adorned with Art Nouveau cast iron work designed by architect Hector Guimard.

flattening of the Fauves, as well as the intensity of emotion expressed in the works of Van Gogh and Norwegian painter Edvard Munch. Expressionism manifested itself in two groups: Die Brucke ("The Bridge"), led by Ernst Kirchner, and Der Blaue Reiter ("The Blue Rider"), led by the Russian-born Vasili Kandinsky. Expressionism was noted for its anti-naturalistic tendencies, expressing extreme emotions of pathos, violence, and rage. Propelling Kandinsky's work was the belief that colour and shape conveyed spiritual meanings, which led him increasingly towards non-representational, abstract painting

Futurism

In 1909, the excitement and possibilities of the machine age inspired the group of Italian artists known as the futurists. The Italian poet Filippo Marinetti launched the movement when he published his manifesto in *Le Figaro*, referring to "the beauty of speed" and threatening to "destroy the museums". Marinetti and the futurists sought to unsettle the public and aimed to represent dynamism and modernity, exalting in the new sensibilities of the era. In his poetry, Marinetti rejected traditional formats, and his plays included such innovations as staging simultaneous yet unconnected actions. The futurist painters, including Umberto Boccioni, Giacomo Balla, and Gino Severini, sought to capture that dynamism in their paintings, emphasizing simultaneity and speed. Their manifesto of 1910 threatened to "destroy the cult of the past". The futurists' calls for a violent overthrow of history were often successful: their performances frequently ended in riots.

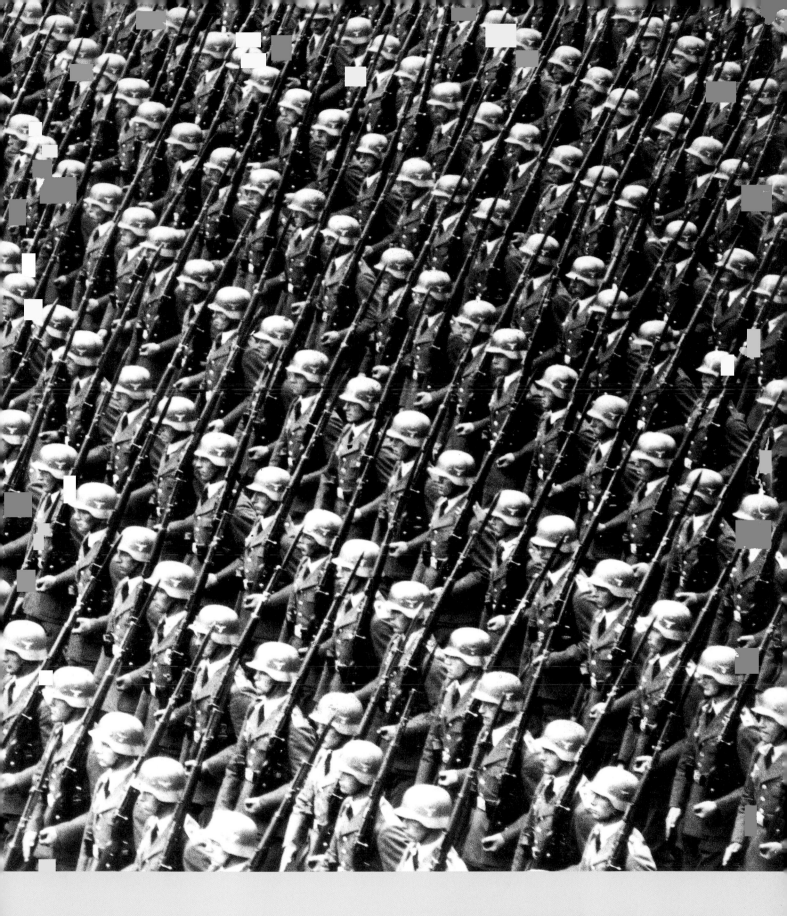

EUROPE AT WAR

1914–45

POLITICS AND GOVERNMENT

1919 After months of negotiation, the victorious Allies place the finished articles of the Versailles Treaty in front of the representatives of the new Weimar Republic.

1918 As resistance crumbles and revolution starts in the naval shipyards, the nascent German Republic signs an armistice on 11 November, ending World War I.

1917 October Revolution in Russia. On 7 November the Provisional Government drifts, and Lenin and his Bolesheviks act and seize power.

1916 The British Grand Fleet and the German High Seas Fleet clash in the North Sea for naval domination at the Battle of Jutland.

1914 Between 1 and 4 August, the two major European power blocs – the Allies and the Central Powers – mobilize. World War I begins.

1928 The majority of the independent nations of the world sign the Kellogg–Briand Pact renouncing war as a means of settling disputes.

1920 The League of Nations is established in Geneva.

1925 The Locarno Treaties secure the Germany's western frontier and set up a system for mediation in case of dispute.

1922 King Victor Emmanuel appoints the fascist Mussolini as prime minister of Italy after he threatens a revolutionary march on Rome.

1910   **1915**   **1920**   **1925**

SOCIETY AND CULTURE

1913 Marcel Proust writes his epic *A la Recherche de temps perdu* (*Remembrance of Things Past*). He pioneers the use of the stream-of-consciousness style later developed by other Modernist writers such as James Joyce and Virginia Woolf.

1916 Dada "anti-art" movement founded in Zurich.

1918 Female suffrage is introduced in Britain for women over 30. The great flu epdemic in Europe kills more people than World War I itself.

1919 The new Weimar constitution grants the vote to women over the age of 20. Walter Gropius founds the Bauhaus school at Weimar. Its aim is to teach its students to unite the different skills of all the arts. First daily flight between London and Paris.

1925 Arts Décoratifs exhibition in Paris gives its name to Art Deco style. Russian director Sergei Eisenstein creates his groundbreaking epic film *Battleship Potemkin*.

1927 First "talkie" films appear.

1921–3 Crop failures in the Soviet Union, lead to an estmated 5 million deaths, the majority in the countryside.

1928 Alexander Fleming accidentally discovers penicillin, leading to the development of antibiotics.

1929 Wall Street Crash triggers the worldwide Depression.

1939 23 August: Nazi Germany and the USSR sign a non-aggression pact. 1 September: German troops enter Poland. The British and French governments' ultimatum that Germany withdraw from Poland is met with silence, and on 3 September, they declare war on Germany.

1938 After agitation by local Nazis, Hitler marches into Austria uniting the two major German-speaking nations on 11 March 1938. Germany is granted the right to the Sudetenland in Czechoslovakia at the Munich Conference.

1933 Hitler, the leader of the largest party in the Reichstag, is appointed chancellor of Germany by President Hindenburg.

1936 Without consultation or permission, Hitler sends troops to remilitarize the Rhineland. Franco and a group of Spanish generals launch their attack against the republican government.

1940 The "Battle of Britain" takes place. Germany invades France, the Netherlands, and Belgium.

1941 Hitler turns his gaze to the East and launches a surprise attack against the USSR ("Operation Barbarossa") on 22 June 1941. The attack on Pearl Harbour by the Japanese, together with Hitler's declaration of war on 7 December 1941, brings America into the war.

1943 The tide turns on the Eastern Front as Hitler's panzers lose the largest tank battle of the war at Kursk.

1944 D-Day. On 6 June 1944, the Anglo–US invasion in the beaches of Normandy opens the long-awaited Second Front.

1945 VE Day. After six years of war, Germany is defeated. Von Keitel surrenders to Marshal Zhukov.

1935   **1940**   **1945**   **1950**

1930–5 The height of the Surrealist movement. The movement explores the expression of the unconscious. Salvador Dalí from Spain and the Belgian René Magritte are the principal exponents.

1936 First regular television broadcast transmitted by the BBC in London.

1937 Picasso's famous painting depicting the bombing of Guernica during the Spanish Civil War is displayed in Paris.

1938–9 Whilst in exile from Nazi Germany, poet and dramatist Bertolt Brecht produces some of his most powerful plays, including *Galileo* (1938) and *Mother Courage* (1939).

1942 Wannsee Conference, at which the Nazis formulate the "Final Solution" to the "Jewish Problem", leading to the Holocaust.

1943 Penicillin first used as a medicine.

1945 The US airforce drop the first atomic bombs on Hiroshima, Japan, killing one third of the population. This is followed three days later by an atomic attack on Nagasaki that leads to the Japanese surrender in World War II.

1944 Germany fires V-2 rockets against Britain. The technology behind the weapon will later be used in developing the space and weapons programmes of the USSR and the USA.

SOCIETY AND CULTURE

A British "Tommy" in his trench on the Somme front in July 1916. The major Somme offensive of that month would see 60,000 British casualties on the first day alone. It was the bloodiest day suffered by any nation during World War I, and the bloodiest day in the history of the British army.

WORLD WAR I

After more than 40 years without a war between any of the great powers, the majority of Europe was convulsed by a titanic clash of arms in 1914. Imperial entanglements, alliances beyond Europe, and the search for fresh allies eventually embroiled virtually the whole world. The impact of the conflict cannot be exaggerated.

The assassination by a Bosnian terrorist of Archduke Franz Ferdinand, the heir to the Austrian throne, at Sarajevo on 28 June ignited a full-scale European war. Earlier diplomatic crises had heightened tension between the great powers, and military and diplomatic alliances already entangled many of them in unbreakable coalitions. If one country became involved, others would have to follow. Intricate military timetables left little room for diplomacy to operate as the crisis deepened during July 1914. Austria-Hungary's declaration of war on Serbia, which it blamed for the terrorist outrage, on 28 July sparked off a chain reaction as the powers came to the aid of their respective alliance partners and declared war in order to sanction the swift implementation of their war plans.

Germany declared war on Russia and France in support of its ally Austria-Hungary, forming the Central Powers. France and Russia were now ranged against them, forcing Britain to honour its close relationship with France by declaring war on Germany, then Austria-Hungary. By 12 August, most of the European powers had ranged themselves with one side or the other; Italy bided its time until 1915, when it joined the Western allies, Britain and France. From the outset, the war had an extra-European dimension. The Turkish Empire, covering much of the Middle East, sided with the Central Powers; Japan followed its long-standing alliance with Britain.

The swiftness with which the war unfolded, however, was not to be matched by an equally swift victory. Four years of war would produce casualties on an unprecedented scale, measured in tens of millions. Economies were destroyed by the strain of the struggle, and attitudes within societies towards representation, gender, and class

were significantly altered in many countries. The appearance of Europe and the balance of power in the world changed. The old Russian Empire disappeared, to be replaced by the new Soviet state that was to dominate so much of the century's history.

The nature of the war was unlike any previous European conflict. This was the first to involve fully developed and industrialized nations, and the scale was vast. The battle lines extended almost continuously from the Channel to the Swiss Alps in the west and along most frontiers in the east. It is estimated that 70 million men were in uniform during the war, of which around nine million were killed. By the end of the war, few households in Europe had not lost a relative.

The stress on the economies of the participants was equally large. Wars had always been expensive, but this was on a scale hitherto unseen. Not only were larger armies involved, but also the armies themselves needed larger quantities of supplies due to the nature of the weapons used. For all of the original participants, central governments took an ever increasing hand in directing their economies to provide for these needs, to the extent of rationing essential goods. Germany was eventually devoting more than 80 per cent of its economy to the war effort. The British blockade would demonstrate how modern nations were built on international trade, with, according to German figures, 750,000 dying from malnutrition by the end of the war.

The financial cost of World War I altered the financial landscape of the world. Great Britain had entered the war as the world's largest creditor nation, but the USA emerged from the conflict with that title due to the large loans that Britain would seek to finance its war effort.

The Western Front

The industrial nature of society had expanded the capacity of governments to organize their populations. In the sphere of defence, this meant an enhanced capacity to put an increased proportion of the population under arms. Most European nations ran a system of conscription. Britain was an exception to this: it traditionally relied on its navy, and conscription was seen as an infringement on personal liberty. Its professional army was dwarfed by its continental neighbours.

Troops on the Western Front "go over the top" at night. In addition to the huge set-piece offensives, night-time raids were used by generals to gather intelligence, disrupt, and demoralize the enemy, and as a means of keeping up the offensive spirit in their own troops. For some, although dangerous, they relieved the stress and boredom of trench life.

The Western Front during World War I was confined to a relatively narrow area. Indeed, the lines of farthest and least penetration occurred at the beginning and end of the war, respectively. For the majority of the war, the trench lines hardly moved, and battles in successive years were contested on the same ground.

Germany had been planning tactics for a two-front war against France and Russia for decades. Britain's role was uncertain. It had no formal obligations to defend France, but had guaranteed Belgium neutrality through the Treaty of London of 1839. The German solution to the unattractive possibility of fighting on two fronts was to employ a modified version of the Schlieffen Plan, developed in the previous century. The German plan was to leave minimal forces on the Eastern Front to guard against the slowly mobilizing Russians, defeat France quickly, then shift the army eastward to meet the advancing Russians by means of its dense railway network.

The opening blows

The attack on France was to be delivered by sweeping through Belgium, outflanking the French front line, and capturing Paris while holding the centre of the line. In August 1914, as the German army advanced to the north, the French advanced

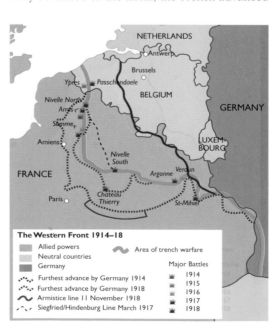

The Western Front 1914–18

- Allied powers
- Neutral countries
- Germany
- ····· Furthest advance by Germany 1914
- ····· Furthest advance by Germany 1918
- ～～ Armistice line 11 November 1918
- ·—· Siegfried/Hindenburg Line March 1917

- ～～ Area of trench warfare

Major Battles
- ✳ 1914
- ✳ 1915
- ✳ 1916
- ✳ 1917
- ✳ 1918

forwards in Lorraine and the Ardennes, only to be beaten back with costly losses. The British sent their Expeditionary Force to link with the left flank of the growing French armies. In contrast, the German army made significant headway through Belgium, pushing back both the French and the British armies. The Schlieffen Plan appeared to be working. Helmut Johannes Von Moltke, commanding the German army, responded by weakening the right arm, believing that he could go on the offensive in Lorraine as well. In addition, certain that victory had already been achieved, he detached a corps for transfer to the east. The situation for Britain and France was critical. Reorganizing and calling up vital reserves, Joseph Jacques Joffre, the French commander-in-chief, prepared a counter-offensive, and the resulting Battle of the Marne on 5 September marked a crucial stage. Casualties were vast on both sides, but the Germans became convinced that they were in danger of becoming outflanked and so withdrew. The Schlieffen Plan had failed. Both sides now attempted to out-manoeuvre the other, by seeking to turn each other's northern flank. By November 1914, an increasingly large system of trenches and fortifications was set up to defend their lines from the Channel to Switzerland. In December 1914, the French and British sought to bludgeon their way through the German lines, seeking a swift conclusion to the war. It was a costly failure: the first months of the war saw approximately one million casualties on each side.

Changing priorities

Having failed to achieve a decisive result against France, in 1915 Germany shifted its focus to the Eastern Front. The French were happy to take up the offensive in their attempts to free French territory under German occupation. The British, whose army was growing through the ready supply of volunteers, looked for a war-winning decision on the Western Front. These attempts were fought along the front in a series of offensives from September to November 1915, at the three battles of Champagne, the Battle of Neuve-Chapelle, the three battles of Artois, the Battle of Loos, and the Battle of Vimy Ridge. The Germans also returned to the offensive. At the second Battle of Ypres, in April 1915, the Germans used poison gas for the first time, but despite this were unable to advance. The defensive power of trenches, barbed wire, and machine-gun nests meant that 1915 ended with little change in the lines. The cost was more than a million casualties for France, half a million for Germany and a quarter of a million for Britain.

Attrition

The focus moved again in 1916. All sides were determined to seek an outcome on the Western Front. The Germans were again on the offensive and the Allies attempted to co-ordinate attacks in the East and West. Falkenhayn, the new German commander, realizing that the Western Front was now a battle of attrition, was determined to exhaust France, even if a breakthrough could not be made. The Germans attacked at Verdun in February 1916, beginning an arduous 10-month battle. Despite suffering enormous losses, the French army did not allow Germany to advance. Relief only came when Russia succeeded in mounting its Brusilov offensive, which drew German divisions away from the Western Front. In July of the same year, Britain and France launched an offensive along the Somme river, attacking after a week-long bombardment aimed at destroying German resistance. It failed. The number of casualties was horrendous: on the first day of the offensive, 60,000 British servicemen were cut down by the German defenders as they left their trenches. By the end of the attack, France had lost just fewer than 200,000 men, Britain around 400,000, and Germany 650,000. The response to the failure of these tactics was to increase the size of the offensives. The Germans withdrew to shorter lines to increase their strength and occupied a fixed line of fortifications running from the coast to Verdun that became known as the Hindenburg Line.

Shifting balance

In 1917, the USA entered the war following the German declaration of unrestricted submarine warfare in an attempt to win control of the seas from Britain. Fresh offensives were also planned by the British and the French. In April, France launched the Nivelle offensive with great optimism. Success was limited, and it proved the

Tanks

The tank was an attempted antidote to the predominantly defensive nature of World War I. Orginally conceived by war journalist Lt Col Swanton, the War Department rejected it and it only received funding due to the patronage of the First Lord of the Admiralty, Winston Churchill. Their massed use at the end of the Somme offensive in July 1916 caused panic in the German lines, but not a total breakthrough. Despite their ability to traverse the broken terrain of No-man's Land and their invulnerability to small arms fire, they were limited by being slow and mechanically unreliable. "Tank" was a codename used to prevent the Germans knowing what was being developed.

breaking point for the French army, with a massive mutiny breaking out. In July 1917, the British attacked at Passchendaele to distract the Germans and prevent them from taking advantage of the weakened French army. Again, heavy losses were suffered by both sides. In November 1917, Britain employed mass tanks, first used at the Somme without an overriding strategy. Now, at the Battle of Cambrai, the use of tanks allowed Britain to break through before mechanical problems stopped their advance. The balance was beginning to shift. Although the USA had begun with a small army, conscription had been rapidly introduced, with plans for an army of five million; by spring 1918, US troops were pouring into Europe at the rate of 300,000 a month. The German High Command realized that victory must be achieved as early as possible in 1918, before the USA could bring pressure to bear.

In 1918, with its strength released from the struggle on the Eastern Front, Germany attacked the combined forces of France, Britain, and the USA on the Western Front. The Germans made progress, advancing all the way to the Marne by July 1918. Once again, they were halted just as they threatened to break through, and the combined counteroffensive using massed tanks drove the exhausted German troops back past the Hindenburg Line, where they had begun their offensives of 1918. Realizing that victory was unrealistic and that terms would only become worse as more of the army was defeated, the new German chancellor, Maximilian, Prince of Baden, agreed to peace on the basis of the Fourteen Points outlined by President Woodrow Wilson in January 1918.

The Eastern Front

The Russian army was large but short of supplies, and its leadership was not as professional as that of the German army. The Austro-Hungarian army was organized along the same lines as Germany's, but was not as strong. Its efficiency was impaired by a language barrier. Most of the officers spoke German, while the majority of men did not. Also, given the nationalist tensions within Austria-Hungary, the loyalty of some of the army was questionable.

In contrast to the Western Front, the front line was more fluid on the Eastern Front, as the Russians advanced and were pushed back over the course of the war. The territory ceded by Russia under the Treaty of Brest-Litovsk was huge, but the treaty was invalidated after Germany was defeated on the Western Front.

The first moves

On the Eastern Front, in accordance with the modified Schlieffen Plan, the Germans were to use an elastic defence, trading space for time, to slow the Russians until men could be transferred from the West. The Austro-Hungarians were to mount offensives against the Russians in Galicia and Serbia.

The start of the war saw matters proceed in accordance with these plans. The Russian steamroller of two armies began to advance slowly into Eastern Prussia in August 1914 under Generals Samsonov and Rennenkampf. The Russians suffered casualties but pushed the Germans back. The Germans made an abortive counterattack that failed to dislodge the Russians. The German commander Prittwitz thought himself in danger of being surrounded by the Russian armies. Prittwitz was relieved, reinforcements were ordered from the Western Front, and the famous combination of General Hindenburg and General Ludendorff was put in command of German forces on the Eastern Front. Before the arrival of the reinforcements using the developed German rail network, they rapidly shifted their forces to establish superiority against the second of the invading Russian armies. At the Battle of Tannenburg in August and September, the commanders devastated the Russian Second Army, inflicting losses of 125,000 men for relatively little loss to themselves. Shifting forces again, Hindenburg and Ludendorff moved against the Russian First Army in Poland in the Battle of Masurian Lakes in September. Again, the Russians were roundly defeated, with losses of another 125,000 men. The German army on the Eastern Front had been more successful than the strategic plan had foreseen, offering some compensation to the Germans for their failure on the Western Front.

The Austro-Hungarian army was less successful in its offensive in Galicia in May 1915, losing a quarter of a million men and being forced back to the Carpathian mountains. The Germans were forced to support their allies to safeguard against a Russian invasion of the vital economic region of Silesia. Although they did not repeat the same remarkable victories of earlier in the year, the Russian invasion was forestalled.

The central push

In 1915, the Central Powers focussed on attempting to defeat Russia, numerically the strongest of the Allied powers. The continued successes of Germany, the aggressive intent of both participants, and the greater spaces in the Eastern Front meant that it had not descended into a war of trench attrition as on the Western Front.

At the beginning of 1915, Hindenburg launched an offensive in heavy winter before the arrival of

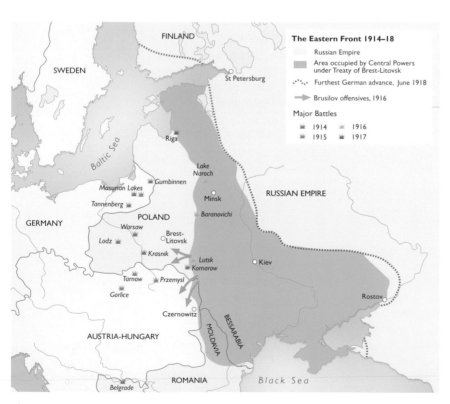

The Eastern Front 1914–18

- Russian Empire
- Area occupied by Central Powers under Treaty of Brest-Litovsk
- Furthest German advance, June 1918
- Brusilov offensives, 1916

Major Battles
- 1914
- 1915
- 1916
- 1917

promised reinforcements. The Russians were again defeated at the second Battle of the Masurian Lakes (7–12 February 1915), costing them another 200,000 men. The arrival of the German reinforcements presented the opportunity for a decisive German victory. Hindenburg achieved a breakthrough of the Russian lines and poured men into exploiting it, beginning a 480-kilometre (300-mile) advance on the Western Front. The Russians were able to withdraw and rebuild their lines, but this defeat caused the tsar, Nicholas II, to take personal charge of the Eastern Front. Later in the year, a combined Austro-Hungarian and Bulgarian invasion succeeded in inflicting major defeats on the Serbians in October 1915.

Costly success

Despite the successes of 1915, the Germans reversed their strategic focus of the past year and placed more emphasis on the Western Front. The progress on the Western and Italian fronts was to have an impact in the East. The French, under pressure from the attack on Verdun, asked the tsar to mount an offensive in the East. The attack, launched in March 1916, was not a success, and Russia suffered another 100,000 casualties. Next it was the turn of the Italians to ask for assistance, as the Austrians exerted pressure on them. This resulted in the Brusilov offensive, an attack on a 480-kilometre (300-mile) front along the Romanian border. This time the Russians enjoyed more success, advancing to the Carpathian foothills and causing the Germans to rush reinforcements from

Verdun and the Austro-Hungarians from Italy. If not for German assistance, the Austro-Hungarian Empire could have been knocked out of the war. The cost to the Russians was vast, as they suffered around one million casualties. In 1917, the Allies had planned for simultaneous offensives on the Western and Eastern fronts, but this was not to be.

Revolution

In February 1917, the revolution in Russia greatly impeded the Russian army's efforts to continue the war. Nevertheless, the provisional government attempted to mount an offensive in the summer of 1917, which had minimal effect. In contrast, the German counterattack that followed was hugely successful, defeating demoralized army after demoralized army. The advance halted on the Galician border when the Germans ran out of forces. In October of the same year, the Bolshevik revolution took place. At the risk of losing territory in the west, the Bolsheviks agreed to an armistice with the Central Powers. However, negotiations over the peace terms were problematic, with the Germans demanding autonomy for several former Russian territories. Because the Bolsheviks were unwilling to accept these terms, the Germans continued to advance in February 1918. A month later, the Treaty of Brest-Litovsk was signed on 3 March 1918, demanding harsher terms than the initial negotiations: Russia would give up Poland and the Baltic states, and the independence of Finland, Georgia, and the Ukraine would be recognized. The war was over between Russia and Germany.

Gallipoli and Jutland

Growing stalemate on the Western and Eastern fronts led to attempts to break the deadlock elsewhere. Opening up the Dardanelles to allow communications with Russia and knock Turkey out of the war looked promising, but failed amidst bitterness and recrimination. Then in 1916, the long-awaited clash of the British and German fleets at the Battle of Jutland promised a decisive encounter, but could not end the stalemate.

Admiral Sir John Jellicoe was a career naval officer who became commander of the British Grand Fleet at the beginning of World War I, having previously been involved in the modernization of the Royal Navy in the pre-war period. He was promoted to First Sea Lord after the Battle of Jutland, but was eventually dismissed following a political disagreement, and went on to become Governor of New Zealand.

On 25 April 1915, after the failure of the Royal Navy to force the Dardanelles with sea power alone, a series of landings was executed. This scene depicts Australian and New Zealand troops ashore at Anzac Cove. The lack of success in pushing inland on the day of the invasion would mean that the landing beaches would remain within enemy artillery fire until withdrawal in January 1916.

The Gallipoli campaign

The Turkish-controlled Gallipoli peninsula commanded the Dardanelles Straits that lead from the Mediterranean to the Black Sea, which had the only clearwater ports of the Russian Empire. It was a vital trade route through which France and Britain could lend aid to their ally if control could be wrested from Turkey. Moreover, with the land war bogged down in the West, a vocal minority in Britain, led by the First Lord of the Admiralty, Winston Churchill, believed that if the Dardanelles were forced and Constantinople threatened, Turkey might be knocked out of the war. Other Balkan states might come into the war on the Allied side and Russia might be allowed to turn all its attention against Germany and Austria.

Initially, only a naval operation was planned, as the British and French commanders were reluctant to divert troops to what they considered a sideshow. But earlier bombardments of the straits' forts had alerted the Turks, who had strengthened their fortifications and mined the straits. In February 1915, a renewed bombardment was followed by an attempt to force a passage with naval vessels, but this was called off when several ships struck mines, even though the Turks were close to evacuation. This lead to an escalation of the plan into an Anglo-French amphibious operation, composed of 78,000 men drawn heavily from the British dominions of Australia and New Zealand. The inevitable delay while the force was assembled allowed the Turks to reinforce their positions.

The first landing took place on 25 April 1915 at Cape Helles and further along the peninsula at Ari Burnu, beyond mutual fire-support range. The landings were a failure; a lack of urgency meant the crucial heights that dominated the peninsula were not captured, despite the fact that they were unoccupied at the time of the invasion. The Turks reinforced, the Allies dug in, and an even more oppressive network of static trenches than those on the Western Front was created. Allied men continued to pour into the campaign, suffering enormous casualties. New landings planned at Suvla Bay for

U-boats

Submarines gave the German navy a weapon with which they could blockade Britain. International opinion prevented the sinking of civilian merchantmen without prior warning being given. This limited the success of the U-boat blockade, although it was assisted by the Admiralty's foolhardy unwillingness to institute a convoy system, which left most merchantmen unprotected and vulnerable to U-boat attack. As the Germans' situation became more desperate, they attempted to tighten their blockade by giving no warning to ships, thus engaging in unrestricted submarine warfare. This increased the German navy's success for a period and threatened the British Isles with starvation, but it also brought the USA into the war. A convoy system was finally introduced and the sinking of merchant tonnage declined, while U-boat sinkings increased.

August repeated the same mistakes as at Cape Helles. The attack lacked drive, the Turks rushed in reinforcements, and the opportunity was lost.

The Allied commander, General Hamilton, was replaced by General Monro, who recommended a withdrawal. After careful planning, the withdrawal began in early December and continued until there was a rump of 35,000 troops left. Although the evacuation was brilliantly executed – not a single soldier was lost – the campaign itself was disastrous, a textbook example of how not to plan a war. Allied casualties totalled 252,000 and Turkish 251,000. Russia remained cut off from Allied war supplies and its trade income.

The Battle of Jutland

The Royal Navy had control of the seas at the outset of the war, in spite of the naval race with Germany that had occurred before World War I. Once war was declared, the Royal Navy took responsibility for the North Sea and the Channel in line with its pre-war agreements with France, blockading Germany and bottling up the German High Seas Fleet in its home ports. But the German navy was a force to be reckoned with. It was the only navy other than that of the USA that could come anywhere near competing with Britain, as it was built to very high standards and anxious to prove its worth. For Britain, the German navy posed an irritating, latent threat, forcing it to tie up the Royal Navy in home waters as long as the German fleet remained undefeated. There was tremendous public expectation in both Britain and Germany about the predicted clash between the fleets. In Britain, nothing less than a "new Trafalgar" was anticipated, but equally it was

recognized that a defeat would have huge consequences – it would possibly be enough to knock Britain out of the war. A major naval defeat would leave Britain open to invasion and the coasts of France vulnerable to attack. Britain's vital supply routes for food and materials could be cut at will. It was little wonder that the British commander of the Grand Fleet, Admiral Jellicoe, was dubbed "the only man who could lose the war in an afternoon".

The long-anticipated encounter occurred between 31 May and 1 June 1916. An expedition by the German High Seas Fleet under Admiral Scheer led to an initial engagement with the scouting group of fast, lighter armoured battle cruisers under Admiral Beatty. Although taking losses, Beatty lured the German High Seas Fleet into the rapidly advancing main British fleet. The result was inconclusive, with nightfall preventing a decisive full-fleet engagement and the German fleet managing to elude Jellicoe and return safely to port. In spite of the British preponderance of ships, their losses were heavier, with three capital ships and three cruisers lost to the German loss of one old battleship and four light cruisers.

Hailed in Germany as a victory, which was how it looked on paper, the battle had brought the German fleet near to disaster, with only nightfall and skilful manoeuvres keeping it from destruction. Strategically, it was a defeat. The German navy never again challenged British naval superiority in the North Sea or attempted to relieve the blockade of Germany. Instead, Germany was forced once again to return to unrestricted submarine warfare on merchant shipping in 1917, even at the peril of bringing the USA into the war. In practice, the battlefleet situation remained in Britain's favour for the rest of the war.

The Napoleonic Wars   290–1 ▶

The Crimean War   316–17 ▶

The Eastern Front   392–3 ▶

Bismarck and Kaiser Wilhelm II   342–3 ▶

The Italian Front

Italy had begun the war allied with Germany and the Austro-Hungarian Empire, having signed the Triple Alliance in 1882; however, the Allies had made concerted diplomatic overtures to Italy. After promises of substantial territorial gains, Italy agreed to declare war on its former ally, Austria-Hungary, on 23 May 1915.

The Italian Front presented some of the most difficult terrain of World War I. While the Eastern Front provided room for manoeuvre despite the vast number of troops deployed, the Alps and the presence of neutral Switzerland largely determined the battlefields and direction of the clash between Austria-Hungary and Italy.

The Italian army numbered around 875,000 men. It was not as well equipped as the French army and was deficient in transport, artillery, and large reserves of supplies. Despite this, the plan was to advance eastwards into Austrian territory, pushing towards the immediate goal of Gorizia, then on to Trieste and Vienna. The sector was held by the Austrians, who had heavily fortified the mountainous border with 100,000 men.

War was declared on 23 May 1915, and, in late June, the Italian army started towards Gorizia. In the first of a series of battles at Isonzo, 200,000 Italians launched themselves against the Austrian defences for two weeks without a breakthrough. With horrific casualties, the Italians continued the offensive. They had no alternative, as the Alps barred any other avenue of advance. Despite using more than six times as much artillery as in the first attempt, the Italian army was again repulsed. By the end of the year the first four battles of Isonzo had cost the Italians 177,000 casualties and the Austrians 117,000.

The first Italian breakthrough

The new year brought new hope and a new offensive for the Italians over the same sector that had been battered for much of the previous year. In the spring of 1916, they launched over two weeks of inconclusive but costly attacks against the deep well-organized defences of the Austrians. The Austrians then launched their first offensive of the war on this front, a change of direction for which the Italian First Army was unprepared. The Austrians captured 40,000 prisoners and inflicted 100,000 casualties, but the hard nature of the terrain slowed progress. An Italian counteroffensive and the need to move men to meet a Russian offensive on the Eastern Front brought it to a halt. The Italians attempted to take advantage of the movement of Austrian troops and shifted men back to the Isonzo Front to launch an attack against the depleted Austrian line. Gorizia was taken, and, although no breakthrough was effected, it was the first morale-boosting victory of the war.

In the autumn and winter of 1916, the war on the Italian Front descended further into a war of attrition. The Italians committed more and more men to continuing offensive pushes against the fortified Austrian lines. In terms of territorial gain, progress was negligible; however, Austrian resources were stretched to breaking point. By 1917, Germany had taken a defensive attitude on the Western and Eastern fronts, while expecting the Austrians to deal a final blow to the Italians. The Allies, worried about the possibility of another successful Austrian offensive, drew up plans for British and French troops to be moved to the Italian

Between 24 October and 12 November 1917, the Italians suffered a massive defeat at the hands of the Austro-German army under General Otto von Below. Using novel tactics developed on the Eastern Front, the Germans broke into the Italian rear, causing massive confusion in the Italian army. The result was retreats such as this one on the Udine–Codroisto road. This defeat would lead to Anglo-French assistance and highlight the need for an Allied supreme war council to unify command and strategy.

theatre in case of an enemy breakthrough. This did not prevent another offensive by the Italians, which went as all those which had preceded it, battling against Austrian lines for little gain. In the summer, the 10th battle at Isonzo saw 157,000 Italian casualties, but the Italians steeled themselves for an ultimate effort. They assembled 52 divisions and, in contrast to the paltry number of weapons for the first offensives of the war, 5000 guns.

The Italians assaulted on two fronts, north and south of Gorizia, achieving a strategic breakthrough that allowed them to push towards their objectives. Eventually, the advance outpaced the artillery support and the ability of the army to supply itself, and it slowed to a halt. The Austrians were in no position to resist any resumption of the offensive and asked the German High Command for assistance.

The Germans poured men into the front. October saw the beginning of the Battle of Caporetto. Using a short bombardment and tactics learnt from battles on the Eastern Front, they infiltrated the Italian lines. The Italians had not built up a full-scale defensive network and were vulnerable to these tactics. They surrendered large amounts of territory and 275,000 prisoners were taken. The advance stopped when the Austro-German army outran its artillery and supplies, and, in accordance with the contingency plans drawn up at the beginning of the year, the French and British shifted 11 divisions to support the Italian front.

The situation changed as 1917 progressed. The Russian Revolution released significant numbers of Austrian troops for other duties. For the 1918 offensives, German troops were withdrawn to concentrate on the Western Front.

The Austrian offensive of 1918 is a fine example of political expediency weakening an attack. The Austrian theatre commander, Archduke Joseph, could not decide whether to focus on a push towards Verona by Conrad, the commander already in place on the front, or Borojevic, the commander coming from the Eastern Front towards Padua. In an attempt at a compromise, they both attacked, meaning that reserves and artillery were split between them. The offensive that was to become the Battle of the Piave began in June. Conrad was halted, but Borojevic threatened a breakthrough, which was slowed by Italian air attack and eventually stopped. Archduke Joseph's earlier indecision meant that Borojevic only had access to limited reserves, so could not fully exploit his attack.

Austria-Hungary surrenders

While there were calls for an immediate counter-strike to take advantage of the stretched nature of the Austrian forces, the Italians opted for a considered offensive. After several months of preparation, the Italians launched the Battle of Vittorio Veneto back across the Piave. They did not suffer the problems that had beset the divided Austrian troops, who were already demoralized by the knowledge that their government was thinking about an armistice. As the British and French broke through the Austrian lines and more troops were brought in to exploit the widening gap, the situation became more desperate for the Austrians. The Allied forces penetrated as far as Trent and Tagliamento. Trieste, the goal of Italian strategy for three years, was captured by an Allied naval expedition on 3 November 1918. Hostilities concluded with the Austro-Hungarian surrender the next day.

Home Fronts

During World War I, the fight on the home front was a critical as that on the battlefield. The war had a deep impact on society. It changed the lives of the people who fought in it and the people who worked to win it. The economy was changed, politics were changed, and the basic values of society were called into question.

Before World War I, there had been increasing pressure for women's emancipation in Britain from the suffragette movement. Women's contribution to the war, while not winning their battle for the vote, significantly reduced the strength of the opposition's arguments. Women voted in a general election for the first time in December 1918.

World War I was the first truly "total war" in history and affected almost every aspect of society. Even before the war, many European states had begun to take a more active role in the lives of their citizens, providing compulsory education, introducing conscription into the armed forces, and developing state welfare services. The rise of democracy and of organized labour also meant that states had to pay some regard to public opinion in carrying on wars that involved immense sacrifice on the part of their peoples. The 1914–18 war intensified the demands that the state put upon its citizens and would require governments to take control of their economies, organize industry, and introduce controls and rationing of goods and services.

Women

While women did not fight on the front line, they assumed many of the positions that men had left behind and took up huge numbers of skilled posts throughout the war. In states with a large agricultural sector, the majority of women were required to work on the land. The first great "battle" of the French home front, for example, was to bring in the harvest of 1914 when most of the male labour force had gone to fight. Women, children, and the elderly had to replace them. This routine and unspectacular work was enacted across agrarian Europe and was less visible than the novel sight of women driving buses and doing skilled work in the factories. However, the place of men in the economy had been threatened by this growth in numbers of female workers. The men returning home from the army expected to and did return to their pre-war jobs. This, coupled with the reduction in the size of the economy at the end of the war, meant that women returned once more to a marginalized economic role.

Women did not accept their relegation to the sidelines quietly. Several countries conceded political rights and greater emancipation to women at the end or shortly after the end of World War I. The new Weimar constitution in Germany, promulgated in 1919, granted the vote to women over 20. In Russia, the October Revolution announced full civil rights for women, along with equal pay and opportunities. In Britain, the Campaign for Women, the movement that from the late 19th century had campaigned for women's suffrage, continued to gather impetus. In 1918, a measure of

The great flu epidemic

In the autumn of 1918, as the end of World War I approached, the world was struck by a disease of staggering proportions – influenza. Now thought to have originated from a mutation in China, it spread across the globe like wildfire. While influenza had existed before, the human immune system seemed unable to combat this particularly strain, and the main complication that accompanied it, pneumonia. One in five people on the planet was infected by the disease. The pandemic is conventionally known as the Spanish flu or *la grippe* and it struck most virulently among the 20–40 age group. It.killed somewhere between 20 and 40 million people worldwide, more people than World War I itself, and is the most devastating epidemic in recorded world history.

The huge armies used by all combatants during the war removed men from their jobs, leaving women to replace them in the workplace. Women now took jobs in munitions factories, managed farms, and worked in responsible positions in banks – jobs from which they had previously been excluded. They were evicted from these jobs when the men returned from the war, but it had given women a new perspective on their capabilities in the economy.

suffrage was afforded to British women, but it would not be until 1928 that women had universal suffrage in Britain. France and Italy had active movements up until the war, but these, as in most of Europe, were put aside during the years of conflict. In both these countries, women would not achieve the right to vote until after World War II.

Wider society

The changing role of women was part of a greater social upheaval, which was due in part to a change in the view of the role that the state should play in the economy. In France, the war saw a sinking of many of the differences between left and right. The declaration of the "sacred union" (*l'union sacrée*) of all French people by President Raymond Poincaré on 4 August 1914 laid the foundation for the state to introduce emergency proposals, giving the government control over the economy, the press, and national defence. In Britain, the formation of a coalition government in 1915 saw the setting up of a Ministry of Munitions and the beginning of much greater regulation of vital sectors of industry. By the end of the war, almost every key part of the war effort was under government direction. In August 1916, the Hindenburg Programme mobilized Germany for total war. All non-essential industry was to cease by 1917 and 300,000 more workers were drafted into munitions production.

But these policies could not prevent further hardships. The Allied blockade caused severe food shortages in Europe, and the bitter "turnip winter" of 1916–17 in central Europe reduced parts of the population to malnutrition, with more than 700,000 deaths in Germany by 1918. The German U-boat campaign of 1917 reduced food supplies to Britain to critical levels, forcing the government to introduce rationing by the winter of 1917–18. Peace on the labour front could not withstand the hardships of many of the domestic populations, leading to a rash of strikes in 1917. In Russia, these would bring about the fall of the tsarist autocracy in February 1917. Out of these discontents there were demands for a better postwar world. Talk of constitutional reform was widespread in Germany by 1917, with calls for universal suffrage and social reform. Even out of defeat in 1918, Germany created one of the most democratic constitutions in the world. In Britain, Lloyd George feared the influence of Bolshevism, and he launched a reconstruction programme. Universal suffrage, enacted in 1918, would be given to men and to women over 30.

It was felt that Britain should be a land fit for its returning heroes, who had been from all social classes. Government continued with the reforming efforts that had begun during the war. There was now free elementary education for all, and a vast house building programme was embarked upon. It was accepted that the state had a role to play in people's health. The end of the war was a time of optimism, and the struggles of war were to result in a prosperous peace.

Internationalism 376–7 ▶
The Russian Revolution 400–1 ▶
The Weimar Republic 408–9 ▶
Interwar Culture 420–3 ▶

The Russian Revolution

The vast Russian Empire was beset with political and social problems. The Russo-Japanese war of 1904–5 had resulted in the consultative assembly of the duma, but the Russian Empire remained an authoritarian state with the tsar at its head.

Vladimir Ilych Ulyanov, who later adopted the revolutionary name Lenin, was born in 1870. He became attracted to the teachings of Marx in his twenties, and from that point started down the road that was to lead to the Russian Revolution. Lenin used his undoubted powers of persuasion to build up a political faction, and it was his leadership that would lead to the Bolsheviks seizing power in October 1917.

In addition, the Russian Empire consisted of a huge number of different nationalities and ethnic groups. Even before the war, there had been separatist movements in many different parts of the Empire. Economically, despite the acceleration of industrialization from the last decade of the 19th century, Russian remained relatively backward.

The strains of war

World War I had placed the Russian economy under tremendous stresses, and disaffection was on the rise throughout society. Casualties on the Eastern Front had been as horrific as those inflicted on the Western; however, despite losing territory, the Russian army remained undefeated. During the course of the war, the liberals, who had pushed for representative government in 1905, agitated for further reform and the appointment of a representative government. Tsar Nicholas II, ideologically committed to autocracy, refused to modify his stance. He continued to take personal charge of his armed forces on the front and was absent from the

tsarist court. Government was left in the hands of Tsarina Alexandra, who was deeply unpopular because of her German origins and because of the importance given to her adviser Rasputin, who had an apparently inexplicable hold over the royal family. Their mismanagement of domestic policy meant that inflation continued, resulting in many peasants reverting to subsistence farming. This in turn created problems in supplying the cities with adequate, affordable food. Some nobles took matters into their own hands and assassinated Rasputin in 1916, thinking then to replace the tsar with his uncle. Army officers met with the aim of forcing the tsar to abdicate. None of these events was the sole cause of the February Revolution of 1917 (March in the Western calendar), but each goes some way towards explaining why it was so successful. The current regime had no unequivocal supporters.

The gathering storm

In February 1917, after a harsh winter with little food supplies, protesters poured onto the streets of

The provisional government in Petrograd, formerly St Petersburg, found the Bolsheviks' Red Guards taking control of key positions in the city. Realizing that their troops were unreliable, government members retreated to the Winter Palace. Lenin brought in sailors from the nearby island naval base of Kronstadt, and, on the night of 25 October 1917, they overcame what little resistance there was and placed the ministers under arrest. Lenin took control of the All-Russia Congress of Soviets, which that night declared it had assumed power throughout Russia.

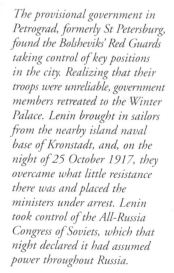

that was still running the Russian Empire. On 15 March, Nicholas II was forced to abdicate. He and his family were later to be assassinated in July 1918.

The coup of the Bolsheviks

The provisional government insisted on continuing to fight the war. This continued to cause stresses on society and was increasingly unpopular, creating an opportunity for those who wanted a more extreme change in regime. The army was weakening through desertions, peasants were disaffected by the slow pace of land reform under the provisional government, and urban workers still laboured under the conditions that had caused the first uprisings. The Bolsheviks, a radical communist faction in the Petrograd soviet, agitated in April for the deposition of the provisional government and the transfer of power to the soviets. They promised what the provisional government was not delivering, namely peace, food, and land. The provisional government was then weakened by the attempted coup by the army under General Kornilov, which failed due to desertions among his own troops. The isolation of the government presented Lenin, leading the Bolsheviks, with a daring opportunity, which he took. On 25 October, using Bolshevik supporters, he arranged for key facilities to be neutralized in Petrograd. In a heavily Bolshevik-weighted All-Russia Congress of Soviets, he issued a proclamation stating that the government was now in the hands of the Petrograd soviet. The provisional government, deprived of support, did not react and its members were arrested in the Winter Palace.

Keeping power

There were elections in December 1918 in which the Bolsheviks polled about a quarter of the vote and were roundly defeated by the more moderate Socialist Revolutionaries. This proved to be irrelevant, as Lenin intended to hold on to power and only allowed the assembly to meet once before having the Bolshevik guard close it down. The struggle then shifted to the Bolsheviks' attempts to consolidate their power.

Lenin offered peace to the Germans, who asked for harsh terms. These were unacceptable to the Bolsheviks, and they responded by the novel approach of refusing to fight. The Germans called their bluff and started to advance further into Russian territory. Confronted with the problems of attempting to gain control of the country, the Bolsheviks caved in and signed the even harsher Treaty of Brest-Litovsk with Germany on 3 March 1918, conceding vast areas of western Russia to Germany and its allies. The treaty would be overturned by the armistice in November.

Petrograd (renamed from St Petersburg to sound less German), and strikes broke out, with protesters calling for peace, bread, land, and freedom. The Imperial Guard attempted to put down the protest by force, then the capital's conscripted peasant garrison mutinied, joining the rioters and depriving the government of the means to end the insurrection. The duma stepped into the void and appointed a provisional government that did not include the tsar. However, it was not alone in trying to fill the vacuum: the socialist factions who had been active during 1905 formed a council of workers and soldiers in Petrograd, called the Petrograd soviet. Thus arose the "dual power" in which the duma and the Petrograd soviet competed for control of the country.

The soviet set about introducing it political programme, issuing orders to other soviets that had formed in other towns and cities. It ordered the army to elect its own soviets, undermining the officer corps and discipline, but preventing the army from being used as an instrument of repression against them. The provisional government called for empire-wide elections of local officials, eliminating at a stroke the authority of the bureaucracy

The early 20th century was still a time of intense superstition and religion in imperial Russia, and it was this atmosphere that allowed Rasputin, a "holy man" from Siberia, the opportunity to gain access to the royal family. While his actual political influence has often been exaggerated, Rasputin was nevertheless a powerful symbol in the arsenal of those trying to undermine the tsar and tsarina.

1914–45

EUROPE AT WAR

The Paris Peace Conference

After the armistice was signed by the Germans and the Austro-Hungarian Empire on 11 November 1918, the terms of the peace had to be decided. The armistice was not a signal for guns to fall silent all over Europe. Russia was in the throes of a civil war, the Austro-Hungarian Empire itself was breaking up, and many nations threatened to join the Russian Empire in revolution. The peacemakers of Paris rapidly had to redraw the map of Europe.

The treaty was the product of months of negotiation and compromise between the victorious powers. It represented 32 countries, accounting for three-quarters of the world's population. The Treaty of Versailles was eventually signed – as illustrated above – on 28 June 1919.

After over four years of bloody conflict, the public mood in France and Britain was unsympathetic: the public wanted vengeance for the suffering they had endured. The French wished to see a dramatic weakening of Germany so that it could not be a threat again. The British wanted a rapid restoration of trade to generate wealth, which meant Germany, a major customer before the war, back on its feet. US president Woodrow Wilson, full of idealism, wanted a settlement on the basis of national self-determination and open diplomacy; however, US domestic opinion did not want the USA to remain involved in European politics. Italy wished to receive the victors' spoils promised in the secret Treaty of London of 1915 for its entry into the war. Russia, the other major victor, was still racked with internal struggle and was excluded from discussions, although its interests were considered. The aims of the victorious powers were not easily reconciled. In addition, the defeated powers were not given a voice, which ultimately led to deep dissatisfaction and accusations of a dictated peace.

A new Europe

To complicate matters, a host of new nations came into existence at the end of the war. The Austro-Hungarian Empire had suffered from growing internal pressures for some years before World War I. The Western powers had attempted to weaken their enemy by encouraging the nationalist aspirations of its component peoples. Coupled with the strain of the war, this meant that even before the war's conclusion there were Slav, Slovak, and Czech nations in waiting. The abdication of Emperor Charles I on 11 November put a seal on the reality. The collapse of the Russian Empire had led to the resurrection of the Kingdom of Poland, admittedly under total German control due to their advances in the east. Poland, Czechoslovakia, and Yugoslavia, as they were not the aggressors in the war, were given representation at the Paris Peace Conference of 1919. The break-up of the Russian Empire had had further consequences, as the central government lost control. Finland, the Baltic states of Latvia, Lithuania,

The conclusion of the peace was of enormous significance to the people of Europe, and the ongoing negotiations generated massive public interest. The very site of the signing ceremony said much about the purpose of the treaty. It was signed, despite vigorous German protests, in the same location that France had signed a humiliating peace after defeat in the Franco-Prussian war – the Hall of Mirrors at the Palace of Versailles.

In common with many of the other combatant nations, Britain organized nationwide celebrations to mark the signing of the peace treaties. The allied commanders, including Foch and Pershing, marched with 15,000 troops through London's Whitehall and past a hastily commissioned Cenotaph memorial on 19 July 1919.

and Estonia, the Ukraine, and Belorussia declared their independence. The Ottoman Empire's collapse meant that the subject of its former territories in the Middle East were heated topics of discussion.

When the conference convened in Paris in 1919, the many nations present represented the majority of the world's population. But in reality, the power lay with the "Council of Four" consisting of the French president, Clemenceau, the British prime minister, Lloyd George, the US president, Wilson, and the Italian premier, Orlando. It was, in effect, a congress of victors called to prepare treaties for the defeated powers to sign.

Compromises and reparations

Each country vehemently pursued its own agenda. France sought particularly harsh terms for Germany, demanding a separate Rhineland state, the return of Alsace-Lorraine, and punitive reparations for the destruction inflicted on its 10 richest provinces during the battles at the Western Front. Further, it demanded the disarmament of Germany and a variety of territorial adjustments that would weaken Germany and strengthen the new nations in Eastern Europe, France's new partners now that Russia, its traditional ally in restricting Germany, no longer had a border with Germany. These aims were modified significantly by the competing aims of the other victorious powers. The idea of a Rhineland state was opposed, and a compromise of military occupation for a period of 15 years was reached. Against a background of worldwide disarmament, Germany was limited to 100,000 troops, no aircraft, and a minor navy. Compromises were reached on the boundaries of the Eastern European states. In return for these compromises, Wilson and Lloyd George gave France a military guarantee in the case of an attack by Germany. In the event, the entire basis of the compromise was swept away when the US senate refused to ratify the treaty or join the League of Nations. Not wishing to bear the financial brunt for the defence of France, Britain refused to guarantee France's eastern frontier if the USA were not involved.

Reparations also proved a difficult topic. The allies had spent two and a half times as much to win the war as the Central Powers had to lose it. Huge loans had been taken out to finance the war, both domestically and with the USA, and popular opinion that Germany should finance these repayments was strong. The British government thought that large payments would be damaging in the long term. The actual figure was so problematic that it was not agreed at the conference, but the principle of reparations was included in the treaty. It was found in the infamous "war guilt" clause that said Germany was responsible for starting the war. This clause was to be the focus for German opposition to the Versailles settlement.

The peace given in the terms of the Treaty of Versailles with Germany, the Treaty of St-Germain with Austria, and the Treaty of Sèvres with Hungary was a result of these compromises. The Treaty of Versailles weakened Germany without destroying it, but caused huge resentment. Italy, a victor, felt cheated by its lack of gains, and Austria was left a German-speaking nation cut off from Germany. Marshal Ferdinand Foch, leader of the French forces, commented: "This is not a peace, this is a 20-year armistice." His words were to prove prophetic.

British delegates at the Washington Armaments Limitation conference in 1921, one of many attempts in this period to prevent another war in Europe.

THE INTERWAR YEARS

The period between the two world wars was dominated by the two conflicts that surrounded it. While there was tremendous hope at the end of World War I, viewing history with hindsight there was an air of inevitability about the march of continental Europe from one Armageddon to another. The fundamental problems that had made Europe such a hotspot before 1914 were never adequately resolved, and the impact of the first war left many potential sources of conflict.

The years immediately following after the conclusion of World War I were occupied with the consequences of the war. The Russian Empire had disintegrated and was in turmoil. The Austro-Hungarian Empire, a major centre of European power, had fallen, and there was the testing question of the future of the defeated Germany.

There was tremendous economic dislocation. The pattern of world trade had been twisted beyond recognition, as had the domestic economies of the main protagonists. In addition, there were the artificially separated economies of the new states that had come into existence as a result of the disintegration of the former Habsburg Empire. The process of shifting all of these economies back to a peacetime footing was a painful and slow one. World War I had caused a fundamental shift in the financial relationships of the European nations, with tremendous debts owed to the USA.

Initially, there were huge contrasts across Europe. Russia was in the grip of civil war from which the Bolsheviks would emerge securely in power. Much of central and Eastern Europe remained severely depressed by the consequences of the war and the reparations burden on Germany. Only after the German economy had experienced a serious hyperinflation in 1923 and put its currency on a new footing would a measure of stability begin to return from the mid-1920s. France and Britain sought desperately to return to pre-1914 conditions. France had the enormous task of renovating the huge tracts of its territory devastated by the fighting and sustaining millions of wounded ex-servicemen and orphaned families.

Britain found its great export trades of pre-1914 permanently reduced because of the drop in the level of world trade and the loss of markets to competitors. A short-lived postwar boom was followed by a rapid rise of unemployment in the early 1920s. Europe's economic recovery during this period was fragile, based largely on a booming USA and vulnerable to any difficulties it might experience.

The effect of World War I had an influence on ideology. Europeans questioned and rationalized the huge sacrifices made during the war. This resulted in new impetuses in art and literature, and scientific advances developed by the necessity of the war. Unsurprisingly, there were lasting antagonisms between countries. Years of struggle raised expectations for the future, which changed the political landscape. Many countries had become mass democracies, effectively for the first time, with the introduction of universal suffrage and, in many cases, votes for women. The communist genie was out of the bottle and threatened to sweep across Europe, encouraging the development of right-wing political thought as a counterpoint to this perceived menace. Different nations dealt with these threats with varying degrees of success.

Whatever the different ideologies, there was a widespread resolve to avoid future sacrifices on such a vast scale. During the 1930s, as the forces of revisionism and totalitarianism began their push towards reconstruction, they were met by populations who were desperate to avoid rushing into a massive conflict, the pain of which was only too fresh in their memories.

A New European Order

The most dramatic changes brought about by the Paris Peace Conference were the redrawing of the map of central and Eastern Europe to create a host of new states to satisfy nationalist aspirations on the principle of national self-determination and the establishment of the League of Nations as a supranational body to arbitrate disputes and prevent war in the future.

The compromise solutions to the Eastern European question: Italy gained territory but not as much as it wanted; Poland split Germany in two through its need for a port, which angered Hitler; The Russian Revolution spawned several new states which Stalin eyed greedily; and Austria was reduced to a small Germanic state on Germany's border.

The new nations

A key feature of the Paris settlement was to conform to the idea of national self-determination. In practice, this meant the amalgamation of different ethnic groups, and, in almost every instance, substantial racial minorities found themselves included in the new states. The result was that Yugoslavia was constructed by amalgamating Serbia, Montenegro, and the area of the former Austro-Hungarian Empire comprising Croatia, Slovenia, and Dalmatia. Czechoslovakia was carved out of the Austro-Hungarian Empire and contained its industrial heartland of Bohemia. Its areas were not just populated by Czechs and Slovaks, but also by Germans, Magyars, and Ruthenes. Poland was given all the lands of the historic Kingdom of Poland; however, this meant that Germans, Jews, Ukrainians, and White Russians were all living within its borders, as it gained land from Germany and the Austro-Hungarian Empire and would go on to win land from Russia in the 1920 war. Austria and Hungary were also technically new states, but their guilt in the war meant that there was no effort by the allies to strengthen them. Hungary, predominately populated by Magyars, lost territory during the peace negotiations to anyone who had a claim against it, a list which included Yugoslavia, Romania, and Czechoslovakia.

The multiracial composition of the artificially created successor states was to cause lasting problems. In Yugoslavia, it was divisive: the Serbs and Croats were in constant conflict, as the Serbs attempted to dominate government. The presence of Germans, Russians, and Magyars meant that territorial revision at Polish and Czech expense was a constant threat. In addition, a number of minor disputes with other new nations always threatened to boil over. With the exception of Czechoslovakia, the new states were economically dependent on agriculture. There were attempts at land reform, but the collapse of agricultural prices in the late 1920s caused extensive hardship. Further pressure was put on their economies by the armies necessary because of their precarious position between Germany and the USSR. Czechoslovakia was more able to cope thanks to its industrial base, which may be the reason that it succumbed last to the threat of dictatorship. It had originally been thought that the new states would become clients of the Western powers, but diplomatically all of the nations attempted to maintain their independence. Czechoslovakia and Yugoslavia joined with Romania to form the Little Entente in 1920.

New States in Europe 1919–23

— 1923 borders
- - - Pre-war borders
1919 Date of independence

PRE-WAR EMPIRES
German
Austro-Hungarian
Russian

The retrieval of its land was to dominate Hungary's interwar years even as its economy struggled and local fascists began to dominate politics. Although Austria was homogeneous in its German population, it was denied the ability to control its destiny and was not to become part of Germany until the Anschluss of 1936. The Austrian economy was particularly vulnerable: it had been the centre of the Austro-Hungarian Empire, but was now a small nation with more than a third of its population living in the capital.

Lithuania, Latvia, and Estonia also achieved independence after World War I which was to survive up until World War II. Finland, likewise, became independent and was to remain so. The Ukraine and the Belorussian National Republic were less fortunate: they were reincorporated with bloody efficiency into the new empire of the USSR during the Russian Civil War.

The League of Nations

The formation of the League of Nations in 1919 had been central to the peace negotiations for President Wilson. The intention was for inter-state relations to be brought into the open, preventing a repeat of the secret protocols and power politics that Wilson believed had led to World War I, and to promote the ideals of his Fourteen Points, namely free trade, disarmament, and self-determination.

There were a number of proposals regarding the League of Nation's powers. France sought a promise that nations would use force to uphold the league's decisions. Britain was opposed to anything that threatened huge expenditure and unpredictable continental entanglements. In the end, it became a loose confederation of nations that would submit international problems for examination under a series of set protocols. Decisions were to be enforced by means of sanctions.

The scheme was severely weakened by the US Senate's decision not to ratify entry into the League, meaning that it was not a true world organization, as two of the major world powers – Russia and the USA – were not involved at the outset.

Despite these fundamental problems, the League was not completely ineffectual. During the 1920s, it was involved in a number of disputes. It helped to solve the disagreement between Sweden and Finland over the Åland Islands, with the League deciding that they should belong to Finland. It also prevented a war in the Balkans between Greece and Bulgaria in 1925. In addition to these territorial disputes, it succeeded in carrying out relief work for those displaced after the war and was instrumental in organizing financial aid for Austria and Hungary, which were suffering extreme economic

dislocation following the break-up of the Austro-Hungarian Empire. The League also monitored the mandate powers who administered the former colonies of Germany and Austria-Hungary and attempted to guide them towards independence.

The weakness of the League of Nations, however, was demonstrated when it came to dealing with disputes involving a major power. The League was bypassed when Italy took Corfu and the problem was dealt with by Britain and France. Germany subsequently joined the League in 1926, which seemed to show promise for the League's future; however, in 1931, it was faced with another test when Japan invaded and conquered Manchuria. Although the League was critical of this action, it did not agree to impose sanctions as the USA would not join them. Japan simply left the League in 1933. The same year, Germany's membership proved short-lived when it withdrew after Hitler had been elected. Despite the USSR joining in 1934, the League was rapidly demonstrating its ineffectiveness. It was powerless to prevent nations intervening in the Spanish Civil War. Its reaction to the Italian invasion of Abyssinia (now Ethiopia) of 1935 was half-hearted, reflecting the conflicting priorities of its leading nations, Britain and France. It was powerless to prevent Hitler's moves into Austria and Czechoslovakia in 1938. By this time, it was relegated to a sideshow, with matters determined in the talks and policies between the major European powers. The last major act of the League was to expel the USSR after its invasion of Poland, a move that did not trouble Stalin unduly. The League of Nations, based in neutral Switzerland and having demonstrated itself powerless to solve the issues it had been brought into existence to control, dissolved in 1946, handing over many of its duties to the newly formed United Nations.

Opposite top: A cartoon from March 1919 shows President Wilson presenting a rather weighty twig of hope to the dove of peace. The League of Nations was the institution that Wilson felt would safeguard the peace and avoid a repeat of World War I. Unfortunately, despite this responsibility, it was far too lightweight an institution to fulfil such a sizeable destiny.

Karl I of Austria was the last Habsburg emperor of Austria-Hungary. A man of principle, his efforts at the end of the war to reconstruct his empire along federal lines failed. He relinquished political power and went into exile in Switzerland, but did make subsequent attempts to regain power in Hungary in the early 1920s. They met with failure and the new shape of Eastern Europe remained.

A Changing Empire   350–1 ▶

The Weimar Republic   408–9 ▶

The Origins of the Cold War   446–7 ▶

The Balkans   484–5 ▶

The Weimar Republic

In Germany, a left-wing revolution led to the abdication of Wilhelm II in November 1918 and a division of authority between a provisional government and various workers' councils. A new National Assembly was elected and voted on a new constitution. Due to the unstable situation in Berlin, the constitution was proclaimed in Weimar.

This photograph of children using blocks of German mark notes as building blocks provides a striking symbol of the hyperinflation during the Weimar period.

The constitution was not revolutionary, and some members of the provisional government had argued that social reform should have been carried out before a constitution was created. In the event, the constitution created a proportionally elected lower chamber, a higher chamber that reflected the traditional separatism of the individual German states while restricting the dominance of Prussia, and the office of a president who had, crucially as it would turn out, the power to issue decrees in the case of emergencies under Article 48.

The first elections produced a variety of parties, a reflection of the many political factions that had already been present in the German Empire. The mainstream parties included the socialist SPD, the Democrats, the Centre Party, and the central powers DVP, with the more extreme parties represented by the Marxist Spartacus Party and the far right-wing DNVP.

Growing pains

"Workers. Vote for the soldier at the front – Hitler." Posters were an essential part of the Nazi method of spreading their message, as seen in this propaganda poster from the 1930 election. It calls on the support of those who had fought at the front for Germany during World War I for the revisionist Nazi Party. It was also an attempt to make Hitler, an Austrian, appear more acceptable to a German electorate by reminding them of his war record.

None of the parties was in a position to form a government by itself, resulting in coalition governments between combinations of the main parties. The unattractive first task of the first Weimar government under provisional president Fredrich Ebert was the signing of the Treaty of Versailles. Vigorous representations against the treaty failed to make a serious impact, and the first government resigned. The threat of violence from the victorious allies prompted the forming of another coalition under Gustav Bauer, which took responsibility for signing the treaty. Because of the public backlash following the signing of the Treaty of Versailles, plans for a popular election had been dismissed, as it had been feared that a far right-wing candidate would be elected. The socialist Ebert, one of the authors of the constitution, was installed as president.

The German public was horrified by the peace terms. This sentiment was to create an atmosphere that, in the long run, would create opportunities for political extremists to argue that such

an unjust peace agreement should never have been signed and that to have done so was to betray the country.

Domestic politics

The first few years of the Weimar Republic saw nine coalition governments preside over a country in economic crisis. In 1918, the economy was in desperate straits due to money borrowed to finance the war. In 1920, the reparations committee fixed the reparations imposed at Versailles at 132 billion marks (33 billion US dollars). Payments began in August 1921, but were stopped in January 1923. As a result, the French occupied the Ruhr in an attempt to take a strong line against this default. The French believed that it was a result of the German government's unwillingness to take harsh measures to stabilize its currency and create a budget surplus.

The German government instituted a policy of passive resistance, which denied the French their spoils, but was twice as expensive to Germany as the reparations. The result was hyperinflation in Germany, which destroyed the savings of many of its people. The government now instituted unpopular policies to stabilize the currency: in tandem with huge loans from the USA under the Dawes plan of 1924 and some mitigation on the size of the reparation payments, the economy grew more stable. The 1920s saw huge amounts of foreign capital flood into the German economy as many saw investment opportunities. This led to a period of great growth, but the impact of the investment was uneven across society and so did not ease the discontent still felt by significant sections of the population. In any case, there was still domestic unease and resentment about the size of the debts owed to Western powers. Despite attempts by the coalition governments to reform the economy, inequities remained within the system. Cartels dominated industrial production, and land remained concentrated in a few hands. This left many with little loyalty to the Weimar Republic.

Foreign policy

Foreign policy was dedicated to the revision of the Treaty of Versailles. After an initial period of open lack of co-operation, there followed a more measured approach designed to modify the provisions in co-operation with France and Britain. There was another strand to German foreign policy: in an effort to support its position, the Weimar Republic attempted to build a relationship with the internationally isolated Soviets. This would lead to the Rapallo Treaty of 1922 to increase trade and facilities for military research and training in breach of the Treaty of Versailles. However, this was only part of German policy, as it alone could not change Germany's isolated position. Under Gustav Stresemann, the foreign minister, much constructive work was done with the Western powers. The Locarno treaties of 1925 guaranteed the western frontiers of France and went some way towards appeasing French security concerns. This in turn led to the evacuation of the first portion of the Rhineland, which, until that time, had been occupied by British and French troops. In 1926 Germany was admitted to the League of Nations and was able to exert some influence in international affairs.

The crisis

This situation was to change with the economic crisis of 1929. There was a flight of capital from

The Wall Street crash

The fragile prosperity of Weimar Germany was undermined by the Wall Street Crash of October 1929. The dramatic collapse of stock market values in the USA followed a period of frantic speculation. It shattered American business confidence and ruined thousands of investors. Its effects rippled across the world as the USA's role in sustaining much of the world economy came to an abrupt end. Loans were withdrawn from Europe, causing a massive downturn in economic activity, which in turn produced a huge rise in unemployment. By July 1931 more than four million Germans were unemployed.

Germany as the USA withdrew behind its protectionist barriers. Every nation had to look first to its own domestic problems. The plummeting economic conditions shook any faith the public may have had in its leaders. As support for the centre parties declined, so extreme parties grew in strength, including the National Socialist (Nazi) Party, formed in the early 1920s under Adolf Hitler. Mainstream parties proved unable to agree on any solution to the economic crisis, and no party was strong enough to enforce a solution by itself. In the 1930 elections, the Nazi Party stepped into this void and achieved massive electoral success, appealing in particular to the middle classes, who had been hit hard by the economic crisis. Despite this, they fell short of a parliamentary majority, and they remained excluded from government. There were attempts to solve the impasse by successive governments asking to use President Hindenburg's emergency powers, which undermined the basis of the democratic state. As the political crisis deepened, several mainstream right-wing politicians decided to use the Nazi's popular support to install themselves in power. The original plan was for Franz von Papen to head up a government with a few token Nazi ministers under President Hindenburg, but Hitler was opposed to this and demanded the chancellorship for himself. Eventually, as other possibilities were exhausted, in January 1933 he achieved his aim and was made chancellor. Von Papen, from his position as Vice Chancellor, mistakenly believed Hitler could be held in check.

Italy: 1918–39

Even before World War I, Italy had been struggling to come to terms with its unification and the changing face of society and politics. Since 1912, there had been almost universal male suffrage. The old liberal ruling politicians were reluctant to accept the growing influence of other sectors of society and the old style of patronage politics was ill-suited to the realities of mass popular politics.

Benito Mussolini, born in 1883, was a qualified teacher. Failing to find work, he edited a socialist newspaper and was at one point arrested for pacifist propaganda relating to the Italian–Turkish conflict of 1911. Influenced by the works of Nietzsche and the syndicalism of George Sorel, Mussolini abandoned his socialist roots and found fascism.

Mussolini and his allies inspect some of the 60,000 supporters who had gathered in Naples in October 1922 for the Fascist Party Congress. Plans were already drawn up to march on Rome to seize power. In fact, preparations for the march were hampered by police action; but the threat of violence and civil war was enough to force King Victor Emmanuel to invite Mussolini to become his prime minister.

There were also pressing social problems that needed to be addressed. Italy had been split politically about its entry to the war. With conscription, five million men had fought at the front. The majority of them were drawn from the agricultural working classes, while industrial workers remained in their jobs. The stimulus of war had skewed the economy in favour of heavy industry; however, with the end of the war, demand was substantially decreased. Shortages and inflation were coupled with the release of the army back into a shrinking labour market, adding to rising unemployment.

In 1919, the introduction of proportional representation resulted in two major political parties: the socialist PSI and the Catholic Party. Neither party was able to achieve outright victory, and both were unwilling to govern in tandem. This left a vacuum occupied by default by the old politicians of the pre-war era. They had to cope with the twin pressures of strikes by the unions and dissatisfaction with the Treaty of Versailles. There were worries that the strikes were the beginning of a Bolshevik revolution, although there was little real

danger of this. However, this fear, together with the militancy of the major political forces, left several sections of society feeling threatened, particularly employers and urban professionals. Yet support for the socialists was not total among the poor, who lost out to union members in the hunt for jobs.

It was to these sectors of society that fascism appealed. Founded in Milan by Mussolini in 1919, the fascist movement adopted as its image the ancient Roman symbol of authority – the *fasci*, an axe wrapped in whips. The movement appealed to notions of ancient Roman greatness, and it was violently anti-communist. As the fascist movement grew, it was formed into squads, who, from their strongholds in the urban centres, carried out violent beatings and arson attacks on the infrastructure and personnel of the socialist unions and Catholic peasant leagues. The success of these attacks raised the fascists' profile and attracted new members. By November 1921, the fascists had become a political party, and, by 1922, membership had expanded to 250,000. However, the organization was not centralized and depended on the

personality of local leaders. Established political leaders felt that they could quell the potential threat of the fascists and, indeed, felt that the fascists could be useful in reducing the socialists' dependency on the extreme left. There were political manoeuvres to bring the fascists into government under the leadership of a traditional liberal. The far left responded by attempting to organize an anti-fascist general strike in 1922. Its failure had the opposite effect: by creating fear of the dangers of socialism, it caused demands for the fascists to be incorporated into the government.

In 1922, Mussolini and 30,0000 of his black-shirted supporters marched from Milan to Rome in a display of the party's strength. Had the government been given permission to implement martial law, the march could have been stopped, but King Victor Emmanuel was worried about mutiny in the army and denied permission. He believed that fascist involvement in the government was inevitable. This show of strength won the fascists additional support, and the premier, Facta, resigned, giving Mussolini the opportunity to lead the next government.

Once in government, Mussolini was voted dictatorial powers for one year by the Chamber. He now had to address the threat from within his own party – the regional squads that had helped the fascists achieve power. Mussolini brought the squads under a central Grand Council, which greatly reduced their influence. In the subsequent elections, Mussolini was able to force through a law that meant the party with the largest vote had two-thirds of the seats, and he used intimidation and violence to secure the result he wanted. One of his most vocal critics, the socialist deputy Giacomo Matteotti, was murdered by fascist thugs in 1924. The socialist opposition in parliament withdrew in protest. The fascist party responded by crushing the opposition, and, in 1925, Mussolini consolidated power by banning trade unions and political opposition and replacing elected officials with appointed officials. Italy was now ruled by a dictatorship, its nascent democracy crushed.

Domestic policy

After the move to dictatorship, growing problems with the economy resulted in a move to higher tariffs and a deflationary policy. The depression that swept Europe after 1929 pushed the state into greater intervention in the economy, and Italy's state sector became second only to that of Soviet Russia, with heavy industry in particular coming under state control. Real spending power declined for the workers, and the suffering of those working in the rural economy led to greater urbanization. A grand programme of public works, such as the

draining of the marshes near Rome, kept employment artificially high.

Foreign policy

Foreign interests under the fascists continued as before, yet the way in which they were pursued was more radical. Territorial gains in the Mediterranean, the Adriatic, and North Africa remained the areas of interest for Italy. Some of Mussolini's domestic policies were geared towards giving Italy the strength to seek readjustment. The Battle for Grain in 1925 was designed to decrease Italy's dependence on other nations for vital supplies. The Battle for Births of 1927 was aimed at increasing Italy's population to allow for more men for the army. Mussolini's success was mixed. The Adriatic port of Fiume was incorporated into Italy in 1924, and he established a protectorate over Albania in 1926, but he failed on a risky venture to establish Italian rule in Cyprus. He intervened in the Spanish Civil War, but gained nothing but notoriety. The resurgence of Germany gave him greater freedom for manoeuvre, as the British and French were worried about driving him into an alliance with Hitler. As a result, in 1936, when Mussolini invaded and conquered Abyssinia, the League of Nations declared half-hearted sanctions. As he tired of the restrictions of the established order, he shifted from a policy against Germany to one supporting Hitler's attempts to change the world order. He pushed for the Axis Alliance of 1939, and, as Hitler dismembered Czechoslovakia in 1939, he signed the Pact of Steel. When Germany invaded France, he belatedly declared war in 1940. He had been drawn into conflict and supporting German war aims.

Mussolini had stated that his objective was to make Italy strong and respected among nations. Colonies were one route to this goal, and, in October 1935, Mussolini invaded Abyssinia (now Ethiopia), an independent kingdom in Africa. While the invasion was a success, the colony was not, and there was little Italian emigration or trade.

The Roman Empire   74–5 ▶
Italian Unification   320–3 ▶
A New European Order   406–7 ▶
The Third Reich   410–11 ▶

Lenin and the Russian Civil War

Although Lenin and the Bolsheviks had nominally been successful in seizing power in the October Revolution, their situation was insecure. Shortly after the signing of the Treaty of Brest-Litovsk, civil war broke out. The harsh terms of the treaty played a part in this, but it was not the only factor. The civil war lasted from 1918–21, and it would cost Russia as many casualties as World War I.

The Russian Revolution was not a clean takeover by the Bolsheviks. The Russian Empire was reduced to a core area by October 1919, as White forces pushed in before Trotsky's armies started establishing their authority over the sizeable area that would become the USSR in 1922.

The Russian Empire had broken up into its constituent parts. Upon formation of the provisional government after the February Revolution, separatist feeling had escalated. In April 1917, the provisional government, confronted with chaos within and the German army without, agreed to independence for the different nationalities of the Empire. The Bolsheviks, although not in agreement, endorsed this policy and proceeded to organize Bolshevik parties within each of the new states.

By the spring of 1918, anti-communist forces known as the Whites, many of them former aristocrats or former members of the Imperial Guard, began to form armies and attack the communist government. Both sides intended to reconstruct the Russian Empire and bring the new states back under central rule once they had obtained power.

The wider conflict

Lenin did not think that Russia could survive by itself as a communist state and fully expected the revolution to sweep across Europe, resulting in other communist states. Although there were attempted revolutions in Germany and Hungary, they were unsuccessful. The flickering of revolution was enough to cause concern in Russia's former allies, and this resulted in armed intervention by French, British, US, and Canadian troops. Further complications were caused by territorial disputes with Poland and the presence of 30,000 released Czech soldiers, formerly part of the Austro-Hungarian army, who had been held as prisoners of war by Russia.

Thus there were many conflicts at the same time: the Whites sought to overturn the result of the October Revolution; Bolshevik parties within the new states were attempting to overthrow their new governments; and international armies, who saw Lenin's government as a puppet of Germany due to its withdrawal from the war, were trying to safeguard their nations' interests.

In reality, the importance of the subsequent allied intervention in the Russian Civil War can be over-emphasized. They landed, in the most part, to prevent supplies delivered to Russia before the revolution from falling into the German army's hands, and, while their sympathies lay with the Whites rather than the Bolsheviks, their presence allowed the Bolsheviks to appeal to patriotism in repelling the foreign invaders.

The Bolsheviks were in a precarious position. They were surrounded by the central protagonists of the Whites, who from early 1918 were using their armies to strike at the nascent communist state. The Czech prisoners of war who were meant to be joining the allies in France took control of the Trans-Siberian Railway, formed an alliance with the right-wing Social Revolutionaries, and seized the imperial gold reserve at Kazan. Finnish Whites in the north were pushing towards Petrograd.

Leon Trotsky was appointed Commissar for War by the Bolsheviks, and he set about building an army from almost nothing. An appeal for volunteers

produced pitiful results. Conscription, mainly among industrial workers, formed an army of 500,000 by April 1919. Discipline was enforced by party members in the ranks; spying by the Cheka, the newly formed secret police; and liberal use of the firing squads. By mid-1920, the army would grow to five million men. Eventually, 50,000 ex-tsarist officers were installed in the Red Army, with their loyalty ensured by keeping their families hostage.

The nadir

As if the Bolsheviks did not have enough problems, they became embroiled in a war with Poland over the Russo-Polish border. Still believing that there were revolutions to come in Germany and beyond, this meant that in order to assist they would have to march through Poland. The Red Army began its move west, and fighting began in February 1919.

In 1918–19, the White generals advanced on the centres of Bolshevik power from the Siberian east, from Estonia, and from the south under General Denekin. Denekin made significant progress and came within 160 kilometres (100 miles) of Moscow. At the same time, the Poles advanced upon the city from the west. The Bolsheviks were in a desperate position, confronted with two enemies. The Poles were worried about the fate of an independent Poland if the Whites succeeded in ousting the Bolsheviks, however, and so did not attack. The Red Army defeated Denekin in November 1919, and the moment of greatest danger for them had passed.

The Poles now felt the might of the Red Army and were driven back from their previous advances. The Red advance continued, reaching to within five days march of Berlin. They were stopped only by a huge cavalry battle at Warsaw in August 1920. Lenin sued for peace, and the Treaty of Riga was signed in 1921.

The recovery

From late 1919, Bolshevik power grew after the defeat of Denekin, and the remaining Whites were defeated by the Red Army under Trotsky. From there, the powerful Red Army reincorporated the new states of the Ukraine, Belorussia, the Caucasus, and Siberia into Russia, creating the Union of Soviet Socialist Republics (USSR) in 1922.

The Red victory was contrary to most expectations. They had been surrounded, outnumbered, and cut off from vital supplies. Their success was due to their interior lines of communication, the divided nature of their enemies, and the fanatical measures they were prepared take. The Civil War had seen the Reds institute war communism, where the state took over the direction of the

Famine

Crop failures in Russia were not unheard of, but the reaction of the government in the nascent USSR to the drought of 1921 led to a natural disaster. The Bolsheviks made no attempts to deal with the impending crisis until it was too late. When food was ordered from abroad, it was fed to the city dwellers, rather than the peasants, reducing the potential to grow more food. Foreign aid was given in vast quantities, but was stopped in 1923 when it was found that the Bolsheviks were busy offering food for sale abroad. By then, however, the worst was over. The estimated death toll was around five million Russians.

economy, and discipline and co-operation were enforced by the Cheka. By 1920, the country was devastated. The struggle had destroyed the economy, and industrial output fell to one-seventh of its 1913 level. The human cost was on an unthinkable scale: precise numbers are impossible to determine, but the number of military and civilian casualties has been estimated at 13 million – more than the entire military dead from World War I.

Victory in the Civil War allowed the regime's consolidation and the establishment of the first communist state in history. The rule of Lenin and the Bolsheviks was unashamedly a dictatorship by the party in the name of the proletariat. The constitutional assembly that had briefly met after the October Revolution was never allowed to reconvene; Party congresses and meetings were the only forms of representation and consultation allowed. Political challenges from within, even of a proletarian character, such as the mutiny by the sailors at Kronstadt in March 1921, were ruthlessly crushed. Within these parameters, however, the early communist regime seemed to possess progressive features.

Artists, writers, and film-makers enthusiastically experimented in the first flush of revolutionary fervour, while the Union Constitution of 1922 was widely hailed as an ingenious attempt to create, on paper at least, a genuine balance between the republics and the central government in Moscow. Most daringly of all, Lenin re-introduced a degree of capitalism into the economy with the New Economic Policy introduced at the 10th Party Congress in March 1921, allowing peasants to sell surplus produce on the open market. But how the regime would develop remained an unknown factor when Lenin was removed from the scene.

Stalin and the Formation of the USSR

Following the end of the Civil War, the withdrawal of foreign troops, and the defeat of the Whites, Lenin set about changing the economy to a more stable footing. His New Economic Policy, adopted in March 1921, put agricultural produce and light industry back on a market basis. This was not a complete success. There were shortages and economic hardship, as prices for food and goods fluctuated widely.

In May 1922, Lenin, the undisputed leader of the Bolsheviks, suffered his first stroke. His health was to decline, and he was to suffer two more strokes before his death on 21 January 1924. This left an enormous vacuum at the heart of the Bolshevik leadership, with Leon Trotsky and Joseph Stalin, Secretary-General, emerging as possible candidates, among others. At this time, Stalin did not look like Lenin's obvious successor: Lenin had written about his doubts as to Stalin's ability to use power wisely and suggested that Stalin should be removed from his post. But the ideological infighting and constantly shifting alliances between the main candidates destroyed their credibility, and

Stalin exploited this disunity. Using his position in charge of the Secretariat – the administrative centre of the Communist Party machinery – he was able to remove his rivals over a period of years. By 1929, Stalin was in control of the Soviet state.

The economy

Stalin did not hold Trotsky's view that the world-wide revolution would materialize in the near future, and saw the consolidation of communism within the USSR as the only realistic policy. In order to make this a reality, he instituted a policy of accelerated industrialization, the timetable for which was established in his Five-Year Plan. The

Labour camps, or gulags, *were a central feature of the political control that Stalin exercised over the USSR. The Chief Administration of Corrective Labour Camps and Labour Settlements was set up in 1934, with an attendant network of camps in remote parts of the country. Those accused of treason or sabotage had to endure relentless work in Arctic conditions in these camps.*

task was to change the Soviet state from an agrarian society to an economic powerhouse, thereby increasing its ability to resist foreign interference. Collectivization of the farms was an essential part of this process, and the peasants were forcibly removed from their lands into the collectives and state farms. Those who refused to comply had property confiscated or were sent to forced labour camps in Siberia. Workers flooded into the cities and were put to work in industry. It was a time of prodigious achievement and economic change, with cities rising from the ground and industries such as coal and steel increasing rapidly.

Despite this, the Soviet economy was beset with difficulty: agricultural production was erratic, productivity per worker was not improving, and it was more a case of reallocating effort than an efficient use of resources. The focus on heavy industry over consumer goods also resulted in very low living standards. The personal demands on workers were enormous: if a machine broke, a worker could be accused of sabotage; lateness could be construed as absenteeism – a criminal offence. Freedom of movement was severely curtailed.

The purges

Stalin set about eliminating potential opposition. Initially, opponents were expelled from the party or exiled. But, as Stalin's grip on power tightened, the purges took on a more deadly dimension. Trials of the so-called "Industrial Party" in late 1930 for sabotage of the Five-Year plan was followed by a large-scale trial of the former leaders of the Menshevik Party (a socialist rival of the Bolsheviks before the revolution) in 1931. The assassination of a Soviet minister, Sergei Kirov, in December 1934, provided the pretext for a directive ordering summary trial and execution without appeal, opening the floodgates for the execution and "disappearance" of those allegedly involved in Kirov's assassination. All Stalin's major opponents and potential rivals were arrested, and most were executed from 1936–8. It was alleged that Trotsky, who had been expelled from the party in 1927 and exiled in 1929, was head of an anti-Stalinist plot. He was later murdered in exile in Mexico in 1940 by a Stalinist agent.

The purges included most senior officers of the Red Army, and extended beyond political circles to figures in the arts and the media. They were used to spur on collectivization, with the population encouraged to denounce rich peasants who stood in the way of state policy. In industry, those who missed their targets were liable to be arrested. Huge networks of prison camps, or *gulags*, were set up in Siberia to house this massive new prisoner population. Precise figures for those who fell victim to the

Stalinist purges and collectivization are unknown, but those who died number many millions.

Foreign policy

Foreign policy was based upon the fact that, while Stalin had declared that "socialism in one country" was practical, it was likely that capitalism and communism would clash sooner rather than later. The economy was being changed to allow the USSR to resist any attack; however, if international relations could give it more breathing space, so much the better. Thus Soviet foreign policy cautiously endorsed the idea of collective security.

France, Britain, and Japan had recognized the USSR by the mid-1920s, although relations with Britain were uneasy. A clandestine relationship with Weimar Germany also allowed the Germans to evade the Treaty of Versailles and train fighter pilots and tank crews in Russia. Stalin built on these contacts, bringing the USSR into the League of Nations in 1934. His principal concern after the rise of Hitler was to build up a "Popular Front" against fascism, using the communist parties of other countries to promote anti-fascism and supporting the republican side in the Spanish Civil War. Frustrated by the West's appeasement of the fascist dictators, however, Stalin was eventually forced into an alliance with Hitler in the Nazi-Soviet pact of August 1939, with which he hoped to buy time.

Stalin and his Companions (1938). *The purges reached their height in the late 1930s. By 1939, Trotsky was the only surviving member – apart from Stalin – of the Politburo of Lenin. Of the 1966 delegates at the Party Congress in 1934, more than 1100 were arrested. Stalin was ruthless in eliminating anyone who might challenge his authority.*

The Russian Revolution 400–1 ►
The Third Reich 410–11 ►
Lenin and the Russian Civil War 414–15 ►
Stalinization and Revolts 456–7 ►

The Spanish Civil War

The civil war that broke out in Spain in 1936 is often seen as an example of the European conflict between fascism and communism. While it is true that this became an aspect of the conflict, as the fascist and communist regimes of Europe intervened to support their chosen allies, the war was also rooted in the nature of Spanish society and its history.

In an ideological conflict that split towns and families, poster campaigns were at the forefront of the battle to win the hearts and minds of the public during the Spanish Civil War. Thousands of posters were designed throughout the war, each addressing a burning issue of the time. This one demands bread and justice for the Spanish people.

The progress of the Spanish Civil War was slow. Despite some international support, the better organized and better equipped nationalist forces steadily reduced the separatist Basques and Catalans and closed in on the remaining republican forces.

By the 1930s, Spain had done little to become a modern industrialized nation. Most of the country was agricultural, with ownership of land concentrated in a few wealthy hands, while the agrarian workers lived in poverty. The country was further divided along regional lines, with the Catalans and the Basques, both with their own culture and language, agitating for autonomy. The Catholic Church provided another divisive issue. Urban liberals were deeply anti-clerical, seeing the Church as the reason for the country's intolerance. In contrast, many of the rural masses and nobility were staunchly Catholic and thus hostile to the liberals.

The monarchy was a final divisive issue. The Spanish Republic had only been formed in 1931, when, after decades of rival claims to the throne, the reigning monarch, Alfonso XIII, left the country after several attempts on his life. The majority of the rural population in support of the monarchy, and, although they were without a set programme of objectives, they had no great loyalty to the republic. The urban population, however, was a different matter and, in general, not opposed to the idea of the republic.

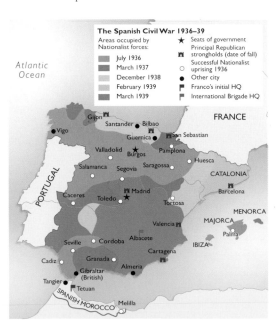

The Spanish Civil War 1936–39

Areas occupied by Nationalist forces:
- July 1936
- March 1937
- December 1938
- February 1939
- March 1939

- ★ Seats of government
- ♙ Principal Republican strongholds (date of fall)
- ○ Successful Nationalist uprising 1936
- ● Other city
- ◾ Franco's initial HQ
- ◾ International Brigade HQ

Atlantic Ocean

FRANCE

Gijon, Vigo, Santander, Bilbao, Guernica, San Sebastian, Valladolid, Burgos, Pamplona, Huesca, Salamanca, Segovia, Saragossa, CATALONIA, Madrid, Barcelona, Caceres, Toledo, Tortosa, PORTUGAL, Valencia, MENORCA, MAJORCA, Palma, Seville, Cordoba, Albacete, IBIZA, Cartagena, Cadiz, Granada, Almeria, Gibraltar (British), Tangier, Tetuan, SPANISH MOROCCO, Melilla

Republican government

The new republican government of 1931, under the moderate liberal premier Manuel Azaña, had begun to institute a series of reforms to address these issues. The privileges of the Catholic Church were attacked, attempts were made at land reform, and some autonomy was granted to the Catalans. All of these measures were unpopular for one reason or another: some were criticized by those that they should have benefited for not being radical enough. A more right-wing government won power in 1933, and the reforms started under Azaña's government were stalled or reversed. There was an attempted general strike in protest, which was put down forcibly by the army.

The 1936 elections were to see another reversal and a victory for a Popular Front government which comprised republican liberals, socialists, and communists, in which Azaña, premier under Zamora's government, was elected president. Even as it gained power, order was breaking down, with strikes and estate occupations growing in number. At this point, the army intervened. The Spanish army, oversized and unenamoured of the republic due to its army reforms, saw itself as the true voice of the people of Spain and believed that the time was right to restore order and stop the danger of a communist takeover.

The army attempted to take control of a number of cities on 19 July 1936. In brutal fighting they overcame Seville, Corunna, Cadiz, and Granada among others, but failed to take Barcelona, Madrid, Bilbao, or Valencia – the real economic centres of Spain. The situation was finely balanced, with the army supported by fascists, monarchists, industrialists, and landowners, and those fighting for the republic made up of Popular Front parties, Catalans, and Basques.

The conflict expands

The growing conflict attracted the attention of the rest of Europe. Both Britain and France remained neutral, while Nazi Germany provided transport aircraft to General Francisco Franco, who was

The International Brigades

The passion aroused by the cause of the Spanish Republic was seen in the flood of volunteers to the International Brigades. Composed mainly of communists and sympathetic socialists and liberals, they were largely recruited through networks organized by the Communist Party. Over 36,000 volunteers came to the aid of the republic, seeing action in the defence of Madrid and the battles of 1937 that saved the republic from imminent defeat, suffering heavy casualties in the process. The International Brigades were withdrawn under the non-intervention agreements made between the great powers.

emerging as the leader of the coup. This allowed the movement of the North African army, previously cut off from the republican navy. An attempt was made to take Madrid using these troops, but it was defeated. International intervention grew. In the absence of support from Britain and France, the USSR was prepared to sell tanks and planes and provide military advisers to the republic in exchange for Spanish gold. Mussolini, trying to increase his influence in the Mediterranean, provided troops to Franco, and Hitler sent the elite Condor Legion. The republic was aided by the International Brigades of volunteers who flooded in from Europe and the USA to support what they saw as a noble cause.

The continuing conflict was characterized by vicious and often confused engagements, reflecting the complicated political background. It also saw an example of the coming barbarity of modern warfare, with the destruction of the undefended, historic Basque town of Guernica by the bombers of the German Condor Legion in April 1937. Madrid, Bilbao, and Barcelona were also bombed, while prisoners of war and known political opponents were regularly shot. Both sides were involved in extensive persecution of political opponents. The Spanish Republic, despite the failure of the army to achieve its objectives swiftly, was gradually losing the war. Under Franco, any divisions of opinion were repressed, achieving a firmness of purpose and direction that was denied to the republicans, who, due to the disparate nature of their objectives were deeply divided. There was infighting among republicans, and much of the direction came not from central government, but from local committees. The moderate ground of politics disappeared, and, by 1938, the republican government was under the sway of the communist President Negrin. Following street fighting in Barcelona between the anarchist (POUM) militias and the communists, the communists took control of the republican war effort, eliminating the militias and executing anti-Stalinist opponents. The war had pushed the country into the very hands that the army's uprising had been designed to prevent it reaching. Within the nationalist side the old conservative parties died away and the fascist Falange, the party adopted by Franco, dominated.

The introduction of conscription by the army and an increasing flow of tanks and guns from Germany and Italy gave the nationalists the edge. Town after town fell to the nationalists, culminating in the sieges of Barcelona and Madrid in 1939. When they fell to Franco, there had been some hope of a unifying peace; instead, those who had been opponents were driven out or arrested. Left-wing parties and unions were banned, regional autonomy was denied, the Church was restored, and prison camps were established. Franco's agenda was not National Socialist, as it would have been understood in Germany or Italy – it was a step back to an older, more conservative Spain.

The cost to Spain was enormous. One of the more economically backward countries in Europe was devastated by a war that cost between 600,000 and one million dead. For a time, Spain engaged the attention of the whole of Europe, but once Britain and France refused formally to intervene, the Spanish Republic was doomed to a slow death as the fascist powers aided a prospective pro-fascist ally and Franco organized the nationalist forces. Stalin was forced to admit defeat in his attempt to stop fascism in Spain.

Interwar Culture

World War I and its aftermath had a massive impact on the thinking, art, and behaviour of European society after 1918. It caused a changing of perspectives and a questioning of society's values. The seismic events of the Russian Revolution also influenced contemporary thought: Marxist revolution was now a reality and was by no means abhorrent to all. Nationalist philosophy also had its supporters across Europe.

The economic revival of the early 1920s saw a party-like atmosphere sweeping across Europe. Freed from some of the restrictions of wartime regimes and relieved at surviving the "War to End All Wars", Europeans partied like there was no tomorrow. The image of young couples dancing the Charleston is a common symbol of the roaring 1920s, yet this was set against a background of political struggle and often violence. Even as the Depression struck Europe and hyperinflation hit Germany, for those with an income, the party continued, as there was little point in saving cash that might be worthless the next day.

It was also in this period that the influence of Sigmund Freud began truly to leave its mark. His work in psychoanalysis at the turn of the century had recognized the importance of the subconscious on human behaviour. This was to influence the many schools of art and literature that proliferated in the interwar period.

The Dadaists wanted to open the way to a new art and a new society by undermining and exposing what they saw as the stale cultural conventions of a decayed European civilization that had led the world into the conflagration of World War I. Many of today's contemporary artistic movements can trace their roots to Dadaism.

Literature

The interwar period was to produce a rich vein of literature across Europe, as authors, influenced by changes in philosophy and society brought about by the war, attempted to find new ways to express themselves and new subject matter to explore. One of the hallmarks of 20th-century culture was restless experimentation with forms. The novel was increasingly seen not as a vehicle for the traditional plot with a beginning, middle, and end, but as something more expressive of states of mind and being. In doing, so many writers took current literary expression almost to the point of incomprehensibility. Thus, in Ireland, James Joyce wrote both *Ulysses* (1922) and *Finnegans Wake* (1929). The former was banned for its sexual explicitness, but was more important for its pioneering use of language. This was developed further in Joyce's second work, where the limits of what could be communicated between author and reader was explored. In France, Marcel Proust produced his epic *Remembrance of Things Past* (1913–27). Both authors used stream of consciousness to compose highly creative, intricate, questioning works.

The aftermath of the war brought about a questioning and criticism of society. In England, the despair at the devastation and loss of life as a result of war was explored through poetry such as T.S. Eliot's *The Wasteland,* as well as the works of those who had lived and sometimes died in the trenches, such as Wilfred Owen and Siegfried Sassoon. There were also attacks on the prevailing values of society. D.H. Lawrence's *Lady Chatterley's Lover* (1928) lambasted English attitudes towards sex and was deemed obscene on publication. In Germany, Thomas Mann produced *The Magic Mountain* (1924), exploring the philosophies of Wagner and Neitzsche, and incorporating modernized German myth. Bertolt Brecht used his plays to question the political values of German society. Across Europe in the East, Franz Kafka's *The Trial* (1926) explored a nightmare vision of bureaucracy in central Europe as an allegory of the human condition. In Spain, the poet and dramatist Federico García Lorca rebelled against the fashionable realism and middle-class ethos of contemporary literature and took up the challenge of representing the tragedy of frustrated womanhood. Women writers took up for themselves the issue of their position in the world. In England, Virginia Woolf, a member of the self-consciously literary and artistic Bloomsbury set, wrote a series of novels of quivering sensitivity.

As the experimental 1920s turned into the 1930s, however, there were divergent currents, such as the nihilism and pessimism of French writers such as Louis-Ferdinand Céline, Albert Camus, and the young Jean-Paul Sartre. Others, like English novelists Christopher Isherwood, George Orwell, and Graham Greene adopted an increasingly documentary style in their novels. But not all literature was aimed at intellectuals: a highly successful genre of publishing revolved around crime fiction, seen in the launch of the Belgian writer George's Simenon's extremely popular Maigret series in 1931. Equally popular were English crime writers such as Agatha Christie and Edgar Wallace, whose crime novels accounted for almost half of all English book sales on the eve of World War II.

Art

In the art world, a continued period of enormous and in many ways fundamental innovation mirrored that of literature. In the immediate pre-war period, cubism had first attempted to break some of the prevailing conventions that had existed since the Renaissance. These developments were to continue through the war and produce further refinements across Europe. In Russia, constructivism used basic materials to create abstract structures in a movement that was initially lauded for embodying socialist values. This seriousness was starkly contrasted by the Dadaist movement, begun in Zurich, but the influence of which spread across Europe. The Dadaists reacted to society with mockery, consciously aiming to produce "anti-art", and emphasizing the importance of the absurd and the unpredictable in creating artworks.

Surrealism, founded in Paris and reaching its height in 1930–5, explored the unfettered expression of the subconscious. Salvador Dalí from Spain and the Belgian René Magritte were the principal exponents, but artists such as Pablo Picasso also went through surrealist phases.

That is not to say artists ignored political reality: the growing strength of the Nazi regime in the 1920s provoked a strong reaction from artists such as Otto Dix and George Grosz, until they were exiled from Germany. Politics and foreign affairs

also affected Picasso: the intervention of the Germans in the Spanish Civil War inspired his depiction of the destruction of Guernica in 1937.

World War II forced many of the surrealists to flee to the USA, influencing some of the later figures in the rise of New York as the centre of the modernist movement in art. The closing down of Paris under German occupation from 1940 ended a chapter in which Paris had served as the forcing house of modern art.

Abstract art had begun to emerge under the Russian constructivists, but was unable to survive under the Stalinist dictatorship. The Dutch artist Piet Mondrian and the de Stijl movement turned observed forms into geometry, producing paintings that were composed of straight lines and patches of colour. First produced in 1917, this remained their dominant style up to World War II. Others took a different route to abstraction, with Hans Arp and Joan Miró introducing biological forms into their abstract painting. By the late 1930s, sculpture had followed the trend towards abstraction with the work of Henry Moore and Ben Nicholson in Britain and the increasingly functionalist products of those influenced by the Bauhaus movement in Germany.

Architecture

The interwar period resulted in radical changes in style, as architecture reflected the artistic and philosophical developments of the period at the same time as using new construction techniques. Modern architecture developed out of various influences, including the arts and crafts movement,

The aim of the Bauhaus school was to teach its students to unite the skills of many different arts and artists. These skills were to be used in the production of everyday items, which were to be art forms as elevated as painting and sculpture. These designs were to be sold to industry to release artists from dependence on government support.

Jazz in Paris

Although originating in the USA, jazz had to cross the Atlantic to be taken seriously. Imported to Europe during World War I, it found wild acclaim in Paris, where many black musicians flocked to escape racial intolerance. The clubs of Montmartre swung to the likes of Louis Armstrong and saxophonist Sidney Bechet, and Josephine Baker, the reigning queen of the Charleston, was fêted equally by high society and the Parisian avant-garde. Paris's fascination with jazz and black culture extended to other art forms: Picasso's study of African masks led to his first experiments in cubism.

with its philosophy of craftsmanship and high quality of materials, and the great engineering traditions of the Industrial Revolution, which had produced stunningly elegant structures based on simple engineering principles. Like story-telling in novels and simple representation in art, architects sought to renounce unnecessary decoration and replace it with "truth to function". The great bridges and railway stations, the first steel-framed buildings, and the monuments to technical daring such as the Eiffel Tower constructed in the 19th century foreshadowed the new movement.

In the immediate postwar period Walter Gropius opened his Bauhaus school of design in the new Weimar Republic. The school reconciled art with industrial techniques and taught many disciplines, from typography to textiles, metalwork to pottery. Gropius was himself an architect, and he designed the building to which the school ultimately moved in the mid-1920s. Its design represented the style that the school would become famous for, with long, clean lines using the new medium of concrete fused with glass. Its influence spread across Europe and to the USA. This developed in the 1930s into the International Style, which derived its name from a book of the same title by Hitchcock and Johnson in 1932 that analysed the style's origins.

The austere International Style did not, however, totally dominate the interwar years – they were also marked by the exuberant eclecticism of Art Deco. Deriving its name from the Arts Décoratifs exhibition in Paris in 1925, it blended exotic, decorative motifs from Ancient Egypt, Latin America, and Moorish art into a colourful style much used in commercial leisure facilities such as cinemas and seaside resorts.

Right up to the beginning of World War II, many architects still chose to work within traditional forms. The grandiloquent structures planned by Hitler's architect, Albert Speer, for Berlin were still neoclassical in form, which was still the favourite style for many public buildings and educational facilities.

Music

In common with the other arts, the music of the interwar period was exemplified by diversity. Classical music underwent a period of significant experimentation, and more populist forms of music started to make a major impact, aided by the development of broadcast radio and the gramophone.

In the classical sphere, there were efforts to break away from the tonal structures of previous composition. Arnold Schoenberg took the lead in the early 1920s by using a twelve-note "serial music" based on an arbitrarily ordered chromatic scale. This continued to develop, becoming more and more ordered, to a point in the 1930s where all musical elements were subject to mathematical procedures. While such experimentation was to carry on into the postwar period, it it had little popular acclaim and was reserved for an elite avant-garde.

Alternatively, jazz, which had started to become popular before the war, continued to grow in acclaim. Spreading from New Orleans throughout the USA and into Europe, the style's boundaries were expanded by performers such as Louis Armstrong and Duke Ellington, who emphasized the importance of improvisation around the original melody. Disdained by the elite in its home country, jazz was taken seriously by classical European composers, with Darius Milhaud creating the first full-length work to combine jazz and classical idioms, *The Creation of the World* (1923). Duke Ellington's moves towards a larger band sound metamorphosed into swing, which proved very popular during World War II.

EUROPE AT WAR 1914–45

422   THE INTERWAR YEARS

Film

The relatively recent development of cinema was taken up with enthusiasm across Europe and the USA, with the first feature-length film produced during World War I. The new medium mixed artistic and populist successes, and they were by no means exclusively one or another. In the USSR, cinema was used for propaganda purposes but was also immensely popular in the hands of one of the geniuses of 20th-century film, Sergei Eisenstein, whose epic *Battleship Potemkin* (1925) served as a blueprint for radical cinematic technique. His later films celebrated the revolution, and his *Alexander Nevsky* (1938) pointedly depicted an early Russian hero who defeated a Teutonic invasion. Other early cinema pioneers such as G.W. Pabst tapped into the psychoanalytical theories of Freud to depict the social and moral disintegration of German society in the 1920s in films such as *Street of Sorrow* (1925) and *Diary of a Lost Girl* (1929). German expressionist cinema represented a serious comment on contemporary society, as did the work of French directors such as Jean Renoir, whose *La Grande Illusion* (1937) presented a powerful anti-war message. It was the USA and Hollywood, however, that would come to dominate film-making, aided by the time it took the European film industry to recover from the war and the economic slump of the late 1920s. Indeed both Eisenstein and Murnau would be attracted to Hollywood for periods of their careers.

During this time, Charlie Chaplin, Laurel and Hardy, Harold Lloyd, and Buster Keaton made the comedies that transformed them into some of the most famous men in the world. This was also the advent of the animated film, as exemplified by the Disney studio creations. During the interwar period, the ability to marry a sound recording to film resulted in the first "talkies" of 1927, expanding cinema's role to news reels and propaganda.

Science and technology

The years after the war were also a time of great scientific and technological advances. Commercial air travel became a reality, with 1919 seeing the first daily flight between London and Paris. Mass production meant that the gramophone and radio were within the reach of ordinary households, allowing the spread of news, ideas, and popular music. The first television transmission took place in Britain in 1927, and nine years later the BBC transmitted the first regular television broadcast. The world was becoming a smaller place.

In medicine, insulin was used in 1923 for the treatment of the previously fatal diabetes, and in the same year a vaccine was developed for diphtheria, previously one of the most common causes of death among small children. The properties of penicillin, discovered by Alexander Fleming in 1928, were later to be developed into the first antibiotic, which was to see widespread use in World War II.

Pabst was one of the three most famous German "Golden Age" directors, along with Murnau and Lang. Pandora's Box *saw him directing Louise Brooks in a film that received both censorship and criticism for its eroticism and scandalous story about an irresistible prostitute who consumes weak men before meeting her end at the hands of Jack the Ripper.*

INTERWAR CULTURE   **423**

The Road to War

The situation in Europe grew ever more complicated as it marched through the 1930s and France and Britain sought a method to deal with a resurgent Germany.

Neville Chamberlain stands at Heston airport having just returned from his discussions with Adolf Hitler in Munich. He believed that the Czechoslovakian problem was solved. He also had a signed undertaking from Hitler to resolve all matters of mutual interest through consultation, which, as he is telling the crowd, represented "peace in our time".

Even before the official outbreak of World War II when Germany invaded Poland, Hitler had already made significant progress in changing the political geography of Europe. He had created a Greater Germany, but he was not content with that.

Conflicting aims

At the beginning of the century, Europe had been kept in balance by the Triple Alliance of Britain, France, and Russia. The Treaty of Versailles had weakened Germany, but the Russian Revolution had created an unknown and feared quantity in the USSR. France was still committed to maintaining its security by keeping Germany weak. Britain was more ambivalent about the Treaty of Versailles and focussed on its imperial obligations. Italy under Mussolini was fiercely anti-Bolshevik, seeking what had been denied it in the Treaty of Versailles by extending its influence in Africa. The USA was entirely isolationist, and Japan was considering expansion in the Pacific. Germany under Hitler wanted a radical revision of the Treaty of Versailles and the European order.

German rearmament

In 1935, Germany, despite being bound by the terms of the Treaty of Versailles, announced its intention to conscript a 36-division army and form an air force. France was horrified by the resurgence of Germany. Britain, while it thought that keeping Germany disarmed indefinitely was unrealistic, was worried about an arms race. Italy was equally concerned, as Germany had almost joined with Austria in 1934, thereby threatening Italy. The

three countries met at the Stresa Conference in April 1935 to condemn German rearmament, although no direct action was taken. France attempted to strengthen the alliance by involving the Soviet behemoth; Britain worried about the effect of this encirclement on Germany; and Italy was outraged at the attempted involvement of communists. The front was further weakened by Italy's unilateral invasion of Abyssinia. Britain was concerned about its stretched naval resources and put the final nail in the coffin of the Stresa alliance, in effect accepting German rearmament by concluding a bilateral Naval Limitation Treaty with Germany. It allowed Germany a navy despite the terms of the Treaty of Versailles. Any attempt at a common front against German resurgence was in tatters. Britain and France began to rearm, although they were deeply worried about the strain on their fragile economies.

At the beginning of 1936, France continued to consider the possibility of involving the USSR as a counterweight to the threat presented by Germany. This was not easy: the USSR no longer had a border with Germany, and the Eastern European states that were under the shadow of these two great European powers and already allied to France were as worried about encroachment by the USSR as they were about Nazi Germany.

A Greater Germany

Hitler continued to push Germany further along the path to a revision of the treaty. He marched troops back into the demilitarized Rhineland on 3 March 1936. The German High Command was deeply worried about the Western response, but this was unfounded. Italy was no longer interested in intervening. Britain, in effect, accepted that the Rhineland was "the Germans' backyard" and not worth going to war over, and France, although deeply worried, was not prepared intervene alone. Hitler's confidence was growing, and he gave Goering orders to prepare the German armed forces and economy for war in four years.

In 1937, there were more problems. Japan illustrated the weakness of the League of Nations as it invaded Manchuria. The USA still remained aloof from the growing turmoil in the world. Mussolini, impressed by the Nazis' demonstration of how

The Expansion of Germany 1933–39

Germany in 1933
Incorporated 1935 (Saar)
Occupied 1936 (Rhineland)

ANNEXED TERRITORY
March 1938
October 1938
March 1939

North Sea — DENMARK — SWEDEN — Baltic Sea — LATVIA — LITHUANIA — Danzig — EAST PRUSSIA — Berlin — Warsaw — GERMANY — POLAND — Frankfurt — SUDETENLAND — Prague — Cracow — Saarbrücken — PROTECTORATE OF BOHEMIA-MORAVIA — PROTECTORATE OF SLOVAKIA — Strasbourg — to Hungary 1938 — to Hungary 1939 — Munich — Vienna — to Hungary — SWITZERLAND — AUSTRIA — Budapest — HUNGARY — Milan — ROMANIA

much could be achieved by threats and unilateral action, threw his lot in with Hitler and signed an anti-communist pact that Japan was later to join.

Hitler, ever looking to expand German *Lebensraum,* now looked towards Austria. Unification between the two countries had been prohibited in the 1919 Treaty of St Germain. Austria itself presented a problem to France and Britain. It was almost entirely populated by Germans, and, in some circles, the Austro-German unification was seen as an inevitability. Hitler began to meddle in Austrian domestic politics, trying to increase the influence of the Austrian Nazis by including them in government. Some of his demands were met, but the Austrian chancellor, von Schuschnigg, attempted to escape Hitler's noose by throwing the issue of independence open to the public in a plebiscite. Hitler was not prepared to risk a setback and, on 12 and 13 March, sent Nazi troops across the border of Austria before the plebiscite. The unification of Germany and Austria – the *Anschluss* – became a reality. The subsequent plebiscite showed substantial Austrian popular support for the move. There was no intervention from France or Britain. Neville Chamberlain, the British prime minister, was determined to find a policy that would remove grievances from the European political scene and thereby reduce the danger of war, and he saw enforced Austrian independence as such a grievance. Chamberlain felt that there was little that could be done to stop Germany from taking this step, short of all-out war. He also feared that such a war would lead to the destruction of the British Empire, as Japan, Italy, and possibly the USSR would annex parts of the Empire as Britain focussed all of its forces on Germany. France, still remembering the Ruhr occupation of 1923, was not going to act without Britain.

The Munich pact

Hitler was not content to stop there, and he looked to the next area where Germans were living outside the boundaries of Germany – Sudetenland in Czechoslovakia. Following Nazi-organized agitation by the Sudeten Germans, Hitler called for Sudeten autonomy and threatened invasion to ensure it. An invasion of Czechoslovakia would almost inevitably have forced France into a declaration of war with Germany, possibly precipitating an all-out conflict. By early September, France had called up its reservists, while seeking a negotiated settlement. Italy, which was not immediately involved, was prepared to act as an honest broker. But it was in fact Chamberlain, the British premier, who took the initiative, seeking to bring Hitler

within the normal channels of diplomacy. In September 1938, Chamberlain flew to meet Hitler personally to propose a conference to decide the Czech issue. On 29 September, Hitler, Mussolini, Chamberlain, and Daladier, the French prime minister, met in Munich and agreed that the Sudetenland area of Czechoslovakia should be ceded to Germany. Believing war had been averted, Chamberlain flew home to be greeted as a hero by the majority of the British public.

A line in the sand

The Munich pact was intended to be the start of a general European settlement, but in fact achieved very little. If anything, it shook Eastern Europe's belief in the West, as neither Czechoslovakia nor the USSR had been present. Six months after the pact, Hitler continued his expansion of Germany, marching on Prague in March 1939 to occupy the rest of Czechoslovakia. This created a storm of protest in Britain and France, and a growing fear in the USSR and other Eastern European governments. This was no longer a question of Germans being incorporated into a Greater Germany, but outright occupation. The move created a much greater acceptance among the public that Hitler should be stopped. Steps were taken to gather an anti-Hitler alliance, and guarantees of aid were made to Poland and other Eastern European states by Britain and France. Despite Britain's distrust, these efforts included diplomatic overtures to the Stalinist USSR, although they were half-hearted and ponderous.

On 7 March 1936 a token force of German troops marched into the Rhineland, breaching the Versailles and Locarno treaties. Any military response from Britain and France would have been decisive, but they merely protested and did nothing. As Lord Lothian put it, "They (the Germans) were only going into their own backyard."

The Third Reich   410–11 ▶
Italy: 1918–39   412–13 ▶
Attack on Poland   428–9 ▶
Assault on the West   430–1 ▶

The aftermath of the Allied
strategic bombing raids on Dresden,
February 1945. It was the
most destructive raid of the war
in Europe. Much of Dresden
was constructed of wood. Estimates
vary, but up to 75 per cent of
the city was burnt to the ground
and up to 135,000 people killed.

WORLD WAR II

In 1939, 21 years after the "War to End All Wars", the world was once again on the the brink of a massive conflagration. Despite the efforts of many to prevent a similar disaster, the legacy of World War I and the diplomatic manoeuvring in its aftermath gave Hitler the platform he needed to attempt a forceful, radical revision of the world order.

The strategic balance was different from the period leading up to World War I. Once again, the USA remained aloof from the growing tension in Europe. Once again, France and Britain were opposed to German expansion. Yet now, the USSR, the third part of the triangle that had been in place to contain the domination of the central European powers during World War I, was no longer aligned with its former allies. In August 1939, Stalin concluded a non-aggression pact with Hitler, and the fundamental problem that had dogged German strategic thinking for decades was no more.

Military thinking in 1939 was influenced by the earlier conflict. France, still haunted by its experiences in the trenches, concentrated on its defence and constructed the Maginot Line – a vast system of fortifications along its eastern frontier. Germany emphasized the importance of the offensive, particularly the potential of tanks to break the stalemate of trench warfare. The third approach focussed on the potential of air power, shown in its in infancy during the earlier war. Strategic bombing had been tried without much success, but now Britain believed that technology had advanced enough to create a potentially war-winning weapon. As a result, Britain, while not forsaking other developments, designed a series of heavy strategic bombers aimed at striking at an enemy's economy.

The impact of World War II was as seismic as the first had been. The casualties and suffering were enormous. In World War I, the massive casualties were among the armed forces; the remaining civilian population felt the effects of war through the loss of relatives and economic deprivations. World War II brought home the destruction of war directly. The strategic bombing of cities caused enormous numbers of casualties and left many more homeless. Almost a million people died from aerial bombardment, the great majority of whom were in Germany. The blitz on Rotterdam and London paled into insignificance compared with the massive and sustained bombing of German cities by the American and British air forces, resulting in the wholesale destruction of cities such as Berlin and Dresden. Moreover, the brutal savagery of the war in the East and the development of partisan and guerrilla warfare brought the civilian population directly into conflict with ruthless occupying forces, and atrocities and death became commonplace. Mass deportations within Stalin's Russia took place to prevent potentially hostile nationalities from joining the Nazi invaders, and the inhabitants of cities such as Leningrad and Stalingrad suffered incredible privations. Most terrible of all, the ideological determination of the Nazis to rid the world of those they deemed racially inferior led to industrial slaughter on a scale the world had never witnessed before. The Holocaust meant that the level of civilian deaths outnumbered those in the military.

Large parts of Europe were devastated economically by the war, and many states were on the verge of bankruptcy or in economic chaos, with populations near to starvation. Millions of Europeans were displaced from their country of origin and had little hope of return as a result of the ideological "iron curtain" that descended across Europe with the ending of the war. The map of Europe was profoundly altered, not just by boundary changes, but also by the Cold War that divided Europe into two ideological camps, one dominated by the communist USSR and the other by the capitalist West.

Attack on Poland

The city of Danzig was German populated, but made a free city within the Polish corridor assigned to Poland at the end of the World War I. It was to Danzig that Hitler turned after the Sudetenland. Hitler was convinced by the example of the Munich settlement that the next German gains could be made without war, while Britain and France thought any further steps would bring conflict.

Hitler and Stalin wash their dirty linen in 1940 – Poland and Finland, two of the countries referred to in the secret protocol attached to the Nazi–Soviet non-aggression pact. Despite the fact that Stalin later became an ally, it shows he was viewed in a similar light to Hitler before the Nazi invasion of the USSR.

The Wehrmacht was a different animal to the Polish army that it faced. In theory, the invading force was fatally outnumbered by the two million-strong Polish army, but in all important respects the Polish army was outmatched. It still relied on cavalry brigades, while the Germans placed emphasis on tanks, planes, and artillery.

Growing tension

In addition to a guarantee of aid to Poland, Britain took steps to create an anti-Nazi alliance which, in order to be successful, would have to include the USSR. Stalin, however, was not enamoured of the status quo and was looking for ways for the USSR to expand its influence. Yet the historical legacy of an overly powerful Germany continued to be a concern, and Poland provided a buffer between the USSR and Germany. However, there was also a long history of antagonism between the USSR and Poland, large parts of which had formerly been part of the Russian Empire. Earlier in the 1930s, the USSR had made overtures about concluding what was in effect an anti-German pact. A result was the non-aggression pact signed between the USSR and France in November 1933, followed by a mutual assistance pact in May 1935 in which both powers

pledged themselves to defend each other against unprovoked aggression. France, however, showed little enthusiasm, delaying its ratification, and no military talks took place. The Little Entente powers of Eastern Europe were reluctant to involve the USSR in any treaties, and Britain was generally unsympathetic towards the communists. Britain also feared provoking a reaction from Germany by encircling it. Now, however, Stalin was not interested in Britain's approaches.

Nazi–Soviet pact

Molotov, the Soviet commissar for foreign affairs, favoured a pro-German line, believing that if Hitler were to engage in a fight with France and Britain over Poland, then the USSR could remain neutral and grow in strength, while the Western powers destroyed themselves in a repeat of the

The Katyn Massacre

The partition of Poland in 1939 created the problem for Stalin of how to run the Soviet section. His solution was an example of a chilling disregard for human life: to remove the leaders. Somewhere between 4000 and 15,000 officers from the Polish armed services, as well as a significant number of influential Polish citizens such as academics, were placed in three prisoner of war camps. After the conflict had ended, the NKVD (the secret police – a forerunner of the KGB) shot the prisoners. When the Nazis invaded Poland, they captured the burial site at Katyn forest and informed the world of what the Soviets had done. The Soviets blamed the Nazis, however, and it was not until *glasnost* in 1992 that the USSR finally admitted responsibility for the atrocity.

Western Front of World War I. Trade negotiations were opened between Germany and the USSR, then, even as France and Britain made belated attempts to revive the Triple Entente of World War I, the German foreign minister Joachim von Ribbentrop made his way to Moscow. Germany wanted to eliminate the potential threat of Poland and make a start on the gain of *Lebensraum* in the East. Hitler was also concerned about a Soviet–French alliance. Whatever his long-term plans regarding the USSR, a pact would allow Germany some freedom to address France. Once negotiations started, it became clear that there were potentially significant gains to be had for both the USSR and Germany, with Poland and Eastern Europe to be divided among them. The Nazi–Soviet non-aggression pact was signed and announced on 23 August 1939. Its real reason was the private protocol attached, detailing the division of Poland and the Baltic states of Finland, Estonia, Lithuania, and Estonia between them.

Invasion of Poland

Hitler now knew that he could invade Poland without Soviet intervention, and, if concluded swiftly, the Wehrmacht – the German armed forces – would be manning the fortified French border if the French attempted to intervene.

Initial preparations to invade Poland began in August. When the attack came, there was no declaration of war. Instead it was based on false accusations of Polish mistreatment of Germans in Danzig. An incident was engineered whereby the SS made it appear that the Polish army had attacked a German radio station on the border, and, under the cover of this "unprovoked" attack, the invasion of Poland began on 1 September 1939. Britain and France issued an ultimatum for Germany to withdraw and declared war when this was ignored.

The Polish army was sizable but not well equipped. Poland did not have the industry to build modern planes or tanks, or the foreign exchange to buy them. No assistance had been forthcoming since the British guarantee of aid. The Poles, despite realizing the dire nature of their predicament in the run-up to the invasion, were determined to put up a fight and were buoyed by the promise of a French offensive 15 days after mobilization was completed.

Defeat

The Polish campaign was to see new tactics employed by the German armed forces. This was the advent of *blitzkrieg*, or lightning war. The antiquated Polish air force was destroyed within a day, leaving the German air force, the Luftwaffe, to provide support for the panzer divisions. The panzer divisions were concentrations of tanks used to punch through frontier defences, then penetrate deeply into enemy territory, encircling enemy formations, disrupting communications and supplies, attacking rear echelon troops, and causing panic. Infantry followed the tanks to mop up resistance and hold captured territory. The hopelessly mismatched Polish army, despite putting up fierce resistance, was on the retreat from day one as the panzers drove deep into Poland. The Polish generals waited for the pressure to be relieved by the French invasion of Germany, but it never came. Instead, two weeks after the invasion, they were assaulted from the east by the Red Army. The Soviet invasion, Stalin declared, was to restore former Russian territory to the USSR, as the Polish state had ceased to exist. The Polish government escaped, and the SS began its work of intimidating the civilian population. Despite continued resistance by the Poles, Poland was partitioned between the two totalitarian states. The conquest had taken a little over a month.

Assault on the West

Poland stood defeated and dismembered by Germany and the USSR. Hitler was poised to fight France and Britain, but the first months of the war were marked by an almost unreal period of inaction known as the "Phoney War". Neither the devastating land battles nor the air battles widely predicted before 1939 were occurring. The calm would soon be smashed as Hitler's blitzkrieg turned west.

A Spitfire of the British RAF attacks a German He-111 bomber. The various models of Spitfire were the best aircraft fielded by either side during the Battle of Britain. , In reality, however, the far less outstanding Hawker Siddeley Hurricane accounted for the majority of British fighters.

There had been no land offensive against Germany since the declaration of war. The failure to secure a solid alliance against Germany had forced France to focus on its defence strategy, resulting in the construction of the Maginot Line, a huge system of fixed fortifications along the French–German border. The plan was for this line to be held against any German attack, until Britain could build up its army and the Germans became weakened by blockade.

The winter of 1939 is known as the "Phoney War". A blockade was put in place, with the aim of doing irreparable damage to the German economy. This was not to be the case, as Germany had concluded deals with the USSR for oil and food. There was the start of a war at sea, whereby German surface raiders and U-boats attempted to destroy as much merchant shipping as possible, but the great clash of arms failed to materialize. The winter of 1939 passed with the Soviets fighting against Finland in an attempt to expand Soviet ter-

ritory in furtherance of the Nazi–Soviet pact. In April 1940, fearful of Allied plans to deny access to neutral Sweden's iron ore, which was important to the German economy, Hitler invaded first Denmark, then Norway. Denmark succumbed rapidly. The Allies rushed to meet the Norwegian invasion, and a period of fierce fighting continued until the beginning of June, at which point the Allies withdrew, and Norway fell to Hitler.

Meanwhile, Germany was planning an invasion of France. The Germans decided that they would attack through the Ardennes, terrain that was popularly thought to be impassable by massed tanks, and swing behind the advancing Allies. In this way, they could simply bypass the Maginot Line, which did not extend across the France and Belgium.

The German army embarked on this plan on 10 May, sweeping into the Netherlands and Belgium using the blitzkrieg tactics that had been so successful in Poland. On 14 May, the Dutch forces

Allied troops wait on the beaches of Dunkirk to be evacuated. Of the 900 ships used, only some 200 were naval. The successful evacuation was hailed as a miracle, but as the British prime minister Churchill pointed out, wars were not won by evacuations.

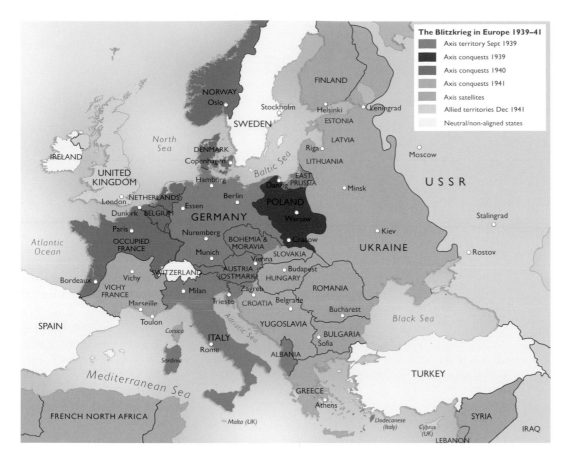

The Blitzkrieg in Europe 1939–41

- Axis territory Sept 1939
- Axis conquests 1939
- Axis conquests 1940
- Axis conquests 1941
- Axis satellites
- Allied territories Dec 1941
- Neutral/non-aligned states

By the end of 1941, Hitler's empire spread across continental Europe. He had conquered territory on a scale and at a pace that had astonished observers. But the seeds of his downfall were already sown. He had failed to conquer Britain in 1940, and in 1941, despite the large amount of territory taken, he had failed to force the USSR out of the war. The bombing of Pearl Harbour by the Japanese in 1941 had led to the entry of the world's largest economy on the Allied side.

surrendered. The German forces advanced through the Ardennes at a rate thought impossible by the French commanders. In 10 days, the German army had reached the French coast, cutting off the northern French armies from Paris and threatening to cut the British off from the Channel ports.

Dunkirk and the defeat of France

There were desperate plans for a French counter attack, but General John Gort, commander of the British Expeditionary Force (BEF), knew these would not succeed and retreated to Dunkirk, where a flotilla of hastily assembled naval and other small vessels started to ferry British and French troops across the Channel. Between 26 May and 4 June 1939, under air attack, 337,000 Allied soldiers were evacuated.

The French attempted to form a line along the Somme and Aisne rivers. Despite stiffened resistance, the panzer advances continued towards Paris and south towards Lyons. Italy, seeing gains, declared war on France on 10 June. US president Franklin D. Roosevelt declared himself powerless to affect the situation, and, on 25 June, a humiliating armistice came into force. The northern half of the country was to remain occupied and 5 per cent of France's population was to stay as prisoners of war. The Germans had lost 27,000 men; the French 90,000. Britain now

stood alone. A French government under Marshal Henri Pétain and centred on Vichy ruled France with the Nazis. Resistance was maintained by General Charles de Gaulle and the "Free French" in London.

The Battle of Britain

Hitler expected Britain to come to terms, but Winston Churchill, premier since May 1940, remained adamant. Hitler therefore planned an aerial assault on Britain as a preliminary to an invasion. The Battle of Britain was fought out above southern England, as the Luftwaffe attempted to wear down the Royal Air Force. Large-scale Luftwaffe attacks failed to destroy the RAF, but by the end of August the situation was critical, with British pilot numbers falling and German bombing of the fighter airfields beginning to cripple the RAF's response. A switch of tactics by the Germans, who began bombing London in retaliation for a raid on Berlin, gave the RAF the chance to inflict even heavier losses on the Germans. After the largest raid was repulsed on 15 September 1940, Hitler was forced to abandon his plans for an invasion. Instead, the aerial bombardment of British cities, the Blitz, was maintained through the autumn and winter of 1940–1. Britain remained in the war, and Hitler had suffered his first defeat.

The Western Front 390–1 ►
The Road to War 424–5 ►
Attack on Poland 428–9 ►
D-Day and German Defeat 438–9 ►

War in the Mediterranean and North Africa

The Mediterranean was a lifeline for the British Empire. The Suez Canal in Egypt allowed movement for trade, supplies, the navy, and the army between the British Isles and its Eastern territories such as India and Australia. Britain's Middle Eastern and North African possessions were therefore vital. The defeat of France left the path open for Mussolini to further his plans for expanding the Italian Empire.

1914–45

EUROPE AT WAR

General Erwin Rommel in the North African desert. Rommel was a general of immense skill, who earned the nickname "Desert Fox" from the Allied troops who opposed him. Although he was ultimately defeated in North Africa by superior force, his performance led to him being promoted and given a command in northern France, where the Allied invasion of Europe was expected.

The Mediterranean

The Italians had built a powerful navy to dominate the Mediterranean Sea. It was not a match for the British Royal Navy, but in this situation it did not have to be. The Royal Navy was divided between guarding home waters, defending convoys, hunting German U-boats, and patrolling the Eastern oceans, guarding its empire. The situation was worsened by the fall of France, which possessed a significant navy. Under the terms of the armistice it was to remain in French hands, but demilitarized. If it fell into German control, it would threaten the Royal Navy's superiority and, by extension, Britain's ability to feed and defend itself. Churchill feared that Hitler would gain control of the French fleet. As a result, in July 1940 an ultimatum was delivered to the French fleet at Oran: sail out of Hitler's reach and scuttle themselves, or be destroyed. The French refused, and the Royal Navy opened fire on their recent allies. The threat of the French fleet falling under German control was removed but the death of 1300 French sailors created lasting resentment. This left the Royal Navy with parity with the Italian navy. This changed when Admiral Cunningham, in a series of engagements culminating at the Battle of Taranto, damaged several Italian battleships, establishing British naval superiority by November 1940. However, ships were still vulnerable to land-based aerial attack. Hitler had hoped that he would be able to close the Mediterranean to the Royal Navy by bribing Spain's General Franco into capturing Gibraltar, but Franco remained steadfastly neutral.

Africa

On land, Italy first attempted to expand from its Abyssinian bases into the Sudan, but a hastily assembled British army consisting of colonial units from around the Empire swiftly defeated the Italian incursion, then proceeded to remove the Italian

presence from Abyssinia by May 1941. A campaign against French-held Syria secured Britain's base in Egypt from every direction except the west. From here, the sizable Italian army of 200,000 men in Libya set about threatening Egypt in the first of three drives starting September 1940. The Italian army marched into Egypt, stretching its lines of communications, but was then sent scurrying back 640 kilometres (400 miles) by a British counterattack in December 1940 under General Sir Archibald Wavell. The British took 130,000 prisoners.

This looked like a decisive victory, but Wavell had his army greatly reduced by Churchill's decision to try to defend Greece in March 1941, which was to be unsuccessful. The balance was further changed by Hitler's decision to send one of his

A German panzer is captured at the Battle of El Alamein in October 1942. The battle was particularly significant, as it marked the first serious defeat for Germany on land and a turning point in the war in North Africa.

generals, Erwin Rommel, with a small force of panzers to North Africa to support the Italians. The Afrika Korps launched an offensive in March 1941, driving the British back to the Egyptian border. There Rommel's army stopped, hampered by the same supply problems that were to beset all the generals in the North African war. Churchill responded by rushing a convoy of precious tanks to Alexandria to counterattack, but the British army was beaten back, largely because of the German 88mm anti-tank gun. General Claude Auchinleck, who had replaced Wavell, launched Operation Crusader in November 1941, which drove the Axis forces back to where Rommel had started his offensive.

In January 1942, the position was reversed again. Rommel drove the British back to El Gazala, north of Bir Hacheim in Libya. Churchill pushed for offensive action, but the Allies were forced to retreat to El Alamein in Egypt in June 1942. Churchill's reaction was to appoint new commanders, and the British position was assisted by the growing bounty of American lend-lease (a system whereby the USA loaned war material to the Allies for free). General Bernard Montgomery, having taken command of the 8th Army, now had a decisive superiority in men and tanks. On 23 October, he launched his attack, and, while the subsequent battle was to prove costly for the 8th Army, it was a decisive victory. There was another 320-kilometre (200-mile) retreat by the Germans.

The situation in North Africa now changed again. Stalin had been pushing for a second front in the West to relieve the pressure on the Soviets ever since the Germans had invaded. The USA, which had joined the war after the attack on Pearl Harbor by Japan in December 1941, engaged in an Anglo-American invasion of Morocco and Algeria in November 1942. Hitler then transferred troops to Tunisia and occupied the southern part of French territory that had been under Marshal Pétain. The Axis forces faced the US and British forces in the west, the Free French in the south-west, and the British 8th Army in the south. The Axis forces put up stiff resistance, but their ability to fight was severely impaired by the difficulty of supplying troops across the Allied-dominated Mediterranean. On 13 May 1943, 275,000 Axis soldiers surrendered.

Italy

The next step for the Allies was to follow up on this catastrophe for the Axis and pursue them across the Mediterranean. After a successful deception campaign, the Allied army invaded Sicily on 11 June 1943. The invasion force outnumbered the Axis defenders and had captured the island by 17 August. Most of the Axis troops had escaped, yet it produced a significant result: Mussolini was arrested by opponents in Italy, and the new government negotiated an almost unconditional armistice with the Allies. Rome had fallen in June, and Florence a month later. On 3 September, Allied troops began to cross the straits of Messina and to land on the main Italian peninsula. Hitler's reaction was to put into action contingency plans whereby the Wehrmacht occupied Italy, neutralized the Italian army, and readied themselves to fight the Allied invaders. A slow, costly drive up the mountainous Italian peninsula began, made slower as forces were diverted away from Italy for the opening of a new front in northern France. Through 1945, the advance continued past Rome and up to the Brenner Pass, although this action was now secondary to the battle in Germany.

The War in the East

Hitler had long desired to secure resources and *Lebensraum* in the East. Yet this was to be a different war from the invasions of Czechoslovakia and Poland: the Slavs were to be regarded by the invading soldiers as inferior and exterminated to allow colonization by Germany in the space vacated.

The capture of Stalingrad had become an obsession with Hitler, and he committed huge numbers of men to costly street-by-street fighting. By the time General Friedrich von Paulus and the surviving 80,000 troops of his 6th Army surrendered in 1942, the Stalingrad debacle had cost the Axis 300,000 men.

The start date for the German invasion, code-named Operation Barbarossa, was delayed due to the Italian army's need for assistance in its invasion of Greece, which imperilled the right flank of any Russian invasion. Hitler had to divert forces to deal with this. The German army swiftly overran Greece, but Operation Barbarossa was delayed by several months until 22 June 1941.

German war aims were divided into three. The northern attack was to advance on Leningrad, which Hitler considered would damage Soviet morale. The central attack was to advance on Moscow, the capital and centre of Soviet communications and government. The southern attack was to capture Stalingrad and the valuable oil fields of the south.

The German whirlwind

No formal declaration of war was given, yet as the date approached, Britain received growing information suggesting that Germany would invade. The information was passed to Stalin, but he ignored it; it is now suspected Stalin was preparing for his own attack against Germany. Whether or not this is true, the Soviet army was lined up close

to the front when 156 divisions of the Wehrmacht crossed into the USSR on 22 June 1941. The panzers, hardened by the invasion in the West, practised blitzkrieg on a vast scale. Entire Russian armies close to the front were surrounded and captured. Stalin and Churchill, diametrically opposed ideologically, signed a mutual assistance treaty in July 1941. As the Germans advanced deeper into the USSR, Stalin gave orders that whole cities with vital industries be uprooted and moved east beyond the Urals. The citizens of the Ukraine and the Baltic nations initially welcomed the invaders as liberators after the atrocities they had endured under Stalin, but their joy was short-lived as the SS and Gestapo that followed the invading Germans treated them harshly. By September 1941, the panzers had penetrated to Leningrad and were within sight of Moscow, at which point the Soviet government went into exile. The civilian population of Moscow erected tank traps and dug trenches around the city as defences. The Germans believed that the entire Soviet army had been destroyed.

Up until now, some of the best Soviet troops had been stationed far to the east on the Chinese

German troops advance on Moscow. Between invasion in June and the point where Arctic temperatures and stiffening resistance finally stopped the German advance, the Axis forces had travelled hundreds of miles and inflicted huge casualties on the USSR – but it was still not enough.

The Battle of Kursk

Kursk was the last real attempt by Hitler to achieve a knockout blow against the Red Army, by cutting off a million men in a salient around the town of Kursk. German preparations, dogged by indecision, lost the element of surprise. Thirty-six German divisions opposed a similar number of Soviet troops when they attacked in July 1943. It was to be the largest tank battle of the war. The Germans made early inroads, but rapidly ground to a halt, exhausted and low in ammunition. Soviet counterattacks reduced the fighting strength of the panzers and drove the Germans back beyond the start line. Germany had lost an irreplaceable proportion of its tanks.

border in Siberia. Stalin received intelligence that Japanese attentions were focused on the USA rather than the USSR, leaving 40 divisions free for transfer. The Soviets counterattacked with these troops, driving the Germans back from Moscow. In 1942, the harsh Soviet winter caught the German invaders unprepared and, without adequate winter clothing, many German soldiers became frostbite casualties. However, with the new year, new offensives were prepared. The Germans shifted the focus of their advance south and made for the Baku (now Baky) oil fields.

While Hitler butchered those Soviet citizens who might have supported him, Stalin changed tack and appealed to Russian nationalism, making allusions to Peter the Great and the Great War, and reopening the previously forbidden churches. The USSR began to tap its seemingly infinite resources of manpower and, with the USA in the war after December 1941, it began to receive increasing supplies of tanks and aircraft from the Allies. The Soviet troops, surviving on supplies that would have appalled their British or US counterparts, hurled themselves with patriotic fervour at the Germans.

The Germans continued to advance in 1942 with less success. German supply lines became stretched as distances from Germany increased and the Allied strategic bombing campaign disrupted German industrial production. Hitler focused on the capture of Stalingrad, as if the capture of his enemy's eponymous city would vanquish him. This lead to a strategic error: Hitler refused to let his 6th Army retreat from Stalingrad as its position became increasingly precarious. Eventually, the German forces were surrounded, and the whole German 6th Army surrendered.

The Soviet juggernaut

The Wehrmacht was now short of men, and 1943 saw its last attempt to defeat the Soviets. It met its end at Kursk, the largest tank battle ever, where the panzers were decisively defeated. This blow was the turning point on the Eastern Front. The Red Army started unleashing ever larger offensives, while the German army struggled to hold back the advance with ever decreasing numbers of soldiers. The offensives pushed at the Dnieper river in 1943, the Vistula at the beginning of 1944, the Danube later in 1944, and on to Berlin in 1945. These offensives simply pounded at the weakened Germans lines, and, although the Red Army paid heavily in casualties, the Germans could not stop the advances. The casualties increased as the front narrowed and Eastern Europe was entered, but the advance ground on. The only pause was when the Polish resistance rose against its occupiers in Warsaw between August and September 1944, awaiting the advance of the Red Army. It never came. The Soviets halted their advance until the rebels had been crushed; the idea of an independent Polish army or government was anathema to Stalin. The pace of the advance was such that, despite the invasion of Italy and eventually Normandy, by the end of the war the Red Army was left in de facto control of much of Eastern Europe. The war on the Eastern Front was incredibly costly in terms of human lives. The number of dead was exacerbated by the treatment of prisoners, who were left to starve to death.

The Napoleonic Wars   290–1 ▶
The Eastern Front   392–3 ▶
Stalin and the
Formation of the USSR   416–17 ▶
Assault on the West   432–3 ▶

The Holocaust

Hitler's aim of creating a strong German state was outlined in *Mein Kampf*. Intrinsic to it was his idea of racial purity and Aryan superiority. The search for *Lebensraum* had led to the German invasion of Poland and the USSR, and millions of East European Jews fell into German hands. Anti-Semitic legislation in pre-war Germany had discriminated against Jews; now Hitler turned to a programme of mass slaughter on a horrifying scale that extended to every country under Nazi control.

1914–45

EUROPE AT WAR

The Anschluss *between Austria and the German Reich in March 1938 meant the spread of Nazi anti-Semitic policies. Here, a young Jew in Vienna is forced to write* Jude *(Jew) on the wall of his father's shop to demonstrate its ownership.*

Persecution

Hitler was vitriolic in his attacks on Jews on his road to power in the 1920s: not only did he see them as a threat to a powerful Germany, but he also considered them part of a shadowy conspiracy that had betrayed Germany during World War I and was ultimately responsible for the shameful Treaty of Versailles.

By the 1930s, there were 500,000 Jews in Germany. When Hitler was entrenched in power after the Enabling Act in 1933, his policies to strengthen the nation were a practical expression of the anti-Semitic ideologies of *Mein Kampf*. In schools, the notion of an historical precedent for the Jewish enemy was reinforced; at universities, theories devised by Jewish intellectuals, such as Albert Einstein, were banned. In April 1933, Jews were banned from the civil service, ejected from the universities, and forbidden to work as journalists. In 1935, the Nuremburg Laws banned Jews from marrying or having sexual relations outside of their own faith, in order to preserve the purity of the German race. They were also deprived of citizenship. The march of exclusion continued, and, in 1938, the Nazis seized Jewish businesses and economic assets. Jews were forced to have obviously Jewish forenames and, in 1941, to wear the Star of David as identification. Mass expulsions became Nazi policy, and anyone with the money to leave was forced to do so. Nazi activists were allowed systematically to attack individuals, synagogues, and any suspected Jewish businesses. Jews were not the only victims: any groups which were designated undesirable, such as Gypsies or homosexuals, were subject to persecution.

As Hitler's foreign policy increased tensions in Europe, he gave a stark warning to Jews across the continent. Blaming a "Jewish Conspiracy" for the last war, he threatened that if they were responsible for another it would mean the end of the Jewish race in Europe. The Nazis were to do their best to make this a reality.

Ghettos provided the Nazis with an intermediate solution to the Jewish "problem". In March 1940, a ghetto was opened in the Polish city of Lodz where, surrounded by troops and barbed wire, Jews deported from all over Europe were segregated and left to starve under incredibly harsh conditions.

The extermination of European Jews was elevated to a gruesome science in the concentration camps. Before execution in the gas chambers, any valuables were taken. Gold fillings were removed, as was clothing – even shaved hair was woven into cloth and put to use in the German economy.

Poland contained Europe's largest Jewish population, and the occupation of Poland in 1939 brought substantial numbers of Jews under Hitler's power. They were housed in ghettos, with many moved to concentration camps such as Auschwitz. At this point, there were no methodical attempts to exterminate the Jewish population of Europe, but there were suggestions that they could be moved from the continent en masse. Madagascar was suggested as a possible destination.

Execution

In July 1941, the tone changed. Many more Jews had come under Nazi control in the formerly Soviet-occupied areas of Poland and in the USSR itself. That month, Goering ordered the Final Solution of the Jewish Question, and, although there is no documentary proof that Hitler ordered it, it is unbelievable that Goering would have done so without the approval of Hitler. The Final Solution was a systematic annihilation of the Jewish population in occupied Europe. At the beginning, this meant that specialist SS units travelling with the Wehrmacht would methodically execute entire Jewish communities as new ground was conquered, claiming tens of thousands of victims at a time. In January 1942, the methods were increased: the infamous Wannsee conference took place to discuss methods to industrialize the extermination of the Jews. From this came the use of gas and cremation chambers at the death camps such as Auschwitz, Treblinka, and Sobibor, and the methods of transporting the victims.

The numbers of deaths accelerated as Jews were cleared systemically from areas under German control. The total number of victims is still by no means certain, but it is estimated that six million people – around 60 per cent of the Jewish population – were sent to their deaths by the Nazis.

Some of the non-Jewish population did what they could in the face of this persecution, and usually at considerable risk. There are numerous examples of Jews being hidden by their gentile neighbours and of individuals such as the Swedish diplomat Ralph Wallenburg organizing the smuggled escape of many of the condemned. The French Resistance attempted to attack the railways in a bid to stop transportation. However, these are still the minority. The majority of the population living under the fear of the Nazi regime did nothing to prevent or stop the persecutions.

Denial

The Allies themselves, during the conduct of the war, refused to believe in the scale or even the existence of the outrage, despite eye-witnesses giving descriptions to the British and US governments. The blinkered approach continued when it was suggested that the rail network leading to Auschwitz could be bombed. At the time, this was treated as a side issue and the suggestion was rejected on the grounds that it would transfer resources from the main aim of bombing German cities. It was only when the Allied armies overran the death camps at the end of the war that the devastating truth began to make itself known.

D-Day and German Defeat

Since the entry of the USA into the war, the ultimate goal was an invasion of Europe across the Channel. The largest amphibious operation ever mounted launched an Anglo-American army against Hitler. Combined with the pounding from the skies and the advance by Soviet forces from the East, Germany was being ground to defeat.

A Soviet heavy tank advances through Berlin on 2 May 1945, stamping out the last vestiges of resistance. Hitler had committed suicide in his command bunker on 30 April, with the Soviets only 183m (200 yards) away, and here the red flag can be seen flying over the heavily damaged Reichstag building.

The beaches of Normandy, which were wide and flat, were selected for the invasion of the summer of 1944. The size of the invasion force was to be bigger than any previous amphibious assault. There were to be five seaborne divisions landing simultaneously and two airborne divisions. Opposing them in France were 60 divisions, but the majority of these were static infantry divisions full of reservists and older troops spread along the coast. Among them was a number of high-quality divisions, including ten Panzer divisions. In addition, under Rommel's direction, a series of formidable fortifications had been built and mines laid in what was called the Atlantic Wall. These forces would be more than enough to inflict a massive defeat on the Allies if the Nazis were able to get their tanks to the beaches on the invasion date. To avoid this, the Allies devised a complex deception scheme to convince the Germans that any coming invasion would come across the shortest route, the Pas de Calais. False radio messages were sent from fictional armies "preparing" for this invasion route. Even as the Normandy landings occurred, the Germans believed that they were a diversion and that a second invasion would come across the Pas de Calais, diverting vital troops from Normandy.

H-Hour

The assault was launched on 6 June 1944 after delays due to bad weather. There had been a huge bombing campaign destroying the railways and bridges that the Germans depended on to move their mostly unmechanized army. Battleships provided shore bombardment. Airborne divisions had been delivered by parachute and glider the night before. There were five beaches used: Omaha and Utah by the USA; Gold, Sword, and Juno by Britain and Canada. The landing went well on most of the beaches, with determined fighting overcoming the German defenders. On Omaha, the Americans came up against the fiercest resistance and came closest to disaster. They were pinned down for most of the day, and it seemed that they would have to be evacuated; however, they eventually succeeded, despite heavy casualties. Most of the 4,500 US casualties on D-Day were suffered on Omaha beach. The success of the operation had been partly due to German indecision. Permission to keep the panzers close to the beaches had been denied to Rommel and there were delays in moving them to meet the invasion. When they did begin to move to battle, they were struck by the overwhelming might of the Allied air forces, which far outstripped the Luftwaffe.

US troops wade ashore at Omaha beach on the morning of D-Day. They were part of the largest amphibious invasion force ever seen. Ten thousand planes, some 4000 ships and over 60,000 soldiers were involved on D-Day. One week later, more than 300,000 troops had been landed.

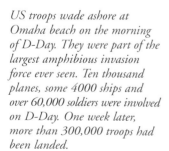

This success gave the Allies a foothold on the continent, but it was still tenuous, and the Germans were trying to bring their strength to bear. The Allies continued to pour men and machines across the Channel. In contrast, the Wehrmacht was hampered by Allied air attack and the damage to their transport infrastructure. By 26 June, there were 25 Allied divisions ashore opposed by only 14 Axis divisions within the immediate Normandy theatre. The Axis troops attempted to prevent a breakout and succeeded in throwing the pre-invasion time-tables off by weeks, but a breakout was just a matter of time, as German casualties and losses mounted.

To cope with the problems of the assault, the Allied engineers designed a number of special solutions. The lack of harbours was compensated for by artificial floating "mulberry harbours"; the fuel problem was solved by a cross-Channel underwater fuel pipe called Neptune. The troops were put ashore by amphibious trucks and specially designed landing ships. To increase confusion among the Germans, dummy paratroopers were dropped across Normandy as a diversion.

German defeat

The situation in August 1944 was becoming a desperate one for Germany. In the West, the army was weakening and struggled to contain the growing menace of the Allied army in Normandy. The German army was on the defensive in Italy, and the seemingly endless Red Army had just captured or killed 350,000 German troops, as well as advancing their lines 480 kilometres (300 miles), almost as far as Warsaw, in Operation Bagration. The strategic bombing campaign was now being carried out day and night, wreaking carnage in city after city.

The Germans had succeeded in slowing the advance of the Allied armies in Normandy, but they had been seriously weakened. Then US General George Patton unleashed Operation Cobra. Preceded by carpet bombing, Patton's US army broke through German lines on 25 July and started to fan out. An encircling manoeuvre at Falaise caught large numbers of German troops. The Germans fled in disorder, leaving 200,000 prisoners, 50,000 dead, and much of their equipment. Paris was triumphantly liberated on 24 August 1944, with de Gaulle given the privilege of entering the city first, and the Allies continued their drive for the Rhine – the next barrier.

Hitler placed his faith in his new superweapons – the V-1 and V-2 rockets. The weapons began to fall on London in the summer of 1944. He believed that they would win the war, but these weapons were never available in sufficient quantities to make that likely. They had come too late.

Bombing raids

The RAF had developed a series of strategic bombers such as the Halifax and Lancaster. After Dunkirk, strategic bombing was the only means that Britain could use to strike at Germany. Daylight precision raids against specific factories proved costly failures, and area bombing against German cities was instituted in an effort to destroy the morale of industrial workers. The effort and destruction were enormous. By dropping a mixture of explosives and incendiaries, firestorms were created in German cities that burnt out vast swathes of territory. In the bombing of Dresden, up to 150,000 people are estimated to have died.

Crossing the Rhine depended on capturing an intact bridge. There was an attempt to use airborne troops to capture the vital Arnhem bridges in the Netherlands. Despite dogged fighting by the Allies, this was a costly failure. Hitler then threw his last die. What was left of the tank troops on the Western Front was concentrated to fight against the USA in December 1944 in the Battle of the Bulge in the Ardennes. It was an attempt to mimic the German success of the 1940 invasion of France. Hitler dreamt of another drive to the French coast, to surround the invading armies. Despite initial success, it failed at great cost, further weakening the Germans' resistance. The Allies eventually crossed the Rhine when General Patton captured the last undestroyed bridge at Remagen.

In the east, on 12 January 1945, Soviet Marshal Georgi Zhukov launched the massive Red Army towards Berlin, from a distance of 640 kilometres (400 miles). German citizens fled before the advancing Soviets, with the German army powerless to stop them. Hitler, in desperation, assembled all able-bodied males over the age of 14 to serve in a people's army to meet the invaders in a final cataclysmic defence.

Meanwhile, the Allied advance gathered pace after crossing the Rhine. The Americans and Soviets linked on 23 April 1945 in Saxony. The Nazis planned for a last desperate stand in the Alps. The Russians besieged Berlin in April 1945. It took three weeks to fall and the number of casualties was enormous. With the Russians advancing on his position, Hitler shot himself on 30 April and the Germans under Admiral Karl Dönitz capitulated soon after. Germany was devastated and occupied by British, American, and Russian armies. Victory in Europe was declared on 8 May 1945.

The Paris Peace Conference   402–3 ▶
Assault on the West   430–1 ▶
The War in the East   434–5 ▶
The Origins of the Cold War   446–7 ▶

THE COLD WAR

1945–1989

POLITICS AND GOVERNMENT

12 March 1947 Truman doctrine: USA promises support to countries under communist threat.
5 June 1947 Marshall Plan for the recovery of Europe announced.
22 September 1947 Soviet founding of Cominform.

February–March 1946 Churchill's "Iron Curtain" speech. Conflict with USSR over Iran.

1953 "Peaceful coexistence" after death of Stalin. Reform and riots behind the Iron Curtain.

July–August 1945 Potsdam conference. Agreement on reparations, but conflicts over communist influence in Eastern European governments.

1952 Establishment of the European Community for Steel and Coal (ECSC).

June 1948– May 1949 The Berlin Blockade.

1949 Establishment of NATO, the FDR, and the GDR. Start of Korean War.

1955 West Germany joins Nato. The Warsaw Pact is established in response.

1956 Anti-Soviet uprising in Hungary. Suez crisis demonstrates decline of Britain and France.

1968 Warsaw Pact tanks crush Czechoslovak reform attempts following the "Prague Spring".

1957 Launch of Sputnik. European Economic Community (EEC) founded.

1961–8 US involvement in Vietnam escalates to all-out war.

1958 Second Berlin crisis as Khrushchev issues ultimatum to Western powers.

1961 Construction of the Berlin Wall.

1962 Cuban missile crisis: threat of nuclear war as USA blockades Cuba.

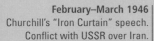

SOCIETY AND CULTURE

1945–9 Wartime destruction brings Europe to the brink of starvation. Political swing to the left; fear of revolution.

1949 The USSR tests its first atomic bomb.

1949–53 Eastern Europe sees Stalinism, collectivization, five-year plans, and shortage economies. In Western Europe, the foundations are laid for the welfare state.

1955–65 Economic growth in Western Europe as reconstruction ends. Birth of the consumer society.

1964–9 Age of protest in Western Europe.

1968 Student protests spark off mass demonstrations in France. Riots by students and "extra parliamentary opposition" in Germany.

1954–5 Rock'n'roll fever travels from the Atlantic with Elvis Presley, and the Bill Haley and the Comets film *Rock around the Clock.*

1962 After their first hit "Love me Do", the worldwide success of the Beatles revolutionizes pop music.

1969–75 Détente between the superpowers: signing of SALT treaty in 1972 and the Helsinki Accords in 1975.

1970–2 Relations improve as West Germany signs treaties with Poland, the GDR, and the USSR.

1985 *Glasnost* and *perestroika* initiated by Gorbachev in the USSR form the impetus for reforms in Eastern Europe.

1980 Strikes, formation of Solidarity, and declaration of martial law in Poland.

1988 Soviet troops start withdrawal from Afghanistan.

1979 Soviet invasion of Afghanistan spells end of détente.

1989 Free elections in Poland sweep communists from power. The end of the one-party state in Poland and Hungary. After the fall of the Berlin Wall in November, the end of communism in East Germany and "velvet revolution" in Czechoslovakia follow. Bloody revolution in Romania.

1989–91 The unification of Germany, the withdrawal of Soviet troops from Eastern Europe, and the disintegration of the USSR mark the end of the Cold War.

70   1985   2000

1973 Oil crisis as the OPEC states quadruple price of oil.

1972 Club of Rome report *The Limit to Growth* warns of catastrophic pollution levels and predicts apocalyptic consequences of unending production and consumption.

1979–85 Heyday of nuclear pessimism. Mass anti-nuclear protest against the stationing of US Pershing II cruise missiles in Western Europe.

1969–77 The rise of the "urban guerrilla" in Western Europe. Terrorists commit bombings, assassinations, and kidnappings.

1976–9 Economic misery expressed in punk youth culture.

1974–85 Recession in Europe: inflation and unemployment lead to social unrest and strikes.

Soviet military might files along under Lenin's watchful eye. Parades such as these were a recurring feature of Soviet holidays such as Labour Day and the anniversary of the Revolution. At the height of its power, the USSR seemed unbreakable. With the fall of the Berlin Wall in November 1989, the illusion was shattered.

A DIVIDED EUROPE

During the Cold War, political and social change swept through Europe. The predominance of Europe as a world power came to an end as the USA and the USSR took the lead in world affairs. In Western Europe, the social struggles of the past were laid to rest by the ascendancy of the welfare state and consumer society.

After 1945, the Grand Alliance of Great Britain, France, the USSR, and the USA against Nazi Germany collapsed, and the erstwhile allies soon confronted one another over Europe. The USSR desired security in the form of communist regimes along its borders, and this expansionism of communism led to fears that Western Europe would be next. The German question stood at the heart of the conflict: the USSR feared a strong Germany tied to the West, and the West in turn feared that a strong, neutral Germany would lead to new German aggression and weaken Western unity against the perceived communist threat.

The conflicts between the allies could not be resolved, and, by 1949, Europe and Germany were divided along the "Iron Curtain" of border posts and barbed wire that separated the ideologies of communism and democratic capitalism. This "Cold War" marked the decline of Europe. Decisions concerning Europe's destiny were no longer made in Paris, Berlin, and London, but in Washington and Moscow. During the 1950s, it became clear that the division of Europe was to last. The re-militarization of West Germany and its inclusion into NATO in 1955 destroyed any possibility of German reunification in the short term. The Soviet invasion of Hungary in 1956 demonstrated that the West respected the balance of power in Europe: it would not risk war to save Hungary.

Two other developments were also connected to the Cold War: decolonization and European integration. As the European powers gradually lost their colonies, the two new superpowers struggled for power and influence in the former dependencies. The desire to prevent a new war, the need for economic reconstruction, the apprehension at a resurgent Germany, and the fear of the USSR induced Western European governments to seek closer political and economic co-operation.

After the construction of the Berlin Wall (1961), the risk of conflict in Europe became too great, and the battlefield of the Cold War moved to the Third World. From the end of the 1960s, détente (relaxation) was established in the form of arms limitation agreements between the superpowers and *Ostpolitik* (West Germany's recognition of East Germany) on the continent. But with the Soviet invasion of Afghanistan in 1979, relations froze again. The Cold War finally came to an end because communism could not sustain itself economically. Centralized production and the lack of private initiative made the communist economies slow, wasteful, inefficient, and unproductive. The endeavours of Soviet leader Mikhail Gorbachev to reform communism instead led to its downfall.

In social and economic developments, Europe was also divided. Planned economy and a focus on heavy industry created shortage economies in Eastern Europe. In Western Europe, on the other hand, the foundations of the welfare state were laid. This, coupled with strong economic growth, cause a consumer culture to arise in the West. Social attitudes to morals and authority changed as a result of modernization, culminating in the almost revolutionary character of the 1960s generation. In 1968, youthful protest gained political expression with students demonstrations in France and West Germany. The Iron Curtain proved permeable, as Western youth culture became popular in Eastern Europe. During the 1970s, student protest made way for the terrorism of groups such as the Red Army Faction. Prosperity in the West came to a halt as recession took a hold in Europe, and the necessary austerity measures put the welfare state under severe pressure.

The Origins of the Cold War

The ideological conflict between communism and capitalism started with the Russian revolution, but the Cold War itself only became possible because of World War II. Hitler had brought the USA and the USSR onto the European continent. They were to remain there for nearly half a century.

At the Potsdam Conference, with Japan as yet undefeated, the Allies still make a public show of unity. It hides the deepening divisions over the future of Germany and Poland lurking under the surface.

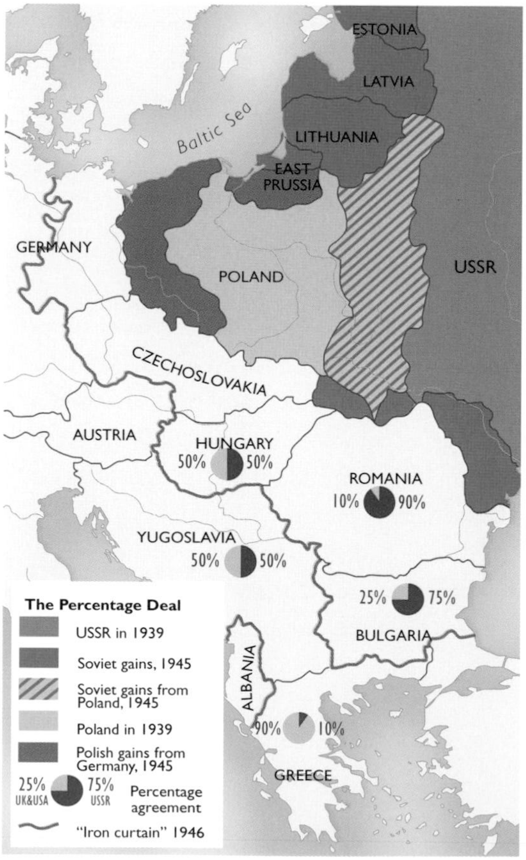

In a note scribbled in pencil, Churchill and Stalin divided postwar spheres of influence. Churchill wrote in his memoirs: "The pencilled paper lay in the centre of the table. At length I said, 'Might it not be thought rather cynical if it seemed we had disposed of these issues, so fateful to millions of people, in such an offhand manner? Let us burn the paper.' 'No, you keep it,' said Stalin."

In the Atlantic Charter of August 1941, the Allies had committed themselves to a war of liberation. After 1945, the peoples of the occupied countries were to decide their own destinies in free elections. This conflicted, however, with the Soviet need for security. Countries bordering the USSR had either joined Germany in its assault (Romania, Hungary), or, like Poland, had functioned as a stepping stone for the invasion. Churchill was inclined to do a deal with Stalin on the division of spheres of influence, leading to the infamous "percentage deal" of October 1944. The USSR would receive 90 per cent influence in Romania, and Great Britain 10 per cent; in Greece, it was the other way round, with the USSR receiving 10 per cent and Britain 90 per cent. Yugoslavia and Hungary were shared equally; and Russia would be given 75 per cent of Bulgaria, with Britain and the taking 20 per cent. However, it was only an informal agreement and not worked out in detail.

At the Yalta Conference in February 1945, the Allies consented to Moscow's insistence on "friendly" neighbouring states. They also published the *Declaration on Liberated Europe*, which promised free elections after the war. In strongly religious, anti-Russian, and anti-communist countries such as Poland, it would prove impossible to combine the two goals.

The liberation of Eastern Europe

Confrontation was fuelled by the rapid rise to power of communists in Eastern Europe, often by undemocratic means and with the help of the Red Army. Western countries soon came to distrust Soviet intentions. Stalin insisted that the "friendly" states would not have to be communist, although that was probably his intention. He told the Yugoslav communist Milovan Djilas in April 1945: "This war is not as in the past; whoever occupies a territory also imposes on it his own social system. Everyone imposes his own system as far as his army has power to do so. It cannot be otherwise."

In all Eastern European countries during World War II, the communist parties presented themselves as democratic and patriotic, fighting for national liberation, and following a peaceful, national road to communism. They established, and quickly dominated, broad "National Front" movements of all forces opposing Hitler. The communists made sure that they obtained key posts in postwar national governments, such as the ministry of the interior, in order to control police and security forces. These were used to intimidate opponents and fix elections, aided where possible by the Red Army.

Salami tactics

In most countries, the communist parties did not attack their enemies all at the same time. In Hungary, a country famous for its sausages, the

The Percentage Deal

- USSR in 1939
- Soviet gains, 1945
- Soviet gains from Poland, 1945
- Poland in 1939
- Polish gains from Germany, 1945

25% UK&USA / 75% USSR — Percentage agreement

"Iron curtain" 1946

(map labels: ESTONIA, LATVIA, LITHUANIA, EAST PRUSSIA, GERMANY, POLAND, USSR, Baltic Sea, CZECHOSLOVAKIA, AUSTRIA, HUNGARY 50% 50%, ROMANIA 10% 90%, YUGOSLAVIA 50% 50%, 25% 75% BULGARIA, ALBANIA, GREECE 90% 10%)

Poland

The Polish government in exile in London would never be a "friendly government" to the Soviet Union because Stalin had been Hitler's partner in carving up Poland in 1939. The hostility between the two countries increased with the discovery in 1943 near Katyn of the remains of 11,000 Polish officers executed by the Soviet secret police. At the Yalta Conference, the Western allies accepted Stalin's own Polish government in exile instead, with the inclusion of some of the London Poles. But in due course, the latter would be isolated and ejected from power.

phrase "salami tactics" was invented to describe this process: opponents were sliced off one at a time, like slices of salami.

First, the communists established alliances with democratic parties to get rid of the nobles and monarchists from the wartime National Front movements. They then allied themselves with progressive parties against the conservatives within the National Front. The next step was to form an alliance with socialists against their progressive former allies. The final move was the defeat of right-wing socialists and a merger with the social democrats. In 1944, there was no blueprint for a takeover: the communists were expected to behave with caution, but push at the doors of power and open them whenever possible. That year, Stalin told the Hungarian communist leader Ernö Gerö, for instance: "… there is no need to work up a scare. But when you get stronger, go full steam ahead."

From the end of 1944, communists in Eastern Europe were forcing down doors. Upon liberation, the Fatherland Front took power in Bulgaria, the National Democratic Front in Romania, and the Hungarian National Independence Front in Hungary. By the summer of 1945, communists were almost in control in Bulgaria and Romania, and the generals of the former regime had been ejected from the Hungarian ruling coalition.

Potsdam

The manipulation of East European governments showed the Western allies that Stalin had no intention of allowing the fair elections that had been agreed upon. Other Soviet actions also infuriated them: without having reached an agreement, the USSR started stripping occupied countries of their assets by way of reparations. The behaviour of the Red Army in the countries it occupied made many politicians change their view of the USSR as a

noble ally. In the enemy countries it conquered, liberation was characterized by widespread looting, executions, and rape.

The Western allies began to feel that they had compromised too much at Yalta, and they took a tougher stance. When Franklin D. Roosevelt died in April 1945, his successor, Harry Truman, met the Soviet foreign minister Vyacheslav Molotov in the same month, and accused him of going back on the promise to hold free elections in Poland. Molotov replied: "I have never been talked to like that in my life." Truman snapped back, "Carry out your agreements and you won't get talked to like that." Truman used US economic strength to increase his bargaining power. Only several days after the war in Europe ended, he halted lend-lease aid to the USSR, to great Soviet indignation.

At the Potsdam Conference, held in July and August 1945, some agreements were reached. Truman recognized the government of Poland. Germany was divided into four zones of occupation by France, Britain, the USA, and the USSR. The USSR had demanded $20 billion in reparations, but instead was allowed to take whatever it wished from its own zone and received a percentage of industrial goods from the Western zones. In return, it would provide the British and French zones with agricultural goods. Polish control over occupied German land was temporarily recognized, pending the signing of a peace treaty.

A number of conflicts remained. Truman did not recognize the governments of Romania and Bulgaria. The USSR rejected Western influence in Eastern Europe, and the Western countries spurned Soviet involvement in Italy and Greece. Soviet requests for control over former Italian colonies and bases in the strategic Black Sea straits were also rejected. Potsdam was to be the last show of harmony of the Grand Alliance.

Towards Containment

The increase of communist power in Eastern Europe led to the fear of communist takeovers in the West, where the political left was on the rise and communism was popular. It also led to a tougher stance against the USSR. Disagreements between the allies over how to approach the question of Germany became more intense.

At Fulton, Missouri, Winston Churchill delivers his "Iron Curtain" speech. It was the first time the former war leader publicly pronounced his misgivings about the USSR. For the time being, the message was ignored. The public remained benevolent towards the USSR.

Germany's cities lay in ruins, its population threatened with starvation, but there was little sympathy for the country; however, for the reconstruction of Europe it would be necessary to rebuild the German economic powerhouse. The fear that a poor Germany would become a breeding ground for communism was another powerful motive in rebuilding the country.

The rise of the Left

As the growth of communist influence in Eastern Europe continued, often through anti-democratic means, communism was also on the rise in Western Europe. Communists had gained respect through their role in the resistance, and the current poor economic situation was a breeding ground for radicalism.

Everywhere in Eastern Europe, there were communist parties jostling for power. Parties outside the communist-dominated National Front were excluded in the Bulgarian elections of August 1945. The Romanian king refused to co-operate with his government due to communist predominance. In Hungary, the Smallholder Party was forced by the Soviets to establish a coalition government, despite winning the November elections with 57 per cent of the vote. In February 1946, the Smallholder Party expelled a large number of deputies after weeks of riots and demonstrations organized by the Communist Party and its allies.

Western Europe seemed ripe for communist takeovers: social and political discontent could soon take hold among the ruins of Europe, where millions of refugees were on the move and millions more were threatened with starvation. The communists benefited from the prestige of the Left in general gained by the war. The war had brought about a sense of national unity, in which the social democratic parties, rejected as revolutionary before the war, were now fully accepted. Left-wing policies were in vogue: many considered that only a planned approach would be capable of tackling the devastation resulting from the war. In many occupied countries, there was a desire to break with the pre-war political systems that had not been able to prevent the catastrophe. Social democrats and communists embodied this desire for rejuvenation. The prestige of the communists was also enhanced by the sacrifice of communist resistance fighters and the role of the Red Army in defeating Hitler. All over Western Europe, the first postwar elections resulted in victories for left-wing parties: in Great Britain, Labour won a landslide election in 1945; elections in France in 1946 produced victories for the socialists and communists; and the social democrats won elections in the Netherlands and Belgium.

The Iron Curtain

The perception of a communist threat in Western Europe coupled with very real communist attempts to gain power in the East caused increasing concern in the West. On 22 February 1946, a high-ranking US diplomat in the Moscow embassy, George F. Kennan, outlined the perceived Soviet threat in one of the most influential documents of the Cold War, the so-called "Long Telegram".

According to Kennan, the "traditional and instinctive Russian sense of insecurity" produced a "neurotic sense of world affairs". Traditional Russian nationalism, combined with Marxism, produced an "uncompromising world view" that could only demand "destruction of the opponent, never coexistence". Winston Churchill expressed himself similarly in his famous speech at Fulton, Missouri, on 5 March 1946: "From Stettin in the Baltic to Trieste in the Adriatic, an Iron Curtain has descended across the continent." Not only were the "ancient countries of central and Eastern Europe" increasingly brought under Soviet control, but also "Communist Fifth Columns", controlled by Moscow, posed a "growing challenge and peril to 'Christian civilization'". These attitudes would dominate foreign policy towards the USSR for the next 40 years.

These growing worries expressed themselves in a more uncompromising attitude, which was to surface later that month when conflict erupted over Iran. The country had been occupied by British and Soviet troops in 1941 to prevent a German takeover. Both powers had agreed to leave the country at the end of the war. By December 1945, however, the USSR was supporting a separatist movement, which made it seem as if it were going to break the deal and stay in Iran. The Soviet troops only left after strong British and US protests in March 1946. This tougher line against the USSR was later to be called the "containment" of communism.

Germany

Concerns relating to the destruction and misery in Germany led to conflicts about its economic management and the payment of reparations. Although the division of Germany had been intended to be temporary, these struggles soon ensured it became permanent. First, tensions arose in 1946 over the formation of the Socialist Unity Party (SED) from the two working-class parties, the communist KPD and the social-democratic SPD, in Germany. Unification was an emotional issue: the failure of both parties to unite against Hitler in 1933 was seen as one of history's great missed opportunities. At last, the split in the labour movement that had occurred during the World War I could be rectified. Yet the KPD did not desire a true unification. It took over the leadership of the new party, and purged it of anti-communist socialists. The SED was forbidden in the Western zones, as it was feared Soviet authorities would use the party to extend their influence to the whole of Germany.

Most problems concerning co-operation in Germany were economic. The initial priority of

"Unity of the Working Class Movement – German Unity". Election poster from 1946. In the Soviet Zone of occupation of Germany, the Communist Party absorbed the Social Democratic Party when both merged into the Socialist Unity Party (SED) in 1946. In the West, this was seen as proof of aggressive Soviet intentions.

all allies was to prevent a resurgence of German power, and, at Potsdam, the Allies had agreed to keep the German economy artificially weak and living standards low. After suffering badly at German hands, the USSR had no qualms about exploiting its zone to the full limit. The French were equally vengeful and determined to keep Germany powerless. The Americans and British, however, were troubled by the Germans' poor living conditions and lack of basic amenities such as heating and food. Humanitarian considerations, and the fear that poverty would be a breeding ground for communism, convinced them of the need to alleviate the suffering of the German people; however, with Germany in ruins, this meant that US and British taxpayers would foot the bill. To avoid this, Germany itself would have to recover, which could be achieved through greater co-operation between the zones. France and the USSR refused to do this, and, in response – and to great Soviet outrage – the Americans and British stopped reparation payment to the Soviet zone, using it instead for the reconstruction of their own zones. Lacking French and Soviet support, the USA and Britain agreed to the economic merger of their zones on 1 January 1947 into "Bizonia". It was the first step towards the political division of Germany. The USSR promoted itself as a champion of German unity, and lambasted the allies as the dividers of Germany. The contest for Germany had started.

The Cominform and the Berlin Blockade

The Marshall Plan was a watershed and marked the beginning of long-term US commitment to involvement in Europe. The Soviet reaction – the establishment of the Cominform – demonstrated that Europe was now well and truly divided. The blocs started to form.

During the Berlin blockade, the besieged city was supplied by a relay of aircraft from the west, with one landing every three minutes. The lifting of the blockade proved the USSR was not willing to fight over Berlin, whereas the West was prepared to risk confrontation over the city.

The Cominform and the Prague coup

In reaction to the Marshall Plan, the Russian Communist Party called for a meeting of Europe's most important communist parties near Warsaw on 22 September 1947. There, the Soviet representative, Andrei Zhdanov, put forward the "two camp theory": the world was divided into two hostile camps, one socialist and one capitalist. The notion of different national conditions and possibly democratic and gradual "national roads to communism" was dropped. Instead, all the parties had to unite in a struggle against American "imperialism". The parties established the Communist Information Bureau (Cominform) to co-ordinate the struggle.

The new hard line became very clear in Czechoslovakia, which alone in Eastern Europe was still governed by a freely elected government. The Communist Party used its possession of the Ministry of the Interior to fill key posts in the police with communists. This caused non-socialist ministers to resign in protest from the National Front government in February 1948. The Communist Party organized mass demonstrations and a general strike,

demanding that the "reactionaries" remain outside the National Front; the Communist Party's paramilitary forces were kept on the side as a threat. The communist prime minister, Klement Gottwald, then accepted a new, left-wing government, dominated by the Communist Party. Czechoslovakia had fallen to communism in a bloodless coup.

In Eastern Europe, perceived enemies of communism were ejected from the socialist parties. Nothing now opposed the absorption of socialists into the communist parties. By the summer of 1948, the one-party state was a reality, and the introduction of socialism following a Soviet model began. One blow marred the communist successes: the Yugoslav communists realized that ideological unity meant subservience to the USSR. Led by Josip Tito, they had liberated Yugoslavia without aid from the Red Army and were not willing to hand over their gains to Stalin. Stalin considered Tito's attempts at provoking communist insurrections in Greece and Albania risky and counterproductive to his plans to carve out a sphere of influence in Eastern Europe. Stalin could not tolerate

Tito's Yugoslavia

During World War II, Marshall Tito (original name Josip Broz 1892–1980) was the leader of Yugoslavia's communist partisans and postwar communist Yugoslavia. Tito was not prepared to subjugate the country to Soviet communism. The split with the USSR went so far that in 1953, Yugoslavia co-operated militarily with the West in a pact with NATO members Greece and Turkey. Tito promoted himself as the leader of non-aligned states that declared themselves outside the orbit of East and West. He built a centralized communist state, and the national aspirations of the peoples of Yugoslavia – Serbs, Montenegrins, Slovenes, Croats, and Bosnians – were suppressed. As a result, opposition to the communist regime quickly took on nationalistic form. Following the death of Tito in 1980, the fall of communism led to the breakdown of the Yugoslav federation, a resurgence of ethnic nationalism, and the bloody wars in the Balkans in the 1990s.

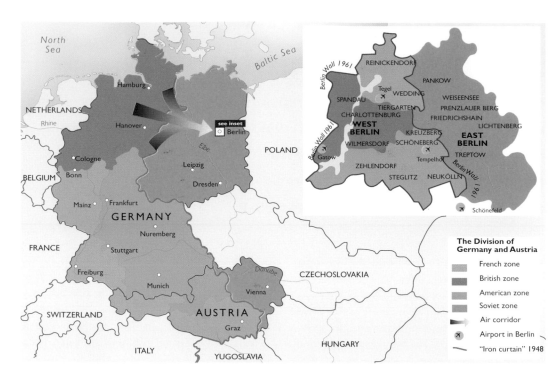

The Division of
Germany and Austria

French zone
British zone
American zone
Soviet zone
Air corridor
✈ Airport in Berlin
"Iron curtain" 1948

At the Potsdam Conference, Germany and Austria were partitioned into zones of occupation. Co-operation between the allies became increasingly difficult, which finally resulted in the division of Germany into two states. The occupation of Austria ended in 1955. Control of Germany and Berlin remained the central issue of the Cold War until 1989.

compromise: in June 1948, Yugoslavia was ejected from the Cominform and its people denounced as agents of the West.

In the West, the Prague coup was seen as Soviet-inspired aggression. Czechoslovakia had never been part of the Soviet sphere of influence vaguely promised at the end of the war. It showed how a country could be brought down by more or less democratic means, without the Red Army, through "salami tactics". Events in Czechoslovakia suggested that the same tactics could be successful in Western Europe. Failed Russian attempts to use the same strategy in Finland seemed to confirm the idea that the USSR was not just consolidating it position, but was instead bent on expansion.

The Berlin blockade

The two blocs confronted each other in Germany. When the launch of a new German Deutschmark for all four occupied zones was blocked by the USSR in June 1948, the Western allies introduced the currency in their own zones on 18 June. They exempted Berlin in order to discuss the matter with the Soviet administration. The latter hoped to use this as an opportunity to claim authority over the whole of Berlin, and forbade circulation of the new currency, on the grounds that the whole city was "economically part of the Soviet zone". On 22 June, the USSR went further and demanded the application of its new East German currency in the Western zones. In reaction, the Western allies introduced their currency in West Berlin. To enforce his claims on the city, Stalin then block-aded the overland routes that connected West Berlin to the Western zones: food and coal could no longer reach the two million inhabitants, and electricity supplies were cut off. Influential voices in the West advocated the sending of an armoured column across Berlin. To put pressure on the Soviets, US president Truman ordered 60 nuclear bombers to US bases in Britain. It was a gesture, as the bomb bays had not yet been adjusted to carry atomic weapons. However, the Soviet blockade was not total: no attempts were made to block the three "air corridors" to Berlin, which meant that the West could supply Berlin by air. Stalin had hoped to pressure the Western allies into giving up Berlin, but it was a half-hearted attempt, and he was not prepared to risk war. The airlift was successful, and the Soviet blockade was called off on 12 May 1949.

The blockade had a deep impact on the division of Europe. In the West, the popular perception of the civilian population of Berlin changed from the enemy to innocent victims; the Soviets shifted from allies to bullies who were starving a city into sub-mission. It was clear the two opposing sides were now deeply entrenched, and a swift solution for the whole of Germany was unlikely. This speeded up the establishment of a West German state on 23 May 1949. Elections were held in August 1949, and the first government of the Federal Republic of Germany (FDR) was installed one month later. In reaction, the USSR created the German Democratic Republic (GDR) from its zone of occupation in October 1949. With the formal division of Germany came the irrefutable fact of a divided Europe.

D-Day and German Defeat 408–9 ▶
The Cold War and European Integration 454–5 ▶
From Suez to Berlin and Cuba 458–9 ▶
The Balkans 484–5 ▶

The Cold War and European integration

World War II turned the idea of European unity from an idealistic dream into a realistic goal. Co-operation, it was hoped, would prevent future wars in Europe, and the Cold War ensured integration would actually happen. Western European unity provided a guarantee against two threats: a resurgent Germany and the USSR.

From the Congress to the Council of Europe

After the War, European unity became part of the national debate in most countries. It was seen as a basic necessity for economic recovery and a shield against threats from both Germany and the USSR. In May 1948, 750 delegates from Western Europe took part in the Congress of Europe in The Hague. Many ideas were put forward, such as a common market and monetary union, which were later to become reality. Early co-operation started on a smaller scale. Belgium, the Netherlands, and Luxembourg established the Benelux in February 1946 to administer tariffs jointly.

Broader European collaboration was established as a direct result of the Cold War, through the handing out of the Marshall funds. While supporting Europe with Marshall aid, the USA left it to the European countries themselves to distribute the funds. For this purpose, the Organization of European Economic Co-operation (OEEC) was formed, which paved the way for more intensive economic co-operation. Military co-operation was also a clear result of the Cold War: in March 1948, Britain, France, Belgium, Luxembourg, and the Netherlands signed the Brussels Pact, promising mutual military aid in case of war. The pact was aimed not only at the USSR, but also against a resurgent Germany. Fearful of an American retreat into isolationism, the Western European states insisted on a binding military treaty with the USA rather than a non-commital pledge of assistance. On 4 April 1949, the USA, Norway, Iceland, Denmark, Canada, Italy, Portugal, and the Brussels Pact members established the North Atlantic Treaty Organization (NATO). American preparedness to sign a treaty and its ratification by the Senate had undoubtedly been helped by the Berlin crisis.

But, despite the Cold War, co-operation still did not go very far. There was broad support for a federal European structure in the Benelux countries, Italy, France, and Germany. Other states, such as Britain and the Scandinavian countries, preferred co-operation to federalism. British participation was believed to be essential for the success of a European project, but Britain would only become a member of a European organization if it did not have too much power over the member states. A compromise was necessary, and the other states scaled down their ambitions. This was evident in the first European body, the Council of Europe, established in May 1949 by the Benelux countries, France, Italy, Denmark, Norway, Sweden, Britain, and Ireland. Although symbolically important, the council did not have any real power.

The Korean War

In 1949, two shocks hit the Western alliance. The first was the explosion of the Soviet atomic bomb

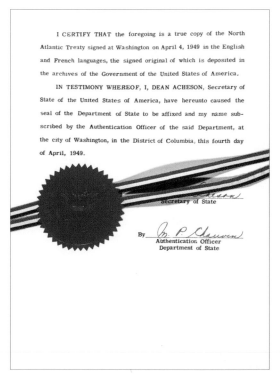

The signatories of the North Atlantic Treaty pledged to consider an attack on one as an attack on all. By signing the treaty, the USA finally committed itself to the defence of Europe. It was the definitive farewell to pre-war American isolationism.

I CERTIFY THAT the foregoing is a true copy of the North Atlantic Treaty signed at Washington on April 4, 1949 in the English and French languages, the signed original of which is deposited in the archives of the Government of the United States of America.

IN TESTIMONY WHEREOF, I, DEAN ACHESON, Secretary of State of the United States of America, have hereunto caused the seal of the Department of State to be affixed and my name subscribed by the Authentication Officer of the said Department, at the city of Washington, in the District of Columbia, this fourth day of April, 1949.

Secretary of State

By _____
Authentication Officer
Department of State

in September 1949, which had not been expected for at least another 10 years. The second was the victory of Mao Ze Dong's communists and the establishment of the People's Republic of China in the same year. At the beginning of 1950, Truman ordered the National Security Council to re-evaluate US defence policy. The resulting document, NSC-68, was the American answer to the Cominform's two-camp theory. The National Security Council perceived global politics as a confrontation between the USA and the USSR, and believed that Stalin was now out to conquer Europe. The USA, therefore, had to lead the struggle against communism across the globe. The first test of this new outlook came later that year when, encouraged and supported by Stalin, communist North Korea invaded South Korea, a Western-oriented dictatorship. Influenced by NSC-68, Truman intervened, and, within three months, a US army under a United Nations flag had beaten back the North Korean forces.

The European Community for Steel and Coal

The first real European institutions that operated independently from national governments were not the result of initiatives such as the Council of Europe, but came about as the result of the security concerns of the two most significant continental countries: France and Germany. France's policy of keeping Germany poor and powerless had failed due to the onset of the Cold War. France continued to fear a resurgent Germany and hoped to keep the country in check by integrating it into Europe. German intentions lay very much along the same lines. The first chancellor of the new Federal Republic, Konrad Adenauer, abhorred the Nazi past and the communists equally. Tying Germany to the West would be the best defence

against the Soviet threat, increased after the Korean War, and it would also prevent the rise of an aggressive Germany. It was only thanks to the fact that the policies of the two largest Western European nations concurred in this way that European integration could truly take place. In 1950, French foreign minister Robert Schuman proposed to create a common Franco-German market for coal and steel that would be administered by a supra-national body. Formed by France, Germany, Italy, and the Benelux countries in April 1952, the European Community for Steel and Coal (ECSC) marked the true beginning of European integration. To Germany, this was proof of Western acceptance, while to France it provided security: Germany's strategically important coal and steel production could be kept under control. It was an important step in European integration, as it was the first time that a multinational body made decisions independent of national governments.

COMECON

In Eastern Europe, integration of a different kind was taking place. The Council of Economic Cooperation (COMECON) was established in 1949 to promote trade throughout the Eastern bloc. The Comecon never became a truly international organization. Trade deals were on the whole concluded bilaterally, with the USSR looking on and ensuring that its interests were safeguarded. Communism was an internationalist ideology, but behind the Iron Curtain this did not lead to the establishment of multi-national institutions. The people's republics defined their foreign affairs not by their relations with their neighbours, but in the first place by their link with the USSR. They were satellites, in orbit around Moscow.

Stalinization and Revolts

Behind the Iron Curtain, the confrontation with the West in Germany and Korea, and Tito's rejection of Soviet communism increased the need for ideological conformity. The imposition of Stalinist dictatorships following the Soviet model began. After Stalin's death, Eastern Europe was shaken by revolts and protest. There was a degree of relaxation between the blocs, but basic Cold War tensions remained.

By 1949, all the Eastern European countries had introduced new constitutions, and had become "people's republics". The communist parties took control of the state, and socialist reforms were implemented. Industries were nationalized; in most countries, agriculture was collectivized, and the private sector shrunk to a minimum. After the Soviet model, Eastern European economies were centrally directed through five-year plans. Stalinism was also spread culturally: the satellites were "Sovietized". National culture was pushed to the background, and socialist culture was given pride of place. Red banners appeared everywhere. Soviet-style military parades and mass meetings were introduced. Statues to Soviet heroes Lenin and Stalin were erected in town squares, and their portraits hung on the walls in classrooms. Stalin was revered as the bringer of peace, the powerful ally and wise teacher. Similar personality cults were created for the national communist party leaders, little Stalins, who were nevertheless always shown to be subservient to the Soviet leader. The Soviet Union was presented as the great example, and Russian was taught in schools instead of other languages. Opponents, both real and imagined, were brutally suppressed: the Church and its leaders were persecuted and tens of thousands of arrests were made. To ensure ideological conformity, prominent communist leaders such as Kostov in Bulgaria, Slansky in Czechoslovakia, and Rajk in Hungary were subjected to lengthy show trials on fake charges of spying for Yugoslavia's Tito and the USA.

Peaceful coexistence

The Soviet bomb, Red China, and Korea all convinced the West that the communist threat was real and immediate, and persuaded Western leaders of the need to rearm Germany. But this idea was very unpopular so soon after the end of World War II. As had been the case with the ECSC, France considered the integration of Germany was the best way to deal with the problem and, in 1952,

proposed the creation of the European Defence Community (EDC). In the EDC, national armies would operate under international control, and in this way, Germany would be contained by the other EDC members. The plan failed: Britain refused to consider putting its military forces under international command, and, in France itself, German rearmament was still so unpopular that the idea was finally shelved in 1954. The USSR also objected to West German rearmament, and proposed the creation of a unified but neutral German state, which was rejected by Chancellor Adenauer as propaganda.

Stalin's death in 1953 reduced tensions; his successor, Nikita Khrushchev, proved more flexible. A ceasefire was agreed in Korea, and, in July 1954, the great-power leaders met in Geneva to discuss arms and the German question. In 1954, the re-militarization of Germany was agreed, and NATO admitted the Federal Republic of Germay in May 1955. Legislation was also passed in 1955 allowing the creation of German armed forces. In response to Germany's NATO membership, the USSR and its satellites established the Warsaw Pact in 1955 for military co-operation within the Eastern bloc. Despite such tensions, in 1956, Khrushchev declared "peaceful coexistence" possible between communism and capitalism – a major climb-down from the "two camp" theory. However, with the re-militarization of West Germany, the creation of a unified, neutral Germany was now definitely off the agenda.

The Hungarian revolt

Stalin's death also brought changes within Eastern Europe. Stalinism had created shortage economies, with the emphasis on heavy industry resulting in lengthy queues for even basic necessities. Workers were dissatisfied with having to attend political meetings after work and working for nothing on "socialist Saturdays". The idolization of the USSR offended nationalist sensibilities. With Stalin's death, unrest was soon expressed overtly. A strike in East Berlin on 17 June 1953 was only curtailed when Soviet tanks intervened. There was widespread discontent in Poland, but, in Hungary, economic difficulties and resentment turned to violence. The USSR replaced Hungary's Stalinist dictator, Rákosi, with the reformist communist Imre Nagy. His government immediately initiated reforms: the concentration camps were closed, prisoners were freed, and peasants were allowed to leave the collectives. Nagy's most fundamental proposal was to share power with other parties. In January 1955, however, he was removed from the party leadership and the reforms were reversed by Rákosi. However, Rákosi was fighting a losing battle: at the 20th All-Union Party Congress in 1956, Khrushchev was critical of Stalin's show trials and his "personality cult". Word of this secret speech leaked out and reverberated throughout the communist system, leading to a summer of unrest in Hungary.

On 23 October 1956, a mass student demonstration demanding Nagy's return to government sparked open revolt. The goal now went farther than the reform of communism and the communist symbol was cut from national flags. When the state radio denounced the protesters as counter revolutionaries, the demonstrators took over the radio headquarters by force. The next day, 24 October, Soviet tanks entered the city from the surrounding countryside. They were met with fierce resistance, mostly from working-class teenagers armed with petrol bombs, and were forced to retreat. After several days of hesitation, Nagy acknowledged the revolution and placed himself at the head of a new

multi-party government. When he demanded that Soviet troops leave the country and announced Hungary's intention to leave the Warsaw Pact, Khrushchev intervened. The Red Army invaded Hungary and quelled the revolt after a week of hard fighting. The uprising left Hungary with 2500 dead and 200,000 refugees. Its leaders were arrested and imprisoned, or, like Nagy, executed.

In retrospect, the great lesson of the Hungarian uprising was that reform of communism in Eastern Europe could soon lead to demands for its complete abolishment, if left unchecked by Soviet power. At the time, it demonstrated the West's acceptance of a divided Europe: the desperate calls for aid had not resulted in military support.

Ideological conformity

To stress Soviet supremacy, the Stalinist dictatorships in Eastern Europe revered the USSR, Stalin, and all things Russian. A joke from Stalinist Hungary at the time could have been told in any socialist country: "A French, British, and Hungarian academic are delivering a paper at a conference on elephants. The title of the French paper is 'The love life of the elephant'. The title of the British paper is 'Elephant and empire'. The Hungarian title is 'Our example – the Soviet elephant!'" At the height of Stalinism, humour was seen as a form of subversion. Such jokes could result in several years' imprisonment in the labour camps.

In the first days of the Hungarian uprising, many Red Army soldiers already stationed in Budapest were sympathetic to the Hungarians and refused to fight. Note the national coat of arms on the tank (front right): this one has been captured by insurgents. Fresh Soviet troops soon quelled the revolt.

STALINIZATION AND REVOLTS   457

From Suez to Berlin and Cuba

Europe's decline was measured not only through its division, but also through its loss of colonies in Africa and Asia. The Suez crisis showed just how far the former great powers had fallen. France and Britain had become dependent on the USA. The era of Europe had most definitely ended.

The Suez crisis

Britain's loss of empire was relatively peaceful. India gained independence in 1947 and was partitioned into the states of India and Pakistan; many of Britain's other colonies followed suit. Other European colonial powers fought lengthy and bloody wars: the Dutch fought for four years before losing Indonesia in 1949. After the decisive French defeat at Dien Bien Phu at the hands of the communist Viet Minh in 1954, Cambodia, Vietnam, and Laos gained independence. Initially, the USA backed the colonial powers, however, when it transpired that they were not capable of withstanding revolution and insurrection, it changed policy. The former colonies became a battleground in the Cold War, with both sides looking for support from the leaders of newly independent countries.

After the Egyptian leader Gamal Abdal Nasser nationalized the Suez Canal in 1956, Britain, France, and Israel intervened and occupied the canal zone. The reaction was almost unanimous disapproval. The USA could not afford to drive Nasser into the arms of the USSR, so it condemned the invasion and threatened to withdraw economic support. Britain and France had no choice but to bow to US pressure and retreat. Britain was so economically dependent on the USA that it could no longer resort to gunboat diplomacy without US consent. The global position once held by Britain and France was in hands of the USA and the USSR. The age of Europe had come to an end.

The Berlin crisis

The West's neutrality during the Hungarian revolt emboldened the Khrushchev government. Soviet confidence received another massive boost with the launch of Sputnik, the first man-made satellite, in an orbit around the earth in 1957. It caused a wave of panic in the USA, as it sent the message that the USSR would soon be capable of creating missiles that could strike continental America. The following years were characterized by relentless Soviet optimism. Khrushchev announced socialism would eventually beat capitalism and predicted that, within 20 years, the standard of living in the USSR would be better than in the USA. Soviet self-assurance led to a new crisis over Berlin.

The division of Europe seemed complete. Further integration of West Germany into the West followed. With the 1957 Treaty of Rome, the

Dissidents in Eastern Europe

After the brutal years of Stalinist dictatorship, opposition to the Communist Party became possible in Eastern Europe and the USSR. The nuclear physicist and nobel-prize winner Andrei Sakharov and his wife, Yelena Bonner, were prominent dissidents, critics of the arms race, and advocates of human rights. Their activities led to exile in the 1980s. The Nobel-prize winning author Aleksandr Solzhenitsyn (right) openly discussed the Soviet system of labour camps in the Gulag archipelago. Playwright and poet Václav Havel became a leading dissident in Czechoslovakia, criticizing life under communism in satirical and absurdist works. Dissidents continued to be harassed and persecuted, but the communist regimes no longer dared punish their critics too harshly: to do so would have meant losing face, especially once they had committed themselves to human rights with the signing of the Helsinki Final Act in 1975.

members states of ECSC established the European Economic Community (EEC), a customs union that over time would be transformed into a common market. Berlin was an anachronism in this divided Europe, as the border between East and West Berlin was still open. Since 1949, two million East Germans had used the open border to escape the dreary dictatorship in the East. It undermined the existence of the German Democratic Republic (the GDR), and the East German communist party leader, Walter Ulbricht, demanded urgent measures. In November 1958, Khrushchev issued an ultimatum: if the West would not withdraw from West Berlin in six months, the USSR would place access to West Berlin under East German control. The allies refused, but consented to hold a summit meeting with all four powers in Paris in May 1960 to discuss Berlin. This was abandoned when an American U2 spy plane was shot down by Soviet missiles over Sverdlovsk. The pilot, Gary Powers, was captured and paraded in front of the press by the Soviets. He was sentenced to 10 years in prison, but was later released in 1962 in exchange for Soviet spy Rudolph Abel. It was a major embarrassment to the Americans and Khrushchev refused to attend the summit.

The outpouring of East Germans to the West continued to pose a serious problem to the East German communists, and Ulbricht closed the border on 12–13 August 1961. The temporary barricade grew into a system of 7-metre (20-ft) walls, barbed wire fences, watchtowers, searchlights, and armed guards. On the Eastern side of the wall, a wide zone was emptied of all obstacles, called the "death strip" after the 191 people that were killed there while trying to escape East Berlin. The Berlin Wall was a tangible symbol of the divisions of the Cold War, but, after its construction, there was no more need to attempt to change the status of Berlin. The situation in Europe had become completely stagnant. Increasingly, the superpowers confronted one another outside Europe.

Crises outside Europe

The first of these conflicts turned into one of the most dangerous crises of the Cold War. In October 1962, American spy planes detected the construction of missile bases on Fidel Castro's communist Cuba. Once completed, they would enable the USSR to strike US cities with nuclear weapons. In response, the United States blockaded the island to prevent Soviet missiles getting through. It seemed that at any moment Soviet ships could attempt to break the blockade or US bombers might destroy the bases in air raids. It was the closest the world had come to war since 1945. After a week of ten-

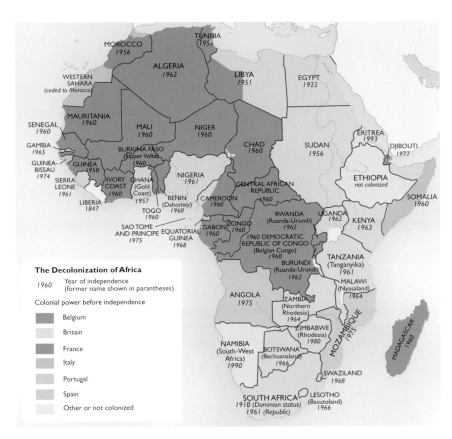

The Decolonization of Africa
1960   Year of independence (former name shown in parantheses)
Colonial power before independence

- Belgium
- Britain
- France
- Italy
- Portugal
- Spain
- Other or not colonized

sion, Khrushchev backed down and called back his ships, and relations between the USSR and the USA became less tense. The shock of having barely escaped nuclear war led to the installation of the "Hot Line", a direct telephone line between the White House and the Kremlin. In Moscow, the party leadership had had enough of Khrushchev's adventures and replaced him in 1964 with the less volatile Leonid Brezhnev.

While the superpowers refrained from conflict in Europe, the Cold War heated up elsewhere in the world. In Asia, the USA feared that one successful communist revolution would inevitably lead to neighbouring states toppling like a row of dominoes. This "domino theory" prompted the USA to take over the role of the French in South East Asia, and supported South Vietnam against the communist North. President John Kennedy stepped up American involvement, and his successor, Lyndon B. Johnson, started bombardments on North Vietnam in 1965. By 1968, there were 500,000 American soldiers in Vietnam, and there was no sign of victory. The USA had committed itself to an undeclared war from which it was impossible to extricate itself. In Europe, the Vietnam War was the focus for anti-American protest and became a central issue in the larger countercultural movement of student demonstration.

Decolonization reflected both the decline of Europe and the global confrontation between East and West. In 1945, almost the whole of Africa was colonized by European states. By 1975, nearly the entire continent was independent. This did not spell the end for foreign interference: the West supported colonial regimes such as Angola and Mozambique, and the USSR and Cuba provided aid to their own client states, such as Somalia.

1945–1989

THE COLD WAR

The Scramble for Africa   356–7 ▶
Nationalism and Empire   358–9 ▶
The Cominform and the Berlin Blockade   452–3 ▶
Culture and Counterculture   470–1 ▶
The Shadow of the Bomb   472–3 ▶

The Prague Spring and Détente

After the Cuban missile crisis, head-on confrontations between the superpowers became rare. With the Berlin Wall, there was no longer any need for struggle in Europe. The USA and the USSR now fought through middlemen in the far corners of the globe. By the end of the 1960s, relations between the two blocs relaxed, and a spirit of reform moved through Eastern Europe, resulting once again in a crackdown in Prague.

The Prague Spring

Changes had occurred in Eastern Europe that made the Soviets seem less threatening to the West. Most importantly, there was no longer a single communist bloc. Disagreements between Mao and Khrushchev led to a split between the USSR and China in 1961.

In Eastern Europe, the Soviet satellites were given more freedom. Romania started to take a more independent line from Moscow. It refused to take part in Warsaw Pact exercises in 1964 and developed a nationalist and occasionally anti-Russian ideology. In Hungary, the party eased political repression, liberalized agriculture, and started placing a greater emphasis on consumer products. Hungary's relative wealth was dubbed "goulash communism" by its envious neighbours.

In Czechoslovakia, a serious economic crisis brought home the need for reform. There were calls for an investigation into the Stalinist purges of the 1950s. The resentment of Slovak communists playing second fiddle to the Czechs put further pressure on the party. Actual reform commenced slowly. The Czechoslovak party had never been de-Stalinized. It had not dealt with the Stalinist past and was more orthodox than the Soviet party. To bring the Czech and Slovak communists in line with the anti-Stalinist policies pursued in the USSR, the Soviet leadership put pressure on the Czechoslovak party to investigate the Stalinist show trials. This occurred only in 1962. Economic changes were introduced in 1964. Events gathered pace when the reformist Alexander Dŭbcek was made leader of the party in January 1967. Following protests from dissident writers such

Peaceful protest in Prague after the invasion by Warsaw Pact forces put an end to the Prague Spring. The USSR would permit no challenges to the rule of the Communist Party.

as Václav Havel, censorship was abolished in March 1968. The Prague Spring had begun.

Dŭbcek wanted to give other parties influence and to restrict the role of party bureaucracy in the economy. Like Imre Nagy before him, Dŭbcek hoped to reform communism, not do away with it, and, like Nagy, he was quickly pushed aside by a public that wanted more. The parallels with 1956 were not lost on Moscow. When the Social Democratic Party re-established itself in Czechoslovakia in the summer of 1968, it was seen as a direct challenge to communist rule. Warsaw Pact troops invaded the country to prevent the introduction of further reforms. The population resisted with mass non-violent protest, and a blood-bath was avoided. To justify the invasion, Brezhnev put forward the "Brezhnev Doctrine": socialist countries had the right to intervene in other social-ist states when developments there threatened the socialist community of states as a whole. The message of the Brezhnev Doctrine was clear: the satellites were allowed freedom of movement to a degree, but the position of the Communist Party was unassailable.

France and NATO

The lessening of tensions between East and West revealed conflicts within NATO. Since World War II, the French Fourth Republic had been racked by crises as a result of the painful decolonization process. An appeal was made to General Charles de Gaulle to end the crisis. Under his leadership, France's Fifth Republic was established in 1958, and France finally abandoned its last colony, Algeria, in 1962. A fierce French patriot, de Gaulle was distrustful of US and British influence in Europe: when Britain finally overcame its fears of federalism and applied for membership of the EEC in 1962, de Gaulle prevented it with a French veto, suspecting British membership a trick to increase American influence in Europe. As the relationship between Washington and Moscow relaxed, de Gaulle feared the USA would fail to use nuclear weapons in defence of Europe and in response, he initiated the development of France's own nuclear weapons. He also withdrew France from the military structure of NATO in 1966, and, although France remained a member of the alliance, its armed forces were no longer under NATO command. Although it was a blow to NATO, it was a sign that the Soviet threat had receded. Ten years earlier, the French move would have been unthinkable.

Ostpolitik

As in France, scepticism about US commitment to European security increased in Germany after the

The dictatorships of Western Europe

Although the Cold War was seen in the West as a struggle between dictatorship and democracy, many Western allies were in fact governed by dictatorship. Portugal was a founder member of NATO, yet the authoritarian dictatorship was not removed until the 1974 "Revolution of Carnations". NATO member Greece was ruled by a military junta from 1967 to 1974. Spain was perhaps the most embarrassing: during World War II, the dictatorship of Franco (pictured right) had shown a benevolent neutrality to Nazi Germany. Domestic protests against Franco's regime continued throughout the 1960s. Although an ally of the West, Spain was not made a member of NATO until 1982, seven years after Franco's death.

Berlin crisis. West Germany's hostile attitude towards "the so-called GDR" to some now seemed counterproductive. During the late 1960s, calls for a new "Eastern Policy", or *Ostpolitik*, emerged as an alternative. Rather than confrontation, Germany should recognize realities and search for accommo-dation in Eastern Europe and with East Germany. The former mayor of West Berlin Willy Brandt was the architect of *Ostpolitik*. As chancellor, he signed non-aggression treaties with the USSR and Poland in 1970. For the first time, West Germany formally recognized the borders in Europe, including the East–West German one. He also reached agree-ments with East Germany. In the "basic treaty" of 1972 on West German–East German relations, the treaty defined Germany as "one nation" living in two states. Two years later, the two countries exchanged permanent diplomatic representatives.

Détente

The USA, in turn, was not completely pleased with *Ostpolitik*. It feared that the USSR might use it to reduce German ties to the rest of the western bloc. The USA also had its own plans for détente. In 1969, the USSR and USA discussed limiting their nuclear arsenals in the Strategic Arms Limitation Talks (SALT). In May 1972, President Richard Nixon and Brezhnev signed agreements freezing the number of nuclear missiles. Talks on conventional armed forces started in 1973. With the signing of the Helsinki Accords at the Conference on Security and Co-operation in Europe in 1975, the superpowers and their European allies recognized the borders of Europe and renounced their change by violent means. The Helsinki Accords also included a promise to respect human rights and political freedoms.

The Paris Peace Conference   402–3 ▶
The Origins of the Cold War   446–7 ▶
The Cold War and
European Integration   454–5 ▶
Gorbachev and the
End of Communism   465–6 ▶

The Reheating of the Cold War

Although communism itself and the relationship between East and West had become more flexible, the basic conflict still remained. At any moment the fragile détente could be reversed. The Soviet invasion of Afghanistan in 1979 precipitated a new round in the Cold War.

The concept of détente was flawed. Although significant, the arms limitation talks did not go far enough. Ideological conflict between communism and capitalism continued across the globe, and occasionally the superpowers clashed openly. Confrontation sometimes escalated to high levels. Following the Yom Kippur War of October 1973 in the Middle East, the USSR threatened to send troops to defend Egypt against Israel. Nixon responded by placing US armed forces across the globe on "Defence Condition III", the last state of alert before actual war. The SALT agreements were lacking in many respects. While freezing the number of certain missiles, the treaties did not stop the development of new ones, or encourage arms reduction. At the beginning of his presidency in 1976, Jimmy Carter had the ambition of bringing nuclear weaponry down to one-third of its then total; however, the final result of the negotiations, the SALT II Treaty in 1979, did not foresee any reductions at all. Détente did not provide a basic change in the antagonistic relationship between the superpowers, and the fragile peace could easily be upset.

Afghanistan

In December 1979, the USSR invaded Afghanistan to prop up the new communist regime. President Carter, in retaliation, put forward the "Carter Doctrine" in January 1980: the Persian Gulf was regarded as vital to American interests, and any threat to it would be countered, if necessary by force. US aid was given to the Islamic opposition against the Soviets. Ronald Reagan, elected president in 1981, promised an even harder line. He considered the USSR an "evil empire" and said so openly. The failure of arms negotiations illustrated this increased tension.

The Strategic Arms Reductions Talks (START) that began in 1982 were suspended after little over a year of discussions. No agreement was reached on medium-range nuclear missiles, and the deployment of American Pershing-II missiles in Europe went ahead despite mass protests. In 1983, Reagan proposed the Strategic Defence Initiative (SDI), a shield of laser and missile weapons in space that could ward off a nuclear attack. While the project was laughed off as "Star Wars", the prospect that it could spark off a very real and costly arms race in space and high-technology armaments alarmed the Soviets. Apart from Britain, most Western European countries reacted less violently than the USA to the invasion of Afghanistan. The British prime minister Margaret Thatcher was anxious to demonstrate the "special relationship" between Britain and the

Soviets attempts to prop up a communist regime in Afghanistan led to 20 years of civil war and a renewed standoff between the two superpowers.

The only organized mass protest movement to exist under communist rule was the Polish union Solidarity. A march by Solidarity supporters is pictured left.

United States. On the continent, on the other hand, a more critical view of US foreign policy had been growing. There was mass opposition to stationing US cruise missiles in Western Europe, and Germany hoped to continue its *Ostpolitik*, however, but the USSR was not able to exploit this to its advantage. It was too enmeshed in problems of its own.

Solidarity

The first crack in the Soviet empire appeared in Poland. Polish agriculture was small scale and beset by periodic crises. Twice in the 1970s, the government had raised food prices to stimulate agricultural production. Twice this had led to strikes by workers. Following a third price hike in 1980, activist Lech Walesa led his fellow workers in a strike at the Lenin Shipyards in Gdansk. Soon the strike was not about food prices: the right to free trade unions and the right to strike were first among the demands of the strikers. The government conceded to the establishment of the trade union *Solidarność* (Solidarity), but continuing police harassment of Solidarity provoked strikes in response. By the summer of 1981, Solidarity had grown into a powerful mass movement of nine million members. When Lech Walesa, now leader of Solidarity, turned down prime minister and party leader General Jaruzelski's proposal to include Solidarity in a Front for National Co-operation under leadership of the Communist Party, Jaruzelski declared martial law on 12 December 1981. Solidarity was suspended, and 40,000–50,000 Solidarity members were arrested.

The problems in Poland were not temporary or unique to Poland, but part of the communist system itself. Communism had brought about substantial social changes in Eastern Europe. It had lifted poor peasants from abject poverty and brought about greater social equality. It provided free or cheap education, childcare, health care, and other social benefits, but the economies were not efficient enough to support these expensive social systems. Party bureaucrats, not businessmen, made economic decisions. Officials had little to lose, and their mistakes were glossed over to protect the infallibility of the party. Corruption was a way of life: many people had a second job on the black market in which they invested all their energy at the expense of their regular jobs. University lecturers worked evenings as taxi drivers; factory workers neglected production to tend their private vegetable gardens. The emphasis on heavy industry meant that there were constant shortages, and queuing for consumer items and even basic necessities was a daily routine. Popular resentment ran high, especially against the party bureaucrats who were seen as corrupt and privileged.

To keep their economies afloat, Eastern European countries resorted to foreign loans. Poland borrowed heavily from the West to prop up its ailing agricultural sector and avert a crisis. Hungary had financed its consumer communism with a foreign debt as large as half its gross national product. Only Romania was able to eliminate its foreign debt entirely, but at the cost of the dismal poverty of its population. These economies were on the brink of collapse and could only be saved by reform. Within the communist systems themselves, there was pressure for change. In Czechoslovakia, dissident writers of the Charter 77 movement such as Václav Havel were at the forefront of protest. Dissidents were also active in East Germany and Hungary. Solidarity in Poland was a highly successful underground organization. There were reform-minded communists to be found in most Soviet satellites, but previous attempts at reform by Nagy and Dŭbcek had quickly escalated to demands for the end of communism altogether, which had been followed by the inevitable Soviet crackdown on protest. By the 1980s however, the situation had changed: the next reformer appeared not in one of the satellites, but at the heart of the system itself.

Russia, Austria, and Poland   270–1 ▶
Attack on Poland   428–9 ▶
The Origins of the Cold War   446–7 ▶
Towards Containment   448–9 ▶

Gorbachev and the End of Communism

The sclerosis at the centre of the communist system was symbolized by the bad health of the old men in charge of the party. Brezhnev died in November 1982, and his successor, KGB chief Yuri Andropov, lasted only a year and a half at the helm. The next secretary general, Konstantin Chernenko, was already dying when he was appointed and was so that weak he could barely speak at Andropov's funeral.

THE COLD WAR   1945–1989

A Romanian soldier photographed through a hole in the Romanian flag during the 1989 revolution. As during the Hungarian revolution in 1956, insurgents cut out the communist symbols from the national flag. In the end, the population regarded the communist regimes as the instrument of a foreign state.

In December 1987 Reagan and Gorbachev sign the Intermediate-range Nuclear Forces (INF) agreement in the White House, ending ten years of fears over tactical nuclear weapons in Europe.

Following Chernenko's death in 1985, Mikhail Gorbachev became party leader. His easygoing manner differed greatly from the gruff exteriors of his predecessors. To this, he added substance: he introduced reforms at home by advocating the restructuring (*perestroika*) of communism, to be accompanied by greater openness (*glasnost*). Most significant were his foreign policy changes: Afghanistan and the large standing armies in Eastern Europe were a drain on the Soviet economy, and the USSR could not afford a new arms race in space. Gorbachev needed détente. In January 1986, he proposed discarding *all* nuclear weapons. This was was seen as a propaganda tactic in the West, but at the Reykjavik Summit of October 1986, Reagan and Gorbachev agreed to deep cuts in their nuclear arsenals. After this, arms reductions quickly surpassed anything that SALT and START had yet produced. In December 1987, Gorbachev and Reagan agreed to eliminate the medium-range nuclear missiles from Europe that had been the source of such mass protest only a few years earlier. At the beginning of 1988, Gorbachev started withdrawal of Soviet troops from Afghanistan and, at the end of the same year, declared that 500,000 Soviet soldiers and 10,000 tanks would be removed from Eastern Europe.

Gorbachev's policies stimulated opposition to communism in Eastern Europe. Like Nagy and Dŭbcek before him, Gorbachev thought that far-reaching reforms would save communism. In reality, they would destroy it.

1989

Like 1848 and 1918, 1989 was to be a year of revolutionary change. Events in one country influenced those in the next, until the entire communist system collapsed. Ironically, it was now the revolutionary communist movement that was swept away by popular dissent.

Dissidents in Czechoslovakia and East Germany took heart from *glasnost* and *perestroika*, but the ruling communist parties were strictly orthodox and tried to limit the changes. In Hungary, however, reformists took hold of the Communist Party and introduced sweeping economic reforms. Opposition movements were formed that now openly challenged the regime. Developments in Poland showed that the rule of the party itself was under threat. After years of conflict with Solidarity, General Jaruzelski finally permitted free elections in June 1989. They were won by Solidarity.

Although communism first fell in Poland, it was in Germany that the Iron Curtain came crashing down. In East Germany, calls to reform the restriction on movement were high on the agenda. East Germans did not demand the right to travel just to go on holiday, but to travel in their own country and to meet long-lost relatives. This was an emotional issue that figured high in the demands of the protesters now demonstrating daily against the

The Fall of Communism in Eastern
Europe 1989–1992

Mar 1990 Date of first multi-party elections

⚔ Major civil uprisings

— "Iron curtain" 1948

North Sea

Baltic Sea

NETHERLANDS

BELGIUM

Gdansk ⚔

POLAND
May 1990

USSR

EAST GERMANY
Mar 1990

Berlin ⚔

Warsaw

1989 Crucial Moments
9 November:
Fall of Berlin Wall

Leipzig ⚔

WEST GERMANY

1989 Crucial Moments
June: Elections won by Solidarity

Prague ⚔

FRANCE

CZECHOSLOVAKIA
Jun 1990

1989 Crucial Moments
28–29 December: "Velvet Revolution"
completed (Havel becomes President)

AUSTRIA

Bratislava ⚔

SWITZERLAND

1989 Crucial Moments
11 September: Releases East
German "tourists"

Budapest ⚔

HUNGARY
Mar/Apr 1990

ROMANIA
Sept 1992

Slovenia
Apr 1990

Croatia
May 1990

Vojvodina

Timisoara ⚔

1989 Crucial Moments
25 December: Trial and
execution of Ceaucescus

Bucharest ⚔

ITALY

Adriatic Sea

YUGOSLAVIA

Bosnia-
Herzegovina
Dec 1990

Serbia
1990

Black Sea

Montenegro

Kosovo

Sofia ⚔

BULGARIA
Jun 1990

Macedonia
Dec 1990

ALBANIA
Mar 1991

TURKEY

Mediterranean Sea

Ionian Sea

GREECE

Aegean Sea

Without Soviet support, the communist regimes in Eastern Europe collapsed in one by one in 1989 like a row of dominoes. Within a year, Germany was united and the standoff between East and West had ended. The Cold War was over.

regime. While the borders to the West were closed, those to the Eastern bloc countries were still open. In consequence, the West German embassies in Prague and Berlin were swamped by refugees in August 1989. By mid-September, 23,000 people had fled the GDR. In cities across the country, hundreds of thousands of people demonstrated to ward off violent retaliation, but the expected response never came. One-party rule formally ended in Poland in September and in Hungary in October. In contrast to Khrushchev in 1956 and Brezhnev in 1968, Gorbachev did not intervene, but instead warned the East German party leadership: "He who comes too late is punished by life." It gave reformists, led by Egon Krenz, the impetus to take control of the party on 18 October.

The German communists finally buckled and opened the borders to West Germany on 9 November. That evening, the first holes in the Berlin Wall appeared, and that breach hastened the end of communism in Eastern Europe. One-party rule in Germany ended on 1 December. Before the end of the year, the Communist Party's hold on Czechoslovakia crumbled, and Václav Havel was elected president of the country. In contrast to the

non-violent "Velvet Revolution" in Czechoslovakia, blood was spilled in Romania. When the army turned its guns on the security forces, the Romanian revolution was over quickly. On 25 December, Romanian dictator Nicolae Ceausescu and his wife Elena were shot after a short, televised trial. A miraculous year in Europe had ended, in which no one would have dared predict that, by the end, European communism would lay in ruins.

With the loss of the Soviet Eastern European empire, the Cold War was over. Germany, key to the conflict, was united in less than a year after the fall of the Berlin Wall. The global military confrontation practically disappeared. In September 1990, Gorbachev promised the US president George Bush co-operation against Iraq's invasion of Kuwait. A treaty reducing conventional forces in Europe was signed in November, and Soviet soldiers soon left Eastern Europe altogether. The Warsaw Pact was dissolved in March 1991. The Cold War was also over as an ideological conflict. Communism did not survive any attempts at reform, including in the USSR. After a failed coup attempt in August 1991, the USSR itself finally fell apart and ceased to exist in December.

Consumer Society

The years immediately following World War II were ones of poverty and gloom. The late 1940s and 1950s were a period of austerity, although aid was available for Western Europe, from the USA in the form of the Marshall Plan. From the end of the 1950s, however, an unprecedented era of wealth began in Western Europe.

The welfare state

In 1945, at World War II's end, starvation threatened many European nations. International aid through the United Nations and the Marshall Plan made recovery slowly possible. Following the immense destruction of the war, there was a popular belief in many western European countries that reconstruction could not be achieved by the market, but only by planned, socialist measures, such as a planned economy and nationalization of industries. In most of Western Europe, social democratic parties were elected into power: they nationalized crucial industries, such as coal mining, steel production, railways, postal systems, and the telephone. The social democrats also laid the foundations of the welfare state. Subsidies for childcare and education, the introduction of comprehensive state health insurance, and pension schemes linked to inflation and past earnings created a society in which the individual was taken care of from the cradle to the grave.

Although for most people in Europe the 1950s were a period of austerity, it was nothing like the mass unemployment and deprivation among the working class of the early 1930s. Reconstruction ensured employment and better working conditions. Because of pressure from trade unions, the postwar average of a 48-hour working week fell further during the 1950s and 1960s.

Consumer society

The consumer society was established through a combination of the welfare state, economic growth, and technological innovation. Because of the social benefits of the welfare state, there were now more people than ever who could afford the products of mass industry. With the protection offered by the state against the costs of old age and disability, there was less need to save and more money to spend. Mass markets for consumer goods had existed since the Industrial Revolution, but the difference now was that the large majority of the population could afford products previously considered luxury items. This development was aided by new mass-production techniques that ensured low prices for high-quality products. The invention of the transistor made the introduction of small, cheap radio sets possible. In the 1930s, owning a car was an impossible dream for a factory worker or schoolteacher. Now, the production of affordable family cars made the dream a reality, and, during the 1960s and 1970s, owning a car became the norm. In the 1950s and early 1960s, the black-and-white television set was still a curiosity, but by the beginning of the 1970s most households owned one. Shorter working weeks and longer holidays meant more leisure time for the worker, allowing more time for daytrips and weekends away. Most holidays were still taken locally or nationally, often at a campsite with the entire family. A drive to a seaside campsite, eating and drinking to the sound of a portable radio, epitomized the beginning of consumer society in many European countries. Holidays to foreign destinations only became common much later. As the purchasing power of consumers increased during the 1960s, there seemed no end to possible growth.

This advertisement for a washing machine from the 1950s typifies consumer society: cheap, mass-produced consumer goods, to save time and labour for recreation.

Servis

YOUR WASHING

The way to modern living

Consumerism as an ideal crossed the Iron Curtain. As this East German advert for a Trabant car shows, governments in the East appealed to the same instincts as the advertising industry in the West. On the whole, they failed to deliver the goods.

Consumerism in Eastern Europe

During their rise to power, the communists promised to do away with wartime poverty and increase the output of basic goods. As a slogan of the Hungarian Communist Party put it: "More eggs! More fat! More shoes! More clothes!" After they gained power, they could not turn these pledges into reality. Conformity to Stalinism demanded concentration on heavy industry, rather than consumer goods. Collectivization of agriculture removed incentives for peasants to produce and led to food shortages. By the time Western Europe was turning from recovery to boom, Eastern European economies could not provide even the basic necessities of life. The protests against Stalinism made it clear that change was necessary. After Khrushchev promised to catch up with the West, many Eastern European countries started to concentrate on the production of consumer products.

The promised overtaking of the West never came: the quality of produced goods was inferior and the choice limited. The production of cars, in particular, illustrated the backwardness of communist economies. Their production relied on the same raw materials as more essential agricultural or military equipment, so cars always remained luxury items. East Germany waiting lists for a car could be as long as 10 years. Even then, they were of substandard quality and extremely polluting. The body of the East German Trabant was made of compressed cardboard, and under the bonnet the car had little more than a motor-cycle engine, which belched out fumes wherever it went. It typified Eastern European consumerism and, after 1989, became the object of Cold War nostalgia – but only in the West.

Pollution

A downside to industrial expansion and consumer society was the immense waste it produced. Heavy industry polluted the environment by poisoning rivers and air with toxic chemicals and heavy metals. Individual consumers caused pollution with the exhaust fumes of all those new cars and through increased demand on electrical energy from mostly coal-based electric plants. The packaging of consumer goods found its way into the environment: ice-cream wrappers, soft-drink cans, plastic bags, and boxes of all kinds littered the side of the road, campsite, or playground where they had been discarded, or were dumped in tonnes at landfill sites. There they were joined by the debris of consumerism: cheap products also meant that they were thrown away quickly.

Concerns about pollution and its effect on natural resources soon started to gain common ground. A group of international businessmen and scientists, called the Club of Rome, commissioned a study into the effects of continuing economic growth on a world of finite resources. The report, *The Limits to Growth*, published in 1972, sketched an apocalyptic future for Western industrial civilization. It predicted that increased population growth, combined with growing industrial production, consumption, and pollution, would put food production under pressure and lead to the exhaustion of natural resources such as oil and coal. Some minerals would already be depleted by the turn of the century. The prophecy may have been exaggerated, but it was taken extremely seriously at the time. It especially hit home when the oil crisis of 1973–4 demonstrated exactly how dependent industrial society was on natural resources.

The Decade of Protest

The second half of the 1960s in Europe was characterized by radical political dissent. This took place against the background of a culture of protest, in which a new generation broke with the values of its parents and rallied against established authority.

The 1960s are famed for the changes that came about on views of authority, sexual morals, and equality of the sexes; but many of these changes were in fact a long time in the making, the process usually starting with the industrial revolution in the 18th century. Strict morals, usually, a product of rural society, were eroded by urbanization: in the anonymous city, the opinions of neighbours became less important. The continuing decline of religious faith meant that the Church was losing its hold on society and its position as an arbiter of moral standards. The world wars also played a key role in the acceleration of changes in moral values. They deprived the older generation of moral authority: their moral codes had not prevented the slaughter in the trenches or the concentration camps. At the same time, the idealization of the anti-German resistance movement made a virtue of any struggle against authority.

The 1960s generation

In the 1960s, these changes in moral code took the form of a struggle between generations. The victory celebrations of 1945 resulted in an unforeseen side effect of liberation: a postwar baby-boom. The children born in the summer of 1946 were the generation of the 1960s. The world they grew up in differed completely from that of their parents in one respect: the rise of the welfare state and consumer society had created a generation for which there were few financial worries. The income of young people working in the 1930s would have been used to support their parents; in the 1950s and 1960s, it was pocket money. Many of the values associated with the 1960s generation were not new at all: both free love and feminism had been propagated in the Victorian age; however, in the 1960s, traditional moral values were no longer strong enough to contain the rise

In 1968, the radical student movement of the 1960s coincided with widespread social discontent. In May 1968, student riots broke out on the streets of Paris, soon leading to strikes across France. Ultimately, the popular unrest brought down French president Charles de Gaulle.

of alternative ones. After World War I, youthful hedonism had been a reaction against the horrors of war, but only among a small elite. In the 1960s, there was an entire generation, young and financially independent, that was capable of defining the spirit of the age.

This youth movement gained ground after the 1967 "summer of love", which produced a hippy culture under the urban, middle-class young that rejected the values of the previous generation. The economic boom and redistribution of wealth in the 1950s had greatly increased the number of students at the universities, and politically motivated student activism was especially strong in Germany and France. Students protested against the Vietnam War and authoritarian structures at the universities, but had broader revolutionary pretensions. They rejected the USSR and traditional Marxism and instead revered the heroes of the third-world revolutionary left: Fidel Castro, Mao Zedong, Che Guevara, and Ho Chi Minh. In France, student demonstrations in 1968 against educational reforms sparked off wider unrest. In May of that year, a spontaneous workers' strike of 10 million people led to the fall of President de Gaulle. In response to the strikes, he called new elections, in which he was defeated. In Germany, the new generation's rejection of the Nazi past of their parents fuelled the general anti-authoritarian attitude. A broad movement, the Extra Parliamentary Opposition (APO), opposed the government on the streets, and, in 1968, Germany erupted into pitched battles between police and students. Student unrest dissipated by the early 1970s, but it had given birth to radical left-wing terrorism. The Italian Red Brigade and the German Red Army Faction both had their origins in the student protest of the 1960s. The more critical attitude of the 1960s was, however, also continued in peaceful protest. In the 1980s, environmental protest, for instance by Greenpeace and in the anti-nuclear energy movement, gained widespread support.

Feminism

Both world wars changed the role of women in society. In countries such as Germany and Great Britain, women replaced the male workforce in the factories and fields as the men fought. In occupied countries, women had fought and suffered in the resistance movement alongside men. In Germany, while men were interred in prisoner of war camps in the USSR, women were left as the sole providers for the family. With the men away, German women became the motor of German reconstruction – as illustrated by the *trümmerfrauen*, or "rubble women", who cleaned up the destroyed

The Red Army Faction

For some student protesters, violent demonstration was replaced by other tactics. But for the Red Army Faction (pictured here on a wanted poster), violence was the only way to shake up the population against capitalism. Supporters dubbed them "urban guerrillas", attributing to them the glamour of third-world freedom fighters. The Red Army Faction began by robbing banks, but lost the limited support it had when it committed bombings, kidnappings, and assassinations. In 1972, its leaders, Andreas Baader and Ulrike Meinhof, were arrested, which sparked off five more years of terror, as their supporters tried to secure their release.

cities of Germany. Even though the return of the male population relegated women once again to a family role, it was enough to start fundamental changes in the views of the role of women. Universal suffrage had ended the struggle for political equality; postwar feminism demanded greater social equality. Feminists demanded the breakdown of traditional perceptions of women as homemakers, the removal of discriminatory laws, the right of women to work, and the right of equal pay to their male colleagues. Feminists demanded a re-evaluation of society's perception of women, attacking the differing sexual standards for men and women as hypocritical. The "sexual liberation" of women was in large part achieved thanks to the invention of the contraceptive pill. For the first time in history, women were able to be sexually active without the risk of pregnancy. A key issue of "women's lib" was the right to abortion, which was defended as the freedom of women to make choices about their own bodies. This issue was just one explored in influential literature such as Simone de Beauvoir's *The Second Sex* (1949), and Germaine Greer's *The Female Eunuch* (1970). In the West, thanks to the large potential electorate, a large part of the feminist agenda was adopted by mainstream politics. Behind the Iron Curtain, many demands – such as free childcare and maternity leave – were already part of the social system, yet the fundamental changes in attitude towards male and female roles demanded in the West did not occur. In the West, Women's Day, 8 March, was a feminist celebration; behind the Iron Curtain, it was a day for the husband do the dishes for a change.

Culture and Counterculture

The postwar world was the age of popular culture. Distinctions between the "high" art of the elite and the "low" culture of the people became less significant. With the rise of mass media, popular culture was moved firmly into the foreground, and rock music became inextricably linked with the youthful rebellion of the 1960s.

Traditional cultural forms struggled with the realities of the postwar world. Bertolt Brecht's theatre group, the Berliner Ensemble, in East Germany grappled with serious political themes and exponents of the theatre of the absurd, like Samuel Beckett in *Waiting for Godot* and Eugène Ionesco in *The Rhinoceros*, expressed some of the major philosophical currents of the era such as existentialism. In Britain, the group of playwrights known as the "Angry Young Men" questioned the assumptions and moral values of a stuffy, complacent postwar society with plays such as John Osborne's *Look Back in Anger* or the social realism of "kitchen sink" dramas. Cinema, too, reflected a changed mood. While Europe's cinema screens were still dominated by Hollywood musicals, westerns, and thrillers, war-time experiences had given films a harder edge. Film noir in American and contiental thrillers displayed darker psychological undercurrents. European film rose from the ashes: led by Roberto Rossellini and Federico Fellini, the Italian film industry enjoyed a renaissance, and French cinema was rejuvenated by the works of "new wave" directors such as Francois Truffaut and Jean-Luc Godard. In Sweden Ingmar Bergman was developing a highly individual approach, creating his masterpieces *The Seventh Seal* and *Wild Strawberries* in the late 1950s. Behind the Iron Curtain, communist regimes fostered the national film industries of Poland, Hungary, and Czechoslovakia, producing some of the classics of postwar cinema, such as Andrei Wajda's *Ashes and Diamonds*. But popular cinema remained dominated by Hollywood, where many of the old formulas were wearing thin. New technologies such as 3-D and CinemaScope proved incapable of halting the slide in cinema audiences faced with the rise of television and a new, vibrant youth culture based on popular music.

It did not take long for mass culture to become influenced by the emerging youth culture. With greater economic freedom and leisure time than their parents, young people had the time and money to instigate their own modes of expression.

Rock'n'roll, blown over from the Atlantic, was different. Derived from rhythm and blues and country music, it was easy to listen to, but exciting; parents hated the wild music and suggestive movements of early rock stars such as Elvis Presley. Their children embraced the newness and rawness of

Elvis, nicknamed "the Pelvis" after his gyrating hips, shocked parents and delighted their teenage children.

rock'n'roll wholeheartedly. Working-class boys with money to spend formed clannish subcultures defined by the music they listened to and the clothes they wore. The velvet jacket, drainpipe trousers, sideburns, and "ducktail" haircuts became the uniform of the teddy boys, a working-class subculture in Britain that quickly gave rock a reputation for rowdiness. Rock'n'roll gave a new generation of young people a soundtrack to rebel to and something to spend their relative wealth and free time on: concerts, dances, clothes, record players, and records were all within their financial reach. The music itself was cheap and easy to play: with three basic chords and instruments such as a tea-chest bass and washboard, anyone could have a go, and skiffle bands popped up everywhere. Many leading pop stars of the 1960s, including the Beatles, started their careers in skiffle bands. Rock quickly took on a variety of different styles but the guitar, bass guitar, drums, and vocals formed the basic set up and rhythm and blues remained the basic influence.

Rock quickly became assimilated into mass culture, initially spread through traditional media, such as newspapers and cinema. As a youth culture, rock managed to be both mass culture and counterculture. For a generation, it succeeded in reinventing itself in new forms that were as shocking as the previous trends they had replaced. Youth culture and the political protest of the 1960s went hand in hand, and other forms of music evolved as accompaniment, with folk singers emerging as the musical voice of protest. If a rejection of the political establishment, vague pacifism, and opposition to the Vietnam War were the recognizable traits of hippy counterculture, in the 1970s, punk was the biggest shock in popular music and was a reaction against the counterculture of the previous generation. Punk's political stance was aggressive and anarchic, and youthful disaffection found its musical voice in the three-chord rock band.

But youth culture continued to mean business: no sooner had a new musical movement or fashion arrived as a form of expression for a new generation than capitalism was eager to exploit it and sell it back to them. Popular music lost its ability to scandalize once it became part of the very institution against which it had protested.

Holes in the Iron Curtain

Although American in origin, rock and the culture around it were truly international in scope. Fashions and music crossed borders as fast as radio and television broadcasts could carry them. The influence was mostly one way, and English started to become the common language of Europe's youth. This was not limited to Western Europe – although almost airtight politically, the Iron Curtain could not prevent Western popular culture and fashion seeping through. Young people in Eastern Europe tuned in to Western radio stations, and, in the GDR, West German television was available. The minority that travelled to the West – truck drivers, train drivers, civilian air personnel, and diplomats – conducted a lucrative trade in records, books, magazines, and clothing. Lacking spending power, people were inventive and made their own clothes following Western magazines. Young musicians built their own instruments and amplifiers, and played rock music in the basement – just like their contemporaries in the West. Despite two political systems that were so utterly alien, family photographs in Eastern Europe of the period show the same long hair, sideburns, bell-bottomed trousers, and pointed collars as appeared in the West. Eastern European authorities were far less tolerant of rock music than their Western counterparts. Like jazz, it was classified as "decadent" Western music, and all too conspicuous followers of fashion, such as teddy boys and hippies, were subjected to policemen with scissors. But it was too popular to be stamped out, and certain rock bands, who trod a fine line between conformity and outrageousness, were tolerated.

As in some parts of the West, folk music rather than rock music became the expression of youthful protest. Not only was playing and dancing to folk music a way of socializing, but it was also a subtle form of national resistance in the face of Sovietized official culture. Dissatisfaction with the regime was expressed in literature and the theatre. This was especially the case in Czechoslovakia, where the writers' movement Charter 77 gained recognition for its protest, and the author and dissident Václav Havel, who had been imprisoned for his writing, would become president of the country at the Cold War's end.

The nihilism of The Sex Pistols, caught smiling in a rare moment, symbolized everything that was grim about the 1970s: industrial action, unemployment, pollution, threat of nuclear war, no future!

The Shadow of the Bomb

When the USA exploded the first atomic bomb at Ground Zero of the Alamogordo test site in New Mexico, on 16 July 1945, Robert Oppenheimer, chief of the project, quoted from the ancient Indian epic the *Bhagavad Gita*: "Now I am become death, the destroyer of worlds." The words later seemed prophetic. During the Cold War, the superpowers built enough nuclear weapons to destroy the world many times over. As long as it lasted, Europe lived under the shadow of the bomb.

The USA soon lost its atomic monopoly. The USSR tested its first bomb in 1949, and both sides began building huge nuclear arsenals. These weapons not only grew in number, but also in their explosive power. The bomb that devastated Hiroshima and killed 100,000 people in 1945 had an explosive strength of 12,500 tonnes of TNT. The first hydrogen bombs, which worked on the principle of nuclear fusion rather than fission, were immensely more powerful, often around 10,000,000 tonnes TNT. The USSR broke the record by testing a 57 megaton nuclear device in 1962. "Small" nuclear bombs were designed to be used on the battlefield; the large bombs were for laying waste to entire cities.

The arms race

The West feared Soviet superiority in conventional weapons such as troops and tanks. American nuclear weapons were initially intended as a deterrent: they would be used immediately, even if the Red Army only attacked by conventional means. The battlefield for nuclear war would be Europe. In the 1950s, a new dimension to the nuclear race evolved: with the Soviet launch of Soyuz, the USA panicked about Soviet missile technology, and Kennedy pledged to reduce the "missile gap". His promise to put a man on the moon before the end of the decade was intended to show the superiority of US missiles. Both sides used German wartime missile technology.

MAD

By the end of the 1960s, both sides had built up impressive arsenals of intercontinental ballistic missiles (ICBMs) and were now capable of destroying each other's cities. In theory, this made nuclear war impossible, as any use of nuclear weapons would automatically lead to "mutually assured destruction", a concept more fittingly known by its acronym, MAD. But still the nuclear

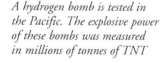

A hydrogen bomb is tested in the Pacific. The explosive power of these bombs was measured in millions of tonnes of TNT

Cultural icons

The leaders of the two superpowers became icons during the 1980s. The second half of the decade was dominated by Mikhail Gorbachev, who gained mass popularity in the West as "Gorby". During the first half of the 1980s, at a time when US popularity had reached rock bottom in Europe and cruise missiles were about to be stationed, President Reagan was, by contrast , an object of caricature, portrayed as the absent-minded "Cowboy Ronnie", capable of setting off disaster as much by accident as intent. Reagan, famous for his gaffes, did little to dispel this image. During a sound check for a radio program, he did not realize that a tape was running and announced to a bemused interviewer: "My fellow Americans, I am pleased to tell you I just signed legislation which outlaws Russia forever. The bombing begins in five minutes."

arsenals increased. Both sides feared that the other would construct enough nuclear weapons to enable a "first strike" – an all-out surprise attack on the enemy, destroying its nuclear arsenal and so any hope of retaliation. Despite MAD, nuclear war remained a feasible threat. Anti-ballistic missile systems were outlawed, as they upset the balance of power. Some strategists suggested that limited nuclear war was possible through a "flexible response", ie a slowly escalating proportionate counterattack.

In Europe, neither MAD nor "flexible response" was acceptable to European leaders. They feared that the USA would not risk its own destruction to save Paris or London. A more measured approach would mean only that Europe would be turned into a nuclear wasteland, while the superpowers remained unscathed.

Protest

High-profile arms negotiations such as SALT I and SALT II created widespread interest in the bomb. Magazines and books described the effects of a nuclear blast in horrifying detail, from the first blinding flash of light to radiation poisoning and nuclear winter.

The atomic bomb quickly became the focus of protest. The Campaign for Nuclear Disarmament (CND), established in Britain in 1958, campaigned for unilateral disarmament of nuclear weapons. It drew thousands of new members after the USA proposed to deploy cruise missiles in Western Europe at the beginning of the 1980s. Around the Greenham Common US airbase in Berkshire, England, a permanent "Women's Peace Camp" was set up. In Western Europe, hundreds of thousands of people demonstrated against cruise missiles,

and, in the Netherlands, one million people signed a petition to prevent their deployment.

Protest was also focussed on a new US weapon, the neutron bomb. Designed for use against tanks, it caused minimum blast damage, but emitted powerful radiation. This protest reflected a growing fear of nuclear arms, and its mass scale put very real pressure on Western European governments. In the end, protest was not enough: the cruise missiles were stationed, and protest fizzled out.

Bomb culture

The bomb was a constant presence in culture and society, and played a part in countless songs and films. In 1964, nuclear strategists were satirized in Stanley Kubrick's film *Dr Strangelove: Or How I Learned to Stop Worrying and Love the Bomb*. Other films and books were less optimistic, such as Nevil Shute's novel *On the Beach* (1957), detailing the spread of radioactive fallout after a nuclear war. The theme of a horrible mistake was worked out in *Failsafe* (1964) and *Wargames* (1983), which scared millions about the possibility of accidental nuclear war. The British government's leaflet, *Protect and Survive*, with advice on how to survive nuclear war, was an unending object of satire, exemplified in Raymond Briggs's *When the Wind Blows* (1985). The bomb also made an impact in popular music, with musicians choosing atomic devastation (Nena's "99 Red Balloons") or the madness of the arms race (Sting's "Russians") as subject matter. Frankie Goes to Hollywood's "Two Tribes" was more overt: the video showed a wrestling match between Ronald Reagan and Konstantine Chernenko, cheered on by the nations of the world, and finally ending with an air raid siren.

The Oil Crisis and Recession

Many of the economic certainties of the 1950s and 1960s vanished in the following decade with the coming of a global economic crisis. Recession, high unemployment, and inflation ended the faith in unending growth. The expensive welfare state now became a burden. Belief in the role of the state on the economy, common even outside socialist circles in the 1960s, decreased.

The 1973 oil crisis brought home precisely how dependent western industrialized society was on fossil fuels and its Middle Eastern suppliers. Pictured right is a scene from the crisis on a German road.

The increasing military build-up of the Cold War was partially responsible for the recession. At the Conference of Bretton Woods in October 1944, the western allies and other states agreed to a new international monetary system, with fixed exchange rates. The pound sterling and US dollar would function as reserve currencies, with the price of the dollar linked to gold. It was soon apparent that sterling was the weaker of the two, and, after 20 years of struggling to uphold its value, the British government finally devalued sterling in 1967. The Bretton Woods system ensured global financial stability until the 1960s, but unrelenting Cold War expenditure in the arms race led to a huge US deficit, which put the dollar under pressure. As a result, President Nixon took the dollar off the gold standard. With the dollar no longer backed by gold, the stability of the global monetary system seemed under threat.

The Oil crisis

Decreasing economic growth and inflation were worsened by the 1973 oil crisis. As a response to western support for Israel in the Yom Kippur War of October 1973, the Arab oil-producing states united in OPEC quadrupled the price of crude oil. Countries that had been especially supportive of Israel, such as the Netherlands and USA, were faced with a complete boycott. The results of the price increase demonstrated just how dependent western economies were on fossil fuels and became a chilling illustration of the doomsday scenario spelt out by the Club of Rome. Shortages resulted in the hoarding of petrol by the public, which was soon followed by rationing in some European states. In the Netherlands, hit worst by the crisis, the government was forced to prohibit driving on Sundays. Countermeasures were taken to make the western states less dependent on the oil-producing countries of the Middle East. Oil was stockpiled; the International Energy Agency was set up in 1974 to co-ordinate policy on energy; and Britain and Norway turned to the North Sea for oil production. Economies in the West were now

characterized by *stagflation*: increased unemployment coupled with rising inflation. This made the crisis all the more acute because economists had always predicted growing unemployment and enhanced inflation could not exist at the same time.

Many of the features that had produced economic growth in the 1950s and 1960s and had contributed to the establishment of the consumer society now turned into structural obstacles. Growing unemployment was worsened by the postwar baby boom: there were more people for fewer jobs. The German and Japanese economies benefited from the total destruction undergone during World War II: they had been forced to rebuild their economies completely. This involved an investment in new technology and production techniques on an unprecedented scale. The other European economies found it hard to compete with the cheaper German and Japanese products, and Japan especially outproduced Western Europe in the high-technology field. In a time of crisis, the expanded welfare states proved a heavy burden on the economy. Unions, used to having their wage

Immigration of workers led to the rise of racism across Europe. In France, anti-racist demonstrators carry an effigy of French extreme right-wing National Front leader Jean-Marie le Pen hanging from a gallows.

demands met, proved formidable opponents. In 1974, inflation led to strikes by miners and electricity workers demanding higher wages. In the wake of the oil crisis, this led to energy shortages and the introduction of a three-day working week in the industrial sector to save power. The wave of strikes and pickets reached a peak in the 1978–9 "winter of discontent". The bleak late 1970s found its expression in youth culture. While the optimistic 1960s had been characterized by the hedonistic hippies, the 1970s were the decade of anarchic punks, with their typical slogan "No future".

Thatcherism

Continuing labour unrest did not bring improvements, but instead diminished confidence in its natural allies, the social democratic parties. In some countries, they were brought down by parties advocating austerity measures and free-market economics. Elsewhere, socialists themselves reluctantly introduced cuts in spending. Margaret Thatcher in Great Britain was the most radical example of this development. Reduced taxes, diminished state spending for social security, and privatization of national industries and services became the calling card of Thatcherism. Partially as a result of these hard measures, economic growth set in once again during the 1980s.

Immigration and racism

From the late 1950s to the early 1970s, economic growth in the industrialized states of Western Europe led to increased immigration. As the indigenous population found employment increasingly in the expanding service sector, cheap labour was required for menial jobs and unskilled work in industry and the service sector support industries. Immigrants typically originated in the former colonies or agricultural Mediterranean states such as Spain, Italy, and Turkey, and usually comprised young men who sent home most of their wages to their families. Initially, long-term settlement was not the intention of most guest workers. But, as years went by, many chose to bring their families to their new homelands rather than return to their country of origin. Racism found its way into mainstream politics: in Britain, the conservative politician Enoch Powell was sacked in 1968 after his "rivers of blood" speech, in which he predicted an apocalyptic future for Britain if immigration were to continue. In the 1970s, emigration from the poorer Mediterranean countries such as Spain and Turkey to the industrialized states of Western Europe increased. As the European economies went into recession, existing resentment against immigrants and tensions between communities increased, leading, in Britain, to race riots in Brixton, London, in 1981. Racist parties such as the British National Party in Britain and the National Front in France, established in 1986 by Jean-Marie Le Pen, gained in popularity. By the late 1980s, both large immigrant communities and organized racism had become part of social and political life in Europe.

THE OIL CRISIS AND RECESSION   475

TOWARDS A UNITED EUROPE

1989–2001

September 1991 Macedonia declares independence.

June 1991 Croatia and Slovenia declare independence from the former Yugoslavia.

Late 1990 Six Balkan republics establish assemblies of freely elected representatives.

October 1990 Re-unification of East and West Germany.

1990 Serbian Communist Party leader Slobodan Milosevic elected Serbian President.

December 1991 The European Council agrees the Treaty on European Union (the TEU; also known as the Maastricht Treaty). The European Union replaces the EEC.

February 1992 TEU signed.

March 1992 Bosnia-Herzegovina declares independence.

April 1992 Serbia and Montenegro establish the Federal Republic of Yugoslavia.

June 1992 The Danish referendum rejects the TEU.

July 1995 Fighting recommences in Srebrenica as Bosnian Serbs enter the town and massacre its Muslim population.

January 1995 Austria, Finland, and Sweden join the EU.

Spring 1993 Vance-Owen Peace Plan Introduced.

May 1993 Second Danish referendum accepts the TEU.

1990

1993

1990s The explosion in technology in the 1990s sees massive changes in telecommunication and popular culture. The use of mobile phones is one key area, as is the increase in online communication through e-mail and the use of the internet, both as a source of information and also a means of conducting business, or e-commerce.

1994 Passenger services begin through Channel Tunnel between France and Britain.

September 1992 "Black Wednesday" sees millions wiped off the value of the pound, forcing Britain to leave the Exchange Rate Mechanism.

1992–3 BSE, "mad cow disease", reaches its peak in Britain, with 100,000 confirmed cases.

1997 Collapse of the Dayton Agreement for peace and the Albanian government leading to the mass movement of Albanians into Kosovo.

1999 Milosevic surrenders.

May 1998 The European Council declares the 11 member states ready to adopt the euro on 1 January 1999.

January 2002 Adoption of the euro as the single currency within 11 member states.

May 2000 Greece joins the eurozone.

January 1999 The euro becomes the official currency of the 11 member states, though national currencies remain in circulation.

August 2001 The euro currency is launched at the European Central Bank and plans for the release of the currency to the general public are revealed.

1996 Yugoslavian war crimes tribunal opens in the Hague.

July 1997 Milosevic elected President of the Federal Republic of Yugoslavia.

May 1999 The Treaty of Amsterdam comes into force, giving the EU a greater role in issues such as employment and combatting crime.

6   1999   2002

March 1996 The European Commission imposes a worldwide ban on all British beef exports.

1997 There is a move to centrist politics in Europe, beginning in Britain with the victory of the Labour Party, ending 18 years of Conservative Party rule.

August 1999 The European Commission lifts ban on British beef, but France continues to enforce the embargo.

2000 Millions of people throughout Europe and the world celebrate the end of the millennium with massive parties staged in all the capital cities.

1996 Lower birthrates and later parenting lead to an aging population in Europe. Italy has lowest birthrate ever recorded.

The Maastrict Treaty

World War II brought terrible suffering to much of Europe, and the immediate priority of the postwar period was to find a way to live together in harmony. For France, following the dreadful land battles it had suffered twice in the first half of the century, the need for peace and security was strongest, which meant containment of the economic and industrial strength of Germany.

The European Community

The key was to find a framework within which all nations could exist peacefully and promote economic development. The result was the European Community (EC), which was ratified by the Treaty of Rome in April 1951. The six original members of the EC were Belgium, France, Germany, Italy, Luxembourg, and the Netherlands. The initial focus of the EC was peace, but, over the next 40 years, economic co-operation and development would play an influential and constructive role.

By 1989, the original six members had been joined by Denmark, Greece, Ireland, Portugal, Spain, and the United Kingdom. Despite their history of different political regimes, all sought the economic modernization that accompanied membership of the EC. The demise of the Eastern bloc in 1989 increased opportunities for enlarging the EC, as it created new markets for expansion. It also provided the opportunity for the reunifica-tion of Germany. This became a key condition of the expansion of market forces in Europe, as a united Germany anchored to the EC would provide the stability for an increasingly federalist Europe.

Under the presidency of Jacques Delors, the European Commission had promoted the idea of a single united Europe throughout the 1980s. With Germany's reunification in 1990 and the support of the pro-federalist German chancellor Helmut Kohl, the idea could become reality. The resulting Inter-Governmental Conferences allowed all member states to discuss political and economic unity, which led to the Treaty on European Union. The treaty was signed in Maastricht in the Netherlands on 7 February 1992.

The European Union

The Maastricht Treaty created the European Union (EU), replacing the old EC. Economic union would be achieved through a single currency, issued by

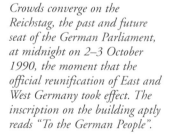

Crowds converge on the Reichstag, the past and future seat of the German Parliament, at midnight on 2–3 October 1990, the moment that the official reunification of East and West Germany took effect. The inscription on the building aptly reads "To the German People".

the European Central Bank (ECB). In addition, the EU added a number of new arms to the old EC and expanded other key areas.

With the creation of the EU, the role of the European Parliament was increased so that it was effectively a joint decision-maker with the European Council (previously the sole provider of policy). The role of the EU in the fields of education, environment, health, and culture was increased. The Amsterdam Treaty in 1999 added employment to this. However, the greatest changes came with the creation of two new arms to the EU: Co-operation in Justice and Home Affairs (CJHA) and the Common Foreign Policy and Security Policy (CFPSP). The former was concerned with cross-border aspects of crime, particularly terrorism, and with citizenship. Member states were to co-operate in these areas, particularly regarding the police, and administrative and customs authorities. Yet this was to be a contentious issue among member states and their own people.

Citizenship was redefined under Maastricht so that any member of a state of the EU is also a member of the EU. This allows freedom of movement between and residency within member states. Foreign residents are not able to vote in national elections, but are free to vote in local elections in the country in which they reside. However, there has not yet been consistent application of the citizenship principles throughout the EU. The policy on border controls is incomplete, with Britain, Denmark, and Ireland retaining their controls. Other states have reinstated border controls to prevent the influx of non-EU citizens.

Police co-operation between member states has increased since the creation of the EU, particularly in relation to cross-border crimes such as drugs trafficking. The EU Courts of Justice and intergovernmental co-operation on judicial matters have also expanded so that citizens' access to courts is now consistent throughout the EU; an additional layer of judicial review is a consequence of this judicial co-operation.

While the Treaty of Rome created the EC on the basis of peace, the Common Foreign Policy and Security Policy provided the opportunity for the EU to create a shared power to rival that of the USA in terms of both foreign policy and defence. An autonomous European defence capacity remains a threat to NATO in the eyes of some member states and its citizens, who feel that a coherent defence strategy should be linked to the USA. Yet the poor performance of UN peacekeeping troops in Yugoslavia resulted in an initiative to improve the EU's ability to react where NATO is not fully engaged.

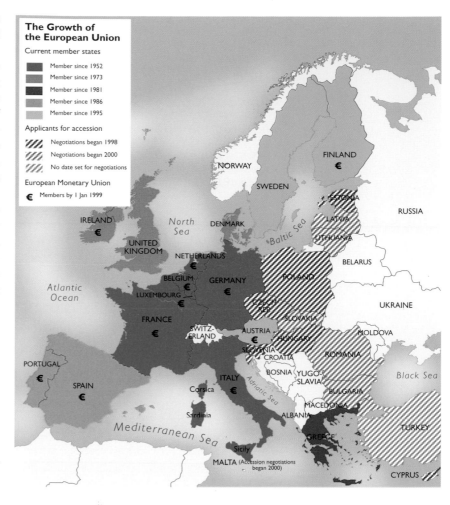

The Growth of the European Union

Current member states
- Member since 1952
- Member since 1973
- Member since 1981
- Member since 1986
- Member since 1995

Applicants for accession
- Negotiations began 1998
- Negotiations began 2000
- No date set for negotiations

European Monetary Union
- € Members by 1 Jan 1999

The result was the EU rapid deployment force, a 50,000-strong unit designed for peacekeeping and crisis management purposes, including humanitarian tasks. The rapid deployment force does not currently present a threat to US hegemony in defence matters, as any member state can opt out of any action. A more federalist structure will be required to provide a single defence policy, but it will provide for greater stability when fully created.

A common foreign policy is not solely adhered to, as the EU is an important trading power. While many member states view trade with the USA as central to their continued economic prosperity, inter-region trade is equally as important. The focus on tariff and non-tariff barriers and the single market programme is central to EU economic policy. Economic interdependence is a cornerstone of EU federalist policy. Disputes often arise, focussed on the supply of agricultural and meat products, as seen in the non-movement of cattle during the outbreak of BSE in the late 1990s.

Yet the EU remains an important trade partner for the member states and with the rest of the world, the mechanism for which may become easier with the introduction of the euro.

The European Union began as the European Economic Community (EEC) in 1957, with six member states. By 1989, another six countries had joined. The fall of the Eastern bloc the same year led to a rush of applications from the former communist countries. The EEC became the EU with the Maastricht Treaty in 1991, which committed the members to the introduction of a single currency. So far, 11 member states have adopted the euro.

The EURO

Economic interdependence was central to the formation of the EU. The European Economic Community (EEC) was designed to promote a single European market and co-operation on economic policy. The initial programme removed tariff barriers between the member states to promote cross-border trade through the EEC customs union, which also set a single external tariff barrier.

Trade across political frontiers grew, and, in the 1960s and even through the recession-hit 1970s, the idea of a single market gained support across the spectrum, from federalists to Euro-sceptics. In the 1980s, the plan to complete the single market was developed. The first task was to remove non-tariff barriers, for example local and national subsidies, indirect taxes, and different regulatory structures, but this required considerably more legislation from the EEC and would take much longer to complete. The logical conclusion to the development of the single market was a single currency within that market, a currency that could move freely across the political frontiers in all forms and where the fluctuation of exchange rates was removed.

Yet while the single economic area promoted the desired economic interdependence, the problems of the international markets continued. Currencies continued to fluctuate against each other within the member states of the EEC, and this instability was a major barrier to monetary union. In 1979, the Exchange Rate Mechanism (ERM) was created. It required national banks of the member states to intervene in foreign currency markets to keep their own currency value within an upper and lower limit. The goal was to stablilize exchange rates, leading to the single currency. Britain did not join the ERM until 1990 and remained in it only for two years, pulling out of it on "Black Wednesday" in 1992, so-called as the value of the pound plummeted on that day.

The ERM led to increased co-operation of member states in the foreign exchange markets, and France and Germany argued favourably that monetary union would lead to monetary stability. The further argument that monetary union should be replicated by economic union became increasingly important. Member states differed in their opinion as to whether macroeconomic policy should be controlled by the federalist community or remain in the control of the individual member state. It is an issue that remains largely unresolved.

The Maastricht Treaty created the European Central Bank (ECB) in 1998, which became the central figure in monetary union. The bank's role was to co-ordinate with the member states' central banks on issues such as the volume of currency in

Wim Duisenberg

Born in 1935 in the town of Heerenveen in the Netherlands, Willem (Wim) Frederik Duisenberg was appointed to an eight-year term as president of the ECB in 1998. Previously employed at the International Monetary Fund (IMF) and having held the position of minister of finance for the Netherlands, Duisenberg was an understandable choice as the new president and was put forwards by Germany, which wanted the ECB to run along the lines of the central German bank, the Bundesbank. Yet his appointment was not without criticism, particularly from France, which had expected Jean-Claude Trichet, governor of the Bank of France, to be appointed.

circulation and member states' interest rates. Yet before a single currency could be introduced, the ECB set a series of performance criteria to be met by each member state willing to join. These were established rates for interest and inflation, ceilings for budget deficits and total debt, and the stability of exchange rates. In order to promote growth, 11 member states – Austria, Belgium, Finland, France, Germany, Ireland, Italy, Luxembourg, the Netherlands, Portugal, and Spain – cut their interest rates in late 1998.

Each member state, while satisfying membership of the ERM, managed its local economic policy to meet the performance criteria by 1 January 1999, when the exchange rates for the single currency would be set irrevocably. During this period, the single currency was changed from the ECU (the European Currency Unit, established in 1979 as a unit for exchange rates among the member states) to the euro. Britain and Denmark negotiated opt-outs to remain outside the "eurozone". Greece, after initially failing to meet the economic criteria to join the euro, did so in 2000.

The euro becomes reality

The new currency was officially introduced on 30 August 2001, to be in circulation on 1 January 2002. The design of the euro symbol was chosen by then president of the European Commission, Jacques Santer, based on the Greek letter epsilon, with two parallel lines meant to symbolize the euro's stability. The banknotes are designed with windows, gateways, and arches on one side, as a symbol of the European spirit of co-operation and openness. The reverse of the note feature bridges to symbolize the close co-operation and communication between Europe and the rest of the world.

Production of the euro is controlled by the European Central Bank (the principal mint), with 12 printing works throughout Europe in early 2002. The first 10 billion notes (of 14.5 billion) were introduced on 1 January 2002 and the remainder held in reserve. The reality of getting the notes into circulation presented sizeable logistical problems, not least as it required a change in the financial awareness of the populations of member states accustomed to their own benchmark indicators. A north-to-south flow of notes during the tourist season in the summer months is expected, and there are plans to redistribute banknotes in bulk from locations with a surplus to those with a deficit.

In 2002, Britain was still not part of the eurozone and had no plans to become so. The issue remains grounds for debate between the main political parties, with no plans for a referendum on the issue.

The Balkans

As Western Europe moved to a more federalist structure in the 1990s, an example of an apparently successful federalist model was collapsing. Since the end of World War II, Yugoslavia, under the leadership of Tito, had struggled to unite the country's many different national identities within one structure. The needs of these ethnic groups have led to political and national unrest throughout its history.

Remembering the dead. In 1994, a woman walks through Sarajevo Cemetery, which holds the graves of thousands of casualties from the civil war in the former Yugoslavia. A decade earlier, this area of the town was host to the 1984 Winter Olympic Games.

At the beginning of the 1990s, the republics that made up the former Yugoslavia sought independence from the Serb-dominated Yugoslav Federation. The government of Serbia, however, wanted to protect the rights of Serbs throughout the region, leading to a vicious war and a huge number of refugees. The 1995 Dayton Peace Agreement, which divided Bosnia-Herzegovina into a Serb Republic and a Muslim/Croat Federation, created a fragile peace. In 1999, the crisis in Kosovo saw another vast exodus – this time of ethnic Albanians from Yugoslavia.

The post-World War II period was one of relative calm for Yugoslavia under Tito's leadership, but his death in May 1980 was the start of the problems that Yugoslavia was to face in the 1990s. It marked a period of economic decline: the country's unemployment levels soared and its debts grew as it attempted to fund its ever worsening economic position. There was still no real nationalist problem, but there soon would be.

As the economic situation worsened, prosperity within each of the different republics changed. Slovenia and Croatia, as wealthier regions, did not experience the growing national unrest of Serbia and Bosnia. Recognizing the strength of their local economies and seeking liberation from the Serbian oppression of Slobodan Milosevic's government, Slovenia and Croatia opted for independence from Yugoslavia in June 1991.

War broke out immediately afterwards. Croatia and Slovenia appealed to the Western powers to acknowledge their independence. The USA, occupied by events in the Persian Gulf, stated that it was a European problem. The UN, however, brokered a deal to send a peacekeeping force to the region.

The possibility of independence for the other republics grew, but the recognition of a state would lead to problems for minority ethnic groups within that state. Without the protective banner of the federal structure, the opportunity for the misuse of power presented itself.

Bosnia

Trouble began in Bosnia-Herzegovina in January 1992, and Bosnia pushed for independence in April of that year, encouraged by the USA, which had begun to take an interest in the problems in the Balkans. Yet the Bosnian Republic was weak financially and militarily, and comprised territory desired by both the Croatians and the Serbs. The Bosnian Serbs rejected independence and fighting began.

There followed one of the worst conflicts of the 20th century. The Serbs targeted the Muslims of the region, particularly outside Sarajevo, resulting in thousands of deaths. As the atrocities continued, the West faced the possibility of intervention on humanitarian rather than economic grounds. The UN imposed sanctions on Serbia, with the support of Russia, a traditional Serbian ally. Isolating Serbia merely exacerbated problems for the region outside Yugoslavia, as it was a key trading route for Romania, Bulgaria, and Hungary. These states were developing their economies, and therefore any disruption would be catastrophic.

As the West focussed its political resources on the Balkans, a tentative peace was brokered in the spring of 1993 – the Vance-Owen Peace Plan. Under the terms of the proposal, Bosnia-Herzegovina would be divided into 10 cantons, similar to the structure of Switzerland. To succeed, the proposal required 50,000 ground troops from the UN and the support of the people. The Bosnian Serbs rejected the proposal in a referendum, and the USA was against sending ground troops.

The plan collapsed, and fighting in the region intensified. The Bosnian Serbs and the Croatians in the Herzegovinian capital of Mostar targeted the

The Former Yugoslavia 1991–9

〰 Boundary of former Yugoslavia, 1991
〜 Boundary established at Dayton Peace Agreement, 1995
(June 1991) Date of secession from Federal Republic of Yugoslavia
➡ Mainly Serb refugees
➡ Mainly Croat & Bosnian Muslim refugees
➡ Ethnic Albanian refugees

Bosnian Muslims. As Muslims were predominantly city based, they prospered most in the period after World War II and became targets for the more rural Serbs, who found their positions threatened. Serbs made up only 33 per cent of the Bosnian population, but occupied over 70 per cent of the territory and had the considerable support of the Serbian army. The Muslims had no allies and were the victims of some of the worst massacres committed on continental Europe since the Holocaust.

Fighting intensified: Sarajevo was destroyed by Serbian shells and Mostar by Croatian. The UN peacekeeping force became the scapegoat, as the Western powers determined the appropriate strategy; the USA was in favour of air strikes, and the EU wanted to commit additional ground force peacekeeping troops. In March 1993, NATO ordered the Bosnian Serbs to withdraw from Sarajevo, and Russia sent in troops to prevent the Bosnian government launching an attack on the Serbs. This respite provided the opportunity to broker peace, and the result was the Bosnian-Croat federation, which permitted increased Croatian intervention into Bosnian affairs. The agreement proposed that the federation would control 51 per cent of Bosnia and a new Serb republic the remaining 49 per cent. To reduce Serbian military superiority, the USA would give Croatia practical support.

Peace lasted until July 1995. All three groups had been preparing for battle earlier in the year, as Croatia stated that it would not accept the renewal of the UN mandate. In July 1995, Bosnian Serbs entered Srebrenica and murdered more than 8000 Muslims. The threat of a NATO air strike forced them to stop at Gorazde. The Croatian army retaliated by launching an attack on Serbs in the eastern regions of Croatia. Consequently, 150,000 Serbs left Croatia, the largest single exodus of refugees in Europe since 1945. Urged on with the support of the USA, this was the first time in the course of the war that the Bosnian Serbs lost ground.

A NATO air strike on Bosnian Serb positions on 30 August 1995 resulted in the signing of the Dayton Agreement, creating the new Bosnian federation. It was an unstable peace, as the federation allowed for three nationalist armies and the UN peacekeeping force. It remains a divided territory, a Bosnian military protectorate where the departure of the UN peacekeeping force will lead to war. All three groups remain dependent on each other for co-operation if the economy is ever to recover.

Kosovo

In spring 1996, the Kosovan Liberation Army pushed for independence from Serbia through a

Slobodan Milosevic

Slobodan Milosevic was born in 1941 in the Serbian town of Pozarevac, close to Belgrade. By 1986, he had become the head of the Serbian Communist Party and, by manipulating the differences between the Serbs and Albanians, he became president of Serbia in 1989. Milosevic ran an authoritarian government that helped reawaken nationalism throughout the region as he pushed for a Greater Serbia in the conflict of the early 1990s. With the crippling of the opposition government, he was the Yugoslav president from July 1997. In 1999, he was indicted by the International Criminal Tribunal for the former Yugoslavia for war crimes committed by his regime in Kosovo. In October 2000, he lost the general election to Vojislav Kostunica. He tried to suppress the new government, but the military finally sided with the new regime and Milosevic was forced to flee. He currently stands trial in The Hague for these war crimes, and his place in Yugoslav history is being rewritten in the local textbooks.

series of localized attacks. The Kosovo Albanians had received little from the Dayton Agreement and continued be dominated by Milosevic's government. As the Kosovars attacked, the Albanian government collapsed in summer 1997, and thousands of Albanian troops flooded into Kosovo. Conflict between Serbs and Albanians increased, and, shortly after the peace in Bosnia, NATO was faced with possible intervention. The possibility of increased instability in Macedonia, with its large Albanian minority, forced the West to intervene. In 1999, air strikes commenced, as Milosevic would not accept the autonomy of Kosovo. Yet NATO would not commit ground troops, and hundreds of thousands of Albanians flooded into Macedonia. Through its intervention on humanitarian grounds, NATO had succeeded in exacerbating the humanitarian disaster that still affects the area. In June 1999, NATO peacekeeping troops entered Kosovo, as Milosevic withdrew from the region.

The economic effects of the fighting in Kosovo will continue for years to come. The Yugoslav surrender in 1999 began a period of reconstruction and redevelopment, and marked the end of one of the bloodiest decades in European history.

Possibilities for the Future

Liberalization of the polities and economies of Eastern European nations provides the opportunity of expanding the scope of the European Union. But to succeed, the EU has many other challenges to meet, both within Europe and internationally.

Presently accession negotiations are proceeding with Cyprus, the Czech Republic, Estonia, Hungary, Poland, Slovenia, Bulgaria, Latvia, Lithuania, Malta, Romania, and Slovakia. However, it is likely that the economic and political performance criteria will prove difficult to meet for the Eastern European states with their relatively short "free market" economic history.

Economic division

Ensuring the full participation of all current member states in the single currency is necessary if Europe is to move to a more federalist structure. Yet Britain and Denmark remain outside the eurozone. While the economic policy of both is structured such that it tracks the value of the euro and the dollar, it is not expected that either member is seeking to join the eurozone within the lives of their current governments. In Britain, membership or otherwise of the eurozone is on the agenda of the major political parties. While there is considerable public support for a referendum – last seen in the UK regarding entry to the EEC in 1975, when the public voted under the Wilson government by two to one in favour of joining – neither the government nor the opposition has pledged to hold one in the life of the current government.

Membership of the eurozone is not the only divisive economic issue within European politics. Within the EU itself, relations between member states often founder over such key issues as the budget stability pact, and the need for state rather than regional control over finances.

Peace and security

As fighting continues in the former Yugoslavia, in Macedonia, and Slobodan Milosevic's trial at the war crimes commission moves on, many of the atrocities committed in the Balkans in the 1990s are being revealed. Peace is by no means certain in this region, as the continued difficulties in securing a lasting peace in Ireland prove.

The terrorist attacks on the World Trade Centre in New York and the Pentagon in Washington DC in September 2001 provide further evidence of the problems in creating a united European response. The UN Security Council declared the event a threat to international peace, making it apparent that an international response was required. Yet should this be a coordinated response for Europe through the EU or will the more traditional bodies NATO

Wreaths are laid in Paris to commemorate the thousands who died in the terrorist attacks in New York and Washington DC on 11 September 2001. While the countries of Europe were unanimous in condemning the terrorists, co-ordinating an official European response to the event has proved difficult.

The euro in use in a French market in 2002. For now, the traders give prices in both francs and euros, but the public is quickly learning to adjust. Britain and Denmark still remain outside the eurozone, however.

and the UN, in which US power is significant, dictate the international action? Incidents such as these highlight the overlap between all these bodies and the balance of power between them. As the G7 economies (USA, Japan, Germany, France, UK, Italy, and Canada) coordinate the international economic response to the incident, with the participation of the European Central Bank and the Federal Reserve in the US, it is clear that the EU will not have exclusivity on the course of action for the member states.

At one level, Europe also has difficulties in playing the role of a full superpower on the world stage to match the United States or even China or Russia. The summit in May 2002 when the American President, George Bush, made a visit to Moscow to agree a major nuclear arms reduction with President Putin had no role for the Europeans. The meeting and the agreement revealed the extent to which the old nuclear superpowers still enjoy their own "special relationship" in which the European states may be consulted but not directly participate. Similarly, Europe can offer its good offices in resolving regional conflicts in places such as the Asian sub-continent or the Middle East, but simply lacks the power to force deals through on its own.

Indeed, more pressing are Europe's relations not with the superpowers, or even lesser states, but with the inflow of immigrants and asylum seekers from all over the world, seeking access to Europe's wealth and opportunities. Like a reverse of imperialism, the poor and upwardly mobile of the Third World now look to Europe for improved opportunities and a better life. The surprising success of the right-wing Jean-Marie Le Pen in the first stage of the 2002 French presidential elections sent shockwaves through liberal and democratic Europe. Was Europe on the brink of a right-wing, possibly fascist future, fuelled by resentments against existing immigrants and fears of an unstoppable flow of new claimants on Europe's prosperity? In practice, Le Pen was easily defeated in the second round and won no seats in the subsequent elections to the French chamber. There were no grounds for complacency, however, and calls grew for Europe's leaders to seek a balance between differing demands. On the one hand, there was some sympathy to offering the opportunity to the poorer inhabitants of the world to migrate and utilize their skills in a Europe that still had jobs to offer and an ageing population. The idea of asylum, written into international codes, was also one that Europe wished to honour, especially with so many repressive regimes in operation around the world. On the other hand, fears of soaring welfare budgets and social disharmony were expressed at the Seville summit of the EU in June 2002, where a coherent agreement on this range of considerations was, perhaps unsurprisingly, hard to achieve.

But Europeans are conscious that they are, with a few exceptions, more peaceful and prosperous that at any time in recent history. Europe is democratic and relatively liberal. If they are to maintain those standards in good conscience, it would seem that they cannot afford not to share them with others, at least to some extent.

The Maastrict Treaty   480–1   ►
The Euro   482–3   ►
The Balkans   484–5   ►

Appendices

Developments in the Arts and Culture

BC c.750 First written copies of the *Iliad* and the *Odyssey* by Homer.

c.480 The beginning of Greek classical art.

387 Plato's Academy is founded in Athens.

c.200 The Dead Sea scrolls are begun.

AD 531–7 Hagia Sophia church built in Constantinople.

c.550 First instance of monks copying out manuscripts by hand.

c.750 The Anglo-Saxon poem *Beowulf* is written down for the first time; *The Book of Kells* is created in Ireland.

1086 Production of the *Domesday Book* in England.

1154 Chartres Cathedral in France becomes the first example of Gothic architecture.

1210 German writer Wolfram von Eschenbach completes the romance *Parzival*.

1248 Construction begins on the Alhambra in Granada, Spain.

1273 Thomas Aquinas writes *Summa theologiae*.

1307 Dante begins work on the *Divine Comedy*.

c.1365 The Bruges School is founded by a group of Flemish painters, including Hubert van Eyck, Jan van Eyck and Robert Campin.

c.1380 Chaucer begins writing the *Canterbury Tales*.

1434 Donatello finishes work on his bronze statue of David.

1485 Malory's *Le Morte D'Arthur* is published by William Caxton.

1503 The *Mona Lisa* is painted by Leonardo da Vinci.

1511 Erasmus publishes *In Praise of Folly*.

1512 Michaelangelo finishes work on the ceiling of the Sistine Chapel in Rome.

1513 Machiavelli writes *The Prince*.

1516 *Utopia* by English writer Thomas More is published.

1520 Martin Luther writes *The Freedom of a Christian Man*.

1533 *The Ambassadors* is painted by German artist Hans Holbein the Younger.

1534 French humanist Rabelais publishes *Gargantua*.

1559 The Catholic Church publishes the *Index of Forbidden Books*.

1575 The baroque period in European art begins with the design of the Il Gesu church in Rome.

1580 The French writer Montaigne begins work on his *Essays*.

1586 El Greco paints the *Burial of Count Orgasz*.

1590 The English playwright Christopher Marlowe completes *Tamburlaine the Great*.

1600 William Shakespeare completes *Hamlet*.

1605 The first volume of *Don Quixote* is completed by Cervantes.

1632 Dutch painter Rembrandt van Rijn completes the *Anatomy Lesson of Dr Tulp*.

1642 Completion of *The Coronation of Poppea*, an opera by composer Monteverdi.

1651 *Leviathan* is published by the English philosopher Thomas Hobbes.

1667 The epic poem *Paradise Lost* is completed by John Milton.

1668 Jan Vermeer paints the *Astronomer*.

1670 Architect Christopher Wren rebuilds 50 London churches, including St Paul's cathedral after they were destroyed by fire.

1689 The English composer Henry Purcell completes the opera *Dido and Aeneas*.

1702 The London-based *Daily Courant* becomes the world's first daily newspaper.

1709 In Italy, an altered version of the harpsichord becomes the first ever piano.

1719 British novelist Daniel Defoe writes *Robinson Crusoe*.

1738 In St Petersburg, the Russian Imperial Ballet School is founded.

1755 Samuel Johnson publishes his *Dictionary* in Britain.

1762 *Le Contrat Social* is completed by French philosopher Jean Jacques Rousseau.

1774 German writer Johann Goethe publishes *The Sorrows of Young Werther*.

1776 The Scottish economist Adam Smith publishes the *Wealth of Nations*.

1786 First performance of *The Marriage of Figaro* by Mozart.

1792 *The Vindication of the Rights of Women* is published by Mary Wollstonecraft.

1798 English Romanticism begins with the publication of *Lyrical Ballads* by Wordsworth and Coleridge.

1804 Completion of Beethoven's *Eroica* symphony.

1810 *The Disasters of War* by the Spanish painter Goya depicts the horrors of the French invasion of Spain.

1813 Robert Owen, the British industrialist, publishes *A New View of Society*.

1830 The French composer Hector Berlioz completes his *Symphonie Fantastique*.

1846 The saxophone is patented in Belgium by Adolphe Sax.

1848 Publication of the *Communist Manifesto* by Karl Marx and Friedrich Engels.

1856 French novelist Gustave Flaubert publishes *Madame Bovary*.

1857 The French artist Jean-Francois Millet paints *The Gleaners*.

1862 Victor Hugo publishes *Les Miserables*.

1867 The first volume of *Das Kapital* is completed by Karl Marx.

1869 *War and Peace* is published by Russian novelist Leo Tolstoy.

1872 Friedrich Nietzsche publishes *The Death of Tragedy*.

1873 In Paris, the first exhibition of Impressionist paintings goes on display.

1876 *The Ring Cycle* by Richard Wagner is performed for the first time.

1880 French artist Auguste Rodin completes his sculpture of *The Thinker*.

1883 Architect Antonio Gaudi begins work on the Sagrada Familia in Barcelona.

1888 Completion of Vincent Van Gogh's *Sunflowers*.

1893 Norwegian artist Edward Munch paints *The Scream*.

1897 *Uncle Vanya* is written by Russian playwright Anton Chekhov.

1900 Freud introduces the concept of psychoanalysis in his *Interpretation of Dreams*.

1905 A group of German painters set up the Expressionist movement.

1907 An exhibition of Cubist paintings goes on display in Paris.

1922 *Ulysses* is published by Irish author James Joyce.

1925 Release of the film *Battleship Potemkin* by Soviet director Sergei Eisenstein.

1927 The film *Metropolis* by Fritz Lang is released.

1936 In Britain, the BBC begins transmitting a regular television service.

1945 British novelist George Orwell publishes *Animal Farm*.

1947 Italian author Primo Levi publishes *If This is a Man*, his account of a Nazi concentration camp.

1949 Publication of *The Second Sex* by French feminist Simone de Beauvoir.

1954 *Under Milk Wood* is published by Welsh author Dylan Thomas.

1955 Irish playwright Samuel Beckett completes *Waiting for Godot*.

1958 *Dr Zhivago* is published by Russian novelist Boris Pasternak.

1961 The Beatles' first British performance is at the Cavern Club in Liverpool.

1967 The Beatles release *Sergeant Pepper's Lonely Hearts Club Band*.

1977 The Pompidou Centre opens in Paris.

1981 Italian author Umberto Eco publishes *In the Name of the Rose*.

1988 Publication of *The Satanic Verses* by British author Salman Rushdie.

1992 British artist Damien Hirst completes his sculpture entitled *The Physical Impossibility of Death in the Mind of Someone Living*.

1996 A restored version of Shakespeare's Globe Theatre opens in London.

Discoveries in Science and Technology

BC c.3400 Invention of potters' wheel in Mesopotamia.
c.3200 First examples of vehicle wheels made in Mesopotamia.
c.2500 First skis appear in Scandinavia.
Four-wheeled chariot invented in Mesopotamia.
c.999–700 First widespread use of iron in Europe.
c.800 Greece begins to use alphabet.
c.700 False teeth invented in Italy.
c.450 Abacus used as calculating instrument in Mediterranean countries.
c.350 Construction of Mausoleum at Halicarnassus, one of the Seven Wonders of the World.
c.292–280 Construction of the Colossus of Helos in Rhodes, another of the Seven Wonders of the World.
c.220 Invention of the three-masted ship in Greece.
193 Romans invent concrete.
c.170 First paved roads are built in Rome.
c.85 Water-powered mill for grinding flour invented in Greece.
46 Julius Caesar introduces the Julian calendar.
AD c.50 Horseshoes invented in Italy.
80 The Colosseum is opened in Rome.
118–28 Construction of the Pantheon in Rome, complete with 43-metre concrete dome.
c.175 Greek physician Galen develops the principles of anatomy and physiology.
200 In Scandinavia, skates are first used for crossing ice.
635 First known use of quill pens, Spain.
c.850 Windmills appear for the first time in Europe.
976 In Spain, the first European use of Arabic numerals is recorded.
1065 First known use of stained glass, Germany.
1150 University founded in Paris.
1167 Oxford University is established.
1174 Construction begins on the Leaning Tower of Pisa.
1200 Magnifying glass invented in England by Robert Grosseteste, the Bishop of Lincoln.
c.1250 In Wales, the longbow is first used in battle.
c.1280 First use of belt-driven spinning wheel in Europe.
c.1300 First known European spectacles are made in Italy.
1340 First European paper factory opens in Italy.
c.1350 Invention of the alarm clock, Germany.
1370 Charles V of France establishes standard time.
c.1400 First oil painting.
1450 In Germany, Johann Gutenberg invents the printing press, producing the first Bible to be printed using moveable type.
1474 Patents protecting inventors' rights are issued for the first time, in Venice.
1500 Leonardo da Vinci designs the helicopter.
c.1505 Invention of the pocket watch in Germany.
1509 First use of wallpaper, at Christ's College, Cambridge.
1528 First use of grenades recorded in France.
1538 In Spain, diving bells are used for the first time.
c.1565 First use of pencils as writing instruments.
c.1590 Invention of the telescope.
1614 Logarithms invented by Scottish mathematician John Napier.
1624 First submarine built in England.
1637 Invention of the umbrella in France.
1643 Mercury barometer invented by Italian scientist Evangelista Torricelli.
1657 First pendulum clock is constructed in Holland.
1661 First European use of paper money recorded in Sweden.
c.1665 Isaac Newton discovers the law of gravity.
1670 King Charles II's mechanic invents the megaphone.
1670 A French monk, Dom Pérignon, invents champagne.
1675 The Greenwich Observatory is established in London.
1680 Discovery of bacteria by Dutch scientist Anton van Leeuwenhoek.
c.1690 Nuremberg instrument maker, Johann Christopher Denner is credited with inventing the clarinet.
1714 Mercury thermometer invented by German scientist Gabriel Fahrenheit.

1733 Design of the first perambulator, or pram, in England.
1759 In Englnd, John Harrison succeeded in making an accurate marine clock, the marine chronometer.
1764 Invention of the spinning jenny in England.
1774 Oxygen discovered by British chemist Joseph Priestley.
1779 William Williams builds the world's first iron bridge at Coalbrookdale, Britain.
1781 British scientist Henry Cavendish discovers that water is a compound of oxygen and hydrogen.
1782 In Britain, James Watt invents the double-action steam engine.
1783 First hot-air balloon for passengers is invented by the Montgolfier brothers.
1789 Martin Klaproth discovers the readioactive element uranium.
1798 Lithographic printing invented in Bavaria.
1800 Alessandro Volta demonstrates the battery.
1802 Gas lighting is used for the first time.
1807 Street gas lighting is used for the first time in London.
1803 Charles Derosne discovers a method for extracting morphine from opium.
1812 Food canning is invented in Britain.
1821 In Britain, fossilized dinosaurs are discovered for the first time.
1839 Photographic processes are invented in France and Britain.
1840 Creation of postage stamps in Britain.
1844 Samuel Morse develops the Morse Code.
1859 Charles Darwin publishes his theory of evolution.
1859 Frenchman Étienne Lenoir builds the first internal combustion engine
1861 First use of colour photography.
1862 Louis Pasteur invents pasteurization, a heating process to preserve milk.
1863 London opens the first underground steam railway.
1867 Swedish chemist Alfred Nobel invents dynamite.
1878 The electric train is invented in Germany.
1886 German engineer Gottlieb Daimler invents first petrol-powered car.
1886 Thomas Crapper invents the first flushable toilet.
1890 Electric trains are used for the first time on the London Underground.
1893 Invention of the automatic pistol in Germany.
1899 First sales of aspirin in Europe.
1905 Albert Einstein publishes his theory of relativity.
1911 Vitamins are discovered by Polish scientist Casimir Funk.
1914 Stainless steel is invented in Germany.
1917 The British army uses tanks in combat for the first time.
1921 The world's first motorway opens in Germany.
1926 Scottish inventor John Logie Baird develops the television.
1927 Britain sees the first public broadcast of a television programme.
1928 Alexander Fleming discovers the first antibiotic, penicillin.
1935 British scientist Robert Watson-Watt invents radar.
1936 Regular television broadcasts begins in Britain.
1939 The insecticide DDT is discovered by Swiss chemist Paul Muller.
1949 Frenchmen, Émile Gagnon and Jacques Cousteau perfect a self-contained underwater breathing apparatus (SCUBA).
1949 First atomic bomb tested by the Soviet Union.
1952 The first jet passenger flight is undertaken by British aircraft.
1959 Hovercraft invented in Britain.
1976 Concorde makes its first flight.
1978 The world's first in-vitro fertilisation (IVF) baby is born in Britain.
1994 The Channel Tunnel opens between Britain and France.
1997 Dolly the sheep is cloned in Britain.

Biographies of Key Figures

Alexander the Great (356–323 BC): King of Macedon, 336–323 BC. Became king on assassination of his father, Philip II of Macedon. Tutored by Aristotle. Took control of Greek States; embarked on war against Persians, 334 BC, destroying them at the battles of Granicus, 334 BC, Issus, 333 BC, and Gaugamela, 331 BC. Took Tyre, conquering Syria, Palestine, and Egypt, 332 BC, and founding Alexandria. Conquests in Persia took him as far as the Indus, defeating the Indian king, Porus, and marrying the Bactrian princess, Roxane. Returning to Persepolis, the Persian capital, quelled a mutiny in his troops but died of fever at Babylon. The greatest military conqueror of the ancient world; conquests spread Hellenic influence into Asia and founded cities as far as the Hindu Kush. His empire was divided among his subordinate commanders.

Alexander I (1777–1825): Tsar of Russia, 1801–25. Son of murdered Paul I. Entered War of Third Coalition against France, 1805. Obliged to conclude Treaty of Tilsit with Napoleon, 1807. Active in Fourth Coalition against France. Leading figure at Congress of Vienna, 1814–15. Secured creation of Polish Kingdom. Established "Holy Alliance" with Prussia and Austria. Early promise of liberal rule gave way to reactionary policy, under influence of Metternich.

Alexander II (1818–81): Tsar of Russia, 1855–81. "The Liberator". Son of Nicholas I. Succeeded to throne during Crimean War. Embarked on wide-ranging modernization of government. Most important reform was liberation of serfs, 1861. Innovations in legal code, 1862, and local government, education, and army administration. Encouraged railway construction and banking. In foreign policy, concerned chiefly with expansion into Balkans, encouraging pan-Slavic movement. In Central Asia, Bokhara and Samarkand acquired, 1868. Russian troops reached Constantinople, 1878. Later in reign, more conservative in response to discontent in Poland, growth of revolutionary societies (e.g. Nihilists) and assassination attempts. Killed by bomb, 1881, before able to implement new constitution.

Aquinas, St Thomas (1225–74): Italian philosopher, theologian, and Dominican friar; known as the "Angelic Doctor". Regarded as the greatest figure of scholasticism. Despite knowing no Greek or Hebrew, and hardly any history, through his commentaries he made Aristotle's thought available and acceptable in the Christian West. His *Summa Theologiae* (1266–73) is the greatest achievement of systematic medieval theology and includes his "five proofs" of the existence of God. His thought, with few exceptions, now represents the general teaching of the Catholic Church. Canonized in 1523. Feast day, 28 January.

Archimedes (287–212 BC): Mathematician and engineer of the ancient world. Born in Syracuse. Mathematical studies led to important discoveries in mechanics. Established principles of the lever and the Archimedes Screw for raising water from a lower to a higher level by means of a screw mechanism enclosed in a cylinder. This facilitated the working of water-pumping device for drainage and was also used for grape and olive presses. Also invented military machines used in the defence of Syracuse. Died in Syracuse when the city fell to the Romans.

Aristotle (384–322 BC): Greek philosopher. Resident of Athens 367–347 BC and from 335 BC. Tutor of Alexander the Great, his influence came mainly through his later period of residence in Athens from 335 BC. Opened a school, but was forced to leave in 323 BC when accused of impiety. Writings cover several categories, including logic, natural science, metaphysics, ethics, politics, and literature. Works largely transmitted through Arab translations and taken up by medieval scholars such as St Thomas Aquinas.

Augustine of Hippo, St (354–430): Major theologian of the early Church. Converted by St Ambrose and baptized, AD 387. Made Bishop of Hippo, 395. Completed his major work *De Civitate Dei* (*The City of God*), 416. He is today best-known for his *Confessions*, a long autobiographical prayer including the memorable "Grant me chastity, lord, but not yet!"

Augustus (63 BC–AD 14): First Roman emperor. Grand-nephew of Julius Caesar; claimed his uncle's inheritance, 44 BC. Was appointed triumvir with Mark Antony and Lepidus, 43 BC. Most successful of a group of competing generals and politicians. Finally defeated Mark Antony and Cleopatra at Actium, 31 BC. Victory in Egypt and its incorporation into Roman rule, his standing in Italy, and his great wealth led to dominant position in Rome. Took on an increasingly central role, with the title "Augustus". Extended the system of direct rule, reformed taxation, and doubled the size of the provincial Empire. By end of his rule, Rome had evolved from a Republican system to a virtually imperial one.

Bach, Johann Sebastian (1685–1750): German composer, born at Eisenach, where he was first employed as a violinist and church organist. His appointment as organist at the Thomaskirche, Leipzig, opened a period in which he became the most prolific and influential composer of baroque music. His cantatas and other chamber works, such as the six *Brandenburg Concertos* (1720–1), are complemented by the great *St Matthew* and *St John Passions*, and the *Mass in B Minor*. He had 20 children.

Balzac, Honoré de (1799–1850): French novelist. After first finding success with *Les Derniers Chouans* (1829), and writing several other novels, he formed the idea of presenting a complete picture of modern civilization in the *Comédie humaine*. Among the works in this scheme are *Le Père Goriot*, and *Eugenie Grandet*. Balzac wrote 85 novels in 20 years, often working 18 hours a day. In 1849, in poor health, he travelled to Poland to visit Eveline Hanska with whom he had corresponded for 15 years. They married in 1850, but Balzac died three months later.

Beethoven, Ludwig van (1770–1827): German composer, born in Bonn. First taught by his unstable and ambitious father, appearing as a keyboard prodigy at Cologne (1778). Settled in Vienna around 1792. Had a series of disastrous love affairs and a domestic life that declined in quality. Despite increasing deafness and bouts of depression his output was prodigious: nine symphonies, 32 piano sonatas, 16 string quartets, the opera *Fidelio* (1814), and the *Mass in D* (the *Missa Solemnis*, 1823). In his *Ninth Symphony* (1824) he broke with tradition in the finale by introducing voices to sing Schiller's "Ode to Joy". A colossal creative force, he is regarded as bridging the Classical and Romantic movements.

Benedict, St (480–550): Founder of Western monasticism; collected his disciples *c.*520–7 and founded his monastery at Monte Cassino, 529, where he drew up the rules relating to monastic life in *The Rule of St Benedict*. This set up the ideal of monastic life as one governed by an elected abbot, residence in one place, and observance of prayers. His ideal of monasticism was carried forward in the Benedictine order and later adapted by other monastic orders.

Bernard of Clairvaux, St (1090–1153): French theologian and reformer. In 1113, entered the Cistercian order. His studious, ascetic life and stirring eloquence made him the oracle of Christendom. Founded more than 70 monasteries. The monks of his reformed branch of the Cistercians are often called Bernardines.

Bismarck, Otto von (1815–98): Prussian-German statesman, architect of German unification. Ultra-royalist member of Prussian parliament, 1847. Hostile to liberal-national Revolution, 1848. Prussian member of German Diet at Frankfurt, 1851–9. Ambassador to St Petersburg, 1859. Ambassador to Paris, 1862. Recalled, 1862, to become Prussian chief minister. Dissolved parliament, undertook reorganization of army. Sought German unification under Prussian leadership, with exclusion of Austria. Engineered wars over Schleswig-Holstein, 1864, Seven Weeks' War with Austria, 1866, and Franco-Prussian War, 1870. Created count, 1866. Chancellor of North German Confederation, 1867–71. Prince and imperial chancellor, 1871–90. Internal political struggles with Catholic Church, 1870s (*Kulturkampf*), and socialists, 1880s. Introduced anti-socialist legislation, universal suffrage, social insurance, and protective tarifs. Foreign policy was geared to securing newly unified Germany. Devised system of alliances (*Dreikaiserbund*, Triple Alliance, Reinsurance Treaty), designed to preserve balance of power and isolate France. Presided at Congress of Berlin, 1878. After disagreements over policy with Kaiser Wilhelm II, resigned 1890.

Blériot, Louis (1872–1936): French airman. Made the first flight across the English Channel on 25 July 1909 from Baraques to Dover in a small 24hp monoplane.

Boccaccio, Giovanni (1313–75): Italian writer, poet, and humanist. Famous for the *Decameron* (1348–58), a collection of 100 tales told by ten young people who have moved to the country to escape the Black Death. Influenced Chaucer, and was a lifelong friend of Petrarch.

Botticelli, Sandro born Alessandro di Mariano Filipepi (1445–1510): Florentine painter. Worked in Renaissance Florence under the patronage of the Medicis. Best known for his mythological works such as *Primavera* (*c*.1478) and *The Birth of Venus* (*c*.1480), both of which are in the Uffizi, Florence.

Brezhnev, Leonid Ilyich (1906–82): Soviet politician. Communist Party official in Ukraine and Moldavia. Held military posts, 1933–4. Member of Praesidium of Supreme Soviet, 1952–7. President of Praesidium, 1960–4, succeeding Marshal Voroshilov. Succeeded Khrushchev as First Secretary of Central Committee, 1964. General Secretary of Central Committee, 1966.

Brueghel, or **Breughel, Pieter the Elder** (*c*.1520–69): Flemish artist. Produced landscapes, religious allegories, and satires of peasant life. His work was highly regarded by Rubens, and his truthful rendering of peasant life and weather conditions sets his work apart from the more Italianate style of his Dutch contemporaries. Principal works include *The Blind Leading the Blind* (1568) and *The Peasant Wedding* (1568).

Caesar, Gaius Julius (102–44 BC): Roman soldier and statesman. Descended from a prominent family; early political career was interrupted by the antagonism of Sulla. Began to establish a political reputation upon return to Rome, 68 BC, but was more noted for his extravagant lifestyle. Sought to reconcile rivals Pompey and Crassus, becoming consul, 60 BC, in first Triumvirate. Obtained command of Transalpine and Cisalpine Gaul and Illyria. From 58 BC mounted a series of campaigns in Gaul. Defeated the Helvetii, the Germans under Ariovistus, the Belgae, and Nervii. Crushed revolt by the Veneti in Brittany; victory over the Aquitani of the south-west gave the Roman Republic complete control over Gaul. A final revolt under Vercingetorix was eventually defeated, forcing complete surrender of rebel forces and reimposition of Roman rule. First exploratory invasion of Britain, 55 BC. Defeated British under Cassivelaunus, 54 BC, forcing them into a tributary relationship. Returned to Italy, 49 BC, to power struggle with Pompey. Caesar subdued Spain then returned to Rome; was elected dictator and consul. Defeated Pompey at the battle of Pharsalus in Greece. Pursued Pompey to Egypt; remained there after the former was murdered. Wars against remaining opponents let to campaigns in Spain and Africa. Jealousy led to conspiracy and his murder in the Senate on 15 March. Great soldier and statesman, also contributed significantly as writer and historian.

Calvin, John (1509–64): French Protestant theologian and reformer. On becoming a Protestant he fled to Switzerland, where he attempted to reorder society and established the first Presbyterian government in Geneva. His *Christianae Religionis Institutiae* (*Institutes of the Christian Religion*) of 1536 was the first systematized account of reformed Christian doctrine and ecclesiastical discipline.

Catherine II, the Great (1729–96): German-born Empress of Russia, 1762–96. Married Peter, heir to Russian throne, 1745. Peter dethroned and murdered, Catherine made Empress. "Enlightened Despot", favouring French philosophers, e.g. Voltaire. Few reforms actually introduced; abolished capital punishment (except for political crimes). During reign, number of serfs in Russia rose, as did economic burdens on peasantry. Turned to repression after Pugachev Revolt, 1773–5. Main development in reign was rapid territorial expansion: three Partitions of Poland, 1772, 1793, and 1795. Wars with Turkey, 1768–74 and 1787–92. War with Sweden, 1788–90. Annexed Crimea and Ukraine.

Cavour, Count Camillo Benso di (1810–61): Italian statesman. Architect of Italian unification. In newspaper, *Il Risorgimento*, called for republican system. Piedmontese minister of agriculture, marine, and commerce, 1850. Succeeded D'Azeglio as prime minister of Piedmont, 1852. Strengthened constitutional government, reduced influence of Church and encouraged economic development. Brought Italian question before Congress of Paris, 1856. Made pact with Napoleon III to expel Austrians from Italy (Plombières Agreement), 1858. Resigned when Napoleon failed to honour agreement. Returned, 1860; negotiated union of Parma, Modena, Tuscany, and the Romagna with Piedmont-Sardinia. Encouraged Garibaldi's sweep through Sicily while occupying Papal States. First prime minister of unified Italian kingdom, 1861.

Ceausescu, Nicolae (1918–89): Romanian dictator. Member of underground Communist Party, 1936. Party Secretariat member, 1954. Deputy leader, 1957–65. General Secretary, 1965. Head of State, 1967. Combined independent foreign policy, notably criticism of the 1968 Warsaw Pact invasion of Czechoslovakia, with authoritarian regime, massive repression, and personality cult. Repressed demonstrations prompted by economic crisis, 1967. Showed little sympathy for the Soviet line instituted by Gorbachev. His corrupt regime and bankrupt economy provoked riots in 1989; their savage repression led to the December 1989 "Winter Revolution". Executed with his wife Elena by firing squad after secret trial, 25 December 1989.

Cervantes Saavedra, Miguel de (1547–1616): Spanish novelist and dramatist. Injured at the Battle of Lepanto, he turned to literature. His *Don Quixote*, published in two parts (1605, 1615), describes the adventures of a poor gentleman with inflated ideas of chivalry. A satire of human folly, it also possesses immense power of human sympathy, and has given the world some of its most famous stories. Immensely influential on European literature.

Chamberlain, Neville (1869–1940): British Conservative politician. Son of Joseph Chamberlain. Lord Mayor of Birmingham, 1915–16. Director general of National Service, 1916–17. Member of parliament, 1918–40. Postmaster general, 1922–3. Paymaster general, 1923. Minister of health, 1923–4, 1931–7. Prime minister, 1937–40. Resigned, 1940, becoming Lord President of the Council in wartime coalition, following rebellion by Conservative MPs in favour of Churchill. Much criticized for attempt to appease Germany and Italy, especially in Munich Agreement, 1938. Retired from politics, due to fatal illness, 1940.

Charlemagne (742–814): Major post-Roman ruler of the West; conquered the Saxons, 772–804, and established his authority over northern Spain and northern Italy. Made his capital at Aix-la-Chapelle and crowned emperor of the West by Pope Leo III in Rome, 800. Regulated Church affairs and effected a general revival of prosperity and peace in the West.

Charles V (1500–58): King of Spain (as Charles I), 1516–56, Holy Roman Emperor, 1519–56. Vast inheritance of lands proved vulnerable to the rivalry of other powers and religious dissent aroused by Reformation. Career dominated by war, defending Christian Europe from the Turkish threat on land and at sea, struggling against Protestantism in Germany, rebellion in Castile, and war with France (1521–44). Defeated French at Pavia (1525), and Protestant forces at Mühlberg (1547). Exhausted by these struggles, Charles handed Naples, the Netherlands, and Spain over to his son Philip II, and the imperial crown to his brother Ferdinand, then retired to a monastery.

Charles X (1757–1836): King of France, 1824–30. Brother of Louis XVIII. Lived in Britain during French Revolution. Returned to France to lead revolt in Vendée, 1795. Appointed Lieutenant-General of France, 1814. After 1815, led reactionary "Ultras" in struggle with Constitutionalists. Ascended throne, 1824. At first, promised loyalty to constitution of 1814. Provoked opposition through his support of clerical party, favourable treatment of former émigrés, and reactionary religious legislation. Appointed Prince de Polignac as head of government, 1829. Dissolved parliament, 1830. "Five Ordinances", July 1830, limiting political and civil rights, led to revolution. Abdicated in favour of Comte de Chambord, but succeeded by his cousin, Louis Philippe, Duc D'Orléans.

Charles XII (1682–1718): King of Sweden, 1698–1718. A legendary soldier who came to the throne aged 15 and initially destroyed the coalition of forces sent against him. The Great Northern War of 1700–21 dominated his reign. Early victories over the Danes and Russians led to his invasion of Russia, which ended disastrously at Poltava in 1709. Continued campaigning and was killed at the siege of Fredriksten.

Churchill, Sir Winston (1874–1965): British statesman. Conservative MP, 1900–4. Became a Liberal in protest at tariff reform policies. Liberal MP, 1906–8, 1908–22. Constitutionalist, later Conservative MP, 1924–45. Conservative MP for Woodford, 1945–64. Under-secretary at colonial office, 1906–8. President of the board of trade, 1908–10. Home secretary, 1910–11. First Lord of the Admiralty, 1911–15. Chancellor of the Duchy of Lancaster, 1915. Minister of munitions, 1917–19. Secretary for war and air, 1919–21. Secretary for air and colonies, 1921. Colonial secretary, 1921–2. Chancellor of the exchequer, 1924–9. First Lord of the Admiralty, 1939–40. Prime minister and minister of defence, 1940–5. Leader of the opposition, 1945–51. Prime minister, 1951–5. Minister of defence, 1951–2. Made K.G., 1953. Resigned, 1955. Chequered career; during World War I involved in disputes over admiralty policy and Gallipoli campaign. Opposed Conservative policies over India and rearmament during 1930s. Advocated prevention of German expansion. Wartime leadership earned him legendary status, though not returned to power in 1945. Negotiated wartime alliance with USA and USSR. After World War II, favoured alliance with USA against USSR.

Cicero, Marcus Tullius (106–43 BC): Roman orator, famous for his defence of the Republic against the threat of ambitious politicians. Letters and speeches among the most widely read and admired of classical literature. As consul, defeated and suppressed Catiline conspiracy, but was unable, as Tribune, to resist the encroachments of the Republic by Pompey, Caesar, and Crassus. After several periods of exile, returned to Rome where delivered speeches denouncing Mark Antony (the *Philippics*), as a threat to the Senate following the death of Julius Caesar. Proscribed by the Triumvirs, he was killed while trying to escape.

Cid, El, properly Rodrigo Diaz de Vivar (c.1043–99): Spanish warrior hero, immortalized as "El Cid" (The Lord). A vassal of Alfonso VI of Castile, he fought constantly from 1065. In 1081 he was banished for an unauthorized raid and began a long career as a soldier of fortune, serving both Spaniards and Moors. Beseiged and captured Valencia (1093–4) and became its ruler.

Clemenceau, Georges (1841–1929): French radical statesman. Mayor of Montmartre, 1870–1. Entered National Assembly, 1871. Elected deputy, 1876, becoming leading of extreme left, 1876–93. Founded radical newspaper, *La Justice*, 1880. Critical of government. Contributed to downfall of several ministries. Instrumental in securing resignation of President Grévy after honours scandal, 1887. Lost seat in Chamber, 1893. Returned after supporting Dreyfus. Senator, 1902–20. Minister of interior, 1906. Prime minister, 1906–9. Completed Church–State separation. Strike-breaking measures aroused Socialist opposition. Attacked military mismanagement during World War I. Appointed prime minister and minister of war, 1917–20. Semi-dictatorial rule. Secured appointment of Foch as Chief of Allied forces, March 1918. Presided at Paris Peace Conference, 1919, pressing for harsh penalties on Germany. Lost presidential election, 1920.

Cleopatra (69–30 BC): Queen of Egypt. Daughter of Ptolemy Auletes. Legendary beauty attracted attention of Julius Caesar, 48 BC. She lived with him in Rome, but returned to Egypt on his death four years later. Formed liaison with Mark Antony, who increased her domains. Committed suicide when Antony was defeated at Actium, 31 BC. The last of the Ptolemaic rulers of Egypt, her death saw Egypt's incorporation into the Roman Empire.

Clovis (465–511): Became chief of the Franks on the death of his father, Childeric, 481; defeated the Roman general, Syagrius, at Soissons and the Germans, 496. Baptized with his army, 496; defeated Alaric, King of the Goths. Fixed his residence in Paris, 508.

Columbus, Christopher (1451–1506): Genoese explorer and discoverer of the New World. Went to sea at 14 and fought in the Tunisian galleys. About 1470, shipwrecked off Cape St Vincent, reached Portugal on a plank. Conceived the idea of reaching India by sailing westward (and thus proving the world was round) as early as 1474, but plans not finally accepted by Ferdinand and Isabella of Castile, until 1492. On 3 August, set sail in the *Santa Maria*, with the *Pinta* and *Niña*, and 120 men. Discovered various Caribbean islands, returning to Spain with full honours on 15 March 1493. Made several other voyages, discovering Dominica in the West Indies, and the South American mainland.

Constantine I, the Great (Flavius Valerius Aurelius) (274–337): Founder of Constantinople. First emperor to make Christianity a state religion of the Byzantine Empire in 324. Son of Constantine Chlorus and Helena. Earned a reputation as a brave soldier and was proclaimed emperor by the troops at York, England. Marched against his rivals, notably Maxentius, for the imperial title, AD 312. According to legend was converted to Christianity by the apparition of a cross in the sky with the message, "By this sign conquer." Establishing his power in the Western Empire, he promoted prosperity and encouraged Christianity. Defeated a rival,

Licinius, in the Eastern Empire, 323, to become master of both Western and Eastern Empires. Assembled the first general Christian Council at Nicaea, 325, which adopted a settled creed of beliefs (the Nicene Creed). Transferred the capital of the Empire to Byzantium, 330, naming it after himself as Constantinople. Breifly reunited the Roman Empire and proclaimed Christianity the official religion of the Empire, 334. Baptized on his deathbed, 337.

Copernicus, Nicolaus (1473–1543): Polish astronomer, and founder of modern astronomy. From 1491 studied mathematics, optics, and perspective at Kracow University, and in 1496, canon law at Bologna. In 1503, began the study of medicine at Padua, and was made doctor of canon law at Ferrara. In 1505, left Italy for Prussia, living at Frauenberg. His *De Revolutionibus Orbius Coelestium*, proving the sun to be the centre of the universe, was completed in 1530, and published just before his death in 1543.

Cortés, Hernán (1485–1547): Spanish conquistador and conqueror of Mexico. Landed on the coast of Mexico early in 1519. Exploited divisions between the Aztecs and their subjects, marching on Tenochtitlán, the site of present day Mexico City. Entered the city, abducted the Aztec king Montezuma, who was forced to submit as a vassal of Spain. In subsequent battles, he defeated Aztec armies, notably at Otumba in 1520, killing Montezuma. He was eventually deposed by his followers, but had established Spanish dominion in Mexico.

Cromwell, Oliver (1599–1658): Soldier and statesman, Lord Protector of England, 1653–8. Emerged as skilled cavalry commander in the English civil war and defeated Royalist forces of Charles I at decisive battles of Marston Moor (1644) and Naseby (1645). A fierce Puritan, motivations were primarily religious. Drawn into politics again by the Second Civil War of 1648–9, and his determination did much to assure the trial and execution of Charles I in 1649. Conducted ruthless campaigns in Scotland and Ireland. Refused the Crown, but took title of Lord Protector. Succeeded by his son, his settlement did not last, leading to the Restoration of the Stuart monarchy in 1660.

Curie, Marie (originally Manya) née Sklodowska (1867–1934): Polish-born French physicist and wife of Pierre Curie. A Sorbonne graduate, married in 1895 and worked with husband on magnetism and radioactivity (a term she invented in 1898). She and Pierre jointly awarded Nobel prize for physics in 1903 with Antoine Henri Becquerel. After Pierre's death in traffic accident, she succeeded him as professor of physics at the Sorbonne. Isolated radium in 1910, awarded Nobel prize for chemistry in 1911. Director of research department at the Radium Institute in Paris (1918–34). Honorary professor of radiology at Warsaw (1919–34). Died of leukaemia, caused by prolonged exposure to radioactive materials.

Dante Alighieri (1265–1321): Italian poet, born in Florence, a lawyer's son of the noble Guelf family. His lifelong love was Beatrice Portinari (c.1265–90); no evidence that she returned his love, and she married at an early age. As one of six priors of Florence, he showed characteristic sternness and impartiality to all the city's faction leaders. Sent on an embassy to Rome to Pope Boniface VIII in 1301, he never again set foot in his native town. Banished from Florence in 1309, and sentenced to death in absentia. Thenceforth led a wandering life, eventually settling in Ravenna, where he is buried. Married to Gemma Donati, Dante had six children. His most celebrated work is the *Divina Commedia*, begun around 1307, his spiritual testament, narrating a journey through hell and purgatory, guided by Virgil, and finally to paradise, guided by Beatrice.

Danton, Georges Jacques (1759–94): French Revolutionary politician. Became an administrator of Paris, 1791. Founded Cordeliers Club with Marat and Desmoulins. Minister of

justice, 1792. Voted for execution of Louis XVI, 1793. Original member of Committee of Public Safety. President of Jacobin Club, 1793. Achieved suppression of Girondins. Later sought conciliation, moving to right wing of Jacobins. Sought to moderate Revolutionary Tribunal. Opposed by Robespierre and the "Mountain". Arrested, 1794, and guillotined.

Darwin, Charles Robert (1809–82): English naturalist, originator of the theory of evolution by natural selection. Studied medicine at Edinburgh (1825–7), then entered Christ's College, Cambridge, in 1828. Naturalist to HMS *Beagle* on a scientific survey of South American waters (1831–6). By 1846, had published several works on geology and zoology which placed him among the eminent scientists of his day. Published his great work *The Origin of the Species* in November 1859. Received throughout Europe with great interest, it was violently attacked and energetically defended, but eventually received recognition from almost all competent biologists. Continued to produce a great series of supplemental treatises, including *The Descent of Man* (1874), until a year before his death.

De Gaulle, Charles (1890–1970): French soldier and statesman. Member of French military mission to Poland, 1919–20. Lectured at Staff College. Sought to modernize army. Published *The Army of the Future*, 1932–4. Ideas subsequently employed by German Army. Briefly a member of Reynaud's government, 1940. Fled to Britain after fall of France. Became head of Committee of National Liberation ("Free French"), 1943. Claimed status of head of government. Led unsuccessful attempt to recapture Dakar. Entered Paris, August 1944. President of provisional government, 1945. Suspected of authoritarian ambitions. Resigned, 1946. Founded political party (Rally of the French People), retiring from its leadership, 1953. During Algerian Crisis, 1958, invited by President Coty to form temporary government with wide executive powers. Won overwhelming victory in referendum on new constitution. Elected first president of Fifth Republic, 1959. Granted independence to former French colonies in Africa, 1959–60. Granted Algeria independence, 1962. Developed independent nuclear deterrent. Encouraged closer ties with West Germany. Twice vetoed British entry to EEC, 1962–3 and 1967. Re-elected on second ballot, 1965. Re-elected after events of May 1968 but resigned 1969, following opposition to his plans to reform constitution.

Disraeli, Benjamin, 1st Earl of Beaconsfield (1804–81): British Conservative politician. Member of parliament, 1837–76. Opposed repeal of Corn Laws, 1846, heading Protectionist group until 1852. Leader of the Commons and chancellor of the exchequer, 1852, 1858–9, 1866–8. Prime minister, 1868, 1874–80. Lord Privy seal, 1876–8. Created Earl of Beaconsfield, 1876. Leader of Conservative party until shortly before death. Introduced franchise reform, 1867, almost doubling electorate. Stressed Tory concern over social and imperial issues. Bought almost half share in Suez Canal Co., 1875. Created Queen Victoria Empress of India, 1876. Aimed to restrict Russian penetration of Eastern Europe. Attended Congress of Berlin, 1878, winning recognition of Britain's right to occupy Cyprus. Failed to resume office after election defeat, 1880.

Dreyfus, Alfred (1859–1935): French soldier. Jewish artillery captain appointed to General Staff. Wrongly accused of espionage and imprisoned. Case revealed depth of anti-Semitism within French establishment and provoked bitter division between "Dreyfusards" (the left, intellectuals, anti-clericals) and "anti-Dreyfusards" (especially Army and Church). Retried and pardoned. Verdict finally overturned in 1906.

Dubček, Alexander (1921–): Czech politician. First Secretary of the Czechoslovak Communist Party and key figure in the Prague Spring reform movement, which culminated in the

Soviet invasion of Czechoslovakia in August 1968; dismissed from his post, he was first president of the New Federal Assembly (August 1968–September 1969) then ambassador to Turkey (December 1969–June 1970) before being expelled from the Communist Party. This attempt to build a national socialism with a "human face" posed a threat to Soviet control of Eastern Europe. By 1989, however, circumstances had changed. In December 1989 Dubček was elected chairman (speaker) of the Czech parliament.

Dürer, Albrecht (1471–1528): German painter and engraver. The leading German artist of the Renaissance, particularly important for his technically advanced woodcuts and copper engravings. Present at coronation of Charles V, who appointed him court painter. Met Luther during his later years, and showed great sympathy with the Reformation.

Eisenstein, Sergei Mikhailovich (1898–1948): Russian film director, born in Riga. Served in the Red Army during the Russian Revolution (1916–18). Appointed to make propaganda films on the history of the revolution with *The Battleship Potemkin* (1925) on the 1905 mutiny, and *Ten Days that Shook the World* (1928), on the October Revolution. His substitution of the crowd for the traditional hero and ability to achieve impressionistic effects greatly influenced film art. His later masterpiece was *Ivan the Terrible* (1944) with its sequel *The Boyars Plot*, the latter being banned in the Soviet Union for many years.

Elizabeth I (1533–1603): Queen of England, 1558–1603. Well-educated, survived early intrigues and imprisonment to emerge as one of Britain's most famous monarchs, principally for her defence of the country against Spanish invasion in the Armada of 1588 (and other later Armadas). Achieved a moderate religious settlement which survived her. Her reign was a delicate balance of negotiation and equivocation, England's European role limited by lack of finance. She never married.

Engels, Friedrich (1820–95): German political philosopher. Associate and colleague of Karl Marx. After 1842, lived mostly in Britain. Wrote *The Condition of the Working Classes in England*, 1844. Involved in revolutionary movement in Baden, 1844. With Marx, wrote *The Communist Manifesto*, 1848. Helped Marx financially. Final years engaged in preparing Marx's writings for publication, completing *Das Kapital* in 1894.

Erasmus, Desiderius (*c*.1469–1536): Dutch humanist and scholar. The foremost Renaissance scholar of northern Europe; reacted against scholasticism and was drawn to the humanists. Although ordained a priest, paved the way for the Reformation with his satires on the Church, including the *Colloquia Familiaria* (1518). However he opposed the violence of the Reformation, and condemned Luther in *De Libero Arbitrio* (1525). Also published many popular, sometimes didactic works like the famous *Encomium Moriae* (*In Praise of Folly*, 1509). He taught in most of the cultural centres of Europe including Paris, Cambridge, and Oxford, meeting all the leading intellectuals of his day.

Ferdinand II (1452–1516): the first monarch of all Spain, as Ferdinand V of Castile, Ferdinand II of Aragon and Sicily, and Ferdinand III of Naples; known as "the Catholic". Marriage to Isabella of Castile united the Christian kingdoms of Spain. Established the Inquisition, 1478–80. Campaigned vigorously against the Moors, finally conquering Granada in 1492. In that same year, he expelled the Jews from the kingdom, and financed Christopher Columbus's expedition to the Americas, thus founding Spain's empire in the New World.

Francis of Assisi, St originally Giovanni Bernadone (1181–1226): Founder of the Franciscan order. Son of a wealthy Italian cloth merchant. In 1208 he rejected the world, adopting the complete observance of Christ-like poverty. His preaching friars travelled throughout Europe, founding new churches and monasteries.

Francis Xavier, St (1506–52): Spanish missionary, "the Apostle of the Indies". Studied, then lectured in Paris, becoming acquainted with Ignatius of Loyola, with whom he founded the Society of Jesus (1534). Ordained priest in 1537. Sent by John III of Portugal as missionary to the Portuguese colonies of the east; arrived at Goa in 1542. In 1548, founded a missionary in Japan that flourished for 100 years. Canonized in 1622.

Francis I (1494–1547): King of France from 151, and notable patron of the Renaissance. Met Henry VIII of England at the Field of the Cloth of Gold in 1520, a costly and portentous exercise that underlined the power and prosperity of France. His wars against HRE Charles V met with failure when he was captured at the Battle of Pavia in 1525, and only released the following year after renouncing his territorial claims.

Franco, Francisco (1892–1975): Spanish soldier and military dictator. Held command of Foreign Legion in Morocco. Chief of staff, 1935. Governor of Canaries, 1936. On outbreak of Civil War, integrated Foreign Legion and Moorish troops into rebel army. Became leader of Nationalist forces, 1936. Defeated Republican government, 1939. Established corporatist, authoritarian stage, acting as "*Caudillo*" ("Leader"), and permitting only one political party, the Falange. Maintained Spanish neutrality during World War II. Presided over Spain's rapid post-war economic development. Faced growing problem of regional separatism in last years. Ensured his own succession by King Juan Carlos I.

Franz Ferdinand (1863–1914): Archduke of Austria. Nephew of Emperor Francis Joseph. Became heir to throne, 1896. Hoped to give autonomy to subject Slav peoples. Assassination by Bosnian Serb at Sarajevo, 28 June 1914, immediate cause of World War I.

Franz Josef (1830–1916): Emperor of Austria, 1848–1916. Succeeded during Revolution. King of Hungary from 1867. Quickly restored order after 1848 in Hungary and Lombardy. Abolished constitution, 1851. Ruled personally until 1867. Favoured government by strong central bureaucracy. Hostile to party politics. Allied monarchy with Catholic Church. Accepted *Ausgleich*, 1867, which gave greater power to the Hungarian Magyars and led to the dual monarchy of Austria-Hungary. Sought to maintain balance of power in Europe, but by annexing Bosnia-Herzegovina, 1908, provoked ill-feeling. Precipitated World War I by attacking Serbia, 1914.

Frederick I, Barbarossa (Redbeard) (*c*.1123–90): King of Germany and Holy Roman Emperor, 1152–90. Made sustained effort to subdue Italy and the papcy, but was eventually defeated at the Battle of Legnano in 1176. This led him to a policy of clemency and concession with his subjects. At the height of his power, led the Third Crusade against Saladin in 1189.

Frederick II, the Great (1712–86): King of Prussia, 1740–86. Son of Frederick William I. Laid claim to Silesia. Encouraged War of Austrian Succession, 1740–8. Made alliances with France and Bavaria. Won military victories at Mollwitz, 1741, and Chotusitz, 1742. Invaded Bohemia, 1744. Acquired Silesia by Peace of Dresden, 1745. Entered Seven Years War, 1756–63, in alliance with England against Austria, France, Russia, Sweden, and Saxony. Position of Prussia greatly strengthened after Peace of Hubertusburg, 1763. Took part in First Partition of Poland with Russia, 1772. Entered War of Bavarian Succession, 1778. Established Furstenbund, 1785, in order to safeguard imperial constitution against Austria. Despite some reversals, a great military commander. Encouraged economic development. Began codification of Prussian law. Some liberalization, e.g. on laws of torture, religion, and censorship. Chief interest was modernization of army.

Frederick William (1620–88): Elector of Brandenberg from 1640, known as the Great Elector. Prussian monarch and army reformer who continued the work of his grandfather to establish Prussia as a formidable military power. Doubled the size of the army and trained it to new levels of efficiency, providing the instrument which his son Frederick II utilized to such good effect.

Galilei, Galileo, known as **Galileo** (1564–1642): Italian astronomer, mathematician, and natural philosopher, born in Pisa. Discovered the constancy of a pendulum's swing, formulated the laws of uniform acceleration of falling bodies, and described the parabolic trajectory of projectiles. Applying the telescope to astronomy, observed craters on the Moon, sunspots, four of Jupiter's satellites, and the phases of Venus. In 1632, published *Dialogo sopra i due massimi sistemi del mondo*, in favour of the Copernican system. After a long trial and imprisonment, sentenced to indefinite imprisonment by the Inquisition; sentence commuted by Pope Urban VIII. Thereafter he lived under house arrest at Arcetri near Florence, continuing researches despite severely impaired hearing and sight.

Garibaldi, Giuseppe (1807–82): Italian patriot. Involved in "Young Italy" movement, 1834. Escaped to South America after sentenced to death for role in attempted seizure of Genoa. Fought against Austrians in Italy, 1848. Joined revolutionary government in Rome, 1849. Voted for a republic, repulsed French troops, but forced to retreat by Austrians. Summoned by King Victor Emmanuel, 1859, and helped to liberate north Italy. Swept through Naples and Sicily, 1860, handing conquests over to Piedmont-Sardinia. Active in campaign against Austria in which Italy acquired Venice. Tried to seize Rome, 1867, but thwarted by French. Eventually secured Rome for Italy during Franco-Prussian War. Supported French Republican government after fall of Napoleon III.

Giotto (Di Bodone) (*c*.1266–1337): Italian painter and architect. Artist in whose work the seeds of the Renaissance are to be found. Broke with the rigid conventions of Byzantine art and introduced a naturalistic style showing human expression. Among most important works are the frescoes in the Arena Chapel, Padua (1305–8), and the Peruzzi Chapel in the church of Santa Croce, Florence (*c*.1320). Appointed master of works for the cathedral and city of Florence in 1334.

Gladstone, William Ewart (1809–98): British Liberal politician. Entered parliament, 1832. Out of office following split over repeal of Corn Laws, 1846–52. Chancellor of the exchequer, 1852–5, 1858–66. Cut government expenditure and advocated free trade. Became leader of Liberal Party, 1866. Prime minister, 1868–74. Introduced national education system. Disestablished Church of Ireland, 1869. Introduced secret ballot in elections, army reforms under Cardwell. Second ministry, 1880–5, formed after success of "Midlothian" election campaign. Widened franchise, 1884. Main preoccupation (as in last two administrations, 1880–5, 1892–4) was Home Rule for Ireland. Issue caused decisive breach in Liberal Party. Both Home Rule Bills, 1886 and 1893, were defeated. Retired, 1894.

Gorbachev, Mikhail (1931–): Soviet statesman who succeeded Chernenko as general secretary of the Communist Party in 1985. His advent to power, after a succession of ailing old-guard leaders, marked a major departure in the Soviet leadership. Succeeded Gromyko as president, 1988. His reforming policies, especially *perestroika* and *glasnost*, have been threatened by nationalism in such areas as Azerbaijan and the Baltic. His

policy of non-interference was vital in the 1989 revolutions in Eastern Europe that overthrew the old communist regimes. He survived the August 1991 *coup* attempt, but his power base was greatly eroded as the old Soviet Union disintegrated. Resigned as president, 25 December 1991, after formation of Commonwealth of Independent States.

Gregory I, the Great (540–604): Consecrated pope in 590; he propagated the faith in Italy and sent Augustine on a mission to evangelize Britain. Established the Gregorian rite to establish uniformity in the Christian West.

Gregory VII, Hildebrand, St (*c*.1020–85): Became pope in 1073. The great representative of the temporal claims of the medieval papacy. Set about amending the secularized condition of the Church, particularly directing efforts against the practice of investiture. In response, the emperor Henry IV declared Gregory deposed, for which the pope excommunicated Henry. Henry set up a Clement III as antipope in 1080 (the Great Schism), and entered Rome in 1084 after a siege of three years. Gregory was rescued, but the wretched condition of Rome forced him to withdraw. He died in Salerno.

Gregory IX (1148–1241): Became pope in 1227. Constantly feuded with the emperor Frederick II, and asserted the highest view of papal power.

Gustavus Adolphus (1594–1632): King of Sweden from 1611, known as "the Lion of the North". Coming to the throne at 17, found the country deeply involved in wars and disorder, but quickly conciliated the nobility, reorganized the government and revitalized the army. Intervened directly in the Thirty Years War on behalf of the Protestants, leaving the government in the hands of his capable chancellor, Oxenstierna. His victories owed much to his innovations in the use of cavalry, and mixed formations of pikemen and artillery. Founded the tradition of military prowess which made the Swedes a formidable power in northern Europe.

Hadrian (76–138): Roman emperor. Adopted heir of Trajan and, although faced with rivals, had the support of the army. Proclaimed emperor of Antioch, AD 117. Long apprenticeship in war and military affairs led him to seek reform and consolidation of the Empire. Established the Euphrates as the eastern boundary of the Empire, then conducted a major tour of Germany and Britain. Erected a continuous palisade (the Limes) on the German frontier and ordered the construction of a wall to mark the frontier of the province of Britannia (Hadrian's Wall). Further travels in Spain, Greece, Syria, and Judea followed. Revolts by the Jews and in Africa were suppressed and he promulgated important legal reforms in his Perpetual Edict of 132. An intellectual, reformer, and effective statesman and soldier, he was buried in the mausoleum he had built himself, the Castel Sant' Angelo.

Hannibal (247–183 BC): Carthaginian leader and general during the Punic Wars with Rome. Son of Hamilcar Barca; forced at an early age to swear eternal hostility to Rome. Commander-in-Chief of the Carthaginian forces at the age of 26. Appointed commander in Spain, 221 BC. Secured Spain, 219 BC; began the Second Punic War against Rome, 218 BC. Crossed the Alps to invade Italy, inflicting crushing defeats on Roman armies at Lake Trasimene and Cannae, 217–216 BC. Marched on Rome, but was deterred from capturing it and harassed by tactics of Quintus Maximus Fabius "Cunctator" (the Delayer). Returned to Africa, 203 BC; defeated by Romans, under the brilliant general Scipio, at Zama, 202 BC, ending Second Punic War. Forced to flee from Carthage, 193 BC, he took refuge in Syria and later Bithynia, where he was forced to commit suicide. A brilliant battlefield commander, Hannibal missed his chance to secure a decisive victory in Italy in 216 BC.

Hegel, George (1770–1831): German philosopher. Became professor of philosophy at Berlin, 1818. Described process of "dialectic", i.e. interaction of two conflicting half-truths (thesis and antithesis), to produce synthesis. At first welcomed French Revolution and Napoleon. His ideas were interpreted as supporting an authoritarian state and being hostile to liberalism. Ideas on dialectic, in modified form, used by Marx. Writings include *The Philosophy of Right*, 1821, *The Science of Logic*, 1812–16.

Henry IV (1553–1610): King of France and Navarre from 1589, first Bourbon monarch. Emerged as foremost Protestant commander in the French Wars of Religion. Succeeded to French throne after assassination of Henry III. Faced with the opposition of the Spanish-backed Catholic League, won important victories at Argues (1589) and Mayenne (1590). Forsook Protestantism to secure his position, but established security for Protestants in the Edict of Nantes. Secured peace with Spain at Vervins (1598), and set about rebuilding his country with his great minister Sully. Assassinated by a religious fanatic.

Herodotus (*c.*485–425 BC): Greek historian. He travelled widely collecting historical, geographical, ethnological, mythological, and archaeological material for his history of the wars between Greece and Persia. Cicero called him "the father of history".

Hindenburg, Paul von (1847–1934): German solider and president. Fought at Königgratz, 1866, and in Franco-Prussian War, 1870–1. Became general, 1903. Retired, 1911. Recalled to duty on outbreak of World War I. Victories won with Ludendorff at Tannenberg, 1914, and Masurian Lakes, 1915, made him a national hero. Became chief of general staff, 1916. Organized withdrawal from Western Front, 1918 (giving rise to myth of undefeated German Army). Advised Kaiser Wilhelm I to abdicate and arranged armistice. Retired, 1919. Elected president of Weimar Republic, 1925–34. Defeated Hitler in presidential election, 1932, but appointed him chancellor, January 1933.

Hitler, Adolf (1889–1945): Dictator of Germany. Born in Austria. Served in Bavarian Army during World War I, becoming lance corporal, twice decorated with Iron Cross. Joined German Workers' Party in Munich, 1919, transforming it into National Socialist German Workers' Party (NSDAP/Nazi Party), based on extreme nationalism and anti-Semitism. Attempted putsch in Munich, 1923, which proved abortive, although made him a national figure. While in prison, wrote political testament, *Mein Kampf*. Began to reorganize Nazi Party, 1925. Established unrivalled position as leader of party. Created efficient propaganda machine and organized elite guard, *Schutzstaffel* (SS). Helped to power by Great Depression. Nazi Party won 107 seats in 1930 Reichstag elections, becoming second largest party. In elections, July 1932, won 230 seats (highest they ever achieved). Appointed chancellor by Hindenburg, January 1933, although Nazis still a minority in Reichstag. Following Reichstag fire and Enabling Act, assumed dictatorial powers. Other political parties dissolved. Nazi Party purged of rivals by 1934. On death of Hindenburg, 1934, became president, uniting position with that of chancellor or *führer* ("leader"). Internal opposition ruthlessly suppressed. Rearmament programme expanded, 1935, aiding economic recovery. Occupied Rhineland, 1936. Rome–Berlin "Axis" negotiated, 1936. Annexed Austria (*Anschluss*), 1938. Gained Sudetenland after Munich Agreement, 1938. Seized remainder of Czechoslovakia, 1939. After non-aggression pact with USSR, August 1939, invaded Poland, 1 September 1939, precipitating World War II. Achieved swift military successes through blitzkrieg campaigns, but fatal error was in attacking Russia, June 1941. Faced combined opposition of USSR, USA, and Britain. Survived assassination attempt, July 1944. Committed suicide during closing stage of war.

Holbein, Hans "the younger" (1497–1543): German painter and engraver. Painted great series of portraits of eminent Englishmen of his time, including Thomas More. Appointed court painter to Henry VIII in 1536, and painted portraits of the king's prospective wives. Most famous work is probably the portrait group *The Ambassadors*, in the National Gallery, London. Died of plague in London.

Homer (*c.*800 BC): Greek poet. Attributed by the ancient world to be the author of two epic works, the *Iliad* and the *Odyssey*. Authorship of these earliest and greatest Greek epics has aroused great controversy, especially over whether Homer was a single figure or responsible for both works. Works are now agreed to be the product of a single author, working in the second half of the 8th century BC. Variations and inconsistencies between the works have been ascribed to the typical forms of oral poetry. The *Iliad* tells the story of the siege and sack of Troy, almost four centuries earlier. The *Odyssey* tells of the wanderings and adventures of one of the participants, Odysseus, on his way back to his homeland in Ithaca. Among the most significance pieces of world literature; nothing is known about the author.

Horace (Quintus Horatius Flaccus) (65–8 BC): Latin lyric poet. Educated in Athens, entered service of Brutus during civil war of 43 BC. Fought at the battle of Philippi. Moved in literary circles with Virgil in Rome during the "golden age" of Roman literature. His *Satires*, *Epistles*, and *Odes* have had a profound influence on Western culture.

Ignatius Loyola, St (1491–1556): Spanish soldier, theologian and founder of the Society of Jesus. Having renounced military life, Loyola pursued the religious life with great zeal, founding the Society of Jesus with St Francis Xavier and four other associates in 1534. Originally aimed at encouraging pilgrimage to the Holy Land and conversion of the infidel, the rule of the order was approved by Pope Paul III in 1540, and Loyola's Spiritual Exercises (1534) is still used in the training of Jesuits today.

Ivan IV (1530–84): Grand duke of Muscovy, 1533–47, first tsar of Russia, 1547–84, known as "the Terrible". Established his personal authority and destroyed privileges of the boyar nobles. Captured Kazan, Astrakhan, and Siberia, but the Tartar siege of Moscow and Polish victory in the Livonian War (1558–82) left Russia weak and divided. Increasingly unstable, he flew into fierce rages, killing his son in 1581. Succession passed to his mentally handicapped second son Fyodor.

Jesus Christ (4–33): Prophet, founder of the Christian religion and believed by Christians to have been divine. Born in Bethlehem in Judea in or about AD 4, he began to preach in 31 and was crucified in Jerusalem on the orders of the Roman governor of Judea, Pontius Pilate, in 33. Christians believe him to have risen from the dead and ascended into heaven at the Ascension. Influence was transmitted through his immediate followers, the apostles, and also by Paul of Tarsus. Life written up in New Testament, consolidating his reputation as a moral teacher and miracle worker, leading to the establishment of Christian communities around the Roman world. Roman Emperor Constantine adopted Christianity, changing its status from an often persecuted sect to a powerful force within the late Roman world, and allowing it to spread as the Roman West disintegrated. In the East, Christianity became an integral part of the Byzantine Empire.

Joseph II (1741–90): Holy Roman Emperor, 1765–90; Archduke of Austria, 1780–90. Succeeded his father, Francis I. Ruled Habsburg possessions jointly with his mother, Maria Theresa. Ruled alone after her death, 1780, as an enlightened monarch. Limited clerical influence, granted religious toleration, 1781. Abolished serfdom, extended education, reformed taxation. Established strong, centralized government. Aroused hostility, expressed in several revolts, 1788. Also in 1788, waged unsuccessful war with Turkey.

Justinian (483–565): Byzantine emperor. Established authority with the assistance of his wife, Theodora, and his commander-in-chief, Count Belisarius, crushing the circus factions in the Nika Revolt and asserting imperial authority. Belisarius defeated the Vandals, reconquering North Africa, and overthrew the Gothic Kingdoms in Italy. In the East he established a stable frontier with the Persians. He rebuilt Constantinople, including the great Church of St Sophia. Produced his law code, the *Corpus Juris Civilis* (*The Body of Civil Law*), 529–35.

Khrushchev, Nikita Sergeyevich (1894–1971): Soviet politician. Joined Communist Party, 1918. Fought in Civil War. Member of Central Committee of Party, 1934. Full member of Politburo and of Praesidium of Supreme Soviet, 1939. Organized guerrilla warfare against Germans during World War II. Premier of Ukraine, 1944–7. Undertook major restructuring of agriculture, 1949. Became First Secretary of all Union Party on death of Stalin, 1953. Denounced Stalinism, 1956. Relegated Molotov, Kaganovich, and Malenkov (potential rivals), 1957. Succeeded Bulganin as prime minister, 1958–64. Official visits to USA, 1959, India and China, 1960. Deposed, 1964, following economic failures.

Lenin, Vladimir Ilyich (V.I. Ulyanov) (1870–1924): Russian revolutionary leader and architect of Soviet State. After expulsion from Kazan University for political activity, absorbed writings of Marx. In St Petersburg, organized League for the Liberation of the Working Class. Exiled to Siberia, 1897. In London, 1903, when Russian Social Democratic Labour Party divided into Mensheviks and Bolsheviks. Led Bolshevik wing and published newspaper, *Iskra* ("The Spark"). Involved in abortive Russian Revolution, 1905. Controlled revolutionary movement from exile in Switzerland. Smuggled into Russia by Germans, 1917. Overthrew Kerensky's provisional government and became head of Council of People's Commissars. Ended war with Germany and concluded treaty of Brest-Litovsk, March 1918. Civil War with "White" armies continued until 1921. As chairman of Communist Party, established virtual dictatorship and dissolved Constituent Assembly. Created Communist International, 1919, to encourage world revolution. Introduced New Economic Policy, 1921, in diversion from planned communist transformation of economy. Recognized dangers implicit in rise of Stalin. Important both as theoretical writer on Marxism and as practical revolutionary organizer. Communist era in Soviet Union officially ended after 1991 coup attempt.

Leonardo da Vinci (1452–1519): Italian painter, architect, scientist, and engineer. Settled in Milan in 1482 where he painted his famous *Last Supper* in the refectory of the convent of Santa Maria delle Grazie. Entered the service of Cesare Borgia in Florence in 1500 as architect and engineer. Around 1504, he completed the *Mona Lisa*. 1506, employed by Louis XII of France; 1516, Francis I of France assigned him an annual allowance and the use of Château Cloux where he lived until his death. The outstanding all-round genius of the Renaissance, Leonardo had a knowledge and understanding far beyond his time in many fields including biology, anatomy, mechanics, and aeronautics, all demonstrated in his many notebooks.

Lloyd George, David, 1st Earl Lloyd George of Dwyfor (1863–1945): British Liberal statesman. Member of parliament, 1890–1945. President of the Board of Trade, 1905–8. Chancellor of the exchequer, 1908–15. Introduced controversial People's Budget, 1909, proposing increased taxation to fund social reform and naval rearmament. Budget rejected by House of Lords, causing constitutional crisis leading to Parliament Act, 1911. Minister of munitions,

1915–16. Secretary for war, 1916. Prime minister, 1916–22. Leader of the Liberal Party, 1926–31. Created Earl Lloyd George, 1945. Dynamic and efficient wartime leader. Attended Paris Peace Conference, 1919. Opposed calls at Versailles for draconian penalties on Germany. Faced economic problems at home in post-war period. Continuing violence in Ireland led to creation of Irish Free State, 1921, weakening Lloyd George's position, as did revelations of his sale of honours. Forced to resign, 1922, when Conservatives left coalition. Never held office again.

Louis XIV (1638–1715): King of France from 1643, known as "The Sun King" (Le Roi Soleil). Established himself as the model of royal absolutism, ruling with authority and increasing ostentation. Defended French interests wherever necessary, maintaining a standing army of more than 150,000 men, and built up the French navy. France was almost constantly at war during his reign, and his commanders, Condé and Turenne, were famous throughout Europe. Finance minister, Colbert, produced a taxation system to support the armed forces and Louis's most famous achievement, the Palace of Versailles. Last years clouded by famine, and the ruinous War of the Spanish Succession (1701–14) bankrupted the state.

Louis XVI (1754–93): King of France, 1774–93. Grandson of Louis XV. In early years of reign, successive ministers (e.g. Turgot, Necker) attempted financial reforms but nobility resisted proposals to include them in taxation net. Costly intervention in American War of Independence spread constitutional theories in France. Summoned Estates General, 1789, on advice of Necker (its first session since 1614). Third Estate's decision to meet separately as National Assembly constituted first act of French Revolution. With death of Mirabeau, 1791, Louis lost a valuable supporter. Fled after the revolution but was captured at Varennes, and appealed to fellow monarchs for help, while France was already at war with Prussia and Austria. Royal family subsequently imprisoned. Republican majority in Convention secured trial and execution of Louis, 1793.

Ludendorff, Erich (1865–1937): German soldier. Entered army, 1882. Major-general by 1914. Planned deployment of German armies at outbreak of First World War. With Hindenburg, won victory at Tannenberg, 1914. Transferred to Western Front, 1916. Shared increasing control of government with Hindenburg after 1916. Conceived spring offensive, 1918. Involved in abortive Kapp Putsch, 1920. Took part in Hitler's Munich Putsch, 1923. Founded extreme nationalist party, 1925. Unsuccessful candidate for Reich presidency, 1925.

Lumière, Auguste Marie Louis Nicolas (1862–1954) and **Louis Jean** (1864–1948): French chemists and brothers. Manufacturers of photographic materials, they invented the first successful cine camera and projector (1895) and a process of colour photography. Also produced the first film newsreels and the first "movie" in history, *La Sortie des usines Lumiére* (1895).

Luther, Martin (1483–1546): German Protestant theologian, the principal figure of the German Reformation. Preached the doctrine of justification by faith rather than by good works, and attacked the sale of indulgences in his famous 95 theses (1517), and papal authority. Excommunicated at Diet of Worms in 1521. His translation of the Bible into High German (1522–34) contributed significantly to the development of German literature in the vernacular.

Magellan, Ferdinand (*c.*1480–1521): Portuguese navigator, leader of the first expedition to circumnavigate the globe. Served in the East Indies and was lamed for life in Morocco. Offering his services to Spain, he sailed from Seville on 10 August 1519 with five ships and 270 men. Having coasted Patagonia, he threaded the strait which bears his name and reached the ocean that he named the

Pacific. By now one ship was wrecked, one had turned for home, a third was scuttled, and a fourth was captured by the Portuguese. Magellan himself was killed by natives in the Philippine islands. His ship, *Victoria*, was taken safely back to Spain by the last surviving Spanish captain, on 6 September 1522, to complete the circumnavigation of the world.

Maria Theresa (1717–80): Archduchess of Austria, Queen of Hungary and Bohemia. Daughter of Charles VI. Succeeded to rule of Habsburg territories, 1740, as result of Pragmatic Sanction. Fought France, Spain and Prussia in War of Austrian Succession, 1740–8. Gained imperial title for her husband Francis, 1745. Ceded Silesia and Italian territories, 1748. Suffered humiliating losses while allied to France in Seven Years War, 1756–63. Ruled jointly with her son, Joseph II, 1756–80. Took part in Partition of Poland, 1772. Introduced economic reforms that strengthened Austrian resources.

Marx, Karl (1818–1883): German philosopher. Father of "scientific socialism". Editor of *Rheinische Zeitung*, 1842. Exile in Paris, 1843–5, and Brussels, 1845–8. Sympathized with early German socialists. Wrote *The Communist Manifesto*, 1848, with Engels. Returned to Cologne during 1848 Revolution. Founded *Neue Rheinische Zeitung*. Expelled from Prussia, settled in London, 1849. European correspondent for *New York Tribune*, 1851–62. Developed philosophy of "class struggle"; described economic laws of capitalism. Derived ideas from dialectic of Hegel, and from materialism of Feuerbach. First volume of *Das Kapital* published 1867. Helped establish International Workingmen's Association (The First International) in London, 1864. Conflicts with Bakunin led to disintegration of Association, 1876.

Mazarin, Jules (1602–61): Italian-born French statesman. Sent to Paris as the Italian papal legate (1634), he became a naturalized Frenchman, and was made a cardinal in 1641, and then chief minister of France (1642) for Louis XIV, succeeding Richelieu. Lover of Anne of Austria, mother of the king.

Metternich, Clemens (1773–1859): Austrian statesman and diplomat. Created prince, 1813. Represented Westphalia at Congress of Rastadt, 1797–9. Entered Austrian diplomatic service, holding posts in Dresden, 1801–3, Berlin, 1803–6, and Paris, 1806–9. Foreign minister, 1809–48. Chancellor, 1812–48. Led Austria into alliance with Russia against France, 1813. Presided at Congress of Vienna, 1814–15. Architect of "Metternich System", i.e. balance of power in Europe in interests of general peace. Politically conservative, aiming at resisting liberal demands and maintaining stability. Led Austria to focus attention on territories in Italy rather than on interests in Germany. Obliged to resign during 1848 Revolution. Returned to Austria, 1849, but not to office.

Michelangelo, properly **Michelagniolo di Lodovico Buonarroti** (1475–1564): Italian sculptor, painter, and poet. The most brilliant representative of the Italian Renaissance. Obsessively interested in the representation of the human body, whether in sculpture or painting. The Sistine Chapel in St Peter's, Rome, and his statue of *David*, in the Academy in Florence, represent these aims, influenced by classical examples, but their form and vitality render them far more than a simple neo-classicist imitation of the past.

Moltke, Helmuth von (1800–91): German soldier. Entered Prussian Army, 1822. Joined General Staff, 1832. Seconded as adviser to Turkish Army, 1835–9. Personal aide to Prince Henry, 1845–6, and to Frederick William, 1855–7. Appointed Chief of Prussian General Staff, 1857. Introduced major reorganization of army, 1858–88. Produced strategic planning that secured Prussian victories against Denmark, 1864, Austria, 1866, and France, 1870. Became chief of Imperial General Staff, 1870. Created field marshal, 1871.

Monnet, Jean (1888–1979): French politician, economist, and diplomat. Member of Inter-Allied Maritime Commission, 1915–17. First deputy secretary-general of League of Nations, 1919–23. Chairman, Franco-British Economic Co-ordination Committee, 1939–40. Became minister of commerce, 1944. Fostered establishment of National Planning Council, becoming head of Council, 1945–7. Architect of European Community. Chairman, Action Committee for United States of Europe, 1955–75. Instrumental in foundation of European Coal and Steel Community. President of ECSC, 1952–5.

Mozart, Wolfgang Amadeus (1756–91): Austrian composer, born in Salzburg. A child prodigy, he was touring Europe by the age of six. Settled in Vienna from 1781, he wrote more than 40 symphonies, nearly 30 piano concertos, over 20 string quartets, and 16 operas, among which are *The Marriage of Figaro* (1786), *Don Giovanni* (1787), and *The Magic Flute* (1791). He wrote his music effortlessly, and his music is regarded as the epitome of the classical era in its purity of form and melody.

Mussolini, Benito (1883–1945): Dictator of Italy. Originally a socialist. Imprisoned for political activities, 1908. Editor of socialist national newspaper, *Avanti*, 1912–14. Resigned from party having been criticized for supporting war with Austria. Founded newspaper, *Il Popolo d'Italia*, Milan, 1914. Organized groups of workers to campaign for social improvements. Amalgamated into Fascist Party, 1919. Elected to Chamber of Deputies, 1921. During period of civil unrest, led "March on Rome", 1922. Appointed prime minister by King Victor Emmanuel III, 1922. Headed Fascist/nationalist coalition, as *Duce*. Acquired dictatorial powers, 1922. Dictatorship established, 1925. Single party, corporatist state instituted 1928–9. Large-scale public works introduced. Lateran Treaty settled Church/State relations, 1929. Expansionist foreign policy: Corfu incident, 1924; invasion of Abyssinia, 1935. Created Axis with Hitler, 1936. Left League of Nations, 1937. Annexed Albania, 1939. Declared war on France and Britain, 1940. Invaded Greece, 1940. Military setbacks in East Africa and Libya. Heavily dependent on Germany by 1941. Forced to resign following coup by Victor Emmanuel III and Marshal Badoglio, 1943. Detained, but freed by Germans. Established Republican Fascist government in German-controlled northern Italy. Captured and executed by Italian partisans, April 1945.

Napoleon I, Bonaparte (1769–1821): Emperor of the French, 1804–15. Entered French army, 1785. Won recognition after campaigns in northern Italy. Laid down peace terms to Austria at Campo Formio. Led unsuccessful expedition to Egypt. Overthrew Directory in "Brumaire" coup, 1799. Created Consul for Life, 1802. Effective dictator of France, 1799–1814. During consulate, introduced legal reforms in *Code Napoléon*, and achieved Concordat with Church. After winning War of Second Coalition, crowned himself Emperor, 1804. Won victories at Austerlitz and Jena during War of Third Coalition, 1804–7. Obliged Russia to accept Peace of Tilsit, 1807. Power reduced after 1808 by failure of "Continental System", and involvement in Peninsular War. Defeated Austrians at Wagram, 1809. Invaded Russia, 1812. Won victory at Borodino, but forced to retreat from Moscow. Defeated at Leipzig during War of Fourth Coalition. Abdicated, April 1814. Permitted by allies to retain imperial title and sovereignty over Elba. Escaped from Elba, February 1815. During "Hundred Days" resumed rule as emperor. Finally defeated at Waterloo, June 1815, and exiled to St Helena.

Napoleon III (Charles Louis Napoleon Bonaparte) (1808–73): Emperor of France, 1852–70. Nephew of Napoleon I. Made two unsuccessful attempts to mount Bonapartist risings against July Monarchy, 1836, 1840. Imprisoned after second attempt, but escaped, 1846, settling in London. Exploited "Napoleonic Legend". Elected president of Second Republic, 1848. Undertook *coup d'état* in order to widen his authority, 1851. Established Second Empire, 1852. Entered Crimean War as ally of Britain, and ensured Peace Congress was held at Paris, 1856. Planned joint campaign to achieve Italian independence after meeting with Cavour at Plombières. Made peace with Austria, 1859, without consulting Piedmont. Founded Catholic Empire in Mexico, 1861. Secured imperial title of Mexico for Archduke Maximilian of Austria, 1864. Diplomatically outflanked by Bismarck during Austro-Prussian War, 1866. Faced Franco-Prussian War, 1870, without allies. After defeat at Sedan, detained in Germany. Exiled in England, 1871–3.

Nero (37–68): Emperor of Rome. Son of Tiberius and Agrippina. Most notorious of the early emperors, responsible for the deaths of his mother, two wives, his stepbrother, and his former tutor, Seneca. Interest in aesthetic pursuits led him to sponsor "Greek" games and to participate in artistic productions. Following the great fire which destroyed much of Rome in 64 he lavished expenditure on his "Golden House" and foreign wars in Britain and Parthia; increasingly paranoid reactions to alleged conspirators led to the Senate decreeing Nero a public enemy. Revolt against him by the Praetorian Guard forced his suicide. Died reputedly lamenting, "What an artist dies with me!"

Newton, Sir Isaac (1642–1727): English mathematician and physicist, considered the greatest single influence on theoretical physics until Einstein. Professor of mathematics at Cambridge in 1669. In his *Principia Mathematica* (1687) Newton gave a mathematical description of the laws of mechanics and gravitation, and applied these to planetary motion. *Opticks* (1704) records his optical experiments and theories, including the discovery that white light is made of a mixture of colours. He constructed reflecting telescopes. His work in mathematics includes the binomial theorem and differential calculus.

Nicholas I (1796–1855): Tsar of Russia, 1825–55. Succeeded his brother Alexander I. Repressed Decembrist plot. Pursued reactionary policies. Introduced codification of laws, 1833. Freed serfs on state lands, 1838. Strengthened autocratic government. Created secret police ("Third Section"), 1826. Through education minister, Uvarov, resisted development of higher education and schools. Crushed Polish Revolt, 1830–2. Helped Austria suppress Hungarian Revolt, 1849. Policy towards Turkey alarmed Britain, resulting in war with Turkey, 1853, and Crimean War, 1854–6.

Nicholas II (1868–1918): Tsar of Russia, 1894–1917. Son of Alexander III. Reluctant to introduce political reforms. Influential in achievement of International Peace Conference in The Hague, 1898. Encouraged building of Trans-Siberian Railway. Forced by revolutionary mood of 1905 (stemming from industrial unrest, poor harvests, and disastrous Russo-Japanese War) to summon elected *duma*. Made gestures of reform under Prime Minister Stolypin. Fell under influence of Rasputin after 1906. Undertook Supreme Command of Russian Armies, 1915. Accused of maintaining communications with Germany during World War I. Abdicated after Revolution, March 1917. Murdered by local Bolsheviks at Ekaterinburg, 1918, together with family.

Nietzsche, Friedrich Wilhelm (1844–1900): German philosopher. Developed ideas of need for social elite of realists, led by a "superman" unhindered by conventional morality. Later association of his writings with political developments (especially Nazism and fascism) has been questioned. Essentially an individualist, suspicious of extreme nationalism. Writings edited posthumously by fanatically nationalistic sister. Insane in later life.

Otto I (912–73): Emperor of Germany. Married to sister of Athelstan, King of England, 930; defeated the invasion of the French, 938, subjugating the Slavonians and Bohemians, 950. Invaded and subdued Italy and expelled the Hungarians from Germany. Crowned Emperor of the West, 962, he deposed the existing pope and nominated his own candidate, Leo VIII. Campaigned in southern Italy and defeated Harold II of Denmark the year before his death.

Pericles (495–429 BC): Athenian statesman. Born in Athens of noble parents. Embarked on a series of successful military conquests, 454–445 BC. Pursued reform in Athens, widening participation, and led Athens to zenith of its commercial and imperial prosperity. Following renewed hostilities with Sparta, during the Peloponnesian War, he was attacked and died shortly afterwards, 431 BC.

Pétain, Henri Philippe (1856–1951): French soldier and politician. Entered army, 1876. Lectured at *l'École de Guerre*, 1906 onwards. Became colonel, 1912. Commanded an army corps, 1914. National renown followed defence of Verdun, 1916. Commander-in-chief of French armies in the field, 1917. Created Marshal of France, 1918. Vice-president, Higher Council of War, 1920–30. Led joint French–Spanish campaign against insurgents in Morocco, 1925–6. Inspector-general of army, 1929. Became minister of war, 1934. Ambassador to Spain, 1939. Became prime minister, June 1940. Became head of state in occupied ("Vichy") France, 1942. Obliged to flee France with retreating Germans, 1944. Sentenced to death for treason, 1945, but sentence commuted to life imprisonment by de Gaulle.

Philip of Macedon (382–336 BC): King of Macedon, Philip II, 360–336 BC. Father of Alexander the Great. Instituted military reforms that enabled Macedon to assert its authority over the Greek city-states, subduing Thrace and defeating the Athenians, 341–338 BC. Assassinated at the marriage ceremonies for his daughter, Cleopatra.

Philip II (1527–98): King of Spain from 1556, only son of HRE Charles V. One of the most powerful rulers of his day, he dedicated himself to the war against heresy (Protestantism), which involved him in ultimately unsuccessful wars in the Netherlands, the failed Armada against England, and expensive and fruitless interventions in France. But successful against the Turks with great naval victory at Lepanto in 1571. An obsessive bureaucrat and a devout Catholic. Built the great palace at the Escorial, where he died, leaving his empire divided, demoralized, and economically depressed.

Plato (429–347 BC): Greek philosopher. Originally named Aristocles, but given the surname "Plato" by Socrates. Founded his "Academy", in Athens, 387 BC, after travel to Egypt and the Greek colonies in Italy, where had met Euclid. Remained largely in Athens after 386 BC, as a teacher and philosopher. Works consist of a series of dialogues in which his mentor, Socrates, is the principal interlocutor. Outstanding reputation ensured that his works are seen as the most famous of Greek philosophy, notably the *Symposium*, the *Ethics*, the *Republic*, and the *Laws*.

Pompey (Gnaeuis Pompeius Magnus) (106–48 BC): Roman general. Became with Caesar and Crassus one of the First Triumvirate, 60 BC. Distinguished military commander from an early age, securing triumphs for campaigns in Africa, 81 BC, and for suppressing slave revolt of Spartacus, 71 BC. Became consul at the age of 36. Suppressed piracy in the Mediterranean, 67 BC. Triumphed over Mithradates VI, securing the Eastern Empire for Rome. Returned to Rome, 62 BC. Following death of Crassus, 53 BC, rivalry with Caesar become more acute, leading to removal of his army from Italy, 49 BC, to recruit more forces in Greece and Macedonia. Pursued by Caesar, after initial success, he was decisively defeated at the battle of Pharsalus, 48 BC. Fled to Egypt but was murdered on arrival.

Proust, Marcel (1871–1922): French novelist, essayist, and critic, born in Auteuil, Paris. A semi-invalid all his life, he withdrew from society after the death of his mother in 1905. He devoted much of his life to writing his great novel *À la recherche du temps perdu* (13 volumes). Its central theme is the recovery of the lost past and the releasing of its creative energies through the stimulation of unconscious memory.

Pushkin, Alexander Sergevich (1799–1837): Russian poet, novelist and dramatist. His first success was the romantic narrative poem *Ruslan and Ludmilla* (1820). Other notable works include the blank verse historical drama *Boris Godunov* (1831) and the verse novel *Eugene Onegin* (1833). Married Natalia Goncharova in 1832, over whose beauty he fought a duel in which he was killed.

Ranke, Leopold von (1795–1886): German historian. Professor of history at Berlin, 1825–72. Established modern critical methods of historiography, stressing need for thorough examination of sources and objective analysis. Made use of documents previously unavailable. Wrote many major works, including *History of the Roman and German Peoples, 1494–1514* (1824) and a history of the papacy in the 16th and 17th centuries (1834–7).

Rasputin, Gregori (1871–1916): Russian mystic. Used hypnotic talents over ailing Tsarevich Alexei (1904–18) to gain influence at court. Interference in politics damaged position of monarchy and provoked opposition among court. Suspected of working on behalf of Germany during World War I. Murdered by aristocrats.

Rembrandt, properly **Rembrandt Harmenz van Rijn** (1606–69): Dutch painter, one of the major figures of the Dutch "Golden Age". Produced work on many subjects, including portraits, landscapes, and large groups. Settled in Amsterdam, married Saskia, who features in many of his paintings. He prospered until her death in 1642, but he died a pauper. *The Night Watch* (1642) is his most famous work. Commonly regarded as one of the greatest artists of all time, his self-portraits are the first psychological studies in the history of art.

Richelieu, Armand Jean de Plessis, duc de (1585–1642): French cardinal and statesman. Minister to Louis XIII from 1624, he dominated French government and was one of the prime architects of French absolutism. Established France as a major rival to Habsburg power. In 1635, he established the Académie Française.

Robespierre, Maximilien de (1758–94): French Revolutionary leader. Dubbed "The Incorruptible". Lawyer, 1781–9. Represented Third Estate of Artois in Estates General, 1789. Emerged as radical in National Assembly, subsequently Constituent Assembly, 1789–91. Drew political inspiration from works of Rousseau. Believed himself to be embodiment of "General Will". Leader of radical Montagnard party. Elected to Committee of Public Safety, acquiring dominant position. Called for death of Louis XVI, 1793. Removed political opponents, e.g. Danton and Hébert, 1793–4. Created political dictatorship and attempted to transform society, involving "Reign of Terror". Provoked opposition among majority of National Convention. Deposed in "Thermidorean Reaction", 1794, and executed.

Rommel, Erwin (1891–1944): German soldier. Served on Romanian and Italian fronts during World War I. Lectured at War Academy. Joined Nazi Party, 1933. Commanded 7th Panzer Division, penetrated Ardennes, May 1940. Became commander of Afrika Corps, 1941, earning nickname "the Desert Fox". Defeated by campaigns of Alexander and Montgomery, 1942–3. Given task of strengthening defences in France, 1944. Active in resistance to Allied landings in Normandy, June 1944. Implicated in plot to assassinate Hitler. Apparently forced to commit suicide, October 1944.

Rousseau, Jean-Jacques (1712–78): Swiss-born philosopher. Attracted interest through his writings which criticized existing social order. *Du Contrat Social* (*The Social Contract*), 1762, described his political views, *Emile*, 1762, his theories on education. *Du Contrat Social* became extremely influential, especially during and after the French Revolution. Saw society itself as source of contemporary ills. Claimed governments only derived their legitimacy from popular consent – "the sovereignty of the people".

Shakespeare, William (1564–1616): English dramatist and poet. Born in Stratford-upon-Avon, he came to London where he worked at The Globe theatre as actor and playwright. His 38 plays are written mostly in blank verse and include comedies such as *A Midsummer Night's Dream*; historical plays, including *Richard III* and *Henry V*; the Greek and Roman plays, which include *Julius Caesar* and *Antony and Cleopatra*; and the great tragedies, *Hamlet*, *Othello*, *Macbeth*, and *King Lear*. He also wrote more than 150 sonnets, published in 1609, which are of equal literary significance.

Smith, Adam (1723–90): Scottish economist. Professor of logic, 1751, and of moral philosophy, 1752, at Glasgow. Friend of Hume. Greatest work, *An Enquiry into the Nature and Causes of the Wealth of Nations*, 1776. Criticized mercantilist economic thought. Proponent of free-market, laissez-faire system. Placed great stress on individual freedom. Devised theory of division of labour, money, prices, wages, and distribution.

Socrates (470–399 BC): Greek philosopher. Born at Athens of well-to-do parents. Lived in Athens during "golden age"; served in military and political roles. Charged with impiety and corruption of youth, found guilty, and sentenced to death by taking poison. Majority of writings lost; best known through Plato's descriptions of "Socratic method" of examining arguments, regarded as the basis of formal logic. Last hours described by Plato in *Phaedo*.

Sophocles (496–405 BC): Dramatist and tragic poet. Born in Athens of noble parents. Successful in tragedian contests. General in the Samian War, 440–439 BC, and took part in civic and ambassadorial tasks. One of a number of famous dramatists who competed in prestigious dramatic contests in Athens; younger rival to Aeschylus and later challenged by Euripides. Caricatured in Aristophanes' play *The Frogs*. Only a fraction of theatrical output survives, in seven out of an estimated 120 plays. Most famous works are *Antigone*, *Electra*, and *Oedipus Tyrannus*.

Stalin, Josef Visarionovitch (J.V. Djugashvili) (1879–1953): Soviet leader. Expelled from seminary for political activities, 1899. Exiled to Siberia twice. Attended conferences of Russian Social Democrats in Stockholm, 1906, and London, 1907. Expert on racial minorities in Bolshevik Central Committee, 1912. Became editor of *Pravda*, 1917. Worked with Lenin in Petrograd during Revolution, 1917. Member of Revolutionary Military Council, 1920–3. People's commissar for nationalities, 1921–3. General secretary of Central Committee of Communist Party, 1922–53. During Civil War, supervised defence of Petrograd. Co-operated with Kamenev and Zinoviev to exclude Trotsky from office, 1923. (Secured Trotsky's exile, 1929.) Gained control of Party at Fifteenth Congress, 1927. Embarked on policy of "Socialism in One Country" through Five Year Plans, 1928. Achieved rapid economic development. Eliminated political opponents in series of "show trials", 1936–8. Chariman of council of ministers, 1941–53. During World War II, as commissar of defence and marshal of the Soviet Union, took over direction of war effort. Present at Tehran, Yalta, and Potsdam Conferences. Established firm control of Eastern European communist "satellites", with exception of Yugoslavia, during post-war period. "Personality cult" of Stalin officially condemned by Khrushchev at Party Congress, 1956.

Stresemann, Gustav (1878–1929): German statesman. Elected to Reichstag, 1907–12, 1914–29. Leader of National Liberals, 1917. Took nationalistic position during World War I, supporting High Command. Became more moderate after war. Founded People's Party (DVP), 1919. Advocated meeting Germany's commitments under Treaty of Versailles, thereby gaining confidence of allies. Became chancellor during crisis year, 1923. Foreign minister, 1923–9. Restored Germany's diplomatic position. Concluded Locarno Pact, 1925. Achieved German entry into League of Nations, 1926. Secured reduction of reparations demands. Negotiated terms for allied evacuation of Rhineland. Supported Dawes Plan, 1924, and Young Plan, 1929. Awarded Nobel Peace Prize, 1926.

Thatcher, Margaret Hilda (née Roberts) (1925–): British Prime Minister. Conservative MP for Finchley, 1959–92. Parliamentary secretary to the Ministry of Pensions and National Insurance, 1961–4, and secretary of state for education and science, 1970–4. In 1975 she was elected leader of the Conservative Party. Between 1975 and 1979 led the party away from the centrist policies of Edward Heath and adopted a monetarist stance on economic problems and a tough line on law and order, defence and immigration. In May 1979 became Britain's first woman prime minister, following her election victory. In spite of considerable unpopularity and very high unemployment, Mrs Thatcher's conduct of the Falklands War and Labour's disarray led to a landslide victory at the polls in 1983. Second term marked by growing emphasis on liberalizing the economy, especially the privatization of major public utilities. In 1987 she achieved a record third term of office with a majority of over 100. Third term marked by economic problems, differences over Europe, and major personality clashes over her style of government. She resigned in November 1990 after a leadership challenge undermined her position.

Theoderic the Great (455–526): King of the Ostrogoths. Succeeded to the throne 474. Defeated the Bulgarians, 485, and rival Gothic chieftains at Verona, 489 and in 493. Major figure in the establishment of Gothic "successor" kingdoms in the West.

Thiers, Adolphe (1797–1877): French politician and journalist. Among group that persuaded Louis Philippe to accept throne in 1830. Politically an Orléanist throughout career. Minister of interior, 1832, 1834–6. Suppressed rioting in Paris and Lyons. Prime minister and foreign minister, 1836, 1840. During 1848 Revolution, advised king to leave Paris, and reassert authority with provincial help. Detained during Louis Napoleon's *coup d'état*, 1851. Re-elected deputy, 1863. Prominent among liberal opposition. Elected "Head of Executive Power" of Third Republic, Bordeaux, 1871. Negotiated peace treaty with Bismarck following Franco-Prussian War. Raised loans to pay war indemnity. President of the Third Republic, 1871–3.

Tirpitz, Alfred von (1849–1930): German grand admiral. Entered Prussian navy, 1865. Won support of kaiser after stressing importance of battle fleet, 1891. Minister of marine, 1897–1916. Expanded High Seas Fleet. Proponent of unrestricted submarine warfare. Resigned when suggestions not acted upon.

Titian, properly **Tiziano Vecellio** (c.1488–1576): the greatest of the Venetian painters. Painted many sensual and mythological works, including the *Venus of Urbino* (1538) and *Bacchus and Ariadne* (1523). He experimented with colour and revolutionized oil techniques. Has been described as the founder of modern painting, and had profound influence on later artists such as Tintoretto, Rubens, Velázquez, and Van Dyck.

Tito, Josip Broz (1892–1980): Yugoslav statesman. Member of Yugoslav Communist Party since early 1920s, becoming its secretary-general, 1937. Led Yugoslav partisan forces during World War II. Became marshal, 1943. After war, secured independence from USSR, 1948. First president of Yugoslav Republic, 1953–80. Pursued independent foreign policy, encouraging co-operation among non-aligned nations.

Trajan (Marcus Ulpius Nerva Trajanus) (53–117): Roman emperor. Adopted by Nerva in AD 97 and succeeded him the following year. Reign was notable for the conquest of Dacia by 106 and the erection of Trajan's column in Rome, one of the most informative records of Roman military operations.

Trotsky, Lev Davidovich (L.D. Bronstein) (1879–1940): Russian revolutionary of Ukrainian-Jewish descent. Exiled to Siberia, 1898. Joined Lenin in London, 1902. Became an independent socialist, 1902. Hoped to achieve reconciliation between Bolsheviks and Mensheviks. Returned to Russia, 1905, and organized first soviet in St Petersburg. Exiled to Siberia again. Returned to St Petersburg from New York, May 1917. Chairman of Petrograd Soviet, November 1917. First commissar for foreign affairs. Delayed conclusion of Treaty of Brest-Litovsk, 1918. Commissar for war during Civil War, creating Red Army. After death of Lenin, and disagreements with Stalin, excluded from office. Theory of "Permanent Revolution" condemned by Communist Party. Lost influence over Party policy, 1925. Expelled from Communist Party, 1927. Deported, 1929. Wrote *History of the Revolution* while in France. Murdered by Stalinist agent in Mexico, 1940.

Turgot, Anne-Robert-Jacques (1727–81): French administrator and economist. *Intendant* of Limoges, 1761–74. Became minister of marine, 1774. Controller-general of finance, 1774–6. One of central figures of Physiocrat school of economics. Abolished *corvée* (forced labour on roads). Encouraged building of roads and bridges. Reformed interest rates and imposed taxes more equitably. Ended some feudal privileges. Tried to re-establish free trade in grain between provinces.

Urban II (c.1035–99): Elected pope in 1088 during the schismatical pontificate of Guibert the antipope Clement III. He laid the emperor Henry IV of Germany under ban and drove him out of Italy, and triumphed similarly over Philip I of France. He inspired the First Crusade (1095–9).

Vesalius, Andreas (1514–64): Belgian anatomist, one of the first dissecters of human cadavers. Professor at Padua, Bologna, and Basle. Court physician to Emperor Charles V and Philip II of Spain. His great work *De Humani Corporis Fabrica* (1543) greatly advanced the science of biology with its excellent descriptions and drawings of bones and the nervous system, and repudiated Galenism. Sentenced to death by the Inquisition for "body snatching" and for dissecting the human body. Sentence commuted to a pilgrimage to Jerusalem; he died on the return journey.

Vespasian (Titus Flavius Vaspasianus) (17–79): Roman emperor. Took control of the Empire after a period of turmoil. Earned his reputation as a soldier, commanding the Legio II Augusta in the south-west of Britain in AD 43–7, then suppressing the revolt in Judea in the years up to 68. Plotting to become emperor, he was proclaimed so in 69 and, arriving in Italy in 70, was given the imperial title. He raised taxation, rebuilt Rome (including the Colloseum), and restored discipline to the army. An industrious and effective emperor, he expanded the frontier of the Empire in Britain, Germany, and the East.

Victor Emmanuel II (1820–78): King of Piedmont-Sardinia, 1849–78; King of Italy, 1861–78. Son of Charles Albert of Savoy. Succeeded to throne when Charles Albert abdicated after Radetsky expelled Piedmontese from Lombardy. Supported moves for Italian unity. Remained a constitutional monarch, upholding liberal Piedmontese constitution, 1849.

Virgil (Virgilus Maro Publius) (70–19 BC): Latin poet. Renowned for 12-book verse epic, the *Aeneid*, (19 BC) an account of the foundation of Rome and the travels of its founder, Aeneas. The work describes how Aeneas came from Troy to found a new home in Rome, the origin of the Roman state. Sponsored by Augustus, *Aeneid* became the founding myth of the Roman Empire and Virgil its Homer. Earlier works, the *Eclogues* and *Georgics*, were concerned with rural life.

Voltaire (François Marie Arouet) (1694–1778): French philosopher. Imprisoned in Bastille, 1717–18, 1726. In *Lettres Philosophiques*, 1734, contrasted French and English institutions. Lived briefly in Potsdam under patronage of Frederick II. Corresponded with Catherine the Great. Philosophical works include *Dictionnaire Philosophique*, 1764. Criticized dogmatic religions, especially Catholicism. Consistent theme in his writings is a lack of respect for authority and institutions, therefore preparing intellectual climate for French Revolution. Campaigned on behalf of victims of religious and political persecution.

Walesa, Lech (1943–): Polish trade unionist. Former Gdansk shipyard worker. Emerged as leader of independent Solidarity trade union. Solidarity comprised some 40 per cent of Polish workers by late 1980. Mounted outspoken opposition to economic and social policies of government. Detained following imposition of martial law, December 1981. Released 11 months later. During his detention, Solidarity was banned. Continued to hold prominent position. Granted audience with Pope John Paul II, 1983. Awarded Nobel Peace Prize, 1983. Guided Solidarity throughout 1980s, but declined to hold office when, in September 1989, Solidarity became part of Poland's first non-communist government for forty years. However, in 1990 elected by direct vote as president of Poland.

Wellington, 1st Duke of, Arthur Wellesley (1769–1852): British soldier and politician. Outstanding military leader during Napoleonic Wars. MP, 1790–5, 1806, 1807, 1807–9. Commanded British force in Portugal, 1808. Created Earl Wellington, then Marquess, 1812. Campaigns in Peninsular War culminated in invasion of southern France, 1813. Created Duke of Wellington, 1814. British ambassador to Paris, 1814. Chief secretary for Ireland, 1807–9. Won decisive victory over Napoleon at Waterloo, June 1815. Commander of British occupying forces in France, 1815–18. Helped ensure moderate treatment of France by Allies. Master-General of the Ordnance, 1819–27. Prime minister, 1828–30. Achieved Catholic Emancipation, 1829. Reluctant to introduce electoral reform, 1830, consequently lost office. Prime minister and secretary of state for all Departments, November–December 1834. Foreign secretary, 1834–5. Minister without portfolio, 1841–6. Commander-in-Chief, 1842–52.

Wilhelm II (1859–1941): German emperor, king of Prussia, 1888–1918. Son of Emperor Frederick III. Dismissed Bismarck from chancellorship, 1890. Implemented "New Course" in policy, aiming to assert German claims to world leadership. Increasingly under control of German High Command. Obliged by them to abdicate following Germany's military defeat, 1918. Went into exile in Holland.

William I (1027–87): Duke of Normandy, 1035–87, and king of England, 1066–87, known as "the Conqueror". Established control over the Duchy of Normandy through formidable fighting prowess. Promised the succession of the English throne, he defeated Harold Godwinson at Hastings in 1066, and secured kingdom with series of brutal campaigns, "harrying the North" in winter of 1069–70. Ordered compilation of the Domesday Book, produced in 1086. After 1072, visited England infrequently, dealing with rebellions in Normandy, where he was eventually killed.

William of Orange, known as **"the Silent"** (1533–84): Count of Nassau and Prince of Orange. A Roman Catholic with moderate and tolerant views. Took leading part in confederation of nobles calling for Philip II to relax heresy laws and suspend the Inquisition. Philip sent the hard-line Duke of Alva to be Regent in Netherlands. William withdrew to Germany, converted to Protestantism, and rallied army to liberate the Netherlands. Invaded in 1572, and through Pacification of Ghent (1576) and Union of Utrecht (1579), the northern provinces became the independent United Provinces. In 1584, the United Provinces formally renounced their allegiance to Spain, and William was assassinated at Delft by Balthasar Gérards.

Witte, Sergei (1849–1915): Russian statesman. Minister of communications during 1880s. Minister of Finance, 1892–1903, with supervisory role over commerce, industry, and labour relations. Principal achievement was construction of Trans-Siberian Railway. Able to stimulate industry with loans from France. Dismissed as a result of military opposition, 1903. Returned to office to negotiate peace at Portsmouth following Russo-Japanese War. Became prime minister after 1905 Revolution. Substantial loans from Britain and France allowed him to by-pass duma. Dismissed after six-month term of office. Strong critic of World War I.

Wycliffe, John (c.1330–84): English religious reformer. Criticized the wealth and power of the Church and upheld the Bible as the sole guide for doctrine. His teachings were disseminated throughout the country by itinerant preachers and are regarded as precursory to the Reformation. Instituted the first English translation of the complete Bible. His followers were known as Lollards.

Index

Acknowledgements

2 Getty Images; 8 Bridgeman Art Library/Vatican Museums and Galleries, Vatican City; 11 Corbis/Araldo de Luca; 14-15 British Museum, London; 16 top The Art Archive/Archaeological Museum, Châtillon-sur-Seine/Dagli Orti; 16 bottom AKG, London/Studium Biblicum Franciscanum, Jerusalem/Erich Lessing; 17 top The Art Archive/Chiaramonti Museum, Vatican/Dagli Orti; 17 bottom Corbis/Vanni Archive; 18 AKG, London/Musée du Louvre/Erich Lessing; 21 Werner Forman Archive/Private Collection; 23 Ancient Art and Architecture Collection; 24 Robert Harding Picture Library/Guy Thouvenin; 26 The Art Archive/Topkapi Museum, Istanbul; 28 AKG, London/Sammlungen Museen Preussische Kutturbesitz, Antikenmuseum, Berlin; 29 Corbis/Mimmo Jodice; 30 AKG, London/Pergamon-Museum, Berlin/Erich Lessing; 31 Ancient Art and Architecture Collection; 32 AKG, London/John Hios; 34 top AKG, London/Akademie der Bildenden Künste, Vienna; 34 bottom The Art Archive/Harper Collins Publishers; 35 AKG, London/The Metropolitan Museum of Art, New York/Erich Lessing; 36 top The Art Archive/National Archaeological Museum, Naples/Dagli Orti; 36 bottom AKG, London/Musée du Louvre, Paris/Erich Lessing; 37 Corbis/Sandro Vannini; 38 top Ancient Art and Architecture Collection; 38 bottom AKG, London/Museo Nazionale, Reggio Calabria; 39 Corbis/Charles O'Rear; 40 top Ancient Art and Architecture Collection; 40 bottom Photos12; 41 AKG, London/Erich Lessing; 42 Corbis/Mimmo Jodice; 43 Corbis/Bettmann; 44 The Art Archive/Archaeological Museum, Salonica/Dagli Orti; 47, 49 Corbis/Araldo de Luca; 50 Corbis/Chris Hellier; 51 top Corbis/José F Poblete; 51 bottom The Art Archive/Tate Gallery, London/Eileen Tweedy; 52-53 Corbis/Hulton-Deutsch Collection; 53 Corbis/Araldo de Luca; 54-55, 56 top Corbis/Archivo Iconografico, SA; 56 bottom Robert Harding Picture Library/Roy Rainford; 57 AKG, London/Antikensammlung, Kunsthistorisches Museum, Vienna; 58 Grazia Neri/Foto Mairani; 60 Corbis/David Lees; 61 Corbis/Araldo de Luca; 62 Bridgeman Art Library/Collection of the Earl of Leicester, Holkham Hall, Norfolk; 62-63 AKG, London/Department of Greek and Roman Antiquities, Musée du Louvre, Paris; 63 Bibliothèque Nationale de France, Paris, Cabinet des Médailles; 65 Corbis/Mimmo Jodice; 66 Corbis/David Lees; 67 Corbis/Christel Gerstenberg; 69 AKG, London/National Archaeological Museum, Naples; 70 Ancient Art and Architecture Collection; 71 The Art Archive/Museo Capitolino/Dagli Orti; 72 top Ancient Art and Architecture Collection; 72 bottom The Art Archive/Galleria Borghese, Rome/Dagli Orti; 73 The Art Archive/Museo della Civiltà Romana, Rome/Dagli Orti; 74 AKG, London/Musée du Bardo/Erich Lessing; 76 The Art Archive; 77 AKG, London/Kunsthistorisches Museum, Vienna; 78 The Art Archive/National Archaeological Museum, Naples/Dagli Orti; 79 The Art Archive/Archaeological Museum, Sofia/Dagli Orti; 80 Werner Forman Archive; 81 Corbis/Christie's Images, London; 82 Corbis/Araldo de Luca; 83 Ancient Art and Architecture Collection; 84 Grazia Neri/Foto Mairani; 85 Corbis/Adam Woolfitt; 86 The Art Archive/Dagli Orti; 87 The Art Archive/Galleria degli Uffizi, Florence/Dagli Orti; 88 The Art Archive/Dagli Orti; 89 AKG, London/Erich Lessing; 90-91 AKG, London/San Vitale, Ravenna; 92 AKG, London/Hagia Sophia, Istanbul/Erich Lessing; 93 top left AKG, London/Monza Cathedral; 93 top right The Art Archive/Musée de la Tapisserie, Bayeux/Dagli Orti; 93 bottom Corbis/José F Poblete; 94 Werner Forman Archive/Academia de la Historia, Madrid; 96 AKG, London/Musée du Louvre, Paris; 97 AKG, London/San Vitale, Ravenna; 98, 99 AKG, London/Hagia Sophia, Istanbul/Erich Lessing; 100 top, 100 bottom Robert Harding Picture Library/Christopher Rennie; 101 Corbis/David Lees; 102 AKG, London/Trinity College, Dublin; 104 top AKG, London; 104 bottom Corbis/Christine Osborne; 105 The Art Archive/San Apollinare Nuovo, Ravenna/Dagli Orti; 106 Bridgeman Art Library/St. Denis, Paris/Lauros/Giraudon; 107 The Art Archive/British Museum/Eileen Tweedy; 108 Ancient Art and Architecture Collection; 109 Bridgeman Art Library/Tretyakov Gallery, Moscow; 110 Bridgeman Art Library/Biblioteca Medicea-Laurenziana, Florence; 111 AKG, London/Stift Kremsmünster/Erich Lessing; 112 AKG, London/Musée du Louvre, Paris/Erich Lessing; 114 top Bridgeman Art Library/Fitzwilliam Museum, University of Cambridge; 114 bottom AKG, London/Erich Lessing; 116 AKG, London/Bayerische Staatsbibliothek, Munich; 117 AKG, London/British Library, London; 118 AKG, London/Nationalmuseet, Copenhagen; 119 Werner Forman Archive/Viking Ship Museum, Bygdoy; 121 The Art Archive/Musée Condé, Chantilly/Dagli Orti; 122 The Art Archive/Public Record Office, London; 123 Bridgeman Art Library/Richard Philp, London; 124 The Art Archive/Archbishops Palace, Ravenna/Dagli Orti; 126 AKG, London/St. Catherine's Monastery, Sinai/Erich Lessing; 127 Werner Forman Archive; 128 Bridgeman Art Library/Biblioteca Nacional, Madrid; 130 AKG, London/Hilbich; 131 AKG, London/Museum des Kunsthandwerks, Leipzig/Erich Lessing; 133 The Art Archive/Bibliothèque Municipale, Castres/Dagli Orti; 134 Corbis/Archivo Iconografico, SA; 135 The Art Archive/Biblioteca Nazionale, Palermo/Dagli Orti; 136-137, 138 Bridgeman Art Library/Bibliothèque Nationale de France, Paris; 139 top AKG, London/Bibliothèque Municipale, Besançon/Erich Lessing; 139 bottom left Corbis/Archivo Iconografico, SA; 139 bottom right Corbis/Gianni Dagli Orti; 140 Copyright The Frick Collection, New York; 142 Corbis/Dave Bartruff; 143 Bridgeman Art Library/Museo Correr, Venice; 144 Bridgeman Art Library/Lambeth Palace Library, London; 145 AKG, London/Arena Chapel, Padua/Cameraphoto; 146 top AKG, London/Heidelberg University Library; 146 bottom The Art Archive/British Library, London; 147 Bridgeman Art Library/Musée Condé, Chantilly; 148 The Art Archive/Biblioteca Nazionale, Turin/Dagli Orti; 149 AKG, London/British Library, London; 150 Bridgeman Art Library/British Library, London; 152 Scope/Philippe Blondel; 153 Corbis/Archivo Iconografico, SA; 154 Bridgeman Art Library/British Library, London; 155 AKG, London/Staatsarchiv, Hamburg; 156 top The Art Archive/British Library, London; 156 bottom Corbis/Cordaiy Photo Library Ltd; 157 Bridgeman Art Library/Hamburg Kunsthalle, Hamburg; 158 Mary Evans Picture Library; 159 top The Art Archive/Dagli Orti; 159 bottom Bridgeman Art Library/Bibliothèque Nationale de France, Paris; 160 top AKG, London/Bibliothèque Nationale de France, Paris; 160 bottom Photos12/Oasis; 162 AKG, London/Bibliothèque Nationale de France, Paris; 164 The Art Archive/Bibliothèque Municipale, Castres/Dagli Orti; 165 AKG, London; 166 top The Art Archive/Real Biblioteca de lo Escorial/Dagli Orti; 166 bottom Bridgeman Art Library/Wallace Collection, London; 167 The Art Archive/British Library, London; 168 top Corbis/Franz-Marc Frei; 168 bottom Corbis/Andrea Jemolo; 169 Corbis/Adam Woolfitt; 170 top Photo Scala, Florence; 170 bottom The Art Archive/Galleria degli Uffizi, Florence/Dagli Orti; 171 Corbis/Jonathan Blair; 172 AKG, London; 174 Scope/Jean-Luc Barde; 175 Bridgeman Art Library/Musée Condé, Chantilly; 176 AKG, London/Bibliothèque Municipale, Besançon/Erich Lessing; 177 Bridgeman Art Library/San Francesco, Upper Church, Assisi; 178 top The Art Archive/Museo Archeologico Nazionale, Cividale del Friuli/Dagli Orti; 178 bottom The Art Archive/British Library, London; 179 Corbis/Cordaiy Photo Library Ltd; 180 Bridgeman Art Library/British Library, London; 181 Bridgeman Art Library/Staatsarchiv, Hamburg; 182 AKG, London/Bibliothèque Nationale de France, Paris; 183 Axiom Photographic Agency/Chris Parker; 184 top AKG, London/Národní Muzeum, Prague; 185 AKG, London/British Library, London; 186-187 AKG, London/Vatican Museums, Rome; 188 AKG, London; 189 top left AKG, London/Museo del Prado, Madrid/Rabatti – Domingie; 189 top right, bottom right Corbis/Bettmann; 190 AKG, London/Doge's Palace, Venice/Cameraphoto; 192 top AKG, London/Biblioteca Ambrosiana, Milan; 192 bottom AKG, London/British Library, London; 193 Bridgeman Art Library/O'Shea Gallery, London; 194, 195 AKG, London/Musée du Louvre, Paris/Erich Lessing; 196 The Art Archive/Bibliothèque des Arts Décoratifs, Paris/Dagli Orti; 197 Corbis/Buddy May; 198 top AKG, London/Museo Navale, Genua-Begli; 198 bottom The Art Archive/Archaeological Museum, Lima/Dagli Orti; 199 Photos12/ARJ; 200 Corbis/Bettmann; 201 Bridgeman Art Library/Johnny van Haeften Gallery, London; 202 AKG, London; 204 The Art Archive/Windsor Castle; 205 Photos12/National Gallery, London/ARJ; 206 top AKG, London/Bibliothèque Publique et Universitaire, Geneva/Erich Lessing; 206 bottom Photos12/Hachedé; 207 AKG, London; 208 The Art Archive/Topkapi Museum, Istanbul; 210 AKG, London/British Library, London; 211 The Art Archive/Musée Céramique, Sèvres; 212 AKG, London/Scuola Grande di S. Rocco, Venice/Cameraphoto; 214 top The Art Archive/Museo de Arte Colonial de Santa Catalina, Cuzco/Dagli Orti; 214 bottom The Art Archive/Museo Tridentino Arte Sacra, Trento/Dagli Orti; 215 AKG, London/Kunsthistorisches Museum, Vienna; 217 The Art Archive/Museo del Prado, Madrid/Album/Joseph Martin; 218 Photos12/ARJ; 219 AKG, London/Erich Lessing; 220 Photos12/National Gallery, London/ARJ; 221 AKG, London/Galleria dell'Accademia, Florence/Rabatti – Domingie; 222 The Art Archive/British Library, London; 223 AKG, London; 224-225 AKG, London/Sammlungen Museen Preussischer Kulturbesitz, Nationalgalerie, Berlin; 226 AKG, London/State Hermitage, St Petersburg; 227 Corbis/Bettmann; 228 The Art Archive/British Library, London; 230 AKG, London; 231 AKG, London/Pinacototeca Querini-Stampalia, Venice; 232 top Bridgeman Art Library/Frans Hals Museum, Haarlem/Peter Willi; 232 bottom Photos12; 233 The Art Archive/Musée du Louvre, Paris/Dagli Orti; 234 The Art Archive/Francesco Venturi; 235 AKG, London/Musée du Louvre, Paris/Erich Lessing; 236 Bridgeman Art Library/City of Westminster Archive Centre, London; 237 The Art Archive/Musée Carnavalet, Paris/Dagli Orti; 238 top Mary Evans Picture Library; 238 bottom AKG, London/Private Collection/Erich Lessing; 239 Photos12/Collection Bernard Crochet; 240 Photos12/Musée du Louvre, Paris/ARJ; 242 The Art Archive/Musée du Château de Versailles/Dagli Orti; 243 The Art Archive/Eileen Tweedy; 244 top AKG, London/Rabatti – Domingie; 244 bottom Photos12/Collection Bernard Crochet; 245 Mary Evans Picture Library; 246 top

Bridgeman Art Library/Private Collection; 246 bottom AKG, London; 248 top Bridgeman Art Library/Centre Historique des Archives Nationales, Paris/Lauros/Giraudon; 248 bottom Corbis/Archivo Iconografico, SA; 249 The Art Archive/Musée du Château de Versailles; 250 Bridgeman Art Library/Blenheim Palace, Oxfordshire; 251 The Art Archive/Museo del Prado/Album/Joseph Martin; 252 AKG, London/Bibliothèque Nationale de France, Paris; 253 Bridgeman Art Library/Hermitage, St Petersburg; 255 Bridgeman Art Library/Topkapi Palace Museum, Istanbul/Giraudon; 256 AKG, London/Museum der Stadt Wien, Vienna; 257 AKG, London/Rijksmuseum, Amsterdam; 258 Bridgeman Art Library/Musée de la Chartreuse, Douai/Giraudon; 260 Bridgeman Art Library/Private Collection; 261 Corbis/Bettmann; 262 top Bridgeman Art Library/Christie's Images, London; 262 bottom Bridgeman Art Library/Fitzwilliam Museum, University of Cambridge; 263 Bridgeman Art Library/Private Collection; 264 top Bridgeman Art Library/Private Collection; 264 bottom Bridgeman Art Library/Fishmongers' Hall, London; 265 AKG, London; 266 The Art Archive/Museum der Stadt Wien/Dagli Orti; 268, 269 AKG, London; 270 AKG, London/Musée des Beaux-Arts, Chartres; 272 Corbis/Bettmann; 274 Bridgeman Art Library/Timothy Millet Collection; 275 Bridgeman Art Library/Courtesy of the Trustees of Sir John Soane's Museum, London; 276 Bridgeman Art Library/Trinity College, Cambridge; 277 AKG, London/Yale University Art Gallery, New Haven; 278 top Photos12/Musée du Château de Versailles/ARJ; 278 bottom The Art Archive/Musée du Château de Versailles/Dagli Orti; 279 Photos12/Oasis/Archives Snark; 280 AKG, London/Musée du Louvre, Paris/Erich Lessing; 282 top left Photos12/Musée Carnavalet, Paris; 282 top centre AKG, London/Musée Carnavalet, Paris/Erich Lessing; 282 bottom AKG, London/National Portrait Gallery, London; 283 top AKG, London/Heimatmuseum, Neuruppin; 283 bottom Photos12; 284 Corbis/Gianni Dagli Orti; 286 AKG, London/Schloß Charlottenburg, Berlin; 287 The Art Archive/Musée Carnavalet, Paris/Dagli Orti; 288 AKG, London; 289 Corbis/Bettmann; 290 Photos12/Musée de la Marine, Paris/ARJ; 291, 292 AKG, London; 293 AKG, London/Maximilianeum Foundation, Munich; 294 AKG, London; 296 top Photos12/Musée Carnavalet/ARJ; 296 bottom AKG, London/Société Historique et Littéraire Polonaise, Paris; 297 Photos12/Musée du Petit Palais/ARJ; 298 Bridgeman Art Library/British Museum, London; 299, 300 AKG, London; 301 The Art Archive/Eileen Tweedy; 302, 303, 304 top AKG, London; 304 bottom Corbis/Hulton-Deutsch Collection; 306 top Photos12/Oasis; 306 bottom AKG, London; 307 Corbis/Bettmann; 308 AKG, London/Städelsches Kunstinstitut, Frankfurt; 309 Corbis/Roger Antrobus; 310 AKG, London/Beethoven-Haus, Bonn/Erich Lessing; 311 top Corbis/Stapleton Collection; 311 bottom The Art Archive/Musée du Louvre, Paris/Dagli Orti; 312-313 Bridgeman Art Library/Château de Compiègne, Oise/Lauros/Giraudon; 314 top AKG, London/Bismarck-Museum, Friedrichsruh; 314 bottom The Art Archive; 315 top Novosti (London); 315 bottom AKG, London; 316 top The Art Archive/Russian Historical Museum, Moscow/Dagli Orti; 316 bottom AKG, London; 317 Bridgeman Art Library/Private Collection; 318 top Bridgeman Art Library/Private Collection/Ken Welsh; 318 bottom Corbis/Vince Streano; 319 AKG, London/Tretyakov Gallery, Moscow; 320 top Photos12; 320 bottom Bridgeman Art Library/Château de Versailles/Lauros/Giraudon; 321 The Art Archive/Museo del Risorgimento, Rome/Dagli Orti; 322 Corbis/Archivo Iconografico, SA; 324 Bridgeman Art Library/Private Collection; 325 Corbis/Underwood & Underwood; 326 top Bridgeman Art Library/Hamburg Kunsthalle, Hamburg; 326 bottom AKG, London/Wehrgeschichtliches Museum, Rastatt; 327, 328 AKG, London; 330 Bridgeman Art Library/Stadtische Kunsthalle, Mannheim; 330-331 Bridgeman Art Library/Musée de la Marine, Paris/Lauros/Giraudon; 331 Bridgeman Art Library/Private Collection/The Stapleton Collection; 332, 333 AKG, London; 334 Bridgeman Art Library/Guildhall Library, Corporation of London; 336 Bridgeman Art Library/Scottish National Portrait Gallery, Edinburgh; 336-337 AKG, London; 337 Corbis/Bettmann; 338 Corbis/Hulton-Deutsch Collection; 339 Hulton Archive; 340, 342 top AKG, London; 342-343 AKG, London/O Tellmann; 343 Hulton Archive; 344 AKG, London/Musée d'Orsay, Paris/Erich Lessing; 346 AKG, London; 347 Hulton Archive; 348, 351 AKG, London; 352 Hulton Archive; 354 AKG, London; 355 Corbis; 357 Hulton Archive; 359 Photos12/ARJ; 360 Corbis/Bettmann; 361 The Art Archive; 362 top AKG, London; 362 bottom Roger-Viollet/Collection Viollet; 363 Corbis/Bettmann; 364 Corbis/William H. Rau; 366 Novosti (London); 367 AKG, London; 368 top Photos12/ARJ; 368 bottom Science Photo Library/Jean-Loup Charmet; 369 Corbis/Bettmann; 370 AKG, London/Albert Meyer; 372, 373 AKG, London/Otto Haeckel; 374 Bridgeman Art Library/Pinacoteca di Brera, Milan; 375 AKG, London/Goethe-Nationalmuseum, Weimar; 376 top Corbis/Bojan Brecelj; 376 bottom AKG, London/Hotel de Ville, Geneva; 377 AKG, London; 378 Corbis/Bettmann; 379 The Art Archive/Richard Wagner Museum, Bayreuth/Dagli Orti; 380 Bridgeman Art Library/Courtauld Institute Gallery, Somerset House, London; 381 AKG, London/Christie's London; 382 Photos12/ARJ; 383 Corbis/Paul Almasy; 384-385 AKG, London; 386 Hulton Archive; 387 left AKG, London; 387 right Hulton Archive; 388 Hulton Archive; 390 Hulton Archive/Library of Congress; 391, Hulton Archive; 393 Photos12/Keystone Pressedienst; 394 top, 394 bottom Hulton Archive; 395 Photos12/Oasis; 396 Photos12; 397, 398 top, 398 bottom, 399, 400 top Hulton Archive; 400 bottom, 401 AKG, London; 402 top, 402 bottom, 403, 404 Hulton Archive; 406 Photos12/Oasis; 407, 408 top AKG, London; 408 bottom, 409 Hulton Archive; 410 top AKG, London; 410 bottom, 411, 412 top Hulton Archive; 412 bottom Photos12/Bertelsmann Lexikon Verlag; 413 Hulton Archive; 415 Corbis/Hulton-Deutsch Collection; 416 AKG, London; 417 Photos12/Oasis; 418 Corbis; 419 Corbis/Bettmann; 420 Photos12/Oasis; 421 AKG, London/Erik Bohr; 422 Hulton Archive/Sasha; 423 Kobal Collection/Nero; 424 Hulton Archive/Central Press; 425 Hulton Archive; 426 AKG, London/Walter Hahn; 428 top Photos12/Oasis; 428 bottom AKG, London; 429 Corbis/David & Peter Turnley; 430 top AKG, London/Jarkowsky-Scherl; 430 bottom Hulton Archive; 432 AKG, London; 433, 434 top Photos12/Keystone Pressedienst; 434 bottom AKG, London/PK-Foto (Grimm); 435 Novosti (London); 436 top, 436 bottom, 437 AKG, London; 438 top Hulton Archive/Slava Katamidze Collection; 438 bottom Hulton Archive; 439 Corbis; 440 Corbis/Bettmann; 442 top, 442 bottom Corbis/Hulton-Deutsch Collection; 443 top Corbis/David & Peter Turnley; 443 bottom Corbis/Alain Le Garsmeur; 444 Corbis/David & Peter Turnley; 446, 447 Photos12/Oasis; 448 top, 448 bottom Hulton Archive; 449 AKG, London; 450 Corbis; 451 Corbis/Hulton-Deutsch Collection; 452 top Photos12/Hadeché; 452 bottom Corbis/Bettmann; 454 Corbis; 455 AKG, London/Erich Lessing; 456 AKG, London; 457 top Corbis/Marc Garanger; 457 bottom AKG, London/Erich Lessing; 458 top Corbis/Bettmann; 458 bottom Agence France Presse; 460 Agence France Presse/Libor Hajsky; 461 AKG, London; 462 Hulton Archive; 463, 464 top Corbis/David & Peter Turnley; 464 bottom Corbis; 466 The Advertising Archives Ltd; 467 AKG, London; 468 Corbis/Hulton-Deutsch Collection; 469 AKG, London; 470 Hulton Archive/Archive Photos; 471 Hulton Archive; 472 Corbis/Bettmann; 473 Corbis Sygma/L.A. Daily News; 474 AKG, London; 475 Hulton Archive; 476-477 Rex Features/SIPA; 478 top Agence France Presse/EPA; 478 bottom Corbis/Adam Woolfitt; 479 top Agence France Presse/EPA; 479 bottom Agence France Presse/Ciro Fusco; 480 Corbis/Owen Franken; 482 Agence France Presse/Boris Roessler; 483 Popperfoto/José Manuel Ribeiro/Reuters; 484 Corbis/Chris Rainier; 485 Agence France Presse; 486 Corbis/Owen Franken; 487 Agence France Presse